Reader's Digest

Complete Guide to Needlework

Reader's Digest

COMPLETE GUIDE TO NEEDLEWORK

PUBLISHED BY THE READER'S DIGEST ASSOCIATION LIMITED

LONDON • NEW YORK • MONTREAL • SYDNEY • CAPE TOWN

READER'S DIGEST COMPLETE GUIDE TO NEEDLEWORK
First edition Copyright © 1981
Reprinted 1991
The Reader's Digest Association Limited,
Berkeley Square House, Berkeley Square, London W1X 6AB

Copyright © 1981 Reader's Digest Association Far East Limited
Philippines Copyright 1981 Reader's Digest Association Far East Ltd

Printed in Italy

ISBN 0 276 00224 5

CONTENTS

CONTRIBUTORS

The publishers would like to thank the following people for major contributions to this book.

Consultant editor Eirian Short

Editorial contributors and designers
Louise Amble   Peggy Bendel   Sherry De Leon   Rosemary Drysdale   Katherine Enzmann   Phoebe Fox   Zuelia Ann Hurt
Barbara H. Jacksier   Joyce D. Lee   Susanna E. Lewis   Claudia Librett   Victoria Mileti   Edna Adam Walker
Monna Weinman   Joanne Whitwell

Technical assistance
Elspeth Arnold   Lesley Arnold   Betty Beeby   Linda Blyer   Barbara Dawson   Janet Eaton   Charlotte Feng-Veshi
Sheila Gore   Jane Iles   Diana Keay   Elizabeth Kerr   Arlene Mintzer   Carole Nolan   Erwin Rowland
Cathie Strunz   Valentina Watson   Joan Webb

Contributing artists
Roberta W. Frauwirth   Susan Frye   Pat Kemmish   John A. Lind Corp.   Marilyn MacGregor   Mary Ruth Roby   Jim Silks
Randall Lieu   Ray Skibinski   Lynn E. Yost

Contributing photographers
J. D. Barnell   Bruton Photography   Joel Elkins   Ken Korsh   Russ McCann/Conrad-Dell-McCrann, Inc.
Michael A. Vaccaro

Research assistance
Aero Needles (Abel Morrall)   Appletons Bros Ltd   C. J. Bates & Son   Emile Bernat & Sons Co.   Bernina Sewing Machines
Boye Needle Company   Brunswick Worsted Mills Inc.   J. & P. Coats   Cowling & Wilcox   Craftsman's Mark
The D.M.C. Corporation   Embroiderers' Guild   Frederick J. Fawcett Inc.   T. Forsell & Son   Harrods Ltd
Harry M. Fraser Company   Hayfield Textiles   Hosiery Machine Co.   Kreinik Mfg Co.   Lowe & Carr   H. Milward & Sons
Newey Goodman   Paternayan Bros Inc.   Paton & Baldwins   Phildar International   Pingouin   Reynolds Yarn Inc.
Royal School of Needlework   Singer Company (UK) Ltd   Sirdar   Talon/Donahue Sales Div. of Textron   Joan Toggitt Ltd
Twilleys of Stamford   Vilene   Whitecroft Scovill   Wm E. Wright Co.

Embroidery

Nineteenth-century bedspread with crewel-work embroidery, Historic Deerfield Inc., Deerfield, Mass.

Embroidery tools and supplies

Yarns and threads
Embroidery fabrics
Hoops and frames
Needles
Design transfer materials
Accessories

Yarns and threads

Embroidery offers an enormous variety of finished effects, and that calls for a wide range of yarns and threads. Several of the types popular for embroidery are pictured below. Although they differ individually in texture, fiber content, number of plies, separable strands, etc., all of the types shown have one feature in common: whatever their character, it remains uniform throughout. Uneven or nubby novelty yarns (see Knitting and Crochet) are generally not recommended, except for occasional special effects.

Some yarns and threads come in more than one fiber, with new ones constantly being introduced, especially synthetic varieties. Some yarns and threads are easier to find than others; you may need to check several sources—needlework departments as well as special shops and catalogs—to find what you want.

In this section, as each form of embroidery is introduced, we specify the yarn or thread traditional for working it. This should not discourage experiment with different yarns and threads—that is what produces original pieces.

Embroidery floss, a loosely twisted 6-strand thread, works well in many types of embroidery. Strands can be separated for finer work. Cotton is most popular; made also in silk and rayon. Many colors (fewer for rayon).

Pearl cotton, a twisted 2-ply thread suitable for all embroidery types, has high sheen, good colors. Comes in sizes 3, 5, and 8 (3 is the heaviest).

Matte embroidery cotton, a tightly twisted 5-ply thread, gives embroidery a muted look. Usually reserved for heavier fabrics. Good color choice.

Crewel yarn, of fine 2-ply wool (also some acrylic), resembles one strand of Persian yarn. For fine embroidery and needlepoint. Many soft, subtle colors.

Persian yarn is loosely twisted 3-strand wool (sometimes acrylic); each strand is 2-ply. Used in needlepoint and embroidery. Good color choice.

Tapestry yarn is a tightly twisted 4-ply yarn appropriate for embroidery and needlepoint. Choice of wool (in many colors) or acrylic (considerably fewer).

Knitting yarn is a 4-ply yarn, like tapestry yarn but less twisted. Usable also for crochet. May be wool or acrylic.

Rug yarn, a thick 3-ply yarn, can also be used for texture variation in embroidered pieces; works best when it is couched down (fastened with small stitches). May be wool, acrylic, or cotton/rayon blend.

Machine embroidery thread is extra fine (size 50 or A). Silk is most popular for its sheen.

Metallic threads, available in many weights and textures, are used only for special effects.

Embroidery fabrics

Embroidery fabrics fall basically into three categories. The first, **plain-weave fabrics,** includes most tightly woven fabrics with a relatively smooth surface. Although medium-weight linens and wools are the traditional preferences, fabrics of other weights and fibres (such as cotton and synthetics) are also acceptable as long as the working thread is not too heavy. Most surface stitchery (including crewel work) is worked on plain-weave fabrics.

Even-weave fabrics, the next of the classifications, are all essentially plain weaves, but with a distinguishing difference: the number of threads per square centimetre is the same for both warp and weft. One type, the *single even-weave*, is made from single strands of intersecting threads; the thread count can vary from a coarse 6 to a fine 14 threads per square centimetre. In *Hardanger,* another of the even-weave types, pairs of threads intersect; 9 pairs of threads per centimetre is the usual count. Still another type is *Binca cloth*, which consists of intersecting thread groups, generally 4 to the centimetre. As a rule, even-weave fabrics are used for thread-counting techniques, such as blackwork and some types of openwork. They may be cotton, linen, wool, or blends of these with synthetics.

What the fabrics in the third group have in common is an evenly spaced **surface pattern** (see examples on right) that supplies guidelines for certain kinds of embroidery, such as cross stitch and smocking. As the samples show, the surface pattern may be printed on or woven in. The method of producing the effect is not important; what matters is its usefulness as a grid. The fabric *type*, however, is important. Select woven fabrics for this purpose; knitted fabrics are rarely satisfactory.

This list of embroidery fabrics is far from complete – silk, damask fabrics and calico, among others, may be used.

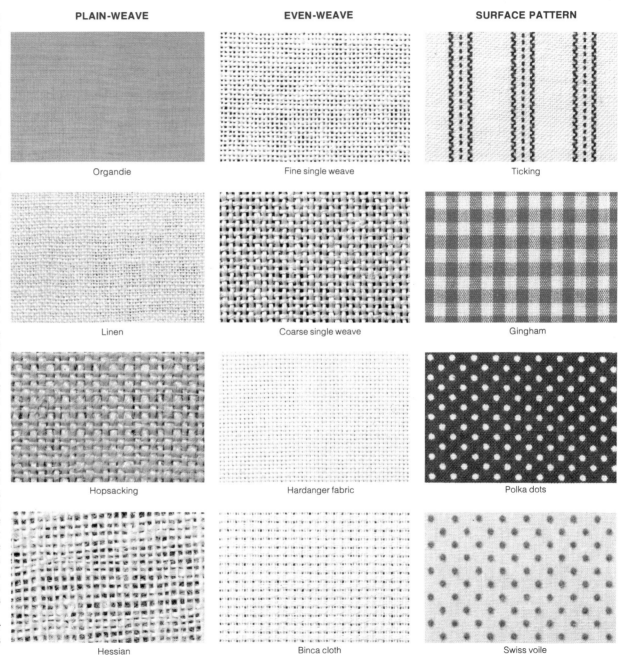

PLAIN-WEAVE

Organdie

Linen

Hopsacking

Hessian

EVEN-WEAVE

Fine single weave

Coarse single weave

Hardanger fabric

Binca cloth

SURFACE PATTERN

Ticking

Gingham

Polka dots

Swiss voile

Embroidery tools and materials

Hoops and frames

A hoop or frame is necessary for most types of embroidery work, to hold the fabric taut for stitching. **Embroidery hoops** keep a section of fabric stretched between two rings. The outer ring usually has an adjustable screw or a spring that allows the hoop to hold different weights of fabric. Hoops come in many sizes and may be hand-held or attached to a stand. **Frames** work by keeping the entire fabric taut. There are two basic types, the slate or square frame and the stretcher frame. *Slate frames* stretch the fabric between top and bottom rollers, which are then tightened. On the *stretcher frames*, which are basically four-sided units that you make with pre-cut wooden slats, the fabric is stretched around the framework and stapled down on the back. For further details about frames, see the Canvas work section.

Needles

Needles for hand embroidery are of three basic types: **crewel, chenille** and **tapestry**. Each has a specific purpose and comes in its own range of sizes (the larger the number, the shorter and finer the needle). Which needle type you should use depends largely on the embroidery technique being worked (see below). Another consideration is the thread; the needle should be large enough that the thread does not fray when it is pulled through the fabric.

Hoop stand is an adjustable stand to hold different-sized hoops. It frees both hands for working.

Slate frames are made in many sizes. The top and bottom rods have webbing stapled to them to attach to the embroidery fabric. Side rods have screws which tighten to keep fabric taut. Slate frames are also available on floor stands (see p. 116).

Standing hoop is made of a hoop fixed to a floor stand. The height can be adjusted for comfortable working.

Hoops come in many sizes, from 15 cm upwards. They consist of two rings that fit inside each other with a metal adjustable screw.

Stretcher frames consist of two pairs of canvas stretchers which slot together to form a rigid frame. They are sold in art and craft shops.

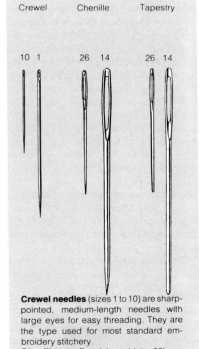

Crewel	Chenille	Tapestry
10 1	26 14	26 14

Crewel needles (sizes 1 to 10) are sharp-pointed, medium-length needles with large eyes for easy threading. They are the type used for most standard embroidery stitchery.

Chenille needles (sizes 14 to 26) are also sharp-pointed needles, but they are thicker and longer, and have larger eyes. They are the appropriate choice for embroidery using heavier threads.

Tapestry needles (sizes 14 to 26) are similar in size to chenille needles, but are blunt rather than sharp. This makes them best for thread-counting embroidery techniques and for canvas work as well.

Design transfer materials

Dressmaker's carbon paper and tracing wheels are used to transfer designs to fabric. Carbon paper is available in a few colours.

Pounce, sometimes called 'inking' powder, is used to transfer designs by the pricking method.

Dressmaker's marking pencils are used to mark fabric, will not smudge and are made in pale colours.

Transfer pencil enables you to make a hot-iron transfer from any design or drawing.

Tracing paper is useful for transferring original designs, and can be bought in many sizes.

Transfers are heat-sensitive patterns that can be ironed on to fabric. There are many types of design available.

Accessories

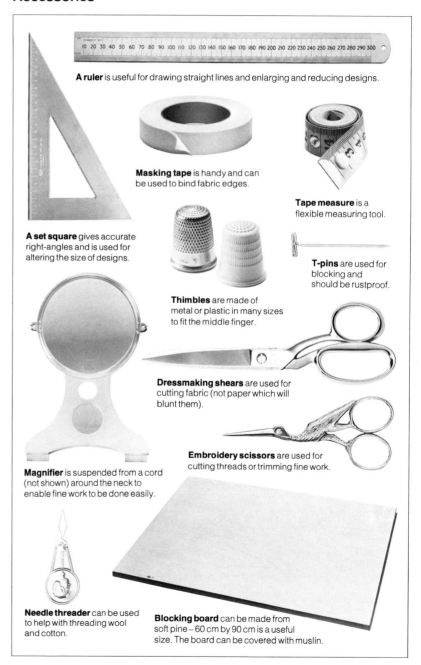

A ruler is useful for drawing straight lines and enlarging and reducing designs.

Masking tape is handy and can be used to bind fabric edges.

Tape measure is a flexible measuring tool.

A set square gives accurate right-angles and is used for altering the size of designs.

T-pins are used for blocking and should be rustproof.

Thimbles are made of metal or plastic in many sizes to fit the middle finger.

Dressmaking shears are used for cutting fabric (not paper which will blunt them).

Embroidery scissors are used for cutting threads or trimming fine work.

Magnifier is suspended from a cord (not shown) around the neck to enable fine work to be done easily.

Needle threader can be used to help with threading wool and cotton.

Blocking board can be made from soft pine – 60 cm by 90 cm is a useful size. The board can be covered with muslin.

11

Designing for embroidery

Design sources and interpretation
Choosing colours
Enlarging a design
Reducing a design

Sources and interpretation

Many needleworkers who have become quite skilled still do not consider themselves designers. Yet all of us, if we try, can manage some degree of designing. One person might take a first creative step by simply changing the thread colours dictated by a kit. Another may go a step further and make all of the colour and stitch decisions. Still another may carry out an original design. It is hoped that this section will encourage more people to try introducing their own ideas into their embroidery.

Many embroidery designs are nothing but personal interpretations of designs from such sources as books, magazines, posters, china, fabric prints, wallpaper and photographs. Examine such possible sources carefully, studying elements *within* a composition as well as the overall composition itself; you may find that you can single out a part of the larger design (see below) with excellent results. Take note of designs that draw the eye naturally up and down or from side to side. This can determine whether the overall line direction of a finished piece will be vertical or horizontal.

When you find a design that you like, place tracing paper over it, and carefully draw its outlines. You may want to omit some of the finer details, perhaps simplify certain lines as well; you can even rearrange elements within the composition. Make several different tracings and select the best one. Remember you are not trying to copy the original design, but to interpret it in embroidery. As you become more experienced at design interpretation, you will begin to recognise what has possibilities for embroidery and – just as important – what does not.

Part of a composition can be isolated for an embroidery design. From design below, bird and flower have been singled out and traced; note the simplifications made in the tracing.

The strong horizontal lines in the full design direct the eye naturally to move from side to side.

Vertical lines draw the eye up and down.

Choosing colours

Once your design is chosen, you are ready to select colours, a decision that will greatly affect your finished project. With colour, as with most design problems, there are guidelines that can help you to make a successful choice. Most colour schemes are one of three basic types. The first, called **monochromatic,** is a colour scheme consisting of different tones (light and dark hues) of the *same* colour (a design done in a 'family' of blues). The second type, the **analogous** colour scheme, uses colours that are *similar*, and 'neighbours' on the colour wheel (blues and greens or violets). A **contrasting** colour scheme, the third combination, brings together two or more *contrasting* colours, the strongest contrasts being those that are opposites on the colour wheel (red and green, purple and yellow).

These colour guidelines, though simple in theory, can be more difficult to put into practice. You will find the task far easier if you make yourself a *colour plan* – a coloured version of your traced design. You may have to colour more than one drawing before you hit upon a satisfactory combination. Once you have one you like, take it along when you go to buy threads. Be ready to make slight modifications in colours when you see what threads are actually available.

 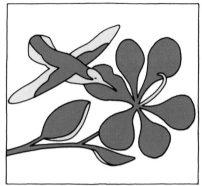 

Monochromatic (one-colour) schemes can achieve surprising variety if the tones (tints and shades) are imaginatively chosen and used, as illustrated.

Analogous schemes combine closely related colours, a characteristic that almost assures a harmonious blend, no matter what combination you choose.

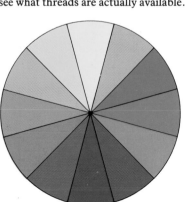

Colour wheel

Contrasting schemes can be much more difficult. Experiment with several different colours until you are satisfied.

Designing for embroidery

Enlarging a design

What do you do if the design you like is not the right size for your project? If there is a commercial photostat service near by, you can give them your drawing or the original artwork and have the size changed to your specifications. The cost for this service is nominal. If there is no such service in your area, or you prefer to do it yourself, you can make your own size change, using the grid methods illustrated – enlargement on this page, reduction on the page opposite. Basically, this method involves simply transposing design lines from one grid to another grid of a different size.

1. Trace design on to centre of paper.

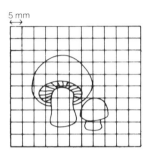

2. Draw a small grid over the traced design.

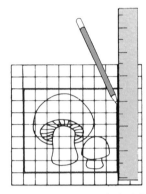

3. Mark perimeters of design to desired shape.

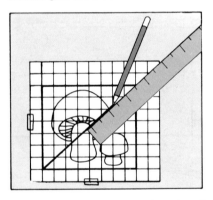

4. Tape grid to lower left corner of a large sheet of paper. Draw a corner-to-corner line diagonally across design area, extending line beyond grid.

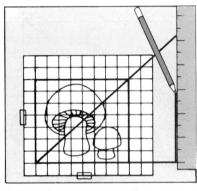

5. Extend the bottom line of the design area to desired width. Draw a line straight up to form a right-angle, extending line to intersect diagonal.

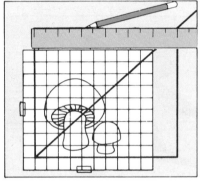

6. Using the finished width and height in Step 5, draw in remaining two sides of rectangle (left-hand line will join line of original grid).

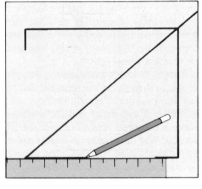

7. Remove grid. Fill in area that was covered by grid, extending diagonal, side and bottom lines to complete enlarged rectangle.

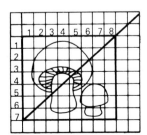

8. Along the design perimeter of the small grid, number each square across top and down side.

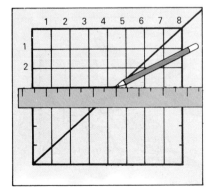

9. Count the squares within marked grid; divide large rectangle into same number of squares.

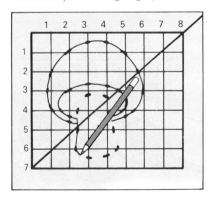

10. To reproduce design, copy lines in small squares on corresponding squares of large grid.

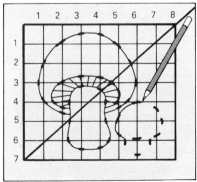

To make copying easier, place a mark where design lines intersect grid lines; connect marks.

Reducing a design

When a design is too large, you have the same choices as when it is too small. It can be reduced to your specifications by a commercial photostat service, as mentioned on the opposite page, or you can reduce the design yourself, by means of the grid technique shown here. The basic principle – copying square by square – is the same for reducing as for enlarging, but the actual steps differ. Essentially, they are the reverse of what is done for enlargement. Follow directions carefully when using either method; for drawing accurate angles, use a plastic right-angled set-square.

1. Trace design on to centre of paper.

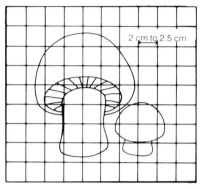

2 cm to 2.5 cm

2. Draw large grid over traced design.

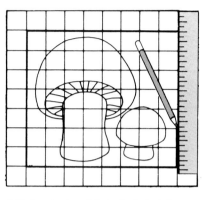

3. Mark perimeters of design to desired shape.

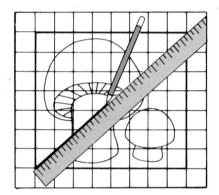

4. Draw a diagonal line from corner to corner of the design area marked off on the grid. Tape a smaller sheet of paper to the lower left corner.

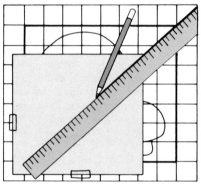

5. Extend the diagonal line at the upper right-hand corner of the grid straight down to the lower left-hand corner of the taped sheet of paper.

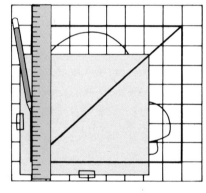

6. Extend bottom line of design area until it intersects diagonal. Connect intersected point with perimeter line on left side to form right-angle.

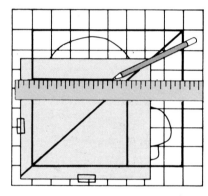

7. Mark off desired width at bottom of small sheet; draw line up at right-angle to intersect diagonal. Mark height on left; draw connecting line at top.

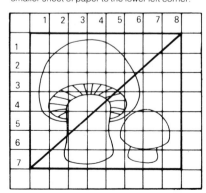

8. Along the design perimeter of the large grid, number each square across top and down side.

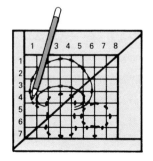

9. Count the number of squares within marked grid; divide small rectangle into same number.

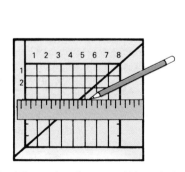

10. To reproduce design, copy lines within large squares on to equivalent squares of small grid.

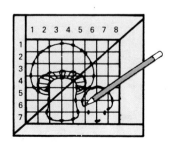

To make copying easier, place a mark where design lines intersect grid lines; connect marks.

General embroidery techniques

Cutting and binding fabric edges
Transferring designs
Using an embroidery hoop
Preparing threads
Threading the needle
Working tips

Cutting and binding edges

To determine cutting size of fabric, measure the overall design and to this measurement add 5 cm all round. Add twice as much allowance if the embroidered piece is to be framed. Cut fabric to the desired size, following the fabric's grainline; a straight grain is especially important for counted-thread embroidery. To keep the fabric from fraying during any lengthy embroidering process, finish off the raw edges, using one of the methods shown below.

Use masking tape over raw edges of fabric.

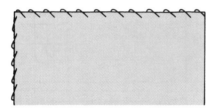

Overcast raw edges by hand to prevent fraying.

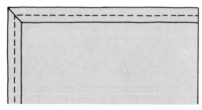

Machine straight-stitch along turned edges.

Machine zigzag raw edges for easy finish.

Transferring designs

Transfer of a design to a fabric can be accomplished by any of three different methods. The first, and probably the easiest, is to use a **hot-iron transfer**, which is simply a printed, heat-sensitive pattern. When the pattern is placed against the fabric and heat from an iron is applied, the design comes off on to the fabric. Commercial hot-iron transfers are produced in a variety of designs. Though most hot-iron transfers are good for only a single printing, there are some specially made to be used more than once. If you prefer to use a design of your own, you can make your own hot-iron transfer with a special transfer pencil (see opposite page).

Another method of design transfer involves the use of **dressmaker's carbon** and a tracing wheel. Do not confuse this type of carbon with typing carbon paper, which can smear badly. The method is basically the same as that used to transfer pattern markings in standard sewing procedures. Dressmaker's carbon is suitable for marking only very smooth fabrics.

Pouncing is one of the oldest and still an effective means of transferring a design. Little holes are pricked along the outline of the design pattern, which is then laid over the fabric and rubbed with *pounce powder*. This is available from artists' suppliers, and is sometimes known as 'inking' powder. When the pattern is lifted away, a fine dotted line remains on the fabric. The dotted lines are then drawn over with a dressmaker's pencil; on fabrics that cannot be pencilled (such as velvet), this step can be done with a fine paintbrush and opaque watercolours. The pricked patterns can be used more than once, and are especially suited to slightly textured fabrics. This method is also suitable for transferring quilting designs.

With all methods of transferring, be sure that the pattern design is properly placed on the fabric (see right).

PLACING DESIGN

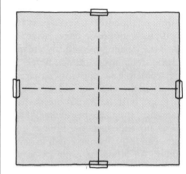

Fold and quarter fabric; crease along folds. If crease will not hold, tack centre foldlines. Pin or tape fabric to flat surface.

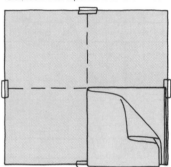

Fold and quarter pattern (design should be centred). Place pattern in one quarter of fabric, centre points aligned.

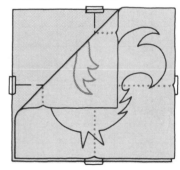

Carefully open out pattern so foldlines match crease lines of fabric. Anchor pattern down, then transfer design.

HOT-IRON TRANSFERS

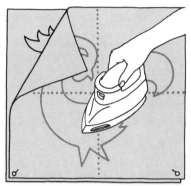

To make your own hot-iron transfer, copy design on heavy tracing paper. Turn paper to back and trace over lines with transfer pencil. With traced side down on fabric, press transfer as described on the right. A wax crayon can be used as a transfer pencil, but usually produces a thick line, so it is recommended only for large designs on coarse fabrics.

To use hot-iron transfer, first cut off any waste lettering and test on scrap of fabric. If test piece takes, position main transfer face down on fabric, and pin at corners. Turn iron to low setting and press down on transfer for a few seconds; lift, then move to next area. Do not glide iron over transfer. Lift up corner to make sure transfer is taking.

DRESSMAKER'S CARBON

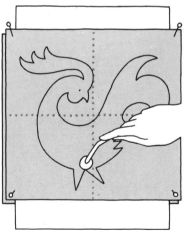

To use dressmaker's carbon, position pattern right side up on fabric, and pin at each corner. Carefully slip carbon paper, carbon side down, between fabric and pattern.

Draw over design lines of pattern, using a tracing wheel. You may find that a knitting needle, used like a pencil, will give you more control when you are drawing over lines.

POUNCING METHODS

To transfer a design by pouncing method, lay pattern on a thick wad of fabric (an old blanket will do). Using a sharp pin or stiletto prick along design lines of pattern; keep holes close together. **To speed up the work,** use your sewing machine. Remove top and bobbin threads, and set stitch length to large. Stitch along the design lines.

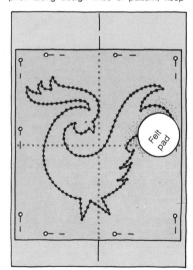

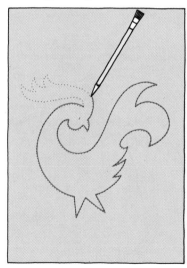

Position design, right side up, on fabric, and pin along all edges. Using a small roll or pad of felt, gently rub pounce (special powder for the purpose) over pricked holes.

Remove pattern carefully to avoid smudging the pounce. Gently blow off excess powder. Use dressmaker's pencil, or a fine brush and water-colour, to connect dots.

General embroidery techniques

Using an embroidery hoop

The purpose of an embroidery hoop is to hold the fabric taut during stitching, so that stitch tension can be kept even and consistent. Hoops may be made of wood or plastic, and are available in different widths and diameter sizes ranging from 10 cm to 30 cm. Both wood and plastic hoops usually have a screw on the outer ring for adjusting the fit as necessary.

To secure the fabric in a hoop, follow the instructions below, making certain that fabric grain is running straight in both directions. When you think the fabric is properly secured, tap it lightly; it should feel like a drum. To protect delicate fabrics, or stitches already worked, use either tissue paper or the tape method, shown bottom right. To secure fabric firmly, even if frame is warped, bind both inner and outer rings with tape.

Although there is no set rule as to which part of a design to centre first, always try to get a full motif within the hoop. For example, if your design is of a flower garden, try centring one full flower within the hoop. If the flower is too large, centre only a portion of it, like three complete petals. Small embroidery motifs can be worked in a hoop if backstitched at the edges to pieces of fabric.

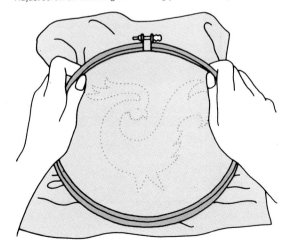

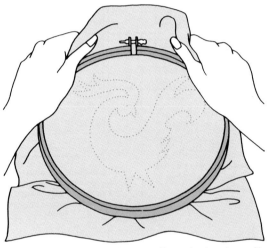

Outer ring

Inner ring

1. With the design side up, place fabric over inner ring of hoop. Adjust screw on outer ring so it fits snugly over inner ring and fabric.

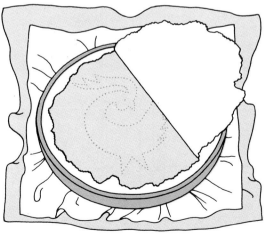

2. Move slowly around the hoop, pushing outer ring down with heels of hands while pulling fabric taut between thumb and fingers.

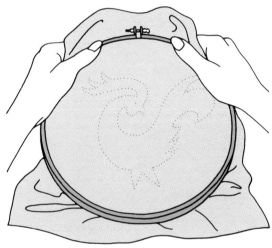

3. Pulling on fabric can make outer ring ride up. To correct this, push outer ring down over inner ring until it is secure.

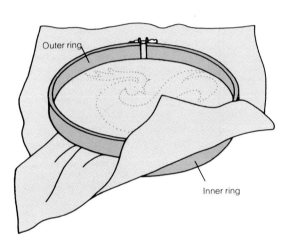

4. Always release fabric from hoop before storing. Press down fabric at edges of hoop with thumbs, lifting outer ring at same time.

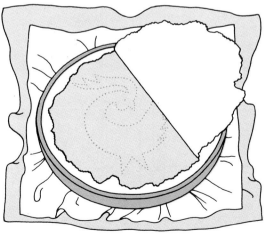

To protect fabric or stitches pressed between rings, place tissue paper over fabric, then fit in hoop. Tear away paper as shown.

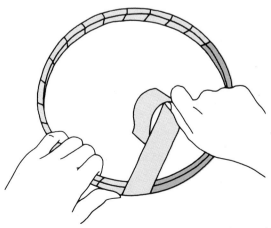

To prevent fine fabric from damage, wrap tape tightly around inner ring as shown; secure ends with masking tape.

18

Preparing threads

Working threads should be no longer than 50 cm; a longer thread, pulled too often through the fabric, tends to fray and lose its sheen towards the end.

Stranded cotton and Persian wool are both loosely twisted threads that can be separated into finer strands (see below for separating techniques). It is best to separate these threads as you need them rather than all at once.

The first step, for either stranded cotton or Persian wool, is to separate from the total strands the number that you want to work with.

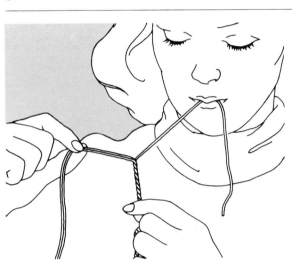

To separate stranded cotton, after dividing strands as shown above, hold one group of strands in your mouth, the other in one hand. Hold rest of cotton length with your free hand. Then gently pull the divided strands apart, moving your free hand slowly down the cotton length to control its twisting action.

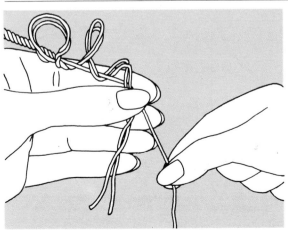

When strands of Persian wool have been undone as in top illustration, lay the wool over your left hand; gently pull out a small quantity of the selected strand with your right hand. Stop, then straighten the remaining strands of wool with left hand to keep them from tangling. Continue pulling and straightening in this way until the entire length is separated.

Threading the needle

There are several ways to simplify needle threading. One is to use a **needle threader,** a handy device specially designed for the purpose. If a threader is not available, try either the **paper strip** or the **looping** method below. Whichever method you choose, be sure that the selected thread can ride easily through the eye of the needle, but not so easily that it will constantly slip out.

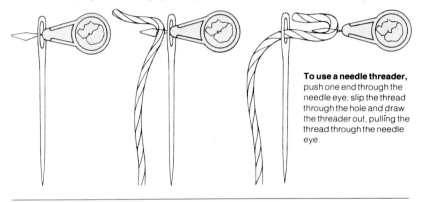

To use a needle threader, push one end through the needle eye; slip the thread through the hole and draw the threader out, pulling the thread through the needle eye.

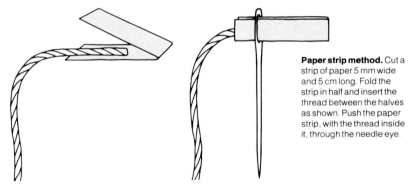

Paper strip method. Cut a strip of paper 5 mm wide and 5 cm long. Fold the strip in half and insert the thread between the halves as shown. Push the paper strip, with the thread inside it, through the needle eye.

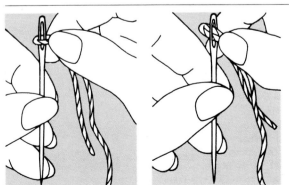

Loop method. Loop end of thread over eye of needle and pull it tight. Slip the loop off the needle and force the fold of the thread through the needle eye.

19

General embroidery techniques

Working embroidery

Above all else, it takes patience and care to create a successful piece of embroidery. Nothing else will produce the characteristic effects in the stitches that make up the design. You should aim for stitches that are executed at just the right tension, and a finished result that is neat and even on the wrong as well as the right side. The illustrations on the right will help you to reach these goals. Some techniques may seem awkward at first, but they will become easier as practice makes you more proficient.

When you are starting or ending a length of thread, never use a knot; it might show through the finished piece or cause lumps on the right side. This is especially true if your embroidery is to be framed. The adjoining illustrations suggest ways of securing thread at the beginning and end. Do not skimp on thread in either process; the ends can begin to work loose after a few washings.

Whether you use an embroidery hoop or a frame, make the most use you can of both hands as you work. You will find the stabbing motion easier to master when your hoop or frame is on a stand – it frees both hands for the push and pull of the needle action.

Before you start to embroider, study your design carefully and notice which of its parts appear to lie on top of other parts. Work first the parts that lie lowest (furthest down), then work the elements above these so that the two overlap. This will give your piece a realistic effect, and also avoid the possibility of fabric showing between parts.

If you are working on one area of the design and would like to move to another in which the same colour thread is used, it is best to secure the thread at the first point and start again rather than trail the thread over a wide space.

Follow the transferred design lines precisely, remembering that they are guides and are not meant to be seen when the embroidery is completed.

STARTING AND ENDING

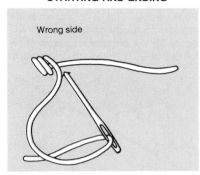

To secure thread at the start of stitching, hold the end of the thread on the wrong side of the fabric and work stitches over 5 cm of thread end.

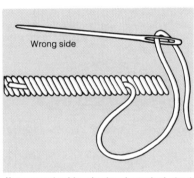

If some embroidery is already worked, simply slide needle under wrong side of laid stitches, securing 5 cm of thread end under the stitching.

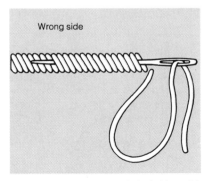

To secure thread at the end of stitching, slide the needle under 5 cm of laid stitches on the wrong side and then cut the thread.

HANDLING NEEDLE

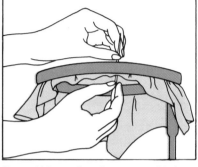

Use stabbing motion whenever possible·for an even tension. Push needle straight down and pull thread through, then bring needle straight up.

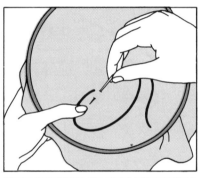

For looped stitches (like chain), bring needle up before thread is pulled through, and use free hand to guide thread around needle.

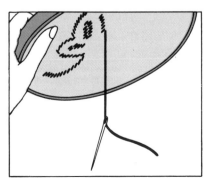

Twisting and tangling often occur with constant needle action. Let needle drop occasionally and dangle freely until thread unwinds.

FOLLOWING DESIGN LINES

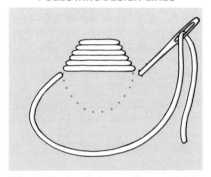

When following design markings on fabric, insert needle on the outside edge of transferred line so that all markings are completely covered.

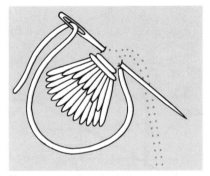

For greater realism in design, work first the parts that lie lowest, then work the parts that lie above them so that the two overlap slightly.

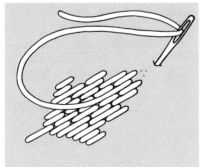

For finer definition of pointed shapes (such as a leaf tip as shown), exaggerate the point by extending the stitch past the transferred line.

Embroidery stitches

Selecting embroidery stitches

Embroidery stitches are the basic components with which a design is carried out. Although the number may seem unlimited, actually each stitch is a part of a stitch family and, as such, has its origin in the basic family stitch. There are 11 such family groups; the pages that follow give step-by-step illustrations for each stitch in each group.

To help you understand the family relationship of one stitch to another, and to provide a means of practicing the stitches, we suggest that you work a sampler of all or some of the stitches you will see on the following pages. You can then keep the sampler as a stitch "dictionary" for future reference or, if you prefer, you can finish it to use as a decorative wall hanging.

Embroidery stitches are used in basically two ways: they either *outline* or *fill*

in a particular shape in a design. The shape can be solidly filled so that none of the fabric shows through, or it can be filled with opened stitches for a lacy effect. Some stitches have natural configurations or textures that make them ideal for particular effects. An example is the Vandyke stitch (see p. 38), which gives a natural impression of a leaf when it is worked.

When you make your first attempt at stitch selection, try to limit your choice to a few stitches, and remember that there is no "right" combination of stitches for a design, only one that pleases you and carries out the design to your satisfaction. Notice how the design below has been interpreted in two different ways. Both are lovely pieces, yet each of them was worked with a totally different stitch combination.

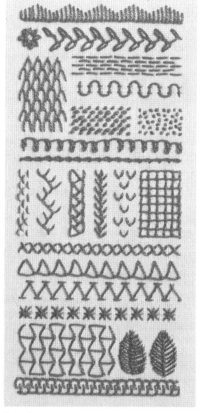

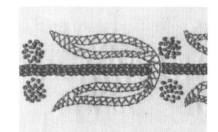

Different stitch interpretations of the identical design can produce two very different impressions.

Sampler can serve as a "dictionary" of stitches.

Charting your design

Prepare a guide for your embroidery work by mapping out a chart that indicates the selected stitches as well as the yarn colors for each part of the design. Use your original traced drawing as the basis for the chart. First assign a *letter* to each stitch and list those stitch symbols at the side. Then print the identifying letters on the appropriate parts of the drawing. Indicate with simple pencil lines the direction in which each stitch will be worked. If colors are not present in your drawing, color-code the yarns in

a similar way: assign a *number* to each colored yarn and put the numbers on the appropriate parts of the drawing. If there are any other variables, such as the number of yarn strands that are to be used with each stitch, indicate those in your list as well. An example of a charted design is shown below.

A – Long and short stitch	1 – Pale orange
B – Wave stitch	2 – Lavender
C – Basic satin stitch	3 – Black
D – Threaded chain stitch	4 – Tan

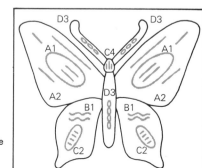

Embroidery stitches

Backstitches

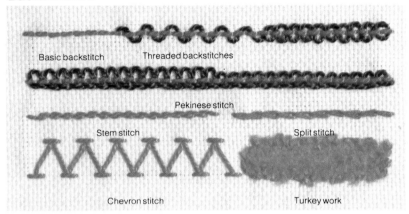

Basic backstitch

Threaded backstitches

Pekinese stitch

Stem stitch

Split stitch

Chevron stitch

Turkey work

Though all of the stitches in the back-stitch group have their own distinctive look, they are related in the stitching motion that produces a stitch row. In every case, the needle must be moved a step backwards before a step is taken forwards along the stitch row. This is true whether stitches are being worked from left to right or from right to left.

Some of the stitches shown are narrow, and so are ideal for outlining. In general, *basic backstitch* is used to outline areas bounded by straight lines, and *stem* and *split* stitches are preferred when the boundary line is curved. Worked in close rows, these thin stitches can be used to fill an area. Some of the other stitches, such as *chevron* and *threaded backstitches*, are wider, and therefore suitable for decorative borders and bands. Most of the stitches shown are flat and not highly textured; the exception is *Turkey work*, which creates a soft pile when trimmed.

When working each stitch, be sure to follow carefully the sequence of steps. Because of the backward movement, the needle will often re-enter at a point already established by a previous step; it is important in these instances to insert the needle exactly in the hole that was previously made.

Basic backstitch is most often used as a straight outline stitch. Its simple line effect is often seen in blackwork embroidery. This stitch also forms the base line for other decorative stitches. Work basic stitch from right to left. Bring needle out at 1. Insert at 2 and come up at 3; distance between 3-1 and 1-2 should be equal. Repeat sequence for next stitch; needle entering at point 2 should go into hole made by thread emerging from point 1 of previous stitch. Keep length of backstitches consistent.

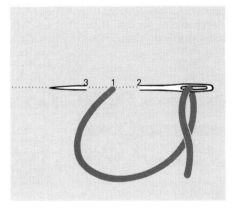
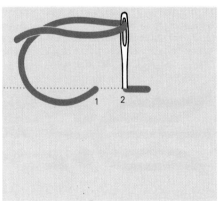
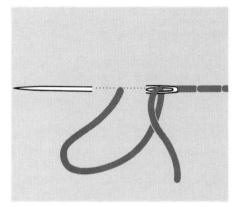

Single or double-threaded backstitches add another dimension to the basic stitch. Worked in contrasting threads, each new row can alter the overall effect. Lay down basic backstitch first. To work *single-threaded* line, use a blunt needle to lace the thread under each stitch; do not catch fabric below. To work *double-threaded* line, lace second thread in opposite direction, keeping loops even on both sides of backstitch line. do not catch or split threads already laid.

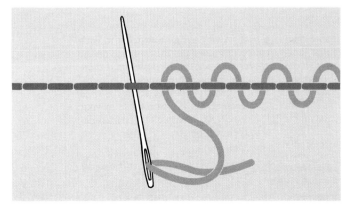
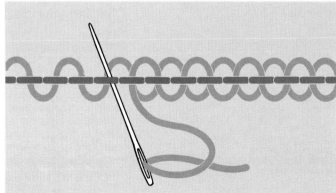

Pekinese stitch (also known as Chinese stitch), like the threaded backstitches, uses simple backstitch as a base. Its interlacing technique, however, produces an effect reminiscent of braid. The stitch is often used for outlining and for decorative borders. Lay down the basic backstitch first. Then, using a blunt needle, lace thread under laid stitches as shown; do not catch fabric below, and keep loops even. Lacing threads can be pulled tighter to eliminate loops above the base line for an even finer braid-like effect.

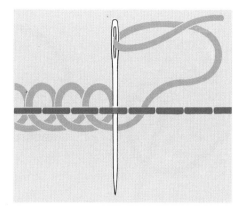 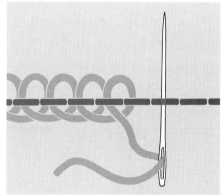 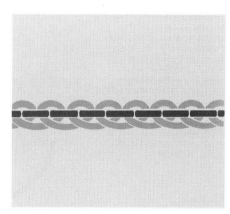

Stem stitch is primarily an outlining stitch, but is often used to work stems. Working from left to right, bring needle out at 1. Insert at 2 and come up a half stitch length back at 3; distance 1-3 and 3-2 should be equal. Repeat sequence. Note that point 3 of previous stitch is now point 1, and the needle emerging at 3 is coming from hole made by thread entering at point 2 of the previous stitch. For a broader stem stitch, angle the needle slightly when entering at 2 and coming up at 3, as shown in the last drawing.

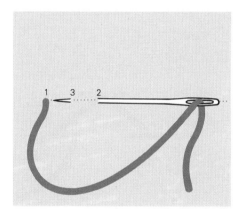 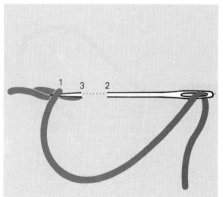 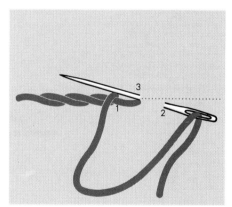

Split stitch is worked like the stem stitch, except when the needle emerges, it splits the working thread. Although outlining is its most common use, split stitch can be used in solid rows as well. Working stitch from left to right, bring needle up at 1 and down at 2. Bring needle back up at 3, splitting centre of laid thread. Repeat sequence. Note that point 3 of previous stitch is now point 1. Keep stitch length even; when going around curves, shorten length slightly. A soft untwisted thread is essential for this stitch.

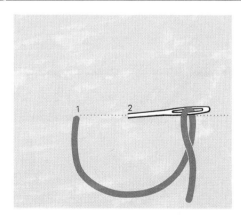 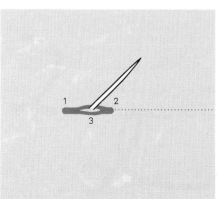 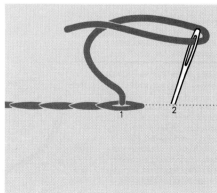

Embroidery stitches

Backstitches

Chevron stitch is often used as a decorative border. The stitch is worked from left to right between double lines. To work stitch, bring needle up at 1 along bottom line. Insert at 2; come up a half stitch length back at 3. Insert needle at point 4 and bring up at 5 along top line; distance between 4-5 is equal to a half stitch length. Bring needle down at 6 (whole stitch length from 5) and back out again at point 4.

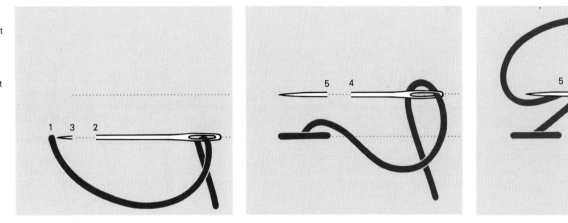

To position needle for repeat, insert needle at 7 on bottom line and come up a half stitch length back at 8; distance between 4-7 is same as 3-4. Continue this 1 to 8 sequence. Note that point 8 is point 1 at start of new sequence.

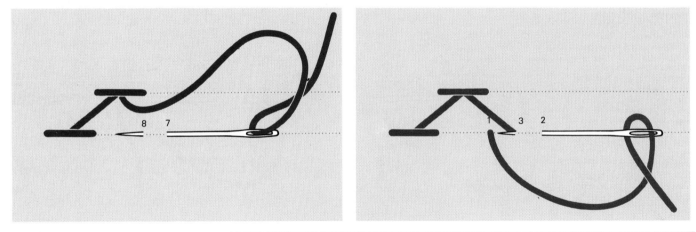

Turkey work is made up of backstitches alternately pulled tight and looped. A series of rows forms a pile, which may be trimmed for a more shaggy effect. Stitch is worked from left to right. Bring the needle out at 1. Insert it at 2 and come up a half stitch length back at 3. Insert the needle at 4, a full stitch length away from 3, and bring it back up at 2; carry thread above stitch line and leave a short loop. Proceed with next backstitch, carrying thread below the stitch line.

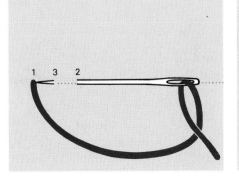

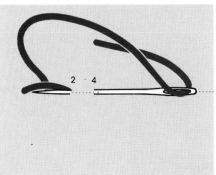

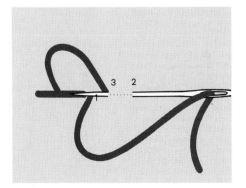

Continue sequence with another looped stitch, then a stitch pulled tight, alternately until row is completed. Cover entire design area with the Turkey work, starting from the top and working towards the bottom. If existing loops get in the way, pin them down. For shaggy pile, cut loops. Do not cut each row individually; instead, trim the entire area at once to a uniform length.

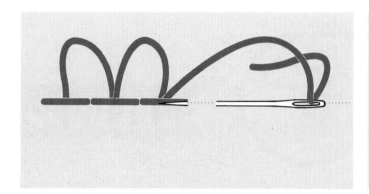

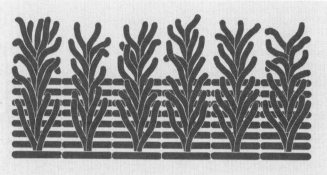

Blanket stitches

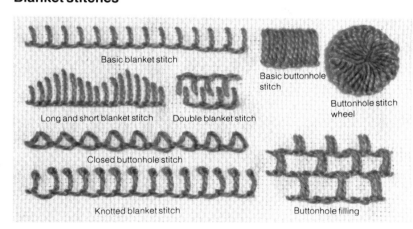

Basic blanket stitch

Long and short blanket stitch   Double blanket stitch

Closed buttonhole stitch

Knotted blanket stitch

Basic buttonhole stitch

Buttonhole stitch wheel

Buttonhole filling

Blanket stitches, which consist basically of edging stitches, comprise the next stitch group. The name probably derived from the finishing worked around the edges of woollen blankets. Today, however, these stitches are often used as outlines and as functional decorative borders as well. One in particular, *buttonhole filling,* can also be worked to cover an entire area, producing an almost crochet-like effect. Blanket stitches are basically flat stitches, neither raised nor textured, and can vary in size depending on the requirements of your design. Because of their adaptability to decorative purposes and the simplicity and speed of working them, they appear in many peasant embroideries, crazy patchwork and appliqué. They are especially useful in hemming embroidery and are also a popular finishing choice for non-woven fabrics, such as felt, that do not require a hem.

You will note that all blanket stitches have a scroll-like base with 'legs' extending from it. This base is formed by looping the thread under the point of the needle before the stitch is pulled up tight. Work carefully to keep stitch height even (unless otherwise specified) and to keep the scroll base at an even tension all the way across.

Basic blanket stitch is a popular finishing stitch for edges. When worked small, it can be used for outlining as well. Stitch is worked from left to right. Bring needle out at 1 on bottom line. Insert at 2 on top line and slightly to the right, then come up at 3, directly below. Before pulling needle through, carry thread under point of needle as shown. Proceed to next stitch. Note point 3 of previous stitch is now point 1. Work entire row in the same way, keeping height of stitches even throughout.

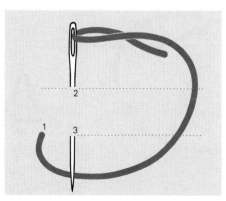

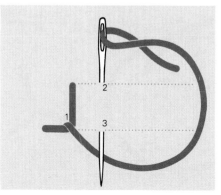

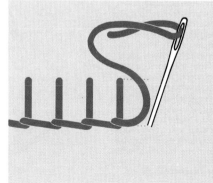

Embroidery stitches

Blanket stitches

Variations of blanket stitch.
The first variation is called *long and short blanket stitch*. It is worked exactly like the basic stitch except that heights of stitches range from short to tall, creating a pyramid effect. *Double blanket stitch* is simply two rows of the basic stitch. Work is turned after one row is completed so that the stitches of the second row can fall between the stitches of the first. Both rows should be the same height and should overlap slightly at the centre.

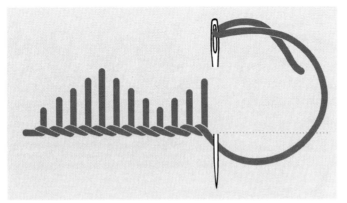 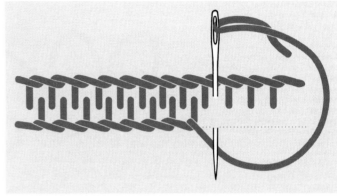

Basic buttonhole stitch is worked like basic blanket stitch, except that the stitches are placed very close together to form a firm edge. This tight little band of stitches is used extensively in cutwork embroidery. For added firmness along an edge, a row of split stitches (p. 23) can be laid along the bottom line first. A *buttonhole stitch wheel* is a popular method for working circular motifs. The basic buttonhole stitch is worked in a circle with the needle entering the same hole in the centre each time.

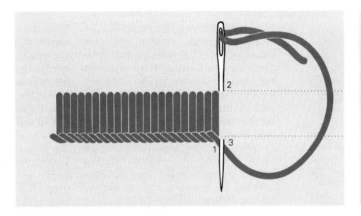 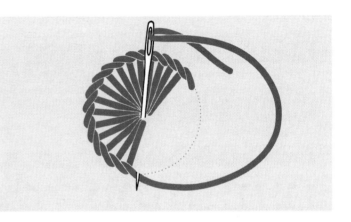

Closed buttonhole stitch is a decorative edging that is worked from left to right. The extending 'legs' form small triangles along the row. Bring needle out at 1 on bottom line. Insert at 2 on top line, slightly to the right, then come up at 3 on bottom line. Before pulling needle through, carry thread under needle point. To complete triangle, insert needle back into 2 again and come out at 4, carrying thread below needle point as usual. Continue sequence as shown. Note that point 4 of the previous stitch is now point 1.

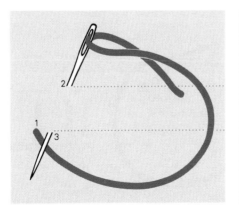 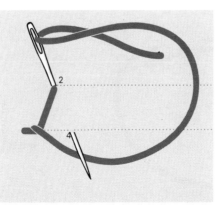 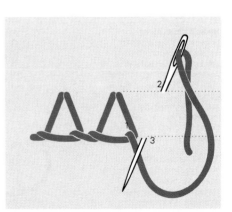

Buttonhole filling consists of several stitched rows that produce a lacy effect. Pairs of buttonhole stitches mesh between other pairs in the row above. (If desired, a group can be three or four stitches.) The buttonhole filling is first worked from left to right, then right to left on the next row. Work the first pair of stitches close together; start the second pair two spaces (width of two stitches) to the right. Continue this way to end of row. Insert needle at end of bottom line, then bring it out at next line directly below to start next row.

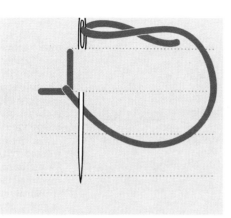 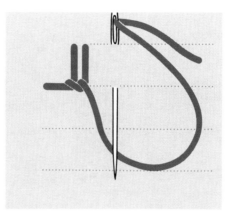 

Work the next row from right to left. The basic 1 to 3 buttonhole stitch sequence is still used, but now the thread is carried under the needle point from right to left as shown. Work the pairs of buttonhole stitches over the open spaces on the row above. At end of second row, insert needle in bottom line, then out at next line directly below. Continue working rows in this way until desired area is covered.

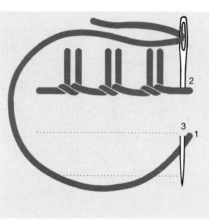 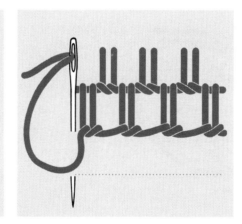 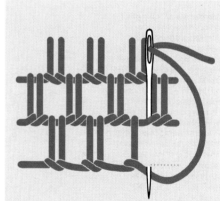

Knotted blanket stitch resembles basic blanket stitch, but with a knot formed at the top of each 'leg'. Working from left to right, bring needle out at 1. Wrap thread around left thumb and place needle point under loop. Slip loop off thumb. With needle inside loop, insert needle at 2 and come up at 3; carry thread under needle point, then pull thread end to tighten loop around needle. Pull needle through to form knot at top of stitch. Continue along entire row. Worked back to back this stitch makes an attractive tree design (see far right).

 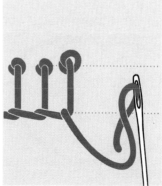 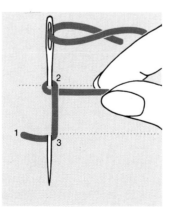 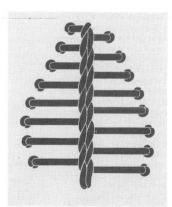

Embroidery stitches

Chain stitches

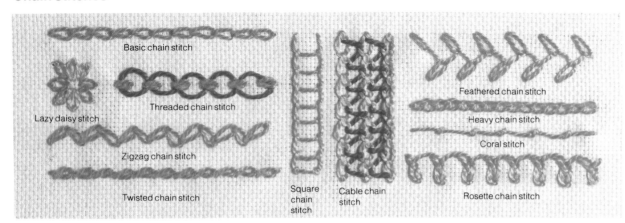

Basic chain stitch
Lazy daisy stitch
Threaded chain stitch
Zigzag chain stitch
Twisted chain stitch
Square chain stitch
Cable chain stitch
Feathered chain stitch
Heavy chain stitch
Coral stitch
Rosette chain stitch

Most of the stitches in this group resemble links in a chain. Each stitch has its own special shape and particular use, but together they form one of the most indispensable of the stitch groups. Chain stitches, like the blanket stitch group, are looped. The working thread is always carried under the needle point before the stitch is pulled tight.

For the most part, these stitches are worked vertically and are used basically for outlining and for decorative borders. If worked in rows to fill an area, all rows are usually stitched in the same direction to give a fabric-like texture. Chain stitch is worked more easily out of a frame.

Basic chain stitch is one of the most popular embroidery stitches for outlining or, if worked in close rows, for filling an area. Bring needle out at 1. Insert back into same hole at point 1 and bring out at 2, carrying thread under needle point, then pull it through. Point 2 is now point 1 of next stitch. Work all stitches the same way, always inserting needle into the hole made by the emerging thread. To end row, take a small stitch over last chain loop to hold it down.

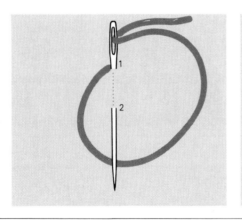
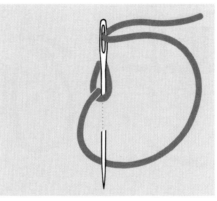
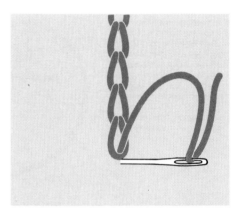

Lazy daisy stitch (or detached chain) is a single unattached stitch, often worked in a circle to give an impression of petals. Bring needle out at 1. Insert back into same hole at point 1, and come up at 2; carry thread under needle point, then pull through. Insert needle at 3 over chain loop, then bring needle out at point 1 for next chain stitch. Continue this way until all petals are completed. Stitches may be scattered at random over an area, provided thread does not have to be carried too far on wrong side.

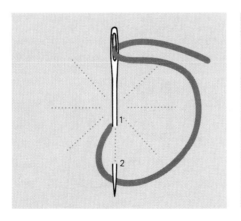
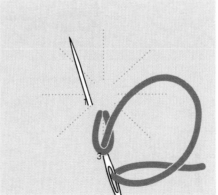

28

Threaded chain stitch
resembles a chain with two link sizes. To achieve this double link effect, detached chain stitches are threaded with a contrasting thread. This makes a pretty border or outline stitch. First work a row of detached chain stitches. Using a blunt needle and contrasting thread, bring needle up under last chain. Lace thread back and forth under each chain; do not catch fabric. Start again at bottom and lace in opposite direction, keeping loops even on both sides of the detached chain stitches.

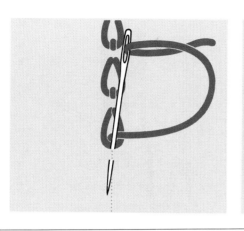 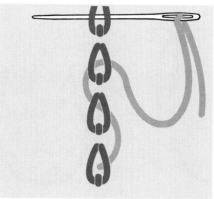 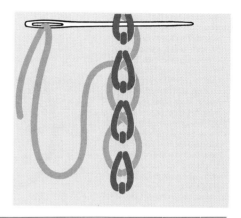

Zigzag chain stitch is worked with the chains positioned at alternating angles to give a decorative zigzag effect. Work first stitch exactly like a basic chain stitch, angling it as shown between double lines. The hole from which thread emerges becomes point 1 for next stitch. Insert needle at 2, piercing loop end to anchor it, and come up at 3; carry thread under needle point, then pull through. Continue sequence, always piercing loop end and keeping angle of stitches consistent. To end, take small stitch over last chain loop.

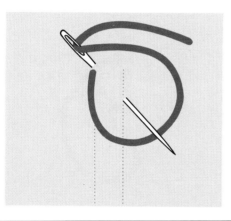 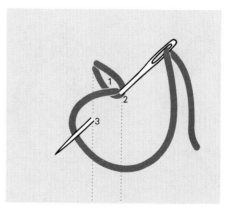 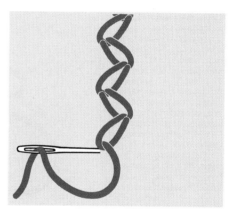

Twisted chain stitch makes an unusual textured outline. To work, bring needle out at 1. Insert needle at 2, which is slightly lower and to the left of 1, then come up at 3, which is in line with 1; carry thread under point of needle, then pull through. Work next stitch the same way. Note that point 3 of previous stitch is point 1 of new stitch. Complete row of chains. To end, take a small stitch over the last chain loop to hold it down.

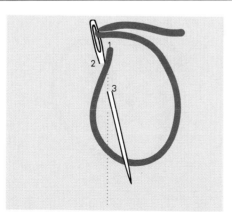 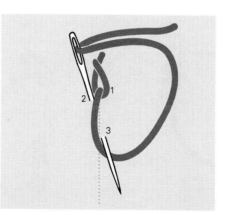 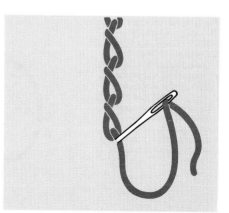

Embroidery stitches

Chain stitches

Square chain stitch (or ladder stitch) provides broad outline that may be laced with ribbon or thread. Stitch is worked between double lines. Bring needle out at 1 on left line. Insert at 2, directly across, and come up at 3; carry thread under needle point, then pull through. Do not pull thread tight; leave some slack so that needle can be inserted inside wide loop for next stitch. Continue this way until row is completed. To anchor last chain, take a small stitch over left side of loop, then take a small stitch over right side.

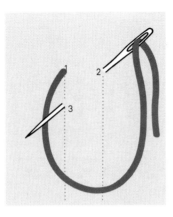 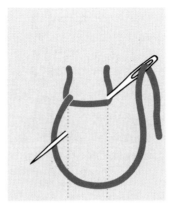 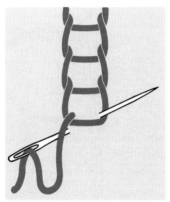 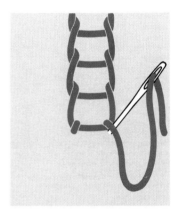

Cable chain stitch resembles a metal chain. It can be used for outlining or interlaced for a filling as in the last illustration. Bring needle out at 1. Loop thread over needle as shown. Insert needle at 2, just below point 1, and come up at 3; carry thread under needle point. As you pull needle through, both small and large links are formed. Continue this way until the row is completed. To interlace, work several rows of cable chain stitch, then use a blunt needle with contrasting thread to weave in and out.

 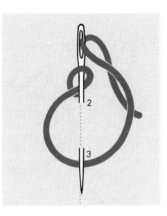  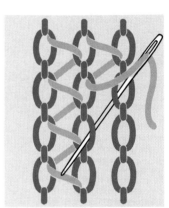

Feathered chain stitch is a delicate border stitch that resembles a vine. It is worked between double lines. Starting at one side of double line, work a slanted chain stitch in the basic 1 to 2 sequence shown. Insert needle at 3, then bring it back up at 4, approximately across from 2. Work subsequent chain stitches the same way, keeping alternating slants of chains consistent on each side.

 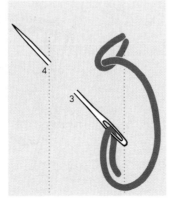  

Heavy chain stitch makes a pretty outline stitch. Because of its plait-like quality, it can also be used for stems, twigs and narrow leaves. To start, work a basic chain stitch by bringing needle out at 1, then inserting needle back in same hole and coming up at 2. Insert needle down at 3 over chain loop, then come back up at 4, which is same distance from 2 as 1 is from 2. Slide needle under first chain stitch from right to left without picking up any fabric. Re-insert needle at 4, and come up at 5.

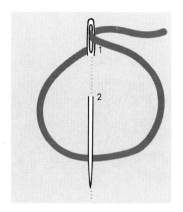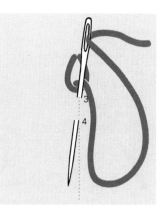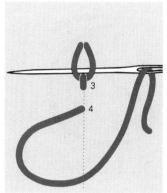

Slide needle from right to left under the second chain stitch and the small anchoring stitch, then re-insert needle at 5, and bring out at 6. Slide needle from right to left under the two preceding chain stitches as shown, then re-insert needle at 6. Continue in this way, always sliding needle under the last two chain stitches.

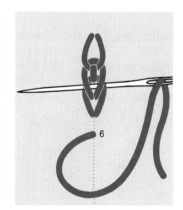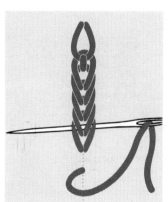

Coral stitch is a simple outline stitch, punctuated with small knots along the row. It is particularly effective used for stems and twigs. If worked in many rows, coral stitch can also fill an area with an unusual texture. Work stitch from right to left. Bring needle up at 1. Insert needle at 2, then take a small bite of fabric slanting needle out at 3. Loop thread over and around needle point, then pull needle through to secure stitch and form knot. Continue in this way for entire row, spacing knots evenly or at random as you wish.

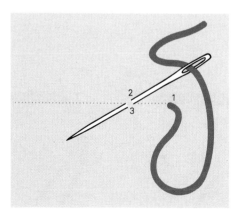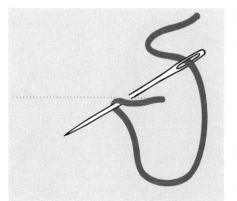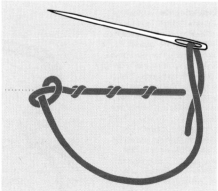

Embroidery stitches

Chain stitches

Rosette chain stitch, a neat edging, is worked small and close together. Work stitch from right to left between double lines. Bring needle out at 1. To make rosette, insert at 2, slightly to the left, then out at 3 directly below; carry thread under needle and pull through. Slide needle under thread at 1; leave a little slack along top. Work next stitch a short distance away, entering at 2 and coming up at 3; slide needle under slack thread at top. To end row, insert needle back into point 2 of last rosette.

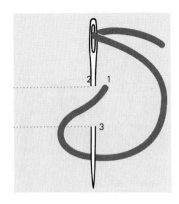 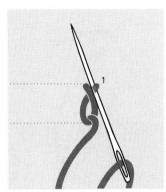 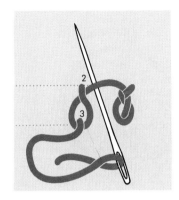 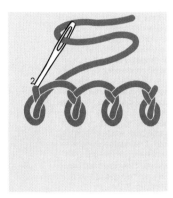

Couching

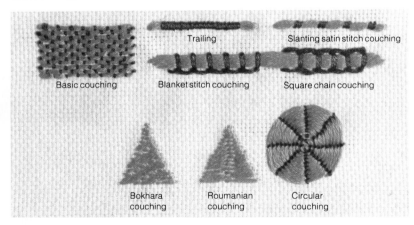

Trailing

Slanting satin stitch couching

Basic couching

Blanket stitch couching

Square chain couching

Bokhara couching

Roumanian couching

Circular couching

This group of stitches, known as couching stitches, is particularly useful in outlining an area or in giving more weight to a single line. Usually, there are two working threads, the laid thread (which can be one or more strands) and the couching thread. The couching thread is stitched over the laid thread to attach it to the fabric. Often the laid thread and the couching thread are of contrasting colours. The actual effect of couching varies with the specific stitch and the number of laid threads that are used.

The more strands you lay down, the heavier the outline. Experiment to determine how many strands should be laid. You will need more strands to outline a heavily embroidered shape than to define a delicate pattern.

In addition to outlining, whole areas can be filled in with couching. This is known as laid work. To create textural variety, lay the threads so that they run in different directions.

Two unusual types of couching are *Bokhara* and *Roumanian*. Both employ only one length of thread for both the laying and the couching.

To create more unusual effects, couch over finished canvas work and appliqué. Or try couching with suitable metallic threads.

Basic couching is used to outline a design. To start, bring up desired number of laid threads on right. Use left thumb to hold and guide laid threads as you couch over them. Bring working thread up at 1 just below laid threads. Insert at 2 directly above laid threads, and come up at 3 further along the line. Point 3 is now point 1 for next stitch. Continue until laid threads are completely anchored; keep distance between stitches consistent. Take ends of laid threads to back of work and secure.

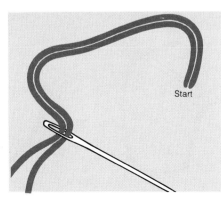 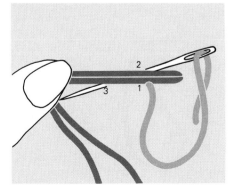 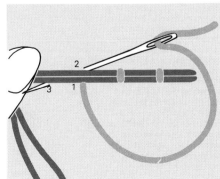

Start

To fill an area, work first line as in basic couching. At end of line, turn trailing laid threads to the right. Take a horizontal stitch at turning point. Turn work *upside-down* and couch second row of threads from right to left, placing stitches between stitches of preceding row. At end of second row, turn trailing laid threads to the right and again take a horizontal stitch. Turn work *upright* and work third row, alternating vertical stitches with those in the row above. Continue this way until entire area is covered.

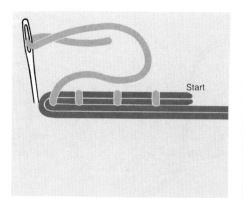 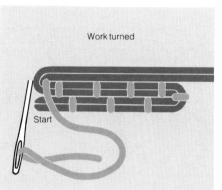 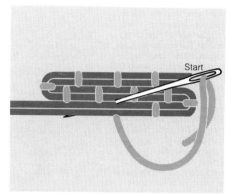

Variations can be achieved by working some basic embroidery stitches over the laid threads. Four are shown on the right. The first is similar to basic couching except that *straight satin stitches* are worked close together to completely cover the laid threads; this produces a raised, textured line known as trailing. The next is couched with pairs of *slanting satin stitches.* The third and fourth types are couched with *blanket stitches* and *square chain stitches,* respectively, over several laid threads.

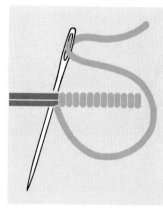 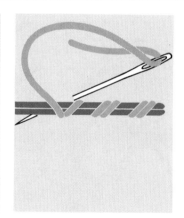 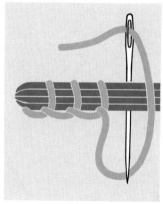 

Bokhara couching is used to fill an area with a woven effect. Unlike the previous couching, both the laid and the couching threads are one and the same. The thread is laid from left to right and couched from right to left. Bring thread up at 1. Insert at 2, and come up at 3 above laid thread. Insert needle at 4 over laid thread and slightly to the left of 3. Come up at 5 (in line with 3). Continue slanted stitches to end of laid thread. Bring needle out at 1 to begin next row. Place slanted stitches in each row between those in previous row.

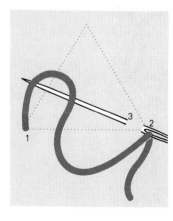 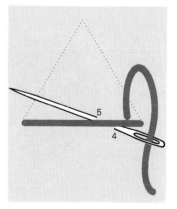 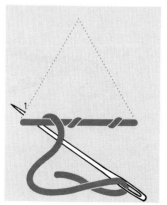 

33

Embroidery stitches

Couching

Roumanian couching, like Bokhara, uses same thread length for laid and couching threads. The two stitches are worked similarly, but the Roumanian stitches are longer. Bring thread up at 1. Insert at 2, come up at 3 above laid thread. Take a long slanting stitch over laid thread to 4; come up at 1 for start of next row. Continue taking laid and couching stitches, keeping threads slack so that the two stitch types appear indistinguishable. Place each new slanting stitch above one in previous row.

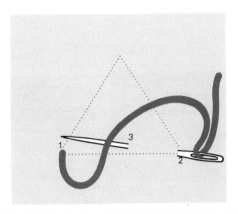
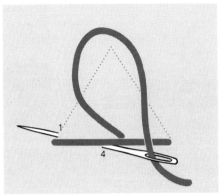
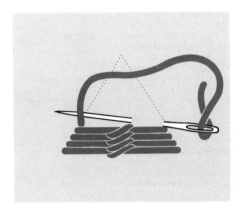

Circular couching produces a solid spoked-wheel effect. It is particularly effective in contrasting threads. Bring couching thread up at 1 in centre of marked circle. Loop laid thread over couching thread as shown, and re-insert needle at 1 to secure laid thread. Bring needle out at 2 along one of the spoke lines, then take a small stitch over the laid threads by inserting needle at 3 directly above 2. Bring needle out at 4 along next spoke line. Take another stitch at 5 over laid threads.

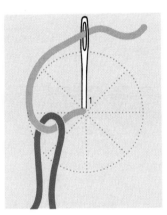
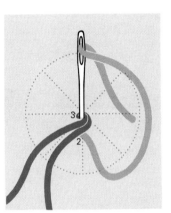
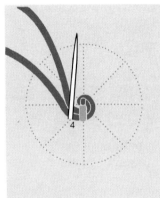
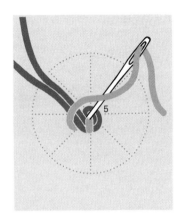

Continue taking small stitches over laid threads at each marked spoke line while guiding the laid threads around centre in a clockwise direction. Be careful not to pull laid threads too tightly or work will pucker. When circle is completed, fasten off couching thread on wrong side. Thread one of the laid threads; take to back of fabric and secure. Thread second laid thread and wind around circle past end of first laid thread (to make circle end gradually). Take to back and secure as before.

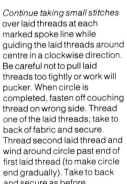
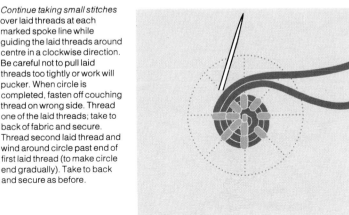

Cross stitches

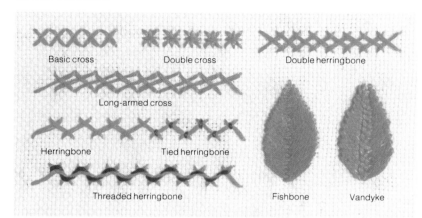

Basic cross   Double cross   Double herringbone

Long-armed cross

Herringbone   Tied herringbone

Threaded herringbone   Fishbone   Vandyke

Cross stitches make up the next group of embroidery stitches. As their name implies, all the stitches in this category are formed in one way or another by two crossing arms. The uses of cross stitches are numerous; they can be worked as outlines, as borders, or to fill in an entire area. Sometimes crossing stitches overlap, as in *herringbone stitches*. Two such overlapping stitches, *fishbone stitch* and *Vandyke stitch*, are particularly well suited to the formation of leaves.

The basic cross stitch is, of course, the best known stitch and in itself qualifies as an embroidery technique. Its even stitch formation makes it ideal for working on even-weave and printed fabrics, such as gingham (see p. 68). Unlike cross stitch variations, basic cross stitches (when worked in a row) can be stitched in two journeys. Half of the stitch is laid on one journey, then the crossing arm is laid on the return. This stitching technique helps to assure an even stitch tension. For a good appearance, make sure that all of the top threads lie in the same direction.

The basic cross stitch can be used to create an intaglio effect (see Assisi embroidery). This is a technique that involves covering the background, leaving the design free of stitching.

Basic cross stitch's simplicity and versatility make it a highly popular stitch. Cross stitches are usually *worked in rows* of even, slanted stitches, first from right to left laying down half the crosses, then back from left to right to complete them. Bring needle up at 1. Insert at 2 and come up at 3 directly below 2. At end of row, work back, entering at 4 and coming up at 5. To *work one cross stitch* at a time, bring needle up at 1. Insert at 2 and come up at 3 directly below 2. Insert needle at 4, above 1.

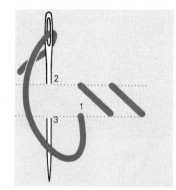  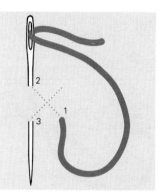 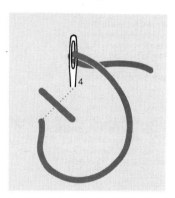

Double cross stitch resembles a star and can be scattered as a filling stitch or worked in a row to provide a decorative border. It is worked very similarly to the basic single cross stitch above. Bring needle out at 1. Insert at 2 and come up at 3 directly below 2. Enter at 4 and come up at 5 (halfway between points 1 and 3). Insert at 6 directly above 5 (halfway between points 2 and 4) and come up at 7 (halfway between 2 and 3). Insert at 8 directly across from 7 to complete stitch.

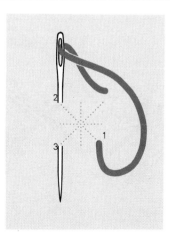 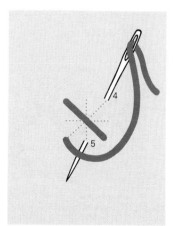 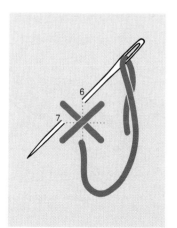 

Embroidery stitches

Cross stitches

Long-armed cross stitch
gives an almost plaited effect
as each cross stitch overlaps
the next. The first arm of the
cross is longer and has a more
extreme slant than the second.
Work stitch from left to right.
Bring needle up at 1. Take a
long slanting stitch to top right,
inserting needle at 2; come up
half a step back at 3. Insert
needle at 4 directly below point
2; then bring needle up at 1
directly below point 3, for start
of next stitch. Repeat sequence.
Note that each stitch touches
the previous one at the top
and overlaps it at the bottom.

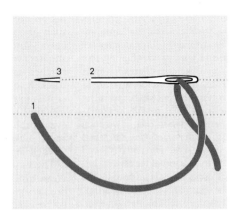
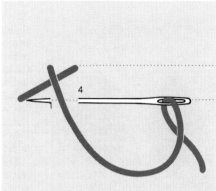
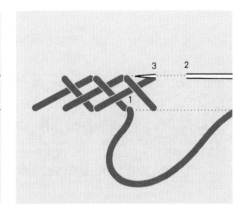

Herringbone stitch is a
popular embroidery stitch often
used for borders. This basic
overlapping stitch forms a
foundation that can be
decorated with a second
colour. Keep the spacing and
length of stitches even. Work
from left to right. Bring needle
up at 1. Take a slanting stitch to
the top right, inserting needle at
2. Come up a short distance
back at 3; insert needle at 4 to
complete stitch. Bring needle
up at 1 to start new stitch.
Repeat sequence for each
subsequent stitch.

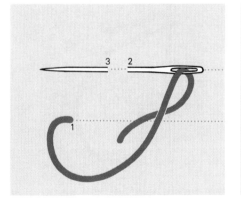
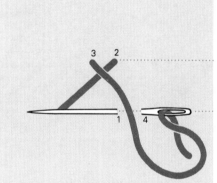
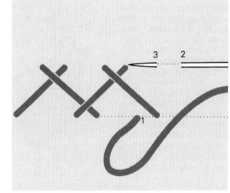

Tied herringbone stitch adds
another dimension to the basic
herringbone stitch above; each
cross of the stitch is tied down
with a small vertical stitch of a
contrasting colour thread.
Work a row of herringbone
stitch first, using the 1 to 4
sequence above. To tie down
crosses, work from right to left.
Bring needle out at A just above
top, right-hand cross. Insert at
B and come up at C below next
cross. Insert needle at D; come
up at point A for the start of a
new sequence. Continue in this
way until all crosses are tied
down.

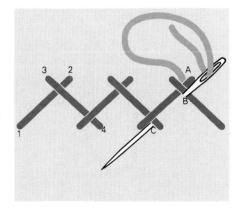
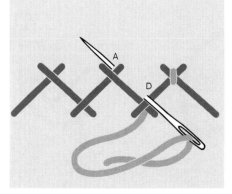
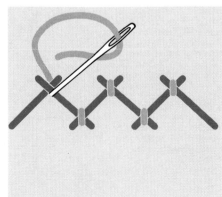

Threaded herringbone stitch is another variation of the basic herringbone stitch. Here, a contrasting colour thread is laced over and under the crosses. The needle does not pierce the fabric, so use a blunt needle for the lacing. Start lacing from the left side so that the needle passes under each arm of the cross and over the intersecting points as shown. Do not pull lacing too tightly or you will distort the basic herringbone stitch.

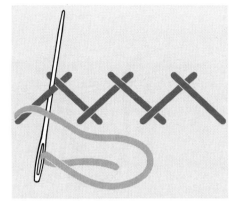
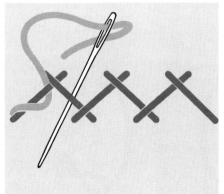
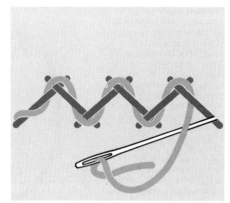

Double herringbone stitch is two rows of herringbone stitches that interlace. Rows worked in contrasting colours are especially attractive. For interlaced look, each row is worked slightly differently from herringbone stitch. Work both rows from left to right. Bring needle up at 1. Take a slanting stitch to top right, inserting needle at 2. Come up a short distance back at 3. Slip needle *under first slanting arm*. Insert at 4 to complete stitch. Repeat sequence, always slipping needle under first slanting arm of each cross.

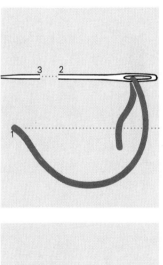
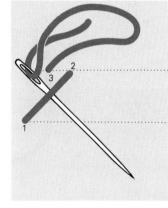

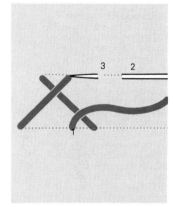

Change to contrasting thread. To get into position for second herringbone sequence, come out at A directly above point 1, and insert at B directly below point 2, crossing over arm 1-2 in original colour. Bring needle out at C directly below point 3, and pass needle under arm 3-4 (original colour). Insert needle at D and come up at E. Pass needle under arm C-D; insert at F. To complete sequence, bring needle out at C for start of next repeat. Continue, repeating sequence C to F, passing each time over and under appropriate slanting arms.

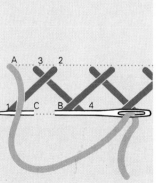
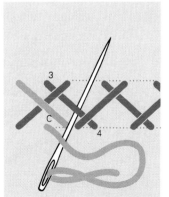
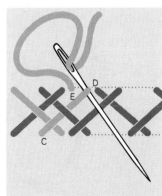
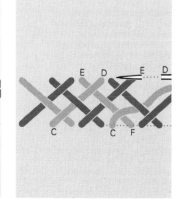

Embroidery stitches

Cross stitches

Fishbone stitch is a type of cross stitch used primarily for leaf designs. The crosses are not immediately evident because the crossing points occur at the base of the arms. To establish tip of leaf, bring needle up at 1 and take a short stitch down centre to 2. Bring needle up at 3 close to first stitch; insert at 4 just to right of middle line. Emerge at 5 directly across from 3. Insert needle at 6 just to left of centre line. Repeat the 3 to 6 sequence by bringing needle up at the new point 3. Continue this sequence until leaf shape is completely filled.

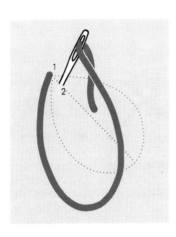
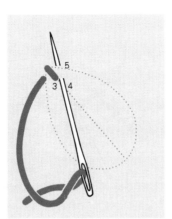
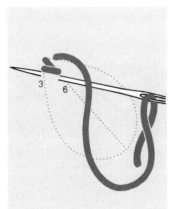

Vandyke stitch is another variation of cross stitch used for leaf designs. As the stitch is worked, a thin plaited line is formed in the centre to represent the centre vein of the leaf. The first four steps in the following series start the design; the fifth and sixth steps are repeated in sequence thereafter. Bring needle out at 1 on left side below tip. Insert at 2 and come up at 3 taking a small bite at leaf tip. Insert needle at 4 directly across from 1. Bring needle out at 5 on left side. Pass needle *under the pair of crossed threads* above.

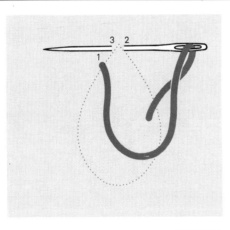
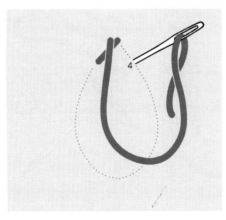
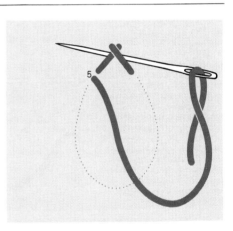

Insert needle at 6 on the right side and bring needle out at left side again for next stitch. Continue 5 to 6 sequence until leaf design is filled, always passing needle under last two crossed threads. Worked between narrow parallel lines, stitch forms a fine raised plait for a decorative outline or border. When worked in adjacent rows, it produces a pebbly texture. Squares or rectangles of this stitch worked at right-angles can convey the texture of bricks or paving stones.

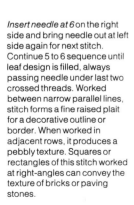
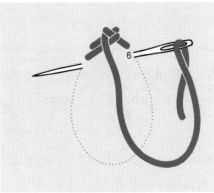
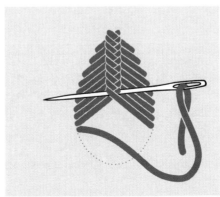
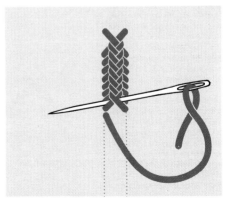

Feather stitches

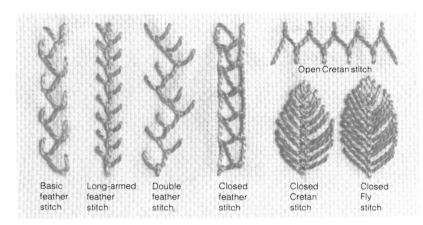

| Basic feather stitch | Long-armed feather stitch | Double feather stitch | Closed feather stitch | Closed Cretan stitch | Closed Fly stitch |

Open Cretan stitch

The feather stitches make up the next category of embroidery stitches. Originally used to decorate 19th-century English smocks, most of the feather stitches are used today for borders on edges and hems. Their feather-like look comes from their being open looped stitches taken alternately to the right and the left from a central core.

Two of the feather stitch variations, *closed Cretan* and *Fly stitches*, are often used for filling leaf and fern designs. When worked, they both have a textured centre that resembles the main vein of a leaf.

The basic feather stitch and its varia-

tions are often seen in crazy patchwork (stitched over the adjoining edges of patches) and in appliqué. They are also used to add a delicate edge to children's and babies' clothes.

Like the earlier blanket and chain stitches, feather stitches are looped; the working thread must be carried under the point of the needle before it is pulled tight. Because of the back-and-forth movement of the needle, care must be taken to keep the stitches even on both sides of the centre line. Before stitching, it is useful to lightly draw guidelines for the centre line as well as the side lines of leaf edges.

Basic feather stitch is a looped stitch that is evenly worked with stitches alternating to the left and to the right. Work stitches from top to bottom. Bring needle up at 1 in centre. Insert needle at 2 slightly lower and to the right. Then angle needle out at 3 along centre line, carrying working thread under point; pull through. Insert needle at 4 slightly below and to left of 3. Angle needle out at 5 along centre line; carry thread under point and pull through. Continue, alternating angle of looped stitches. To end row, take a small stitch over last loop.

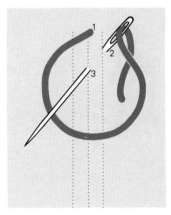   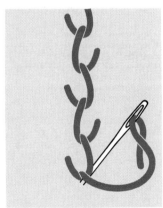

Long-armed feather stitch (or Cretan stitch) is worked like the basic stitch except that the longer half of each loop is on the outside. Bring needle up at 1 in centre. Insert needle at 2 slightly higher and to the right, then angle needle out at 3 along centre line. Carry thread under needle; pull through. Insert needle at 4 slightly higher and to left of 3 (distance between 1-2 and 3-4 should be equal), then angle needle out at 5 along centre. Carry thread under needle and pull through. Repeat 1-5 to end.

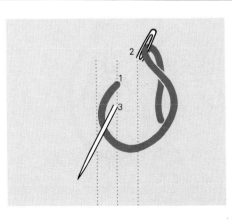 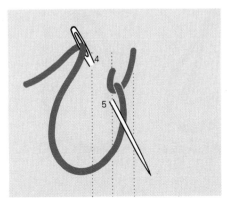 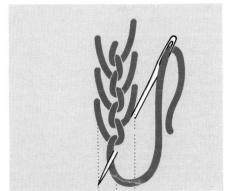

39

Embroidery stitches

Feather stitches

Double feather stitch makes an airy, zigzag border. Instead of a single looped stitch placed alternately left and right, two stitches are made consecutively to one side and then to the other. Keep the loops even. To start, bring needle up at 1 in centre. Insert at 2 directly across. Angle needle left and out at 3; carry thread under point of needle and pull. Insert at 4 directly across from 3. Angle right, coming out at 5; carry thread under needle and pull. Insert needle at 6. Angle right, coming out at 7; carry thread under needle and pull.

To complete sequence, insert needle at 8 directly across from 7 and below 3. Angle left and out at 9; carry thread under needle point and pull. Two sets of looped stitches are now complete. Repeat sequence from start. Note that point 9 of last sequence is point 1 of the new sequence. Continue with 1 to 9 series until row is completed.

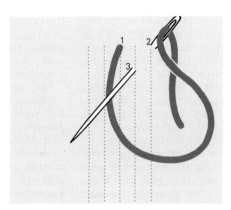 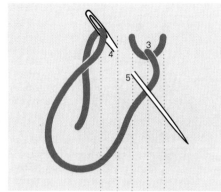 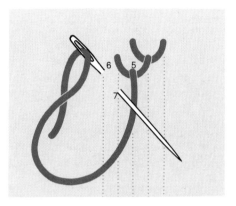

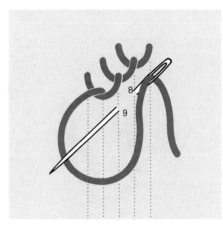 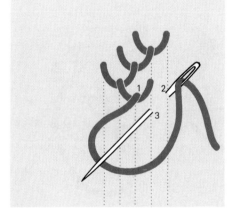 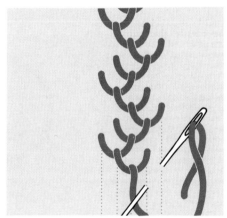

Closed feather stitch is a simple variation of the basic stitch in which each stitch *touches the previous one,* leaving no space between. To achieve this, the stitches are made *vertically* rather than at an angle. Bring needle up at 1. Insert at 2, half a step up and to the right of 1; emerge at 3 a full step below. Carry thread under needle point and pull through. Insert needle at point 4 just below 1, so that the threads touch. Emerge a full step below at 5. Repeat sequence, always inserting needle just below previous stitch to form an unbroken line.

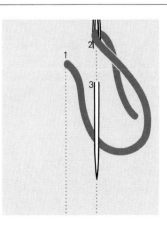 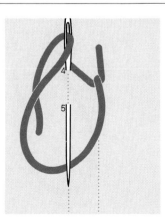 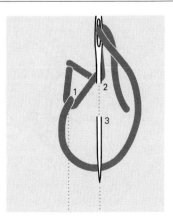 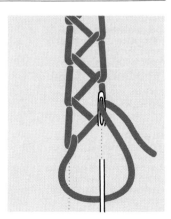

Open Cretan stitch is a type of feather stitch that produces a decorative border. Unlike most feather stitches, it is worked horizontally. Bring needle up at 1. Insert at 2 above and to right; come up at 3 directly below 2. Carry thread under point and pull through. Insert needle at 4 on bottom and further to the right; come up at 5 directly above 4. Carry thread under point and pull through. Continue in this way, always placing each stitch to the right of the last one and keeping the distance between stitches even.

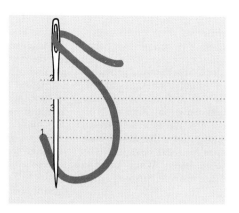
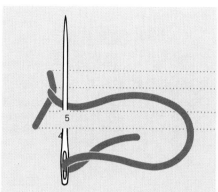
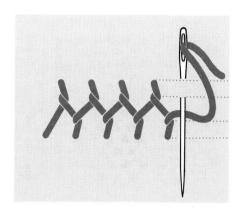

Closed Cretan stitch is usually used as a leaf-filling stitch as it forms a natural plait down the centre. Bring needle up at leaf top, 1. Insert at 2 and come up at 3, slightly to the right of the centre line. Carry thread under needle point and pull through. Insert needle at 4 directly across from 2; come up at 5 directly across from 3 and slightly to the left of centre. Carry thread under needle and pull. Start next stitch on right side, then alternate, bringing needle out either to the left or to the right of the centre line to create centre plait.

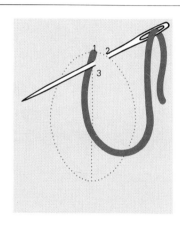

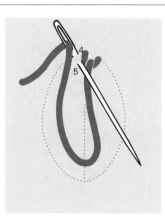

Closed Fly stitch is another leaf-filling stitch. It has a spine down the centre. Bring needle up at 1 and take a small stitch down centre to 2. Bring needle up at 3; insert at 4 directly across from 3. Come up at hole originally made at 2; carry thread under needle point and pull through. Proceed to next stitch. Note that point 2 of previous stitch (where thread emerges) is point 1 of next stitch. Continue this way until leaf design is filled.

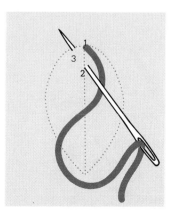

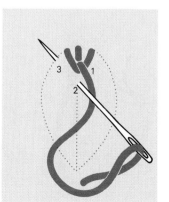

Embroidery stitches

Filling stitches/detached

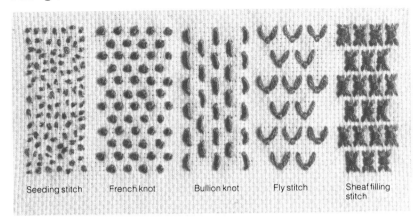

Seeding stitch   French knot   Bullion knot   Fly stitch   Sheaf filling stitch

Although all the stitches in this next set are quite different from one another, each having its own unique look, they have one thing in common – they are all detached, single stitches used primarily as a means of filling in a design area. All the stitches presented here contribute great textural variation to an embroidered piece. Certain especially raised stitches, among them the *French knot* and the *bullion knot,* can be flattened by an embroidery hoop. When using a hoop, take care to avoid crushing raised stitches (see p. 18).

Because each of these stitches has such an individual look, it can serve many purposes besides filling. The French knot is a particular favourite of embroiderers. It can be used singly to represent a feature such as an eye, or a number of knots can be grouped to form a texture. Another versatile stitch is *seeding stitch*, which can be scattered lightly or heavily to give a shaded effect. *Fly stitch* and *sheaf filling stitch* both require a little more planning in the placing. Worked in rows, they can be used as a border. They can also be worked singly. Scattered fly stitches resemble distant birds in flight; sheaf filling stitches look very much like bundles of wheat.

Seeding stitch is one of the simplest filling stitches. It can be used in clusters or scattered. If worked close together, groups of seeding stitches can even be a means of shading. Bring needle up at 1 and take a tiny stitch down at 2. For a heavier stitch, bring needle up at 3 and take another small stitch at 4 close to the first stitch. Scatter seeding stitches as desired, changing the direction of the stitches for a varied effect. If all stitches are worked in one direction, filling will be uniform.

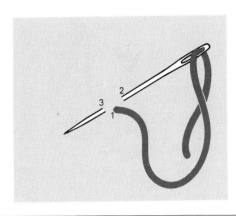
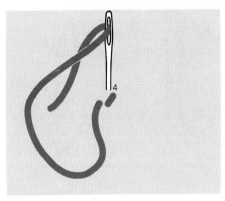
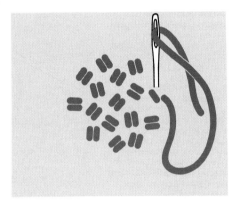

The French knot is used like the seeding stitch, but it is considerably more textured and raised. Knots can be worked close together to fill an area completely, producing a knobbly effect. Bring needle up at 1. Holding thread taut with left hand, wrap thread around needle twice as shown; gently pull the thread so the twists are tightened against the needle. Carefully insert needle near point 1 and pull through; be sure thread end is still held taut. Scatter knots as desired within design area. French knots can be made larger by using a thicker thread.

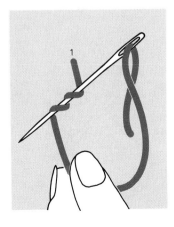
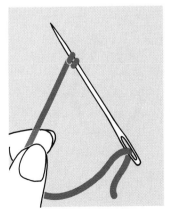
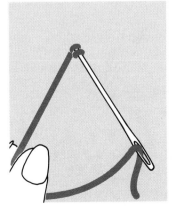
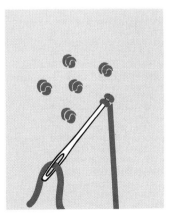

Bullion knot can be used as a filling or as an outline stitch. Bring needle up at 1. Insert at 2 and come up at 1 again, but leave needle in fabric. Twist thread around needle point five to seven times depending on length of stitch (distance from 1 to 2). Then carefully pull needle through both fabric and twists; take care not to distort twists. Pull thread towards point 2 so that coil can lie flat. Pull working thread tight and use point of needle to pack threads in coil together evenly. Re-insert needle into point 2.

 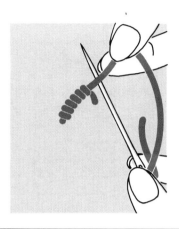  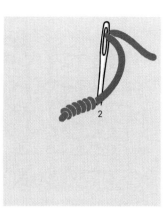

Fly stitch is a single, looped stitch not unlike the basic feather stitch. When completed it resembles a Y. It can be scattered about as a filling, lined up for a border, or used as a leaf filling (p. 41). Bring needle up at 1. Insert at 2 directly across, then angle needle out at 3. Points 1, 2 and 3 should be equidistant. Carry the thread under the needle point and pull through. Complete stitch by inserting at 4 over loop. Work as many fly stitches as necessary to fill design area.

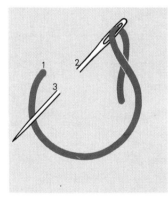 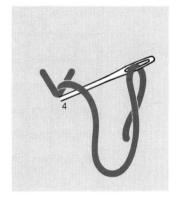  

Sheaf filling stitch resembles a tied bundle of wheat. Stitches can be arranged in alternate rows or set close together, one right below another. Bring needle out at 1. Work three satin stitches, following numbered sequence shown. Bring needle up at point 7, midway between 5 and 6. Pass needle around the stitch bundles twice without piercing fabric and pull thread taut. Insert needle under bundle and through fabric; secure stitch on back of work. For a different effect, work the tying stitches in a contrasting thread colour.

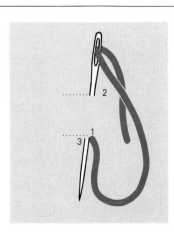 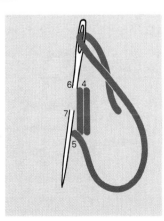  

Embroidery stitches

Filling stitches/laid work

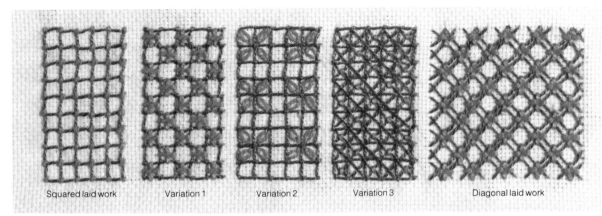

Squared laid work   Variation 1   Variation 2   Variation 3   Diagonal laid work

A fairly large design area can be attractively filled with this next group of embroidered filling stitches. These stitches are longer than the preceding detached ones and are laid to create the effect of a grid or lattice. The basic lattice is laid down, then anchored down at its intersections to keep them in place.

Embellishments can then be added: this is usually done with contrasting thread. In laying down the long, grid-like stitches, take care to ensure even and consistent spacing. Do not pull thread too tight as work will pucker.

It is essential for laid work that the fabric be stretched taut in a frame.

Squared laid work is made up of long stitches that form a lattice over which other stitches are worked. This basic structure is anchored by small, slanting stitches at each thread crossing. To form lattice, bring needle up at 1; take a long stitch to 2. Bring needle up at 3 below 2; insert at 4 below 1. Work stitches until area is covered, keeping spacing even. Lay vertical stitches over the horizontal ones the same way. Take small slanting stitch over each intersection. Start at upper left. Work across and back, up at A, down at B.

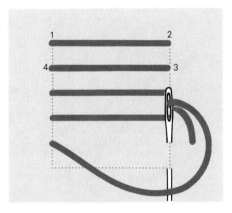

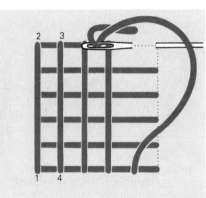

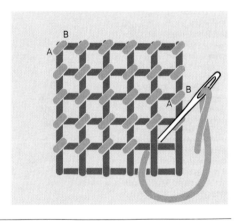

Variation 1. Here upright cross stitches are worked over alternate squares of the lattice made from the basic laid work shown above. Work entire lattice with one colour, cross stitches with a contrasting colour. Starting at upper left corner, bring needle up at 1; insert at 2. Come up at 3 and complete stitch at 4. Work the second row using the same numbered sequence, moving from right to left. Continue in this way, working each row until the laid work is filled.

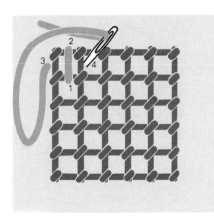

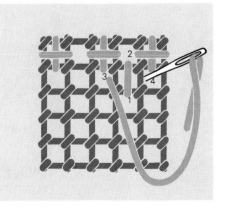

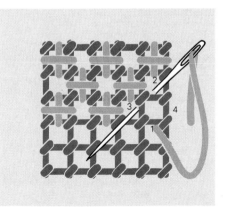

Variation 2. Here a series of four detached chain stitches is worked within a set of four lattice squares. Depending on the number of squares, the position and number of sets will vary. Make each chain stitch so that the anchoring stitch over the loop is at the centre of the four lattice squares. Bring needle up at 1; insert back into 1 and emerge at 2. Carry thread under point and pull through. With thread over loop, insert at 3. Work the next and subsequent stitches anti-clockwise until the set is complete.

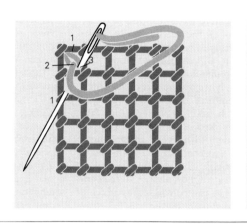
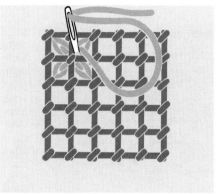
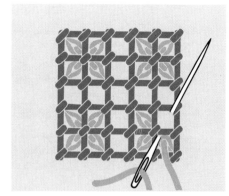

Variation 3. This time, diagonal threads are laid over basic threads, then anchored down at each intersection. Starting at top left corner of laid work, bring needle up at 1; insert at 2. Bring needle up at 3, two squares to the right. Take a diagonal stitch to 4, two squares below 1. Work remainder; keep spacing even. Lay diagonal threads in opposite direction. Start at top right and follow same sequence. At each crossing, take a small vertical stitch, A to B. Start at upper left corner; work across, then back, until all intersections are covered.

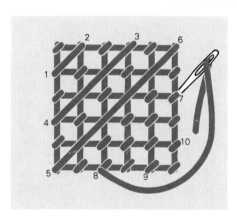
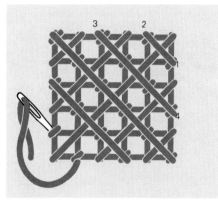
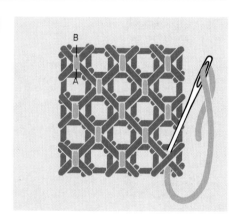

Diagonal laid work is made up of pairs of threads laid diagonally to form a lattice base. Each intersection is anchored down with four small straight stitches. To form lattice, bring needle up at 1 in upper left corner; insert diagonally at 2. Bring up at 3 near 2; take another stitch to 4. Work pairs of stitches back and forth, keeping spacing even. Then, starting at upper right corner, lay pairs of threads on the opposite diagonal. At each intersection, take four stitches, all out at A and in at centre point B. Work these sets across and then back.

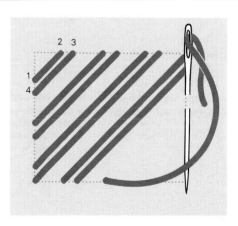
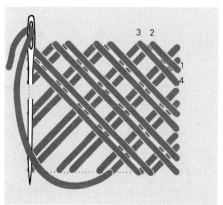
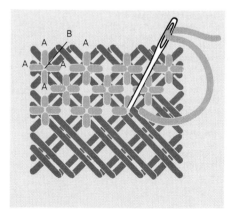

Embroidery stitches

Running stitches

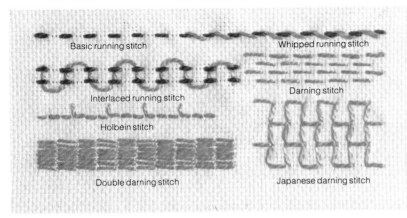

Basic running stitch
Whipped running stitch
Interlaced running stitch
Darning stitch
Holbein stitch
Double darning stitch
Japanese darning stitch

Running stitches would appear to be the simplest of all the stitch types to work, and in many ways they are. There is nothing at all complicated about the basic movements of the needle. Care is required, however, to keep the stitch lengths uniform. This is why the running stitch and its variants are frequently worked on fabrics that have an even weave, with every stitch length covering a predetermined number of fabric threads. Unlike the majority of embroidery stitches, almost all the running stitches can be worked by picking up several stitches on the needle before pulling the needle and thread through.

This speeds up the work considerably.

Basic running stitch is primarily used for outlining, and it is the basic stitch in quilting. Worked in rows with contrasting threads laced through it, it can also be used as a border or band. *Holbein* or *double running stitch* is often used for outlining. Carefully worked, a piece embroidered with only Holbein stitch can be reversible; right and wrong sides will be identical.

Darning stitches are usually used to fill a space. By changing the lengths and arrangements of the stitches, many different patterns are possible (see Blackwork, p. 56 and Pattern darning, p. 70).

Basic running stitch, the easiest outline stitch, can be same length on right and wrong sides or longer on right side. Work basic stitch right to left. Bring needle up at 1; down at 2. Pick up several stitches on needle before pulling it through. *For whipped variation,* weave contrasting thread through stitch base (second illustration); do not pick up fabric below. *For interlaced variation,* work two rows of running stitches and thread contrasting thread up and down through rows (last illustration).

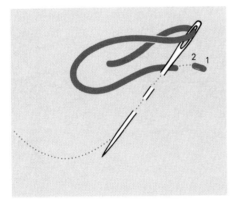
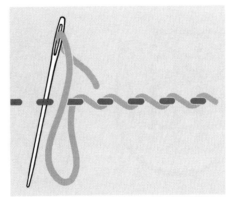
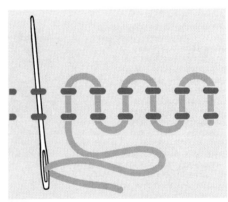

Darning stitch is basically several rows of running stitches of any desired length. Surface floats usually form a design like the type found in blackwork embroidery. We show a 'brick' design. Each row of running stitches consists of a long float on top with only a few fabric threads picked up by the needle. The long floats of each row are evenly stitched so that they lie just below short spaces of row directly above. Work rows as needed to fill area.

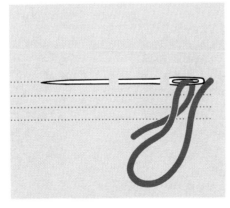
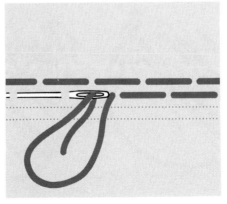
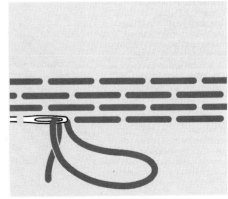

Holbein or double running stitch is an outline stitch used often in blackwork and Assisi embroidery. This stitch is worked with two journeys of running stitches. On first journey, work evenly spaced running stitches. Turn work and stitch second journey so top floats are stitched over spaces left by first journey; enter and come up at same holes.
If design has offshoot stitch, work it on first journey. Bring needle up at 3, base of stray stitch. Insert at 4; come up at 3 again. Continue to next stray stitch. Turn, and work back.

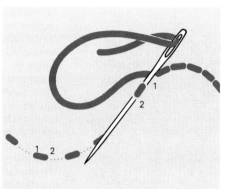
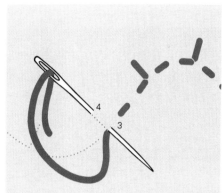
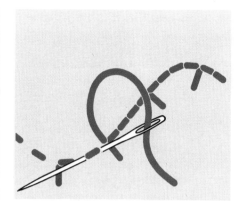

Double darning combines the techniques of both darning and Holbein stitches. This entails working several rows of evenly spaced Holbein stitches. To start, work the first journey of the first row with evenly spaced running stitches. Turn work, then stitch second journey over first so top floats are over spaces left by first journey. Work each subsequent row in the same manner, lining up stitches of each row directly below the stitches in the row above. Leave enough space between rows so the threads do not overlap each other.

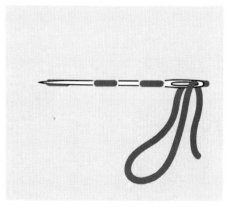
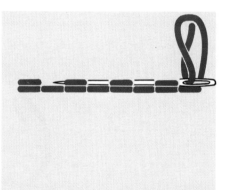
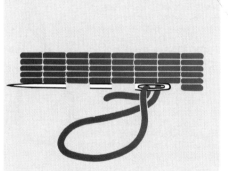

Japanese darning can be a filling stitch or a border. Work several rows of darning stitch in 'brick' pattern, but with more space between rows than in darning shown opposite. Work each row so the top float of each stitch is slightly longer than the intervening spaces. To connect rows, come up at 1 on top row. Insert at 2; come up at 3, with needle picking up fabric between 2 and 3. Continue, alternating pick-up stitches from row to row. Connect the subsequent rows in the same way until all have been joined.

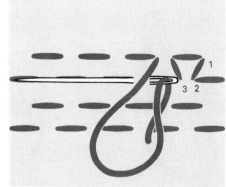

Embroidery stitches

Satin stitches

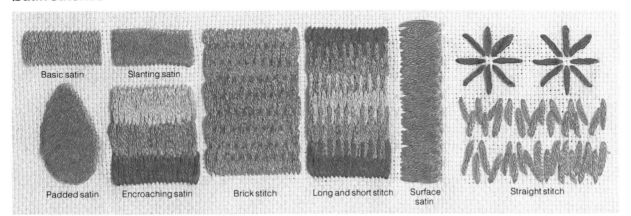

Basic satin

Slanting satin

Padded satin

Encroaching satin

Brick stitch

Long and short stitch

Surface satin

Straight stitch

This group of satin stitches is the most popular set of embroidery stitches for solidly filling in a design with a smooth surface. Although the main stitch movements are fairly simple, it still takes practice to get the floats to lie flat and close together, and the edges of the stitches to align evenly. When working satin stitches, be sure none of the fabric below shows through. An important aspect of satin stitching is the direction in which the stitches fall within a design. Decide this before starting; the stitch direction will influence the way the light reflects on the filled area, and will determine its ultimate look.

Basic satin stitch is a solid filling stitch that covers the design area with long, straight stitches placed close together. Care must be taken to keep the stitches smooth and at an even tension. This simple version of satin stitching is the basic stitch in Hardanger embroidery. The stitch is usually worked from left to right. Bring needle up at 1. Insert at 2 directly above; come up at 3 close to point 1. Continue until area is filled. The stabbing method of stitching (see p. 20) will help to keep the stitches even.

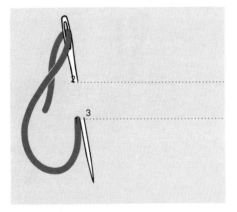

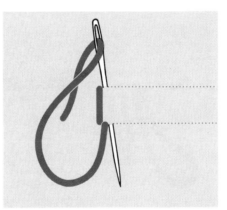

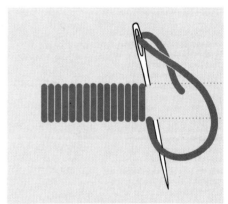

To slant satin stitches, start work in the centre of the shape to establish the angle of slant. Work across to fill one side, then start again at the centre and work across the other way to fill other side. When shape is large, slanting stitches tend to flatten out (becoming too horizontal) by the time you reach the end. To prevent this, work satin stitches so that needle is always inserted at upper edge (point 2) *very close* to preceding stitch; come up at 3 *slightly further* from exit point of preceding stitch.

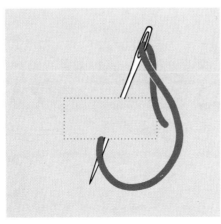

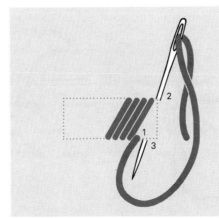

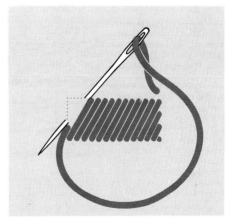

Padded satin stitch gives the same effect as the basic satin stitch, except that the stitched area is slightly raised for texture variation or design emphasis. The padded area consists of an outline of split stitches and two 'layers' of satin stitching. Work one row of split stitches (see p. 23) around the shape. Carefully work basic satin stitch horizontally across, covering the split stitches. Then work upper satin stitch layer in desired direction. Take special care to keep the outline edges even; work slowly.

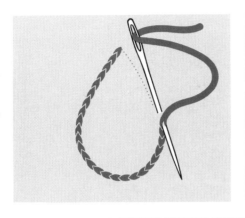 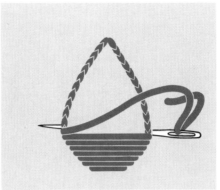 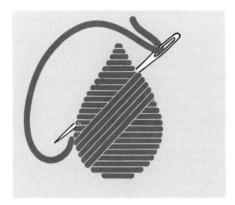

Encroaching satin stitch offers systematic colour shading within a shape. Several rows of basic satin stitches are worked to give an almost woven effect. The colours of the rows can go from dark to light. Work a basic satin stitch along first row. Start second row so that its first stitch falls between first two stitches in row above. Continue stitching second row so that stitches fall between the stitches above them. Work next rows the same way. If you use shaded thread, and want precise shading, start each row at the same colour section.

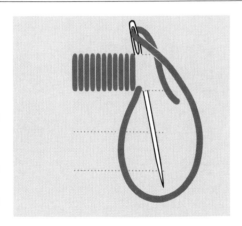 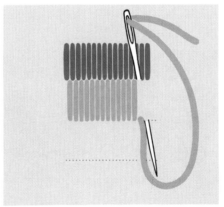 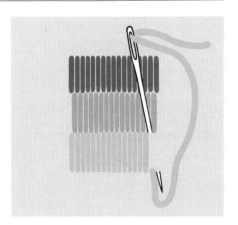

Brick stitch is a type of satin stitch with a texture like that of a woven basket. Stitching is done alternately left to right, then right to left. To work first row, alternate long and short satin stitches across; each short stitch should be approximately half the length of the long stitches. Work all other rows in long satin stitch. On last row, fill in the half-spaces with short satin stitches. Make sure that the top of each stitch touches the base of the stitches directly above it.

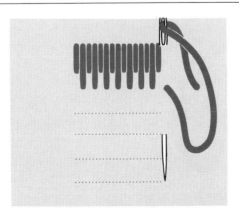 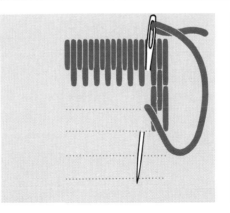 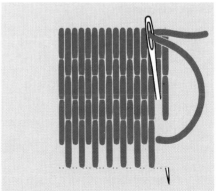

Embroidery stitches

Satin stitches

Long and short stitch is a popular stitch for shading areas in a design. The stitch is worked very similarly to brick stitch, but there is more stitch blending. Each stitch from the second row onwards pierces the stitch above it in the preceding row. Work first row as for brick stitch (preceding page). Change colour and work long satin stitches along second row, staggering them so top of each stitch splits base of stitch directly above. Work each subsequent row in this way. Fill in the last row with short satin stitches.

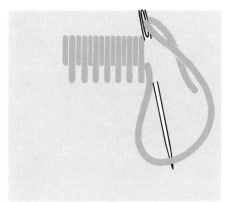 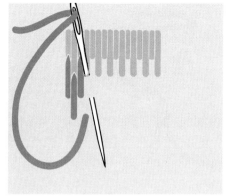 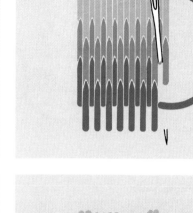

The direction in which long and short stitches fall is very important for proper shading effect. Before starting, decide direction stitches will take within each separate shape. Pencil in some direction lines. Here are three designs that have been partially worked with the long and short stitches running in different directions. Note the radiating coloured effect achieved in the first and last illustrations by fanning the first row of stitch colour.

 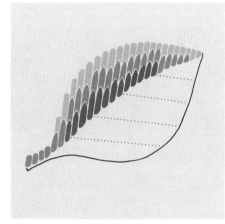 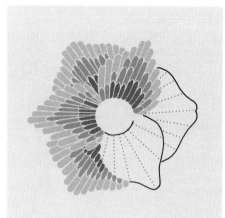

Surface satin stitch is an economical way to obtain the look of the basic satin stitch; it eliminates the long floats on the wrong side. It needs care to get the stitches to lie close together. Use the stabbing motion (see p. 20) to work this stitch. Bring needle up at 1. Insert at 2 directly across; bring needle up at 3 as close as possible to 2 (no more than a fabric thread away). Insert needle at 4 directly across from 3. Or space the stitches slightly further apart and fill in with a second sequence of stitches for a smoother effect.

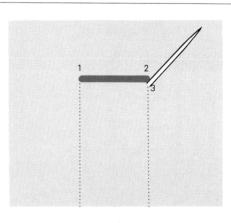 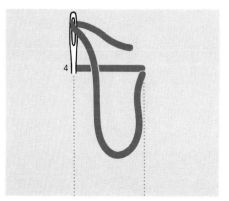 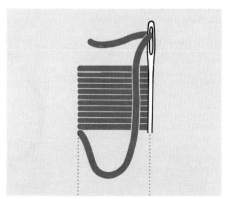

Straight stitch is a single satin stitch that can be of any length and worked in any direction. It can be used to cover straight design lines or scattered for an open filling. Be sure thread is not carried too far on wrong side between stitches. Worked in a circle (last illustration), the cluster of straight stitches resembles a stylised flower, the centre of which can be filled in with French knots (see p. 42). Bring needle up at 1; insert it at 2. Work as many as needed for desired design.

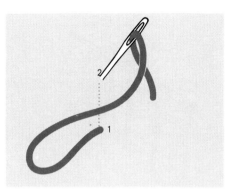

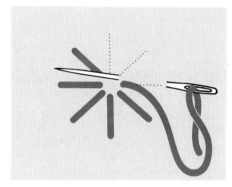

Weaving stitches

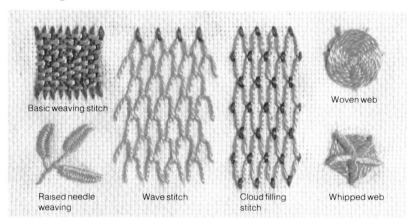

Basic weaving stitch

Raised needle weaving

Wave stitch

Cloud filling stitch

Woven web

Whipped web

The next embroidery stitch group, the weaving stitches, consists entirely of stitches based upon a network of threads that are first laid down and then woven over. The thread used for weaving may be the same or a contrasting colour. The effect, and therefore the choice, varies considerably from one stitch to another. The *basic weaving stitch,* for example, can fill an area solidly with its subtle texture; *raised needle weaving,* on the other hand, produces a particular motif, such as a leaf or petal. *Spiders' web stitches* are special in that the finished stitch assumes a definite circular shape. Both *wave stitch* and *cloud filling stitch*

will serve as lacy fillings for different areas in a design. The filling can appear closed or quite open, however, depending on the placing of the base threads. The weight, too, affects stitch appearance, the same stitch looking very different in two different weights of thread. Experiment until you find the particular effect you want.

Although a pointed needle is used for laying down the base threads, it is recommended that you exchange it for a tapestry needle when you come to the weaving portion of these stitches. This will help to avoid piercing the fabric or splitting the laid threads.

Basic weaving stitch is a solid filling stitch with a basket-like texture. Lay down the vertical threads first, working right to left. Bring needle up at 1; insert at 2 directly above and come up at 3 on left. Insert at 4 and repeat for as many threads as needed. Change to tapestry needle. Starting at upper right corner, come up at A and weave across, going over and under alternate vertical threads. Insert needle at B; come up at C for next horizontal run. Continue to weave vertical threads.

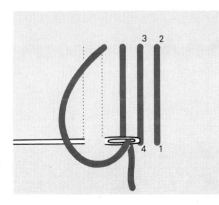

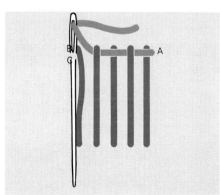

Embroidery stitches

Weaving stitches

Raised needle weaving is a weaving stitch that lies on top of fabric with only laid threads attached. Bring needle out at 1. Insert at 2 directly below; emerge at 1. Insert needle at 2 again and bring needle up at 1. Change to a tapestry needle; begin weaving over and under the two laid threads alternately without picking up any fabric below. Continue to work back and forth over the laid threads until they are completely covered. Take care to keep the tension even so the shape of the stitches is not distorted.

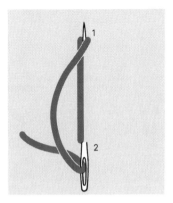 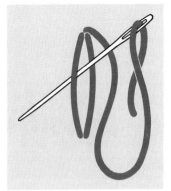 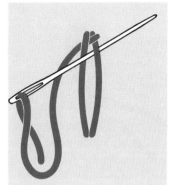 

Wave stitch is a lacy filling stitch that gives a honeycomb effect. Depending on the spacing of the stitches, this lace-like effect can look open or closed. To start, work a row of small, vertical satin stitches that are evenly spaced. Come up at 1; insert at 2. At end of row, bring needle up at 3, below and to right of last satin stitch. Pass needle back under satin stitch without picking up any fabric below; insert at 4. Bring needle up right next to point 4 and repeat the sequence until all satin stitches are threaded.

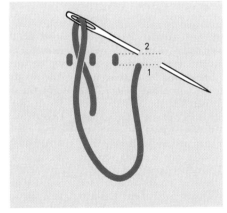 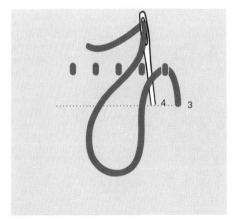 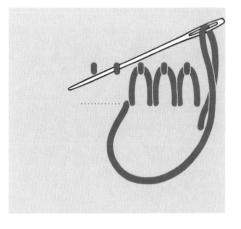

To work next row, bring needle up at 5 slightly to the left of the last stitch above. Pass needle under stitch above without picking up fabric. Insert at 6. Bring needle up right next to point 6 and repeat the sequence across, this time slipping needle under the pairs of stitch bases directly above. On following row, bring needle up at 7 directly under end stitch of first weaving row, and end at point 8, directly under end stitch of first weaving row. Work subsequent rows the same way, passing needle under the stitch bases in row directly above.

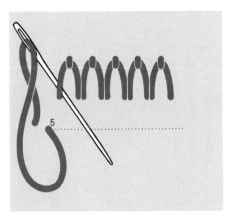 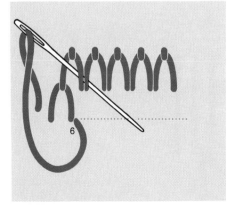 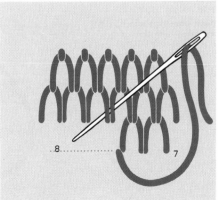

Cloud filling stitch is much like the wave stitch in texture. To start, work several rows of small, vertical, evenly spaced satin stitches as shown on the right. Change to tapestry needle and contrasting thread. Bring needle up at A; lace thread back and forth through satin stitches of first two rows. End lacing at B, securing thread at back. Lace second and third rows (C to D) and all subsequent pairs of rows. Different impressions can be achieved with contrasting threads and by varying spacing.

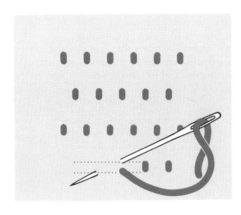

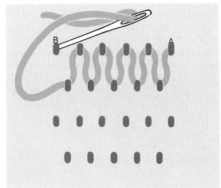

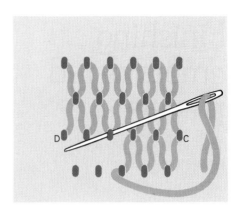

Spiders' webs are embroidered circular motifs that can be used as design accents or to represent stylised flowers. Spokes of the web are laid, then *woven over and under* for a smooth surface or *whipped* to produce a pronounced rib. Before starting, divide circle into nine equal parts; mentally number each. Bring needle up at spoke 1. Insert at 4 and bring out at centre; carry thread under needle and pull through. Insert at 7 and bring out at 9. Insert at 3 and bring out at centre; carry thread under needle and pull through. Insert at 6 and bring out at 8.

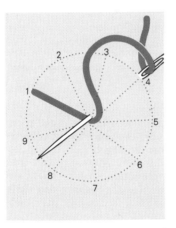

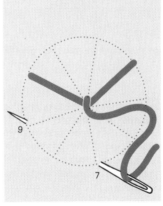

Insert needle at spoke 2 and bring out at centre; carry thread under needle, pull through. To complete last spoke, insert needle at 5 and come up at centre. To *weave* over spokes, start from centre and pass needle over and under spokes, moving around and outwards anti-clockwise until spokes are covered. To *whip* over spokes (last illustration), carry needle under and back over a spoke, then under that spoke and next spoke ahead. Work around, always moving needle back over one spoke and forward under two in a backstitch until all spokes are covered.

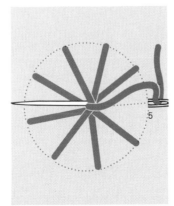

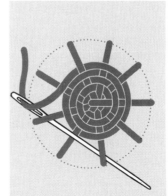

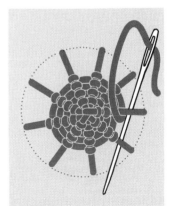

Finishing embroidered pieces

Cleaning, pressing and blocking embroidery

Cleaning

Because of all the handling involved in the embroidering process, your finished piece may get very dirty and need cleaning before it is pressed or blocked. Embroidered pieces made with washable fabrics and threads can simply be washed as illustrated below. Swish the embroidery around in the cool, soapy water – never scrub embroidery harshly – rinse thoroughly, and roll in a towel to blot up the excess water. If the piece is not washable, you can use a good stain remover – which you have first tested on a scrap of fabric – or take the piece to a reliable dry-cleaner.

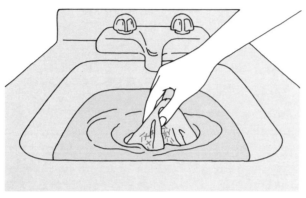 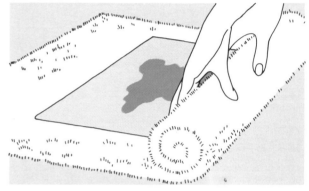

Gently wash the embroidered piece in cool water and mild soap. Rinse thoroughly (do not wring or twist); **roll in towel** to absorb excess moisture.

Pressing

When an embroidered piece is completed, it must be either **pressed** or **blocked** to help remove any wrinkles and to straighten fabric distortions that may have been caused by embroidering. If a piece is not seriously distorted, pressing is usually sufficient. Pressing, rather than blocking, is also recommended for embroidered clothing. Before pressing, pad the ironing board with a folded towel. If your board is too narrow to take the work satisfactorily, lay the towel over your blocking board. Place the embroidered piece face down and cover it with a cloth. If the article has been washed (see above) and is still damp, you can use a dry cloth; if the piece is dry, use a damp cloth. Press very lightly over the embroidered area, letting the iron just touch the cloth. Press surrounding fabric in usual way.

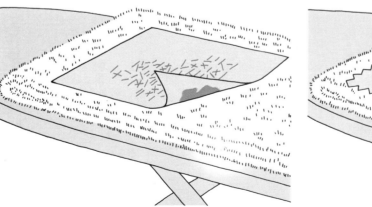 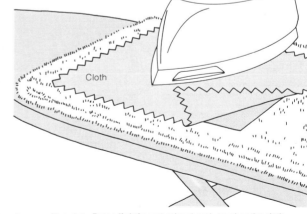

To press an embroidered piece, lay it face down on a padded ironing board, and cover with a cloth. **Press lightly** so that iron barely touches the cloth.

Blocking

Blocking is a corrective process in which embroidery pieces are stretched over a board to remove fabric wrinkles and distortions. To make a blocking board, see below. If you would like to pad the board, cut an old mattress cover into pieces to fit the board, and place a couple of them between the board and the covering of muslin.

To block embroidery, first soak the piece in cold water. If the stitches are flat, lay the piece face down on the board; if many stitches are raised and highly textured, lay it face up to prevent crushing. Stretch the fabric and hold it in place with heavy-duty T-pins or drawing pins placed close together. Pieces that cannot be soaked should be stretched dry. Moisten areas around embroidery with a damp sponge, and use tip of iron to press moistened areas lightly; let fabric dry before removing.

If the piece has been worked on a frame it should not require stretching.

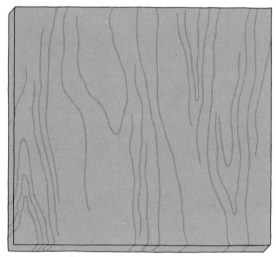

1. To make blocking board, buy a piece of 1.5 cm thick pine or soft composition board that is approximately 60 cm by 60 cm.

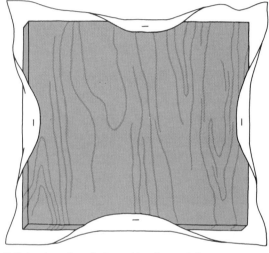

2. Cut a piece of muslin 5 cm wider all around. Centre board over fabric, and stretch fabric over edge, stapling at centre of each side.

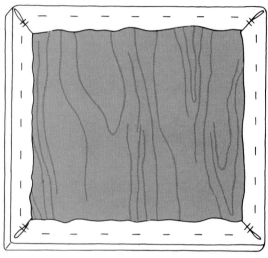

3. Working out from the centres, stretch and staple fabric along each edge. Neatly fold excess fabric at corners and staple.

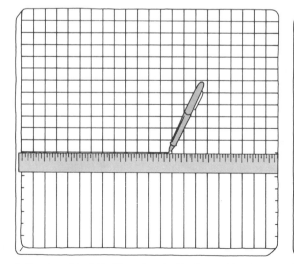

4. Turn board to right side and mark off a 2 cm grid, using an indelible marking pen that will not run when wet.

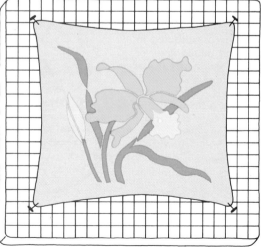

5. Soak embroidered piece in cold water and lay on top of board, face up or down as explained above. Pin at each corner.

6. Pull sides out to desired measurements, using grid as a guide, and pin in place. Leave it to dry before removing.

Blackwork embroidery

Introduction to blackwork
Basic stitches
Examples of blackwork patterns
Creating your own blackwork
pattern
Working block designs
Working blackwork fillings

Introduction

Blackwork is a special category of counted thread embroidery in which repetitive patterns are used to fill design areas. It is called blackwork because, traditionally, black silk thread was worked on white linen.

Blackwork is said to have originated in Spain, becoming very popular in England during the 16th century when Catherine of Aragon married Henry VIII. At that time, blackwork appeared on clothing and pillow covers.

The play of one diaper pattern upon another creates dark, medium and light areas within a design; a mixture of all three tones adds interest to a piece. Today, blackwork patterns are used in working two different types of designs: **block designs,** in which the patterns themselves form a simple geometric shape; and **free designs,** in which the patterns are used to fill predetermined shapes in a design.

Blackwork is done on even-weave fabric (see p. 9), typically even-weave linen or Hardanger fabric. For exact pattern repetition, stitches are counted over a precise number of threads. The more threads there are per centimetre of fabric, the smaller (and darker) the embroidered blackwork area will be.

Stranded cotton is usually used in blackwork; depending on the weave of the fabric, the number of strands can vary. Finer pearl cottons and cotton à broder are also suitable. Although black thread on white linen is the traditional colour choice, other colours can be used to give blackwork a more modern look. Brown thread on beige linen or deep blue on eggshell are popular (see examples on the right). Metallic threads add richness to a design.

Because blackwork is worked over an exact number of threads, the needle must go between threads rather than pierce them. For this purpose, fine tapestry needles are best. Select a size that corresponds to your thread.

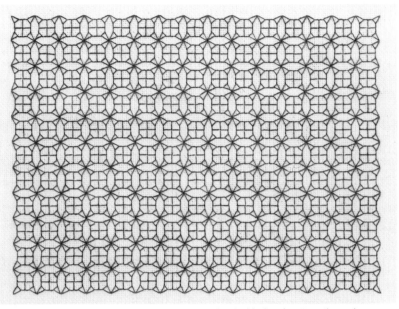

Block designs consist of simple geometric units formed by the blackwork patterns themselves.

Free designs make use of outline stitches with blackwork fillings.

56

Basic stitches

Blackwork patterns are built upon a few basic embroidery stitches worked over a definite number of threads. The stitches that are used most often are shown below. Included are **backstitch, Holbein** and **running stitch, double cross stitch** and **Algerian eye stitch**.

In addition to the stitches that create the patterns, other stitches are often used as embellishments to add textural interest and variety to the overall design or to outline shapes. The free design on the opposite page features such supplementary stitching. One excellent contrast to the intricate blackwork lines is a solidly filled area; **satin stitch** will provide a smooth, solid filling where such an effect is wanted. To add definition to a free shape, outline it with a linear embroidery stitch. **Stem stitch, chain stitch** and **couching stitches** are all good for this purpose.

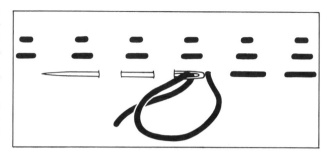

Darning stitch is often used alone in blackwork patterns. A running stitch worked in parallel rows, its floats may be any length. Stitch rows create the patterns.

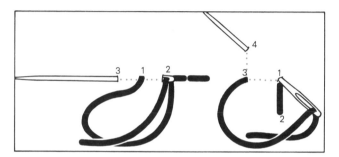

Basic backstitch is worked right to left. Bring needle out at 1, go in at 2 and out at 3. To stitch corners, come up at 1, take a backstitch at 2 and come up at 3. Insert at 1; come up at 4; re-insert at 3 to complete stitch.

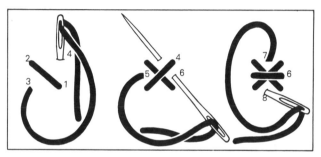

Double cross stitch is star-like. To work, bring needle up at 1, go in at 2 and out at 3 below 2. Enter at 4, come up at 5 between 2 and 3. Insert at 6 across from 5; come up at 7 between 2 and 4. Insert at 8 below to complete stitch.

 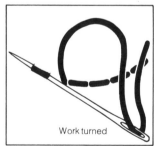

Holbein stitch is worked in two runs. The first consists of a simple running stitch. The return run is made along the same stitching line with running stitch filling in spaces left from the first.

Work turned

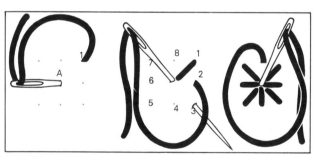

Algerian eye stitch produces an eyelet effect. To work, bring the needle up at 1 and insert at centre, A. Bring out at 2 and insert at A. Continue to work in clockwise direction until all points are stitched.

Additional stitches

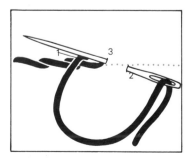

Stem stitch is worked left to right. Bring needle out at 1. Insert at 2 and bring out at 3. The distance between 1-3 and 3-2 is the same. Repeat sequence for next stitch. Keep length of stitches even.

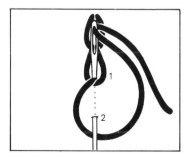

Chain stitch is worked as follows. Bring needle up at 1. Holding thread down to left of 1, re-insert needle at 1, bring out at 2, looping thread around needle point. Pull needle through and repeat the sequence.

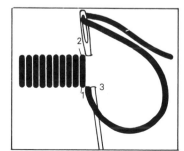

Satin stitch is used to fill small areas. Bring needle up at 1, down at 2. Emerge at 3 next to 1. Repeat same sequence until area is filled. Keep thread smooth and even.

Blackwork embroidery

Examples of blackwork patterns

Blackwork patterns consist of repetitive geometric motifs made from basic embroidery stitches. The original blackwork patterns probably were derived from Arabic embroidery designs. Later, when blackwork reached the height of its popularity in 16th-century England, the original geometric patterns were influenced by English design. At that time, fruits and figures were used as repeated motifs, with twining stems giving a cohesive look to the design. Elizabethan portraits of both men and women show this kind of blackwork pattern covering sleeves and collars. Some patterns are reminiscent of engravings or wrought iron work.

Even in the 16th century, blackwork was not always done in black thread on white or cream linen. Sometimes gold and black thread were used together in one piece. Even red thread, on occasion, was substituted for black.

We have selected 12 patterns to illustrate the range of possibilities. The number of patterns, however, is infinite. They are simple to design on your own (see p. 63) or to adapt from an existing design. Look at fabric prints or mosaic tile designs for inspiration. Or choose any blackwork pattern that appeals to you and simply change its scale or the thickness of the thread.

Each pattern will tend to have a dark, medium or light tone according to the relative openness or compactness of its lines. Note the differences on the sampler. A sampler like this one will serve as a pattern dictionary for future use and will provide you with practice in working the patterns. Any pattern can be adapted to either free designs or block. The best pattern combinations are those that create textural contrast.

To show the order of steps necessary to work the patterns, each sequence begins in black and continues in colour. On the grids, the spaces between dots represent individual fabric threads.

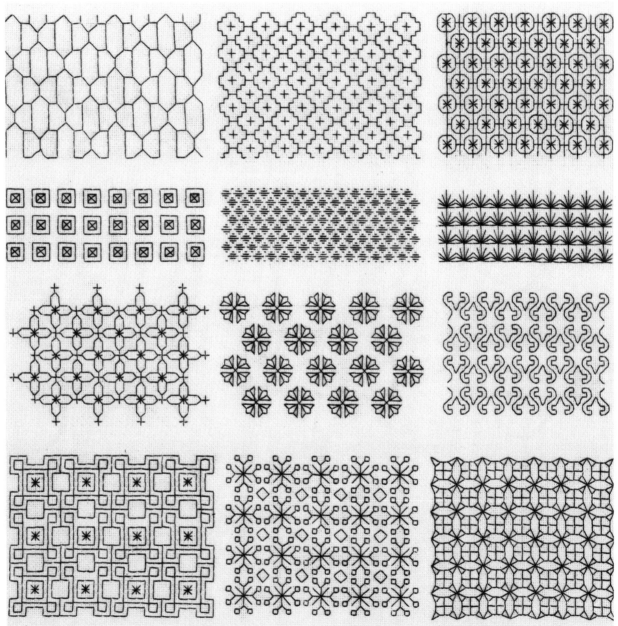

Representative sampler of 12 blackwork patterns illustrates the three tones of light, medium and dark.

This light, honeycomb pattern is worked completely in *backstitch* or *Holbein*. Work the pattern from left to right, stitching vertical rows in stitch lengths as indicated on grid (second illustration). For backstitch, work first line from top down, and second line (shown in colour) from bottom up. Continue in this way until desired area is completely filled. For Holbein stitch, work first stage of each line from top down, and second stage from bottom up.

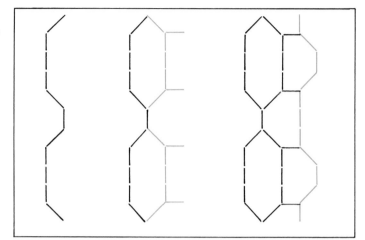
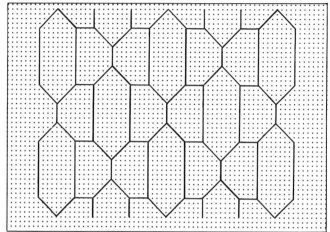

Step design is darker than the honeycomb because its lines are closer, its motif smaller. Work the basic shapes in *backstitch* in the sequence shown. Then fill centres with a single, vertical *cross stitch*. This pattern can be used as a border or filling.

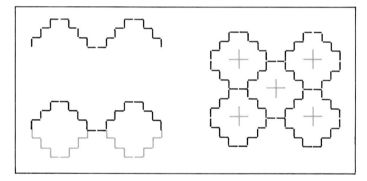
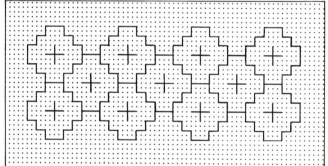

Octagonal trellis is a compact pattern worked in *backstitch* and *cross stitch*. The vertical lines and octagons are worked in backstitch. The octagons are then filled with cross stitch. The horizontal stitches add a third arm to the crosses and connect the octagons.

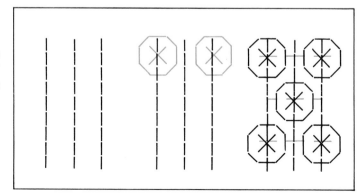
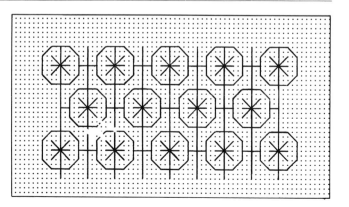

Blackwork embroidery

Examples of blackwork patterns

Delicate diamonds are worked entirely in *darning stitch*. The top floats, worked in rows, create the patterns. To begin, work the top row of either pattern from right to left, spacing stitches as shown on grid. Work subsequent rows, following stitch pattern, until desired area is filled.

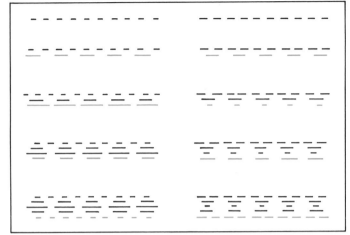

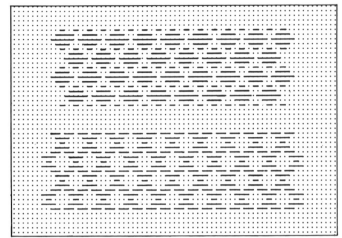

Dark fern pattern is made of closely stitched motifs. Each motif is worked like *Algerian eye stitch*, coming up at the end of each line and entering at same centre hole. Work across one row and return on next row until area is filled. Note stitch lengths as indicated on grid.

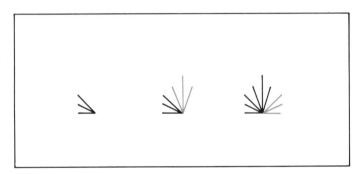

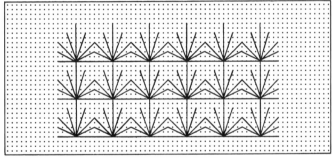

A simple geometric shape like this filled double square can be given a light or dark tone depending on its filling. To work this pattern, stitch the squares in *backstitch* and fill with *cross stitch*. For a darker pattern, use *double cross stitch*. Work blocks closer together, or use a heavier thread.

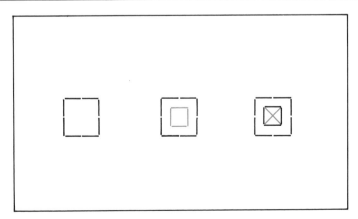

This Greek scroll, though it looks complex, is easy to work. *Backstitch* or *Holbein* can be used. Work the first row as shown. For the next row, invert motif to create a mirror-image effect. This pattern can be used as a filling or as a border.

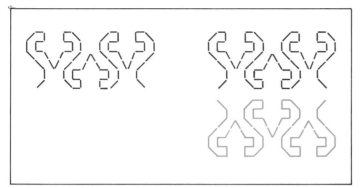

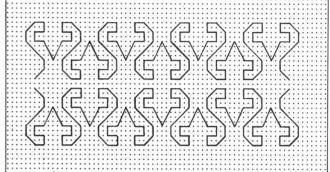

Crossed star motif is composed of a network of intersecting stars. Begin each star with a central *double cross stitch*. Add the points in *backstitch* and join the stars with a single vertical-horizontal *cross stitch* at each point.

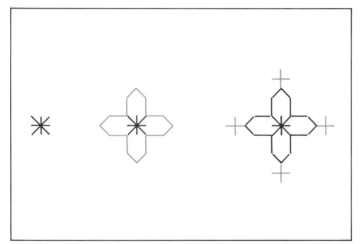

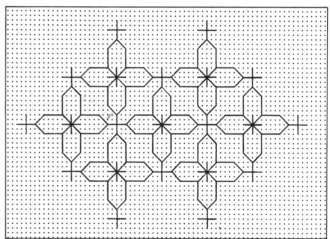

Flower arrangement. To work this pattern, stitch centre *cross stitch* of each group, suitably spaced. Then work the outline of one motif, in *backstitch*, adding the detail lines last. Work the other three motifs in the same way.

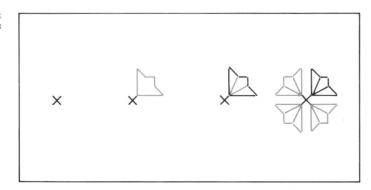

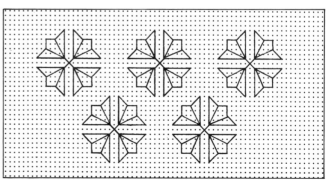

Blackwork embroidery

Examples of blackwork patterns

Scattered snowflakes. Work snowflake centre in *Algerian eye stitch*. Then work the adjoining lines and shapes in *backstitch*. When all rows of pattern are complete, add the diamond shapes in backstitch.

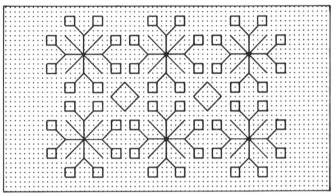

Stacked 'H' shapes are worked from the outside. The main motifs are worked in *backstitch* (see p. 57 for the way to work corners). Fill in the centres of the 'H' shapes with *Algerian eye stitch*.

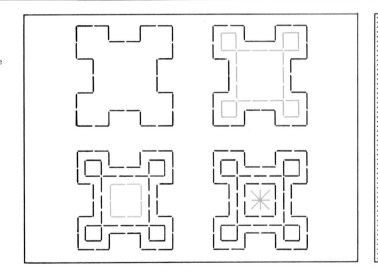

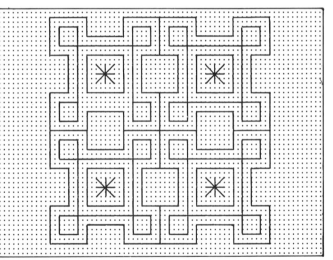

Stained-glass pattern. Though the lines look intricate, this pattern is easy to work. Begin by stitching a *backstitch* cross. Add an octagonal ring and four corner triangles (all backstitch).

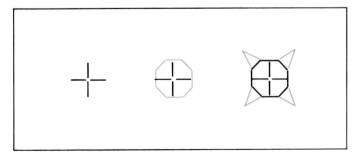

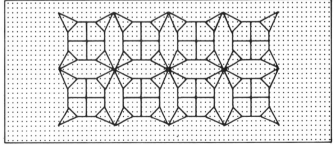

Creating your own blackwork pattern

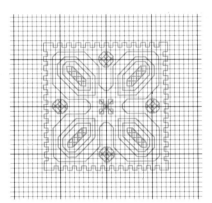

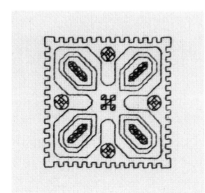

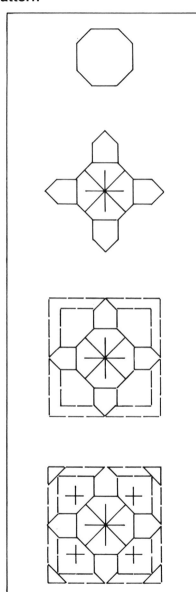

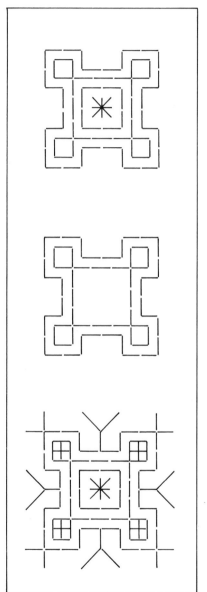

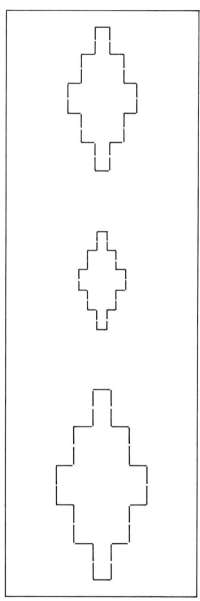

A geometric motif from a fabric print or a ceramic tile can be used by 'squaring' all curved lines, with the help of graph paper. To suit blackwork technique, all parts of the design must take a horizontal, vertical or diagonal direction.

Develop your own pattern from any simple geometric shape, adding lines and other shapes to fill in or extend the original shape. Pattern above combines Algerian eye stitch, backstitch and cross stitch.

Modify an existing blackwork pattern to your taste. Simplify the motif by removing some of its lines. Or add lines for a larger or more complex pattern. Algerian eye stitch, backstitch and cross stitch are used above.

Change the scale of an existing pattern to give it a new look. Enlarge the motif by lengthening the stitches. To make the motif smaller than the original, shorten the stitches. Motif shown is worked in backstitch, over 2, 4 or 6 threads.

Blackwork embroidery

Working blackwork in block designs

When working a blackwork piece to form a block or all-over design (see block design on p. 56), the blackwork pattern must be symmetrically placed. To accomplish this you must carefully measure and divide the area to be stitched.

First determine the approximate size the finished blackwork design is to be. Then cut even-weave fabric on grain to the dimensions of the projected design plus 10 cm on all sides. Bind or finish the raw edges of the cut fabric to prevent fraying as you embroider (see p. 16). Count the threads within the area to be worked and mark the perimeters clearly. Since blackwork patterns are worked from the centre out, the centre point of the design must be located and marked. Place the initial motif in relation to the centre point so that as many *whole motifs* as possible fit into the worked area. This positioning is particularly important if the motifs are large.

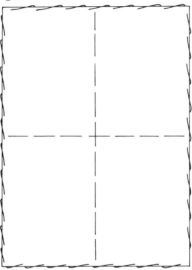

1. Fold fabric in half vertically; tack along centre line with thread. Fold fabric in half across and tack along that centre line. Intersecting tacking lines mark centre of fabric.

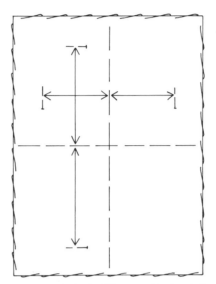

2. Measure desired width on one side of vertical centre line; mark with pins. Count same number of threads from centre on opposite side and mark. Mark length from horizontal centre.

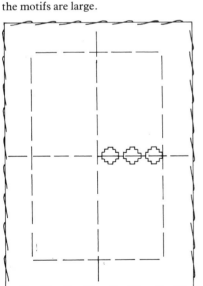

3. Tack along pinned lines for perimeter of design. Start from centre point and work one horizontal row of pattern outwards from vertical centre line. Work other half in opposite direction.

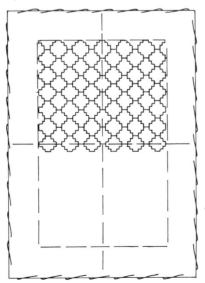

4. To fill remaining area, repeat rows of pattern above and below first row. Using it as a guide, subsequent rows can be worked from edge to edge, rather than from centre out.

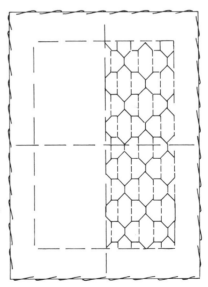

5. If the selected pattern is worked vertically, stitch first row out from horizontal centre line. To fill remaining area, stitch subsequent rows, using first completed row as a guide.

POSITIONING LARGE MOTIF

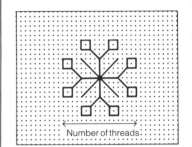

Number of threads

If a motif is large, whether it will be worked horizontally or vertically, as many motifs as possible should be worked on a line. To accomplish this, count fabric threads in a row, then fabric threads in one motif. Divide number of fabric threads by the number in one motif.

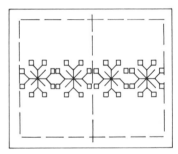

If the result is an even number, start motif *at* centre line, working a complete motif on either side of centre.

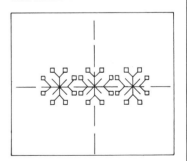

If result is an odd number, work half a motif *on either side* of centre line so that one full motif is centred.

Working blackwork fillings

When blackwork patterns are used as fillings within freely drawn shapes, they must be selected carefully. Choose patterns that have different tones of light and dark, distinct enough so that the shapes in the piece do not become blurred. When combined thoughtfully, the lights and darks can add depth and interest to a free design.

In choosing a pattern to fill any shape, consider the size of the shape in relation to the scale of the pattern. Make sure that there is enough space within the area to repeat the motif several times. Otherwise, the pattern will not be shown to its best advantage.

In addition to the basic stitches used to work patterns, consider working other embroidery stitches. Use *chain stitch*, *stem stitch* or *couching stitches* to emphasise and outline shapes that need definition. Or incorporate very dark areas of contrast into the design by filling small shapes with *satin stitch*.

1. Trace or draw design on heavy tracing paper. Colour in different tones of grey to represent light, medium and dark patterns. Arrange them for balance and contrast. Select the patterns that best represent the greys in the drawing.

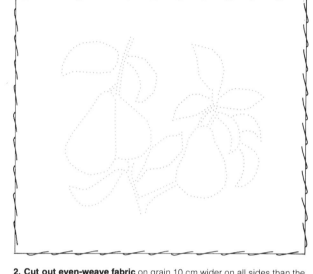

2. Cut out even-weave fabric on grain 10 cm wider on all sides than the desired finished size of design. Bind or finish the raw edges of the fabric to prevent fraying while the design is being worked (see p. 16). Transfer the design to the fabric (pp. 16–17).

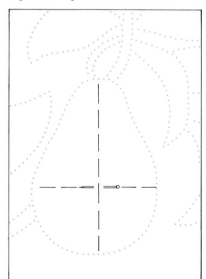

3. Determine approximate centre of each shape to be filled; mark with a pin. Block designs must be centred by thread counting; centre of a free shape can be determined by eye.

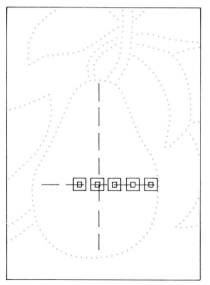

4. Start pattern at centre, working the row out to marked edges. At edges where a whole motif may not fit, use part of a motif, perhaps shortening stitches, to keep pattern within outline.

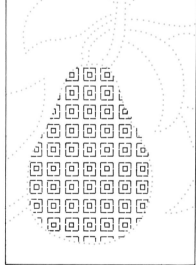

5. Repeat the pattern rows, using the first completed row as a guide. As before, at edges where a whole motif does not fit, work a partial motif, shortening stitches as necessary.

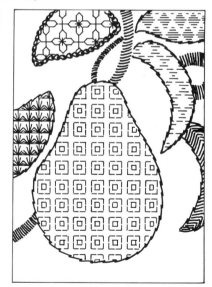

6. When all shapes in design have been filled, outline them, using such stitches as *stem stitch*, *chain stitch* or *couching stitches*. Fill in solid areas with *satin stitch*.

Cross stitch embroidery

Introduction to cross stitch
Basic cross stitch
Cross stitch guides
Cross stitch on gingham
Assisi embroidery

Introduction

Cross stitch is a traditional type of embroidery which is adaptable to either simple or intricate designs. Cross stitch designs are often worked exclusively in basic cross stitch, as on the right, though variations of the stitch can also be used.

Cross stitch can be worked on almost any fabric suitable for embroidery. The even-weave types are especially good because their even threads help guide the stitches. Gingham is popular for cross stitch for a similar reason – its squares form a natural grid (see p. 9).

Stranded cotton is the usual choice for working cross stitch, but other embroidery threads can be used. Just be sure the thread you select is compatible with the weight of your embroidery fabric.

Choose a needle according to your fabric: a tapestry needle for an even-weave, to slip between threads; for other fabrics, a sharp-pointed needle (crewel or chenille) to pierce the fabric. To keep stitch tension even, it is best to use an embroidery hoop or frame.

Versatile basic cross stitch fills shapes, forms geometric motifs and outlines designs.

Forming the basic cross stitch

Basic cross stitch can be formed in two ways. It can be worked **in rows** of even, slanted stitches, with one arm of the crosses laid down in one movement, the other in a second, return movement.

Cross stitches can also be worked **one at a time**. Work cross stitches in a row when they are adjacent in a design. When they are scattered, it is best to work them singly; this way no long threads will be trailed on the wrong side. Make sure that the top threads all lie in the same direction. This is important to obtain the even, neat look that is characteristic of cross stitch.

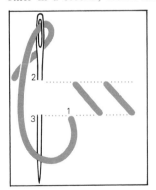
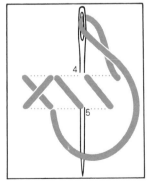
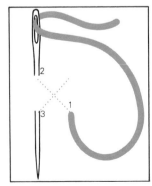
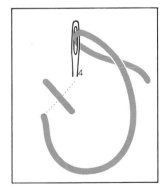

Cross stitches in a row. Starting on the right, come up at 1, insert at 2 and come up at 3. At end of row, work back, inserting at 4, coming up at 5.

To work one cross stitch at a time. Bring needle up at 1, insert at 2 and come up at 3 below. To complete, insert needle at 4 above 1

Cross stitch guides

There are two sources for cross stitch designs, **hot-iron transfers** and **charted designs**. Hot-iron transfers can be applied to any smooth, tightly woven fabric. Use charted designs on any fabric that offers a natural grid (even-weaves, or plain weaves with an even surface pattern, such as gingham).

With an iron-on transfer, your finished embroidery will be the same size as the transfer. If you use a charted design, finished size will depend on the number of fabric threads or surface lines you work over.

Charted designs (both the coloured key and symbol key types) are printed on a grid. Each square in the grid represents a single cross stitch. The scale of each stitch is your choice.

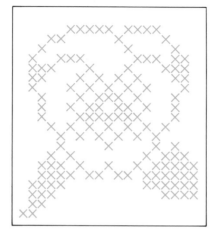

With iron-on transfers for cross stitch, simple crosses indicate stitch position.

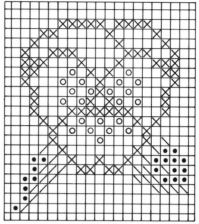

In charted designs with symbol keys, symbols represent stitch position and colour.

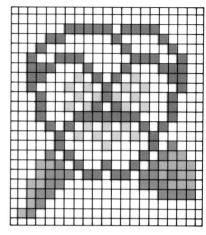

Charted designs with colour keys show stitch position and colour with coloured squares.

Natural grids

Fabrics with natural grids (even-weaves, and plain weaves with even surface patterns) are ideal for cross stitch. With charted designs, fabrics of this type are essential. When the weave pattern is large, as in Binca fabric, each cross stitch can cover one thread inter-

section. When it is smaller, as in Hardanger fabric, each cross stitch can cover several fabric strands or thread intersections. Be sure each stitch crosses the same number of fabric threads horizontally and vertically.

When a fabric does not have a natural

grid, a **single-thread canvas** can supply one. Choose a suitable size, making sure the mesh is not interlocked, and tack it to the embroidery fabric. Work the cross stitch design over the canvas grid. When the design is completed, remove the tacking stitches and trim the excess

canvas close to the design without cutting into the cross stitches. Carefully draw out the canvas threads with tweezers. Start from one corner and pull all parallel threads in one direction. Then, working from another corner, pull out the remaining threads.

Cross stitch on Binca fabric shows each stitch worked over one thread group.

Cross stitch on a fine even-weave shows each stitch worked over two threads.

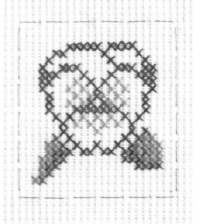

Canvas, tacked to embroidery fabric, can substitute for a fabric grid.

When the design is finished, the canvas threads are pulled out with tweezers.

Cross stitch embroidery

Cross stitch on gingham

Gingham is a highly popular fabric for cross stitch because of its natural grid. One cross is worked within each square, which keeps stitches uniform.

Any charted design that requires a fabric with a natural grid can be worked on gingham, but some designs are particularly effective on this fabric. The three tones of gingham (dark, medium and white) can be used to advantage (see below). A motif worked on only the dark squares will create a different effect, for example, from the same motif worked on the medium or the white squares.

Gingham comes in check sizes from one to three per centimetre. Since the check size determines the size of each cross, the larger the squares, the larger the overall design.

Cross stitch on gingham design features a repeated geometric motif, a favourite use of the technique and ideal for decorative borders.

Crosses worked on the dark squares enhance the contrast between whites and darks.

Crosses worked on the white squares give a one-tone look to the gingham.

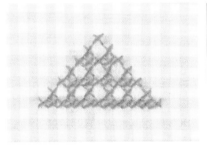

Crosses on both dark and white squares make shape more solid, whites more emphatic.

Variations of the basic cross stitch can be incorporated into the main motifs of a design or used to embellish a border pattern. The variations above are *herringbone stitch* (p. 36) and *double cross stitch* (p. 35).

Working sample motif

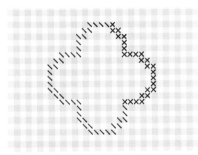

Individual flowers are stitched separately. Work outline as a row (in two journeys).

Next fill in centre petals, working one petal at a time, again as a row.

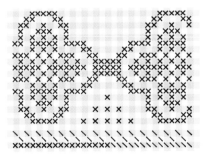

Work connecting blocks and border stitches as rows. Stitch triangle crosses one at a time.

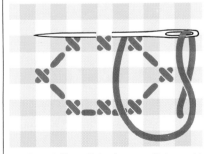

Work medallion with basic cross stitches, adding running stitches to connect them.

Assisi embroidery

Assisi embroidery is a variation of basic cross stitch, in which design areas are left open and the background filled with cross stitch. Designs are usually outlined with Holbein stitch (see p. 47). Details and highlights within the open forms are also worked with either Holbein or cross stitch.

The technique is named after the town in northern Italy where it originated. (Assisi is also the birthplace of St Francis, founder of the Franciscan order.) A revival of this traditional Italian embroidery took place at the beginning of this century. The designs were adapted from centuries-old embroidered pieces preserved by local churches. The motifs in these early 20th-century pieces were of primitively drawn animals. As the embroidery became more popular and greater variety of design was needed, elaborate patterns were adapted from the woodcarvings in the churches of Assisi. The adaptations include animals, figures, geometric and floral motifs. Traditionally, only one colour was used. Today, colours can be mixed. A particularly effective way of combining colour is to use one for filling and another for outline and detail.

Most cross stitch charts can be adapted for Assisi work. Simply select designs with strong shapes and reverse the open and filled areas.

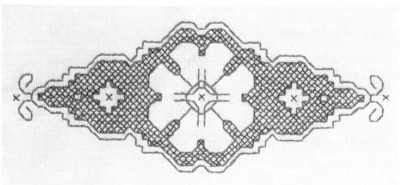

The first Assisi designs were naively drawn animal shapes. Later, the designs were refined into more delicate shapes, abstract, floral and geometric shapes, and intertwining figures.

To work an Assisi piece, first stitch the outline of the shape in *Holbein stitch,* worked as two journeys of running stitches. On the first journey, stitch evenly spaced running stitches. Work the second journey so that top floats are stitched over the spaces left by the first journey. Enter and come up at the same holes. When the outline is complete, fill in the background areas with cross stitch, worked in rows (see p. 66).

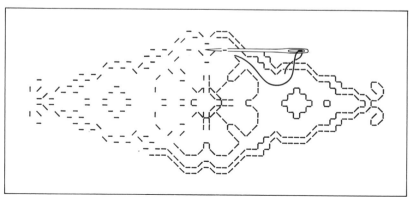

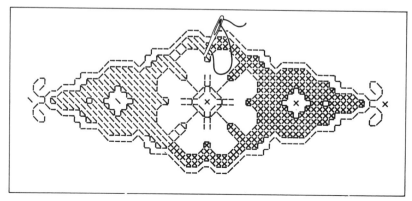

69

Pattern darning

Introduction to embroidery
Motifs
Basic stitch movements
Working pattern darning

Introduction

The type of pattern darning shown here is traditionally worked on Huckaback linen, a towelling fabric with well-defined vertical floats in the weave. This fabric is now difficult to obtain, but with a little ingenuity the method can be adapted to even-weave or to honeycomb fabric.

A look at the magnified insets on these two pages will show how pattern darning looks on even-weave fabric. It does require some planning if you wish to stagger some rows (see bottom left motif, p. 71). As even-weave does not have floats already spaced out, you will have to devise your own system. You could, for instance, pick up every fourth vertical thread in a straight row of darning. This would leave three clear threads in between (an odd number) which makes it possible to stagger the next row by picking up the middle of the three threads. This would not be possible if you picked up the third or fifth thread, leaving an even number of threads in between.

In honeycomb fabric, the vertical floats lie in straight rows up and down, with horizontal floats in alternate rows. To follow some of the stitch diagrams on pp. 71–73 you will have, on alternate lines, to pick up two warp threads which lie between the horizontal floats.

Threads used for pattern darning are usually pearl cotton and stranded cotton; sometimes Persian wool and soft embroidery cottons are used. Because the needle picks up the floats rather than piercing the fabric, a tapestry needle, in a size that suits your thread, is recommended. An embroidery hoop is not needed. Designs for pattern darning are usually geometric shapes, used as a *single motif*, a *border, all-over or repetitive patterns* or *stylised figures*. Examples appear on the far right, with drawings that show the order of working each type. For drawings of the basic stitch movements, see p. 72.

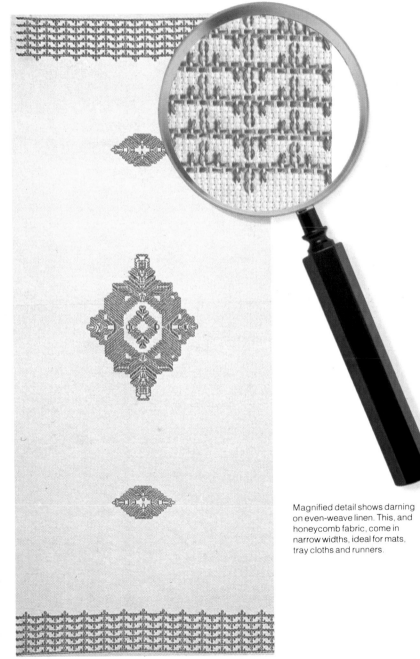

Magnified detail shows darning on even-weave linen. This, and honeycomb fabric, come in narrow widths, ideal for mats, tray cloths and runners.

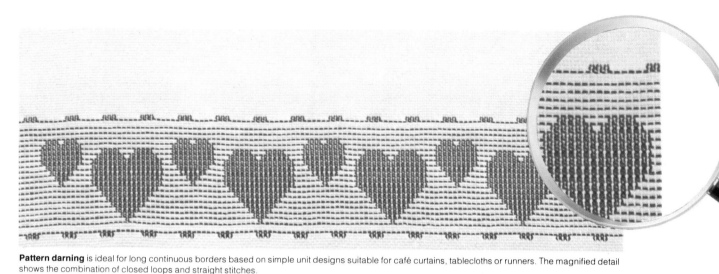

Pattern darning is ideal for long continuous borders based on simple unit designs suitable for café curtains, tablecloths or runners. The magnified detail shows the combination of closed loops and straight stitches.

Four basic motifs

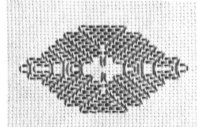
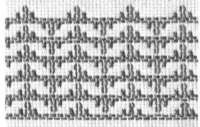
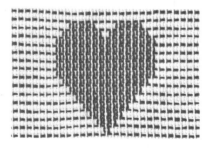
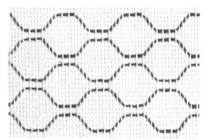

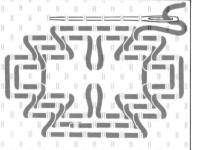
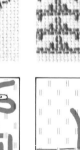

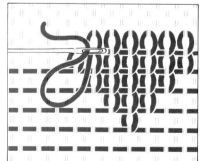
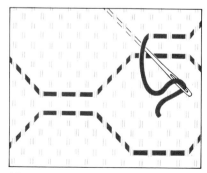

Single motif is worked from centre out. Design above consists of straight stitches, offsets and open loops.

Border is worked from bottom upwards in rows from right to left. Stitches used are straight stitches and figure-eights.

Stylised figure is worked from right to left in rows. The heart shape above is worked in rows of closed loops and straight stitches.

All-over pattern is worked in rows from right to left until desired area is filled. Pattern above is worked entirely in straight stitch.

For detailed stitch instructions, see next page.

Pattern darning

Basic stitch movements

Straight stitches are the type used most often in pattern darning. To work, move needle from right to left, picking up warp threads in a straight line. Needle can also move diagonally.

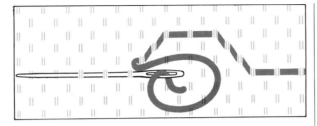

Offsets are darning stitches that create a stairway effect. To work, always move needle from right to left, and forwards.

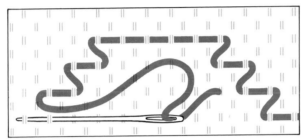

Open loops are darning stitches that are looped at the top and open at the base. Move needle from right to left, and forwards at each pick-up point, to keep the loops open.

Closed loops are like open loops, but the stitch base is closed. To work, move needle from right to left at the base and from left to right at the top. *Re-enter under same thread* at base, moving right to left.

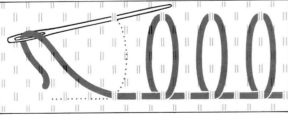

Figure-eights are a combination of open and closed loops. Move from right to left at base, and at top of loop. Figure-eight is formed by *re-entering under same warp thread on base line* to complete the stitch.

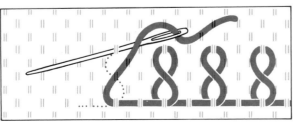

Working pattern darning

Most darning designs are worked in rows of stitches that start at the bottom and are built upwards. The first row of a design, however, is worked from the centre out to make sure the design is balanced on both sides. After this line is laid, rows can be worked from right to left. Many darning patterns consist of large motifs that are repeated. In order to fit as many full motifs as possible within the width of the fabric, the initial motif must be carefully placed.

To determine position of the first motif in relation to the centre of the fabric, count the number of warp threads that are spanned by one motif, then the number across the fabric. Divide the number of warp threads per motif into the number available in the fabric. Drop all fractions from the result. If the answer is an even number, place the edge of a motif on the centre line and work a complete motif on either side. If the answer is an odd number of floats, centre the first motif – that is, work half a motif on either side.

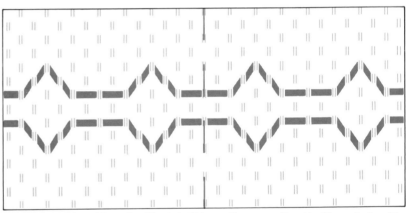

For an even number of darned motifs, start with two motifs, one on either side of the centre line of the fabric.

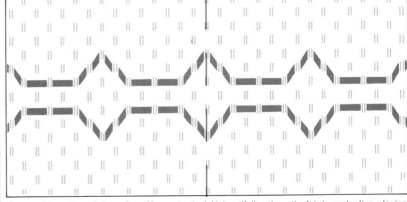

For an odd number of darned motifs, centre the initial motif directly on the fabric centre line, placing half on either side.

To start, fold fabric width in half; mark fold. Cut thread to suitable length (for one row across fabric without a join). Do not knot thread end. Leaving half of thread length free at centre, work first row from centre to left.

Finishing ends

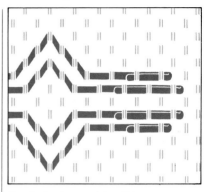

If a design is complete within an open area, weave thread ends back into final stitches.

Turn work upside-down. Thread needle with free thread and work the other half of the row from the right to the left.

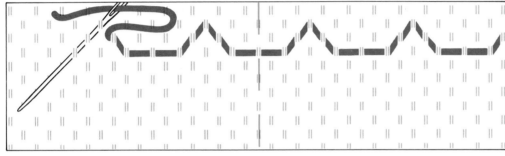

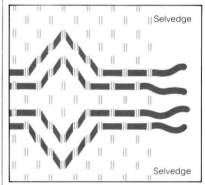

Selvedge

Selvedge

If a design runs all the way to a seam, leave ends free; they will be caught in seam.

Turn work right side up again and work next row, going from right to left, using a continuous length of thread.

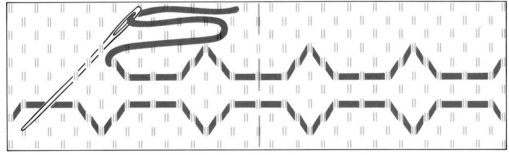

Work all other rows from right to left, using continuous lengths of thread. Stitch carefully, using the laid rows as a guide.

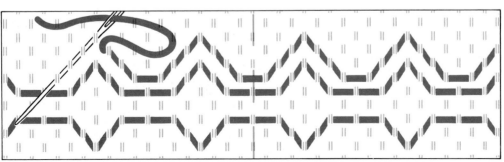

To join thread ends within pattern, run thread to very end. Start new thread 2.5 cm back.

Openwork/ Pulled thread embroidery

Introduction to pulled thread work
Working a pulled thread work piece
Stitch patterns

Introduction

Pulled thread embroidery (or drawn fabric work) is a type of openwork often employed to decorate linens. In pulled thread work, each stitch pulls the fabric threads together, creating open, lace-like patterns. Simple embroidery stitches are used also to outline motifs or to add textural interest.

Being a form of counted-thread embroidery, pulled thread work is usually stitched on even-weave fabrics. Select a thread similar in weight to a single fabric thread drawn from the fabric. Use the largest tapestry needle that will slip easily between fabric threads. This will exaggerate the openings. Use an embroidery hoop or frame, but do not stretch fabric too tightly or the stitches will not 'pull' effectively.

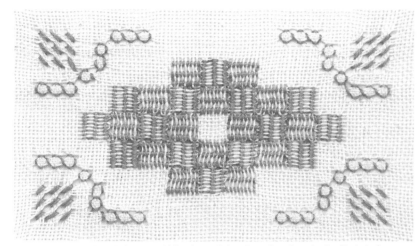

Pulled thread work piece combining three stitch patterns from the selection illustrated.

Working a pulled thread work piece

For any pulled thread work piece, first find the fabric centre and mark with tacking. Then position motifs, counting threads from centre point out. If outer edges of motif will be covered with an embroidery stitch, you can *draw* the outline on right side of fabric. If outline will not be covered, use tacking stitches. Work motifs one at a time, from centre one out; work stitch patterns in rows (see next three pages). Always secure row ends as shown below. Work all patterns, then add embellishments.

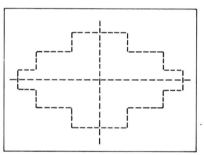

Mark centre of fabric, then draw or tack motifs on fabric, counting threads from centre.

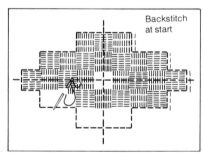

Backstitch at start

Work motif groups one at a time, from centre of piece out; work stitch patterns in rows.

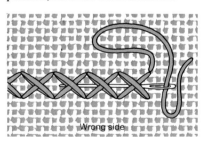

Always secure row ends by passing needle under worked stitches on wrong side. Then pull out the backstitches worked at the beginning and secure those thread ends the same way.

To tie in new thread. Make loop for simple knot; hold twisted part with thumbnail close to last stitch; pull to small circle; insert thread end to form second loop. Thread new thread; pull

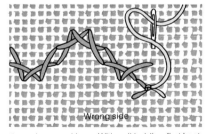

through second loop. With nail holding first knot, tug on second loop to pull first partly closed. Pull old and new threads opposite ways until second loop disappears and clicks through first. Trim.

Stitch patterns

Pulled thread embroidery offers quite a choice of stitch patterns. Here and on the next two pages we show step-by-step instructions for six of the most popular. Each stitch pattern is worked in rows.

Depending on the pattern, rows may run from side to side, horizontally or vertically. The needle movements are simple, though changing rows can be confusing. Follow each sequence carefully, noting the needle movements and direction in which the fabric is held. (Often it is turned for easier handling.) The last illustration in each sequence shows the look of the pulled threads.

Begin with a few backstitches outside the area to be worked. End by weaving thread into back of work. Finally, pull out the first backstitches and weave those, too, into the back of the work.

Four-sided stitch is worked in horizontal rows, always moving from right to left. To start, come up at 1, go in at 2 and out at 3 to the left of 1. Go in at 1 and come up at 4 above 3. Go in at 2, come up at 3. Pull each stitch tight. *Repeat sequence* until row is complete. For next row, turn fabric upside-down and work second row as you did first. At end of row, turn fabric again for start of third row.

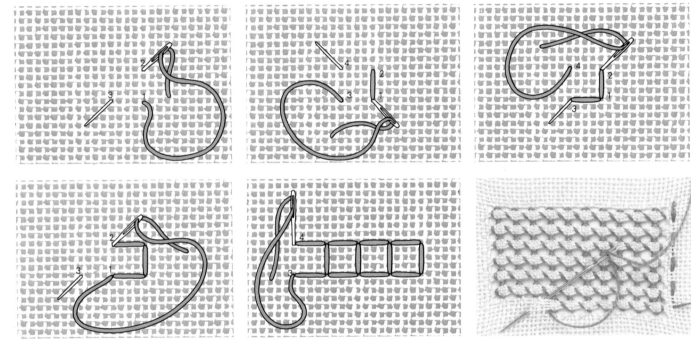

Coil filling stitch is made of groups of satin stitches worked in horizontal rows. To start, come up at 1 and work three satin stitches. Move to next group, four fabric threads to left, repeat Steps 1 to 6. At end of row, come up at 1 below for start of next row. Work second row left to right, third right to left.

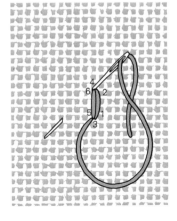
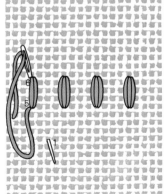
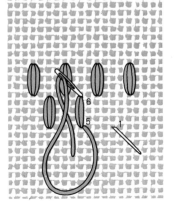
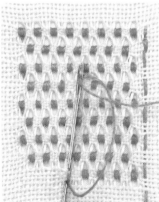

Openwork/Pulled thread embroidery

Stitch patterns

Chessboard filling stitch is worked in blocks. Each block is worked in three rows (eight stitches each) alternately right to left, then left to right. At end of third row, turn as shown and come up at 1 to start new block. *Work all subsequent blocks like the first, turning as shown for each new block.*

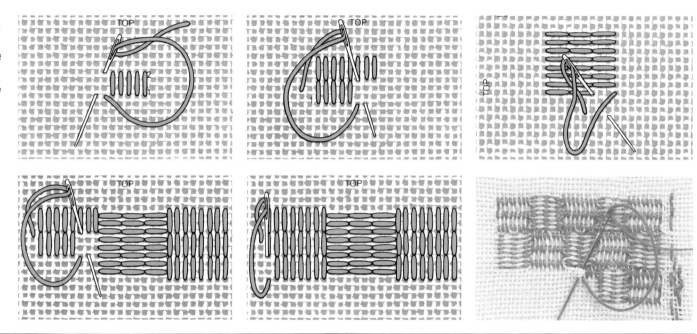

Framed cross is worked in two parts. First work the vertical pairs of stitches in rows alternately from right to left, then left to right, until desired number of rows are completed. *Then turn fabric* as shown and work pairs of stitches perpendicular to the first set, working rows alternately right to left, then left to right.

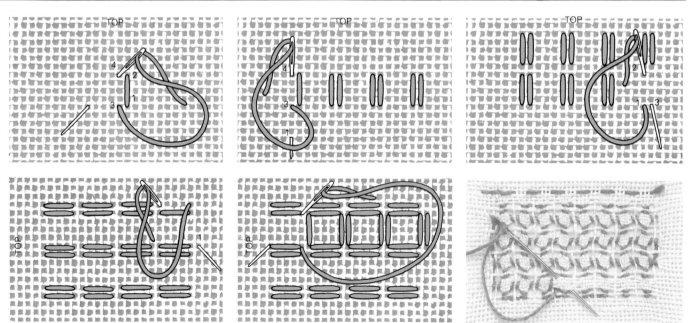

76

Ringed backstitch is worked in two journeys. In the first, a series of half-rings are formed. In the second journey, the rings are completed. To start, come up at 1, go in at 2 and out at 3. Continue working backstitches through Step 9. (A 1 to 9 sequence forms two half-rings or eight stitches.) *Repeat sequence* until desired number of half-rings are formed. At end of row, turn fabric and work other half of rings as shown. Always move from right to left; turn fabric to accomplish this.

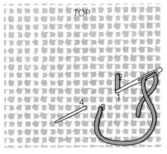 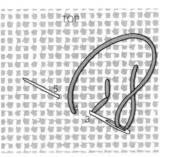 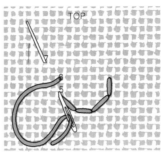 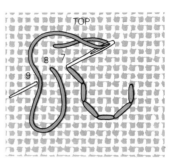

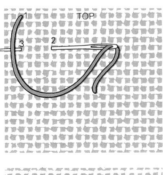 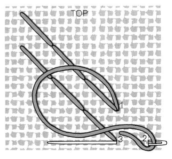 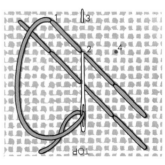

Reverse faggot stitch is worked in pairs of diagonal rows. Worked as shown, stitch fills a square area. Square is worked one half at a time. To start, come up at 1, go in at 2 and out at 3 directly across from 2. Go in at 4, come up at 2. Repeat the sequence until two rows are formed, having four and three stitches respectively. (Subsequent rows shorten similarly to form a corner of the square.) Turn fabric to begin next rows. *Using same 1 to 4 sequence*, work second pair of rows. Turn fabric upright for third pair. Work the other half of the square the same way. Note that because the second set of rows uses some of the same holes as the first set, double lines of stitching are formed.

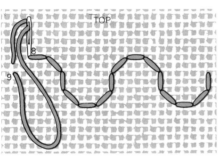 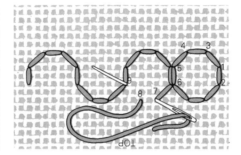 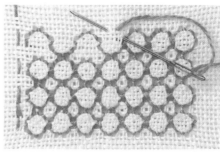

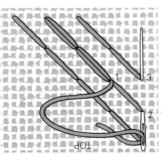 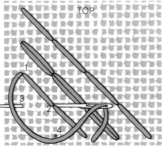 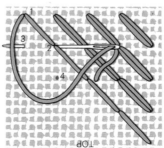 

77

Openwork/ Drawn thread work

Drawn thread work techniques

Drawn thread work is a type of openwork embroidery in which some of the weft and warp threads are drawn out or removed from the fabric. The remaining threads in the drawn area are then grouped together by means of different stitches, creating an open, lacy effect. There are two basic types of drawn thread work, **hemstitching** and **needleweaving**, both used primarily for border decorations on table linen. Fabric threads are drawn out the same way in both hemstitching and needleweaving. They differ in the way the remaining threads are decorated.

Introduction to hemstitching

Hemstitching is the most common type of drawn thread work. It is called hemstitching because as it groups threads within a drawn border, it may also hem the edge below the border. It can also be used solely to group threads in a drawn border, without a hemmed edge.

Almost any woven fabric can be used, though an even-weave is easiest to handle. Select a thread of a thickness comparable to one strand of your fabric. Use stranded cotton or fine pearl cotton and work with a tapestry needle.

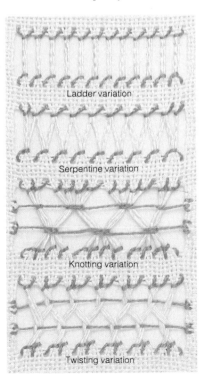

Ladder variation

Serpentine variation

Knotting variation

Twisting variation

Preparing fabric for hemstitching

To prepare an edge for hemstitching, you must first decide how deep and wide the border will be. Exact width and depth depend on the stitch variation you select (see pp. 80–81). Each one calls for the grouping of a certain number of vertical threads; a border's actual width will be a multiple of the threads in one group. Stitch variations differ, too, in depth, as the illustrations show.

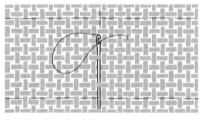

Determine border width

and depth

Allow for double hem plus 5 mm for turning

Decide distance of border from edge. If hem is needed, allow twice hem depth plus 5 mm for turning. Tack mark as explained below.

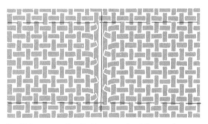

After drawing threads, press raw edge under; press hem up so top edge is one fabric thread from bottom of border. Pin and tack hem.

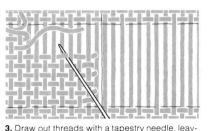

Drawing threads. 1. Tack along top and bottom of border between two horizontal threads. Tack-mark approximate width, then the centre.

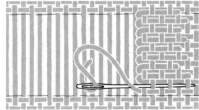

2. Using a pair of sharp embroidery scissors, carefully cut the horizontal fabric threads at the centre of the marked border.

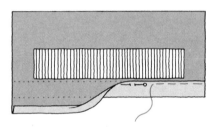

3. Draw out threads with a tapestry needle, leaving free the exact number of vertical threads for the stitch variation you plan to work.

4. At border edges, weave fabric threads back into the wrong side of the fabric for 2.5 cm. Trim excess after weaving.

Working basic hemstitch

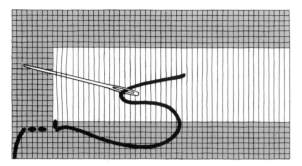

Without a hem, basic hemstitch is usually worked from wrong side of fabric. To start, leave 15 cm of thread and work backstitches up to left edge of border. Take a small vertical stitch to right of edge. Then pass needle from right to left under fixed number (3-5) of vertical threads. Pull together into bundle.

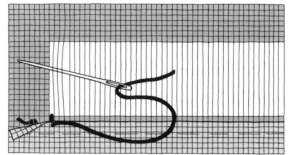

With a hem, too, basic hemstitch is usually worked from wrong side. To start, bring needle up at left edge of border, securing thread in hem fold with a simple knot. Take small vertical stitch just to right of edge, being sure to catch hem. Then pass needle under fixed number of vertical threads (3-5) and pull together into bundle.

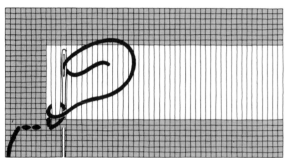

Take a small vertical stitch under two horizontal threads to the right of the bundle. Continue working in this way over the entire width of the border, keeping the small vertical stitches even throughout.

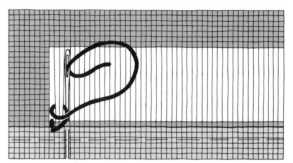

Take a small vertical stitch through right side, emerging at hem fold, to right of thread bundle. Continue working in this way across entire width of border.

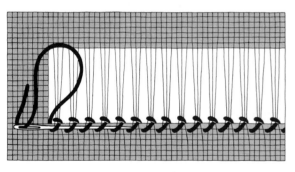

At end of border, still on the wrong (working) side, pass needle through completed stitches to secure. Pull out the backstitches at left edge of border and secure these as well by passing the thread through the completed stitches there.

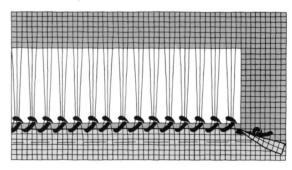

When the stitching is complete, secure it by passing needle through hem fold and hem stitches. Trim excess thread.

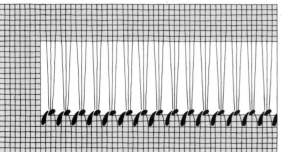

The finished effect on the right side (when work is done on the wrong side) is shown on the left. If you prefer the look of the small loops formed on the working side, as shown immediately above, work hemstitching from right side of fabric. Secure thread ends on the wrong side; they should, of course, be invisible.

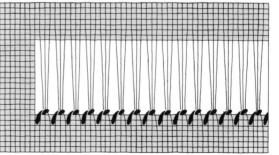

Look of right side (when worked from the wrong) is shown on the left. If you prefer the looped effect shown above, work hemstitching from the right side of the fabric, being sure to catch hem, which will not be visible as you work. Finish off thread ends, of course, on the wrong side.

Openwork/Drawn thread work

Grouping variations

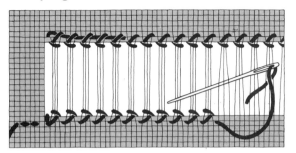

Ladder variation. To work, complete a row of basic hemstitch. Turn work upside-down and work basic stitch on opposite edge. Stitch from left to right, catching the same threads in each bundle as were caught above to form a ladder-like pattern. Secure thread at both ends as for basic hemstitch.

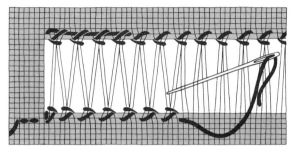

Serpentine variation. To work, complete a row of basic hemstitch, making sure each bundle has an *even* number of threads. Turn and work basic stitch on other edge, grouping halves of adjacent bundles together. First and last bundles will contain half as many threads as other bundles.

Knotting variations

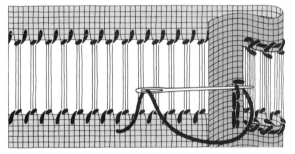

Simple knotted effect. To work, begin with a ladder variation on a border at least 1 cm deep. (Number of bundles must be a multiple of number grouped in second step.) Secure thread by working backstitches along right edge of border. Then oversew as shown, emerging at centre, from wrong side, for next step.

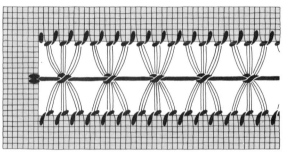

Continue working over remaining groups of bundles. When border is complete, oversew at left edge to fasten, then weave end of thread invisibly into back of fabric. Pull out the backstitches at opposite end and secure them the same way.

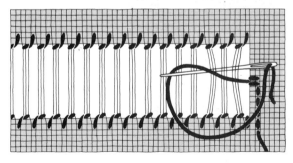

Working from right side of fabric, group the desired number of bundles (here three) as follows: loop thread as shown; pass needle behind thread and under bundles; bring needle out with thread under point.

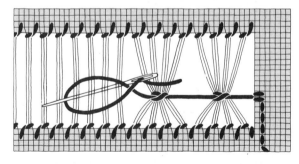

Double knotted effect. To work, draw out border at least 1.5 cm deep. Work a ladder variation. (The number of ladder bundles must be a multiple of 4.) Then work a simple knot, grouping four bundles one-third of the way up the drawn border.

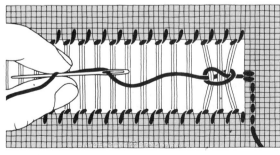

Pull needle through to form knot around bundles at the centre of the border depth. This is a version of coral stitch (p. 31).

Work the same knot two-thirds of the way up the border, taking adjacent halves of the bottom bundles in each knot. The first and last groups will contain half as many bundles as the others.

Twisting variations

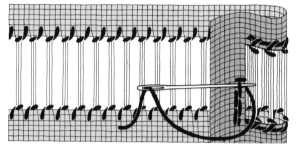

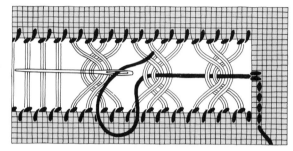

Simple twisted border. To work, complete ladder variation on a border at least 1 cm deep. (Work an even number of bundles.) Then, on right side of fabric, secure end of thread by backstitching along the right edge. Oversew as shown, emerging at centre, from wrong side, for next step.

Multiple bundles can be twisted in the same way that two are twisted. (For the variation shown here, number of bundles must be a multiple of 4.)

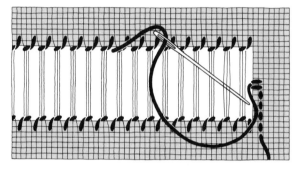

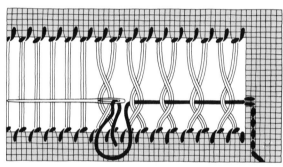

Working from right side of fabric, place needle over first two bundles. Then angle it down and towards the right, going under the second bundle and over the first with the tip of the needle.

Double twisted effect. Draw out a border at least 1.5 cm deep and work a ladder variation. (The number of bundles must be a multiple of 2.) Then work a simple twisting stitch one-third of the way up, grouping two bundles together.

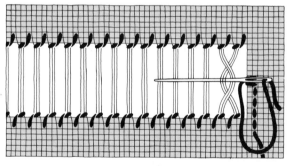

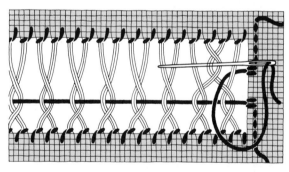

Press tip of needle against the first bundle and scoop it to the left, under the second bundle. Pulling the first bundle under the second causes the two to cross as shown.

Work the same simple twisting stitch at the top one-third of the border, but go under the first bundle before beginning actual twisting. The first bundle is missed in order to stagger twisting points of the top and bottom rows.

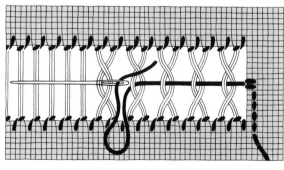

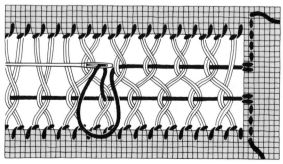

Pull the needle through, keeping thread taut to hold bundles in position. Continue working over pairs of bundles until entire border is twisted. At left edge, fasten thread with oversewing, then weave end invisibly into back of fabric. Remove backstitches at opposite end; secure the same way.

Continue twisting in this way until border is completed. Be sure to keep thread taut to hold intricate pattern in place. Fasten end of thread on left edge of border with oversewing. Weave end invisibly into back of fabric. Remove backstitches at opposite end and secure them in the same way.

Openwork/Drawn thread work

Handling drawn corners

Often a drawn thread border of hemstitching (or of needleweaving) will run along all four edges of an article such as a napkin, a tablecloth or a handkerchief. This will result in completely open corner areas where both warp and weft fabric threads have been drawn out. Drawn corners, depending on their size, can either be left open or decoratively filled with additional stitches. A small corner can be left open. A larger one should be filled to give it stability.

Decorating drawn corners

When the hemstitched border is shallow (less than 1.5 cm), the open corners will be small and can be left open. The outer edges of the corner, however, should be reinforced with the **basic buttonhole stitch** or **tailor's buttonhole stitch**.

When the border is deep (1.5 cm or more), the corners will be larger. These should be reinforced with a buttonhole stitch, then decorated as well. Decora-tive stitches help to strengthen large corners. Two such stitches are shown on these pages, **loopstitch** and **dove's eye filling**. Loopstitch forms a simple, flower-like motif and can be used with basic hemstitch or any hemstitch variation that has a straight bundle at each corner edge. Dove's eye filling forms an 'X' with a circular centre and can be used with any form of hemstitching.

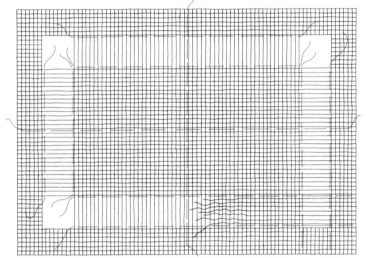

To prepare for corners, cut fabric to desired size, including hem allowance (see p. 78). Tack through horizontal and vertical centres. Measure and tack border's outer edges, then its inner edges; keep tackings between fabric threads. Draw threads (p. 78), being sure that all sides contain the correct number for the stitch variation chosen. Hem as described at far right on opposite page.

BUTTONHOLE STITCHES

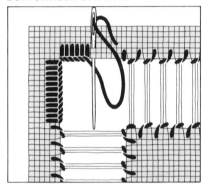

Basic buttonhole stitch. Work on outer edges of all corners, whether to be open or filled. Stitch from right side, two to three fabric threads deep, catching hem if there is one.

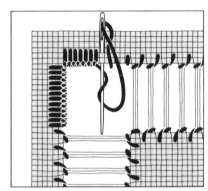

Tailor's buttonhole stitch. An alternative to the basic buttonhole stitch, and worked like it except that the thread is wrapped around the needle as shown before it is pulled through.

Hemstitching to and around corners

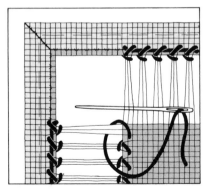

Hemstitch outer edges first, ending with small vertical stitch at last bundle of threads. To secure, pass thread through completed stitches; secure other end the same way, removing backstitches.

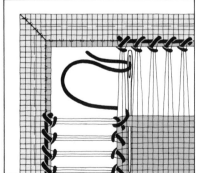

Hemstitching at the **inner edges** turns corners. Notice that thread simply wraps the last bundle on the left edge, then the first one on the top edge, before the small vertical stitch is taken.

DOVE'S EYE FILLING

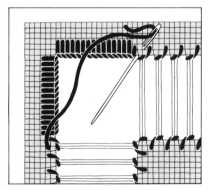

Dove's eye. 1. First reinforce edges with buttonhole stitch. Then bring needle up at lower left corner. Insert needle in fabric at upper right corner, coming out at corner opening.

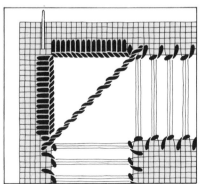

2. Oversew the laid thread, working from upper right to lower left corner. Take needle to back of fabric and slip it through the buttonhole stitches, coming up at top left corner of square.

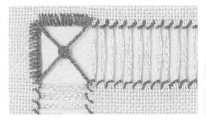

Buttonhole stitch reinforcing corner edges.

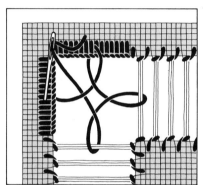

Loopstitch worked in large open corner.

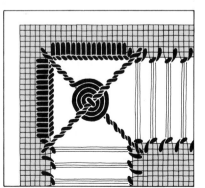

Dove's eye worked in large open corner.

Hemming corners

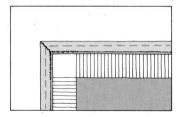

To hem corners, press under 5 mm on raw edges. Press hem so fold is just below border edge. Unfold pressed hem.

LOOPSTITCH

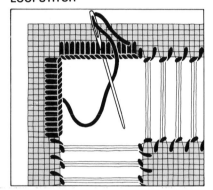

Loopstitch. 1. Work buttonhole stitch on outer edges. Then draw thread through underside of stitches, coming up at left centre. Take a stitch at top centre (thread passes under needle).

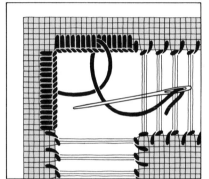

2. Loop needle over and under bundle at right edge; keep thread under needle. Do not pull thread too tightly; leave some slack to create open-looking loops and to avoid distortion.

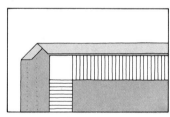

3. Loop needle over and under bundle at bottom edge. Pass needle under thread at left edge and take a stitch at left centre. Run needle through buttonhole stitches on wrong side to secure.

Trim off each corner diagonally as shown above, cutting along the diagonal of the corner square formed by the creases.

DOVE'S EYE FILLING–continued

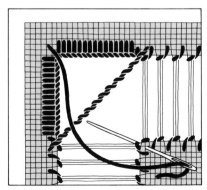

3. Bring needle over laid thread and insert into fabric at lower right corner. Come out again at the opening, pulling the thread tight enough to form an even 'X' with the other laid thread.

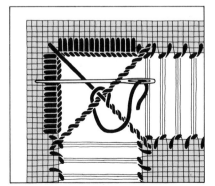

4. Oversew second laid thread to the point where the two threads cross. Weave under and over the laid threads at centre point, going anti-clockwise, until dove's eye is desired size.

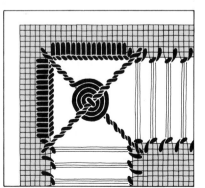

5. Oversew remainder of diagonal yarn to upper left corner. Secure stitching thread at back of fabric by running needle through buttonhole stitches along top edge of open square.

Turn down trimmed corner first. Then re-fold hem edges along the pressed lines to form neat, mitred corners.

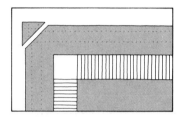

Pin and tack hem. Slipstitch mitred edges, also tack hem edge along outer corner. Hemstitch hem in place (p. 79).

Openwork/Drawn thread work

Needleweaving

Needleweaving, like hemstitching, decorates threads in a drawn thread border. In needleweaving, however, thread bundles are covered, with the thread ends secured under the covering.

The basic stitches are *overcast stitch* and *darning stitch*. Overcasting wraps the drawn threads, forming vertical bars. Darning weaves over and under them, giving a braid-like finish.

If needleweaving is 'attached' (covers the bundles), the border is not usually hemstitched. (The hem, if there is one, must then be slipstitched.) Hemstitching is advised for 'detached' types (see darning variation on opposite page).

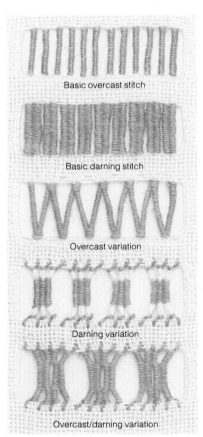

Basic overcast stitch

Basic darning stitch

Overcast variation

Darning variation

Overcast/darning variation

Basic needleweaving stitches

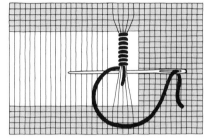

Basic overcast stitch. Place end of working thread over the five threads to be overcast. Wrap working thread over threads and thread end.

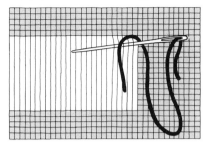

Pull threads taut as you work. Place them close together with the needle from time to time. Take care not to let wrapping threads overlap.

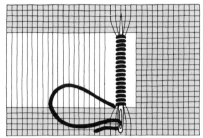

When bar is completed, run needle through it to secure thread. If fit is tight, change to a thinner, sharp-pointed needle. Trim excess thread.

Needleweaving variations

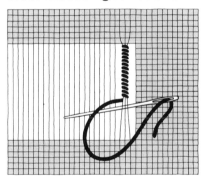

Overcast variation. Prepare drawn border, with total threads a multiple of three. **1.** Work one basic overcast bar over three threads.

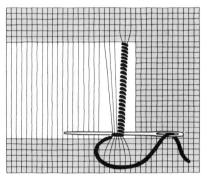

2. Just above bottom edge of border, overcast twice over six threads as shown, pulling first and second bundles together.

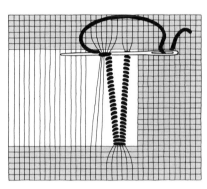

3. Work up over second three-thread bundle. At top, overcast twice over six threads, pulling second and third bundles together.

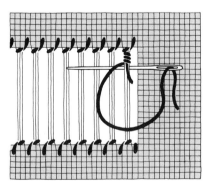

Overcast/darning variation. Bundles multiple of four, three threads each in ladder hemstitch. **1.** Overcast top quarter of first bundle.

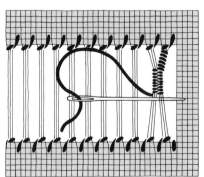

2. Change to darning stitch and darn over and under first and second groups of threads until three-quarters of the border depth is covered.

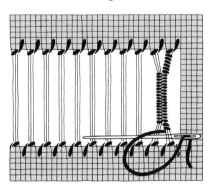

3. Change back to overcasting stitch and wrap the remainder of the first group of threads to the bottom edge of the border.

84

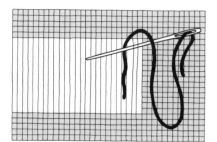

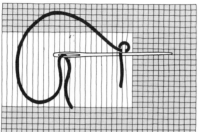

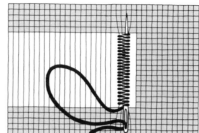

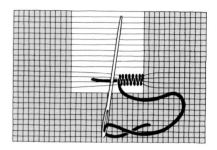

Basic darning stitch. Lay thread end along first four threads. Pass needle under first two (have thread behind needle); pull it through. Then pass needle back under second two threads, grouping four threads and thread end together, in figure-eight movement. Continue weaving needle over and back until bar is covered. To secure thread, run needle through woven bar; if fit is tight, change to thinner needle. Trim. If working across vertical bars is awkward for you, **turn the work** so that the bar lies **horizontally,** and work darning stitch as shown.

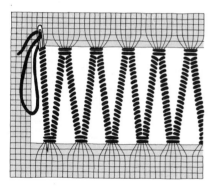

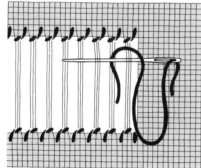

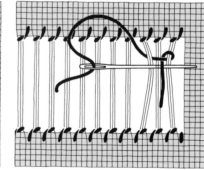

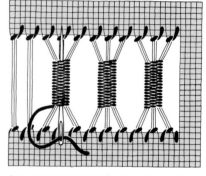

4. Continue this way to end of border, creating a zigzag effect. Run needle through last bar to secure yarn; change to thinner needle if fit is tight.

Darning variation. Work ladder hemstitch (see p. 80), with ladder bundles a multiple of 3. **1.** To begin, place needle as shown above.

2. Darn three bundles together along centre half, moving needle right to left, left to right until centre half is darned. Pull thread taut as you weave.

3. As each bar is completed, run the needle up through it to secure thread; trim excess. If fit is tight, change to a thinner needle.

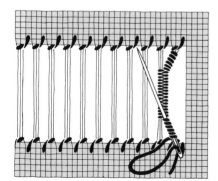

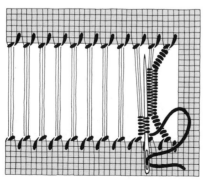

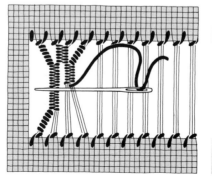

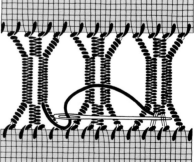

4. Slip needle up through these last overcasting stitches to get into position for next step. If fit is tight, change to thinner needle.

5. Darn second and third groups together to bottom edge. Run thread through just-darned area; use thinner needle if necessary. Trim.

6. Turn work upside-down and, using new length of thread, repeat entire sequence to fill in other half of pattern. Turn right side up for next one.

7. Continue working individual units by halves, the first half right side up, the work turned for second half, until border is filled.

Openwork/ Hardanger embroidery

Introduction to Hardanger
Kloster blocks
Working a motif
Covered bars
Filling stitches
Decorating a motif

Introduction

Hardanger embroidery is a type of openwork named after the district of Hardanger in Norway. Similar work was done in Persia centuries ago.

Hardanger is characterised by precisely worked blocks of satin stitch called **kloster blocks**. These are arranged to form the outer shapes of motifs and are often worked within these shapes as well. When blocks have been stitched, warp and weft threads are cut and drawn out in appropriate places (where there are kloster blocks opposite each other to secure ends). Remaining fabric threads within the motifs are covered to form either **overcast** or **woven bars**. The open squares between bars can be decorated with various filling stitches. Often surface stitching is added to enhance the overall design.

Because Hardanger is a type of counted thread embroidery, it is advisable to plot a piece on graph paper – first the shapes and placings of motifs, then bars, fillings and embellishments. To prepare the piece for working, tack the outline of each motif on the fabric.

The work is generally done on Hardanger fabric, which has double warp and weft threads. Almost any evenweave fabric will do, however. Because kloster blocks are worked over a uniform number of fabric threads, the finer the fabric (the more threads per centimetre), the smaller a motif will be.

Ideally, two sizes of thread are used. Thread for kloster blocks should be slightly thicker than the threads of the fabric; the usual choice is a medium-weight pearl cotton. To cover bars and work filling stitches, thread should be thinner – either a fine pearl cotton or a suitable number of stranded cotton strands. Originally, Hardanger was worked with white thread on white fabric; today both thread and fabric are often coloured.

Always do this work in an embroidery hoop or frame.

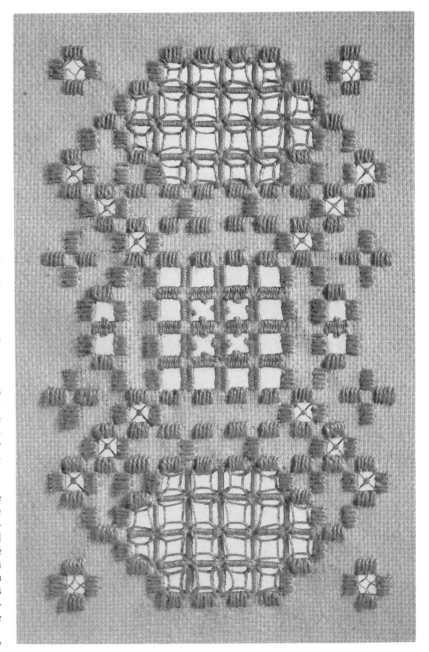

Hardanger piece of overcast bars, woven bars, loopstitches and dove's eyes (pp. 88–89).

Kloster blocks

The basic kloster block consists of five satin stitches worked over four fabric threads. In a motif, the blocks may be worked across in rows or diagonally in steps. In placing the blocks, remember that they must be opposite each other where warp and weft threads will be cut. While the basic kloster block is always worked in the same way, the movement from block to block varies with the arrangement. When blocks are in steps (see drawings below), stitching direction alternates from row to row.

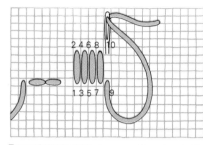

To work kloster block, secure thread end with backstitches; come up at 1 and work five satin stitches, each over four fabric threads.

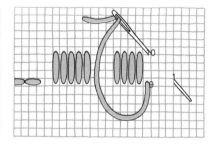

To work blocks in a row, stitch first block as usual. At end, come up four fabric threads to the right of point 9 to start the next block.

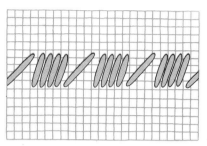

When kloster blocks are worked in a row, there should be single slanting threads from block to block on the **wrong side** of the fabric.

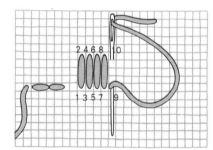

To work blocks diagonally in steps, stitch first block as usual. At the end, come up again at point 9 where the last satin stitch began.

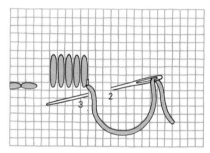

Point 9 of first block is point 1 of the second block. Start the second block by working a *horizontal* satin stitch over four fabric threads.

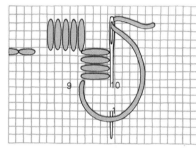

Work last stitch of second block as usual (up at 9, in at 10). Come up four fabric threads below 10 to start *vertical* stitches of third block.

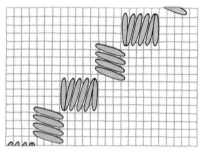

When kloster blocks are worked diagonally, there should be no trailing threads between blocks on the **wrong side** of the fabric.

Working a motif

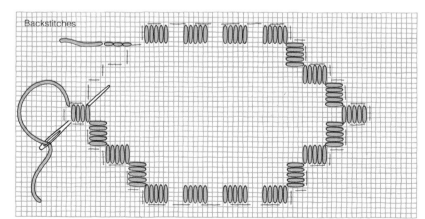

To work a motif. Tack shape on to fabric. Secure thread end with backstitches. Working clockwise, go from block to block as instructed above. For every block where threads will be cut, another must be worked directly opposite, in the same direction, enclosing the same fabric threads. At end of motif, run thread under five blocks to secure. Pull out backstitches and secure thread the same way.

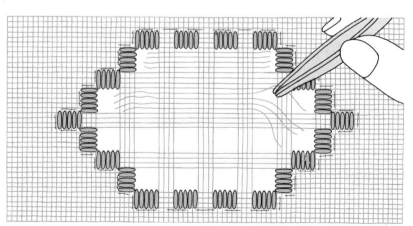

To remove threads. With sharp embroidery scissors, cut four threads at the base of a kloster block; cut *same* four threads at base of opposing block. (All cut threads must be secured at both ends by blocks.) Cut only threads that run the same way as satin stitches – never those the satin stitches cross. Remove threads with tweezers. Draw all appropriate threads running one way, then those running the other.

Openwork/Hardanger embroidery

Covered bars

When kloster blocks have been worked and threads drawn, motifs are usually decorated. The loose threads are **overcast** or **woven** into covered bars; *picots* (loops) can be added to woven bars during weaving. Open areas are generally embellished with filling stitches. Secure beginning thread with backstitches. To start a new thread, secure thread end under next bar as you cover it.

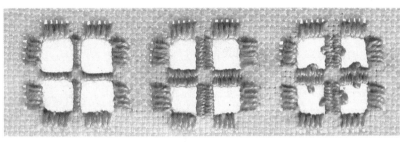

Overcast bars   **Woven bars**   **Woven bars with picots**

Filling stitches

The three filling stitches shown in the sampler on the right and explained below are **oblique loopstitch, straight loopstitch** and **dove's eye filling**. These are basic filling techniques that, like other aspects of Hardanger embroidery, can be and are varied in many ways.

Fillings differ, too, in their usage. They can be worked to fill all the open areas in a motif, as suggested in the illustrations on the far right. Or squares can be filled selectively. An area can be filled with one kind of stitch, or several.

The directional and other advice given earlier applies equally to the working of filling stitches. The recommendation that bars and fillings be worked diagonally is simply for convenience; it is generally easier to pass from bar-to bar in this direction. If an area is to be worked in bars alone, many needleworkers recommend working all bars in one direction, then all bars in the other.

When all work on a motif is finished, run the thread through the backs of five or more kloster blocks to secure it; remove the beginning backstitches and secure them the same way. Start a new thread by working over its beginning end as you cover the next bar. For details of this manoeuvre, and some other useful similarities between Hardanger embroidery and needleweaving, refer to pp. 84–85.

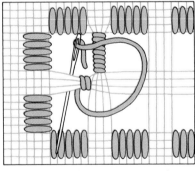

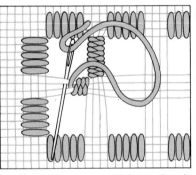

To overcast a bar, wrap thread compactly around thread bundle; **to weave a bar,** bring needle up in centre of bundle and weave thread over and under pairs of threads. As bundles are covered, move in diagonal steps from bar to bar, passing thread behind threads or through backs of kloster blocks.

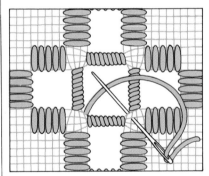

Oblique loopstitch. Come up at lower left, go in at lower right, come up at opening. With thread under needle, pull it through, leaving a loop.

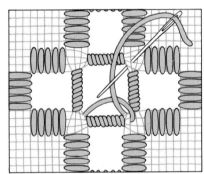

Insert needle into fabric at upper right corner, come up at opening. Making sure thread is under needle, pull it through, again leaving a loop.

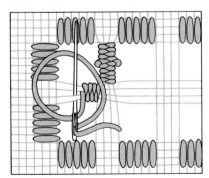

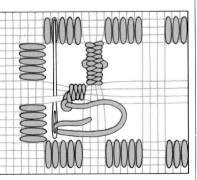

Woven bar with picot. Weave half of bar. Bring needle up through centre; loop thread under it as shown. Pull thread through to form small loop.

Insert needle under same two threads and pull it through. Work another picot through two threads on opposite side. Weave rest of bar.

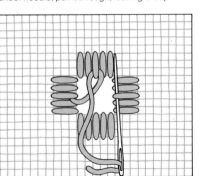

Straight loopstitch in area enclosed by kloster blocks. Come up at left below centre stitch; loop thread right to left through top centre stitch.

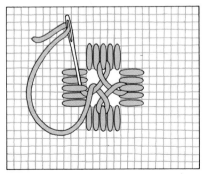

Continue working around square, looping thread through centre stitch at each side. Always carry thread under needle. Stitch last loop as shown.

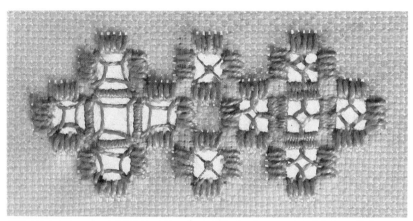

Filling stitches shown are, left to right, **oblique loopstitch, dove's eye** and **straight loopstitch.**

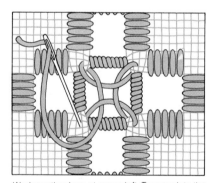

Work another loop at upper left. To complete the stitch, pass needle under first laid thread and insert it into fabric at lower left corner.

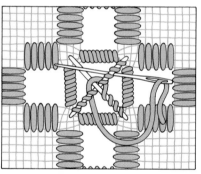

Dove's eye filling. Crossed laid threads are woven over and under at centre to form circular filling. For instructions, see pp. 82–83.

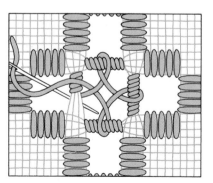

To work **straight loops with overcast bars,** work 3½ bars. Before working last half, make loops as on the left. Finish overcasting of last bar.

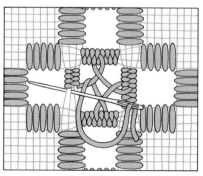

To work **straight loops with woven bars,** work 3½ bars. Then work loops, going through centre of bars (over two threads). Weave last half of bar.

Decorating a motif

Because Hardanger designs vary so widely, it is difficult to give precise rules to suit all of them. It will help, however, especially on the first try, to understand some general principles that can be applied to most typical motifs. With those, and some practical experience, it should not be long before you can work Hardanger embroidery with the traditional precision and delicacy.

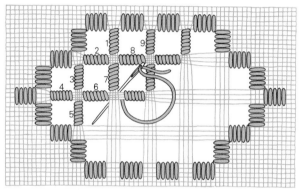

To work bars, most experts recommend the procedure shown, which progresses in diagonal steps from the upper left over four bars (1-4), then up in similar steps over five bars (5-9), and so on until all thread bundles are covered. Bars can be worked in two journeys: first all bars across, then, with work turned, all bars in the other direction.

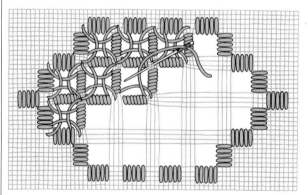

Oblique loops worked with bars go in the same general direction, the thread being passed behind adjacent fabric threads to reach the next opening. It is important to pass the threads in such a way that they are hidden. To start a new thread when needed, secure it in the most convenient bar.

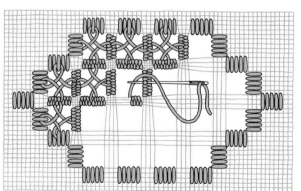

Straight loops with bars vary according to the sides of the opening that they are to fill – that is, whether individual loops go to a woven or overcast bar, or to a kloster block. The drawings on the left will refresh your memory.

Openwork/ Cutwork embroidery

Introduction to cutwork
Basic procedure
Making a cutwork piece

Introduction

Cutwork is a form of openwork embroidery that became fashionable in the 16th century and is still popular today, primarily for table linens and clothes. Despite its delicate look, cutwork is quite sturdy because each part of the design is outlined in close buttonhole stitch. After outlining, certain portions are cut away, giving the embroidery its characteristic airiness. Large cut-out areas are reinforced with embroidered bars, worked to bridge the areas and strengthen the work. Surface stitches are often added to enhance a cutwork design.

Closely woven fabrics (those not likely to fray) should be used for cutwork. Stitch with pearl cotton or stranded cotton and a sharp-pointed needle in a size that accommodates your thread. Use an embroidery hoop or frame while working the outline stitches. Remove work from frame before cutting.

Generally, the motifs in cutwork are floral, but other kinds can be used. In choosing a design, consider what areas will be cut away. If you are designing your own cutwork piece, think of the cut areas as negative and the uncut areas as positive, and try to balance the two.

There are three basic ways of arranging these positive and negative spaces. One is the stencil design, in which a motif is established by cutting away its main sections. (The small flowers in the sample are stencil designs.) Or a motif can be left intact and the background cut away, silhouetting the motif. (The stems and leaves in the sample are handled in this way.) Buttonhole-stitch outlining gives the shapes further definition. The third approach leaves some of the motif whole, with only small, interior sections cut away. This technique must be employed to achieve the shaped edge that is so attractive a feature of cutwork – it is the only one that permits a motif to be positioned at the very edge. (See the large corner flower in the sample.)

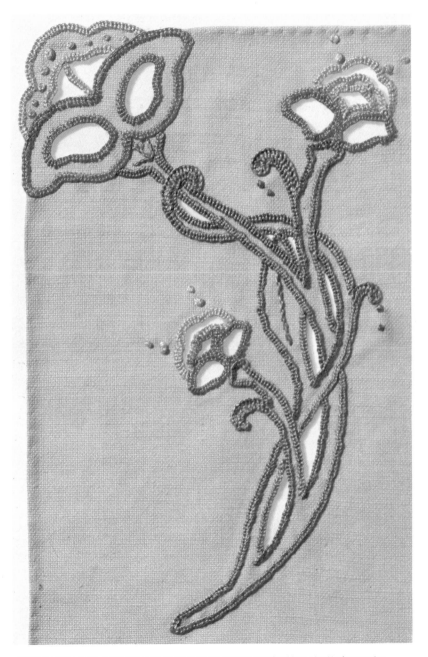

Cutwork piece features floral motifs. All outlining (in buttonhole stitch) is worked before cutting.

Basic procedure

The basic procedure for cutwork is quite simple, but the steps must be taken neatly and carefully to get professional results. The two main stitches in cutwork are **buttonhole stitch** and **running stitch.** The motifs are first 'drawn' with running stitches, then buttonhole stitch is worked over these lines. Be sure you know which side of a motif line will be cut away; the buttonhole stitch must be worked so that the ridge lies along the edge to be cut. If the fabric will be cut away on both sides of a line, outlining can be done with a **double buttonhole stitch** (two facing rows of the basic stitch, slightly overlapped at the centre).

To be sure that you will recognise the areas that are to be cut away, mark them before beginning to work the buttonhole stitch. On commercial transfers, open sections are often indicated by an 'X' that transfers on to the fabric. If you are creating your own design, you may wish to use a similar method.

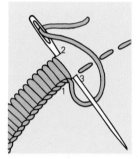
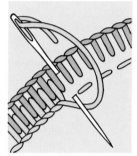

Buttonhole stitch is worked from left to right. Come up at 1, insert at 2, and come up at 3 directly below 2. Carry thread under needle point, pull through. Take care to keep stitches close together.
Double buttonhole stitch is two rows of the basic stitch. Work stitches in first row so that those of second row can go between them. Turn work to stitch second row.

Making a cutwork piece

First outline the design with *running stitches* (using either stranded cotton or pearl cotton). **Then cover the stitched shape** of the motif with a fine, close *buttonhole stitch*. Make certain that the ridge of the stitch falls on the side of the line that is to be cut away. Tailor's buttonhole stitch may also be used for this purpose. **Cut away design areas** indicated after removing work from frame or hoop. Work from the *wrong side;* this makes it easier to cut close to the base of the stitches. Be careful not to cut into the buttonhole stitches.

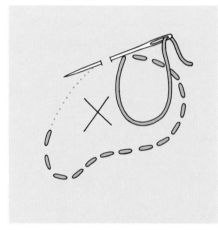
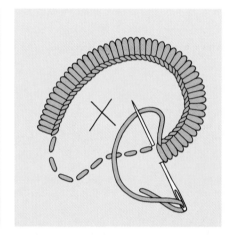
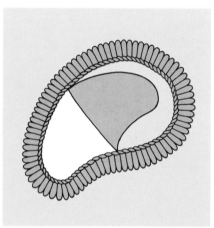

To work bars across an area, outline the design with running stitches until you come to a position for a bar. Carry thread across the area, take a small stitch, bring the thread back and take another stitch. **Work buttonhole stitch** over the laid thread *without catching fabric beneath.* Continue the running stitch around the rest of the motif, then outline it with fine buttonhole stitch. Cut away the fabric as above, taking care not to cut stitches.

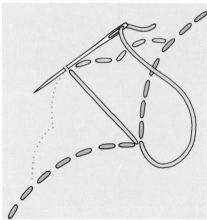
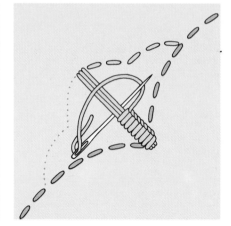
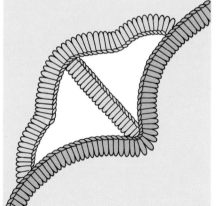

Smocking

Introduction

Smocking is a type of embroidery that decorates as well as gathers the fabric on which it is worked. It is based on a grid that is marked on the fabric in evenly spaced dots. Hot-iron transfers of smocking dots can be bought, or you can make your own dotted grid.

There are two basic smocking methods, **'mock' smocking** and **traditional.** In mock smocking, dots are marked on the *right* side of the fabric. The smocking stitches are worked from dot to dot, with the fabric gathered in each stitch. In traditional smocking, dots are marked on the *wrong* side of the fabric. Rows of uneven running stitches are worked from dot to dot, forming small, even pleats (known as 'tubes' or 'reeds'). Smocking stitches are then worked from the *right* side of the fabric, with a small stitch taken at each tube formed by the gathering. The look of the stitches is the same, regardless of the smocking method. The traditional method is particularly useful when combining different stitches (see p. 97).

Fabrics and grids

Smocking, as a rule, is worked on soft, lightweight fabrics (cotton, lawn, fine wool) with pearl cotton or stranded cotton and a crewel or chenille needle.

Since smocking gathers the fabric, you should work on a piece two and a half to three times the desired finished width. This proportion of flat to gathered width is approximate. How much is actually drawn up depends on fabric weight, stitch tension and the spacing between dots.

A smocking grid can be produced by

To use a transfer, cut it to fit the flat area to be smocked. Align the edges of the transfer with the fabric, leaving a seam allowance above the top row of dots. Press carefully.

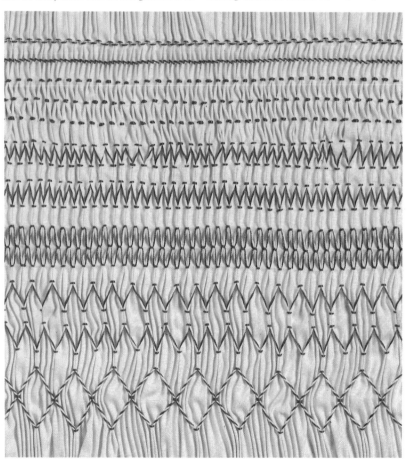

Smocking sampler of cable, stem, honeycomb, surface honeycomb, Vandyke, wave, trellis stitches.

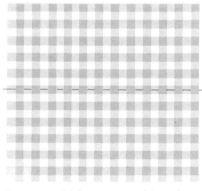

Even-weave fabrics, or even prints such as polka dots or gingham, need not be marked with transfer. The natural grid can guide your running stitches and gathering proceeds quickly.

Adding smocking to a garment

means of a hot-iron transfer. You can also plan your own on graph paper, or use an even-weave or an evenly printed fabric as a guide. Space between dots is usually from 3 to 5 mm; between rows of dots, from 3 mm to 1 cm. The closer the dots, the more elasticity the finished smocking will have.

While most stitches can be worked on any smocking grid without their appearance being markedly altered, some stitches require grids of a specific proportion.

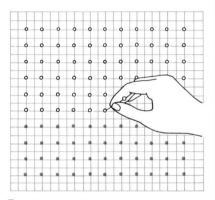

To use graph paper, cut it to fit fabric. Using a sharp stiletto or a needle or pin, pierce dots in paper to desired spacing. Place paper on fabric and mark dots with a hard pencil.

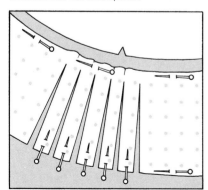

To mark curved area, use either a transfer or graph paper. On the grid, slash between dots to the top row. Align top edge of grid with curve, pin in place, and mark as usual.

Smocking can be a most attractive decoration for a garment. It is easiest to apply in areas that have simple, rectangular pattern pieces – a yoke, stand-up collar and cuffs – and it may be used to gather the neckline fullness of a dress for a baby.

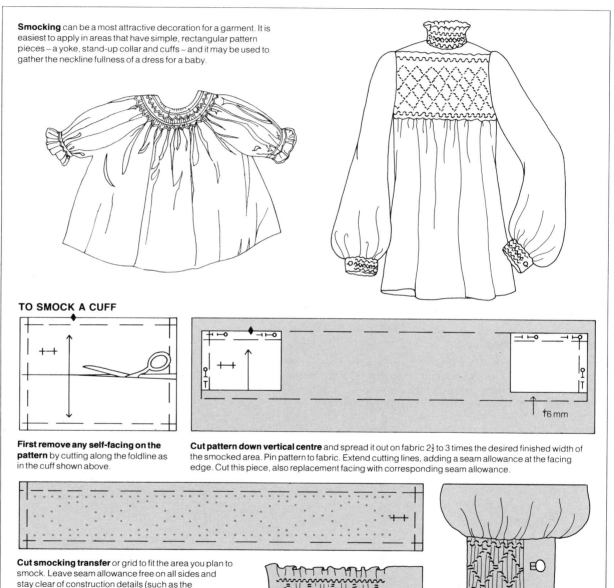

TO SMOCK A CUFF

First remove any self-facing on the pattern by cutting along the foldline as in the cuff shown above.

Cut pattern down vertical centre and spread it out on fabric 2½ to 3 times the desired finished width of the smocked area. Pin pattern to fabric. Extend cutting lines, adding a seam allowance at the facing edge. Cut this piece, also replacement facing with corresponding seam allowance.

↑6 mm

Cut smocking transfer or grid to fit the area you plan to smock. Leave seam allowance free on all sides and stay clear of construction details (such as the buttonhole on the cuff shown). Mark as usual.

Work smocking stitch or desired stitch combinations (pp. 94–97).

Construct garment according to pattern instructions, attaching smocked piece and replacement facing.

Smocking

Traditional smocking

Traditional smocking is recommended for use by beginners because preparatory gathering into tubes makes the actual smocking stitches easier to work. The rows of running stitches form even, secure pleats, gathering the fabric uniformly. This regulates the tension of the smocking stitches. Preparatory gathering does not, however, determine the width of the completed smocking.

When the running stitches are removed, the area will relax, how much depending on how tightly the smocking is worked. To prepare for gathering, mark the dots on the wrong side of the fabric. Be sure that the grid you mark is appropriate for the stitch you plan to work (see smocking stitches). Do the gathering by hand and work smocking stitches from right side of fabric.

To gather fabric, start thread with a knot at right end of top row of dots. Pick up fabric between dots, making small floats over dots (as shown), or make even running stitches from dot to dot. At end of row, leave a loose thread a few centimetres long. Work all other rows like the first.

Pull all thread ends together at left edge, forming parallel vertical tubes. Pull the threads only tight enough to form even, stable rows. Leave a small space between tubes.

Tie pairs of threads together until all threads are secured at left edge of fabric.

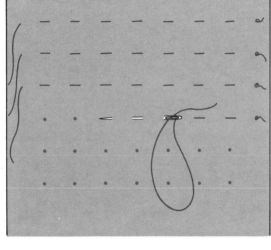
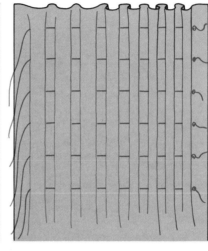
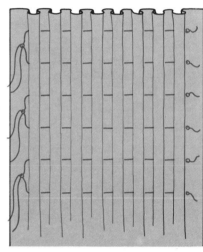

Smocking stitches

The stitch instructions that follow are illustrated in steps for mock smocking. The five stitches on these pages can be worked over any smocking grid. The last two stitches (stitch variations, p. 96) require grids of specific proportions; the grid proportions for these are indicated in the first step of their respective instructions. Be sure to follow these proportions carefully.

All of the stitches can also be worked in traditional smocking. The grid is the same (though the markings are placed on the wrong side of the fabric), and so are the stitch movements. Instead of taking a small stitch at a dot, however, take a stitch at the top of each tube along a row of running stitches. Pick up only a couple of fabric threads at a uniform point on the top of each tube. The last illustration in each sequence shows the stitches worked over the gathered tubes of this method and is intended to help you visualise this way of working.

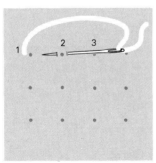
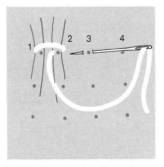
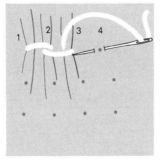
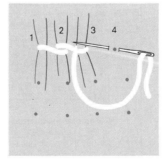
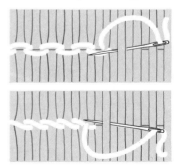

Cable stitch. Work this stitch from left to right. Come up at 1. Then take a small stitch at 2, keeping the thread above the needle.

Pull the thread taut so that points 1 and 2 are drawn together. Take another small stitch at 3, keeping the thread below the needle.

Take a stitch at 4, keeping thread above the needle. Continue this sequence, alternating position of thread above and below the needle.

Stem stitch (also known as outline stitch). Worked as for cable stitch except that the thread is always held below the needle.

Traditional method of working cable and stem stitch. Work across the rows of gathering, taking a small stitch through the top of each tube.

94

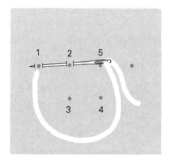 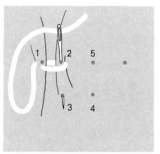 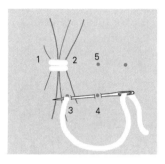 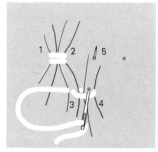 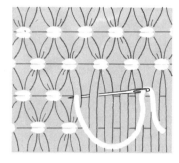

Honeycomb stitch. Work from left to right, with the needle pointing left. Come out at 1, take a small stitch at 2, another at 1. Pull thread taut.

Re-insert the needle at 2, come out at 3 on the row below directly below 2. (This stitch is worked back and forth along two rows of smocking dots.)

Take a small stitch at 4 and another at 3, keeping the needle pointing to the left. Pull the thread taut so that 3 and 4 are drawn together.

Re-insert the needle at 4 and come up in the top row at 5, directly above 4. Point 5 is now point 1 for the start of the next sequence.

Traditional method of working the honeycomb stitch. Work stitch back and forth along two rows of gathering stitches, catching the tube top as shown.

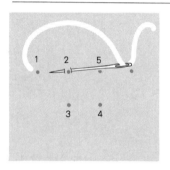 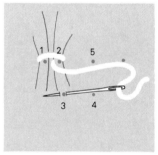 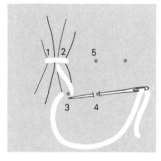 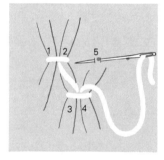 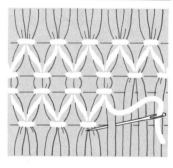

Surface honeycomb stitch. Work left to right, with needle pointing left. Come up at 1 and take a stitch at 2, keeping thread above needle.

Pull thread taut, drawing points 1 and 2 together. Then take a stitch at 3 directly below 2 on the second row of smocking dots.

Take a small stitch at 4, to the right of 3 on second row. Keep thread below needle. Pull thread taut, drawing points 3 and 4 together.

Return to top row and take a stitch at point 5 directly above 4. Point 5 is now point 1 for the beginning of the next sequence.

Traditional method of working surface honeycomb stitch. Work back and forth along two rows of gathering. Note the pattern created by two rows of this stitch.

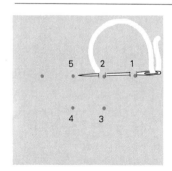 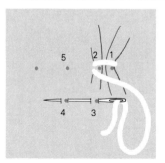 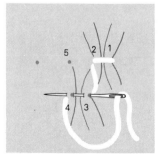 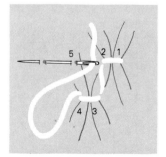 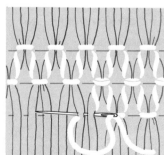

Vandyke stitch. Work from right to left, with needle pointing left. Come up at 2. Take a stitch at 1, another at 2. Keep thread above needle.

Pull the thread taut so that 1 and 2 are drawn together. Then take a stitch at 3 directly below 2 and a stitch at 4 to the left of 3.

Take another stitch at point 3 and at point 4, keeping the thread below the needle. Pull the thread taut so that 3 and 4 are drawn together.

Return to the first row of dots and take a stitch at 5 (point 1 for the next sequence). Repeat Steps 1 to 5 until the row is complete.

For traditional smocking, work Vandyke stitch along two rows of gathering. Note how two rows are worked with the centre stitches overlapping.

Smocking

Chain stitch 28   Cross stitch 35
Lazy daisy stitch 28   Satin stitch 48

Stitch variations

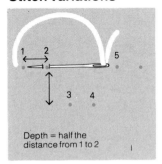 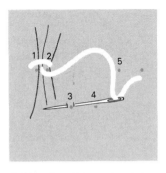 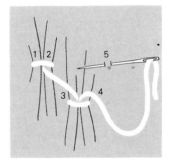 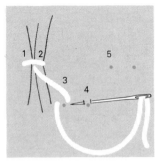 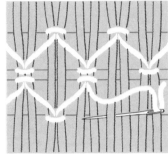

Depth = half the distance from 1 to 2

Wave stitch. Mark dots *only* where stitches will be taken. An all-over grid cannot be used. To work, come up at 1, take a stitch at 2.

Pull thread taut. Take another stitch at 3 below and to the right of 2 in the second row of dots. Wave stitch is worked along two rows of dots.

Keeping thread below needle, take another stitch at 4, directly to the right of 3. Pull thread taut to draw 3 and 4 together.

Return to top row, taking a stitch at point 5. Point 5 is now point 1 for the beginning of the next sequence. Continue pattern to end of row.

For traditional smocking, you can use an all-over grid as the dots do not show once the tubes are drawn up. Work stitch as on left.

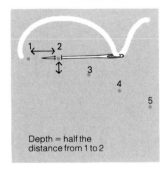 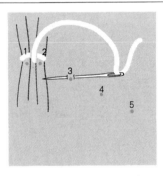 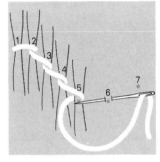 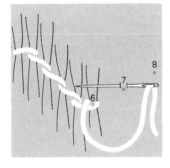 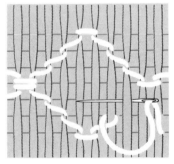

Depth = half the distance from 1 to 2

Trellis stitch. Mark dots as shown. An all-over grid cannot be used. To work, come up at 1, take a stitch at 2. Keep thread above needle.

Pull thread taut. Take another stitch at 3, keeping thread above needle. The distance from 1 to 2 is the same as the distance from 2 to 3.

Take stitches at point 4 and at point 5, still keeping thread above needle. Then take a stitch at 6, this time keeping thread below needle.

Take a stitch up at 7 and continue working diagonally upwards to the top row of dots. Repeat the sequence as needed to complete row.

In traditional smocking this stitch is known as Chevron stitch and can be worked over tubes drawn up in the normal way.

Embellishing stitches

Embroidery stitches are sometimes added to smocking for embellishment. The four stitches shown here (from left to right, lazy daisy, cross stitch, satin stitch and chain stitch) are worked between rows of smocking stitches or in the open areas formed by such stitches as trellis. Work all embellishments over two or more tubes. For detailed instructions, see basic embroidery, pp. 22–53.

 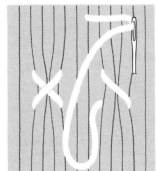 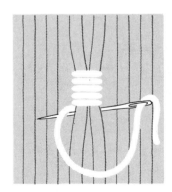 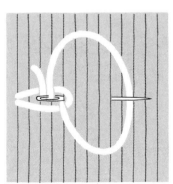

Working stitch combinations

Stitch combinations make the most interesting smocked pieces. If the stitches being combined can all be worked on the same grid, no special treatment is needed. Use mock smocking or the traditional method, as you wish. If, however, the stitches to be combined require different grids, as is true of the combination on the right, smocking must be done by the traditional method, applied in a specific way. The combination on the right is worked as follows: a row of cable stitch, two rows of overlapping wave stitch, and another row of cable, forming the borders; six rows of trellis in the centre; satin stitch embellishments.

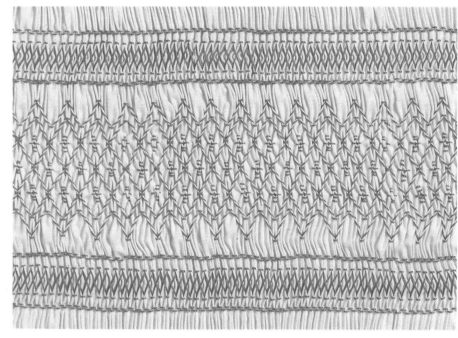

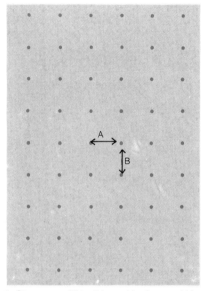

1. Choose a grid for this combination on which the distance between dots and between rows of dots is equal (above, A and B). Mark fabric and gather for traditional smocking.

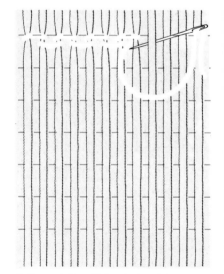

2. To work the stitches in the photographed sample, start at the top row of dots and work a row of cable stitch (refer to p. 94 for detailed instructions) along a row of gathering stitches.

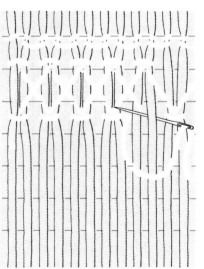

3. Place the wave stitches that follow so that they span *1¾ times* the distance between rows of gathering stitches. This adjusts the proportions of the grid to those of the stitch.

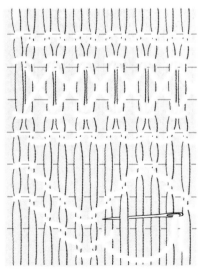

4. For the trellis stitch that forms the centre pattern, place diagonal stitches to span *half* the distance between gathering rows. This adjusts grid and stitch proportions.

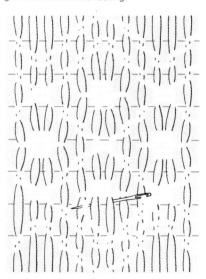

5. Complete six rows of trellis as shown. Repeat border pattern below. Then add embellishments in indicated positions. Satin stitches are used here; for other possibilities, see the facing page.

Machine embroidery

Introduction to machine
embroidery
Straight stitching
Zigzag stitching
Decorative stitch patterns
Free-motion embroidery
Machine hemstitching
Machine cutwork
Machine smocking

Introduction

Though machine embroidery effects are rooted in, and usually named after, traditional hand techniques, each has its own look and style. Except for a few that require a highly sophisticated machine, most of them can be achieved with any efficient zigzag model.

Even the *straight stitch*, the basic stitch on any machine, can produce several embroidery effects (including some free-motion embroidery, see p. 100). Most machine embroidery, however, calls for a *plain zigzag stitch*. Most present-day machines include both a zigzag and a straight stitch. In addition, there is an increasing number of *'automatic' stitches* that can only be worked by a machine equipped with the necessary adjustments or attachments.

Machine embroidery can be worked on almost any type of fabric. If the fabric you choose is lightweight, stitch through paper (which afterwards can be torn away), to prevent puckering. Use machine embroidery thread or normal sewing thread for basic stitching, lurex, pearl cotton or silk twist for special effects. Make sure you know how to use your machine properly; consult the instruction booklet.

Straight stitching

Border motifs can be worked on any straight stitch machine. Use a heavy thread such as silk twist, set stitch length to medium. Mark design on fabric, adjust tension (work a test piece first), and stitch along design lines, pivoting at corners. (To turn corners, see drawings at lower right.)

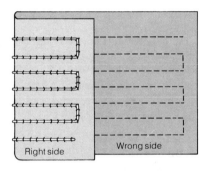

Right side / Wrong side

Mock couching can be achieved with straight stitching. Hand-wind a heavy thread (such as pearl cotton) on bobbin and loosen bobbin tension to accommodate thread. (Not all machines have this adjustment.) Then tighten upper tension. Stitch from wrong side to give couched effect on right side.

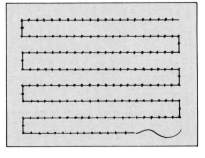

Textured fillings can be worked to resemble hand-embroidered laid work. Use the cross-hatching method shown. Stitch lines horizontally; stitch vertical lines over them. Add diagonal lines on top, following grid formed by the first stitching lines.

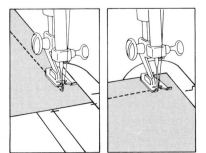

Right side / Wrong side

A looped stitch can be worked simply by adjusting (drastically reducing or completely disengaging) bobbin tension. Wind a heavy thread on bobbin. Then slowly stitch from wrong side of fabric. Small loops will form on right side. (Work a test piece; some machines also need top tension loosened.)

A beaded effect can be created by adjusting top tension so it is slightly tighter than usual. Stitch along design lines. Note how the tightened tension pulls the bobbin thread up, forming tiny beads.

To turn corners, stop machine at corner with needle in fabric. Lift presser foot and turn fabric. Lower foot and continue stitching along design.

Zigzag stitching

Satin stitch, a plain zigzag with a *very short* stitch length, is popular for working along borders and bands. Stitch width can be varied to produce either *wide bands* of stitching or delicate *narrow lines* of satin stitch.

To turn corners, stitch to corner, stopping with needle in fabric at outer edge (for precise point, see drawings, far right). Lift presser foot, turn fabric. Lower foot, resume stitching.

Border design worked in a wide satin stitch.

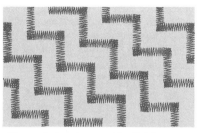

All-over design of narrow satin stitch lines.

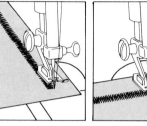

Turn a corner by stopping and pivoting.

Zigzag filling can be produced with cross-hatching (near right). Work stitches horizontally, cross over these vertically, then diagonally.

A 'wishbone' effect (centre illustration) can be achieved by tightening top tension. Experiment until a satisfactory adjustment is found.

For couching, zigzag over heavy thread or cord. Adjust stitch width to thread thickness; lay thread as you stitch. Thread can match or contrast.

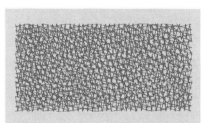

Zigzag filling done with cross-hatching.

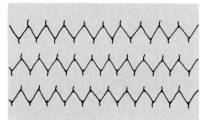

For 'wishbone' effect tighten top tension.

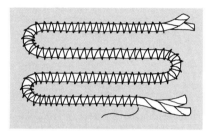

Zigzag couching over heavy thread or cord.

Decorative stitch patterns

Sophisticated machines can work all the straight stitch and zigzag embroidery, and produce fancy patterns as well. Each machine offers its own selection; some of the most common are shown below. Though these stitches are attractive on their own, they can be enhanced in various ways. We show several; these may suggest others. See your instruction booklet for basic stitching information and use of special embroidery feet.

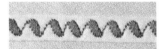

Embroidery over ribbon or braid increases texture and colour impact. Select a stitch of appropriate width, centre the ribbon or braid under the presser foot, and begin stitching. Guide the ribbon carefully so that the embroidery is worked evenly along its length.

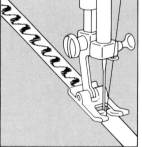

Working with a twin needle produces parallel rows of decorative stitching in one step. Carefully test for stitch width; it must be narrow enough for both needles to clear sides of hole in zigzag throat plate. Use either the same colour thread for both rows, or contrasting colours.

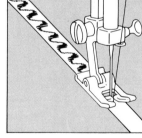

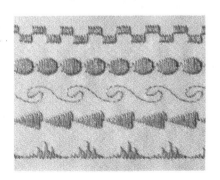

Stitching over a cord is another way to create texture. For the cord, select a contrasting shade of pearl cotton or wool. Keep the cord centred under the presser foot, and guide it carefully as you stitch. There are machine feet with guide holes designed to hold cord in the proper position.

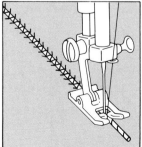

For a heavier stitching line, work a decorative stitch with heavier thread in the bobbin. Fill the bobbin by hand with pearl cotton, loosen bobbin tension (if there is an adjustment), and tighten upper tension slightly. Stitch slowly from the wrong side of work. Use a simple, open stitch pattern.

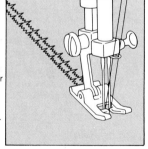

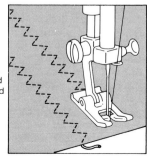

Machine embroidery

Free-motion embroidery

Free-motion embroidery offers unlimited stitching possibilities because fabric motion is not restricted by the presser foot (not used) or the feed dog (either lowered or covered depending on the machine). An embroidery hoop holds the fabric taut and is moved in the desired stitch direction. Control of the hoop movement requires practice. Before beginning any kind of free-motion piece, experiment with thread tension, threads and fabrics to create different effects. Free-motion embroidery can be worked on all machine types. For machine preparation, see below, and read your instruction booklet.

To prepare machine for free-motion work, remove presser foot and its shank. Drop feed dog or cover it with a plate. Set stitch width to 0. Loosen top tension slightly. Be sure needle is a proper size for thread.

Place fabric in embroidery hoop. (Be sure hoop is thin enough to clear presser bar.) Do not use a hoop larger than 20 cm in diameter. Place fabric and backing right side up over larger ring and press inner ring down into outer ring so fabric rests directly on machine bed.

To stitch, lower presser bar to engage upper tension. Holding upper thread taut, turn handwheel towards you to bring up bobbin loop.

Pull bobbin thread up and out so thread ends can be held taut. Hold both top and bobbin threads to the left of the needle as shown.

Take a few stitches to secure threads. Cut off ends as close as possible to stitching.

To manoeuvre hoop, hold it between fingers at edges. Keep elbows down and relaxed. Gently move and guide hoop in the desired direction. Keep machine running at an even, moderate speed. If machine has a speed range, set it at slow until you acquire some expertise. Keep the hoop moving evenly at all times to avoid a pile-up of stitches on the wrong side and possible thread breakage. Length of stitch is controlled by speed at which the work is moved.

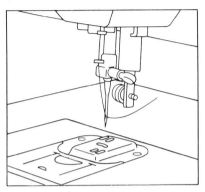
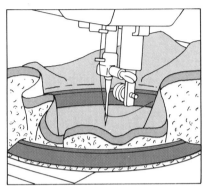
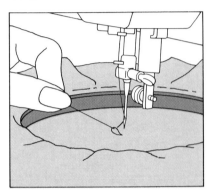
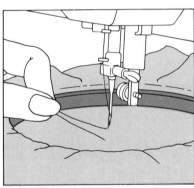
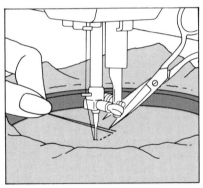
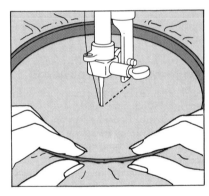

LINE DRAWING

Line drawing is one type of free-motion embroidery. It uses the machine needle to create linear designs. For line drawing, first mark a basic design outline on the fabric. Then improvise the details as you stitch. By altering the machine tension and by using different threads in upper and lower tensions, subtle textures can be created. Heavy threads (pearl cotton or lurex) set in the bobbin also result in interesting surface effects. (Wind heavy bobbin threads by hand, taking care not to stretch them.)

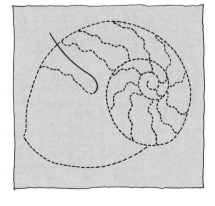

Simple stitch lines can create contour in a design, giving it a three-dimensional look. A shell is an excellent subject for line interpretation. First stitch along marked outline of design. Then stitch interior design lines, improvising as you go.

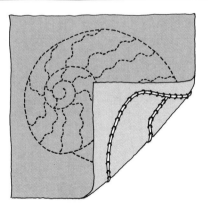

A couched effect can be produced by stitching a design from the wrong side of the fabric, with pearl cotton wound on to the bobbin by hand (do not stretch thread as you wind it). Tighten the upper tension slightly. Move hoop slowly as you work.

SATIN STITCHING

Satin stitch can be worked in free-motion embroidery by setting a zigzag stitch, and moving the frame very slow-ly, so that the stitches lie close together. The width can be varied during stitch-ing by altering the stitch width lever, but this entails using only one hand to guide the hoop and should only be attempted by an experienced machine embroiderer.

The direction in which the stitches are worked varies the look of the line or filling; hoop movement determines the direction in which the stitches run. Keep the machine in constant motion.

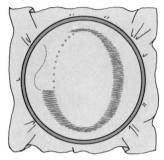

To outline with satin stitch, merely move along design lines. As lines change direction, contour will automatically be formed.

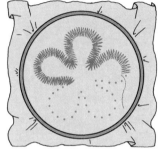

For designs with several parts, rotate hoop continually to work an even line of consistent width along all parts of the design.

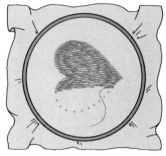

To fill a shape, move hoop slowly from one side to the other and backwards. If you should miss a spot, go back and cover it. Keep the hoop moving.

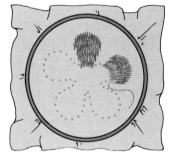

If a design has several parts, fill each part individually, rotating the hoop to move from one part of the design to another.

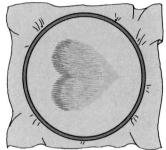

To shade, work several compact rows of satin stitch. Make edges jagged so that the next colour will blend imperceptibly into the previous one.

Machine hemstitching

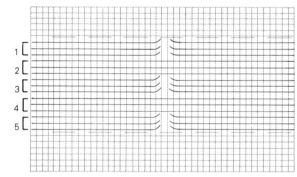

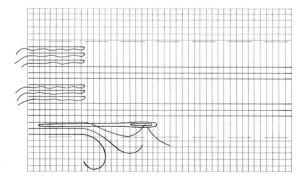

Machine hemstitching requires only a plain zigzag stitch. As in hand hemstitching, threads must be drawn out in a border.

1. Hand-tack upper edge of border. Count off 10 or 15 threads and tack lower edge. Divide threads into 5 groups (2 or 3 threads per group). Cut 1st, 3rd and 5th groups of threads at centre of border, leaving 2nd and 4th intact.

2. Draw out cut threads (groups 1, 3 and 5) to the edges of the border. To stabilise border edges, weave each drawn thread back into wrong side of fabric for 2 cm. Trim the excess thread length.

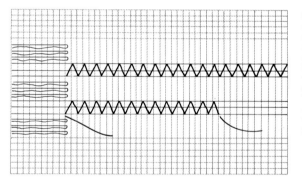

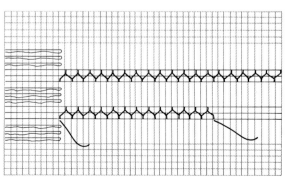

3. Stitch intact threads (groups 2 and 4) within drawn area. Use a normal machine needle, matching or contrasting thread. Hoop is not needed. Set machine to narrow zigzag; stitch over group 2, then group 4. This stitching decorates the border and fastens the threads in each group together.

4. For added texture, tighten the top tension so the zigzag is off-balance (see p. 99). Work this stitch over groups 2 and 4 as for a plain zigzag stitch shown above.

Machine embroidery

Transferring a design 16–17   Hand smocking 92–97
Embroidery scissors 11   Stencil designs 90   Zigzag on curves 197

Machine cutwork

Machine cutwork can be done on any sewing machine that is equipped for zigzag stitching. It is best to keep designs fairly large; very small and intricate ones can be difficult to work. Stencil designs (also used for hand-embroidered cutwork) work best for machine cutwork. A satin stitch is used to outline the motifs; their centres are then trimmed away close to the stitching. Because of the heavy satin stitching that is worked around the shapes, the fabric needs backing for extra body. A lightweight iron-on interfacing is a good backing choice. Stitch with machine embroidery cotton, number 30 or 50.

Transfer the design to the right side of the fabric. Cut a piece of interlining large enough to cover the entire design. With wrong sides together, tack the interlining to the fabric.

Set the sewing machine to a fine straight stitch (about 7 stitches to the centimetre). Then, working from the right side of the fabric, stitch carefully along the lines of the motif.

Remove tacking and trim away excess interlining, leaving about 3 mm around stitching lines of design. Press interlining that remains; it will provide the necessary body around each shape.

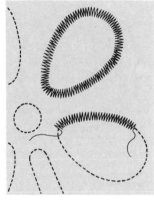

Set the machine for a satin stitch. Work over the straight stitching around each shape. (See Appliqué section for zigzag stitching around curves and corners.)

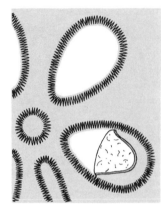

Carefully trim design areas, using a pair of sharp embroidery scissors. Trim as close as possible to satin stitching without cutting the threads. Press entire piece on wrong side.

Machine smocking

A form of mock smocking can be done on any machine. Though machine smocking is similar in appearance to hand smocking, it does not offer the same elasticity, and so is best worked on garments or in areas where elasticity is not needed. Simple smocking can be produced with a straight stitch, a zigzag, or one or more 'automatic' stitches. Fabric to be smocked must first be gathered on several rows of straight machine stitches (select a long stitch length on your machine; about two stitches to the centimetre is appropriate). The mock smocking stitches are then worked using the rows of gathering as a guide.

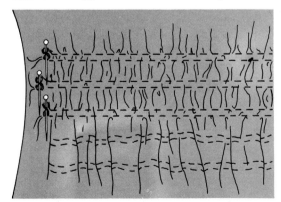

Work rows of gathering stitches in multiples of two, 5 mm apart. Work as many pairs of rows as needed to gather area to be smocked. Space the pairs 1.5 cm apart. Gather to desired width.

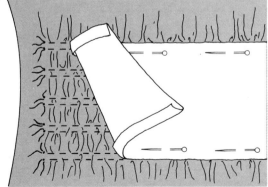

Cut an underlay 3 cm wider than gathered area; fold long edges under 1.5 cm and pin or tack underlay to wrong side of fabric. Test decorative stitches (or plain zigzag) for maximum width of 5 mm.

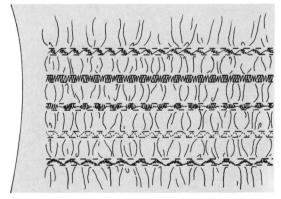

Work 'automatic', plain zigzag or straight stitches between pairs of gathering stitches. Work two rows of stitching when using straight stitch between the pairs of gathering stitches.

Monogramming/Machine embroidery

A monogram adds an individual touch to a towelling robe and is quick to do on a zigzag sewing machine. To make the letters easy to read, choose a thread colour that contrasts strongly with the colour of the robe.

Materials needed

Paper and pencil for enlarging initials
Tissue paper
25 cm interfacing
Machine embroidery thread *or* normal sewing thread
Embroidery scissors

Enlarging the initials

To enlarge the desired initials, make a grid with 2.5 cm squares and copy the letters square for square (see p. 14). Arrange the initials with the second one lower than the first, as shown on left, or place them side by side; trace them on to the tissue paper. Put the robe on and pin the traced monogram to the robe wherever it looks most pleasing to you.

Stitching

Pin the interfacing to the inside of the robe directly behind the monogram. Pin-tack the three layers together around the edges. Outline the letters with a straight stitch, then carefully tear the tissue paper away. With a pair of sharp embroidery scissors, trim the interfacing close to the stitching on the inside of the robe. Stitch over the straight stitches with satin stitch (see p. 99). This outlines the letters with a strong, straight edge. Bring the thread ends to the inside of the robe, knot them and trim off the ends.

Initials personalise a robe above; they could also be stitched on a skirt pocket or blazer lapel.

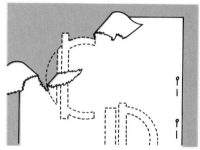

Straight stitch around the traced letters, stitching directly on top of the paper. Carefully tear away paper; trim interfacing close to stitches.

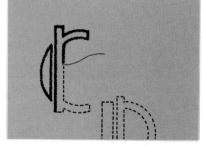

Carefully satin stitch around the letters, covering the straight stitching. This creates a strong outline with contrasting fabric showing through.

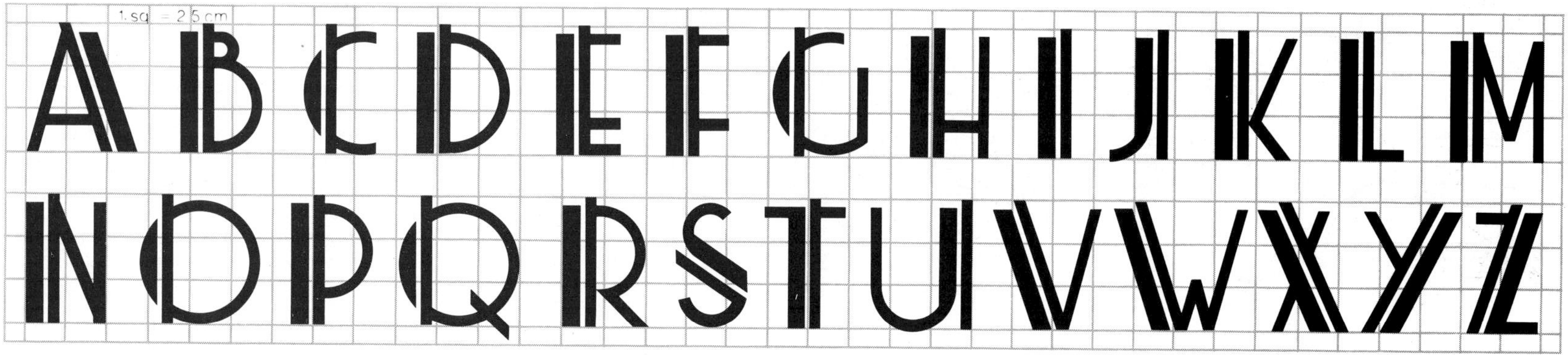

1 sq = 2.5 cm

A B C D E F G H I J K L M
N O P Q R S T U V W X Y Z

To enlarge the desired initials, make a grid with 2.5 cm squares and copy the letters square for square (see p. 14). You can use one, two or three initials, depending on the area you want to cover.

Crewel-work picture

The fine wool and soft colours give crewel embroidery its distinction. The design was adapted from the print fabric on p. 12

1 sq. = 2.5 cm

To enlarge design, see p. 14. Add 2.5 cm to each side of enlarged (25 by 40 cm) size to fit mount.

Colours and wool amounts

▨	Brown
▨	Dark leaf-green
▨	Light leaf-green
▨	Mauve
▨	Dull rose
▨	Pink
▨	Fuchsia
▨	Light mauve
▨	Light pink
▨	Dark red
▨	Signal green
■	Black

One skein of each, except two of light leaf-green.

List of stitches

A	stem stitch (p. 23)
B	slanted satin stitch (p. 48)
C	long and short satin stitch (p. 50)
D	coral stitch (p. 31), worked over satin stitch on odd-colour petal of each flower
E	squared laid work (p. 44)
F	padded satin stitch (p. 49)
G	Turkey work (pp. 24–25)

Framing crewel embroidery or any type of needlework is an attractive way of displaying and protecting your work.

Materials needed
50 cm linen twill
Crewel wool (see below)
Crewel needle
Paper and pencil to transfer design
Embroidery hoop
Masking tape
Mount: 40 by 60 cm with 25 by 45 cm opening
Cardboard: 40 by 60 cm
Polystyrene board, same size as above
Glass (optional), same size as above
Frame, same size as above
Straight pins
2 screw eyes
Wire for hanging

The embroidery
Needlework that is to be framed usually needs to be stretched on to a backing for support and to ensure that the work does not wrinkle or pucker. When planning a project, allow a few centimetres of fabric beyond the stitching area for stretching purposes. If you plan to add a mount, allow extra so the fabric can be stretched on to a board that is the size of the embroidery and the mount combined.

The enlarged design (see p. 14 for instructions) will be 25 by 40 cm; to fit the 25 by 45 cm mount opening, add a 2.5 cm margin on both ends. Cut a 45 by 66 cm piece of linen (large enough to stretch on to a 40 by 60 cm board) and bind the edges (p. 16). Transfer the design to fabric (pp. 16–17). Work embroidery, following the chart below; use a hoop or frame to keep the fabric taut. Wash and block finished embroidery (pp. 54–55) if necessary.

Mounting the embroidery
Certain forms of wood, such as plywood or wood stretchers, contain acid that will discolour fabric and thread in time. For mounting any needlework, use polystyrene or cardboard, which are acid-free. Place the crewel work face down on

a clean, flat surface. Centre the board on top. When you are stretching the fabric, work two opposing sides at once so the fabric has something to pull against. Start in the centre and work towards the corners. At the centre of one side, pull the excess fabric around the board and put a pin into the edge of the board. Pull fabric at centre of opposite side and pin it. Repeat with the other two sides. Turn the piece over to see if the embroidery is properly centred. If it is not, pull out the pins and start again. When centres are satisfactorily pinned, work towards corners, working as before on opposite sides. Turn the piece over occasionally to make sure that the grain of the fabric and any straight lines in the design are straight. Fold fabric at corners into pleats (see Step 3, below).

Assembling the frame

Whether you use glass to cover framed needlework is a personal decision. Glass will keep the piece clean and free from handling marks, but it tends to obscure the texture, which is why we chose not to use it. If you decide to use glass, clean both sides. Place the frame face down and put the glass in it first; if you are not using glass, place the mount and the embroidery, in that order, in the frame first. Place the cardboard on top; seal the edges with masking tape. Insert screw eyes at back of frame, one-third of the way down the sides, and attach a hanging wire (Step 6, below).

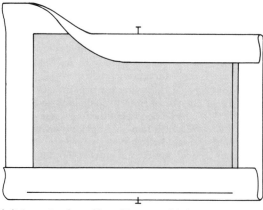

1. At the centre of one side, pull the excess fabric around the board and put a pin into the edge of the board. Pull the fabric at centre of opposite side and pin it. Repeat with two remaining sides.

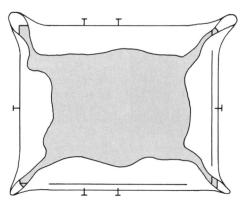

2. When all four centres are anchored, start pinning the area adjacent to the centre pins, always working from the centre out to the corners, and pulling opposite sides against each other.

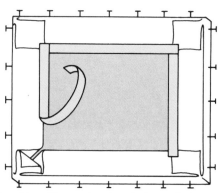

3. When all four sides are pinned taut, fold corner fabric into pleats as shown. Secure fabric to the board with masking tape, taping from pleat to pleat along the edges. Remove pins.

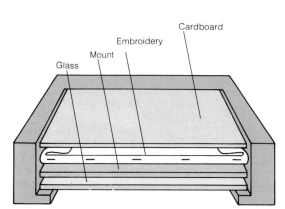

4. To assemble, place frame face down on a flat surface. Insert glass first if you are using glass. Then place mount and mounted embroidery face down; put cardboard backing on top.

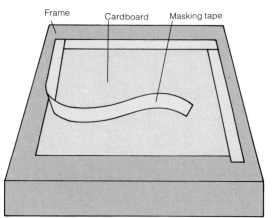

5. Carefully turn the assembled unit over to check that everything is correct from the front. Turn the unit to the back. On the back, secure the edges of the cardboard to the frame with masking tape.

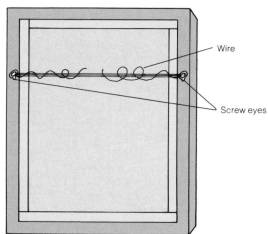

6. To attach a hanging wire, insert a screw eye on either side of frame one-third from top. Run a length of wire between screw eyes several times; wrap end of the wire around itself.

105

Place mat and napkin (Pulled thread)

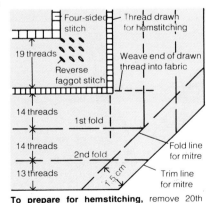

The design for the place mat and matching napkin was adapted from the pulled thread design on p. 74.

A pulled threadwork place mat and napkin are finished with a hemstitch edge.

Materials needed

75 cm even-weave linen, 7–10 cm per centimetre, for one place mat and one napkin

1 ball No. 8 pearl cotton

Embroidery hoop

Tapestry needle

Sharp needle and sewing thread

Pulled thread embroidery

Cut out a 60 by 45 cm rectangle for the place mat and a 60 cm square for the napkin; bind the edges (see p. 16). Mark with a pin the vertical grain of the napkin. Cut sizes allow 5 cm beyond the hem allowance for a 47 by 33 cm mat and 40 cm square napkin.

To place the motif in the upper right corner of the place mat, tack one line 21.5 cm down from the top edge and another line 18 cm in from the right edge. The intersection of fabric threads where these tacking lines cross is the centre of the lower motif. Tack motif outline, following thread counts given below, left. Find the centre of upper motif; tack its outline. Work both in chessboard filling stitch (p. 76).

To begin four-sided stitch (see p. 75) that outlines place mat, count 28 threads down and 28 threads to the right of centre of lower motif (see below, left). Stitch is 4 threads high by 4 threads wide; each square in the drawing represents one stitch. Work the stepped line under the motifs from right to left, using the drawing to count the number of stitches. Along the top of the mat, work 53 stitches including corners; turn the mat so the left side is on top and work 52 stitches. With bottom edge on top, work 83 stitches. Work 34 stitches along right side to meet stepped line. Work a reverse faggot stitch (see p. 77) in the other three corners.

To embroider the napkin, tack a line 12 cm in from two adjoining sides. At intersection begin the four-sided stitch. Work all four sides, placing 64 stitches along the two sides that parallel the vertical grain, 65 stitches on the other sides; this compensates for the fact that even-weave fabric has more warp threads than weft per centimetre. Work a reverse faggot stitch in one corner.

Hemstitching

To hemstitch both place mat and napkin, draw out the twentieth thread outside the four-sided stitch on all four sides (see p. 78). Weave thread ends into wrong side of fabric for about 3 cm. With your fingers, press a crease 14 threads beyond the drawn-out thread on all four sides, folding towards the wrong side (see below, right). Make a diagonal crease at each corner at the point of the first crease. Trim corners 1.5 cm beyond this diagonal crease. Make a second crease 14 threads from the first. Trim away excess fabric 13 threads beyond second crease. Fold second crease, then fold first crease; pin and tack. Fold should line up with bottom of drawn-thread space. With sewing thread and needle, slipstitch mitres (see p. 83). Work hemstitching over groups of two threads (see p. 79), catching hem fold. Remove tackings.

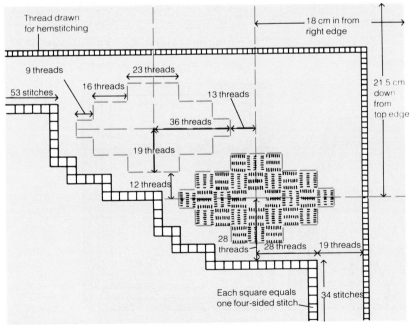

To begin pulled threadwork, tack lines 18 cm in from right side and 21.5 cm down from top. All embroidery is worked by counting threads from *intersection* where these two lines meet.

Thread drawn for hemstitching

9 threads

53 stitches

23 threads

16 threads

13 threads

36 threads

19 threads

12 threads

28 threads

28 threads

19 threads

18 cm in from right edge

21.5 cm down from top edge

34 stitches

Each square equals one four-sided stitch

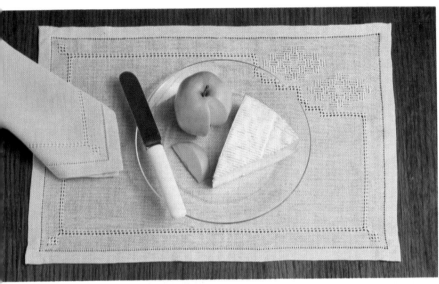

To prepare for hemstitching, remove 20th thread beyond four-sided stitch. Re-weave ends into fabric for 3 cm. Make two folds beyond drawn-out threads for hem. Mitre corners.

Four-sided stitch

Thread drawn for hemstitching

19 threads

Reverse faggot stitch

Weave end of drawn thread into fabric

14 threads

1st fold

14 threads

2nd fold

Fold line for mitre

13 threads

1.5 cm

Trim line for mitre

Table runner/Pattern darning

The design of hearts on this table runner was adapted from the design on p. 71.

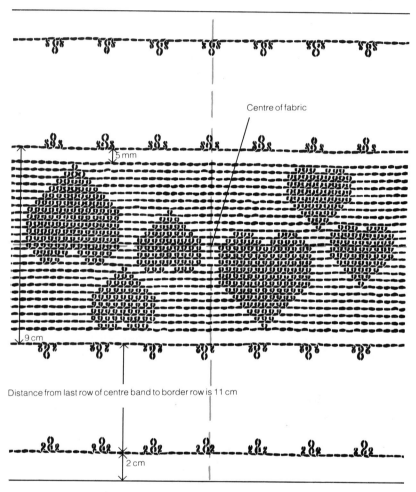

Centre of fabric

5 mm

9 cm

Distance from last row of centre band to border row is 11 cm

2 cm

Pattern darning is ideal for table runners and tray cloths.

Materials needed
1 metre of honeycomb fabric, even-weave, or huckaback when available
8 skeins of stranded cotton
Tapestry needle

The fabric
The widths of suitable fabrics vary. Honeycomb fabric is 35 cm wide, even-weave cotton 45 cm and huckaback, when available, 38–43 cm wide.

Pattern darning can be worked to any length. Thread ends are secured and new threads joined on the fabric front, and the joinings show. In this 82 cm runner, rows are worked fully with a single thread length (half at a time, which is easily manageable), avoiding the problem of joinings.

The embroidery
Bind both cut edges with masking tape; you need not bind selvedges. Embroidery is started at centre and worked out to sides row by row; rows build from the centre up to top and down to bottom.

Find the centre by folding the fabric in half both ways (diagram right). Heart motif combines straight and closed loop stitches (see pp. 71–72). Cut a 1.20 cm length of thread (about one and a half times as long as the row). Start first row at fabric centre, leaving half of the thread free; work first to left (see p. 73). Then turn the fabric around and, with free end of thread in needle, work other half of row. Work all rows the same way so you are always stitching with half a thread length. If you decide to make a longer runner, cut threads to different lengths so that joinings do not appear in the same place on each row. To work borders, see drawing on the right and figure-eight stitch, p. 72.

Hemming
When using narrow fabric, selvedges only need to be turned under and hemmed. Trim cut ends about 2.5 cm beyond the edge of the embroidery, turn under, tack and hem. If the runner is cut from a wide fabric, make a hem all round. Iron on the wrong side.

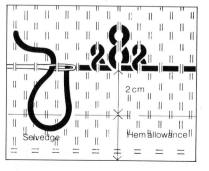

Selvedge

Hem allowance

2 cm

Diagram above shows the design components and their relationship on the fabric. The design consists of right-side-up and upside-down hearts in a centre band. Each motif is a grouping of one large and two small hearts that spans about 9 cm. Allowing for three floats between motifs, nine units fit within the length of the runner.

Detail on left shows border row of figure-eight stitches (p. 72); same stitch edges centre panel as well. Allow for side hems; work border on each side, 2 cm from point where hem fold will be.

Cutwork embroidery on caftan

Cutwork embroidery adds an elegant touch to a caftan; cut-out areas contrast with solid buttonhole-stitch outlines.

Materials needed

Commercial dressmaking pattern for caftan, and length of white cotton
Dressmaker's carbon paper
Tracing wheel
No. 8 pearl cotton:
  1 ball blue
  1 ball rust
  1 ball green
Crewel needle

Preparation

To enlarge the design to the appropriate size, make a grid with 1 cm squares; copy the design square for square (see p. 14). Place the enlarged design under the front pattern piece of the pattern you are using to be sure the design fits within the seamlines. If it does not fit, adjust the design slightly, or re-draw grid using 1.25 cm squares. Then trace it directly on to the pattern piece.

The embroidery is worked on the fabric before pattern is cut out. To trace design on to fabric, pin pattern piece to fabric. Insert dressmaker's carbon between the two and trace around pattern piece and design with tracing wheel (see p. 17). To trace the other half of caftan front, turn pattern over, line up centre front edge, and trace around pattern and design again (see below left).

Embroidery

Work cutwork embroidery, following the directions on pp. 90 and 91. Press the completed embroidery with a damp cloth, placing embroidery face down on a thick towel. Cut the open areas carefully from the back; press the embroidery again. Cut out the pattern pieces and construct caftan, following pattern directions.

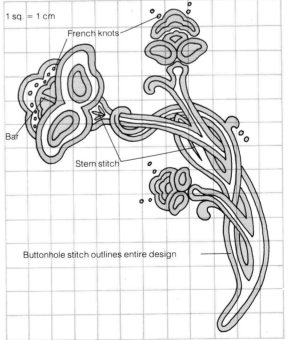

1 sq. = 1 cm

French knots

Bar

Stem stitch

Buttonhole stitch outlines entire design

To enlarge the graph, make a grid with 1 cm squares and copy the design square for square (see p. 14).

To work the embroidery, see the cutwork section on pp. 90 and 91. The design is outlined in buttonhole stitch, and embellished with French knots and stem stitch. To work the bar of buttonhole stitch that supports the large cut-out area, see p. 91. The grey areas indicate areas to be cut away when the embroidery is completed.

Caftan embroidery is the cutwork design on p. 90; both the design and its mirror image are used.

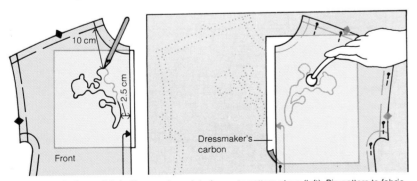

10 cm

2.5 cm

Front

Dressmaker's carbon

To transfer design to fabric. Trace enlarged design on to pattern piece (left). Pin pattern to fabric. With dressmaker's carbon between pattern and fabric, trace around pattern and design with tracing wheel. Turn pattern over, align front edge, and trace mirror image of pattern and design (right).

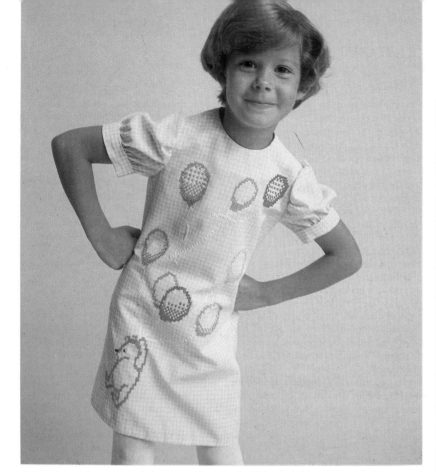

Cross stitch on gingham, a technique especially suited to children's clothing, see pp. 66–68.

Cross stitch for a child's dress

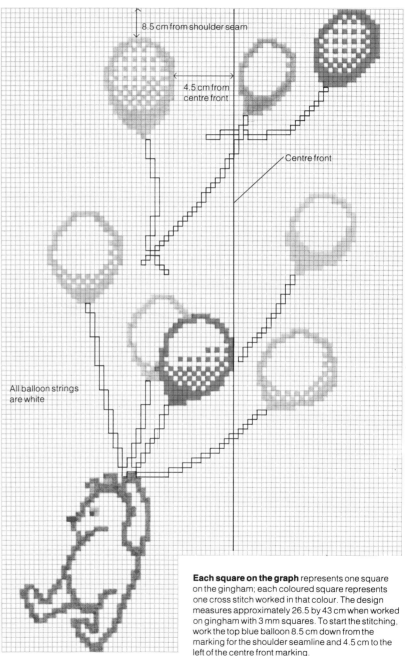

8.5 cm from shoulder seam

4.5 cm from centre front

Centre front

All balloon strings are white

Each square on the graph represents one square on the gingham; each coloured square represents one cross stitch worked in that colour. The design measures approximately 26.5 by 43 cm when worked on gingham with 3 mm squares. To start the stitching, work the top blue balloon 8.5 cm down from the marking for the shoulder seamline and 4.5 cm to the left of the centre front marking.

Cross stitch on gingham is used for a child's outfit.

Materials needed

Gingham with 3 mm squares; amount indicated on pattern envelope

1 skein stranded cotton in each colour: red, blue, yellow, green, orange for balloons; white for string; light brown, dark brown, black, for bear

Embroidery hoop

Crewel needle

Design position

The cross stitch design on the right measures about 26.5 by 43 cm when worked on gingham with 3 mm squares. It was stitched on a child's size 4 dress; however, it will work on any pattern with a straight front, such as a sun dress, pinafore or apron. To work the design on dungarees that have a centre front seam, work each half of the design on the corresponding front piece, keeping stitches within the seamlines, and making sure design parts meet at centre front marking.

To be sure the design fits your pattern, measure the length and twice the width of the front pattern piece (which represents half the dress front), staying inside seamlines and hemline.

The embroidery

Trace around front pattern piece on to the fabric with tacking stitches; do not cut it out. Mark seamlines and hemline. Using an embroidery hoop and following the chart, work design in cross stitch (see p. 35). Then cut out pattern pieces and sew the dress.

Piped cushion/Blackwork

A simple way to show off embroidery – canvas work, appliqué or patchwork. The backing and piping instructions apply equally to other covers.

Materials needed

50 cm even-weave cotton
6 skeins stranded cotton
Tapestry needle
1 m fabric for backing and piping
2 m of 5 mm piping cord
30 cm zip
36 cm square cushion form

Preparing design for embroidery

To enlarge the design to the appropriate size, make a grid of 2.5 cm squares and copy the design square for square (see p. 14). Cut out a 45.5 cm square of fabric, bind the edges (p. 16), and mark the horizontal and vertical centres with lines of tacking. Transfer design to fabric.

Embroidery

Work the design, following the chart and key below for stitch placing and identification. Block the embroidery (pp. 54–55). Trim fabric to 38 cm square.

Piping

Cut two 20 by 38 cm rectangles for cushion backing; set aside. To make piping, cut 5 cm wide bias strips (see p. 199) from remaining backing fabric. Seam them together into a 1.48 m length. Fold the bias strip in half along its length with the wrong sides facing. Insert piping cord in the fold and tack; stitch close to cord, by hand, or by machine using zip or piping foot. Trim piping seam allowance to 1 cm. Tack piping to the right side of top at seamline (Step 1 below). Where the piping ends meet, join them as shown in Step 2.

Backing

Pin the two backing rectangles together with right sides facing. To prepare the seam for inserting zip, follow Step 3 below. Clip the tacking threads at both ends to simplify later removal of tackings. Press the seam open. Insert zip according to package directions. Remove tacking stitches; partly open the zip. Join backing and embroidered top as specified in Step 4. Clip corners as illustrated to reduce bulk. Open zip and turn the cushion cover inside out, squaring corners. Insert cushion form.

The design for this piped cushion was adapted from the blackwork design shown on p. 56.

1 sq. = 2.5 cm

To enlarge design, follow instructions on p. 14. Two basic embroidery stitches are used: stem stitch (A), described on p. 23; satin stitch (B), on p. 48. Directions for the seven blackwork stitches are given in that section: C & D, p. 59; E, F, G, p. 60; H, p. 61; I, p. 62.

To construct cushion. 1. Trim raw edges of piping to 1 cm; pin piping to cushion top at the stitching line and with raw edges aligned. At corners, clip into piping seam allowance so piping will turn corner neatly. Tack along stitching line of piping. To join piping see Step 2.

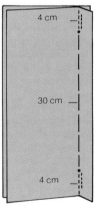

2. Trim cords so they butt. Trim fabric to 1 cm overlap; fold the edge under 5 mm and wrap around starting end. Sew across join.

3. To prepare zip seam, place backing pieces face to face. On one 38 cm side, stitch 4 cm, tack 30 cm, stitch to the end.

4 cm

30 cm

4 cm

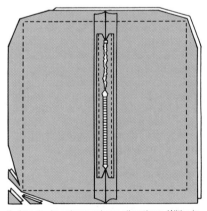

4. Attach zip using package directions. With zip partly open, place backing and top fabrics together, with right sides facing and raw edges aligned; tack. Stitch around all four sides 1 cm from raw edge. Remove tackings; clip corners to reduce bulk. Open zip; turn cover inside out

Canvas work

'Fleurs de mon pays', designed by Shirley Brickendon for Montreal Museum of Fine Arts.

Canvas work basics

What canvas work is

Canvas work is the technique of forming stitches on a special open-weave fabric known as canvas. Canvas is constructed of *vertical* and *horizontal* threads that are woven together to produce precisely spaced *holes* between threads. The points at which these threads intersect are known as *meshes.* All canvas work stitches are worked to make use of the grid-like structure of the canvas.

Basically, any canvas work stitch can go in only two directions, either diagonally across or parallel to the canvas threads and meshes (see the stitch direction sample below). The direction the thread takes is dictated by the kind of stitch that is being worked. Several canvas work stitches fall in only one direction; others require threads to be laid in several directions or even to be crossed over each other.

The size of a stitch depends upon two things. One of these is the character of the stitch. Certain of the stitches span only one canvas thread or mesh; other stitches span two or more. Stitch size also depends on the gauge of canvas that the stitch is being worked on. (The gauge of a canvas is the number of meshes to each 2.5 cm of that canvas.) The more meshes per 2.5 cm a canvas has, the smaller the stitches worked on it can be. Canvas is available in many gauges (see p. 114); this wide overall range breaks down into two subgroups, **petitpoint** and **grospoint**. A petitpoint canvas is one with 16 or more meshes; a grospoint canvas has fewer than 16 meshes. Because a petitpoint canvas has more meshes per centimetre than a grospoint canvas, any stitch worked on a canvas in the petitpoint range will be smaller than it would be on a grospoint canvas. Petitpoint and grospoint stitching are shown actual size in the two samples below, right. The same stitch,

tent stitch, is used in both, and the area of canvas is also the same. The first sample is done on a 24-gauge canvas, which is well within the petitpoint range of canvases; the second sample is on a 12-gauge canvas, which falls in the grospoint range.

Stitch size affects the amount of working time and the durability of the finished item. In general, the smaller the stitches, the more time will be spent in working them and the more durable the finished item will be. More time is required for small stitches, of course, because it takes more of them to cover the canvas. Small stitches are more durable than large ones because they are less likely to be snagged or broken when the finished canvas work is in use. How hardwearing an item needs to be depends on its end use. A cushion, for example, will be subject to more hard wear than a wall hanging.

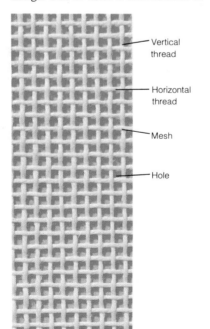

Construction of single thread canvas

Directions stitches can take on canvas

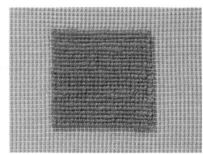

Petitpoint stitches

Grospoint stitches

The three types of canvas work

The interpretation of the overall drawn design on which a finished canvas work is based depends upon the stitches. They can affect a design in two ways. First, the stitches can alter the drawn lines of the design. Differences between drawn and stitched lines occur because the stitches must be worked to conform to the grid-like structure of the canvas. Drawn lines, of course, are free of such restrictions. How much deviation there is between the two lines depends on the character of the stitch and its size. The other way the stitch can affect a design arises from the texture or pattern the stitching produces. Interpretation in texture changes design elements drastically, greatly altering the design's visual impact. Canvas work offers a wide choice of texture possibilities. For illustrations and explanations of a comprehensive assortment of canvas work stitches and the many textures and pat-terns they produce, see pp. 118–61.

When you are deciding which stitches to use, bear in mind that three distinct visual impressions can be produced by means of canvas work stitches (see the three stitched samples below). The first sample illustrates the effect of **tent stitches** on a design. Tent stitch is a small diagonal stitch that spans only a single canvas mesh. Though there are different ways of working tent stitches, each method produces the same stitch and even texture on the right side of the canvas. Because tent stitches are small, they can interpret a drawn line fairly precisely; the smaller the stitches, the truer the stitched line will be to the drawn line. A design to be executed in tent stitches, therefore, can be fairly detailed and include varying degrees of subtle shading.

All other stitches could be categorised as **ornamental stitches.** This group em-braces many stitches, each varying in size, texture and pattern. A design intended for ornamental stitches tends to be less detailed than one meant for tent stitches, usually relying on the structur-al elements of a design rather than on its details. There are two reasons for this. First, virtually all ornamental stitches are large, and so less suited to following drawn lines. Second, the textures pro-duced by ornamental stitches interpret and enhance the physical reality of de-sign elements exceptionally well. The second sample below follows the same basic design used for the tent stitch sam-ple next to it. Notice how much more prominent than design details major ele-ments have become, and how well the knotted stitch (see p. 145) suggests the texture of wood for the barn, the diamond eyelet (p. 153) the window of the barn, the leaf stitch (see p. 154) the tree. Stitch selection, however, is just one factor to consider when composing a design that will be carried out in canvas work. For a more thorough explanation of designing, see pp. 162–3.

Included in the ornamental stitch classification are the **Florentine stitches** that produce the third type of canvas work. Florentine stitches are straight canvas work stitches placed parallel to the threads of the canvas. Many patterns can be produced with Florentine stitches, but one of the most familiar and classic is the chevron design (see third sample below). Florentine stitch is based on the customary straight stitches, but they are placed in a zigzag line across the canvas. With many Florentine embroideries, the overall finished design is determined by the structure of the stitch rather than the selection of a stitch to fill in a predeter-mined shape. For more details on Florentine work, see p. 173.

Design done in tent stitches

Same design worked in ornamental stitches

Arrangement of Florentine stitches

Canvas work basics/Tools and materials

Canvases

Canvas is fundamental to the success of any canvas work project, and so should be selected with the utmost care. Be sure the threads are free of knots and cuts. Most canvases are made of cotton or linen. Some newer ones are made of synthetic fibres; some fine-gauge canvases come in silk. The gauge should be suitable for the item and design being worked (see pp. 162–3).

To determine the gauge of a canvas, hold a ruler along a horizontal thread and count the meshes in 2.5 cm. In the photograph above, this is being done on a 10-gauge single canvas.

There are several different types of canvas. Those used most often are plain single, interlock single, and double. Both **plain and interlock single** canvases have a single-mesh structure; the construction of the mesh, however, is different in each. A single mesh of the plain canvas is formed by the intersection of a single vertical and a single horizontal thread. With interlock canvas, each vertical thread is actually two thinner threads that have been twisted around each other and a single horizontal thread to produce a 'locked' single mesh. The locked construction of the interlock canvas is more stable than the merely intersecting mesh of plain canvas. All canvas work stitches can be formed successfully on an interlock canvas; plain single canvas, however, is not suitable for use with certain canvas work stitches, such as the half-cross stitch (see p. 120). Both the plain and interlock canvases are available in a wide range of gauges.

Double canvas (sometimes known as Penelope) has a double-mesh construction. The double mesh is formed by the intersection of pairs of vertical threads with pairs of horizontal threads. Besides being strong, a double mesh has a second advantage – it can be adjusted so that stitches of different sizes can be worked on the same piece of canvas (see photograph below). Used as is, a double

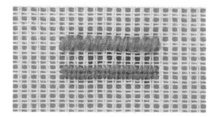

mesh can accept one size of stitch; when the pairs of threads are separated, four plain meshes are formed that are capable of receiving four smaller stitches. The double-mesh adaptability is advan-

tageous when your design calls for finely stitched areas. The gauge of a double canvas is given as two numbers separated by a line, for example, 10/20. The smaller number designates the number of double meshes per 2.5 cm; the larger number, the meshes per 2.5 cm if threads are separated. Double canvas is readily available in 5/10 to 14/28 gauges.

In another type, **rug canvas**, each mesh is formed by two vertical threads that are twisted around each other and a pair of horizontal threads. Threads cannot be separated. Rug canvas comes in 3 to 5 gauges, and is used primarily for rugs.

Canvas may be bought with the design printed or painted on in full colour. Subjects range from abstract patterns to naturalistic pictorial scenes.

Plastic canvas is moulded rather than woven into a stiff, medium-gauge canvas-like form. Sold in cut pieces in kits used for items such as rugs.

Plain single canvas

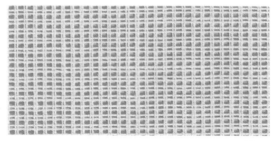

Double canvas

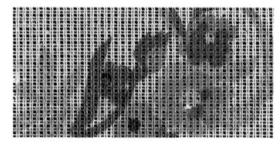

Printed canvas

Interlock canvas

Rug canvas

Synthetic canvas

Threads

Threads for canvas work come in several fibres, weights and textures, as well as many lovely colours. Shown below are the types of threads most often used. The weight of thread varies with the type: tapestry wool, for example, is thinner than rug wool. The thread should be thin enough to slide through the holes of the canvas easily and without distortion, but thick enough to cover the canvas in stitch form. In general, the larger the canvas gauge, the heavier or thicker the thread should be. Appropriate thread weight depends also on the stitch that is being formed (p. 118).

Strand and *ply* are two terms relating to thread structure that need to be understood. A strand is the unit; a ply is a part of a strand. For example, Persian wool is made up of three strands of wool, but each of these strands consists of two plies. Strands are easily separated, which allows you to decrease or increase the number of strands as necessary to produce wool of a particular thickness. Plies are not easily separated. Canvas work threads are made of several different fibres, such as wool, cotton, silk, rayon and metallic threads. Wool is used most often. This is because it is an inherently strong fibre that has proved very durable for canvas work.

A thread selected for use in canvas work should have the capacity to withstand abrasion both while the stitch is being worked and when the finished item is in use. If the canvas work item will not get hard use, less sturdy fibres, such as rayon and metallic, can be used.

Another strength factor is the length of the fibres used in manufacturing the thread. The fibres in canvas work wools are longer, and therefore stronger, than those that are used in the wools made especially for knitting. This is why knitting wools are not recommended as substitutes for canvas work wools.

Needles

The needle type recommended for use in canvas work is the tapestry needle. It has a large eye that allows for easy threading, and a blunt point that prevents the needle from piercing the canvas threads. Tapestry needles are available in a range of sizes from 14, the heaviest, to 26, the finest. The finer the size, the shorter the needle and the smaller its eye. Select the needle size according to the gauge of the canvas that is being worked. The needle should be thin enough to be passed easily through the holes of the canvas without distorting them. The 18 needle is used most often, since it is suitable for the popular 10 and 12-gauge canvases. Needles from 20 to 26 are used on the finer-gauge canvases; those from 13 to 16, on heavier canvases. Test any needle to make sure it is the correct size. Tapestry needles are usually sold in packages of several needles; they may be one size only or an assortment of sizes.

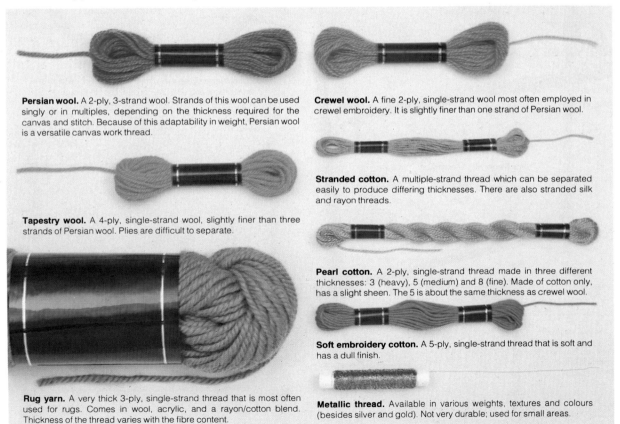

Persian wool. A 2-ply, 3-strand wool. Strands of this wool can be used singly or in multiples, depending on the thickness required for the canvas and stitch. Because of this adaptability in weight, Persian wool is a versatile canvas work thread.

Tapestry wool. A 4-ply, single-strand wool, slightly finer than three strands of Persian wool. Plies are difficult to separate.

Rug yarn. A very thick 3-ply, single-strand thread that is most often used for rugs. Comes in wool, acrylic, and a rayon/cotton blend. Thickness of the thread varies with the fibre content.

Crewel wool. A fine 2-ply, single-strand wool most often employed in crewel embroidery. It is slightly finer than one strand of Persian wool.

Stranded cotton. A multiple-strand thread which can be separated easily to produce differing thicknesses. There are also stranded silk and rayon threads.

Pearl cotton. A 2-ply, single-strand thread made in three different thicknesses: 3 (heavy), 5 (medium) and 8 (fine). Made of cotton only, has a slight sheen. The 5 is about the same thickness as crewel wool.

Soft embroidery cotton. A 5-ply, single-strand thread that is soft and has a dull finish.

Metallic thread. Available in various weights, textures and colours (besides silver and gold). Not very durable; used for small areas.

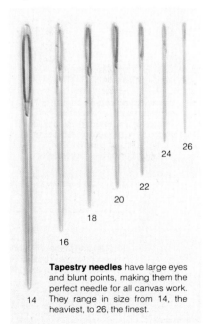

Tapestry needles have large eyes and blunt points, making them the perfect needle for all canvas work. They range in size from 14, the heaviest, to 26, the finest.

115

Canvas work basics/Tools and materials

Frames and holders

In working canvas work, use of a frame or some other kind of canvas holder can be a great help. Such devices help to keep canvas neat and to allow the stitches to be properly laid on to the canvas. They also prevent the canvas from being severely distorted by the stitches. The best device to use is a slate frame; a frame attached to a stand will free both your hands for stitching. Several varieties are shown below. Most canvas work frames work on the same principle. The top and bottom edges of the canvas are first sewn to tapes on rods. Then the canvas is rolled on to the rods and the rods are fastened to the side arms of the frame. The canvas can be narrower but not wider than the tapes. In length, the canvas should not be too much shorter than the side arms; it can be longer, however, since excess length can be rolled on to the rods.

Another device that can serve as a frame is a canvas stretcher. It must be large enough to accommodate the entire piece of canvas. Once the canvas is fixed in place, it should not be re-positioned.

A hoop is best reserved for finer-gauge, softer canvases, which are less likely to be creased by the pressure of the rings.

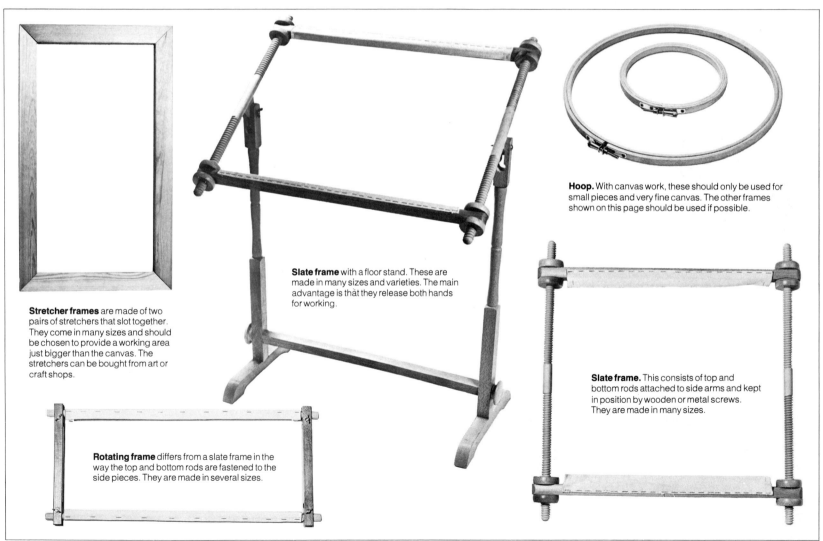

Hoop. With canvas work, these should only be used for small pieces and very fine canvas. The other frames shown on this page should be used if possible.

Slate frame with a floor stand. These are made in many sizes and varieties. The main advantage is that they release both hands for working.

Stretcher frames are made of two pairs of stretchers that slot together. They come in many sizes and should be chosen to provide a working area just bigger than the canvas. The stretchers can be bought from art or craft shops.

Rotating frame differs from a slate frame in the way the top and bottom rods are fastened to the side pieces. They are made in several sizes.

Slate frame. This consists of top and bottom rods attached to side arms and kept in position by wooden or metal screws. They are made in many sizes.

Design transfer needs

If you intend to design your own canvas work, certain tools will be essential, others will make the job easier and more professional. The most necessary tools, of course, are the papers and pens. If you are copying a design from a book, tracing paper is helpful. Graph paper is needed for charting a design; see-through graph paper, for tracing a chart or design. When a design is being coloured on paper, the pen need not be waterproof; it must be, however, when you want to colour a design on canvas. To paint on canvas, choose acrylic paints, thinned with water. When dry, acrylic paints are permanent.

Miscellaneous equipment

Shown below are some pieces of equipment that you will find yourself needing or wanting at different points in the canvas work process. Some you may already have, others you may have to buy. The blocking board and indicator pins will be necessary for stretching the stitched canvas work back into its original shape. The large scissors are for cutting the canvas, the embroidery scissors for cutting threads. Masking tape is ideal for binding canvas edges. A needle threader will make it easier to thread wools; a magnifier will help you do a better job with fine details. A tape measure will be useful.

Graph paper. Available as opaque or transparent paper in centimetre squares.

Tracing paper is sold in many sizes and usually in pads or rolls. It is used to trace designs from drawings or other sources.

Felt-tipped markers are available with fine or broad tips. Waterproof markers should be used.

Paints and brushes are needed if you paint a design on canvas. Acrylic paints are waterproof when dry.

T-square. This is a ruler with a head at right-angles to the body. It is used for drawing grids by sliding the head along the side of a drawing board.

Tape measures are flexible, and usually 1.50 m long. They are often marked in both centimetres and inches.

Masking tape is used for binding the raw edges of a canvas.

A magnifier can help to reduce eye strain, especially when you work on very fine canvas.

Embroidery scissors are small and have sharp points, making them ideal for close, fine work.

Dressmaker's shears are needed to cut out the canvas. A left-handed model is also available.

Indicator pins (rustproof) will be needed for blocking. Large-headed pins are easiest to handle.

Needle threader helps with threading.

Blocking board is a piece of soft wood, such as a pastry board, large enough to hold the canvas while it is being blocked.

Canvas work stitches

General information

The most familiar canvas work stitch is the small, slanted stitch known as tent stitch (see first sample below). It is also the most basic stitch, and one that every embroiderer should master and use. There are many other canvas work stitches, each with its own application. A working knowledge of a variety of stitches can add greatly to the scope and originality of your canvas work projects.

You will find a great many stitches illustrated and explained in the 40-page section that follows. For ease in learning, they have been grouped according to the direction that the thread takes while the stitch is being worked. There are five stitch groups: **diagonal**, **straight**, **crossing**, **composite** and **pile**. An actual-size sample of each stitch accompanies a detailed step-by-step explanation of how that stitch is worked.

The best way to learn the stitches, however, is to do them. Working the stitches yourself will show you, too, which ones can be worked quickly and how much thread is taken up by each. Also, of course, this will give you your own stitch samples. Do this stitching in sampler form, and it will be a permanent and handy reference to help in selecting stitches for a particular project. On p. 162 you will find additional tips on choosing stitches for the enhancement of a particular design. If you decide to make your own sampler, a 10-gauge interlock single canvas and Persian wool will be suitable for most of the stitches. There are only a few, as you will see, that should be done on double canvas. Wool thickness will depend on the stitch that is being done. A discussion of proper stitch tension and thread weight appears on the immediate right; general stitching techniques are explained on the facing page.

The stitches contained in this section are geared to right-handed people. For guidance on how to work if you are left-handed, turn to p. 161.

Stitch tension and thread coverage

As you work canvas work stitches, two things must be observed simultaneously: maintenance of a correct stitch tension and use of a weight of thread that satisfactorily covers the canvas. A good stitch tension allows the thread to be held tautly around the threads of the canvas; when the correct tension is maintained, all the stitches will be formed evenly. Tension that is too loose causes the thread to stand out more than it should from the surface of the canvas. This affects the durability of the stitch; loose threads are susceptible to snagging when canvas work is in use. Tension that is too tight will distort the canvas threads, and stretch the thread too thin as well. If thread is too thin, the canvas will not be well covered. This result is illustrated by the second sample of tent stitches below. In general, the larger the gauge and the longer the stitch, the

heavier the thread should be. To combine different stitch sizes successfully on the same piece of canvas, you will most likely have to use different weights of thread. All of the stitches shown below were done on a 10-gauge, interlock single canvas. The first two samples are of tent stitches, both worked with two strands of Persian wool. Coverage is good in the first sample because the stitch tension was correct. In the second tent stitch sample, tension was too tight. The adjoining samples (below right) are of straight Gobelin stitches. Both were worked with the proper tension, but the two strands of Persian wool used in the second sample were too thin for adequate coverage. The first sample was worked with four strands, which, as the result shows, is the proper weight of yarn for the stitch and canvas. Always experiment before beginning a design.

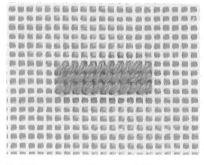

Tent stitches, proper tension/weight

Straight Gobelin, proper tension/weight

Tent stitches with too-tight tension

Straight Gobelin with too-thin thread

General stitching techniques

There are a few working techniques common to all canvas work stitches. The most basic of these are separating strands of thread and threading a needle; these are explained fully in the Embroidery chapter. Before threading the needle for any canvas work stitch, cut the thread to a 50 cm length. A thread longer than that tends to become frayed as the stitches are being worked. The number of strands will depend on stitch and canvas (see facing page).

In canvas work, there are special methods for **securing thread ends.** When starting, allow 3 to 5 cm of thread to remain at the back of the canvas. Hold this thread end against the canvas and catch it with the first few stitches. When the end is secured, clip off the excess and continue to work the rest of the stitches. To end a thread, bring needle and

thread to the back of the canvas; weave the thread through the underside of the last few stitches, then clip it. Avoid starting and ending threads in line with each other. Instead, stagger their positions; this will avoid the formation of a ridge on the right side of the canvas.

What makes each canvas work stitch different from the other is the way the thread is laid on to the mesh of the canvas. In order for the thread to be properly laid, the **canvas must be held correctly** while the stitch is worked. Most of the canvas stitches are worked with the canvas held so that the lengthwise threads lie vertically, and a horizontal thread marks the top edge of the canvas. The technique for some stitches requires the canvas to be turned while you are working. With several of the stitches, among them tent stitch (as

shown on p. 121), the canvas is turned around for each new row. When these are finished, however, all the stitches lie in the same direction. Sometimes the canvas is given only a quarter-turn. This may be done to produce a particular textural effect (see p. 163), but quite often the quarter-turn simply makes it easier to work a particular stitch. Examples are those stitches, like triangle stitch (see p. 155), in which the thread is laid in four directions.

Almost all of the stitches included in this section are shown worked on single canvas. It should not be assumed from this, however, that a stitch cannot be done on another type of canvas. Where it is necessary to use a particular canvas, this requirement is pointed out. The illustrations also show the stitches being formed by the **sewing method,** in which

the point of the needle is inserted and brought out in a single scooping movement. There is another method, the **stabbing method,** that involves two separate motions for each stitch. The stabbing method is recommended when the canvas is on a frame; it is difficult to scoop under the canvas threads when a canvas is stretched taut. Both of these methods of forming the stitches are shown below.

With either working method, there is a possibility that the thread may become too twisted. Excessive twist causes thread to kink and knot and to appear thinner than it would in its normal, relaxed state.

To untwist the thread, discontinue stitching and allow the needle and thread to dangle freely. When the thread has unwound itself, resume stitching.

SECURING THREAD ENDS

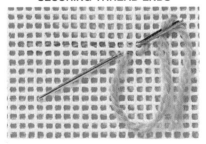

When starting, leave 3 to 5 cm of thread at the back of the canvas. Catch the thread end with the first few stitches; then trim off the excess.

When ending, bring the needle and thread to the back of the canvas. Weave the thread through the backs of the last few stitches; then cut it short.

HOLDING CANVAS WHILE WORKING

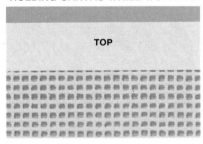

Canvas is held with the top edge at the top to work most canvas stitches. Before beginning, label the top edge of the canvas.

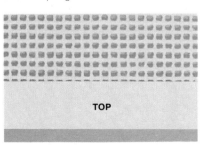

For some canvas stitches, the canvas is turned while you are working. With tent stitch (p. 121), turn canvas for each new row.

METHODS OF STITCH FORMATION

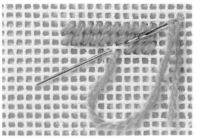

With the sewing method of stitch formation, the needle, in one motion, scoops in for the end of one stitch and out for the start of the next.

The needle is then pulled through the canvas and the thread of the last stitch is positioned over the proper canvas thread or meshes.

The stabbing method requires two movements for each stitch. First, needle and thread are pulled through to right side of the canvas.

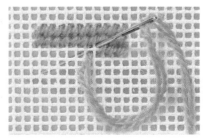

Then the needle and thread are pulled through to the back side of the canvas. The thread of the stitch is laid with the second motion.

Canvas work stitches

Diagonal stitches

The canvas work stitches in this first group are classified as diagonal stitches because all of them are worked to slant diagonally across the threads of the canvas. Included in the diagonal group are the tent stitches, the most familiar and frequently used of all canvas work stitches. Tent stitches produce an even texture applicable to any type of design. They are often used to produce the subtle effect of shading in a flower petal by using several tones of one colour. Each of the other diagonal stitches has its own distinctive texture or pattern. Whether you use any diagonal stitch will depend, first, on whether you find it appealing, and second, on how well its size and pattern meet the requirements of your canvas work design.

Diagonal stitches over one mesh can be formed with either a half-cross or a tent stitch. Tent stitch, which can be worked horizontally, vertically or diagonally, is more hard-wearing than half-cross, but uses up more thread. The diagonal method is often preferred because it distorts the canvas less. Half-cross stitch is difficult to work on single canvas, as the stitches slip at the mesh points. Half-cross can be made more durable by working over a laid thread.

Half-cross stitch (front and back views)

Tent stitch (horizontal, front and back views)

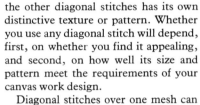

Tent stitch (diagonal, front and back views)

Half-cross stitch (done horizontally). Starting at the upper left, work each row of stitches from left to right. Form each stitch by bringing needle out at 1, then in at 2. At the end of each row of stitches, finish the last stitch and leave the needle at the back of the canvas. Then turn canvas completely around and form the new row in line with the stitches just completed.

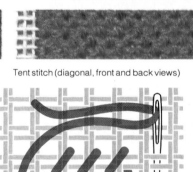

CANVAS TURNED

Half-cross stitch (done vertically). Begin at the lower right and work each row of stitches up the canvas. For each stitch, bring needle out at 1, then in at 2. At the end of each row, finish the last stitch and leave needle at back of canvas. Turn the canvas all the way around and form the new row of stitches next to those just done.

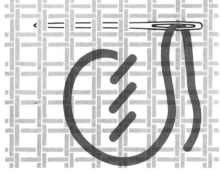

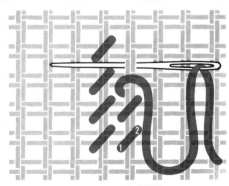

CANVAS TURNED

120

Tent stitch (done horizontally). Start at upper right and work each row of stitches from right to left. Form each stitch by bringing needle out at 1, then in at 2. At the end of each row of stitches, finish the last stitch and leave needle at back of canvas. Then turn the canvas completely around and work stitches of the new row directly in line with those in the row just completed.

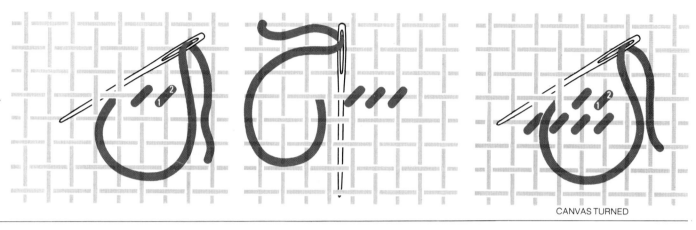

CANVAS TURNED

Tent stitch (done vertically). Start at the upper right and work each row of stitches down the canvas. To form each stitch, bring the needle out at 1, then in at 2. At each row's end, finish the last stitch and leave needle at back of canvas. Then turn the canvas completely around and form new row of stitches next to the row just completed.

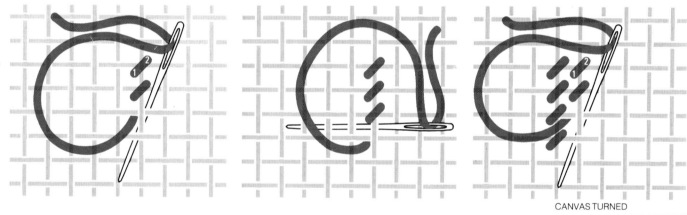

CANVAS TURNED

Tent stitch (done diagonally). Begin a few meshes from upper right and work rows alternately down, then up the canvas. For each stitch, bring needle out at 1, in at 2. Place stitches next to each other in a diagonal row; miss one canvas hole between. To work down, hold needle vertically to go from stitch to stitch. Below last stitch of a down row, form first stitch of an up row. To work up, hold needle horizontally between stitches. Form first stitch of down row next to last stitch of up row. Turn canvas to fill in corner above first row.

Canvas work stitches

Diagonal stitches

Slanted Gobelin stitch

Encroaching slanted Gobelin stitch

SLANTED GOBELIN STITCHES

Each of the individual slanted Gobelin and encroaching slanted Gobelin stitches is formed in the same way; each can vary in size to the same degree. The visual difference between the two is caused by the way the rows of stitches are placed. The rows of slanted Gobelin stitches are kept separate, producing a definite, row-by-row configuration. Rows of encroaching slanted Gobelin stitches overlap, resulting in a single, uniform texture. Both stitches can be adapted in size to suit confined or background areas of a canvas work design.

Slanted Gobelin stitch. Start at upper right and work rows alternately right to left, then left to right. For each stitch, bring needle out at 1, pass it up over canvas, down into 2. Space between 1 and 2 can be from two to five horizontal canvas threads by one to two vertical threads. Spacing here is two horizontal by one vertical thread. At the end of each row, reverse working direction; place new stitches so their bases (1) are one stitch length below bases of stitches in preceding row.

Encroaching slanted Gobelin stitch. Starting at upper right, work rows alternately right to left, then left to right. For each stitch, bring needle out at 1, up over canvas, and down into 2. Space between 1 and 2 can vary as for slanted Gobelin stitches. Space shown here is three horizontal by one vertical canvas thread. At end of each row, reverse the working direction. Position tops (2) of new stitches one canvas hole above and to the right of the bases of the stitches in the preceding row.

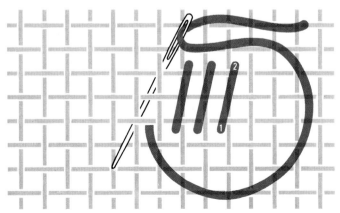

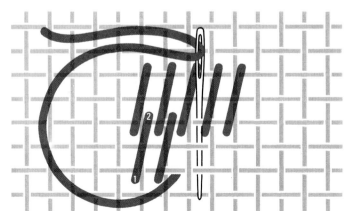

Byzantine stitch

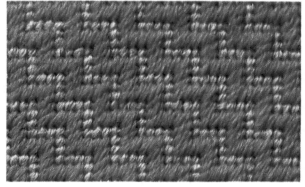
Jacquard stitch

BYZANTINE STITCHES

Byzantine stitch and its variation, jacquard stitch, form striking patterns of diagonal, uniformly stepped rows of stitches. Each stitch in the Byzantine pattern is long and slanted; the jacquard pattern alternates rows of Byzantine stitches with rows of horizontal and vertical tent stitches. The size of both the long stitches and the steps can vary (see below). Both patterns are ideal for use as background in canvas work. A second colour can easily be introduced into either pattern by alternating the colour of thread used for the rows.

Byzantine stitch. Start at upper left corner, work first row, in steps, diagonally down the canvas. Each row is a repetition of six or eight stitches (six here). Half are placed next to each other horizontally, the other half vertically, to form the steps. Form stitches consistently over two to four canvas meshes (two used here, 1 to 2). Subsequent rows are worked alternately up, then down the canvas to first fill in upper, then lower areas. Fit the steps of a new row into steps of preceding row (far right illustration).

Jacquard stitch. Here, too, canvas is covered with rows of Byzantine stitches, but rows are spaced one mesh apart, leaving stepped rows of blank meshes. On each row of exposed meshes, form tent stitches (p. 121). Work rows from bottom up, turning canvas completely for each new row. On horizontal steps, form stitches in the usual way, bringing needle out at base of stitch (1) and in at top of stitch (2). On vertical steps, reverse the direction of stitch formation, bringing needle out at top of stitch (A) and in at base (B).

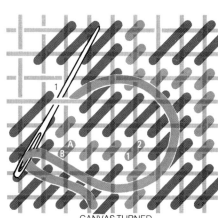
CANVAS TURNED

Canvas work stitches

Diagonal stitches

Mosaic stitch

Condensed mosaic stitch

MOSAIC STITCHES

Mosaic stitch produces a block-like pattern through repetition of the same three stitches. Rows of these stitches can be worked either horizontally or diagonally across the canvas. When only one thread colour is used, both methods result in the same pattern; when two colours are used, because the colours are differently placed with each method, the resulting patterns will differ greatly (p. 160). Condensed mosaic stitch produces an overall texture by repeating the same two stitches. It is always worked diagonally. Use mosaic and condensed mosaic stitches in small or large areas.

Mosaic stitch (done horizontally). Begin at upper right; work rows right to left. Each is a repeated grouping of three stitches worked to form blocks. Form block as follows: work one tent stitch, 1 to 2; next, a longer stitch across two canvas meshes, 3 to 4, then another tent stitch, 5 to 6. Begin next block one canvas hole to the left. At end of each row, leave needle at back of canvas, then turn canvas completely around. Align blocks of new row with blocks of preceding row.

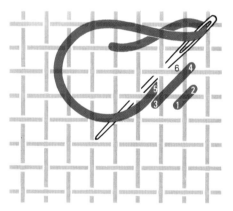

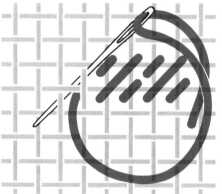

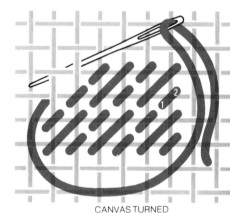

CANVAS TURNED

Mosaic stitch (done diagonally). Start at upper left and work first row diagonally down to lower right. Work successive rows alternately up, then down the canvas, filling in first the upper, then the lower areas. Each row is a repeated formation of mosaic stitch blocks (1 to 6), but blocks are placed diagonally next to each other, missing one canvas hole between. At end of row, reverse working direction and fit new blocks between blocks of preceding row.

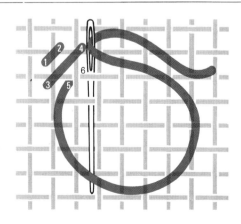

Condensed mosaic stitch.
Start at upper left; work first row diagonally to lower right. Work subsequent rows up, then down canvas; fill in first upper, then lower areas. For each row, alternately form a tent stitch, 1 to 2, then one stitch diagonally across two meshes, 3 to 4. Form the next tent stitch over the mesh opposite the centre of the 3–4 stitch. At end of each row, change working direction; place new stitches so that the tent stitches are next to the long stitches of preceding row.

Scotch stitch

Condensed Scotch stitch

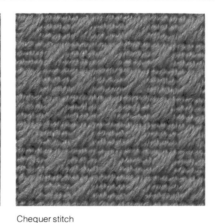

Chequer stitch

SCOTCH STITCHES

Like mosaic stitch, Scotch stitch can be worked horizontally or diagonally across the canvas to produce a block-like pattern. Blocks are formed, however, of five rather than three stitches. Condensed Scotch stitch is always worked diagonally: it repeats a group of four rather than five stitches. There is also a variation of Scotch stitch called chequer stitch. It alternates blocks of Scotch stitches with same-size blocks of tent stitches (diagonal tent stitches here). Scotch stitches, being slightly larger than mosaic stitches, cannot fit into as small a canvas area.

Scotch stitch (done horizontally). Start at upper right; work each row from right to left. Each row is a repeated group of five stitches worked to form blocks. For each block: form a tent stitch, 1 to 2, then a stitch over two meshes, 3 to 4, follow with stitch over three meshes, 5 to 6, another over two, 7 to 8, then a tent stitch, 9 to 10. Place next block to left of this. At each row's end, turn canvas around; place new blocks in line with those of preceding row.

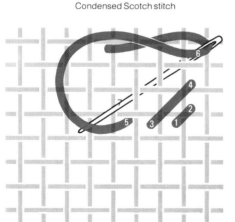

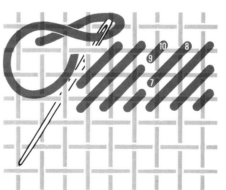

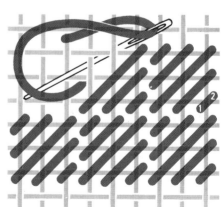

CANVAS TURNED

Canvas work stitches

Diagonal stitches

Scotch stitch (done diagonally). Start at upper left and work first row diagonally to lower right. Work the remaining rows alternately up, then down canvas, first filling in upper right, then lower left. Each row consists of blocks of Scotch stitches (1 to 10). Place blocks diagonally next to each other with one canvas hole missed between blocks. At the end of each row, reverse working direction and fit blocks of new row into indentations in preceding row.

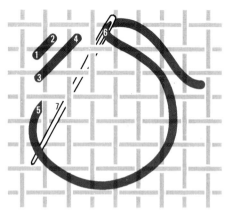

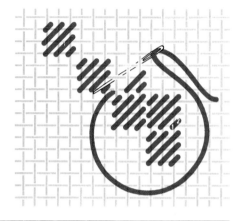

Condensed Scotch stitch. Start at upper left and work first row diagonally to lower right. Work subsequent rows up, then down the canvas to fill in first the upper, then the lower halves. For each row, repeat the following four stitches: a tent stitch, 1 to 2, a stitch over two meshes, 3 to 4, another over three meshes, 5 to 6, a fourth over two meshes, 7 to 8. Start new repeat over mesh opposite centre of last stitch. At end of each row, change working direction; form new tent stitches next to longest stitches of preceding row.

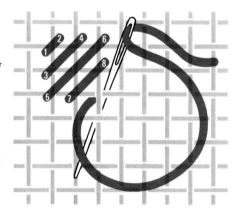
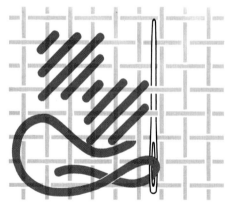

Chequer stitch. Start at upper right; work each row right to left. Each row alternates a block of Scotch stitches with a block of tent stitches. Start with a block of Scotch stitches; next to it, work a block of tent stitches to cover same area (three by three meshes). Diagonal tent stitches (p. 121) used here are formed in the order indicated by the letters A to I. At the end of each chequer-stitch row, turn the canvas around; align new tent-stitch blocks with the Scotch-stitch blocks of the preceding row.

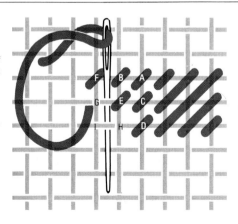
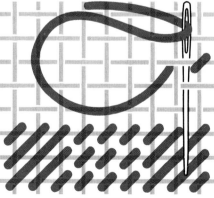
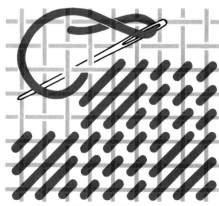

CANVAS TURNED

CANVAS TURNED

Cashmere stitch

Condensed cashmere stitch

CASHMERE STITCHES

Cashmere stitches, like mosaic and Scotch stitches, form a block-like pattern on the canvas. The blocks in this case, however, are rectangular, not square like those formed with the other two stitch types. Each block of cashmere stitches consists of four stitches; rows of cashmere stitches can be worked either horizontally or diagonally across the canvas. In the condensed cashmere stitch, each repeat is three stitches; the rows are always worked diagonally. Cashmere stitches can be used in most parts of a canvas work design, but they are especially good for backgrounds.

Cashmere stitch (done horizontally). Start at upper right and work each row from right to left. Each row consists of rectangular blocks that are formed by identical groups of four stitches. Form each group of stitches as follows: work a tent stitch, 1 to 2, two long stitches, each over two meshes, 3 to 4 and 5 to 6, then another tent stitch, 7 to 8. Place the next block to the left of this. At the end of each row, turn canvas around; align new rectangular blocks with those of the row just completed.

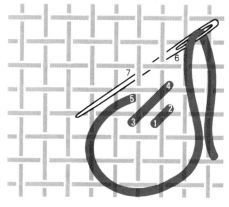

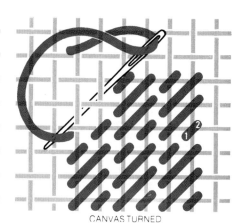

CANVAS TURNED

Cashmere stitch (done diagonally). Work first row of stitches from upper left corner diagonally down to lower right. Work subsequent rows alternately up, then down canvas, filling in first upper right, then lower left areas. Each row is made up of units of cashmere stitches (1 to 8). Each unit is placed diagonally next to the other, with one canvas hole missed in between. At the end of each row, reverse the working direction and fit new units into indentations made by units of the preceding row.

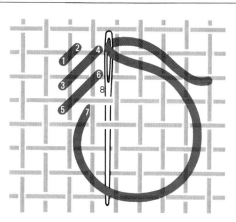

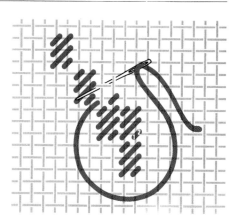

Canvas work stitches

Diagonal stitches

Condensed cashmere stitch.
Start first row at upper left; work to lower right. Successive rows are worked alternately up, then down the canvas first to cover upper right, then lower left areas of canvas. Each row is a repeated series of the same three-stitch unit: one tent stitch, 1 to 2, then two long stitches each over two meshes, 3 to 4 and 5 to 6. Start next unit over mesh that is opposite last stitch. At end of each row, change direction; fit new units into indentations formed by preceding row.

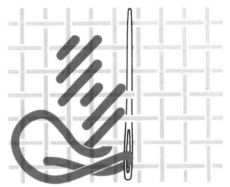

Milanese stitch

Oriental stitch

MILANESE STITCHES

Both Milanese stitch and its variation, Oriental stitch, form large and very dramatic patterns on canvas. Neither stitch should be used for a small area. Milanese stitch is composed of rows of triangular units of stitches. Oriental stitch starts with rows of Milanese stitches, but these rows are spaced to allow for the addition of groups of long diagonal stitches. When all rows of the Oriental stitch are done in one colour, a large, stepped pattern develops. But when the rows are done in alternating colours, the two different patterns frame one another (see left).

Milanese stitch. Work first row diagonally, upper left to lower right. Do subsequent rows up, then down canvas; fill in upper, then lower areas. Each row is a repetition of a group of four stitches worked to form triangular units. For each unit, form one tent stitch, 1 to 2, then a stitch over two meshes, 3 to 4, another over three meshes, 5 to 6, the last over four meshes, 7 to 8. Start next unit over mesh opposite centre of last stitch. At each row's end, change direction. Form new tent stitches diagonally next to longest stitches of previous row; reverse direction of triangular units.

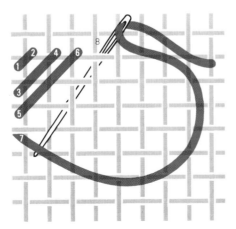
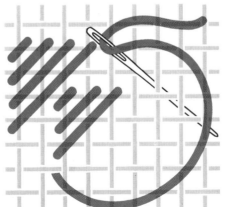

Oriental stitch. Begin by laying down rows of Milanese stitches in the following manner. Starting at upper left, work rows down, then up the canvas, filling in first upper, then lower halves. Reverse direction of the triangular units with each row. Space these rows so that the longest stitches of all units lie next to each other diagonally. This particular row-to-row arrangement of the units leaves open rectangular areas of canvas between the rows; direction of the open areas alternates from vertical in one row to horizontal in the next.

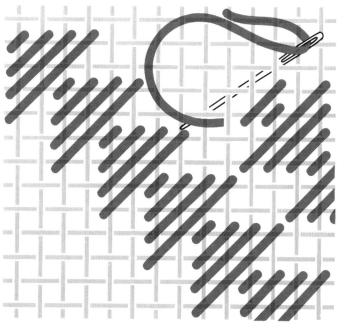

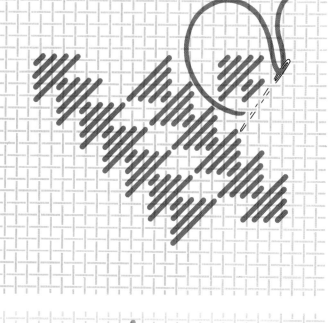

Fill in the open areas as follows: starting with the first open space in the upper left corner, work the rows diagonally down, then up the canvas. Work the vertically shaped rows down the canvas; those that are horizontal, up the canvas. In every area, form three diagonal stitches, each over two meshes, 1 to 2. Form stitches in the vertical areas below one another; place the stitches in horizontal areas next to each other. All of the stitches should slant in the same direction, from lower left to upper right. All groups of stitches hug the edges of Milanese stitches. When using filling-in stitches (p. 161) to complete the outer edges of the stitched area, maintain the pattern of separate rows of stitches.

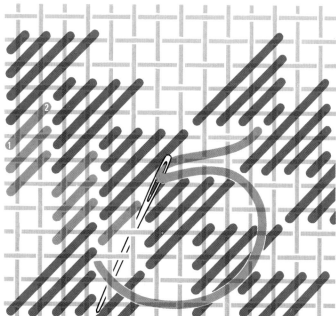

Canvas work stitches

Diagonal stitches

Kelim stitch

Stem stitch

KELIM STITCHES

Kelim stitch and its variation, stem stitch, form plait-like patterns on the canvas. The pattern that emerges from Kelim stitch, as shown here, travels across the canvas; stem stitch pattern goes up and down. Both patterns are composed of rows of diagonal stitches, with the stitches in each successive row slanted the opposite way from the stitches in the preceding row. Stem stitch also involves backstitches between paired rows of diagonal stitches. Both Kelim and stem stitches can be used for small or large design areas; Kelim stitch is suitable for use in rugs.

Kelim stitch. Begin at upper right and work rows alternately from right to left, then left to right. Each stitch is taken over one horizontal by two vertical canvas threads. When working rows from right to left, bring needle out at base of stitch, 1, and in at top of stitch, 2. When working rows from left to right, reverse the slant of the stitches by bringing the needle out at top of stitch, 3, and in at base of stitch, 4. Rows of stitches are formed directly below one another.

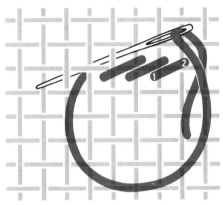
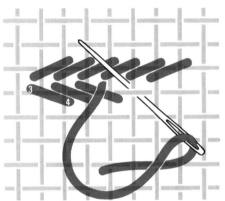
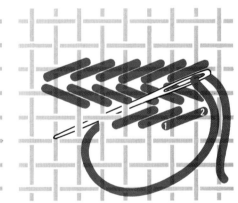

Stem stitch. Start at upper left and work in groups of three rows. One row of diagonal stitches is worked down the canvas, a second up; a third row, of backstitches (see p. 138), is worked down the canvas, between the first two rows. Form each diagonal stitch over two meshes. When working stitches down the canvas, slant them up to the left, 1 to 2; when going up the canvas, slant them up to the right, 3 to 4. Work a backstitch, A to B, over every horizontal thread between bases of diagonal stitches. Form next repeat to right.

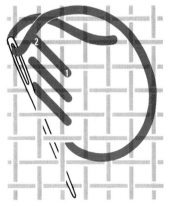
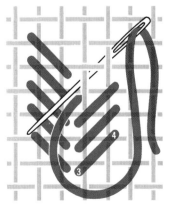

Straight stitches

The stitches in this group are called straight stitches because all of them, except for the backstitch done diagonally, are formed to lie parallel to the threads of the canvas. In most instances, the stitches are parallel to the vertical canvas threads. Two exceptions are darning stitch and backstitch done horizontally; these lie parallel to the horizontal threads. The straight-stitch group also includes Florentine stitch and its variations. These produce the familiar zigzag stitch patterns that are associated with Florentine work. The techniques for this are explained in more detail starting on p. 173.

STRAIGHT GOBELIN STITCHES

Straight Gobelin and encroaching straight Gobelin stitches are comparable in their formation, but not in the patterns they produce. The visual difference is caused by the way the rows of stitches are placed. Straight Gobelin stitches result in a definite row-by-row pattern because each row of stitches is separate from the other. Encroaching straight Gobelin stitches form a uniform texture because the rows overlap. Both stitches can be varied in length (see below) to suit canvas areas of any size.

Straight Gobelin stitch

Encroaching straight Gobelin stitch

Straight Gobelin stitch. Start at upper right; work rows alternately right to left, then left to right. For each stitch, bring needle out at 1, pass it up over the canvas, down into 2. Space between 1 and 2 can be from two to five horizontal threads. Spacing here is two horizontal threads. At the end of each row, reverse working direction; place new stitches so their bases (1) are one stitch length below bases of stitches in preceding row.

Encroaching straight Gobelin stitch. Start at upper right and work rows alternately right to left, then left to right. For each stitch, bring needle out at 1, pass it up over the canvas, down into 2. Space between 1 and 2 can vary as for straight Gobelin stitches. Space shown here is three horizontal canvas threads. At each row's end, reverse working direction. Position tops (2) of new stitches one horizontal thread above, but consistently to the left or right of the bases of the stitches in preceding row (tops here are to the left).

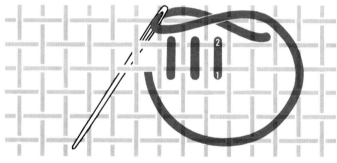

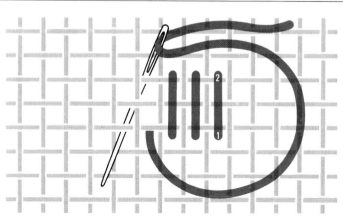

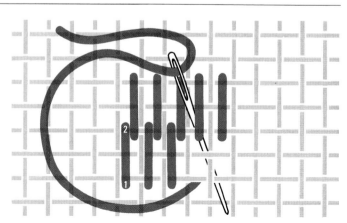

Canvas work stitches

Straight stitches

Brick stitch

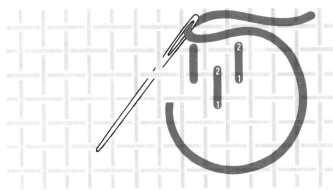

Gobelin filling stitch

BRICK STITCHES

Brick stitch and Gobelin filling stitch are alike in that each produces a very similar pattern. Each individual brick stitch, however, is only two canvas threads long, whereas each Gobelin filling stitch is six threads long. Another similarity between the two is that the methods of row formation (shown below for both of the stitches) are interchangeable. The row method illustrated for the brick stitch produces single rows of stitches, each of which forms a zigzag pattern across the canvas. With the row method that is shown for Gobelin filling stitch, this same zigzag effect is produced after two rows.

Brick stitch. Starting at upper right, work rows alternately right to left, then left to right. Each row makes use of three horizontal canvas threads, but each stitch spans only two of these threads. Position of stitches alternates in each row, first being over the top two threads, then over the lower two. For each stitch, bring needle out at 1, insert at 2. At each row's end, reverse working direction. Position bases (1) of new stitches one stitch length below bases of stitches in preceding row.

Gobelin filling stitch. Start at upper right and work rows alternately from right to left, then left to right. For each stitch, bring needle out at 1, up over six horizontal canvas threads, then down into 2. Position bases (1) of stitches one canvas hole apart. At the end of each row, reverse working direction. Position new stitches so that their top halves are between the stitches of the preceding row.

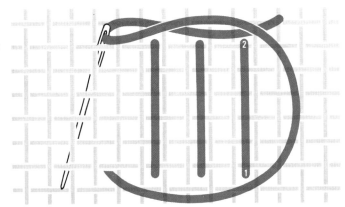
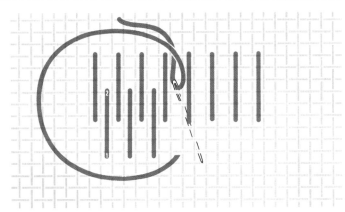

FLORENTINE STITCHES

Florentine stitch and its variations form the zigzag patterns used so often in the type of canvas work known as Florentine embroidery. The high points of the zigzag are referred to as peaks, the low points as valleys. Each row consists of straight stitches placed next to each other in a diagonal arrangement up and down the canvas. The diagonal effect results from the 'step' between stitches. **Step** is the term for the number of horizontal canvas threads between the bases of neighbouring stitches. A kind of shorthand is used to specify stitch length and step. Given as two numbers separated by a full stop, for example, 3.1, the first number means stitch length, the second number stands for the step between the stitches. The amount of step is always less than the length of the stitch. The pattern of a Florentine stitch is arrived at by manipulating the number, length and steps of the stitches. In its basic form, Florentine stitch has an even peak-and-valley pattern. Two variations are shown here. For more on Florentine stitches, see p. 173.

Florentine stitch

Two variations of Florentine stitch

Florentine stitch. Work first row in two movements across horizontal centre of canvas, from vertical centre to left, then from centre to right. Work subsequent rows in one movement, from right edge to left, or left to right. Place rows above or below first row, fitting stitches of each new row into jagged edge of preceding row. Overall pattern is usually a repeat of several rows; three-row repeat is shown here with second two above the first. In each row, there can be from three to eight stitches between valley and peaks (four shown). Stitches can be two to eight horizontal canvas threads long; step must be at least one less than the stitch-length number. Stitches in all of these rows are four threads long with step of two between stitches (4.2).

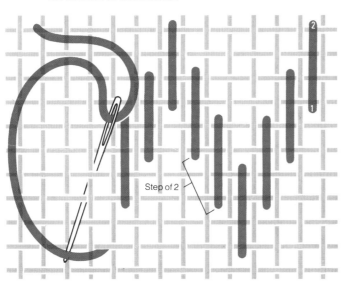

Step of 2

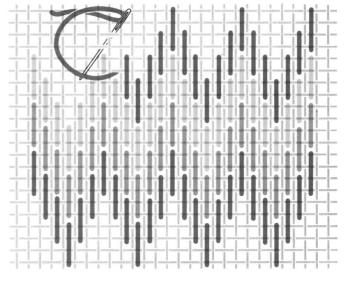

Canvas work stitches

Straight stitches

One way to vary Florentine stitch is to work rows that form peaks and valleys of varying sizes. This general pattern of uneven points is called flame stitch. There is no set pattern; you can design your own. In general, the more stitches used between peak and valley, the longer those stitches, and the greater the step between stitches, the higher the point will be. Usually, the stitches of any one row are the same length; the step between them can vary to give an even more undulating look to the row. The stitch length used for each subsequent row can be different from the first, but the step plan established by the first row should be maintained. On the immediate right the first row is being done; in the compressed drawing, far right, the first row is the centre row. Notice how the step change is maintained even though a different stitch length is used for each row.

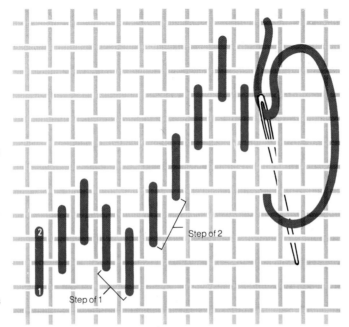

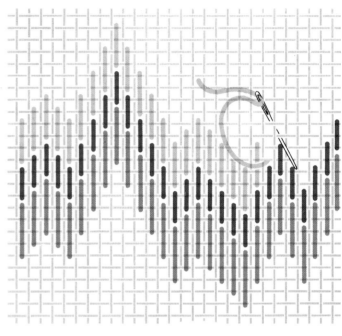

Another way to vary Florentine stitches is to round off the peaks (and valleys, not shown). This is achieved through the use of blocks of stitches. There can be two or more (usually up to six) in each block. The number of blocks used to round off the point can vary. In general, the more blocks used, and the more stitches in each block, the rounder the point will be. The stitches in each block are the same length; the step between blocks can vary with the length of stitch used. The row pattern can include pointed and rounded peaks and valleys. The block and step plan established by the first row (top row in compressed drawing) is maintained by the other two. It is not necessary, however, for the stitch length to be the same in each row.

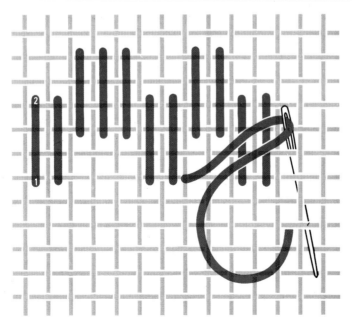

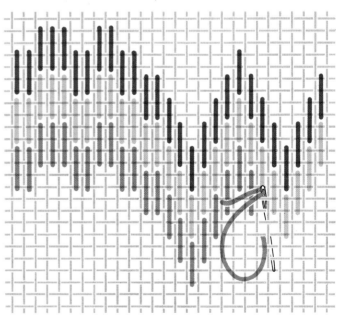

HUNGARIAN STITCHES

Both Hungarian stitch and Hungarian diamond stitch produce patterns of diamond-shaped units across the canvas. Each of the diamond-shaped units of Hungarian stitch is small and consists of three stitches. The diamonds of Hungarian diamond stitch are larger because each unit consists of five stitches. The pattern of Hungarian grounding is achieved by alternating rows of Hungarian stitches with rows of Florentine stitches. Any of these stitches is excellent for filling in large or background areas of a canvas work design.

Hungarian stitch

Hungarian diamond stitch

Hungarian grounding

Hungarian stitch. Start at upper right; work rows alternately right to left, left to right. Each row is a repeated grouping of three stitches to form diamond-shaped units. For each unit, work one stitch over two horizontal canvas threads, 1 to 2, next a stitch over four threads, 3 to 4, then another over two threads, 5 to 6. Miss one canvas hole to start next unit. At each row's end, reverse direction; work new units so tops of long stitches are between units of preceding row.

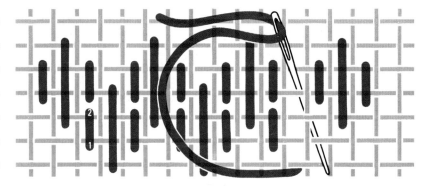

Hungarian diamond stitch. Begin at upper right and work rows alternately right to left, then left to right. Each row is a repeated grouping of five stitches to form large diamond-shaped units. Form each unit as follows: work one straight stitch over two horizontal canvas threads, 1 to 2, a longer stitch over four threads, 3 to 4, another over six threads, 5 to 6, followed by a stitch over four threads, 7 to 8, then another over two threads, 9 to 10. Miss one canvas hole to start next unit. At end of each row, reverse working direction. Position new diamond units so that the tops of the longest stitches fall between the diamonds of the preceding row.

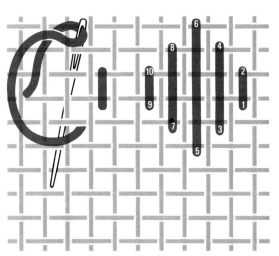

Canvas work stitches

Straight stitches

Hungarian grounding. Start by working a row of Florentine stitches across centre of canvas (p. 133). Form its even peaks and valleys three stitches deep, using stitches four threads long with a step of one between them. Then work a row of Hungarian stitches, placing longest stitches of each unit below the peaks of the Florentine. Below this, work a row of Florentine, placing its valleys below longest stitches of the Hungarian-stitch units. Continue alternating stitch rows; turn canvas to stitch open area of canvas in the same way.

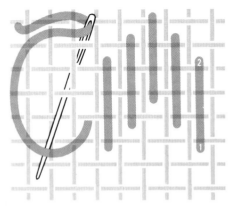 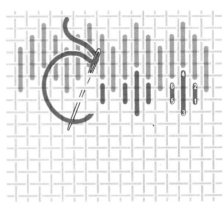 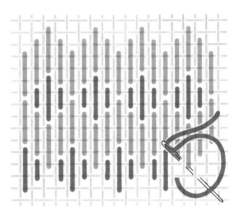

Parisian stitch

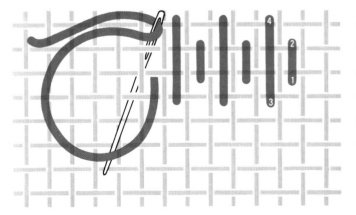

Old Florentine stitch

PARISIAN STITCHES

Parisian stitch forms an irregular texture across the canvas; old Florentine stitch produces a very large pattern resembling the surface of a woven basket. The size difference between these two patterns is caused by the size of the individual stitches, Parisian stitches being shorter than old Florentine. The row structure for both Parisian and old Florentine stitches is very similar (see below and facing page). Stitches in each row of Parisian alternate from one short to one long stitch; stitches in each row of old Florentine alternate two short stitches with two that are very long.

Parisian stitch. Start at upper right and work rows alternately right to left, then left to right. For each row, alternately form a short stitch over two horizontal canvas threads, 1 to 2, then a long stitch over four threads, 3 to 4. At end of each row, reverse working direction. Position new stitches so that the tops (2) of the short stitches are in the same canvas hole as the bases of the long stitches in the preceding row.

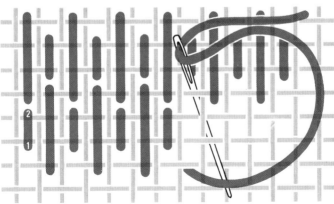

Old Florentine stitch. Start at upper right; work rows alternately from right to left, then left to right. For each row, alternately form two short, then two long stitches. Work each short stitch over three horizontal canvas threads, 1 to 2 and 3 to 4; form each long stitch over nine threads, 5 to 6 and 7 to 8. At end of each row, reverse working direction. Position new stitches so that the tops of the short stitches (2 and 4) are in the same canvas holes as the bases of the long stitches of the preceding row.

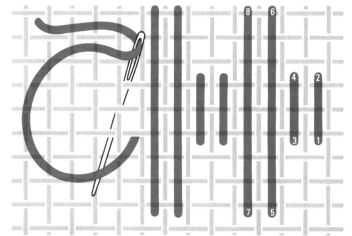

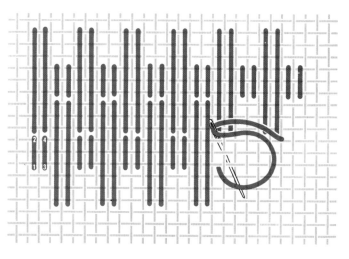

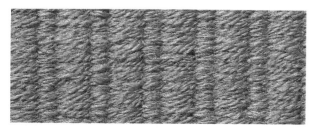

Darning stitch

Enlargement of darning stitch

DARNING STITCH

Darning stitch produces a very tightly stitched surface on the canvas. For each row of darning stitches, the thread is woven across the canvas in four journeys (complete spans) to form interlocking long and short stitches within the space of two horizontal canvas threads. The sample has been enlarged to make the stitches easier to see.

Darning stitch. Work each row in four journeys (full spans) across the canvas, within the space of two horizontal canvas threads. Starting at upper left, work first journey to the right, forming long stitches as follows: bring needle out at 1, over four vertical threads (1 to 2) then under two (2 to 1). At end of journey, reverse direction. Work second journey to the left, forming short stitches as follows: with needle out at 1, pass over two vertical threads (1 to 2) then under four (2 to 1). Work third journey like the first; work the fourth like the second. Form the next set of journeys between the next two horizontal canvas threads (1).

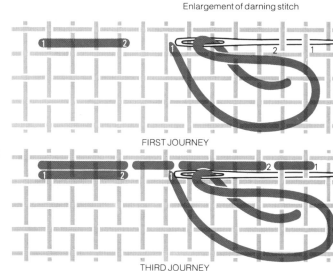

FIRST JOURNEY

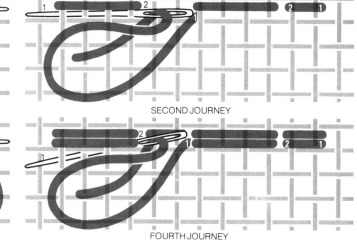

SECOND JOURNEY

THIRD JOURNEY

FOURTH JOURNEY

Canvas work stitches

Straight stitches

Backstitch (done horizontally)

Backstitch (done vertically)

Backstitch (done diagonally)

BACKSTITCHES
In canvas work, backstitches are never used to cover an entire area of blank canvas. Rather, they are used as single rows of stitches to outline a stitched area of a canvas work design, or to cover the canvas threads left exposed by another canvas work stitch (see diamond eyelet, p. 153). They can be worked in all directions on the canvas.

Backstitch (done horizontally). Work rows either right to left or left to right. When working right to left, point needle to left; when working left to right, point needle to right. For each stitch, bring needle out at 1, pass it back over one vertical thread, into 2. To start next stitch, pass needle under two vertical threads.

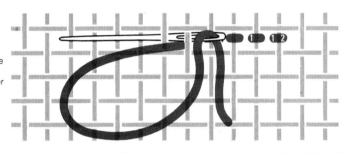

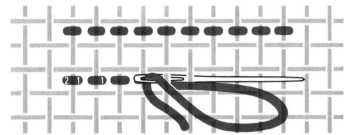

Backstitch (done vertically). Rows can be worked down or up the canvas. When working down, have needle pointing down; when working up, have needle pointing up. Form each stitch as follows: bring needle out at 1, pass it back over one horizontal canvas thread, then into 2. Pass needle under two horizontal threads to start the next stitch.

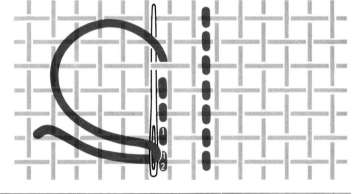

Backstitch (done diagonally). Rows can be worked diagonally up or down the canvas, to span canvas right to left, as shown, or left to right. When working down, have needle pointing down; when working up, have needle pointing up. For each stitch, bring needle out at 1, pass it back over one mesh, into 2. Pass needle under two meshes to start next stitch.

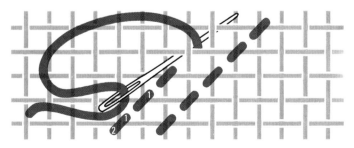

Crossing stitches

The stitches in this group are classified as crossing stitches because each of their patterns is achieved through the use of stitches that cross over each other. Some stitches are diagonal, some straight. Some of the stitches involve only two stitches for each unit; cross stitch is an example. In others, there are more than two, eight in double leviathan stitch, for instance. The crossing of the stitches occurs, for the most part, within each individual unit or within a row of units. Exceptions are the plaited and perspective stitches; in these two cases, the crossing takes place between two rows of diagonal stitches.

CROSS STITCHES

A cross stitch consists of two diagonal stitches crossing at the centre. Generally a cross stitch spans only one canvas mesh, and its upper stitch slants the same as a tent stitch. Cross stitches can be formed in two ways. Use either method to form any size cross stitch on interlock or double canvas; to form one-mesh cross stitches on single canvas, use Method 1 below. To alter the slant of the upper stitch of any cross stitch, see bottom of next page.

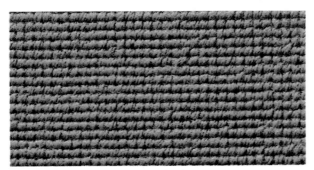

Cross stitch with upper stitch slanting same as tent stitch

Cross stitch variation (upper stitch slanting opposite to tent stitch)

Cross stitch (Method 1, done horizontally). Start at upper left; work rows alternately from left to right, then right to left. For each cross stitch, form the lower stitch first, coming out at 1 and going in at 2. Then form the upper stitch, bringing the needle out at 3, up over the 1–2 stitch, then inserting it at 4. At end of each row, reverse working direction and form the new stitch row directly below the stitches just completed.

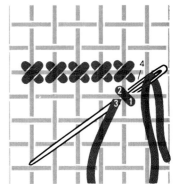

Cross stitch (Method 1, done vertically). Start at upper left; work each row down the canvas. For each cross stitch, form the lower stitch first, coming out at 1, going in at 2. Then form the upper stitch over the lower, coming out at 3 and going in at 4. At end of each row, finish last stitch, but leave needle at back of canvas. Then turn the canvas completely around and form the new row of stitches next to those just completed.

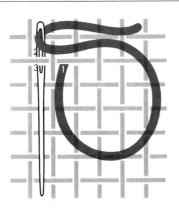
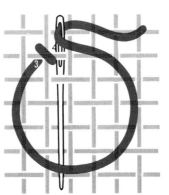
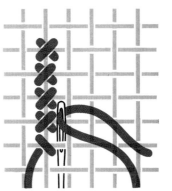
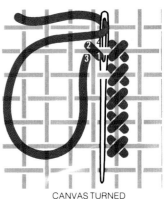

CANVAS TURNED

139

Canvas work stitches

Crossing stitches

Cross stitch (Method 2, done horizontally). Start at upper right; work each row of cross stitches in two spans – first from right to left, then left to right. When working from right to left, form lower stitches of the cross stitches by bringing needle out at 1, inserting at 2. At end of span, reverse work direction. Working from left to right, form the upper stitches of the cross stitches by bringing needle out at 3, over the 1–2 stitch, then in at 4. Work next row of cross stitches below those just completed.

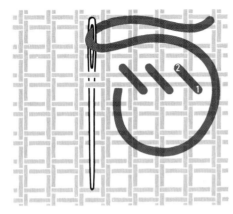 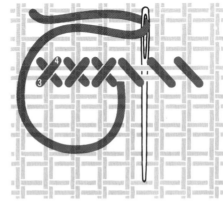 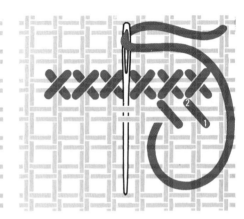

Cross stitch (Method 2, done vertically). Start at upper right; work each row of cross stitches in two spans – first down, then up the canvas. When working down, form the lower stitches of the cross stitches by bringing needle out at 1 and inserting it at 2. At end of span, reverse working direction. Working upwards, form the upper stitches of the cross stitches, bringing needle out at 3 and over 1–2 stitch, then inserting it at 4. Work next row of cross stitches to left of those just completed.

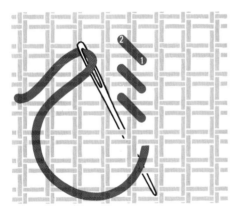  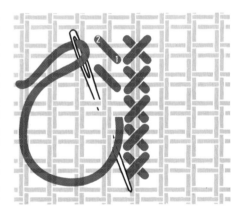

To reverse slant of upper stitch, change way of forming the upper and lower stitches of the cross. The easiest way to understand this is by comparing steps 1 to 2 (the lower stitch) and steps 3 to 4 (the upper stitch) on the right with the 1–2 and 3–4 steps shown above (Method 2) and on preceding page (Method 1). If you use Method 1, the working direction of rows, whether horizontal or vertical, stays the same. With Method 2, reverse directions, starting at upper left to work rows horizontally; at lower left to work rows vertically.

 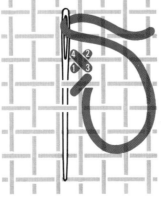 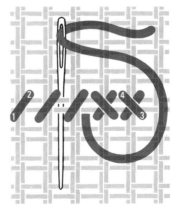 

Oblong cross stitch

Oblong cross stitch with backstitch

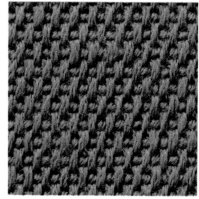
Double stitch

OBLONG CROSS STITCHES

Oblong cross stitch is an elongated cross stitch consisting of two diagonal stitches that cross each other to span a rectangular area of the canvas. All three of the stitch samples shown here use oblong cross stitches either by themselves or in combination with other stitches. First sample is of plain oblong cross stitches. The middle sample is of oblong cross stitches each of which has a backstitch across its centre. The last sample is of double stitch, in which oblong cross stitches alternate with one-mesh cross stitches. For a two-colour version of double stitch, see p. 160.

Oblong cross stitch. Starting at upper right, work each row in two spans across the canvas. First work from right to left, forming lower stitches of each oblong cross stitch, 1 to 2. Space between 1 and 2 is two horizontal by one vertical canvas thread. Then, at end of span, work row back to right, forming upper stitches of each oblong cross stitch, 3 to 4. Space between 3 and 4 is same as between 1 and 2. With each new row, position bases of new stitches (1 and 3) one stitch length below the stitches of the preceding row.

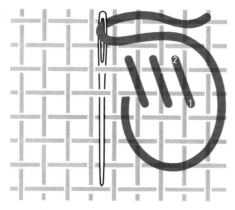
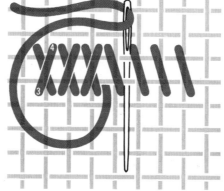
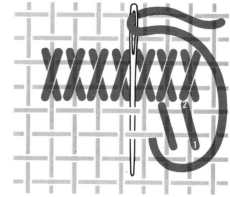

Oblong cross stitch with backstitch. Start at upper right; work rows alternately from right to left, then left to right. For each stitch, form an oblong cross stitch, 1 to 2 and 3 to 4, then work a backstitch over the centre of the cross stitch, 5 to 6. Size of oblong cross stitch is same as above; 5–6 stitch is over one vertical canvas thread. At each row's end, change work direction. Place bases of new stitches (1 and 3) one stitch length below stitches just done; reverse direction of 5 to 6 so a backstitch is formed.

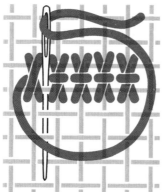
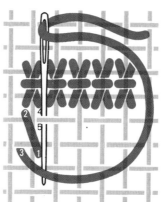
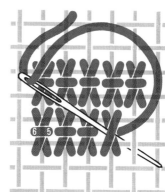

Canvas work stitches

Crossing stitches

Double stitch. Start at upper left and work rows alternately left to right, then right to left. For each row, alternately form oblong and normal cross stitches. Work each oblong cross stitch over three horizontal by one vertical canvas thread, 1 to 2, 3 to 4; work each normal cross stitch over one mesh, 5 to 6, 7 to 8. At end of each row, reverse working direction. Place new stitches so that tops of oblong cross stitches (2 and 4) are in same canvas holes as bases of the normal cross stitches of the preceding row.

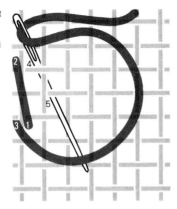

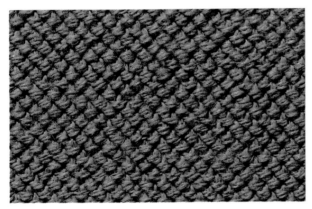

Upright cross stitch

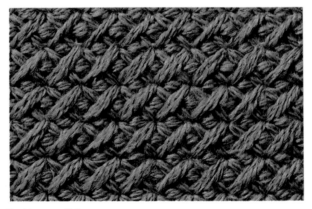

Double cross stitch

UPRIGHT CROSS STITCHES

Each upright cross stitch is composed of two straight stitches that cross at their centres. The lower stitch lies parallel to the vertical threads of the canvas; the upper stitch is parallel to the horizontal canvas threads. By themselves, upright cross stitches produce a pebbly texture on the canvas. Used in combination with large normal cross stitches, they become the double cross stitch pattern. Double cross stitch creates a lovely latticework pattern, which can be made even more interesting by working it in two colours. For two-colour working techniques, see p. 160.

Upright cross stitch. Start at upper left and work rows alternately from left to right, then right to left. For each upright cross stitch, bring needle out at 1, in at 2, then out at 3 and in at 4. Each upright cross stitch can span two or four vertical by horizontal canvas threads (span of two is shown). At each row's end, reverse working direction. Place new stitches so their tops (2) share a canvas hole with neighbouring horizontal stitches in the preceding row.

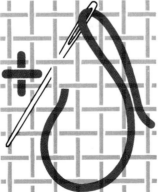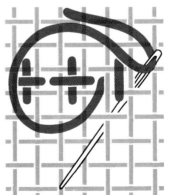

Double cross stitch. Start at upper left; work rows left to right, then right to left. For each row, alternately form a large cross stitch to span four by four canvas threads, 1 to 2 and 3 to 4; then form an upright cross stitch over two by two threads, 5 to 6 and 7 to 8. At each row's end, change work direction. Place tops of new large cross stitches (2 and 4) in canvas holes of bases of large cross stitches in preceding row. Cover canvas with double cross stitch; form upright cross stitches between rows (A to B and C to D).

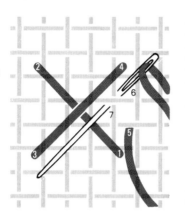 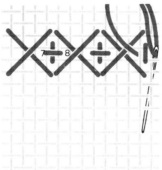 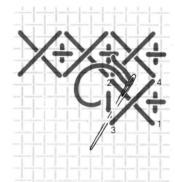 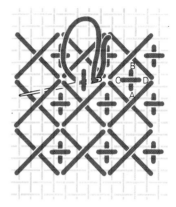

Double straight cross stitch

Leviathan stitch

Double leviathan stitch

DOUBLE STRAIGHT CROSS STITCH/ LEVIATHAN STITCHES

All three of the patterns in this group form large, raised stitch units, each consisting of multiple layers of crossing stitches and spanning four horizontal by four vertical canvas threads. The resulting units, however, are different in shape. Units of the double straight cross stitch are diamond-shaped; those of both the leviathan and double leviathan stitches are square. These are very precise stitches, and to achieve their neat layering and distinctive look, you must follow the sequence of steps with great care.

Double straight cross stitch.
Start at upper left and work rows left to right, then right to left. Form each stitch as follows: first, a large upright cross stitch that spans four by four canvas threads, 1 to 2 and 3 to 4; then, a large cross stitch, over centre of upright cross stitch, spanning two by two threads, 5 to 6 and 7 to 8. Miss three canvas holes between bases (1) of stitches. At each row's end, change work direction. Place new stitches so that tops (2) share canvas hole with neighbouring horizontal stitches in row above.

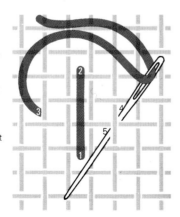 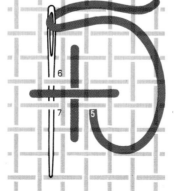  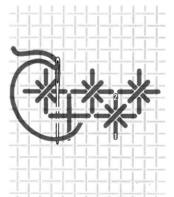

Canvas work stitches

Crossing stitches

Leviathan stitch (also known as double cross stitch and Smyrna stitch). Start at upper left and work rows from left to right, then right to left. Form each stitch as follows: first, a large cross stitch that spans four by four canvas threads, 1 to 2 and 3 to 4; then, a large upright cross stitch, over centre of large cross stitch, that spans four by four threads, 5 to 6 and 7 to 8. At end of each row, reverse work direction. Place new stitches so tops (2, 6 and 4) share canvas holes with bases of stitches in row above.

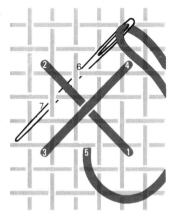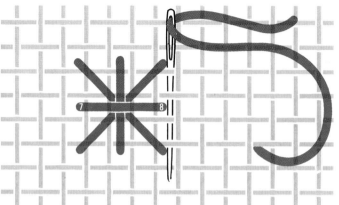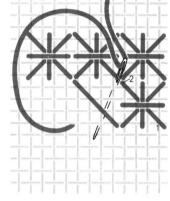

Double leviathan stitch. Start at upper left; work rows alternately left to right, then right to left. For each stitch, first form a large cross stitch over four by four canvas threads, 1 to 2 and 3 to 4. Then bring needle out at 5, up over the cross stitch and in at 6, out at 7. Pass needle down over cross stitch, in at 8, out at 9. Bring needle up over cross stitch, in at 10, out at 11. Pass needle down over cross stitch, in at 12, out at 13.

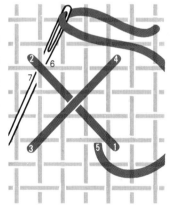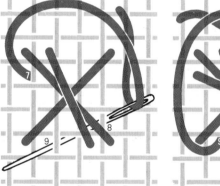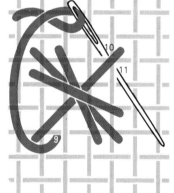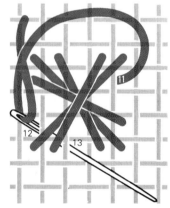

To complete the stitch, form a large upright cross stitch as follows: bring needle from 13 up over the stitch and in at 14; then, out at 15, across the stitch, and in at 16. At the end of each row, reverse the working direction. Position stitches of new row so their tops (2, 6, 14, 10 and 4) share canvas holes with the bases of the stitches in the row just completed.

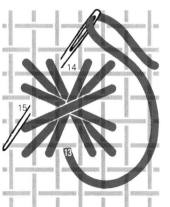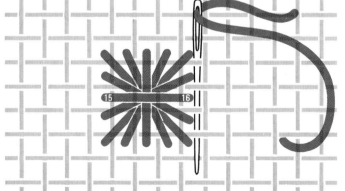

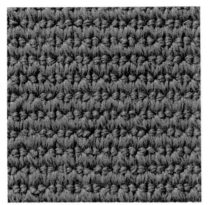

Knotted stitch

French stitch

Rococo stitch

KNOTTED STITCHES

These three patterns – knotted stitch, French stitch and rococo stitch – all involve long stitches that are held down to the canvas by short crossing stitches. In knotted stitch, both the long and the short stitches cross diagonally over each other and over the canvas. In the French and rococo stitch patterns, long straight stitches are crossed by short straight stitches, but the long straight stitches become bowed in shape when the short crossing stitches have anchored them to the canvas. Of the three knotted types, the rococo stitch pattern is the largest and most dramatic.

Knotted stitch. Start at upper right; work rows alternately right to left, left to right. For each stitch, bring needle out at 1, over three horizontal and one vertical canvas thread, in at 2. Bring needle out at 3, over the 1–2 stitch, and in at 4. When working rows from right to left, work 3–4 stitch down over 1–2 stitch; working left to right, work 3–4 stitch up over 1–2 stitch. At each row's end, change working direction. Place tops of new stitches (2) one canvas hole above and to the right of bases of stitches just done.

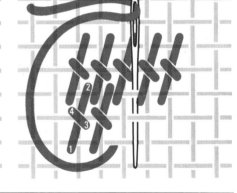

French stitch. Begin at upper right; work rows from right to left, then left to right. For each French stitch, form two tied-down straight stitches, both within the space of two vertical canvas threads. Work first stitch, 1 to 2 and 3 to 4; then second, 5 to 6 and 7 to 8. Start next stitch in second canvas hole from base of stitch just done. At each row's end, reverse working direction for rows and for horizontal stitches. Place new stitches between those of row above, so that their tops share canvas hole of neighbouring horizontal stitches.

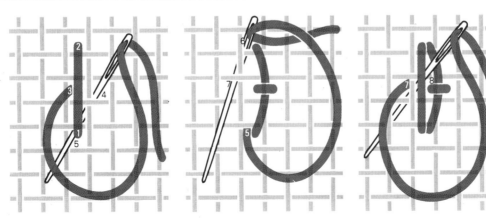

Canvas work stitches

Crossing stitches

Rococo stitch. Begin upper right; work rows from right to left, then left to right. For each rococo stitch, form four tied-down straight stitches, all within the space of two vertical canvas threads, but fanned to span four threads. Work as shown, starting with the first stitch, 1 to 2 and 3 to 4, then the second, 5 to 6, 7 to 8, the third, 9 to 10, 11 to 12, then the fourth, 13 to 14, 15 to 16. Start next stitch in fourth canvas hole from base of stitch just done. Work new rows as shown (explained in French stitch, p. 145).

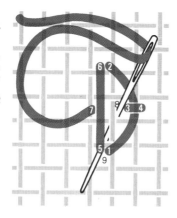 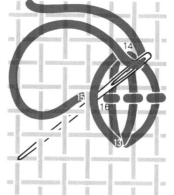 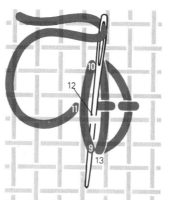 

Rice stitch

Enlargement of rice stitch

RICE STITCH
Rice stitch produces a very tightly stitched, well-covered canvas area. Each stitch unit consists of one large ordinary cross stitch and four additional small stitches, each of which crosses a corner of the larger base cross stitch. The sample on the far left shows rice stitches actual size; in the sample on the immediate left, an area of those stitches has been enlarged to show the pattern more clearly. If you wish, rice stitch can be worked in two colours, the large cross stitches first in one colour, then the smaller crossing stitches in the other (see p. 160 for two-colour techniques).

Rice stitch. Start at upper right; work rows alternately right to left, then left to right. For each rice stitch, first work a large cross stitch over two horizontal by two vertical canvas threads, 1 to 2 and 3 to 4. Form four small crossing stitches, each over a corner of the large cross stitch, 5 to 6, 7 to 8, 9 to 10 and 11 to 12. At end of each row, reverse working direction. Place new stitch units directly below those just completed

 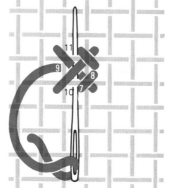  

FISHBONE STITCH/FERN STITCH

Though these stitch patterns are different in result – the fishbone stitch produces a wavy pattern across the canvas, the fern stitch up-and-down stripes – they are quite similar in technique. Both are worked in vertical rows; stitches in each row are crossed, this time off centre. The rows of fishbone stitching are worked alternately down and then up the canvas; all fern stitch rows are worked down. Each fishbone stitch consists of a long diagonal stitch crossed at one end by a short crossing stitch. Fern stitch is made up of two stitches that cross one another at their lower ends.

Fishbone stitch

Fern stitch

Fishbone stitch. Start at upper left and work rows down, then up the canvas. Each fishbone stitch consists of a long diagonal stitch that is crossed at one end by a short diagonal stitch. Each long stitch is over three horizontal and two vertical canvas threads; each short stitch is over one mesh. When working row down, work long stitch up, 1 to 2, and cross its top, 3 to 4. When working up a row, work long stitch down, 5 to 6, and cross its bottom, 7 to 8. Rows of stitches are formed next to each other.

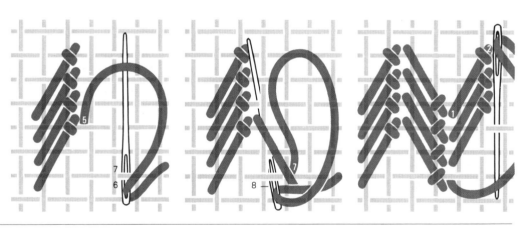

Fern stitch. Start at upper left; work all rows down the canvas. For each stitch, bring needle out at 1, down over two canvas meshes and in at 2; pass under one vertical thread, out at 3, up over two meshes and in at 4. Begin next stitch in canvas hole below the start of the stitch above (1). Form next row of stitches to the right of those just done.

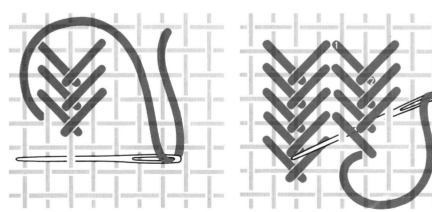

Canvas work stitches

Crossing stitches

Herringbone stitch

Double herringbone stitch

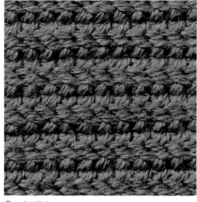
Greek stitch

HERRINGBONE STITCHES/ GREEK STITCH

Both herringbone stitch and its variation, double herringbone stitch, form a tightly woven texture on the canvas. Greek stitch produces a plait-like pattern. All three of these stitch patterns are worked in rows across the canvas; all rows consist of stitches that cross off centre. Both of the herringbone stitches are strong enough to be suitable choices for rugmaking. Greek stitch, however, is not as durable. Double herringbone stitch is usually worked in two contrasting colours as shown on the left and explained below.

Herringbone stitch. Start at upper left; work all rows left to right. Consistently form stitches as follows: bring needle out at 1, down over two canvas meshes and in at 2; then under one vertical thread, out at 3, up over two meshes and in at 4. Pass needle back under one vertical thread to start next stitch. Begin each new row of stitches in the canvas hole below the start of the stitches in the row above.

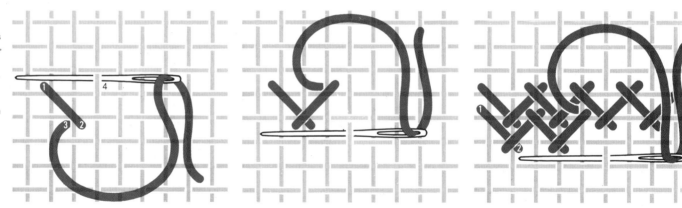

Double herringbone stitch. Begin at upper left; work all rows left to right. Cover the entire canvas area with rows of herringbone stitches (above) but space them by beginning each new row in second canvas hole below the start of the row above. Then go back and cover each of these rows with rows of 'upside-down' herringbone stitches. Bring needle out at A, up over two canvas meshes, in at B; then back under one vertical thread, out at C, down over two meshes, in at D. Pass needle under a vertical thread to start next stitch.

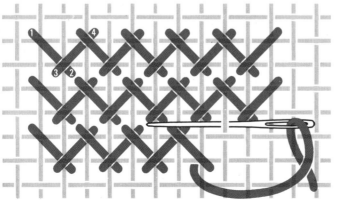

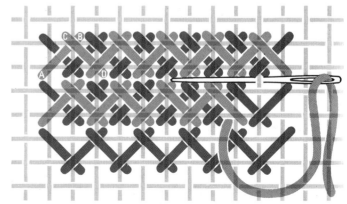

Greek stitch. Begin at upper left; work all rows from left to right. Form each stitch as follows: bring needle out at 1, up over two canvas meshes and in at 2; then under two vertical threads, out at 3, and down into 4, the fourth canvas hole from start of stitch. Pass needle under two vertical threads to begin next stitch. End each row with a 1–2 stitch, then turn canvas completely around to work the next row of stitches. Start each row with a 1–2 stitch.

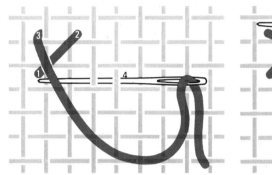
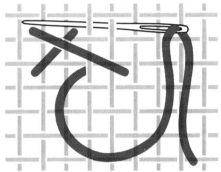
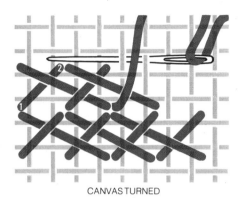

CANVAS TURNED

Plaited stitch

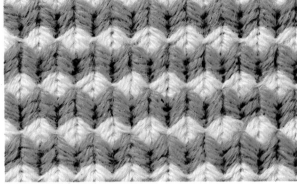

Perspective stitch

PLAITED STITCH/ PERSPECTIVE STITCH

Plaited and perspective stitches are unique in the way that their individual stitches cross each other. With these two stitch patterns, the crossing of the stitches does not occur within single rows of stitches. Instead, the stitches of one row become crossed by the formation of the stitches in the next row. Plaited stitch produces the texture of a thick, woven fabric; perspective stitch results in a pattern of three-dimensional boxes. The three-dimensional effect is strongest when done in varying tones of a single colour.

Plaited stitch. Start at upper right and work rows right to left, then left to right. For each stitch, bring needle out at 1, up over four horizontal and two vertical canvas threads, then in at 2. Start next stitch in second canvas hole from base (1) of stitch just done. When working rows right to left, slant stitches back towards the right; when working left to right, slant stitches to the left. At each row's end, change working direction. Position new stitches so their tops (2) are in second canvas hole above bases of stitches just done.

Canvas work stitches

Crossing stitches

Perspective stitch. Worked in series of four rows, each consisting of vertical groups of three diagonal stitches. Each stitch is over two canvas meshes; the working direction, and the slant of the stitches, alternate from group to group. Usually worked in contrasting colours as shown. Overall effect is best if the colours alternate with each row.

For first row, start at 1 to 2 and work a group of three stitches, down the canvas, slanting each stitch from lower left to upper right. Then, at 3 to 4, work up the canvas, forming three stitches that slant from lower right to upper left. Continue to work across canvas, alternately working 1–2 and 3–4 stitch groups. At end of row, leave needle at back of canvas and turn canvas around.

Begin second row with a group of stitches slanted in a direction opposite to last group of preceding row. Start with a 1–2 or 3–4 group, as needed; place all stitches of all groups to overlap groups of preceding row as shown. At end of row, turn canvas around.

Start third row with a group of stitches slanting the same way as the last group of row just completed. Start with a 3–4 or 1–2 group, as needed; position all stitches of all groups to 'nest' below those of the preceding row. At end of row, turn canvas around.

For fourth row, begin with a group slanting in the opposite direction to that of the last group of the row just completed (3–4 or 1–2, as required). Overlap all stitches in this row with those in the preceding row (see far right). At end of fourth row, turn canvas. Following the same four-row procedure just described, cover the entire canvas area with perspective stitches.

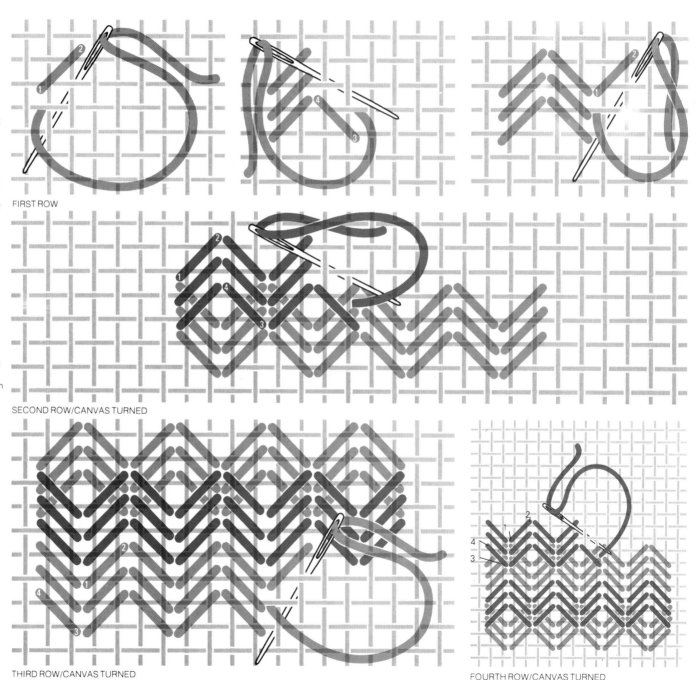

FIRST ROW

SECOND ROW/CANVAS TURNED

THIRD ROW/CANVAS TURNED

FOURTH ROW/CANVAS TURNED

150

Composite stitches

The stitches in this group are classified as composite stitches because each uses more than one of the other types of canvas stitches. For example, Algerian eye stitch (below) makes use of straight and diagonal stitches; triangle stitch (p. 155) contains straight and cross stitches. Except for the normal size Algerian eye stitch, all the composite stitches are large, and produce definite shapes rather than overall textures. As can occur with any large stitch, the thread may not completely cover the canvas mesh. To lessen the amount of canvas exposure, do not pull thread too tight while forming stitches.

Algerian eye stitch

Large Algerian eye stitch with backstitch

ALGERIAN EYE STITCHES

Algerian eye stitches form star-like units on the canvas. Each unit, whether normal size or the enlarged version, consists of eight small stitches worked around a common canvas hole. When selecting thread for this stitch, be sure that the thread will be able to pass through the common canvas hole eight times without distortion. If the selected thread does not adequately cover the canvas mesh, form backstitches around each unit as shown on left and below.

Algerian eye stitch. Begin at upper right and work rows alternately right to left, left to right. For each stitch unit, form eight small stitches, in a 1 to 8 sequence, around a centre hole, A. Bring needle out at a number, over one mesh or thread, then in at centre. When working rows right to left, work the eight stitches in a clockwise direction; when working rows from left to right, work them anticlockwise. Place the stitches of each new row below those of the preceding row.

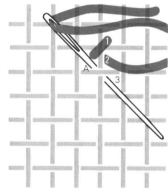

Large Algerian eye stitch. This is a large version of Algerian eye stitch (above). Row formation and stitch unit construction are the same; the difference is that each of the eight stitches is now taken over two canvas threads or meshes. With a large Algerian eye stitch, it can be difficult to cover the canvas completely. To cover canvas threads still exposed, form backstitches (see p. 138) around the stitch units. Use either the same or a contrasting colour thread (contrasting colour used here).

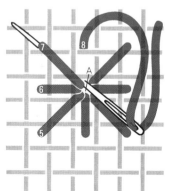
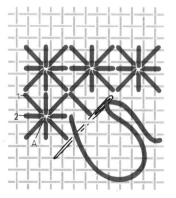
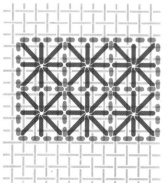

151

Canvas work stitches

Composite stitches

Ray stitch

Expanded ray stitch

RAY STITCHES

Each ray stitch and expanded ray stitch consists of several stitches that radiate from a common canvas hole. Ray stitch consists of seven stitches that form a square; an expanded ray stitch comprises 13 stitches that produce a rectangle. When selecting thread for either of these stitches, choose one that is thin enough so that the thread of the multiple stitches will fit through the common canvas hole without distortion. While working either of these stitches, do not pull the thread tight. For additional variety, alternate the colour with each unit or row of units.

Ray stitch. Begin at upper left and work rows alternately left to right, then right to left. Each ray stitch consists of seven stitches, fanned out around a common canvas hole, to cover a canvas area of three vertical by three horizontal canvas threads. Working anticlockwise and following a 1 to 7 sequence, begin each stitch at a number, end each in the common canvas hole, A. Fan each of the units as shown in the illustrations. At each row's end, reverse working direction; place new stitch units below those just done.

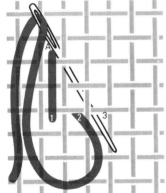
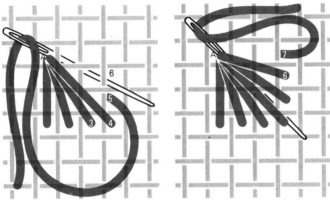

Expanded ray stitch. Start at upper left and work rows alternately left to right, then right to left. Each stitch unit consists of 13 stitches, fanned out around a common canvas hole, to cover six vertical by three horizontal canvas threads. Work stitches in a 1 to 13 sequence. For each stitch, bring needle out at a number, in at A. When working row from left to right, work anticlockwise; when working row from right to left, work clockwise. Place stitch units of each new row below those of preceding row.

Diamond eyelet stitch

Diamond eyelet stitch with backstitch

DIAMOND EYELET STITCH

Diamond eyelet stitch is a pretty but large stitch. In fact, one diamond eyelet stitch can be used alone as a detail in a canvas work design. Each unit is composed of 16 stitches, all emanating from one centre canvas hole. Select thread weight carefully so that it will pass through the same canvas hole 16 times with no distortion. If the stitches do not adequately cover the canvas threads, backstitches can be worked over them (see left and below). Because of its long stitches, the diamond eyelet stitch is not recommended for items that will be subject to hard wear.

Diamond eyelet stitch. Begin at upper left and work rows alternately left to right, then right to left. Each diamond eyelet stitch consists of 16 stitches that form a diamond-shaped unit over eight vertical by eight horizontal canvas threads. Start first stitch, 1, in the fifth canvas hole from the corner. Then, working clockwise, form the other stitches, 2 to 16, as shown. Begin each stitch at a number; end each in the centre canvas hole, A. Start each new stitch unit in the eighth canvas hole from the start (1) of the unit just completed.

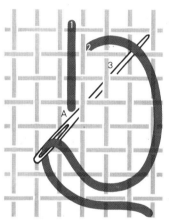
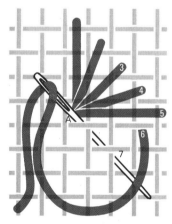
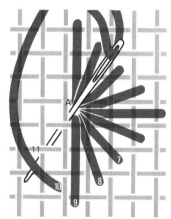
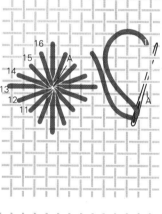

With each new row, reverse the working direction. Place new stitch units so that the first stitch, 1, shares a canvas hole with the horizontal stitches of the units in the preceding row. If desired, add backstitches (see p. 138) to cover the exposed canvas threads between the stitch units. Use the same or a contrasting colour.

153

Canvas work stitches

Composite stitches

Leaf stitch

Leaf stitch with backstitch

LEAF STITCH

Leaf stitch is another relatively large stitch that can be used alone or in groups. Each leaf stitch uses 11 stitches to form a leaf shape. Five stitches are fanned to form the top of the leaf shape and there are three stitches, in a vertical row, on each side of the unit. If you want to make the leaf shape longer, increase equally the number of stitches in each vertical (side) row; the five stitches at the top remain the same. To give the leaf shape some additional detail, work backstitches in centre of each unit; use the same or a contrasting thread.

Leaf stitch. Start in upper left corner (at 1); work rows alternately left to right, then right to left. Each leaf stitch unit shown here consists of 11 stitches – three side stitches; five fanned out to form the top of the leaf; then three stitches for the second side. (Units can be made longer by working more but equal numbers of stitches on each side.) Work side stitches first, 1 to 6, then top stitches, 7 to 16, then other side stitches, 17 to 22. For each stitch, bring needle out at an odd number, in at an even number. When working rows from left to right, work stitches clockwise; when working right to left, work anticlockwise. Begin each new unit in the sixth canvas hole from the start (1) of the unit just completed.

With each new row, reverse direction for working rows and units. Position new units so their top parts are nested as shown along the lower edges of the units in the preceding row. For extra detail, backstitches (see p. 138) can be formed up or down the centre of each leaf stitch unit. Colour of thread for the backstitches can be the same as or a contrast to the colour used for leaf stitches.

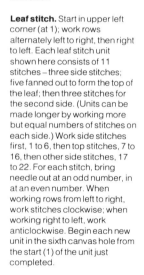

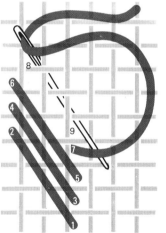

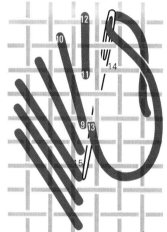

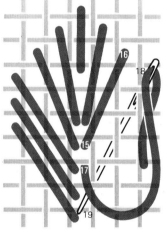

154

Triangle stitch (one colour of thread used)

Triangle stitch (two colours of thread used)

TRIANGLE STITCH

Triangle stitch, which is square in its overall shape, is made up of four triangular shapes placed point to point. A large cross stitch in each corner completes the unit and squares off its shape. The patterns produced by triangle stitches can be very interesting. When all the stitches are worked in the same colour, the basic square shape of a unit will sometimes appear to go back, while neighbouring groups of triangles come forward to form secondary patterns. The use of a second colour increases the range of possible patterns.

Triangle stitch. Each stitch unit (see the fourth drawing below) consists of four triangles placed point to point to produce straight outer edges. Cross stitches at corners square off and complete unit. Start first row at upper left; work rows alternately left to right, then right to left.

For each inner triangular unit, work seven stitches, 1 to 14 as shown, bringing needle out at an odd number, in at an even number. Stitch top triangular unit first; work all units and stitches in an anticlockwise direction. Place triangles as shown, bringing needle out of the same canvas hole for each of the four 7's. Although not shown, canvas can be turned a quarter to work each triangle.

Complete triangle stitch unit by working a large cross stitch (see p. 139), over two by two canvas meshes, in each of the four corners. Start in upper right corner and work cross stitches as shown, A to D. (Note: working order of first cross stitch is different from other three.) Begin next triangle stitch in tenth canvas hole from start of stitch unit just done. With each new row, reverse direction for working row. Place new stitch units below those just completed.

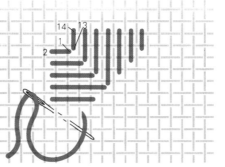

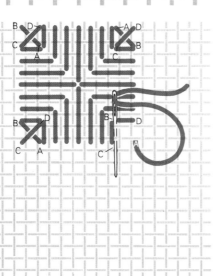

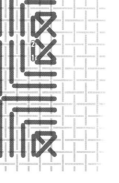

Canvas work stitches

Composite stitches

Brighton stitch (one colour of thread used)

Brighton stitch (two colours of thread used)

BRIGHTON STITCH

Brighton stitch is produced by rows of diagonal stitches; these are worked in blocks, and the slant of the stitches alternates from block to block. Each new row of stitches is a mirror image of the row above; sets of rows form a pattern of diamond shapes. An upright cross stitch in the centre of each diamond completes the Brighton unit. The upright cross stitches can be worked in the same or a contrasting colour, as shown in the samples on the left.

Brighton stitch. Rows consist of blocks of diagonal stitches. Each block has five stitches; the slant alternates with each block. Sets of rows form diamond-shaped units. An upright cross stitch is worked in centre of each diamond.

Start at upper left; work all rows from left to right. Begin first row with a block of five stitches that slant from lower left to upper right, 1 to 10. Then work the next block of five stitches, slanting them from lower right to upper left, 11 to 20. Continue to work across the canvas, alternately forming 1–10 and 11–20 stitch blocks. At end of each row, leave needle at back of canvas and turn canvas around.

Begin each new row with a block of stitches that slant in a direction opposite to the slant of the last block in the row just completed. Start with either a 1–10 or an 11–20 block as required.

Cover entire canvas area with rows of stitches. Then, form an upright cross stitch in the centre of each diamond, A to D, as explained on p. 142.

FIRST ROW

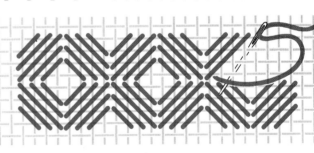

SECOND ROW/CANVAS TURNED

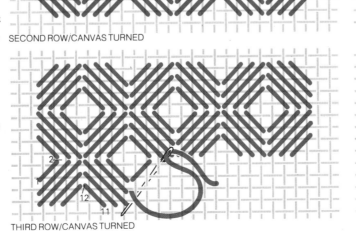

THIRD ROW/CANVAS TURNED

Pile stitches

There are only three stitches in this canvas work stitch group. They are all alike in that each produces a texture that extends out from the surface of the canvas. This extended surface, referred to as a pile, is produced by the loops of thread formed with the stitches. These loops may remain in their uncut form or they can be cut. The loop-cutting technique is explained on the next page with the velvet stitch; it can be used, however, for any of the three stitches in this group. Pile stitches are most commonly used for rugs, but they are suitable for any type of canvas work item that calls for a pile surface.

RYA (OR GHIORDES KNOT) STITCH/ VELVET STITCH/SURREY STITCH

Though these three stitches are alike in forming a pile surface, they differ in individual construction. Additional differences, due to different positioning, can occur with each of the three. These stem from the type of canvas (single, rug or double) the stitch is being worked on, and are explained as they arise. For more about canvases, see p. 114.

Rya stitch

Velvet stitch

Surrey stitch

Rya stitch (on single or rug canvas). Begin at lower left; work all rows left to right. For first stitch of each row, hold thread end on right side of canvas. Work each Rya stitch as follows: pass needle under one vertical canvas thread, 1 to 2, and pull thread through. Curve excess thread up, pass needle under next vertical thread, 3 to 4; pull thread through. Form loop of desired length; hold in place while forming next and each successive Rya stitch. Work stitches of new row above row just done. If desired, cut loops (see next page).

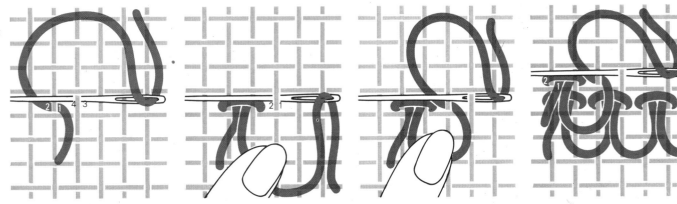

Rya stitch (on double canvas). Stitch and row construction are same as above, but the position of the stitch can vary. When using double canvas, each Rya stitch can be formed above two canvas meshes, like stitches above, or one mesh, as shown on the right. To work a Rya stitch above one mesh of double canvas, spread double set of vertical threads and treat as single threads while forming the stitch. Pass needle under one thread, 1 to 2, then under the next thread, 3 to 4.

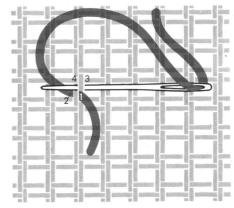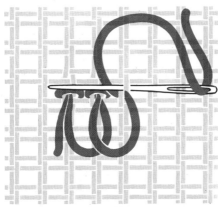

157

Canvas work stitches

Pile stitches

Velvet stitch (on single or rug canvas). Begin at lower left; work rows left to right. Work each velvet stitch as follows: bring needle out at 1, up over two canvas meshes, in at 2, then out at 3 (same hole as 1). Form a loop of desired length; hold in place. Insert needle at 4 (same hole as 2), under two horizontal threads (or two sets of threads if using rug canvas), and out at 5 with point of needle under loop. Then pass needle back over two meshes and in at 6. Begin next stitch in same canvas hole as the 5 of the stitch just done.

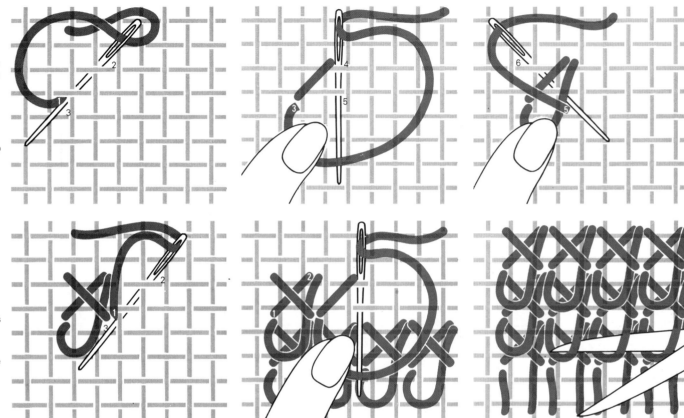

Work velvet stitches across the canvas, placing them next to each other. For each new row, begin at the left; place new stitches above those in the row just done. When all rows are completed, the loops can be cut, if so desired.

To cut the loops, open scissors and slide blade through a few loops (illustration on the far right). Cut the loops while slightly tugging on them with the scissors blade. Proceed to the next group of loops and cut them in the same manner.

Velvet stitch (on double canvas). Both row and stitch formation are the same as above. The only difference is another stitch-position possibility permitted by the double-mesh canvas. Each velvet stitch can be worked over two meshes, as on single canvas above; or over only one mesh, as on the right, following this procedure: bring needle out at 1, over one double mesh, in at 2; out at 3, over the same mesh, and in at 4. Then under a set of horizontal threads, and out at 5; back over the double mesh, and in at 6.

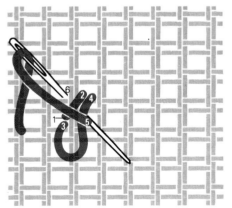

Surrey stitch (on single or rug canvas). Start at lower left; work all rows left to right. For first stitch of each row, hold thread end on right side of canvas. Work each Surrey stitch as follows: insert needle at 1, pass under two horizontal threads (two sets of threads if using rug canvas), bring out at 2. Pull excess yarn through and curve up as in the second illustration. Bring needle over two meshes, in at 3, under two vertical threads, then out at 4 with point of needle over excess curved thread. Pull thread through. Form a loop of desired length; hold in place while forming the next and each successive Surrey stitch. For each new stitch, start in the same canvas hole as the 3 of stitch just done; make sure that when needle is brought out at 2, its point passes over the loop of thread (far right).

With each new row, start again at the left and place the new stitches above those in the row just done. When all rows are finished, the loops may be cut if so desired. Cutting of loops is explained on opposite page.

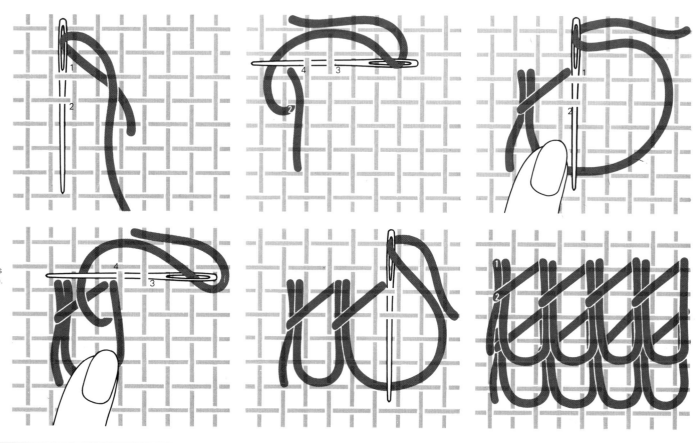

Surrey stitch (on double canvas). Row and stitch formation are the same as above. The only difference that can occur is in the placing of stitches. With double canvas, each Surrey stitch can be done over two meshes, as above, or over only one mesh, as are the stitches on the right. When working a Surrey stitch over only one mesh of double canvas, consider the pairs of threads as single units and work stitch as shown, 1 to 2, then 3 to 4.

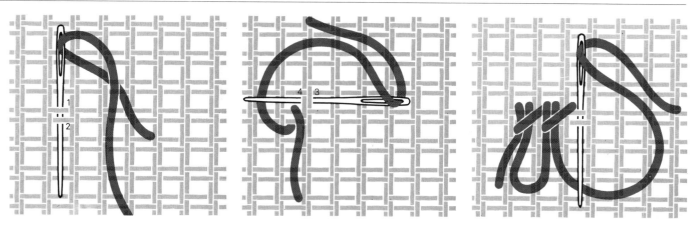

Canvas work stitches

Additional stitching techniques

The technique discussed below, **multi-colour** stitching, is a process of forming a colour pattern while working a canvas work stitch pattern. The colour designs can be formed by changing the thread colour with each row or by placing the various colours within the same row. The technique at the top of the opposite page, **filling-in stitches,** concerns the formation of partial stitch patterns along the edge of an area. The last technique, **left-handed** stitching, is at the bottom of the facing page. It explains how the instructions and illustrations given for stitches in this section can be adapted by a left-handed person.

MULTI-COLOUR STITCHING

The use of more than one thread colour to work an area of stitches actually produces two patterns. One is the pattern created by the stitch itself, the other results from the arrangement of the various colours. There are two ways of introducing different thread colours: row by row (Method 1) or within a row (Method 2). With both methods, the individual stitches are formed in their usual way, but the procedure for working the rows of stitches is altered.

In **Method 1,** the new thread colour is introduced with each row of stitches and the rows are worked in row-units, with each unit consisting of as many rows as there are colours. When rows are being worked normally, the working direction is reversed or the canvas is turned at the end of each row. When you are working with row-units, this change occurs with the first row of each new unit. With Method 1, each colour is threaded into a separate needle. If there is excess thread at the end of a row, it is brought up to the right side of the canvas and secured away from the working area. When you are ready to work a new row in that colour, the excess thread is brought to the wrong side of the canvas to the point where the new row begins.

Method 2 places the different colours within a row of stitches. It works best when only two thread colours are used for a stitch pattern that contains two stitch types. One such pattern is the double stitch, in which oblong cross stitches alternate with one-mesh cross stitches. First, all the rows of one stitch type and colour are worked, leaving spaces for the other stitch type. Then, the other stitch type is worked in the spaces left, with the second colour.

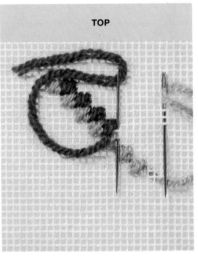

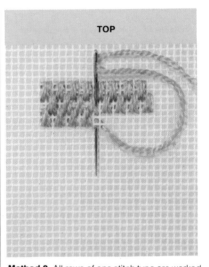

Method 1. Stitch is worked as usual; colours change with each new row; rows are worked in units. The examples (both mosaic stitches) are worked in two colours so that two rows constitute a unit. Both rows in left sample are worked right to left; both in right sample are worked diagonally down.

Method 2. All rows of one stitch type are worked as usual, leaving spaces for the second. Base stitches here are oblong cross stitches.

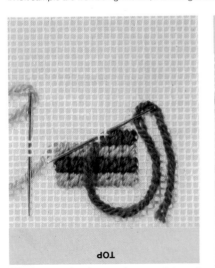

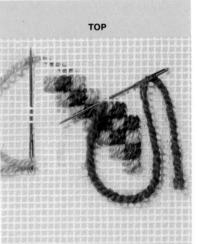

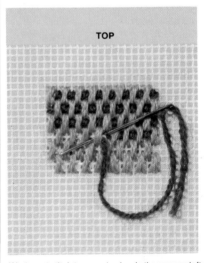

With first row of each new unit, canvas is turned around or the direction for working rows is reversed. Which it is depends on the way the rows of the stitch are usually done. Left sample was turned to work new unit; working direction was reversed in right sample.

Work next stitch type and colour in the spaces left by first stitches. One-mesh cross stitches here complete the double stitch pattern.

FILLING-IN STITCHES

The photographs below (details of the ornamental stitch barn shown on p. 113) illustrate filling-in stitches in use.

Filling-in stitches are partial stitch patterns worked along the edge of a design area. They cover the open spans of canvas that are too small to hold full stitches

of the pattern in that area. Their purpose is to maintain the effect of the area's stitch pattern (and colour pattern) all the way out to its edges. They are formed

along with the full stitches, and the length of each filling-in stitch is equal to the span of canvas left between the edge and a full-size stitch.

LEFT-HANDED STITCHING

All of the stitches in this section are illustrated and explained for the use of a right-handed person. If you are left-handed, these illustrations and explanations can be adapted for your use.

To begin with, read and familiarise yourself with the way the stitch is done by a right-handed person. Then, when you are ready to work, turn the book and your canvas upside-down. Begin working your stitches in the same corner that now appears in the upside-down illustration, and work the row in the direction that it shows. Read the upside-down numbers in numerical order and follow that sequence for forming the stitch. If the instructions say to turn the canvas or reverse the working direction with each row of stitches, do so. If they indicate that all the rows are to be worked in one direction, work all your rows in the one direction that now appears in the upside-down illustration. Shown on the right are three canvas work stitches. The top three illustrations show the stitches in the right-handed working order. The lower three show these same illustrations but turned to an upside-down position for left-handed use.

Tent stitches, done horizontally. Work from right to left; turn canvas with each row.

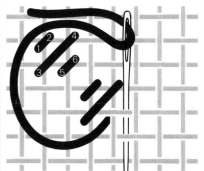

Mosaic stitches, done diagonally. Work first row down; reverse direction with each row.

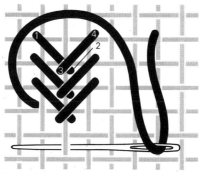

Fern stitches. Start at upper left and work all rows down the canvas.

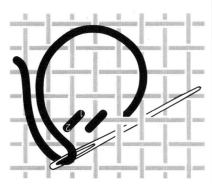

If left-handed, turn canvas upside-down. Work from left to right; turn canvas with each row.

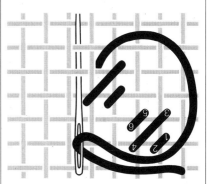

If left-handed, turn canvas upside-down. Work first row up; reverse direction with each row.

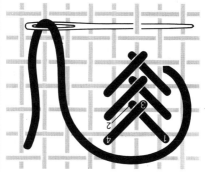

If left-handed, turn canvas, start in lower right corner and work all rows up the canvas.

Designing and making canvas work

Design elements

The design used for any canvas work is affected by several elements. With a kit, these elements have already been correlated so that all you have to do is stitch the design according to the instructions. When you are creating your own design, you must be aware of many things. First, you should know about the three different appearances that canvas work stitches can achieve (see p. 113). Also important is a basic knowledge of the materials (pp. 114–15), and the stitches (pp. 118–61) used in canvas work. The more you know about these, the easier it will be for you to combine the design elements discussed on these two pages. (The elements described here do not apply to the design of Florentine embroidery; for information about Florentine work, see p. 173.)

The most important element is the **design** itself. It should complement and be in proportion to the size and shape of the finished item. A design can consist of one motif on a plain background, or it can be a composition that fills the entire space. (Many compositions are repeats of a single motif, see pp. 170–1.) Most canvas work designs are asymmetrical, that is, their components are different from area to area (barn design on p. 113 is asymmetrical). Some canvas work designs are symmetrical in that their parts (halves or quarters) are mirror-images of each other (pp. 168–9). If you are good

at drawing, you can create a design. If you are not, trace the design from an existing source, such as a book, a plate or a piece of fabric. While you are still working out the design, keep your drawing to a manageable size. It can be enlarged or reduced later, when you are ready to transfer it to canvas. (See Embroidery chapter for more on composing designs and on enlarging and reducing.)

The amount of detail in the design must also be considered; this determines the **gauge of canvas** you should use. A design with simple shapes or large masses of colour can be carried out on a large-gauge canvas (under 10). A simple shape with moderate curves and some detail and colour shadings can be done on medium-gauge canvas (from 10 to 14). Whether simple or complex, a design with strong curves, small details and considerable shading will require a fine-gauge (16 to 20). An extremely delicate or small design could require a canvas even finer (over 20 gauge). The gauge of your canvas will affect the amount of time you spend stitching and the durability of the finished item. In general, the finer the gauge, the more time spent in stitching, but the more durable the final result. If you do not want to use the recommended gauge, you can either select another design better suited to the canvas you prefer, or adapt the design you have to the limita-

tions of that canvas gauge. For example, a very fine design can be re-drawn with larger details and less definite curves so that it will be suitable to a medium-gauge canvas.

How much detail your stitched design has will depend on the size and texture of the **stitches** you select. There are basically only two stitch categories, tent stitches and ornamental stitches. Tent stitches are the smallest of the canvas work stitches, and so are best for translating drawn lines or details. If you plan to use tent stitches, your design can be as detailed as the intended canvas gauge will allow. The ornamental stitches (except for the one-mesh cross stitch) are larger than tent stitches and therefore less suitable for expressing drawn lines and small details. The beauty of the ornamental stitches, however, is in the texture that each produces, and the way that these textures interpret design motifs. When drawing a design for ornamental stitches, keep the lines simple and eliminate small details. How simplified these should be depends on the area of a particular stitch. Some of the smaller ornamental stitches are capable of creating simple colour shadings. The samples and illustrations in the stitch section will help you to determine the space requirements of particular stitches. Remember also that you can mix tent and ornamental stitches in the

Drawing of a leaf

Tent stitches on 18-gauge canvas

Tent stitches on 12-gauge canvas

same design. When drawing any design, place the lines and details as best you can; they can be refined further as you work the stitches on to the canvas. If you want to be very accurate in your placing, the design can be charted (see p. 172). If your design is symmetrical or a multiple repeat, it should be charted.

Shown below is a leaf shape stitched on to four different gauges of canvas. The first three are worked with tent stitches, the fourth with Byzantine stitch, an ornamental stitch. All four were based on the same drawing, and each spans the same area of canvas. The first tent-stitch leaf is on an 18-gauge canvas, the second on a 12-gauge, the third on a 7-gauge; the ornamental-stitch leaf is on a 10-gauge canvas. Notice how the leaf shape becomes less detailed and its lines simpler as the gauge and the stitches grow larger. For another example of the change that stitches can make in design lines and areas, compare the differences in the two stitched barns that are shown on p. 113. Both samples were based on the same drawing of a barn scene.

With any canvas work stitch, a part of the textural effect comes from the way light strikes the thread on the canvas. If you alter the direction the thread (stitch) takes on the canvas, you also change the way the light hits the thread. Changing the direction of a stitch is a simple work-

ing procedure, explained on the far right. This technique will affect any stitch except those, like the diamond eyelet, in which the thread is laid in all directions. It will also change the direction of some stitch patterns. For example, when fern stitch is worked normally (p. 147), it produces a pattern of up-and-down stripes. When the fern stitch is worked with the method explained on the right, the stripes go across the canvas.

The type of thread used to work a stitch will also affect its texture. Loosely twisted types, such as Persian wool, produce a softer surface than do those that are more tightly twisted, such as tapestry wool. Those that are inherently shiny, such as pearl cottons and the metallic threads, will add a bit of sparkle to the stitches. When deciding on the type of thread to use, also consider its durability. Threads that are made of wool, cotton or acrylic are stronger than those made of rayon or synthetic metal.

When selecting the **colours** for your design, choose a scheme that you like and that will enhance the design. Colour schemes and their effects are discussed in the Embroidery chapter. After you have selected your colours, colour in the drawing so that you can see how they look together. When you go to shop for threads, use the colours in the drawing as a general guide.

Changing the direction of a stitch

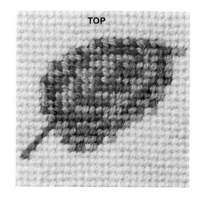

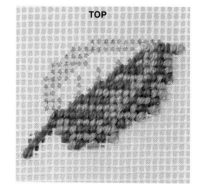

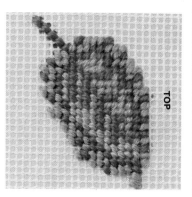

To change the direction of a stitch or of its pattern on the canvas, work the stitch as usual, but hold the canvas so that its top edge is at the side. If the canvas needs to be turned around to work each new row of stitches, do so, but turn it so that the top edge alternates from right to left sides. The finished leaf on the left shows tent stitches slanting in opposite directions. The first illustration below shows the canvas with its top edge in the normal position to produce tent stitches with a normal slant (for the lower half of leaf). The second shows the canvas with its top at the side to produce tent stitches with the opposing slant (for the upper half of leaf). To avoid confusion while using this technique, label the top edge of the canvas.

Selecting working techniques

There are many different working techniques in canvas work; it is up to you to select the ones you will need to use. Many of the techniques apply to the way the design is transferred to the canvas. These can be divided into methods for transferring uncharted designs (pp. 164–5) and charted designs (pp. 166–71). Techniques applying to Florentine work, another class of charted designs, begin on p. 173. Read all of these pages and choose the technique recommended for the type of design you are using. Before any design can be transferred to the canvas, the canvas

must be prepared (p. 164). General working techniques that can be used with any type of design are described on the last few instructional pages of this chapter. The information on estimating thread amounts enables you to calculate the quantities of threads needed to stitch any design, especially one that you designed yourself. The other techniques – setting canvas into a frame, removing stitches, repairing canvas and blocking – will help you to make your canvas work as near perfect as possible. For ideas on canvas work items, see the projects at the end of the chapter.

Tent stitches on 7-gauge canvas

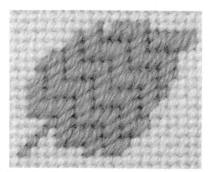

Byzantine stitch on 10-gauge canvas

Designing and making canvas work

Design transfer needs 117   Calculating thread amounts 183
Miscellaneous equipment 117   Blocking 185

Basic preparations

To begin canvas work, you must first prepare a piece of canvas large enough to receive the design. 'Large enough' means the finished size of the design plus a margin of at least 5 cm along each edge. When you are working with an uncharted design, finished size equals the dimensions of the drawing you will follow. When a design is charted, finished size depends upon the number of canvas threads called for by the chart in relation to the threads per centimetre in the canvas. If the canvas is too narrow, lengths can be joined to get the necessary width (centre right). Make a pattern of the prepared canvas (far right); it will be needed when it is time to block the worked canvas.

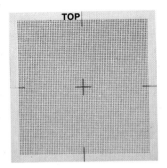

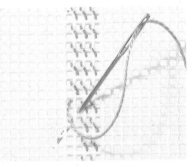

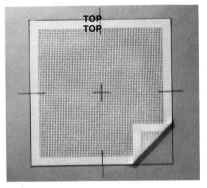

Basic preparation of canvas. Cut canvas to finished size of design plus a margin (5 cm minimum) along each edge. Bind edges with tape; label top edge. Mark vertical and horizontal centres. If centres are on threads, mark at middle of canvas and on each side as above. If centres are between threads, tack with wool (see p. 167).

To join lengths of canvas to produce necessary width. Cut two pieces to required length. Place side by side and cut off neighbouring selvedges. Overlap cut edges by 3 to 4 vertical threads and match all threads and meshes. Using strong thread, work down each row of matched threads, oversewing around every other matched mesh.

To make a pattern of prepared canvas. Place canvas on a piece of brown paper and trace its outlines. Indicate top edge on paper and mark centre of each edge. Keep pattern; it will be needed to block the worked canvas.

Placing the design on canvas / Method 1

This design transfer method places both the shapes and the colours of the design on to the canvas. The stitches are then worked right over the painted design. This method is recommended for use with any uncharted design, especially one that uses tent stitches only. Before a design of this type can be transferred, both the drawing and the finished size of the canvas must be equal to the finished size of the item for which the canvas work is being done. To transfer the design to the canvas, use only waterproof colouring pens or paints. If you are not absolutely sure about any pen, do not use it; colours that are not waterproof are likely to run while the worked canvas is being blocked. Use the painted canvas as a guide to calculate the amount of thread that will be needed.

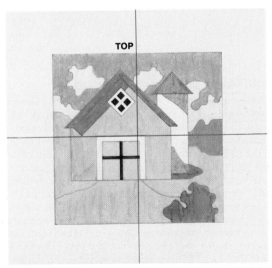

1. Draw a line down and another line across the centre of the drawing. If necessary, label top edge and establish outer lines of design area. Prepare canvas as explained at top of page.

2. Place prepared canvas over drawing; match its centre lines to those in drawing. Pin layers together and paint design on to canvas. Copy shapes in drawing; use matching or similar colours.

3. When canvas is dry, work stitches right over the design. Work an area or a colour at a time. Place stitches at the edges of an area as close as you can to its painted edges.

Placing the design on canvas/Method 2

This method of transfer puts the lines of a design, but not its colours, on the canvas. It is recommended for use with any uncharted design, particularly one calling for some ornamental stitches.

Both the canvas and the drawing of the design are prepared as for Method 1; if ornamental stitches are being used, the name of the stitch is noted in appropriate areas on the drawing. To transfer the lines to the canvas, use markers that are waterproof and neutral in colour. As you work an ornamental stitch area, modify the size or shape of the area to conform to the space needs of the selected stitch. If you would prefer to check and perhaps adjust an ornamental stitch area before transferring its lines to the canvas, chart the area and the stitch as explained at the bottom of this page.

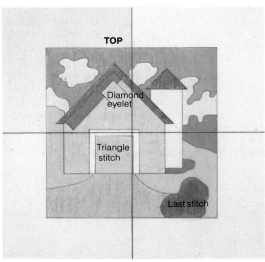

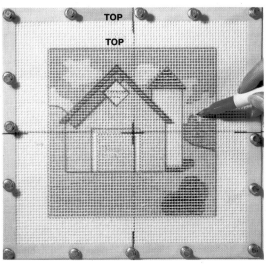

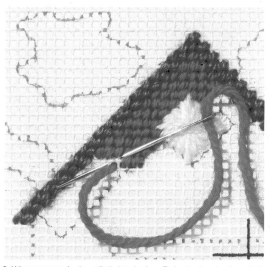

1. Draw a horizontal and a vertical line through centre of drawing. Label each ornamental stitch area with its name. Prepare the canvas as explained at the top of the preceding page.

2. Place canvas on top of drawing and match centre markings. Pin layers together and transfer lines of design to canvas. To chart an area before transferring its lines, see below.

3. When canvas is dry, stitch the design. Refer to drawing for stitch and colour placing. When you work ornamental stitches, use filling-in stitches to fill gaps, or alter area to fit stitch.

TO CHART AN AREA

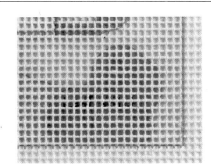

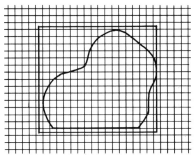

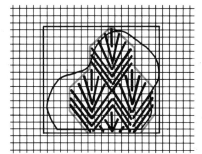

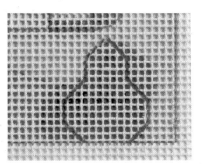

1. With the design area in position under the canvas, count out, at its widest points, the number of canvas threads that the area spans across and up and down. The area being checked is the bush in the lower right corner of the design. Leaf stitches are planned.

2. On a piece of graph paper (any gauge), count out these same totals in graphed lines and draw a box to enclose them. Then, referring to the area under the canvas, sketch shape on graph paper, crossing its lines in same way as lines cross canvas threads.

3. Sketch stitch pattern in outlined area. For help, see illustration in stitch section. If stitches nearly fill area, gaps can be filled with filling-in stitches. If they cover too much or too little, adjust lines to fit stitch (above) or use a stitch better suited to the area.

4. Referring to the graph paper, transfer the area's outline (with changes, if any) to the canvas. Make sure that the lines cross the canvas threads the same way they cross the graph paper lines. When stitching this area, refer to its chart for guidance in placing the stitches.

Designing and making canvas work

Understanding charts

Some canvas work designs are presented in chart form, that is, the position of each stitch in the design is recorded on graph paper. Graph paper is used for charting because it is structurally similar to canvas. Its vertical and horizontal lines correspond to the canvas threads; the squares and intersections made by the crossing lines are like the holes and meshes of the canvas. Both come in several gauges, related to the number of sub-divisions (squares with graph paper; threads with canvas) to the centimetre. There are two ways to make use of these similarities, and each produces a different type of chart.

With a **box chart,** the squares on the graph paper represent the threads and/or meshes of the canvas. For a tent stitch, one square means one mesh. With straight or ornamental stitches, a square means one thread or mesh of the stitch's total span. The total span is represented by the requisite number of squares, heavily outlined. For example, a straight Gobelin stitch, four threads long, is represented by an outlined row of four squares. A large Algerian eye stitch, which spans four by four meshes, is represented by a group of four by four squares with a heavy outline.

Line charts are an exact duplication of how the stitches will be laid over the canvas threads and meshes. A tent stitch is a slanted line over one intersection of a pair of lines. A straight Gobelin stitch, four threads long, is a straight line over four lines. A large Algerian eye stitch is represented by eight lines drawn over a group of intersections and lines and converging in a centre square.

In either type of chart, the colour of the stitch is indicated with actual colours or with symbols in black and shades of grey. With a box chart, the square is filled with either the colour or the symbol. With a line chart, the indications are incorporated in the drawn line. If the chart is in colours, the line is drawn in the colour. If symbols are being used, the symbol is made a part of the drawn line. Since there is no standardisation of the character and meaning of symbols, they will differ from chart to chart. Sometimes the colour symbols also indicate a type of thread. With other charts, letters or numbers represent colours, stitches or threads.

An integral companion to a chart is a listing, or key, that translates the meanings of the symbols in the chart. There can be one or more keys. In addition to a key, some charted designs also include a simplified (schematic) line drawing to explain some aspect of the design that is not covered by the chart or key. For several typical examples of symbols and keys used with box and line charts, refer to the symbol chart below.

In order to work a charted design on canvas, you will need a piece of canvas that contains at least the total number of threads needed to stitch the entire design. This thread number is based on the number of threads the chart calls for across and up and down, and the number of times the chart must be followed to produce the complete design. If the chart depicts a *full design* (see next page), it will be followed only once, and the total number of threads needed is just the amount contained in the chart. If it is a *partial design chart,* of which there are several types, it must be followed more than once to produce the total design, and the total thread requirements will therefore be a multiple of the number called for by the chart (see pp. 168–71).

After total thread requirements have been calculated, cut and prepare canvas. Be sure to add a minimum 5 cm margin along each edge before cutting the canvas. The measurements of the prepared canvas will of course vary according to the gauge of the canvas, since it is by the number of threads per centimetre that canvas gauges differ.

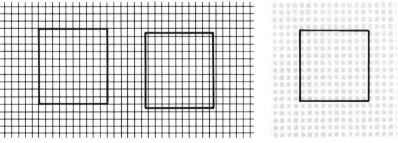

To calculate canvas thread requirements of a charted design, first count the threads across and up and down that the chart calls for. Then match these numbers with same number of canvas threads across and up and down. First chart area above represents 10 by 10 threads on a box chart; the second represents 10 by 10 threads on a line chart. Area of canvas on the right has 10 by 10 threads.

TYPES OF CHARTING SYMBOLS

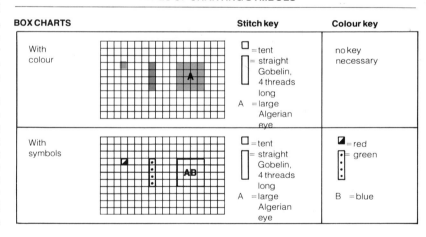

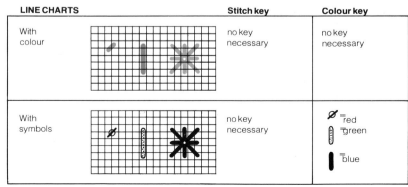

Full design charts

A full design chart is one in which all areas of the total design are represented. A partial design chart (pp. 168–71) lays out only one area; this one area, repeated, makes up the total design. The need for a full charting comes from the asymmetrical structure of a design, that is, from all of its areas being different. When you are using a full chart, the number of canvas threads necessary to stitch the design is the same as the number of threads in the chart. With a kit or chart that does not supply the canvas, you will need to determine the span of canvas that is required by the design. To do this, first determine whether the chart is a box or a line chart, and then notice how each represents threads (see preceding page) so that you will understand how to interpret yours. Once this is understood, count the threads across and up and down called for by the chart. Then calculate the quantity of canvas that will be needed to supply these same numbers of threads across and up and down, and add to this a minimum 5 cm margin along each of the edges. The overall dimensions of the canvas will vary according to its gauge; the finer the gauge being used, the smaller the finished size will be. The gauge of canvas should also be suitable to the design (see pp. 162–3) as well as to the size of the item it is intended for. If the chosen gauge of canvas will produce too small or too large a finished size, you have several options. You could change to a different gauge of canvas that would give you a more suitable finished size. If the design has a background area, it can be enlarged or reduced by using more or fewer stitches in the background. If a design needs enlarging and has no background area, one can be added if this would be appropriate to the design's character. There is no way to reduce such a design except to change the canvas gauge.

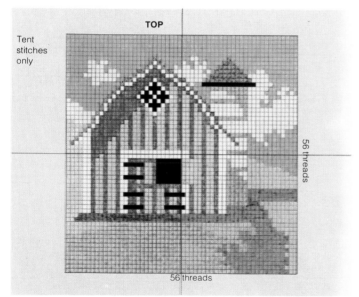

Tent stitches only

TOP

56 threads

56 threads

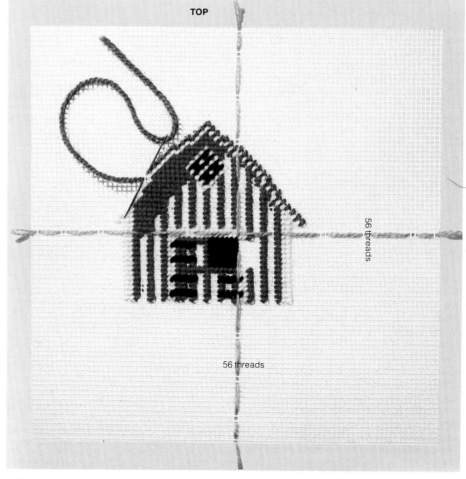

TOP

56 threads

56 threads

1. First locate and then draw horizontal and vertical centre lines on the chart. If necessary, also label the top edge of the charted design. Count the number of threads across and up and down that are called for by the chart.

2. Prepare canvas for work. Calculate its measurements to be sure it contains the same number of threads across and up and down as called for by the chart. To this add a margin (minimum 5 cm) along each edge. Cut canvas to these overall measurements. Bind the edges with tape and label the top edge. Locate and mark the vertical and horizontal centres of the canvas. If the chart calls for an uneven number of threads, the centre falls on a thread, as shown on p. 164. If the chart involves an even number of threads, the centre is between threads and is marked with tackings in wool (see right). Use a pale colour for tackings; stitch over or remove them as you work.

3. Stitch the design on the canvas. Refer to chart (and to keys, if necessary) for the stitch type, placing and colour. Use the centre markings on chart and canvas as reference points for locating areas. Work design from the centre out, an area or colour at a time. If there is a background, work this part last.

Designing and making canvas work

Partial design charts

A partial design chart presents only a portion of the total design. The reason for the partial representation is that the total design consists of repeats of that portion. There are several types of partial design charts. One type is used to form a multiple-repeat design (p. 170); another is the row chart used to work Florentine embroidery (p. 173). The two partial design charts that are discussed here are half-charts and quarter-charts; it is these that are used to form symmetrical designs.

A symmetrical design consists of two or four repeats that meet and mirror each other at the design's centre. If there are two repeats, one on each side of a centre line, the design has two-way symmetry. A half-chart, followed twice, will produce a two-way symmetrical design. If the parts are on each side of a horizontal centre line, as in the fish design on the right, the chart used is a **horizontal half-chart**. If they are on each side of a vertical centre line, as is the butterfly shown below, the chart used is a **vertical half-chart**. When there are four units that are arranged around horizontal and vertical centre lines, the design has a four-way symmetry (see the tile design on the opposite page). A **quarter-chart**, followed four times, will produce a four-way symmetrical design.

The total number of canvas threads required to work a symmetrical design is a multiple of the number called for by the chart. These calculations are explained with the individual charts. When working the half or quarter represented by the chart, place its areas in the same positions as shown on the chart. When working the non-charted halves or quarters, place their areas so they mirror the comparable areas on the other side of the centre. It is not necessary to start and stop stitching at the centre lines. An exception to this: when you are alternating the direction of the stitches in each repeat (see opposite).

Horizontal half-charts

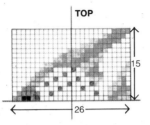

1. Label top of chart. Draw a line down the vertical centre of the design, another line across its horizontal centre. The total number of canvas threads required for the entire design is the *same* as the number of threads that the chart calls for across the design but *double* the number of threads indicated on the chart from the horizontal centre to the design's edge. Prepare canvas for work. Label its top edge and mark its vertical and horizontal centres as well (p. 167).

2. Work the top half of the design on canvas. Use the centre markings on the chart to locate areas and work them in exactly the same positions on the canvas, using its centre markings as guides.

3. To work the lower half, use the chart to locate areas; place them on the canvas in the same relation to the vertical centre of the canvas but in the reverse position in relation to its horizontal centre.

Vertical half-charts

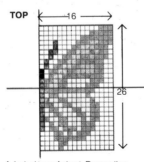

1. Label top of chart. Draw a line across the horizontal centre of design, another line down its vertical centre. Total number of threads needed for the entire design *equals* the number of threads the chart calls for from top to bottom of the design but *is double* the number from the design's vertical centre to its edge. Prepare canvas. Label its top edge and mark its vertical and horizontal centres (p. 167).

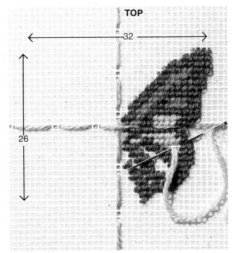

2. Work the right half of the design on the canvas. Use the centre markings on the chart to locate areas and place these areas in the same positions on the canvas, using its centre lines as guides.

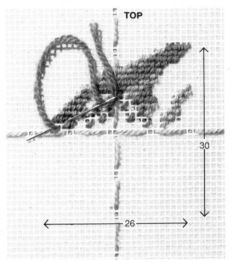

3. To work the left half, use the chart to locate areas. Place the areas on the canvas in the same relation to the horizontal centre but in the reverse relation to the vertical centre.

Quarter-charts

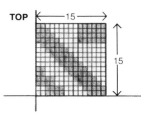

TOP ← 15 → / 15

1. Label top of chart. Draw a line down the vertical centre of the design, another line across its horizontal centre. The total number of canvas threads necessary for the entire design is *double* the number of threads that the chart calls for from the vertical centre to the edge and from the horizontal centre to the edge. Prepare the canvas. Label its top edge; mark its vertical and horizontal centres (p. 167). To work the upper quarters, hold chart with its top edge up and use it to locate areas.

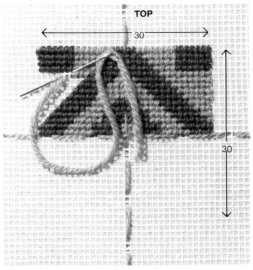

2. Place areas in the right quarter as charted. Place areas in the left quarter in the same relation to the horizontal centre, but in reverse relation to the vertical centre.

3. To work the lower quarters, hold the chart upside-down (as it is shown in the illustration below) as you use it to locate the areas at the bottom.

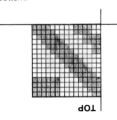

4. Place areas in the left quarter as charted. Place areas in the right quarter in the same relation to the horizontal centre, but in reverse to the vertical centre.

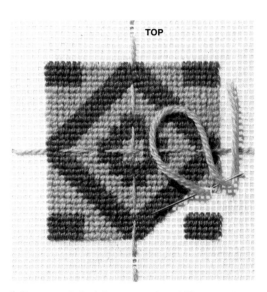

TO ALTERNATE STITCH DIRECTION WITH EACH QUARTER

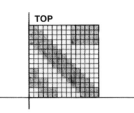

1. Work the upper right quarter with top edge of chart at top. Locate areas on chart; work them in same positions on canvas.

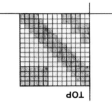

2. To work lower left quarter, turn chart upside-down. Find areas on chart; work them as they are positioned on upside-down chart.

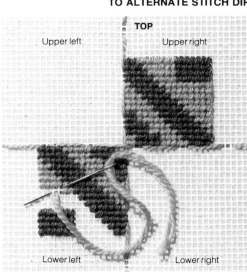

3. To work the upper left quarter, hold the canvas with its top edge at the side. Read the worked upper right quarter to locate areas, and place them in the upper left quarter in the same relation to the horizontal centre of the canvas but in the reverse relation to its vertical centre.

4. To work the lower right quarter, hold the canvas with its top edge at the side. Read the worked lower left quarter to locate the areas, and place them in the lower right quarter in the same relation to the horizontal centre of the canvas but in the reverse relation to its vertical centre.

Designing and making canvas work

Repeat patterns

A motif repeated a number of times according to a planned arrangement is a repeat pattern. The motif can be anything you like that makes an attractive pattern when it is repeated systematically. Before a design is worked, the arrangement must be planned and the basic motif charted. The chart must have a thread count that, when multiplied, permits the arrangement to fit a finished canvas size. To calculate motif size for charting, see opposite page.

The motif can be your own design or a tracing from an existing source, perhaps a ready-made chart. If the source is a chart, it may turn out that its thread count will fit or can be altered to fit the arrangement. If it is a half-chart or quarter-chart, follow the procedures on the right to obtain a complete shape. Make several copies of the motif, either by re-tracing it or using a photocopying machine. Trim away excess paper, leaving a border if you want a background. Position the copies different ways until you find a satisfactory arrangement.

Although many repeat arrangements are possible, the three at the bottom of the page are the most common. In the first, a **straight** arrangement, the units in the rows line up horizontally and vertically. In the second and third arrangements, the units are staggered. To achieve a **horizontally staggered** arrangement, line up the vertical centres of the units in every horizontal row with the ends of the units in the row above. For a **half-drop** arrangement, line up the horizontal centres of the units in every vertical row with the ends of the units in the row to the left. Be prepared to encounter partial motifs, which can occur with any arrangement, particularly those that are staggered.

When you have an arrangement you like, place tracing paper over it and trace all lines. Use this tracing when calculating the size of the motif and working the arrangement on canvas.

Producing a single motif

A complete motif can be your own original drawing, or a motif traced from a book, a piece of fabric, or even a ready-made full design chart.

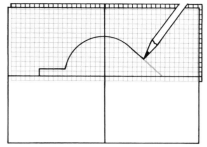

If motif is in half-chart form, draw horizontal and vertical lines on tracing paper and align them with centre lines on chart. Trace charted half.

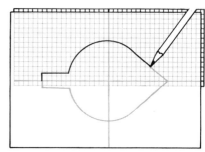

To form second half, turn tracing paper, positioning unmarked half over chart. Match lines on tracing paper and chart; re-trace chart.

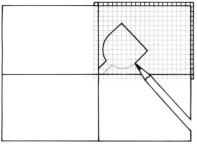

If motif is in quarter-chart form, draw horizontal and vertical lines on tracing paper and match them with lines on chart. Trace charted quarter.

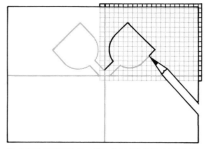

To trace second quarter, turn tracing paper so that unmarked quarter is over chart. Match lines on tracing paper and chart; re-trace quarter.

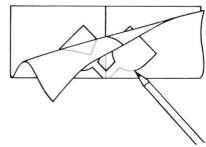

To form second half, fold tracing paper in half so that unmarked half is over drawn half of design. Re-trace design half; open tracing paper.

Types of arrangements

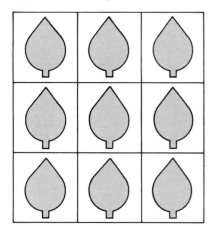

Straight arrangement

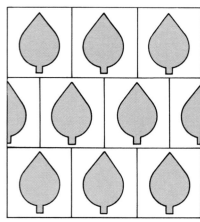

Horizontally staggered arrangement

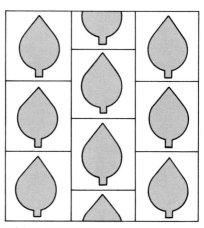

Half-drop arrangement

170

Calculating unit size; working repeat patterns

To chart an original motif for a repeat-pattern design, you must first decide its area in the arrangement, then its thread size. The area is the length and width of one unit; thread size is the number of canvas threads spanned by this area. To calculate the length of a unit, divide the finished length of the canvas by the number of unit rows up and down. To determine the width, divide the finished width of the canvas by the number of rows across. To find the thread size of the unit, multiply its length and width by the gauge of the canvas. Canvas gauge should be suitable to the needs of the design and to the durability requirements of the finished item (pp. 112, 162–3). Once thread size is known, the motif can be charted (next page). Example A is a lesson in simple calculation. If you have traced an existing chart to obtain your motif, its thread size may fit exactly into the finished size of the arrangement. If it does not, perhaps the thread count of the finished size or of the chart can be altered. If the charted motif has no background, try changing the

arrangement's finished size or select a different gauge of canvas (Example B) to provide the number of threads needed for the chart's repetition. For a chart that has a background area, try increasing or decreasing the number of background threads to arrive at a new thread size that will fit the finished thread count (Example C, background area was increased). Sometimes, no matter what you do, the ready-made chart will not fit. If you find yourself in this situation, choose another motif.

To prepare to work a repeat-pattern design, cut canvas to contain the total number of threads needed for the arrangement plus a minimum 5 cm margin at each edge. Tape all edges; label the top edge. Also mark the horizontal and vertical lines of the arrangement; units are worked within their boundaries. Use the chart to work at least the first unit; to work the others, follow either the chart or a worked unit. For partial units work just the portion required by the arrangement (see Example B, on right).

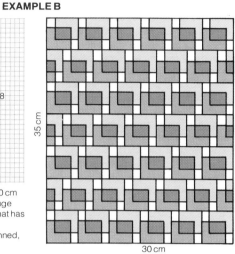

Problem: finished design must measure 30 cm wide by 35 cm long on either a 12 or 14-gauge canvas. Motif is from a ready-made chart that has a thread size of 28 across by 28 down. A horizontally staggered arrangement is planned, with 6 units across by 7 down.

Solution: since each of the units as charted requires 28 threads by 28 threads, the planned arrangement of 6 units across by 7 down will need a total of 168 threads across by 196 up and down. A piece of 12-gauge canvas measuring 30 cm wide by 35 cm long (size of finished design) contains 144 threads across by 168 up and down; this is not enough threads for the units as charted and planned. A piece of 14-gauge canvas 30 cm wide by 35 cm long contains 168 threads across by 196 up and down; this is the exact number of threads needed for the units as charted and planned. It makes sense, therefore, to use the motif as charted and work the arrangement as planned on a 14-gauge canvas. When working the partial units in the staggered rows, be sure to work the chart's right half at the left end of the row and the chart's left half at the right end of the row.

EXAMPLE A

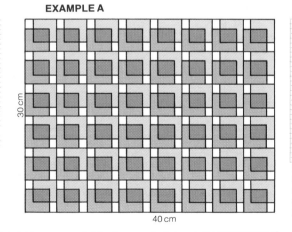

Problem: finished item must measure 40 cm wide by 30 cm long on a 10 or 12-gauge canvas. Motif is original and in a straight arrangement of 8 units across by 6 down.

Solution: in order for a planned straight arrangement of 8 units across by 6 down to fit a finished area of 40 cm wide and 30 cm long, each unit must measure 5 cm by 5 cm. If a 10-gauge canvas is used for the entire design, each unit will span 20 by 20 threads; if canvas is 12-gauge, each unit will span 24 by 24 threads. Chart motif according to the gauge of canvas that the entire arrangement will be worked on. For instructions on charting, see next page.

EXAMPLE C

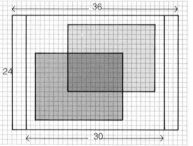
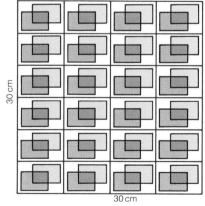

Problem: motif is charted and has a background; thread size is 30 across by 24 down. Finished design must measure 30 cm square on a 12-gauge canvas. A straight arrangement, 4 units by 6 down, is planned.

Solution: a 30 cm square of 12-gauge canvas contains 144 by 144 threads. If the chart (thread size of 30 across by 24 down) is used to work the arrangement as planned (4 units across by 6 down), it will span 120 threads across by 144 down (24 threads short of the finished width; correct number for length). If 6 threads of background are added to the width of each of the 4 units (3 on each end of each unit), the 144 threads will be spanned. Add 3 threads to each side of chart.

Designing and making canvas work

Charting a design

Before charting your own design, you should familiarise yourself with the types of designs and how they are presented in chart form. You should also understand the two ways canvas threads are represented in charts and how symbols and keys are used to indicate the stitch and colour. All of this information is on pp. 166–71.

To chart your own design, first decide on its finished size and then determine the number of canvas threads that will be required to carry out the full design

or the repeated part. This procedure has already been explained for a repeat pattern (p. 171). Single-motif designs usually must be enlarged or reduced to fit the finished size (see Embroidery chapter). Draw one line across and another line down the centre of the re-sized drawing; label its top edge. Decide what gauge of canvas is suitable for the needs of the design (pp. 162–3) and cut a piece to the finished size plus a minimum 5 cm margin on each edge. Bind its edges with tape; label the top

edge; mark vertical and horizontal centres (p. 167).

Centre the prepared drawing under the prepared canvas, then count the canvas threads spanned by the entire design or the repeated part. If the design is *asymmetrical*, count the number of threads across and up and down the entire design. For a *horizontal two-way symmetrical* design, count only the top half from side to side and from the centre up. For a *vertical two-way symmetrical* design, count the right half

from top to bottom and from the centre out. For a *four-way symmetrical* design, count threads only for the top right quarter of the design, from its horizontal centre to the top and from its vertical centre out to the right edge.

When the thread size of the design is established, you duplicate it within the same number of squares or lines on graph paper. When charting the motif for a repeat pattern, place a finished-size drawing of it under its prepared canvas and proceed with Step 2, below.

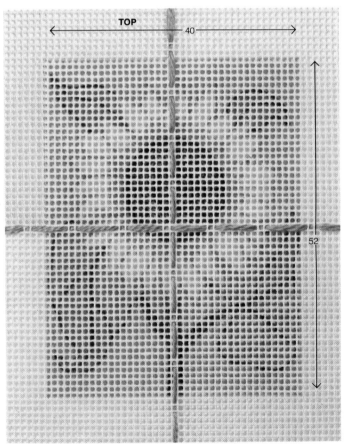

1. Centre finished-size drawing of design under prepared canvas. Pin layers in place; count canvas threads spanned by design or design part across and down.

2. On graph paper (any gauge), count the threads called for by design or part being charted. On a box chart, a square is a 'thread'; on a line chart, a line is a 'thread'. Draw box around this number of threads; draw centre lines for design or part being charted: both lines for full design, as above; for horizontal half, a vertical centre line from bottom of box; for vertical half, a horizontal centre line from left side of box.

3. Referring to the design under the canvas, draw the lines of the design over the lines on the graph paper, making sure they cross the graph paper lines just as they do the canvas threads. Use a pencil and draw an area at a time, using the centre lines on canvas and graph paper as reference points.

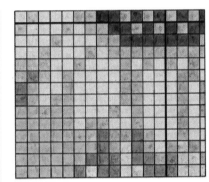

Make a box chart if you intend to use only tent stitches. Re-draw the lines in steps along the nearest squares. Fill squares with intended colours or use symbols and make a colour key.

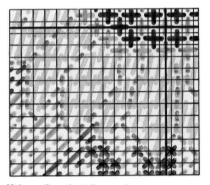

Make a line chart if you will use ornamental stitches. Sketch intended stitch in design area, then modify the area's lines to fit the stitches (p. 165). Draw stitches in actual colours or use symbols to denote colour and make a colour key.

Designing and working Florentine embroidery

Types of Florentine work
Florentine stitch patterns
Colour
Equipment
Row designs
Motif designs
Four-way designs

Types of Florentine work

Florentine work is defined, in the most general terms, as any design worked on canvas with straight stitches. By this broad definition, any design, even the sunflower opposite, becomes Florentine work if straight stitches are used to work it on to the canvas. Traditionally, however, the name Florentine work signifies a unique form of canvas work in which Florentine stitch or one of its variations is used to produce dramatic patterns on canvas. It is this traditional kind of Florentine embroidery that is described on the following pages.

There are three fundamental types of Florentine-based designs, represented by the three examples on the right. Each of the three overall designs is formed through the repeated working of a single unit (for clarity, the repeated unit is outlined in each example). To ensure that the unit is the same each time it is worked, the unit is charted; such a chart is called a *row chart*. The three designs differ mainly in the character of their repeat units. In a **row design** (first example), the repeat unit consists of several rows of Florentine stitches that follow the pattern established by the top row. For a more detailed explanation of designing and working a row design, see pp. 176–7. In a **motif design** (second example), the top and bottom rows of the repeat unit mirror each other and together form an enclosed intervening area. This area is filled with Florentine stitches or other straight stitches that conform to the area's shape. Motif designs are explained on pp. 178–9. The third type is a **four-way design,** in which the overall design is produced by working each triangular quarter of the design at right-angles to the others. Although a row design repeat is the basic unit in the four-way design shown, a motif design unit can also be used to form this type of Florentine work. The design and working of four-way Florentine designs are dealt with on pp. 180–2.

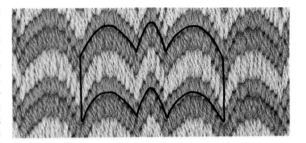

Row designs are the easiest of the Florentine types to design and work. The repeat unit consists of several rows of Florentine stitches that follow the pattern of the top row of the repeat. The overall effect is bands of mirror-imaging repeats across the canvas.

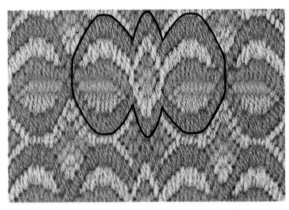

Motif designs form medallion-like repeats across the canvas. The repeat consists of a top and bottom row that mirror each other and form an enclosed area. This area is filled with Florentine or other straight stitches.

Four-way designs are produced by working the triangular quarters of the overall design at right-angles to each other. Either a row or motif type of repeat can be used to form the design. The design shown here is based on a row type of repeat.

173

Designing and working Florentine embroidery

Forming Florentine stitch patterns

Even though there are only three fundamental types of Florentine-based designs, the number of possible patterns among them is almost limitless. This is because the span of Florentine stitches on which a repeat unit is based can be varied in many ways. Some knowledge of how these variations are achieved will help you to design your own project, or more easily to understand and work a design from a ready-made row chart.

The zigzag pattern of any Florentine stitch is formed by combining two elements: straight Gobelin stitches and a stitch-placing device known as *step*. Step allows the stitches to be placed diagonally next to each other so that the stitches can rise to form the peaks or descend to form the valleys of the zigzag pattern. The illustrations below show the effects of stitch length and step on the height of a peak. Under each example is a set of

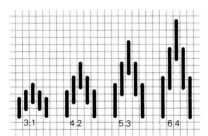

Effects of stitch length and step on peak height.

numbers. The first number denotes stitch length; the second, the amount of step between stitches. Stitches can be from two to eight threads long. Step, which is the number of threads between the bases of neighbouring stitches, must be at least one less than the stitch length number. As the examples show, the greater the stitch length and step, the higher the peak (or lower the valley). The extremes would be even greater if more than three stitches were used between peak and valley.

The row pattern of a Florentine stitch

is formed by combining peaks and valleys. If peaks and valleys are all the same size, the result is an even zigzag pattern, which is the Florentine stitch at its most basic. When pointed peaks and valleys of different sizes are combined, a variation of the Florentine stitch, known as flame stitch, is produced. Additional

The basic Florentine stitch produces an even zigzag pattern. This is achieved by combining peaks and valleys of the same size. To form a deep zigzag pattern, use high, same-size peaks and valleys; for a shallow zigzag, use short, same-size peaks and valleys.

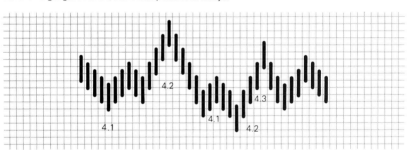

To form an uneven zigzag pattern, combine peaks and valleys of different sizes. Stitches in example above are all four threads long, but heights of peaks and valleys are varied by using different numbers of stitches between them, and changing the amount of step between the stitches.

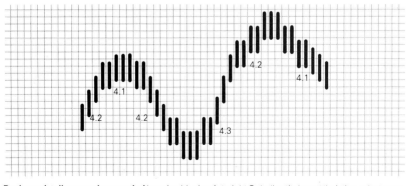

Peaks and valleys can be rounded by using blocks of straight Gobelin stitches at their tips or between them. Step is retained between blocks but not between the individual stitches of a block.

variation can be achieved in a zigzag pattern by rounding the points. This is done by using blocks of straight Gobelin stitches. There can be from two to six stitches in a block; the blocks can be placed at the tip of a peak or valley or between the two. The step is kept between blocks but not between stitches.

Colour

The most basic role of colour in Florentine work is identifying rows or areas in the repeat unit, a natural result of each row or area usually being assigned its own colour. Properly selected and placed in the repeat unit, however, colour can also add depth or movement to the overall design. Colours cause different visual responses; you can control these by assigning colour to a row or area according to how much you want it to stand out in the design. To select colours so that they will perform to your satisfaction, it helps to know something about colour theory.

There are six basic colours in a colour wheel – red, yellow, orange, blue, green and violet. The first three (red, yellow and orange) tend to stand out in a design; the last three (blue, green and violet) tend to recede. Each of these colours has a range of tones, that is, degrees of lightness and darkness. A light tone, or *tint*, is achieved by adding white to the colour. To produce a dark tone, or *shade*, black is added to the colour. As a general rule, tints appear to come forward and shades to go back. How much a tint comes forward or a shade goes back will depend on the intensity of the pure colour from which it was derived. For example, pink, which is a tint of red, will advance more than will pale blue, which is a tint of blue.

The power of any colour or tone is affected by colours and tones around it. A harmonious combination is one in which colours are close, producing a relaxed visual response. A contrasting combination, in which the colours are not close, produces an active response. Most harmonious of all is a combination involving variations of a single colour. Also harmonious is a scheme of related colours, such as blue with blue-green and green. Contrasting schemes may consist of contrasts in tone (very light against very dark) or in colour (violet, green and orange).

SHADES AND TINTS

Shades (darker tones), formed by adding black.

Pure red

Pure blue

Tints (lighter tones), formed by adding white.

KINDS OF COLOUR SCHEMES

Harmonious colour schemes. To form a monochrome harmony, combine several close values of one colour as was done in the first sample above. To create an analogous harmony, combine several related colours as in the second example above.

Contrasting colour schemes may be produced by combining distant tones of one colour as shown by the example on the left. Or, to get a complementary contrasting scheme, combine unrelated colours as was done in the example on the right.

RELATED/UNRELATED COLOURS

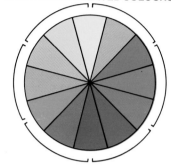

Related colours are those that are next to each other on the colour wheel – red, red-orange and orange; blue, blue-violet and violet.

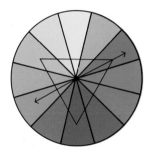

Unrelated colours are those that are opposite or separated on the wheel. Red and green are unrelated; so are green, orange and violet.

Equipment

To work a Florentine embroidery, you will require a chart of the design, canvas and thread. Since this embroidery is a type of repeat pattern design, the amount of canvas needed will be a multiple of the number of threads in the chart. The procedures for estimating canvas amounts are explained on the next few pages. If you are designing your own Florentine embroidery, you will need graph paper and colouring pens. A very handy designing tool is a set of projection mirrors. You can make a set yourself (see right) with felt, glue and two identical small mirrors.

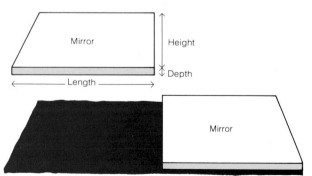

To make a set of projection mirrors, proceed as follows. Cut a piece of felt that is as wide as the mirror is high and equal in length to twice the mirror's combined length and depth (thickness).

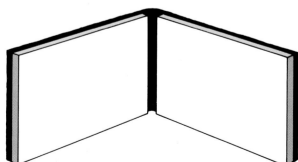

Spread glue on wrong side of both mirrors. Position a mirror at each end of the felt, glued side down. Press both of the mirrors in place and wipe off any excess glue. Leave to dry before using.

175

Designing and working Florentine embroidery

Row design charts

The first step in designing any of the three types of Florentine embroidery designs is to establish the row pattern on which the repeat unit will be based. The easiest way to find a row pattern is to slide projection mirrors (see p. 175) along a predetermined row of Florentine stitches. Though any row of Florentine stitches can serve this purpose (even a photograph of a finished sample), you can improve your chances of discovering a unique pattern by experimenting with

a stitch row that you designed (p. 174). The way the mirrors should be held to reflect the kind of establishing row pattern you need will depend on the type of unit you are designing. The plotting of row design units is explained here; for motif and four-way design units, refer to pp. 178, 180 and 181.

To plan a row design unit, you need to establish a side-to-side pattern for the top row. You can find one by sliding a mirror along a charted row of stitches

(Steps 2 and 3 below). Slide it from right to left and from left to right; patterns will differ each way. More patterns can be produced by turning the row upside-down. When you have found a satisfactory top row, make a line chart of it (p. 166) on a new piece of graph paper; then chart the other rows of the repeat under the first (Steps 4, 5 and 6). Each new row can have a different stitch length so long as the length used will maintain the step arrangement established by the top

row. When charting, use a different colour for each row. Colours need not match those in which the design will be worked on the canvas; once the actual colour arrangement is decided, however, it should be indicated on the chart.

When designing your own unit, it is recommended that you chart the entire side-to-side pattern of all the rows of the unit, this lets you see the actual pattern. Many ready-made charts depict only half of the side-to-side pattern.

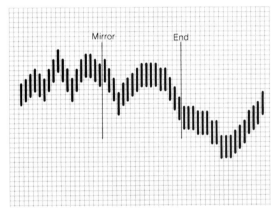

1. Begin by charting a row of Florentine stitches. Make the row long enough to include peaks and valleys of several different sizes and shapes. The red lines indicate position of mirror and end of side-to-side pattern established in Step 3.

2. Position one mirror parallel to the charted stitches. Slowly slide the mirror along the row, looking, as you do, at the charted stitches and their mirrored images. Stop when you come to a section that forms a pleasing pattern on each side of the mirror.

3. Holding the mirror in place and still looking at the charted stitches and their images, slide your finger along charted stitches until you come to a suitable end to the side-to-side pattern. Mark the end with a line; make another line along edge of mirror.

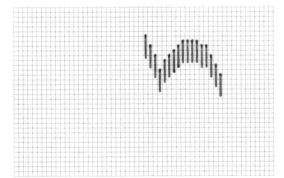

4. On a new piece of graph paper, chart the stitches that lie between the marks drawn in Step 3. When making the new chart, be sure to draw the stitches to the same length and step, and in the same positions, as they were on the original chart.

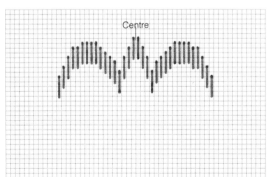

5. Then chart the mirror images of the stitches. These are charted in the opposite direction from those in Step 4 but in the same order. Make sure that you also chart them to the same stitch length and step. Mark the centre of the side-to-side charted pattern.

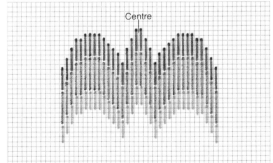

6. Using a different colour for each, chart the other rows of the unit under the first. For each row, use a stitch length that will maintain the step arrangement established by the top row (note that 3-stitch length is too short for the 3-step in centre peak).

Preparing for and working a row design

Florentine designs look best with units centred on the canvas. You can centre a row design by centring the top row at the vertical centre of the canvas (drawing A), or by placing a top row on each side (drawing B). Because of unevenness in heights, most row patterns will cross the horizontal centre irregularly.

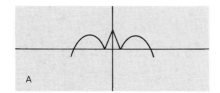

A

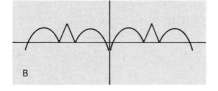

B

With the centre position determined, decide on the number of units you want across and up and down for the total design; then calculate the canvas threads needed to work the design. To find the number of threads needed across, multiply the number of units across by the number of threads across one unit. To find the number needed for length, multiply the number of row units up and down the design by the number of threads needed for each row. Divide these totals by your canvas gauge; the resulting numbers are the measurements of the finished canvas. If the arrangement and gauge produce too small a finished size, add full or partial units to enlarge it. If they produce too large a size, reduce the number of units or select a finer canvas gauge. Prepare canvas for work by cutting it to finished size plus a minimum 5 cm margin along each edge; tape all edges and label the top; mark centres (p. 167).

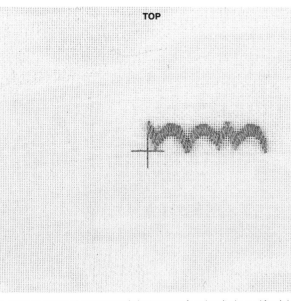

TOP

1. Start at centre of canvas; work the top row of each unit planned for right half of design. Refer to chart for colour and stitch placing.

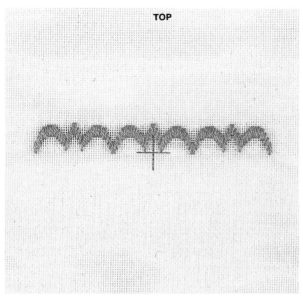

TOP

2. Begin again at centre and work the top row of each unit planned for left half of design. Check entire span for accuracy of stitch placing.

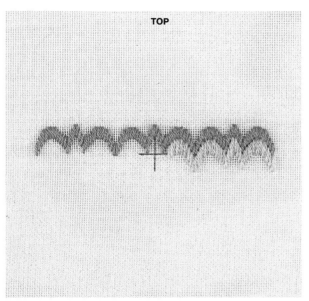

TOP

3. Using the row just completed as a guide, work the second row of all units in one journey across the canvas. Refer to chart for row colour.

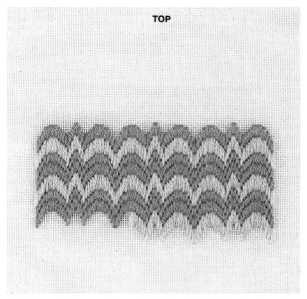

TOP

4. Work remaining rows of lower, then upper half of design. Begin each row at right or left edge; refer to chart for its correct colour.

Designing and working Florentine embroidery

Motif design charts

To design a repeat unit of the motif type, you need to establish patterns for both top and bottom rows. The rows are identical, and are found simultaneously by holding projection mirrors (p. 175) at right-angles to each other and to a row of Florentine stitches. As shown in Step 2 below, a side-to-side pattern is formed on each side of the vertical mirror and this same row pattern is also seen upside-down in both mirrors. When top and bottom rows are in this relationship, an open area is formed between them. This area is filled with Florentine or other straight stitches. With many of the motif patterns, open areas between rows will themselves form secondary motifs. When designing your own motif, it is recommended that you chart several motifs, as shown in Step 4, so that you can see and plan the design of the secondary motifs. Many ready-made charts show only half of both primary and secondary motifs.

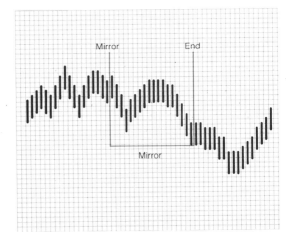

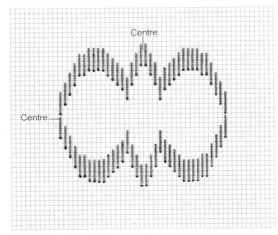

1. Chart a row of Florentine stitches long enough to include various sizes and shapes of peaks and valleys (p. 174). Red lines indicate the positions of the mirrors and the end of the side-to-side pattern established in the next step.

2. With mirrors at right-angles to each other and stitches, slide them along row until you find a suitable motif pattern. To adjust motif depth, slide mirrors up and down. Mark end of side-to-side pattern; trace right-angle formed by edges of both mirrors.

3. Re-chart stitches between marks; draw stitches intersected by horizontal line to the length above the intersection. Chart other half of side-to-side pattern and mark centre (p. 176). Chart bottom row to mirror top row; mark horizontal centre of motif.

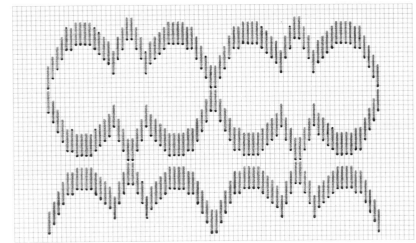

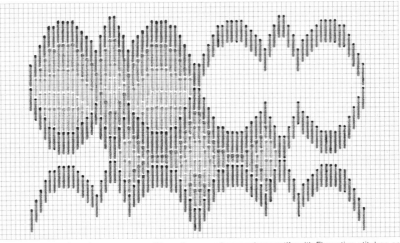

4. To determine if open areas between rows of motifs will form secondary motifs, chart another motif next to the first; under these, chart the top row of two corresponding motifs, aligning their vertical centres with centres of motifs above, and abutting highest points below with lowest points above.

5. Fill in on your chart the open areas of the primary and secondary motifs with Florentine stitches or other straight stitches that make interesting patterns and conform to the shapes of the open areas. Use a different colour for each row or area.

Preparing and working a motif design

The centring of motif design units is usually achieved either by centring a motif at the exact centre of the canvas (drawing A), or by placing full motifs at each side of the centres (drawing B).

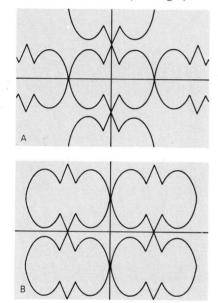

Some motif designs, however, combine these two arrangements. For example, the design on the right centres the motifs horizontally, but places full motifs on each side of the vertical centre. When the centring is determined, decide how many units you want across and up and down to form the total design. Then calculate the amount of canvas needed, and prepare it for working.

As shown in Step 1 on the right, the first row to be worked is the top row of the motifs that run across the centre. If you want the centres of the motifs to be at the horizontal centre of the canvas, then work this top row along the horizontal centre. If you prefer to have whole motifs above the horizontal centre, you will need to work the top row a full motif above that centre line.

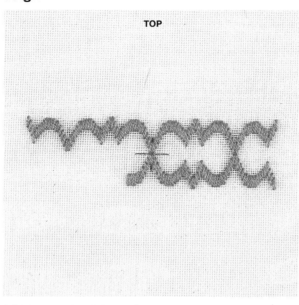

1. Work top row of motifs from vertical centre out to each edge; work bottom row in one journey across. Placing depends on unit centring plan.

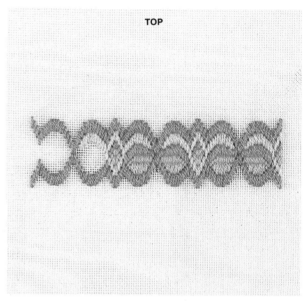

2. Referring to chart for colour and stitch position, work middle areas of motifs – either one at a time or parts of all progressively.

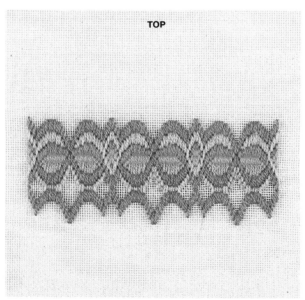

3. Work top row of next span of motifs in one journey across canvas. Work the middle areas of secondary motifs one at a time or progressively.

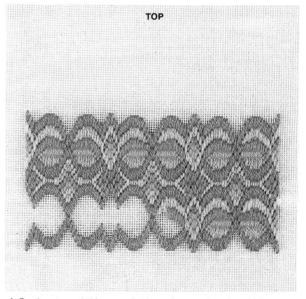

4. Continue to work this way – that is, work a row, then the middle areas – until lower half of the design, then upper half, are completed.

Designing and working Florentine embroidery

Four-way row design charts

Four-way Florentine work consists of four identical triangular quarters that meet and change direction along diagonal lines. Because of this structure, it is also known as mitred Florentine. To design your own four-way Florentine, you need only chart one whole quarter; you then follow it four times to work the design. The design of the quarter can be based on a row design unit, as on this page, or a motif design (opposite page). The main difference between the charting of the two types is the way the row or motif is established and centred in the triangular quarter. To work either type of four-way design, see p. 182.

1. Design a row of Florentine stitches (row above is the same as on p. 176). Hold one mirror parallel to stitches; other at a 45° angle to first. Move mirrors along stitches to find a four-way side-to-side row pattern; up and down to alter length of pattern and its distance from centre of design. Trace 45° angle along mirrors to mark first half of row pattern and its distance from centre.

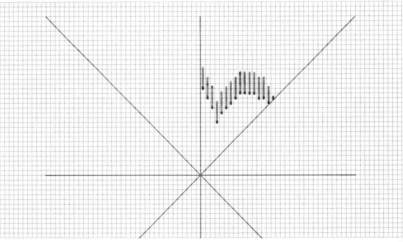

2. On a new piece of graph paper, draw vertical and horizontal centre lines; mitre quarters as shown. If row pattern has one stitch at centre, draw lines *between* graph lines; if row has same number of stitches on each side of centre, draw lines *on* graph lines. Chart first half of row same distance above centre as marked in stage 1; draw stitches intersected by diagonal mark to length above intersection.

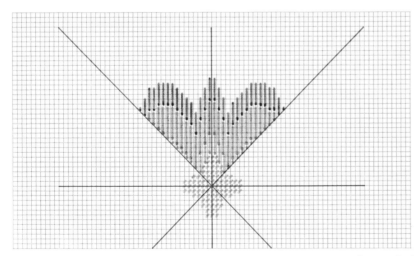

3. Chart second half of row to mirror first half (p. 176). Maintaining pattern set by the first row, chart progressively shorter rows towards centre of design. If space between diagonals becomes too short to chart an acceptable row pattern, design an arrangement of tent or ornamental stitches to fill rest of centre area. Chart all quarters of centre design; for another treatment, see next page.

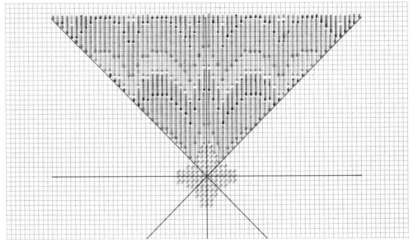

4. Design wide end of triangle to form a straight outer edge. Ornamental or tent stitches can be used (see next page), or you can chart increasingly longer side-to-side row patterns as shown here. If charting rows, maintain pattern set by first; make rows longer by charting stitches to mirror the ends of the row patterns. Use filling-in stitches and parts of rows to form straight edge.

Four-way motif design charts

The primary consideration, in charting a four-way design, is that the establishing row or motif be centred in a triangle. A row design is automatically centred in the process of designing four-way row patterns (Step 1, facing page). When a motif is used for a four-way design, design the top and bottom rows of the motif first (Step 1 below) and then establish its centre position in the triangle (Step 2). This must be done in two stages because there is no way to hold projection mirrors so that they simultaneously reflect both the top and bottom rows of a motif and the motif's arrangement in a four-way pattern.

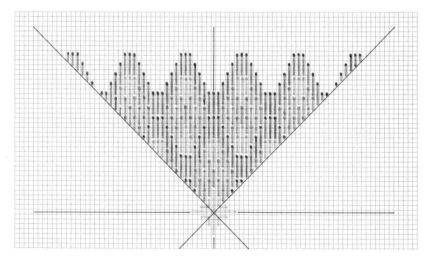

1. Design a row of Florentine stitches (the row used above is different from the one on pp. 176 and 178). With mirrors at right-angles to each other and to the stitches, slide them along the stitches until you find a suitable motif. Slide mirrors up and down if you wish to alter motif depth. Mark the end of the side-to-side pattern; trace the right-angle formed by the mirrors.

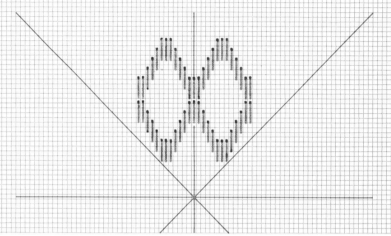

2. Chart top and bottom rows of motif (see p. 178); draw a line down vertical centre of motif. Directly under motif, draw diagonal mitre lines. Mitre lines should meet at the vertical centre line and form a 45° angle on each side of that line; they should not intersect any stitches of the motif. Draw a horizontal centre line through point where diagonals meet vertical centre line.

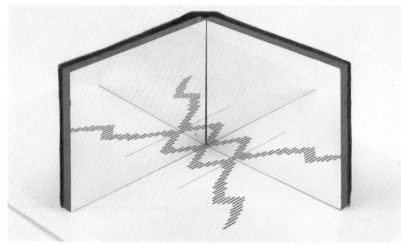

3. If upper portion of motif does not fully span the distance between diagonals, chart partial motifs to fill spaces. Chart middle of each motif, then chart rows and a centre treatment to fill the space (if any) between motif and centre of design. Chart all four quarters of the centre treatment (ornamental stitches are used here; design on facing page has tent stitches at its centre).

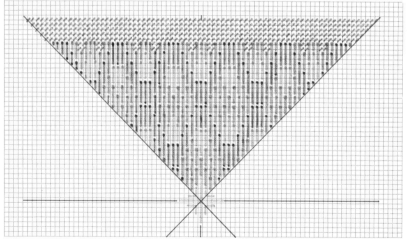

4. Design the wide end of the triangle, making its outer edge straight. Depending on the effect you want, either chart full, then partial rows above motif (as was done above establishing row in Step 4, opposite page), or plan to fill the space above the motif with tent or ornamental stitches, or use a combination of partial rows and other stitches, as was done here.

Designing and working Florentine embroidery

Preparing for and working a four-way design

The centring of the units in a four-way Florentine design is established in its chart and should be maintained in all four quarters of the design as you work them. To work the full design, you have to determine the amount of canvas needed to contain it. To do this, first calculate the number of threads at the outer edge of the triangle, then divide this number by the gauge of your canvas. This one measurement is all that is needed because the outer edges of the triangles are the same on all four sides of the finished design. Some ready-made charts show adjacent halves of triangles separated by a diagonal or mitre line (see the illustration of such a chart below). If you are using this type of chart, calculate the total number of threads for the outer

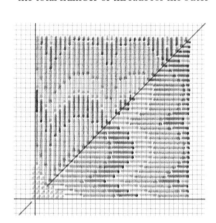

edge of a whole triangle by doubling the number of threads charted for the outer edge of one of the halves.

Cut a piece of canvas to measure the finished length and width plus a minimum 5 cm margin along each edge. Tape all edges and label the top edge. Mark the centres of the canvas (see p. 167). Use wool tackings to mark the lines of the design. Although a row design is being worked on the right, the same procedures apply for a four-way motif design.

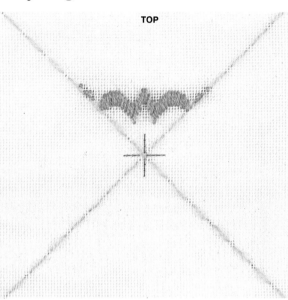

1. Begin with top quarter and work its middle row from vertical centre out to each mitre line. Refer to chart for colour and stitch position.

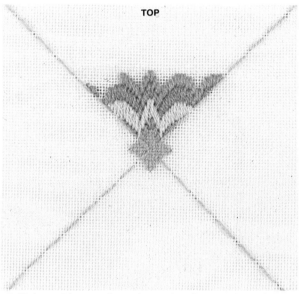

2. Work remaining rows from mitre to mitre; first those from middle row down; then entire centre treatment; finally top rows to outer edge.

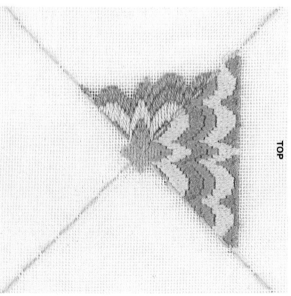

3. Turn canvas clockwise and work rows of next quarter in any convenient sequence. Be sure rows match their counterparts along the mitre.

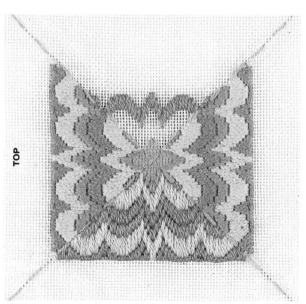

4. Work third and fourth quarters as the second quarter was done. Refer to chart or a worked quarter for colour and stitch position.

General working techniques

Calculating thread amounts

The amount of thread needed to work a particular design will depend on the stitches and the gauge of the canvas as well as the planned finished size of the design. In order to calculate the total thread requirements, you have to determine the amount of thread each stitch uses to cover a square centimetre of canvas. If you plan to use only one stitch, only one test is necessary; if several stitches are being used, you must test them all. All stitch tests must be done on the same gauge of canvas as the design will be worked on. You must also use the proper weight of thread for the stitch and the canvas gauge (see p. 118).

To do a stitch test, cut your thread into several 50 cm (half metre) lengths. Using the pre-measured lengths, work a 2 cm square of the stitch. Record how many lengths were used and convert this number into metres; if a partial length was used, count it as a full length. Use the test result amount to calculate the total amount of thread needed for that particular stitch over the entire design.

Estimate how many square centimetres of that stitch will be worked in the design and multiply that number by the test result amount. Apportion this total amount among the different colours in which the test stitch will be worked. Apply the test result amount of each stitch test in the same way. Add the amounts for individual colours to arrive at the total amount needed for each. To allow for mistakes in calculation or during the work, increase each colour's amount by 10 per cent.

Removing stitches

Stitching mistakes are likely to happen, and are no cause for alarm. If you notice the error while you are stitching and it involves only two or three stitches, the correction is easy. Unthread the needle, pull out the incorrect stitches and re-stitch them with the same thread. If the mistake involves more than just a few simple stitches, or if you discover it after the area is finished, the procedure is different. In this case, you have to carefully cut the incorrect stitches from the canvas, as shown and explained on the right, then, with new thread, re-stitch the area where stitches were cut.

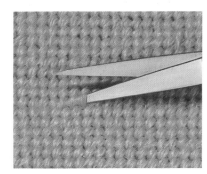

1. From right side, slip scissors blade under a few incorrect stitches; pull thread up from canvas and cut. Clip a few at a time until all are cut.

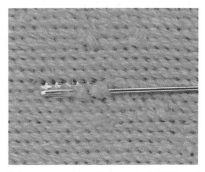

2. From wrong side, with eye end of needle, pull out cut thread. To secure intact stitches, unstitch a few; catch thread into backs of new stitches.

Repairing ripped canvas

You may discover that in the process of removing stitches you have accidentally cut the threads of the canvas. If this happens, you can easily repair the cut with a patch of the same canvas type and gauge. To prepare the area for the repair, pull out enough stitches around the cut to allow ample space for the patch. A patch needs to be a few meshes larger each way than the cut; the space for the patch must be slightly larger than the patch. When the area is ready, apply the patch as shown and explained on the right. Re-stitch the area through both layers; trim threads that protrude.

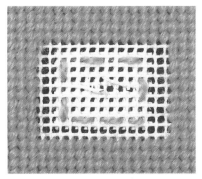

1. Position canvas patch under the cut. Align the threads of both canvases; tack patch in place.

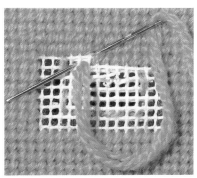

2. Re-stitch area through both layers of canvas. Carefully trim any protruding canvas threads.

General working techniques

Setting canvas into a frame

It is best to do canvas work on a frame or other holding device. Work that is done this way will stay neat and be less distorted when it is finished. As explained on p. 116, there are different types of frames and stretchers, each with its own use and limitations. Basic instructions for setting canvas into most of the frames are given below. A fine-gauge canvas can be set into a hoop if you prefer; for instructions, see the Embroidery chapter. Because there will be slight variations among different brands of frames, you should use these instructions as guides, adapting them if necessary to your needs. If your frame is equipped with a stand, you should attach it before starting to work.

Slate and rotating types are the most versatile of all the canvas work frames. Each consists of top and bottom rods and two side arms (see the illustrations below). The canvas is attached to fabric tapes on the rods, and the rods are then inserted into the side arms. If your slate or rotating frame does not have fabric tapes, you should add them.

To add fabric tapes, cut two lengths of rug binding or webbing, each slightly longer than rod after insertion into side arms. Centre tape on rod with one edge lapped and the other extending; turn raw edges of tape under flush with working ends of rod. Secure lapped edge with staples or small tacks. Attach the second tape the same way.

SLATE FRAME

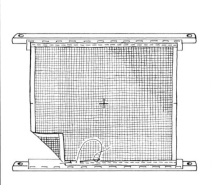 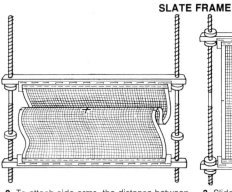 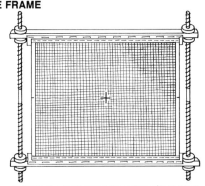 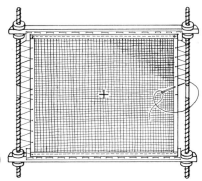

1. Centre and lap the top canvas edge over the tape on the top rod; hold in place. Sew the canvas firmly to the tape with a needle and strong thread (such as button thread) using backstitches. Use several backstitches in one place to start to secure the thread, and several more at the end to prevent the canvas becoming undone when under tension.

2. To attach side arms, the distance between rods must be less than the side arms' length but no less than half that length. If necessary, roll canvas on to one or both rods. Place a locking nut on each end of each side arm; bring to centres. Insert top ends of arms into ends of top rod; slip arms through and insert other ends into bottom rod.

3. Slide the rods along the arms with canvas centred in the frame. Bring the centred nuts out to hold the rods in place, holding the canvas taut. Attach a nut to each end of each arm; bring towards the rods. Tighten all the locking nuts. Some slate frames have slat side arms with spaced holes. The canvas is held taut by pegs through rods in the appropriate holes.

4. To hold canvas taut at the sides, oversew each side to an arm. Begin and end by winding thread between nut and rod. When finished, adjust thread to hold canvas evenly. If preferred, use tape and pins, see p. 383. To reposition canvas, remove oversewing and repeat Steps 2 to 4. Keep canvas evenly tensioned to prevent unnecessary distortion.

ROTATING FRAME

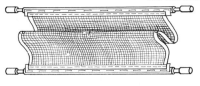

1. Secure top and bottom edges of canvas to webbing on top and bottom rods as explained in Step 1 of slate frame instructions (see above). Loosen wing nuts at ends of side arms and slip the rods through openings in the arms.

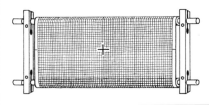

2. Turn rods to take up slack canvas; secure by tightening nuts. Edges can be oversewn to side arms (Step 4 above). To re-position canvas, remove oversewing and loosen nuts; re-roll canvas and tighten nuts.

CANVAS STRETCHER

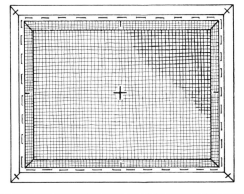

Arrange the four strips as they will be set together, each with its shorter edge towards the inside of the frame. At each of the four corners, fit ends of adjacent strips together and staple across each join to secure it. Mark centre of each strip. Centre canvas over frame, making sure that the entire working area is clear of the frame's inner edges. Allow a margin of 2 cm all round. Staple or pin each edge of the canvas to the frame. Canvas should not be re-positioned after work has begun. This would mean stapling or pinning through some of the worked area.

Blocking canvas work

Blocking is the process that brings the stitched canvas work to its original size and alignment. It is made necessary by the almost unavoidable distortion that occurs as the canvas is worked. The primary cause of distortion is the stitches themselves, with the diagonal and crossing stitches generally distorting the work more than straight stitches. Stitch distortion can be compounded by using too tight a stitch tension or too thick a wool for the canvas gauge; it can be minimised by working the canvas on a frame. There are three methods of blocking; which one you use will depend on how misshapen your canvas is. Before blocking, check for any missed stitches.

Use Method 1, below, for canvases with little or no distortion. For these, all that is needed is a light steam-pressing to straighten up the shape and even out the stitch surface. Method 2, top right, is

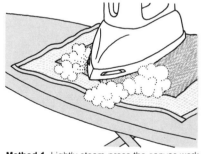

Method 1. Lightly steam-press the canvas work from the wrong side; let it dry thoroughly.

for canvases that show noticeable distortion; Method 3, on the immediate right, is for those that are extremely distorted. With either of these last two methods, the canvas is stretched to match the pattern made of it before it was worked (p. 164). With any method, it is important to let the canvas dry thoroughly before it is moved. If it is still out of shape after drying is complete, block it again.

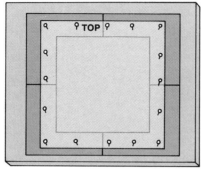

Method 2: 1. Place pattern of prepared canvas right side up on blocking board; cover it with a sheet of tissue paper. Pin both to board.

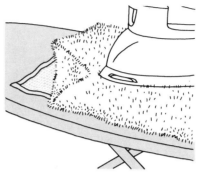

2. Place canvas work face down on ironing board. Dampen a towel and use it to steam-press and dampen the canvas work.

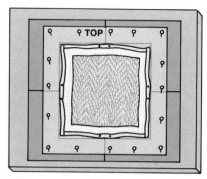

3. Place canvas work face upwards on the pattern and stretch so that its centres and edges match those on pattern. Pin every 2 cm; let dry.

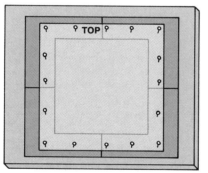

Method 3: 1. Place pattern of prepared canvas right side up on blocking board; cover it with a sheet of tissue paper. Pin both to board.

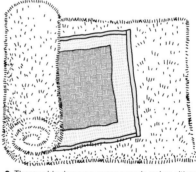

2. Thoroughly dampen canvas work, using either of the following methods. Roll canvas work in a damp towel and leave it rolled until moisture has penetrated both the stitches and the canvas (above left); or sprinkle or sponge the canvas work with enough warm water to dampen it (above right).

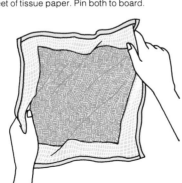

3. Stretch canvas in the direction opposite to the distortion. Begin by pulling at opposite corners; then pull along opposite edges.

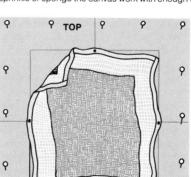

4. Place the canvas work face upwards on the pattern. Stretch canvas so that the centre markings at its edges match those on pattern. Pin.

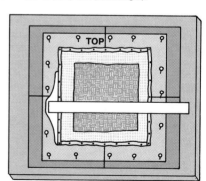

5. Stretch canvas to align its edges with those on pattern; pin in place every 2 cm. Use a T-square to check straightness of canvas threads.

185

Spectacle case/Florentine work

Mark spectacle case with initial for a gift.

A row-repeat Florentine pattern (pp. 176–7) and tent stitches create a colourful spectacle case in an unusually generous size. It is shown with one initial here, but could have more.

Materials needed
14-gauge canvas, 28 cm by 29 cm
21.5 cm by 20 cm of soft lining fabric
Skeins of each of the following colours in Persian or tapestry wool: 3 light turquoise; 2 medium blue; 2 royal blue; 1 gold and 1 burnt sienna
Size 20 tapestry needle
Sewing thread to match lining
Hand-sewing needle

Preparation
Cut canvas piece to the required size. Tape edges; label top. Mark centres of canvas between threads (p. 167). Vertical centre is foldline between front and back of case. Mark outside shape of case. For top and bottom edges, draw a line on the 50th thread above and below the horizontal centre. For each side of case, draw a line on the 53rd thread on each side of vertical centre.

The canvas work
Following row chart on facing page, form two consecutive peaks across front of case. Begin at vertical centre and place base of first stitch over the 20th thread above horizontal centre. Then, working from vertical centre out to left, form two peaks across back of case. *Note:* there is a single stitch at each peak and valley. Referring to chart, work as many row repeats as necessary for the length of the case; form a straight edge along bottom. Using tent stitches and following appropriate chart, work chosen initial between the two peaks on front of case. The outlined square area on row chart locates centre area between peaks; centre your letter in that area. Fill unstitched areas with tent stitches. Block the canvas work (p. 185).

Finishing the case
Trim each edge of canvas to 1.5 cm. Turn back all edges. Mitre corners (see right). With wrong sides together, fold case along vertical centre; match threads along bottom and side edges. Sew together with oversewing, first across bottom, then along side of the spectacle case. Reinforce the top corner by oversewing three times in the same hole, fanning the stitches around the corner.

Take piece of lining fabric, 21.5 cm wide by 20 cm long. With right sides together fold lining in half vertically. Make a 1.5 cm seam, trim. Turn top edge back 5 mm. Slip lining into case, align seams of lining and case. Stitch lining to case along top edge.

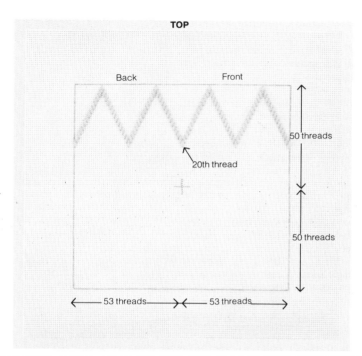

Canvas is cut 28 cm long by 29 cm wide, which allows for a 5 cm margin around canvas work. Dimensions of case, and starting point for Florentine work, are determined by counting threads.

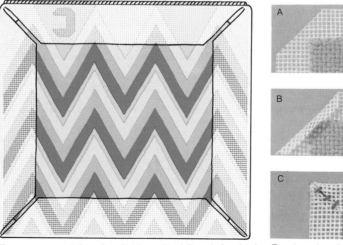

Excess canvas at the edges is trimmed to 1.5 cm before turning. Turn top edge along the canvas work; turn other three along thread next to the stitches. **To mitre corners,** trim canvas diagonally across corner (A); fold back across corner (B); turn back edges on each side of corner and tack (C).

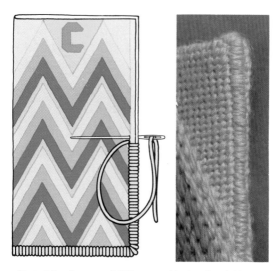

Assembling the case. 1. With wrong sides together, fold canvas work vertically in half. Align edges and match threads along bottom and sides; stitch together with oversewing. Begin stitching at fold and work first across bottom, then along side. Reinforce top corner by forming 3 stitches through the same hole, fanning them around the hole.

2. With right sides together, fold lining vertically. Stitch 1.5 cm seam along bottom and side; trim. Turn top edge back 5 mm. Slip lining into case; sew to case at top edge.

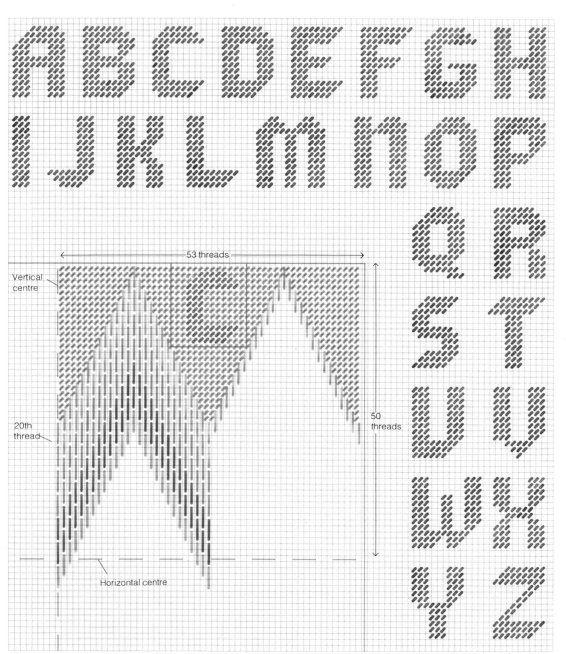

Line charts are used here (p. 166); the colour of the drawn stitches represents the colour of thread in which they should be worked.

Oriental-design footstool cover

This Oriental design was first painted on the canvas and then worked in tent stitches.

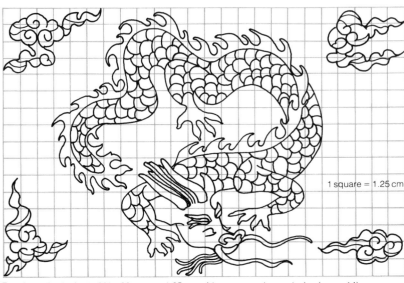

1 square = 1.25 cm

To enlarge the design to 20 by 30 cm, use 1.25 cm grid squares and copy design (see p. 14).

To make a canvas work footstool like the one shown here, the stool must have a removable top; footstools of this type are available in many needlework and craft shops. Both instructions and materials are based on a 23 by 36 by 5 cm stool top, and on the design being worked in tent stitches. The instructions can be adapted to cover any stool top; if measurements differ, canvas and thread needs must be re-calculated (see on the right and p. 183), and the design elements may need rearranging.

Materials needed
Footstool with top measuring 23 by 36 by 5 cm
60 cm 14-gauge canvas (for the stool shown here)
Persian or tapestry wool skeins: 11 light grey; 1 light mustard; 2 rust red; 1 dark green; 1 turquoise; 1 dark mustard
22 tapestry needle
Staple gun
Unbleached muslin, wadding and masking tape if stool top needs re-padding
Paper and pencils

Preparation
Remove stool top (usually attached with screws on underside of footstool). If it needs to be re-padded, first remove old padding from mounting board. Then, lay several layers of wadding over board and staple in place to underside of board; trim excess at corners or curves. Cover with muslin and staple in place to underside of board, gathering excess at corners or curves. Measure stool top – length plus depth at each end and width plus depth at each end. Add 2.5 cm to each of these measurements to achieve the total area needed for design and background, plus 1.5 cm along each edge. Cut canvas to these measurements plus an 8 cm margin on each edge. For a 23 by 36 by 5 cm stool top, cut canvas to 50 by 63 cm. To decide the position of the design and its dimensions, measure the top surface of the stool. Enlarge the design (p. 14), using the grid drawing above as a guide. To produce an enlarged drawing of 20 by 30 cm, a size suitable for a 23 by 36 cm top, use 1.25

cm grid squares. To make it significantly smaller or larger, assign a different measurement to the grid squares. To adapt the design for a square or circular area, either re-position the corner motifs or eliminate them. Place design on canvas (pp. 164–5).

The canvas work
Stitch design on canvas, using any of the forms of tent stitches (p. 121). Two strands of Persian wool should provide a

suitable thread coverage (p. 118). Block the canvas (p. 185); remove while it is still slightly damp.

Mounting the canvas work
Centre right side of stool top to wrong side of canvas work. Working opposite edges at the same time, wrap canvas work to underside of stool top, stretch taut and staple in place. Gather fullness at corners. Trim excess canvas. Allow to dry. Attach top to footstool.

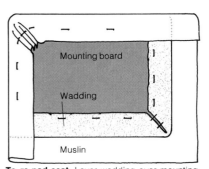

To re-pad seat. Layer wadding over mounting board; staple to underside; trim excess. Cover with muslin; staple to underside; gather excess.

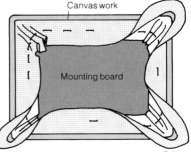

Canvas work

Mounting board

Centre seat to wrong side of canvas work. Bring edges of canvas work to underside; staple in place; gather fullness at corners or curves.

Man's belt

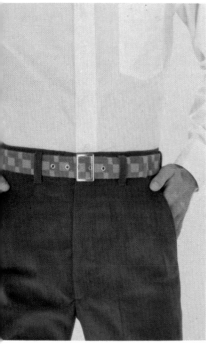

This canvas work belt makes an unusual gift.

Man's belt

The overall design of this canvas work belt is formed by the repetition of a single charted motif. The number of units will depend on the waist size of the man for whom it is being made; the belt here is made for an 82 cm waist.

Materials needed

Strip of 14-gauge canvas, 14 cm wide by waist measurement plus 25 cm
Petersham ribbon, 4 cm wide by waist measurement plus 15 cm
Persian or tapestry wool skeins (for sizes 84–86 cm): 3 rust; 3 olive; 2 light olive; 2 camel
22 tapestry needle
4 cm centre-bar buckle
Stiletto
Metal eyelets and eyelet pliers

Preparation

Cut canvas to measure 14 cm wide by a length equal to the waist measurement plus 25 cm. If necessary, join lengths (p. 164), or cut along the selvedge to produce desired length. Tape edges of canvas. Draw one line across canvas 5 cm below top edge, another line parallel to and 20 threads below the first line. These mark top and bottom of belt. To mark right end of belt, draw a vertical line 5 cm in from right end of canvas. To mark left end, draw a line that is the waist measurement plus 16 cm away from the right-end mark. Next mark several points along horizontal centre of belt. Place first mark 4 cm in from left end – this marks place where buckle prong will be set. Place next mark, for centre eyelet, the waist measurement minus the length of the prong away from the prong mark. Make additional marks, for more eyelets, to right and left of centre eyelet, spaced about 3 cm apart.

The canvas work

Following the chart for Example A on p. 171, and using tent stitches, stitch design on to canvas. Tapestry wool or two strands of Persian wool should provide suitable thread coverage (see p. 118). Work first unit to right of prong mark, then work units towards right end of belt, leaving four meshes unworked around each eyelet marking. Work last unit to left of prong mark; leave four meshes unworked around prong mark. (All unworked meshes should align with each other.) Block the canvas work as described on p. 185.

Finishing the belt

Trim each edge of canvas to 1.5 cm. Turn edges back along canvas work; mitre corners (p. 186). To attach buckle: using a stiletto, spread unworked meshes at prong mark. Slip end of belt over bar of buckle; push prong through hole. Fold belt end back over bar of buckle. Align outer edges of fold-back to outer edges of front of belt; stitch together along edges. Cut petersham same length as belt; turn ends under 1.5 cm. Lay petersham on to wrong side of belt and match one folded end to right end of belt; lap other end over end of fold-back. Pin in place; using small stitches, sew along all edges. From right side and using a stiletto, push apart the four unworked meshes at each eyelet marking; then, push the stiletto through the petersham at each mark. Using eyelet pliers, attach the eyelets.

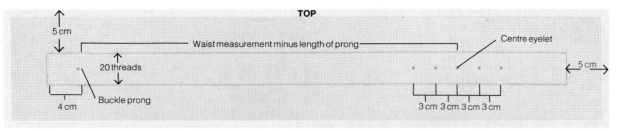

Strip of canvas should measure 14 cm by the waist measurement plus 25 cm. Markings include, besides edges of belt, points for buckle prong and eyelets.

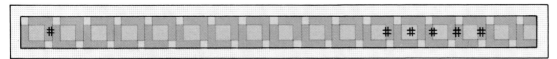

Units are worked with tent stitches, from prong mark to right, then final unit to its left. Four meshes are left unworked at prong and eyelet marks.

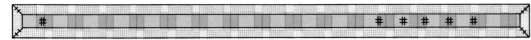

After stitching is completed, excess canvas at edges is turned back along the last row of stitches; corners are mitred as explained on p. 186.

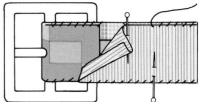

Petersham is same length as belt; ends are turned under 1.5 cm. One end aligns with belt's right end; other laps over fold-back at left end.

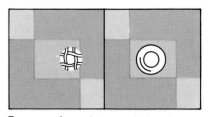

To prepare for eyelets, unworked meshes are spread and petersham is pierced with a stiletto. Eyelets can then be attached with eyelet pliers.

Address book cover

Barn is charming motif for an address book.

Address book cover

Barn design is 56 threads square – about 14 cm on 10-gauge canvas.

Materials needed

Binder (one shown is 23 cm long by 18 cm wide with a 3.5 cm wide spine)
10-gauge canvas (length of binder plus 15 cm by twice width of binder plus width of spine plus 15 cm)
Persian or tapestry wool in skeins, 12 beige, and 1 each of the following colours: medium blue; pale orange; dark red; salmon; light blue; light green; white; dark green; sand; black; medium green; blue-green; cream
18 tapestry needle
Lining fabric (length of binder plus 3 cm by twice the width of binder plus width of spine plus 6 cm)
Sewing thread to match lining
Hand-sewing needle

Preparation

Cut canvas the length of the binder plus 15 cm, by twice the width of the binder plus width of the spine plus 15 cm.
For a 23 by 18 by 3.5 cm binder, cut canvas 38 cm long by 55 cm wide. Tape the edges of the canvas. Label the top. Open the binder and centre it on the canvas. Mark canvas as follows: draw a line 5 mm above and below the binder; then draw a line along each side of the binder. Mark the width of the spine at both top and bottom. Remove binder and mark front edge of spine from top to bottom marks. Mark the centre of the front cover (see right).

Cut one strip of lining fabric that is the length of the binder plus 3 cm, by the width of the spine plus 6 cm. This strip will be used to face the spine area; for the binder shown, facing is 25 cm long by 11 cm wide. Cut two strips of lining fabric, each measuring 3 cm more than the length of the binder but the same as the binder in width. These pieces will be used to face the front and back covers; for the binder shown, each of these pieces measures 25 cm long by 18 cm wide. Turn under all of the edges of all three of the facing pieces 5 mm. Machine-topstitch the folded edges.

The canvas work

Stitch the barn design on to the centre of the front cover. Follow the chart on p. 167 using tent stitches and a three-strand thickness of thread. Cover the remaining area with an ornamental stitch (Hungarian stitch is used here); change the thread weight if necessary for adequate coverage (p. 118). Block (p. 185).

Finishing the cover

Trim the excess canvas to 2.5 cm. Turn back each edge along the canvas work, mitre the corners (p. 186). Apply facings as shown on the right. To insert binder into finished cover, fold covers of binder and canvas work back, then slip each binder cover under a cover facing.

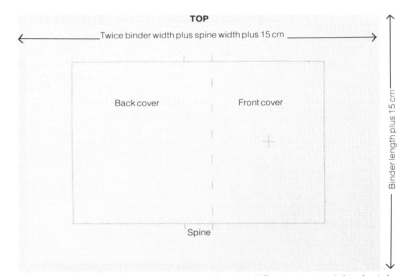

Canvas is cut and prepared as shown above and explained on left. Front cover extends from front of spine to right edge of canvas work, back cover from back of spine to left edge of canvas work.

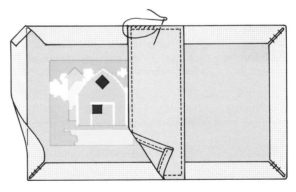

Attaching facings. With wrong sides together, centre spine facing over spine area of cover. Align its top and bottom edges with top and bottom edges of canvas work. Stitch the two together along these edges.

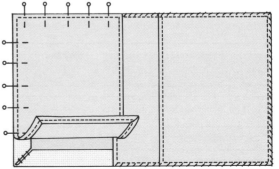

With wrong sides together, place a cover facing to the front cover area of the canvas work. Align its top, side and bottom edges with those of the canvas work. Stitch the two together along those three edges. Apply a facing to the back cover area the same way.

Appliqué

Wall hanging 'Landscape with Mountain' © Madge Huntington 1976

Appliqué basics

Tools and materials

Appliqué work is basically a sewing craft, and so it calls for much the same tools and materials. **Fabrics** are of course essential, but not necessarily in great quantities; scraps and pieces are usually adequate for a small project. Easiest to handle are smooth natural fabrics in a light to medium weight. Be sure that all the fabrics used are of the same type if they are to be laundered. Try to avoid loosely woven or extremely bulky fabrics; they can be very difficult to manage. If, despite this limitation, you still want to use a particular loose weave, back it with iron-on interfacing (see p. 199). Before using any fabrics, press out all wrinkles and creases.

To stitch an appliqué in place, use an all-purpose (size 50) sewing **thread.** For additional decorative stitching, you can use stranded cotton or pearl cotton. Sharps are a type of medium-length **needle** excellent for hand stitching. They come in different sizes to accommodate different fabric weights. Other needle types, such as crewel and chenille, have larger eyes, permitting thicker threads to be used.

Another essential tool in appliqué work is a sharp pair of **scissors.** Ideally, you should have two pairs, medium-size dressmaker's shears for general cutting, and small, pointed embroidery scissors for close trimming.

Other useful sewing aids include fine **dressmaker's pins** for holding appliqué in place, and a dressmaker's **marking pencil** or hard lead pencil for marking fabrics. **Thimbles** are handy if you are accustomed to using them. **Frames** and **hoops** are optional and should be used only if they will make your work easier. **Heavy tracing paper** and **coloured stiff paper** are helpful for copying or cutting out designs.

As an alternative to stitching appliqué down, you can use **fusible webs,** which you can buy in packets. See p. 197 for the fusing technique.

Design ideas

Inspiration for appliqué designs can be found in many sources, among them colouring books, greeting cards and everyday objects. Traditionally the designs are quite primitive and childlike, rather than works of art. A typically simple design can consist of a central motif cut from a single piece, or perhaps made up of two or more pieces. A composition, in contrast, is somewhat more difficult and consists of many motifs that together form a complete picture. If you are a beginner, start with designs consisting of one or a few large pieces.

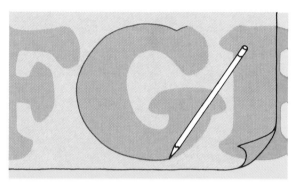

The monogram letter is a typical one-piece design. It is being *traced*, which is the simplest method for obtaining a design. If traced drawing is not the desired size, enlarge or reduce it to your liking by methods described in the Embroidery chapter.

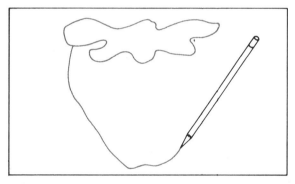

The single strawberry exemplifies a simple design of two main pieces. It is being *drawn freehand*, which is another way to obtain a design. Freehand designs can come from your imagination or from a model. Drawings need not be precise; in fact, simplified lines and details work best.

This sheep design is a composition created by first *cutting free shapes* of stiff paper, then arranging them to form a pastoral scene.

Making templates

If you have cut out some shapes from stiff paper to arrive at a design, or if you have cut out pattern pieces from a book or pattern, those pieces become the actual templates. If, however, you have traced or drawn a design, you will have to make templates for each separate shape in the design (see below). When appliqué is employed in patchwork, a single design may be duplicated many times over, which means the patterns are used again and again. In such instances, it is wise to re-cut the patterns from very heavy paper so that the templates will not become too worn to use.

To make a template from a tracing or drawing, simply cut along the drawn outline of the appliqué piece. If the template is to be used many times, re-cut it from heavy paper or thin card.

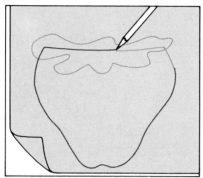

If your design consists of two or more pieces, re-trace each piece separately. Straighten out edges that will be covered by another piece instead of trying to fit the two pieces together.

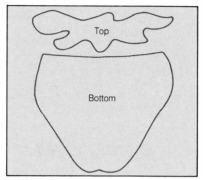

Cut out each separate piece along the drawn outlines. To avoid any errors when cutting the actual appliqué, mark the right side of each pattern piece with an identifying word or symbol.

Transferring designs

Before transferring a design, cut background fabric, which may be a patchwork block or even a garment section, to desired size. In order to centre the design accurately, mark vertical and horizontal centre lines through the background piece. The centre lines are especially helpful in patchwork because they enable you to position the appliqué in exactly the same spot for each of the blocks involved. A single appliqué may be placed in position on the centre lines by eye only, but for greater accuracy position marking is recommended.

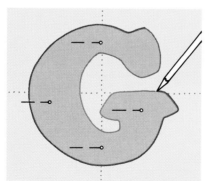

To determine centre lines, fold and crease background fabric in half, then in quarters. Open fabric out, and for a firm guideline, tack along vertical and horizontal creases.

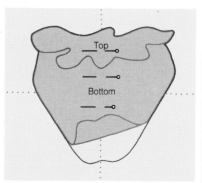

To transfer your design, position template, right side up, on background fabric and pin in place. Trace around template, using either a sharp dressmaker's pencil or a hard lead pencil.

If a design has two or more pieces, carefully assemble all pieces in position, then pin them to the background fabric. Trace around design formed by the combined templates.

Other design possibilities

Paper cut-outs are another good source of designs. This kind of snowflake is often seen in traditional Hawaiian quilts. Because of its intricacies, hand stitching is advised and it is usually accompanied by echo quilting (see p. 200).

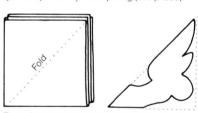

To make a paper cut-out, fold square sheet of paper in quarters, then in half diagonally. Cut out pieces through all thicknesses, then open out.

Using a fabric print is a quick and easy way to obtain an appliqué design. Simply cut 1 cm to 2 cm outside design silhouette and machine-stitch appliqué print to background fabric (see p. 196).

Appliqué basics

Cutting appliqué

The first step, if you will be cutting much appliqué, is to assemble your fabric scraps and decide which ones will be used for each piece. Try to achieve a balance of colours as well as a balance of printed and plain areas. If the fabrics you have selected have a dominant print or weave, consider carefully how you want that print or weave placed on each appliqué piece. For example, if a fabric is striped, it can be cut so that the stripes run vertically or horizontally. Always cut appliqué to follow the grain of the background fabric. This will give the best results.

Another consideration is the compatibility of the appliqué fabric and the background fabric in terms of care. Generally speaking, if the appliquéd article will not be laundered, almost any combination of fabrics is acceptable. If it will be laundered, be sure that all of the fabrics you plan to combine can take the same kind of washing and drying.

To cut out an appliqué, follow the step-by-step instructions given on the right. Note that staystitching is recommended to make it easier to turn edges under. If an appliqué has curves or corners, the seam allowances need to be clipped or notched to facilitate turning.

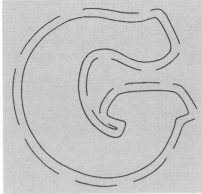

1. Pin template to right side of fabric. Trace around pattern with dressmaker's pencil. Remove template. Mark a 3 mm to 5 mm seam allowance outside the drawn seamline. Use the wider seam allowance on fabrics that are loosely woven.

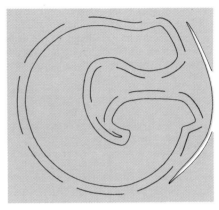

2. Cut appliqué outside marked lines so that an ample fabric width is left. This wider margin will make it easier for you to staystitch in the next step.

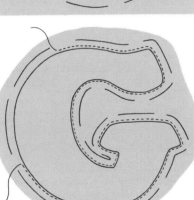

3. To facilitate turning under of edges, staystitch just outside inner marked seamline. Set sewing machine to sew short stitches.

4. Trim margin by cutting appliqué on outer marked lines as shown. Clip seam allowances around curves and corners so edges can be properly turned (see below).

Handling curves and corners

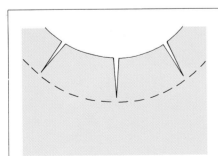

Along inner curves, clip seam allowance to staystitching to aid turning. Space the clips closer together along deeper curves.

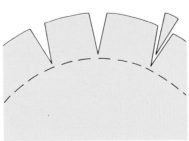

Along outer curves, notch out pieces along seam allowances to keep bulky pleats from forming when edges are turned under.

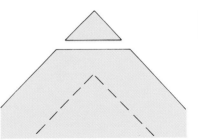

At outside corners, blunt seam allowance as shown to help reduce bulk in the point when the edges are mitred (see opposite page).

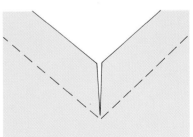

At inside corners, make a single clip into the point of the corner (up to staystitching) so that the edges can be turned under.

Securing appliqué by hand

An appliqué can be hand-stitched in place by either of the two methods shown below. The first method, though somewhat more time-consuming, is recommended for beginners. It calls for an additional tacking step that holds the turned-under seam allowance in position, making it less awkward to secure the appliqué to the background. The second method omits the initial tacking of edges; instead the appliqué is pinned in place, and the edges turned and stitched.

To secure the appliqué, a fine slip-stitch is recommended; it holds the appliqué securely and is almost invisible when carefully worked. Oversewing stitches, though not invisible, should be used in small areas that tend to fray; these little straight stitches can keep the short fabric threads from popping out (see below). Embroidery stitches such as running stitch and cross stitch can also be used to fasten down an appliqué. Remember that these are decorative stitches, meant to be seen; they will become part of the design (see p. 200).

The use of a hoop or frame is optional. Some find stitching easier without one, while others find it a necessity.

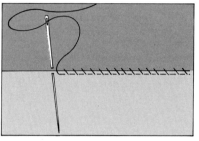

Paris stitch. Work from right to left. Bring needle out of appliqué just above the edge. Insert needle below and make a horizontal stitch to left. Replace needle in hole it came out of and make a diagonal stitch up and to the left.

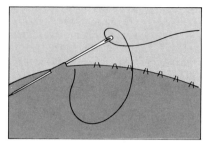

Slipstitch. Work from right to left. Bring needle up through folded edge of appliqué. Pick up thread opposite on background fabric then slip needle through folded edge for 3 mm. Bring needle out and pull thread tight.

Methods of sewing appliqué

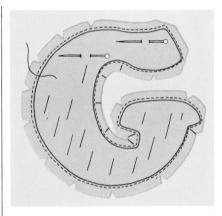

Method 1. Along marked seamline of appliqué, fold and finger-press seam allowance to wrong side; tack folded edge as you finger-press. Keep staystitching within the seam allowance width.

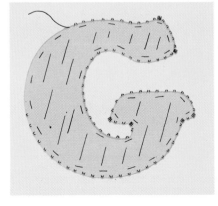

Pin appliqué to background and, if necessary, hold in place with vertical tacking stitches. Secure appliqué with a fine slipstitch along folded edges. Remove all tacking.

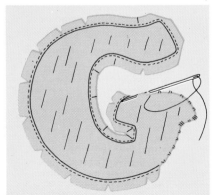

Method 2. Pin cut appliqué to the background (edges are not yet turned under). If needed, hold appliqué in place with vertical tacking. Be sure that stitches do not extend into seam allowance; edges must still be turned under.

Using point of needle to tuck seam allowance under, slipstitch turned edges in place. Be sure staystitching is turned in with seam allowance. Continue to turn and stitch in this way until appliqué is fully secured. Remove all tacking.

Outside corners should be mitred to avoid bulk at point. Fold down trimmed corner first, then neatly fold in each adjacent side.

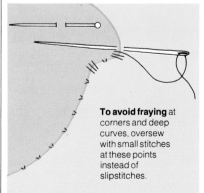

To avoid fraying at corners and deep curves, oversew with small stitches at these points instead of slipstitches.

Appliqué basics

Securing appliqué by machine

The sewing machine is used extensively in appliqué work today because it makes it possible to complete a project in less than half the time it would take to do a similar project by hand. A decision to stitch an appliqué by machine instead of by hand can depend upon several factors. First, if the fabrics you are working with are relatively substantial rather than fine and delicate, they will be easier to handle with the sewing machine. Another consideration is the ultimate use of the appliquéd article. If it is likely to get a great deal of wear (a child's dungarees, for example), a machine application is undoubtedly more practical.

There are basically two methods of machine appliqué. One is done entirely by means of straight stitching; the other, which is considerably faster, uses a combination of straight and zigzag.

Before starting, test and adjust the machine so its tension is balanced and the pressure is correct for the fabrics being used. For straight stitching set the machine to medium stitches. When using thin fabric, zigzag stitching is usually narrow, with a short stitch length.

Straight-stitch method

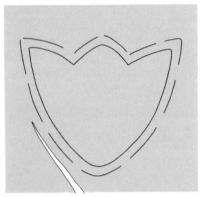

Pin template to right side of appliqué fabric. Trace around pattern and remove it. Mark 5 mm seam allowance outside marked line. Cut outside marked lines, leaving ample fabric width.

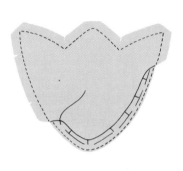

Staystitch just outside inner marked seamline. Trim excess margin by cutting on outer marked lines. Clip and notch curves and corners. Fold seam allowance to wrong side; tack in place.

Position and pin appliqué to right side of background fabric; if necessary, tack appliqué down with vertical tacking as shown to keep appliqué from shifting during stitching.

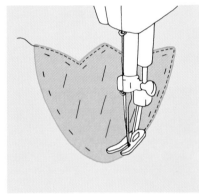

Set sewing machine to medium stitch length. Carefully stitch along folded edges of appliqué. Pull thread ends to wrong side and knot. Remove all tacking threads.

Zigzag method

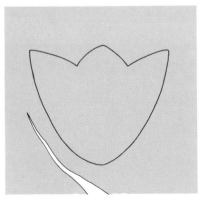

Pin template to right side of appliqué fabric and trace around it. Remove pattern. Cut out appliqué outside marked lines, leaving an ample seam allowance (approximately 1 cm to 2 cm wide).

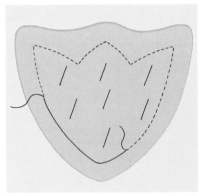

Position and pin appliqué to right side of background fabric; if necessary, tack appliqué down with vertical tacking as shown. Straight-stitch directly over the marked seamline.

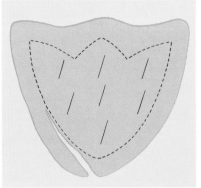

Using a sharp pair of pointed embroidery scissors, trim away seam allowance, cutting as close to stitching line as possible; be careful not to cut the stitches or the background fabric.

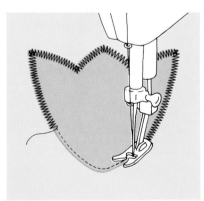

Select suitable width and length for zigzag and sew over raw edges and straight stitching. Pull thread ends to wrong side; knot. Remove tacking.

Zigzagging around corners and curves

Right-angle corners.
Zigzag down one side of corner and stop at point shown by dot. For *outside* corner, position needle outside of point. For *inside* corner, position needle inside of point. Pivot and zigzag down other side of corner.

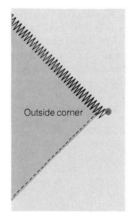

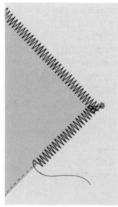
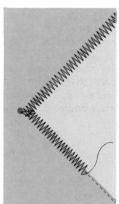

Outside corner

Inside corner

Wide-angle corners.
Imagine a line running through centre of corner. Zigzag down one side of corner and stop when needle hits imaginary line at dot. For *outside* corner, position needle on dot outside of corner. For *inside* corner, position needle on dot inside of corner. Pivot and zigzag down the other side.

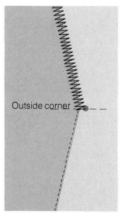
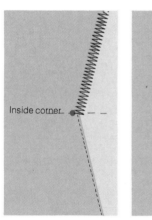
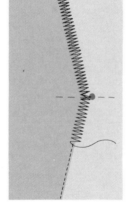

Outside corner

Inside corner

Sharp-angle corners.
Zigzag down one side of corner. Shortly before reaching point, start narrowing zigzag width. Continue stitching to just beyond corner (zigzag by then will be very narrow). Pivot and zigzag down the other side, gradually widening zigzag back to original width. Technique is the same for both outside and inside sharp corners.

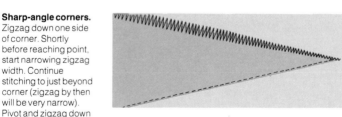
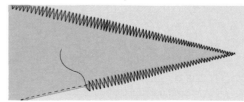

Tight curves. Zigzag down one side towards curve. To get around curve, stop and pivot work often, positioning needle on the narrower side of the curve each time work is turned. The technique is the same for both outside and inside curves.

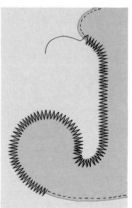

Securing by fusing

Appliqué can be secured with a fusing web, a bonding agent that holds two fabrics together when it is melted between them. Fusing works best on large appliqué pieces; alignment of appliqué and web becomes difficult with small or intricate shapes. Follow manufacturer's instructions carefully for a bond that will hold during normal cleaning.

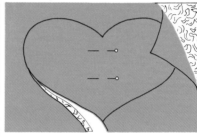

Pin fusing web to wrong side of fabric; treat two as one layer. Pin template to right side of fabric; trace around. Cut out appliqué on marked line.

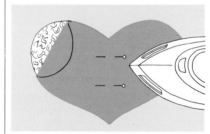

Pin appliqué and web to right side of background; be sure they are perfectly aligned. Heat-fix appliqué by pressing between pins with tip of iron.

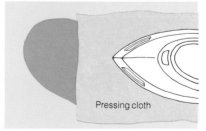

Pressing cloth

Remove pins. Place damp cloth over appliqué. Hold iron on cloth until area is dry. Lift iron and move to next area; do not slide iron.

197

Appliqué basics

Planning appliqué layering order

If the design of your appliqué is made up of two or more pieces, a certain amount of planning must be done to work out a numerical *order of layering*. This plan of action establishes the order in which the appliqué pieces will be laid down so that elements that should appear below others are properly positioned to do so.

This type of planning is especially important if the design consists of many pieces (see example, below right).

Use a drawing of your design as a map for your layering plan. Number each piece in the order in which it should be laid down. The elements that lie lowest are number 1, and subsequent layers

building upwards are numbered 2, 3, and so on. When layering order is established, each piece is stitched down in numbered sequence. All the pieces numbered 1 are stitched first, then pieces numbered 2 and 3, until the design is completed. An exception can be made to sequential stitching if you are

making several such appliqués. With this method, all pieces are pinned in layering order, then stitched at random. The result is not as neat as with sequential stitching, nor as secure, since hidden edges are not finished. But it is faster and, if the item is quilted, the incomplete stitching will not matter.

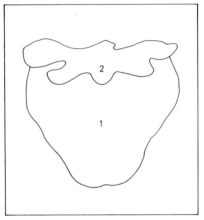

1. Make a layering plan on your drawn design by numbering each piece from lowest layer up. Following numbered plan, lay out actual appliqué pieces on marked background fabric as a check.

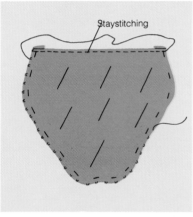

2. Remove all pieces except those numbered 1. Secure layer 1 in position, leaving unturned the edges that will be completely covered by another piece (top edge in the example above).

A layering plan is especially important in intricate compositions such as the sheep design shown here. As the numbering shows, six separate layers have been established in this design.

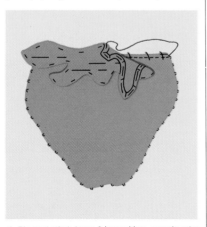

3. After the turned edges have been secured, use oversewing along the unturned edge of the appliqué as shown; this will prevent a bulky ridge showing through at the overlap.

4. Pin and stitch layer 2 in position, covering the raw edges of layer 1. If the design has more layers, continue layering and stitching in this way until the composition is completed.

In this illustration, layers 1 (cloud and mountain), 2 (meadow), and 3 (feet) have been appliquéd; layer 4 (bodies of sheep) is being pinned. Note how composition is being built from bottom layer up.

Using bias strips in appliqué

When a design calls for a thin, gently curved strip of fabric (for example, a stem), use a length of bias strip instead of cutting a thin, curved appliqué piece that can be difficult to manage. The bias strip has some stretch and can be shaped to the curve. Commercially packaged bias tapes are convenient, and are made in a range of colours.

To make your own bias strip, find the true bias by folding it diagonally so that a straight edge on horizontal grain is parallel to vertical grain (1). Press fabric on diagonal fold, open it out and use crease as a guide to mark parallel lines the desired width of the strip plus 1 cm for seam allowances (2).

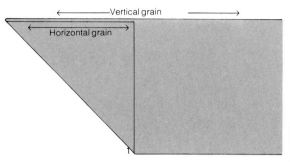

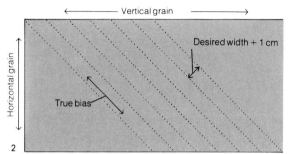

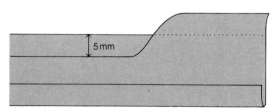

Cut bias strips along marked lines. Press under 5 mm seam allowance along both long edges of the cut bias strips.

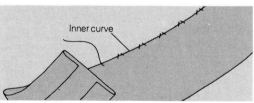

To secure, pin bias strip to background fabric, stretching it as necessary to conform to the desired curve. Secure the inner curve of the strip first.

Gently stretch outer edge of bias strip to shape to the curve; secure in place. Press bias strip after it is secured.

Interfacing an appliqué

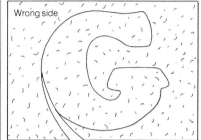

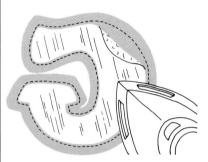

Appliqué fabrics that are limp or loosely woven usually need interfacing to give them stability and body for easier handling. Lightweight iron-on interfacings are usually the most convenient and can be bought by the metre. The wrong side of the interfacing is covered with a special bonding agent that will melt and adhere to another fabric when a hot iron is applied.

To interface appliqué, cut out appliqué as usual (see p. 194). Place template on *wrong* side of interfacing and trace. Cut out interfacing along marked line; do not leave any seam allowances.

Centre the interfacing over the appliqué so that wrong sides are touching, then press interfacing in place following the manufacturer's instructions. The appliqué is now interfaced and can be handled as you would a normal appliqué piece.

Stuffing an appliqué

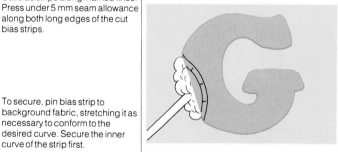

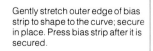

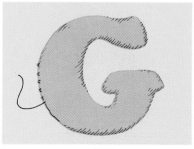

To add dimension to some appliqué designs, you can stuff the appliqué or parts of it with a soft wadding, thereby bringing the appliqué into relief. Either cotton or polyester wadding is suitable for this type of work.

To stuff an appliqué, first cut and secure it in place as described on pp. 194–5; instead of completely fastening the appliqué down, leave a small opening in a strategic area, and carefully stuff wadding through opening with a blunt needle or stick. Distribute the stuffing equally, but do not overstuff; this might distort the appliqué.

When you have finished stuffing the appliqué, stitch the opening down. Manipulate stuffing in this area if it has become flattened.

Appliqué basics

Decorating appliqué

Decorating with embroidery or quilting can greatly enhance the overall look of any appliqué design. Even though you may not deliberately plan on any such embellishment, possibilities may occur to you after your appliqué is completed. There is a vast array of **embroidery** stitches to choose from; you can use them to work out original details or special effects, or simply as a decorative means of securing the appliqué in place.

Quilting is another decorative device that can add immeasurably to appliqué, particularly for patchwork appliqué.

Before quilting is begun, a layer of wadding and one of muslin are placed under the appliqué background and all three are tacked together. The simplest form of quilting is called *outline quilting* – a single row of running stitches sewn around the entire design, or parts of it, to emphasise its silhouette. Several quilting lines stitched concentrically following the outline are known as *echo quilting*. These can add a whole new dimension to a design. Quilting stitches can even be part of a composition (see sheep illustration, lower right).

Embroidered details add a touch of realism to the simple appliquéd strawberry.

Embroidered cluster of grapes gives originality and charm to the appliquéd block initial.

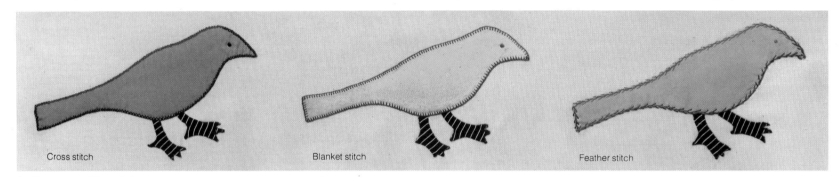

Cross stitch

Blanket stitch

Feather stitch

A different embroidery stitch is used to edge each of these appliquéd birds. The decorative stitches not only hold the appliqué in place, but also contribute colour and texture to the individual designs.

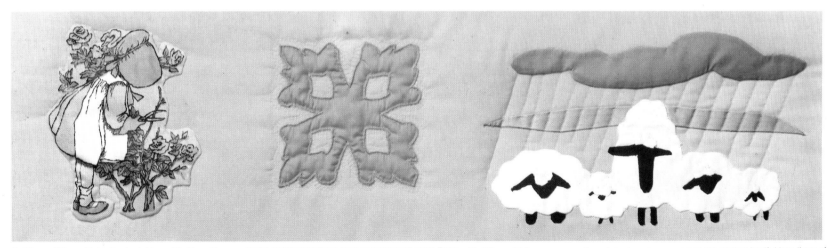

Outline quilting, stitched just outside motif, silhouettes and emphasises appliqué cut from fabric print.

Echo quilting radiates from an appliquéd motif. Technique is popular in Hawaiian quilts.

Quilting stitches are sometimes introduced as a part of the design itself. Here lines of quilting have been stitched to simulate falling rain.

Reverse appliqué

General introduction

Reverse appliqué, like surface appliqué, involves multiple fabric layers, but they are handled differently.

Reverse appliqué is known, in its traditional form, as **San Blas appliqué**, in honour of its best-known practitioners, the Cuna Indians from the San Blas Islands off the Panama coast. Even today, their colourful primitive designs decorate the front and back panels of the blouses, or *molas,* of the San Blas women. Their motifs are usually radiating, silhouetted shapes of people, plants and small creatures. These, plus slits that add strokes of colour, give this intriguing appliqué form its unique look.

Aspects of this traditional technique have been adapted to create a modern form of reverse appliqué that is known as **cut-through appliqué**. This technique can be successfully used with large, simple, bold designs like the sun design illustrated.

The basic difference between the traditional and modern forms of reverse appliqué is the order in which layers are cut and stitched, and the relative complexity of technique that this imposes. To produce the intricate channels of San Blas appliqué, you must work from the bottom layer up, cutting and stitching as each layer is added. Simpler cut-through designs require far less exacting techniques than those of the traditional method. For cut-through work, all fabric layers are tacked together at once, and shapes are cut out from the top layer down, producing larger to smaller 'shaped holes'. Special colour effects are made possible by variations on each technique; these are explained on the following pages.

Fabrics for either technique, ideally, should be tightly woven, lightweight, 100% cotton, and opaque. (Synthetic fabrics are too springy to turn under.) When you have chosen a pleasing combination of plain colours, find a matching thread for each fabric colour.

San Blas appliqué is distinguished by the radiating shapes and random slits. Surface appliqué and embroidery can also be used. This animal design was worked from the bottom layer up.

Cut-through appliqué is stencil-like in appearance. The fanciful sun design was systematically stitched and cut from the top layer down (see p. 266).

201

Reverse appliqué/San Blas

Basic technique

San Blas appliqué can be improvised, but to do this without losing the characteristic look, you must understand the basic technique, and the equal importance of the areas both *inside* and *outside* the drawn shape. When you work with only two layers of fabric, the drawn shape is cut from the top layer; at this point, depending on how the cutting was done, three different effects can occur (see variations on right). By interchanging these effects, you can get a variety of images, whether you use two layers, or decide to add a third. The total is rarely more than three, even in the most seemingly complex designs.

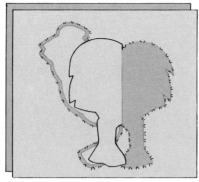

When a drawn shape is cut on the top layer, **the area inside can be removed,** and cut edges of outside area turned and stitched to bottom layer.

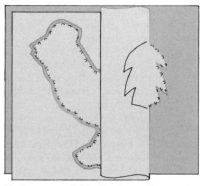

Or the area outside the drawn line can be removed. This time the cut edges of the inside area are turned and stitched to the bottom layer.

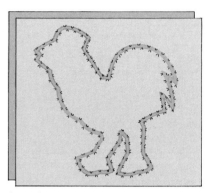

As a third alternative, **both inside and outside areas can be kept,** and cut edges on each side turned and stitched to create a channel.

Using two fabric layers

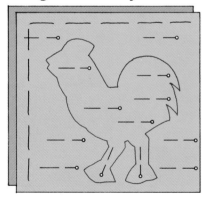

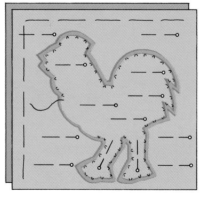

Using a total of only two fabric layers, you can still achieve the distinctive linear effect typical of San Blas appliqué.
1. Lay second fabric layer on first layer and tack them together around two edges. Draw or trace the main shape on to the top layer, and pin the two layers of fabric together inside and outside the drawn line.
2. Cut along the marked line, being careful not to cut layer below. Using point of needle, turn under the cut edges of the inside shape and slipstitch it to the layer below; clip curves. Cut and sew a small piece at a time for the best results.
3. Now turn and stitch the cut edge of the outside area the same way to produce the coloured channel that defines the shape. Remove pins.

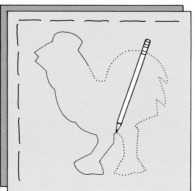

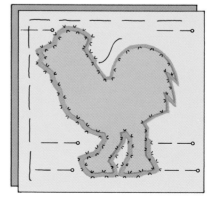

As a variation, a *third colour* can be added without adding a full third layer of fabric. This new colour can cover either the inside or outside areas of the drawn shape. In the example, the third colour covers the outside area.
1. Follow Steps 1 and 2 in instructions above. Remove tackings and take away parts of the top layer that are not stitched down.
2. Lay the third fabric over the first pair and tack fabrics together around two edges. With a sharp pencil, feel edges of main shape below and trace around it. Pin the layers of fabric together outside the traced line.
3. Cut along line of top layer only. Remove inside area to expose second colour below. Turn and stitch cut edges to bottom layer. Result is three colours, but only two full fabric layers.

Using three fabric layers

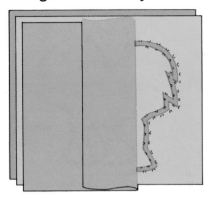 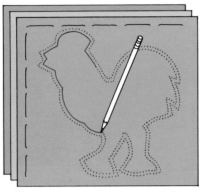 

Using a total of three fabric layers, you can achieve more elaborate linear effects.
1. After working first two layers (see opposite page), place third fabric layer over them, and tack all three together around two edges.
2. Using a sharp pencil, feel edges of finished channel below and trace around it. Pin all three layers of fabric together inside and outside the drawn channel lines. Now you must decide which part of the layer will be cut away and which part will remain (see Basic technique). Example shown is just one way to handle this third layer.
3. Cut along the inner marked line first. Turn under cut edges of the inside shape and stitch to layer below. Cut along outer marked line; turn and stitch the cut edges, turning enough to expose a total of three different channels.

Using slits in San Blas designs

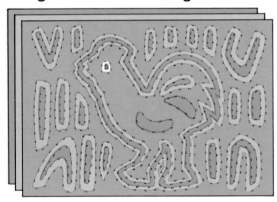

The series of elongated slits within the main motif and in the background is a typical feature of all San Blas appliqué. The slits are either *straight, angular* or *curved,* and are used at random according to the design's configuration. Slits can be worked on the second layer as well as the third.

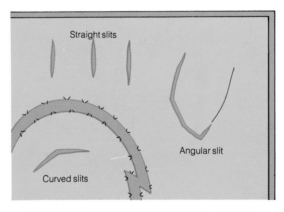

Straight slits

Angular slit

Curved slits

1. Draw desired slit lines on the uppermost fabric layer. Slits can be positioned in any direction. Cut on marked line through top layer only.

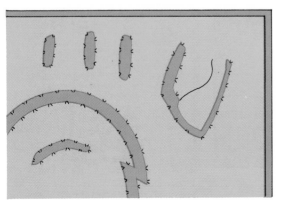

2. Using point of needle, turn cut edges under and stitch to the layer below, clipping as necessary to get around the curves and corners.

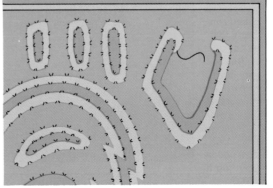

If third layer of fabric is added to piece already worked with slits, proceed first with the channelling of the main shape as described above. With a sharp pencil, feel edges of slits and trace around them. Cut along marked lines, then turn under and stitch cut edges to fabric layer below. An additional channel of colour will be revealed around the original slits as shown. New slits can be added to the top of the third layer as well.

203

Reverse appliqué/San Blas

Using coloured patches

Coloured fabric patches are another way of getting more colour into your San Blas piece without adding whole layers of fabric. This technique, like most of the San Blas methods, is intended to be improvised and can be introduced whenever you would like to add an extra colour. Merely tack fabric patches of the desired colours and sizes between any two layers of fabric; then cut away small shapes and slits to expose the additional patch colour below. In the examples shown, patches are applied to both the first and second layers. Select colours that will give you a strong contrast.

1. Cut and secure main motif (bottom left, p. 202). Position patches as desired; tack in place.

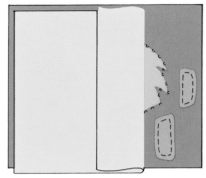

2. Lay next fabric layer over first layers and tack together around two edges.

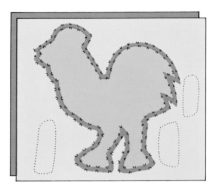

3. Complete the channelling of the main motif as described on p. 202.

4. Feel patched areas below; cut and stitch slits or shapes over them to reveal their colour.

5. Position more patches over the top layer of fabric and tack around each.

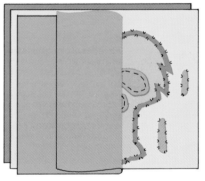

6. Lay another fabric layer over the first group and tack together around two edges.

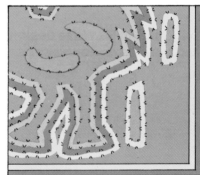

7. Complete channelling of main motif, then of the slits and smaller shapes over patched areas.

Using shaped patches

Another patch possibility in San Blas appliqué is a shaped patch. Its edges are meant to produce a predetermined contour, and are revealed to achieve that. This requires the patch to be cut to a definite shape and its edges finished neatly before the next layer is put down. Shaped patches, like standard patches, can be used between any two layers. A shaped patch along the edge of a major motif will change its overall silhouette and add interest to the colour (see example). The patch in the example is added to the first layer, with the main motif already stitched down (see p. 202).

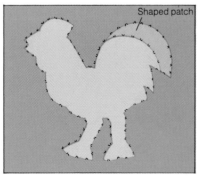

1. Cut patch to appropriate shape. Position over desired area; turn and stitch edges in place.

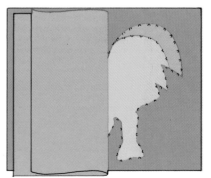

2. Lay next fabric layer over first layers and tack together around two edges.

3. Trace around motif, and complete channelling as desired to reveal edges of shaped patch.

Reverse appliqué/Cut-through

General introduction

Cut-through appliqué is worked with all layers tacked together first, then shapes cut away to expose the layer below; five layers are the maximum number used.

The first shape that is cut from the uppermost layer must be large enough to accommodate each subsequent shape to be cut within it. Cut-through designs are usually free and bold, and have an almost sculptured look. Because of the bolder designs, this technique can also be done by machine (see next page).

Sometimes a layer can be exposed out of sequence by cutting through one or two layers above it. Additional coloured patches can also be added if desired.

Basic technique

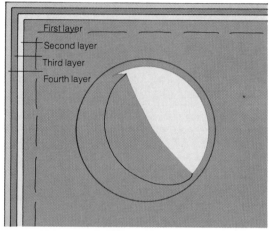

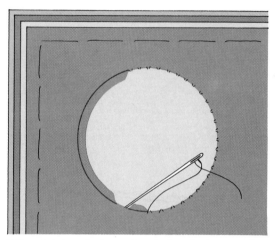

Cut desired number of layers to same size and stack them; tack together around outer edges. Trace or draw main shape (face) on top layer. Cut 3 mm inside marked line; do not cut layer below.

Using point of needle, turn under cut edge, clipping seam allowance as necessary to turn it under. Slipstitch turned edge to fabric layer below, letting a few stitches go through all layers.

Draw smaller parts of design that lie within the main shape. Decide which shape or shapes will expose third layer (in this instance, the mouth). Cut and stitch shape the same way as before.

Special cut-through techniques

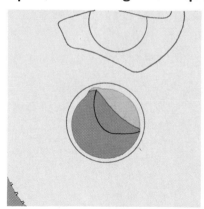

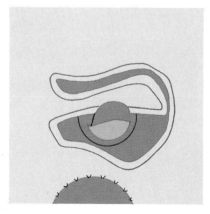

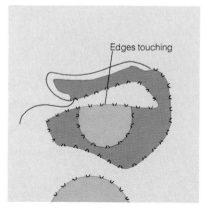

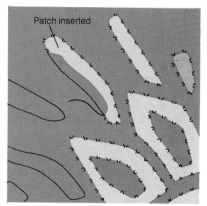

To miss a layer, cut shape (cheeks) from *two* top layers; cut brown one slightly deeper so edges lie under upper cream layer. Turn and stitch edges of upper layer to orange below.

With this multiple layer procedure, you can work a detailed area so that two shapes touch one another (rather than one lying inside the other). First cut away the larger shape (eye unit)

from top layer; do not secure edges yet. Draw and cut the smaller shape (eyeball) from newly exposed layer. Turn and stitch edges first of the smaller shape, then of the larger shape.

To add another colour, draw and cut shape (sun ray) from top layer. Cut a patch 5 mm larger than cut piece. Insert patch under upper layer, then turn and stitch cut edges to patch below.

Reverse appliqué/Cut-through

Basic machine technique

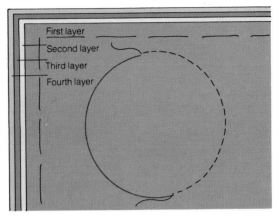

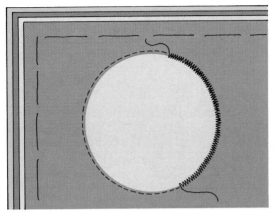

Cut desired number of layers to same size and stack; tack together around outer edges. Draw main shape (face) on top layer. Set short stitch length and straight-stitch on marked line.

Cut top layer just inside stitched line. Adjust sewing machine to suitable length and width of zigzag, then sew around cut shape to cover the raw edges and straight stitching.

Draw smaller parts of design that lie within the main shape. Decide which shape or shapes will expose third layer (in this case, the mouth). Stitch and cut as described for larger shape.

Special machine cut-through techniques

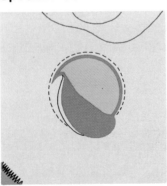

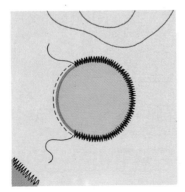

To miss a layer, straight-stitch around drawn shape. Cut away the shape (cheeks) from the two uppermost layers to expose the fourth layer below.

Zigzag over the cut shape to cover the raw edges and the straight stitching.

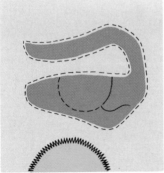

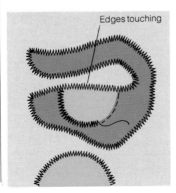

To work multiple layer procedure so two shapes touch, straight-stitch along larger marked shape (eye unit). Cut away shape just inside stitching line. Mark and straight-stitch the smaller shape (eyeball) on newly exposed layer.

Cut away small shape inside stitching line. Zigzag over cut edges of both large and small shapes.

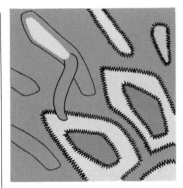

To add patch for extra colour, draw shape (sun ray) on top layer. Cut 3 mm inside the marked line. Cut a patch that is 5 mm larger than the cut-out piece.

Insert patch under cut edges of upper layer. Straight-stitch on marked line. Trim seam allowance even closer to stitching line. Zigzag over the raw edges.

Patchwork

Quilt, 'Aurora' © 1976 Michael James

Patchwork basics

Types of patchwork

Patchwork is the joining of pieces of fabric to form a larger unit of fabric. The most interesting characteristic of any patchwork is the design that the joined fabric pieces produce. Some patchwork designs are simple and easy to analyse, others are so intricate that it is hard to tell how they were achieved.

The easiest type of patchwork to understand is the **one-shape** patchwork, in which all the pieces are the same shape and size. A one-shape patchwork can be worked in a single colour, but two or more colours, carefully arranged, pro-duce a more interesting design. An example of the one-shaped patchwork is the Shell design (first illustration below).

All other patchwork can be classified as **block-unit** patchwork, so called because the fabric pieces are first joined into a block that itself becomes the basic shape. There are two kinds of block units, pieced ('mosaic' patchwork where the patches are inlaid or joined edge to edge) and appliquéd (where the patches are sewn in layers to a background fabric). Most pieced block units consist of precisely shaped pieces that form a definite design within a square; when several such units are joined, a secondary overall design can be formed as in Simple Star (below). Crazy patchwork is also a pieced block patchwork using random patches. An appliquéd block unit consists of an appliqué and the base fabric to which it is stitched. Appliqués tend to be stylised versions of realistic objects. For additional examples of patchwork designs, and instructions for producing geometric shapes, refer to pp. 210–15.

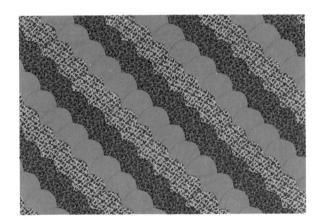

Shell design, a one-shape patchwork

Simple Star, a block patchwork of precisely shaped pieces

Crazy patchwork, a random-pieced block patchwork

Rose design, an appliquéd block patchwork

General considerations

Before any patchwork is started, two decisions need to be made simultaneously: the purpose of the patchwork, that is, whether it will be used for a skirt, a cushion, a quilt, etc.; and the patchwork design. Certain considerations can influence both choices. One is your level of experience. If you are a beginner, it is best to start with a comparatively small project, and a simple design that does not have too many pieces. Also, you might find it easier to copy an existing design than to create one.

Another influential factor is the construction techniques advised for different types of patchwork. There are basically only two methods of construction, both explained briefly on the right. The first is recommended mainly for one-shape patchworks because the shapes associated with them are difficult to join accurately by any other sewing method. Hand sewing here is preferable to machine; it adapts better to the variations involved in preparing and joining the pieces (see pp. 232–4). The second method is used for block-unit patchwork; in this case, joining may be done either by hand or by machine. Shapes that can be joined with straight seams will be easier to sew than those requiring cornered or curved seams. For more details on sewing block-unit patchwork, see pp. 220–31.

Also to be considered are the size and number of pieces that will be needed to produce the finished patchwork. Both of these are determined in the course of charting the entire patchwork (p. 217). In general, the more pieces a design involves, the longer it will take to make the patchwork. It should not be assumed that a large finished size necessarily means a great many pieces. A single block of Simple Star (opposite page), for example, can be made quilt or cushion size. Regardless of its size, each block would take the same number of pieces; in this particular case, 17.

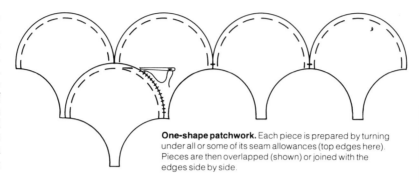

One-shape patchwork. Each piece is prepared by turning under all or some of its seam allowances (top edges here). Pieces are then overlapped (shown) or joined with the edges side by side.

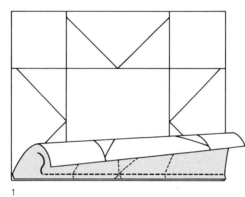

Block-unit patchwork. This type of patchwork can be sewn by hand or machine. First, the pieces are joined to form the individual block units (illustration 1). If it is a pieced block, the pieces are seamed to each other; for an appliquéd block, the appliqué is stitched to the base fabric. Next, the blocks are sewn together into strips of blocks (illustration 2). Finally, the strips are joined to complete the patchwork (illustration 3).

1

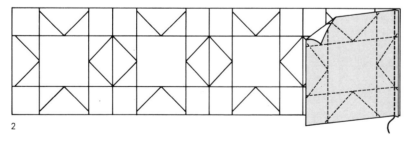

2

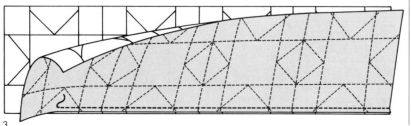

3

Fabrics and equipment

The fabrics for a patchwork should be compatible in weight, construction and care requirements. Similar weight and construction makes them easier to join and ensures that, when the fabrics are joined, one will not overpower and weaken the other. Medium-weight, evenly woven natural fabrics work best. When fabrics have common care requirements they can all be cleaned in one way, either laundering or dry cleaning, with no fear of some being ruined.

Before buying any fabrics, chart the entire patchwork (p. 217). A chart gives you a preview of the finished patchwork design, and it becomes the basis for experimenting with and deciding on suitable colour and print combinations. With a chart, you can also determine the exact size of each piece and then make templates (patterns) for cutting them out. Templates are also used to calculate how much of each fabric is needed to carry out the patchwork (p. 219). When you buy fabrics, try to find colours and prints that match or come close to those on the chart. If you are not sure how the fabric colours and prints will work together, buy a small amount of each and make a test patchwork. If you like the result, you can then buy the necessary quantities.

Certain drawing and sewing tools are needed. For designing and charting, you will need pencils, graph paper, a rubber, a ruler and colouring pens. A compass will help you to draw curves and circles; a protractor is used to divide a circle. Use heavy paper or thin card to make the templates. Scissors, pins, hand or machine sewing needles and thread will be needed for cutting and sewing. Thread should be either white or a colour that blends with the fabric colours. To mark fabric shapes and their seamlines, use a dressmaker's pencil. A white pencil is recommended for marking dark fabrics; a pink or blue pencil is best for marking light-coloured fabrics.

Patchwork basics

Designing with squares and diagonal lines

Of all the shapes used in patchwork, the most frequent is the **square**. It is possible to draw a very accurate square on graph paper, using its lines as guides.

During the designing of a pieced block, the square can be any size, but before templates are made it must be drawn to finished size (p. 218). In both design and template stages, the square is divided into smaller squares equal in size and number, across and up and down. These inner squares form the grid used to produce the shapes of the pieced design. The simplest division of a square is two squares across by two down, or a 2 × 2 grid, but other and finer divisions are possible (see below). The more squares in a grid, the greater the number and the variety of potential shapes. The pieced block designs on these two pages show the development from simple to complex patterns. To make it easier to 'see' the basic structure, the underlying grid of each has been emphasised in the drawings.

Some pieced block designs consist of just the grid squares, for example, the Chequerboard (1). In other designs, grid squares are grouped to form rectangles or larger squares; one such block design is Patience Corner (9).

Diagonal lines are introduced to form more intricate shapes. A diagonal may be drawn through a square or a rectangle; in either case, it is a straight line drawn from one corner to the diagonally opposite corner. When a diagonal line is drawn through a square, two half-square triangles are formed; when drawn through a rectangle, it produces two half-rectangle triangles. The triangles may be used as they are, or grouped with other triangles, squares, or rectangles to create shapes. Half-square triangles are the basis of the Windmill (2). Pairs of half-square triangles with their diagonal edges in opposing directions form the four larger triangles along the edges of the Simple Star (4). Pairs of half-square triangles with their diagonal lines parallel produce the rhomboid shapes that represent the 'scraps' in the Basket of Scraps (6). The centre piece of the Sally's Windmill block (14) results from joining two half-rectangle triangles to a grid square. The unusual shape in each corner of Crusader (15) is a grouping of three grid squares and two half-square triangles. Much of the effectiveness of pieced block designs hinges on the assignment of colours to shapes. For guidance in this, turn to p. 216.

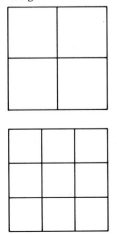

A grid is formed by dividing a square into smaller but equal squares. To do this, measure, then divide equally each side of the square; mark each dividing point. Draw grid by connecting sets of marks with straight lines from top to bottom, side to side. Shown left are a 2 × 2 grid (top) and a 3 × 3 grid (bottom). Right are a 4 × 4 grid (top) and a 5 × 5 grid (bottom).

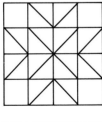

A diagonal line drawn between two diagonally opposite corners of a square or rectangle will form two triangles. The triangles can be used for the shapes of a design or grouped with other triangles, rectangles or squares. First illustration shows diagonals for Eight Point Star shapes (p. 222); the second, diagonals for shapes of Sally's Windmill (14, next page).

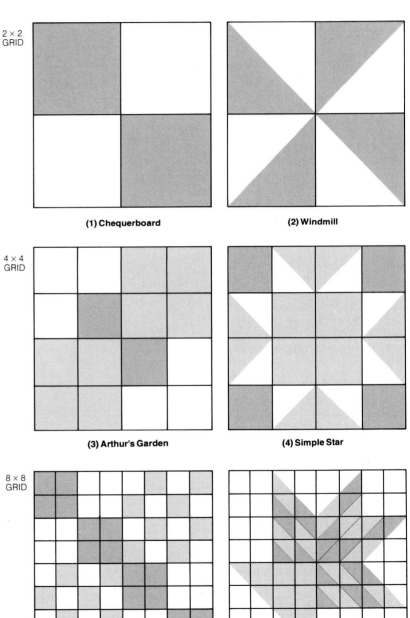

2 × 2 GRID

(1) Chequerboard

(2) Windmill

4 × 4 GRID

(3) Arthur's Garden

(4) Simple Star

8 × 8 GRID

(5) Mixed Squares

(6) Basket of Scraps

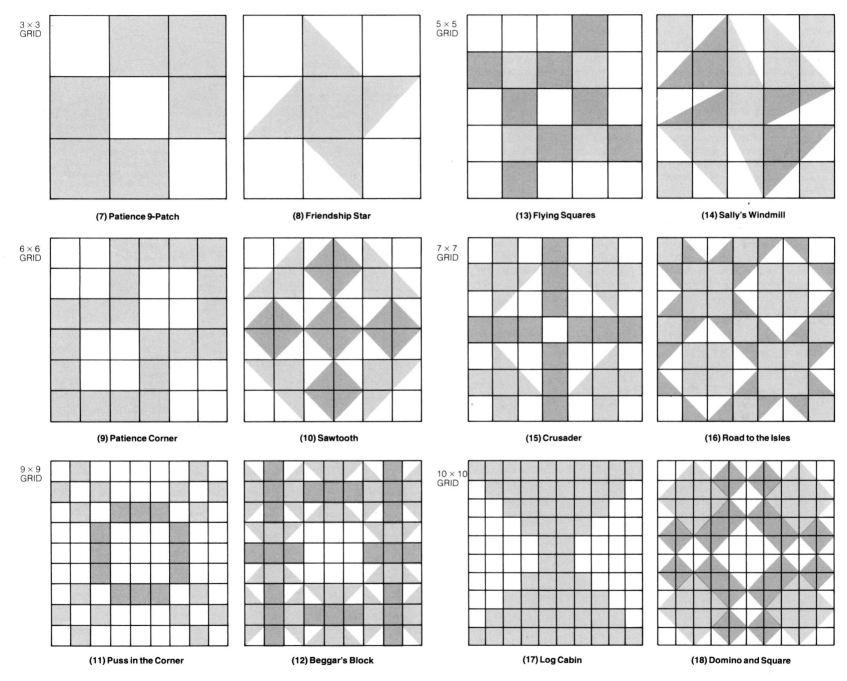

3 × 3
GRID

(7) Patience 9-Patch

(8) Friendship Star

5 × 5
GRID

(13) Flying Squares

(14) Sally's Windmill

6 × 6
GRID

(9) Patience Corner

(10) Sawtooth

7 × 7
GRID

(15) Crusader

(16) Road to the Isles

9 × 9
GRID

(11) Puss in the Corner

(12) Beggar's Block

10 × 10
GRID

(17) Log Cabin

(18) Domino and Square

Patchwork basics

Designing with circles and parts of circles

The use of circles and their parts to produce shapes is demonstrated by the patchwork designs on these pages. The techniques for forming the shapes accompany each design and are based on certain basic facts about circles.

A *circle* is a closed curve, of which all points are equidistant from a centre. Its perimeter is called the *circumference*. The distance from the centre of a circle to one edge is a *radius*, and equals half the circle's width. The *diameter* is the distance from edge to edge through the circle's centre (in effect, two radii); it equals the width of the circle. Any circle contains 360°.

A compass is used to draw a circle. Formation of a circle to a certain size is best accomplished by drawing it within a square. The size of the square and of the circle within it depend on the design

(see Dresden Plate; Grandmother's Flower Garden). Their common centre is located with vertical and horizontal lines that also act as diameters.

A portion of the circumference, called an *arc*, is also used to form shapes. A six-part division, with straight lines between division points, produces a hexagon (top of next page). An arc bounded by two radii creates a *sector*. Its shape depends on the length of the arc; that is determined by the degrees between radii. An arc equal to half a circumference and bounded by a diameter is a semicircle, containing 180° (see Shell). An arc equal to a quarter of a circumference and bounded by two radii at right-angles is a quarter-circle, containing 90° (see Shell; Drunkard's Path). To form a sector containing less than 90°, use a protractor (see Dresden Plate).

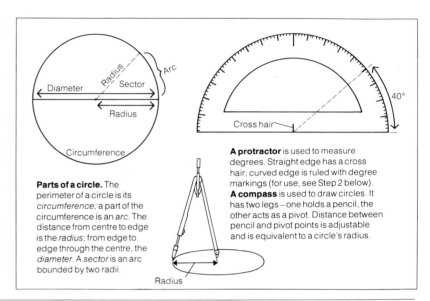

Parts of a circle. The perimeter of a circle is its *circumference*; a part of the circumference is an *arc*. The distance from centre to edge is the *radius*; from edge to edge through the centre, the *diameter*. A *sector* is an arc bounded by two radii.

A protractor is used to measure degrees. Straight edge has a cross hair; curved edge is ruled with degree markings (for use, see Step 2 below).
A compass is used to draw circles. It has two legs – one holds a pencil, the other acts as a pivot. Distance between pencil and pivot points is adjustable and is equivalent to a circle's radius.

Circles/Small sector

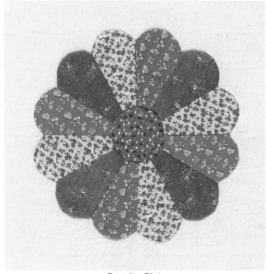

Dresden Plate
Concentric circles within a square supply the shapes for this appliquéd block design. The square determines the base block, also the large circle; from the large circle comes the **sector** for the wedge-shaped pieces. Small circle is the centre piece.

1. Draw a square (if you are making templates, draw it to finished size). Locate and mark the centre of each side. Connect marks on top and bottom edges with a vertical line, those on the sides with a horizontal line. The point where these lines intersect is the exact centre of the square. Place pivot point of compass on centre of square. Extend pencil leg out horizontally to a point close to the side of the square (if you are drawing a template to finished size, point is about 4 cm from side). Draw the circle.

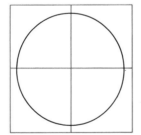

2. To determine the degrees in each wedge, first decide on number of wedges, then divide this number into 360 (circle contains 360°). Appliqué on left has 12 wedges; each wedge contains 30°. To form a sector with the desired number of degrees, proceed as follows: align straight edge of protractor along horizontal centre line; align its cross hair with vertical line. Find desired degree marking along curved edge of protractor and mark (30° in this case).

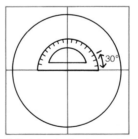

3. Remove protractor. Using a ruler, align the exact centre point of square and the angle marking. Hold ruler in place and draw a radius from the centre, through the angle measurement mark, to circumference of circle. Remove ruler. The horizontal centre line of the square serves as the second radius for the sector.

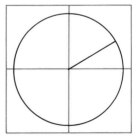

4. Working freehand, curve the outer edge of the sector as shown. Then place pivot point of compass on centre of square, and spread pencil leg enough to draw a small circle. Small circle is the finished shape for the centre piece of the appliqué. The sector, from its newly curved outer edge to the small circle, is the finished shape of each of the wedges in the appliqué. If making templates, only these two shapes need be drawn. If still in the design stage, roughly sketch in the other wedge shapes.

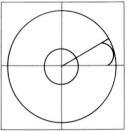

Circle/Small arcs

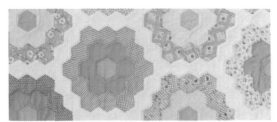

Grandmother's Flower Garden

Baby Blocks

A circle divided into six arcs underlies a **hexagon,** the six-sided figure repeated in both patchworks on the left. *Grandmother's Flower Garden*, the first example, consists simply of small hexagons; the hexagons in *Baby Blocks* are large, and each is composed of three equal size **diamonds.** The first step in constructing a hexagon is to draw a square with sides equal to the height of the desired hexagon. The finished hexagon will be the same height as the square, but narrower. In general, the hexagons for Grandmother's Garden are 4 cm high by 3.5 cm wide, and the hexagons for Baby Blocks are 15 cm high by just over 13 cm wide.

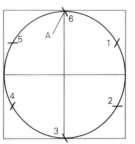

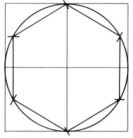

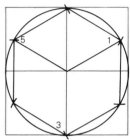

To draw a hexagon. Draw a square and find its centre (Step 1, facing page). Draw a circle same width as square. With compass at same setting, divide circumference into six equal parts by means of six arcs, 1 to 6. Draw first arc with pivot of compass at point A; draw each new arc with pivot at point where arc just drawn intersects circumference.

Then draw the six sides of the hexagon. For each side, line up two adjacent arc intersection points along the edge of a ruler and draw a straight line from point to point.

For Baby Blocks, start by drawing a hexagon. Then divide the hexagon into three equal diamonds as follows: draw a straight line from intersection point 1 to the centre; another line from intersection point 5 to the centre. Bottom of vertical centre line from centre to intersection point 3 acts as the other dividing line.

Semicircle/Quarter-circles

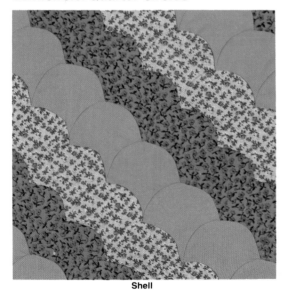

Shell

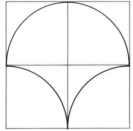

Draw a square and find its centre (Step 1, facing page). With pivot point of compass on centre, extend pencil leg along the horizontal centre line to side of square; form a semicircle in upper half of square. With compass at same setting, place pivot on lower left corner and form a quarter-circle; move pivot to lower right corner and form another quarter-circle.

A semicircle and two quarter-circles produce the shape repeated in the *Shell* patchwork. To form the shell to a desired finished size, begin with a square the height and width of the shell (the most common actual size being 8 cm).

Drunkard's Path

A quarter-circle smaller than a square is what must be drawn to produce the repeat in this pieced block design. The block begins with a square divided into a 4 × 4 grid; identical quarter-circles are drawn with compass, guided by 16-square grid.

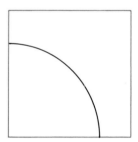

Draw a square; divide into a 4 × 4 grid (p. 210). With pivot of compass on corner of grid square, extend its pencil leg along one side of the square to a point about three-quarters along the side. Draw a quarter-circle by swinging the pencil to the opposite side. For templates, only one quarter-circle need be drawn. When designing, form a quarter-circle in each grid square, keeping the compass at a uniform setting; follow illustration on left for placement of quarter-circles.

213

Patchwork basics

Designing appliqué

The appliqué block units used most often consist of a **single** or **multiple-layer** appliqué and a square of base fabric. As the names imply, the first appliqué type consists of one layer of fabric, the second of several layers. Because of the one fabric layer limitation, single-layer appliqué can have only one colour and the shapes are usually those of simple, recognisable objects that you can trace or draw freehand. Maple Leaf is a single-layer appliqué. A more intricate design, such as the Snowflake, can be formed by cutting a design through a folded piece of paper (p. 193). Multiple-layer appliqué can have more than one colour; the designs, which can be drawn or traced, can be more realistic than single-layer designs. The Rose and the flowers in the Basket of Flowers are examples.

When designing appliqué, draw the base square and appliqué any size; at the template stage, draw them to finished size. The appliqué must fit within the square; some space can be left between the appliqué and the edges of the square as background. To draw designs to their proper size, see pp. 14–15; for a folded-paper design, use a piece of paper the size of the appliqué.

There are two other types of appliqué block units. One consists of a **pieced** appliqué and a square of base fabric. The appliqué is designed to fit in the square; the area for the appliqué is sub-divided to form the shapes of the appliqué. An example is the Dresden Plate, see p. 212. The last type of appliqué block unit combines a single or multiple-layer **appliqué** with a **pieced block**. An example is the Basket of Flowers. To design such a unit, draw a square, sub-divide it into a grid, and form a pieced block design (pp. 210–11). Then design an appliqué to fit an area of the block. Basket of Flowers is based on a 6×6 grid; appliqué fits its upper part.

Maple Leaf

Snowflake

Rose

Dresden Plate

Basket of Flowers

Crazy patchwork

Crazy patchwork design is unique among pieced block patchworks in that the pieces that form the design are random sizes, shapes and colours. Originally, crazy patchwork was worked as one large block unit. An easier way of working is to sew the pieces to form small block units, then sew these blocks together. The only element that has to be exact in size and shape is the block of base fabric to which the pieces are sewn, this is decided during charting (p. 217). For a method of deciding the arrangement of the pieces, see right.

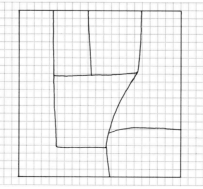

A sketch of an arrangement of shapes for one or all of the blocks can be helpful in designing and working a crazy patchwork. The most difficult aspect of crazy patchwork is imagining how random shapes will work together. By drawing an arrangement of shapes, you can see the design they form, and alter any of the shapes before they are cut out. You can even colour in the sketch to see how colours will work in the design. A tinted sketch can serve as both a shape and a colour guide when you are cutting out the pieces. If you like, you can make a finished-size replica of the sketch, cut it apart, and cut the fabric pieces from the paper pieces. Remember, if you do this, to add a 5 mm seam allowance to each piece.

Dividers and borders

Two other elements in patchwork are dividers and borders. Made of strips of fabric, they are joined to other patchwork units to become part of the overall patchwork fabric. Dividers are sewn between blocks and strips of blocks; borders are sewn to the outer edges of the joined patchwork units. The best time to plan for them is when you are charting the design (p. 217). It is then that you can see the needs of the overall patchwork design; you are also able to decide if the addition of a border or divider or both will produce a more desirable finished size for the patchwork. Although their main function is to 'frame' other patchwork units, an interesting patchwork fabric can be formed by sewing these strips to each other. This is known as a *strip quilt.*

Depending on the effect you want, the strips can be made of continuous fabric lengths or of pieced lengths. Strips made from continuous fabric lengths do not require finished-size templates; just calculate their length and width and add a 5 mm seam allowance at each edge. If necessary, plan to join lengths to achieve the measurement you require. Additional decoration can be supplied by appliqué. If using appliqué, decide where it will be placed and design it to fit that area. Appliqué will need finished-size templates.

Pieced fabric strips are made up of small and relatively simple pieced block units. To design a pieced strip, decide on a suitable block design and plan to repeat it for the length of the strip. Some designs are shown on the right; for more information, turn to pp. 210–11. While designing, pay attention to corners and other points where strips will meet. Some pieced designs will not match at these points; the easiest remedy is to use a plain square at corners or intersections. With other pieced designs, a different colour arrangement in the block will make the design work.

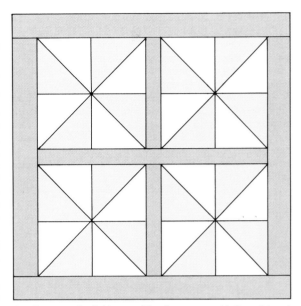

Continuous-strip dividers and borders are used in the patchwork above. They can be left plain (as above) or decorated with appliqué. Several examples of appliquéd strips are illustrated below.

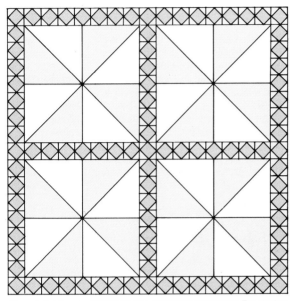

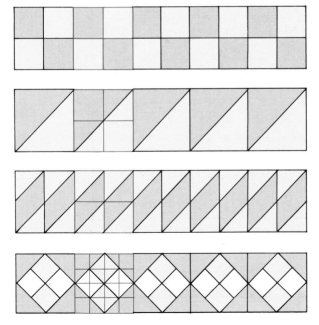

Pieced dividers and borders are used in this patchwork. The design of a pieced strip is formed by the repetition of a small pieced block. Notice the base block units outlined in the pieced strips below.

Patchwork basics

How colour can influence a patchwork design

Colour selection and arrangement are central to the overall design impression of a patchwork. It is simple to choose and arrange colours for a single pieced block, but for a multi-block patchwork you must consider the effect of colours on one another when many blocks are joined.

Choose colours carefully. Their arrangement depends on the area you want emphasised – whether you want the design of the *individual units* to stand out, or prefer to develop a *secondary overall pattern* from the combined units.

Supposing you like the idea of a secondary pattern, should it have more impact than the individual units? Or would you like to create the illusion of an interplay between the two, with first one and then the other predominant?

Getting the effect you want calls for experimentation with colours and their arrangement. A good way is to try out colour plans over a charted patchwork (see far right, opposite page). Bear in mind, as you do, these general colour theories as they apply to patchwork.

The dominant colours – reds, yellows and oranges – stand out more than do blues, greens and violets. Thus in combining, say, red and green, put red where you want emphasis.

Lighter tones, as a rule, show up more than darker ones, depending on the original colour they come from. Pink, derived from red, will stand out more than a comparable tone of blue. **The more space a colour covers,** the greater its strength will generally be.

Place emphasis in a patchwork *within* the units if you want their design more obvious; *at their edges* if you prefer to stress the secondary pattern. To equalise the two, balance colour strength and quantity among all pieces of all units.

Position of units, too, can affect a design's look. Notice below the dramatic result of setting blocks diagonally. On the opposite page, plain blocks and dividers separate the pieced blocks, emphasising their design but also creating another kind of secondary pattern.

Printed fabrics For patchwork, the small patterns are best. Small prints create an impression of dots. Prints with straight lines produce striping.

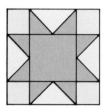

Concentration of one colour over the entire star shape gives that area great impact, strong enough for the block unit to remain dominant in the total design. The colour itself, being moderate in value and having yellow and red as its major components, contributes to this emphasis.

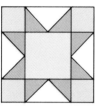

The colours here are balanced in mass and comparative impact; their weight evenly distributed over the patchwork piece. Let your eye move naturally from shape to shape, and you will perceive the play back and forth from unit design to secondary pattern.

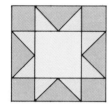

Blocks set on the diagonal, with strong colour emphasis at their edges, show the striking difference unit arrangement can make. The eye is drawn diagonally, making the secondary pattern more prominent than the unit design. It takes effort, in fact, to find the block design in the pattern.

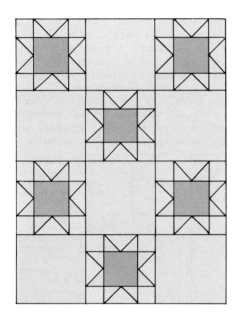

Alternating plain and pieced
blocks is undoubtedly the surest
and easiest way to make unit
designs stand out, if that is your
preference. In every sense of the
words, the plain blocks set the
pieced blocks apart, giving them
great clarity and definition. This
idea is worth considering for a first
try at design because it avoids the
extreme colour reactions that can
occur when pieced blocks are set
edge to edge. The plain blocks
could be a totally different colour
from any in the unit design, but it is
simpler and more effective to pick
up one of those in the pieced block.

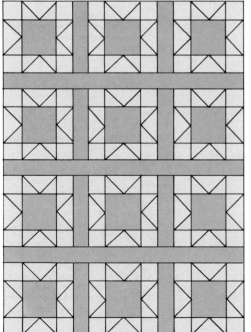

Dividers emphasise unit designs
as a frame does a painting. They
are made of continuous fabric
strips, but they could also be
pieced (see p. 215). Dividers are
often introduced into patchwork to
bring it up to a required size. If you
preferred to place the pieced
blocks edge to edge, you could
use borders instead of dividers to
increase the size. It is also possible
to combine the two. For details
about these and other possibilities
offered by borders and dividers,
see p. 215. Techniques for joining
them to blocks appear on pp.
230–1.

Charting a patchwork

Before actually charting a patchwork
design, assign measurements to all the
different units and see how they will fit
into the approximate finished measurement of the patchwork. Then, if the
combined measurements do not add up
to near the desired finished size, alter
the size or number of the units. Sup-
pose, for example, you want your
finished patchwork to measure approximately 2 m × 2.40 m and you plan to
use five Simple Star blocks across by six
down, with dividers between blocks and
strips of blocks. If 30 cm blocks are
used, they total 1.50 m × 1.80 m; if the
dividers are 8 cm wide, the total is only
1.82 m × 2.20 m, smaller than the
desired 2 m × 2.40 m. Add a 10 cm
border, and the total measurement
would be 2.02 m × 2.40 m, almost

exactly the right size. Another plan,
which would produce exactly 2 m ×
2.40 m is shown below. It uses larger
(40 cm) but fewer blocks (four across by
five down) and a 20 cm border. The
blocks total 1.60 m × 2 m; the border
brings the total to 2 m × 2.40 m.

If the combined units produce a satisfactory design, chart them to scale on
graph paper and record the finished size
of each. Then decide the best colour
plan for the design. Place tracing paper
over the chart and colour in all pieces.
Use a new piece of tracing paper for each
colour plan; leave the selected one on the
chart. In buying fabrics, try to get as
close a colour match as possible. Refer to
the chart when making and using templates (pp. 218–19). Use the chart as a
guide when you sew the patchwork.

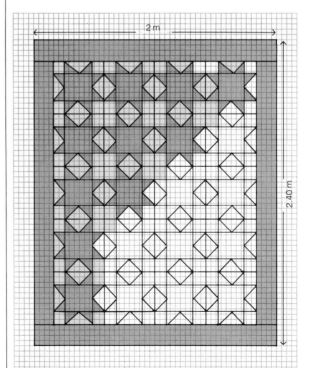

Finished size:
2 m × 2.40 m
Units:
20 Simple Star blocks
each 40 cm square and
coloured as shown

4 brown border strips,
each measuring 20 cm
× 2 m. (When cutting
out, add 5 mm seam
allowance to each side)

Preparing and sewing a block-unit patchwork

Making and using templates
Choosing a joining sequence
General sewing techniques
Straight seams
Cornered seams
Curved seams
Seams through a base fabric
General techniques for appliqué
Single-layer appliqué block units
Multiple-layer appliqué block units
Pieced appliqué block units
Appliqué-pieced block units
Joining blocks, dividers
and borders

Making templates

The first step in the construction of a patchwork is to make a cutting and a marking template (pattern) for the different shapes in the design. To make templates of the correct size and shape, first draw to finished size each of the units in the patchwork that require templates. (All but crazy patchwork and continuous strip dividers or borders, pp. 214–15, will need templates.) For guidance in drawing patchwork units, see pp. 210–15. When units are drawn to finished size, study each one to determine the combination of shapes that can be most easily joined to form the unit's design. For example, when a Simple Star block is coloured as below, the first impression is of a one-piece star surrounded by separate triangles and corner squares. If you look more closely, you will see that the star, too, is composed of several pieces – namely, a large centre square, with small triangles making the points. Though it may seem otherwise, the second of the two combinations will be easier to join. To understand why, see p. 220 on choosing a joining sequence. When the shapes have been decided, make templates using sturdy paper or thin card (see below).

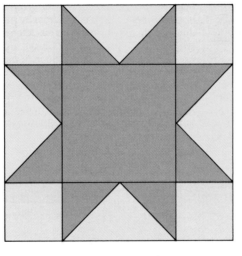

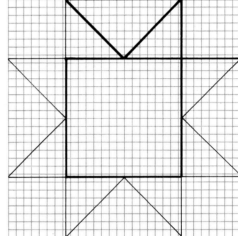

To make templates,
proceed as follows:
1. On graph paper, draw the patchwork unit to its finished size.

2. Study the unit and determine the shapes that will need templates.

3. Carefully cut out one of each of the required shapes from the finished-size drawing. For example, the shapes needed for a Simple Star block are a large and a small square and a large and a small triangle. These shapes are indicated on the left by heavy lines.

4. Place cut graph-paper shapes on sturdy paper or thin card, trace around each. Remove shapes and cut out new pieces along traced lines. These are your *marking* templates.

5. Place graph-paper shapes back on the heavy paper, leaving 2 cm to 4 cm between them; tape in place. Mark several points 5 mm beyond each edge of each shape. Draw lines to connect marks; cut out new pieces along these lines. These are your *cutting* templates. The 5 mm between graph-paper shape and edge of template is the seam allowance needed to sew the pieces together.

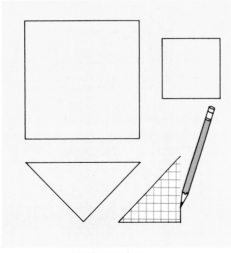

Marking templates

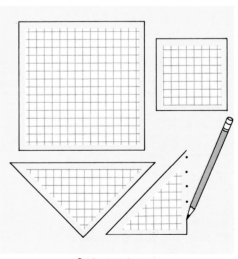

Cutting templates

Using cutting templates

Cutting templates are used first to determine the amount of fabric needed for a patchwork, then to cut out the pieces (see right).

Look at your charted patchwork and list the number of times each shape appears in each colour. Then, using one of the templates, see how many times it can be repeated across the fabric width (usually 90, 115 or 150 cm). Divide the number of times each shape appears in one colour by the number of units that fit across one fabric width; multiply the answer by the depth of one row (actually of one shape) to get the total length needed. Repeat for each shape; add the totals for each colour to determine the amount required of each. To allow for mistakes, always buy a little extra of each colour.

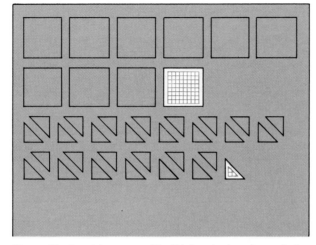
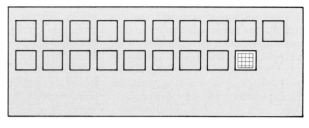
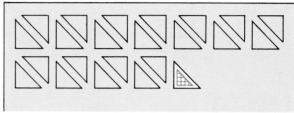

Place cutting template on wrong side of fabric and, using a dressmaker's pencil, draw its outline. Repeat until all of the pieces are drawn; be sure to draw the correct shape on the correct colour fabric. To save fabric, pieces can be drawn closer together than as shown here.

Special layout and cutting plans

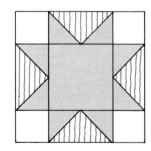

If using a one-way print fabric, such as a stripe, draw the shapes to reflect the direction you want the print to take in the finished block. Triangles were laid out as below so that the stripes would be as shown above in the finished block.

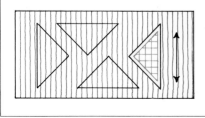

Shapes, too, can have a one-way direction. Two examples are the Dove appliqué (above, left) and the rhomboids in the Eight Point Star (above, right). When tracing the template of a one-way shape, place it on the wrong side of the fabric but in the direction opposite to its finished direction. The resulting cut piece, when it is turned to its right side, will face in the proper direction. The illustrations below show the shapes traced on the wrong side of the fabric, then the resulting cut shapes when turned to the right side.

Using marking templates

Marking templates are used in preparing cut fabric pieces for sewing; how they are used depends on the method of joining the pieces. Since most are joined with plain seams, a marking template is used mainly to mark seamlines (below). In appliqué pieces, marked seamlines are used as guides for staystitching and for turning seam allowances under; sometimes the marking template itself is used as a guide for pressing seam allowances back (p. 227). The marking templates of some one-shape patchworks are used to make paper pieces (p. 233).

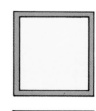

To mark seamlines, centre marking template on wrong side of cut shape; hold it in place and, using a dressmaker's pencil, draw outline of marking template on fabric.

Preparing and sewing a block-unit patchwork

Choosing a joining sequence

Before doing any sewing, you must decide the best sequence to follow in putting the separate pieces together. With an appliqué block unit, you must decide on a layering sequence (p. 226). With a pieced block, you need a sequence for joining smaller pieces into progressively larger units. Look, first, for small units 'built' by repeated joinings of the same shapes. Then check the shapes adjoining these for another repeated joining that will make those small units larger. The small units, with additions, form strips that, when joined, produce many blocks. Simple Star and Drunkard's Path, below, are examples. Some block designs are built from the centre (see the Eight Point Star, below).

Test whether your sequence will work by sewing one block. If it is not satisfactory, modify it until you find one that works, then follow it to sew all of the blocks simultaneously – that is, form all of the *smallest* units of all the blocks; then add the pieces that make them *progressively larger;* and finally, join the *larger strip units,* block by block, until all the blocks have been formed.

General sewing techniques

The pieces in a block unit may be joined with either hand or machine stitching. If it is an appliqué block, the appliqué is topstitched, usually by hand, to its base block (pp. 226–9). The pieces of pieced block units are generally joined with plain seams (exceptions: Log Cabin and Crazy blocks, pp. 224–5). **To form a plain seam,** place the pieces that are to be joined with right sides together and seamlines matched; pin and stitch through both layers on the seamline. Remove pins as you approach them; do not stitch over them. Hand-sew with a small running stitch (see below); set the machine to short stitches. The thread colour should blend with fabric colours. The character of a seam – that is, whether straight, cornered or curved – will depend on the shapes of the pieces. (See straight seams below and on the facing page; cornered and curved seams on pp. 222–3.) Press seam allowances to one side (except certain cornered seam allowances, which are pressed open). At cross seams, alternate the direction of the seam allowances; this will distribute the bulk more evenly.

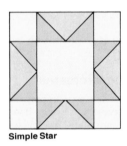
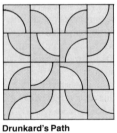

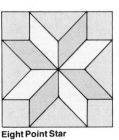

Simple Star

Drunkard's Path

Eight Point Star

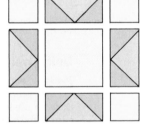
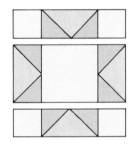
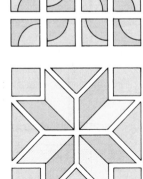
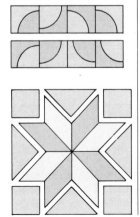
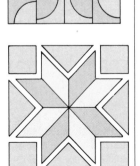

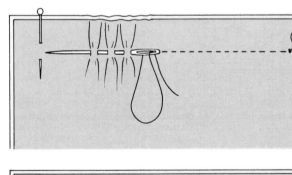

Machine sewing. Test stitch length, tension and pressure before starting to sew the blocks. Place stitches on seamline. Do not backstitch to secure stitches; tie thread ends if necessary (p. 222).

Hand sewing. Use running stitches. Weave needle in and out of fabric several times before pulling needle and thread through. Keep stitches and spaces between them short and even. Knot thread end to secure the start of the seam.

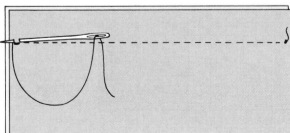

To secure the end of a seam, form a few small backstitches on top of each other.

220

Straight seams

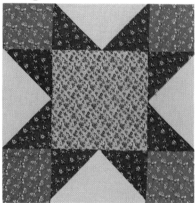

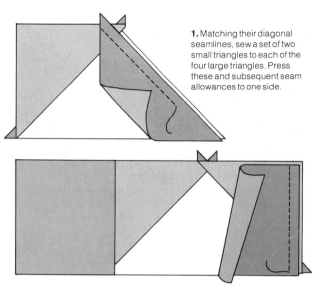

1. Matching their diagonal seamlines, sew a set of two small triangles to each of the four large triangles. Press these and subsequent seam allowances to one side.

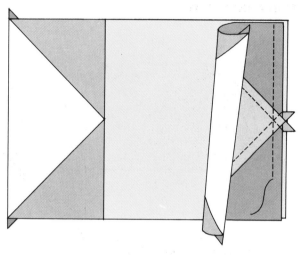

A large proportion of all the pieces in pieced block designs have straight edges and will therefore be joined with plain straight seams. An example of a block in which all of the pieces are joined with straight seams is the Simple Star. This block consists of 17 pieces – a large centre square, four small corner squares, four large and eight small triangles. The pieces are joined in the sequence shown on the right.

2. To form the top and bottom strips of the Simple Star block, sew a small square to each end of two of the triangle units that were formed in Step 1 above.

3. To form the centre strip of the block, sew the two remaining triangle units made in Step 1 to opposite edges of the large square. Take care to position the point of the large triangle and stitch across it exactly as shown above. This will ensure that the point of the triangle will be visible and will face towards the centre of the block when it is finished.

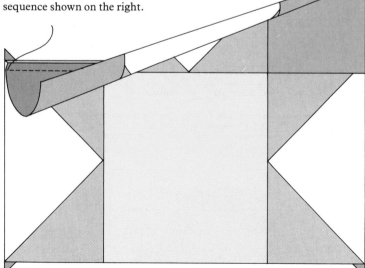

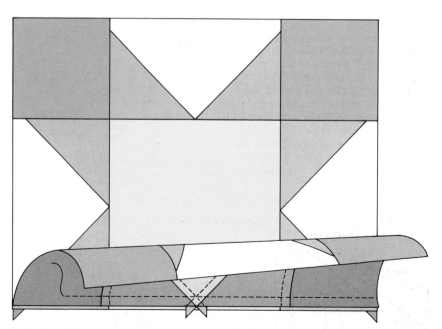

4. Sew the top strip to the centre strip. Match all cross seamlines and position and stitch across the point of the large triangle as was done in Step 3.

5. Complete the Simple Star block by sewing the bottom strip to the free edge of the centre strip. Be sure to match all cross seamlines and carefully position and stitch across the point of the triangle.

Preparing and sewing a block-unit patchwork

Cornered seams

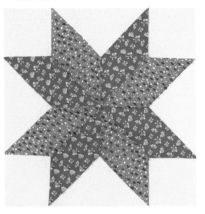

A cornered seam is used to join a piece having an outward-cornered edge to a piece with an inward-cornered edge. One will occur between each of the triangles and squares (outward corners) and the star unit (inward corners) of the Eight Point Star shown on this page. To prepare for a cornered seam, the inward corner is split; this allows the piece to be spread so its edges can be matched to the edges of the outward corner. If the inward-cornered piece is formed by the seaming of two pieces (as happens in the Eight Point Star), the split will automatically be formed by stopping the seaming of the two pieces at the inward-cornered seamline (Steps 1, 3 and 4). If a *continuous piece of fabric* forms the inward corner, the corner will need to be stay-stitched and clipped (see the first column of the next page).

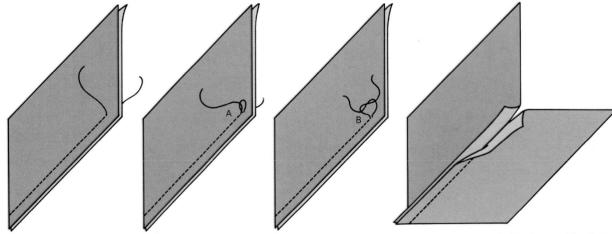

1. With long edges matched, sew a set of rhomboids together from edge of narrow corner to cross seam of wide corner. Pull top thread to bring up bobbin thread (A); tie together (B).

2. Form three more rhomboid units as explained in Step 1; press open the seam allowances of all four.

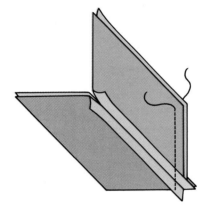

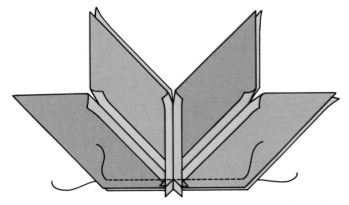

3. Sew two rhomboid units together; end stitching and tie threads as in Step 1. Press seam open. Sew remaining two units together the same way.

4. With right sides together, match seamlines and cross seams at lower edges of units made in Step 3; pin in place. Stitch units together, starting and stopping at the cross seamlines at each end of the matched units. Tie threads as in Step 1; press the seam open.

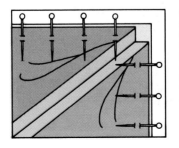

Squares and triangles are pinned and stitched to outer edges of star as follows. With right sides together and star uppermost, spread inward corner of star so its edges match those of piece being joined. Pin the two together, keeping seam allowances open.

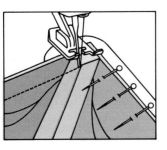

To sew first half of seam, stitch from edge of seam to corner; leave needle in fabric at corner. Lift presser foot; pivot fabric on needle to bring it into position for sewing the second half of the seam.

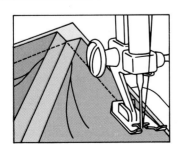

To sew second half of seam, lower presser foot and stitch from corner to end of seam.

222

If a continuous piece of fabric is used as the inward-cornered portion of a cornered seam, it must be reinforced with staystitching and clipped for flexibility as shown and explained below.

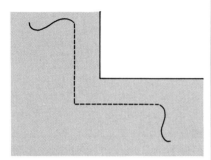

Reinforce the inward corner by placing a row of staystitching, just inside the seamline, for 2 cm on each side of the corner.

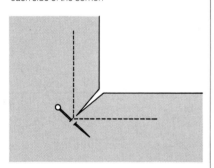

Clip the corner, being careful not to cut the staystitching. To avoid cutting these stitches, place a pin across the corner.

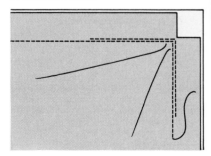

Spread clipped piece so its edges match those being joined to it. *Pin and stitch* through both layers as explained at bottom of facing page.

Curved seams

A curved seam is used when a piece with an outward-curved edge must be joined to one with an inward-curved edge. Such a seam forms each of the 16 small repeated units in the Drunkard's Path design illustrated here. To make the curved edges match, it is necessary first to staystitch and clip the inward-curved edge (Step 1). Then spread it to match the outward-curved edge and stitch through both layers on the seamline (see Step 2). To make the curved seams lie quite flat, press their seam allowances towards the inward curve. When all of the individual units have been stitched, they are joined to form four strips (Step 3); these strips are then joined with straight seams (Step 4).

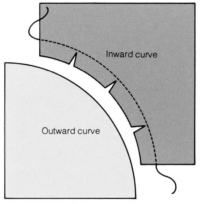

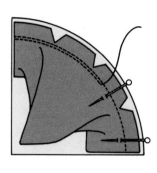

1. Prepare each inward-curved edge as follows: place a row of staystitching just inside the seamline. Then clip the seam allowance in a few places without cutting into the staystitching.

2. With right sides together and clipped piece uppermost, spread clipped edge to fit the outward curve. Pin and stitch along the seamline. Do the same for remaining 15 sets of pieces.

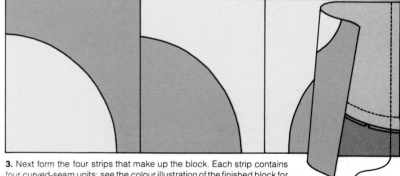

3. Next form the four strips that make up the block. Each strip contains four curved-seam units; see the colour illustration of the finished block for their position in each strip. Join units with plain straight seams.

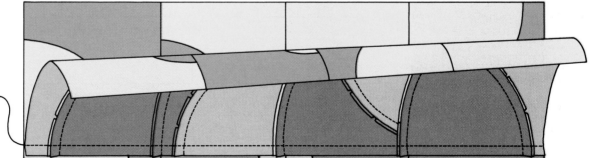

4. Sew the four strips to each other with plain straight seams, again referring to the coloured block for the position of individual strips. Be sure to match their cross seamlines exactly before stitching any of the strips together.

223

Preparing and sewing a block-unit patchwork

Seams through a base fabric/Log Cabin blocks

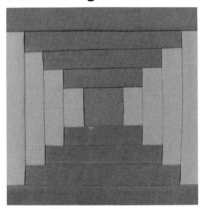

The pieces that make up Log Cabin blocks are seamed through a base fabric block as they are seamed to each other. Blocks are built from the centre out; the sewing sequence for the pieces (strips of graduated length) depends on the Log Cabin design. This design suggests an hour-glass.

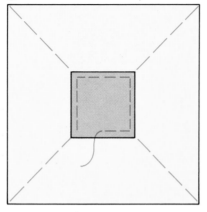

1. Fold block of base fabric diagonally in half, then into quarters; lightly press folds. Open up block, mark the folds with tackings; then press block flat. With its right side up, centre the centre square of the pieced design on the block; use the tackings as guides for position. Pin and tack square to base block.

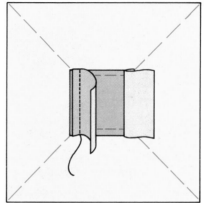

2. Sew the two shortest strips to opposite edges of the centre square. With right sides together, match, pin and stitch one strip to the right edge of square. Then turn the strip back to its right side and press it flat. Sew the other short strip to the left edge of the centre square. Turn it back to its right side and press it flat.

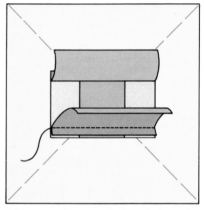

3. Sew the next larger set of strips to the top and bottom edges of the centre square and the strips sewn to it in the preceding step. Turn each strip to its right side and press flat. Continue sewing progressively larger sets of strips to the block, alternating their position from side to side, then to top and bottom. When all the strips have been sewn to the block, tack the free edges of the final strips to the base block of fabric.

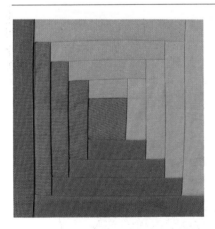

In another popular Log Cabin design, dark and light strips are grouped on opposite sides of a diagonal centre. The design here differs from the one shown above mainly in the sequence used for sewing the strips to each other through the base block of fabric (see right).

1. Mark base block of fabric and tack centre square in place as explained in Step 1 above. Then, with right sides together, match, pin and stitch the shortest light-coloured strip to the top edge of the centre square. Turn the strip to its right side and press it flat.

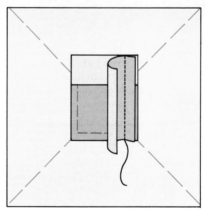

2. With their right sides together, match, pin and stitch the next longer light-coloured strip to the right edge of the centre square and the strip sewn to it in the preceding step. Turn the strip to its right side and press flat.

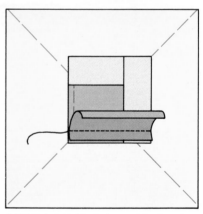

3. With their right sides facing, match, pin and stitch the shortest dark strip to the bottom edge of the centre square and the strip sewn to it in Step 2. Turn strip to its right side and press. Working clockwise, sew gradually longer sets of dark and light strips to block. End with the longest dark strip; turn and press each strip before sewing the next. Tack free edges of last round of strips to base block.

Seams through a base fabric/Crazy patchwork

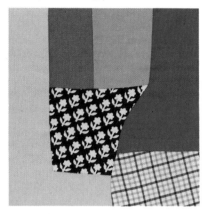

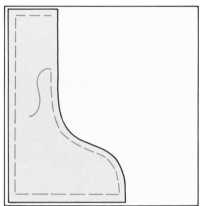

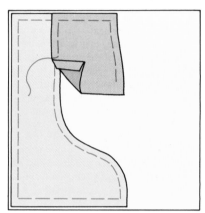

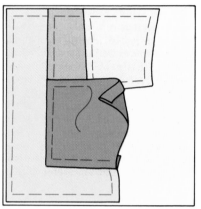

Crazy patchwork is different from other patchwork designs in that the only guide used for cutting the pieces is a sketch of the block's design (see p. 214). Also unique to crazy patchwork is the way in which the pieces are sewn to each other and to a base block of fabric (see the detailed instructions on the right).

1. Referring to your rough sketch of the block design (explained on p. 214), decide which piece should be laid down first. In general, it is best for the first piece to be laid along an edge of the block (left edge here). Cut a piece of fabric like the drawn shape, plus at least 5 mm seam allowance along each edge. Position the fabric piece, right side up, on base block of fabric; pin and tack it in place.

2. Decide which piece will be laid down next and cut a piece of fabric to that approximate shape, with 5 mm seam allowance along each edge. Position this piece, right side up, on the block, lapping it appropriately over the piece tacked in Step 1. Turn under the seam allowance of any lapped edge that will be exposed in the finished block; tack the piece in place along all of its edges. To turn under curved or cornered edges, see p. 227.

3. Continue to cut out and lap pieces one at a time and in the order of their relationship in the design. When cutting a piece, always remember to include 5 mm seam allowance along all of its edges; before tacking any piece in place, turn under the seam allowance of edges that will be exposed when the block is finished. When all of the pieces have been tacked in place, trim off any edges that extend beyond the edges of the base block.

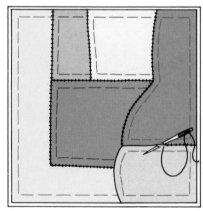

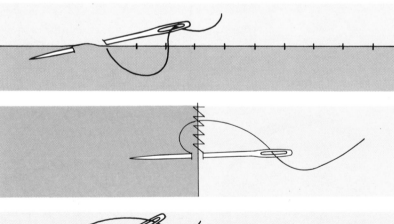

4. Secure each turned edge with hand stitches. If you want the stitches to be almost invisible, use either the slipstitch (p. 195) or the blindstitch, shown and explained on the right. For a more decorative finish, use the featherstitch (bottom right) or farmer's shirt stitch, to span both sides of the seamline. Finally, remove all tackings except at edges of block.

Blindstitch. Work stitches from right to left. Begin by bringing needle and thread through turned-under edge, back to front. Form stitches as follows: directly opposite point where thread comes out of folded edge, insert needle into block, take a small (about 5 mm) stitch, and bring needle out through turned-under edge. Pull needle and thread through, and repeat.

Farmer's shirt stitch. Hold seam vertical. To begin, bring needle and thread up on left side. Make a horizontal backstitch through the right side and bring the needle up the original hole. Make the next stitch a few threads down, from right to left, producing a slanted stitch. Continue making backstitches and slanting stitches.

Featherstitch. Hold seam vertical and work stitches down the seamline. To begin, bring needle and thread up on one side of seamline. Pass to opposite side, then, holding thread in place, point the needle diagonally down towards seamline and take a small stitch; keep thread under needle point. Pull stitch through, letting thread under it curve slightly. Cross to opposite side; repeat.

Preparing and sewing a block-unit patchwork

General techniques for patchwork appliqué

The first step in constructing an appliqué block unit is to make finished-size templates (p. 218) for all of the shapes in the appliqué as well as for the block if it is pieced (Basket of Flowers). If the base block is a continuous piece, no template is needed, only its finished measurement. Other elements, such as stems (in the Rose below) and the basket handle in the Basket of Flowers, can be made from bias fabric strips (p. 199). They are also exceptions and do not require templates; their finished measurements are sufficient.

Once all the pieces have been cut out and marked, the next step is to plan a **layering sequence,** that is, the order in which the pieces of the appliqué should be laid on top of each other. If it is a single-layer appliqué (for example, the Snowflake), no sequence is involved. For appliqué consisting of more than one layer, such as multiple-layer appliqué (Rose) or certain pieced appliqué (Dresden Plate), lay the pieces down in this order: the lowest layer first, and from the centre of the block out. Notice the sequence planned for the Rose

below. More examples of layering, as well as traditional construction techniques for appliqué block units, are given on pp. 228–9. For other appliqué methods, see pp. 192–206.

When planning a layering sequence, identify those edges that can be lapped under other pieces, and those that will be exposed and therefore must be turned under. The dotted lines in the schematic drawing of the Rose (below) signify lapped edges; all other edges will be turned under. It is usually easier to turn under the edges of the pieces before

they are positioned on the base block. When **turning an edge under,** turn it along its seamline and crease the seamline with either finger-pressing or an iron. If you have difficulty turning the edge, place a row of staystitching along the seamline or use the marking template as a pressing guide (next page). If the edge is cornered or curved, clip or notch it. After all the pieces have been tacked on to the block, hand-stitch the appliqué. Use either the slipstitch (p. 195), blindstitch or farmer's shirt stitch for a more decorative finish (p. 225).

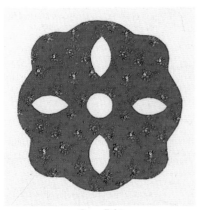

Snowflake

Rose

Dresden Plate

Basket of Flowers

Plan a layering sequence, that is, the order for laying down the pieces (indicated by numbers). Then decide which edges will be *overlapped* (dotted lines) and which *turned under* (all other edges).

Turning edges

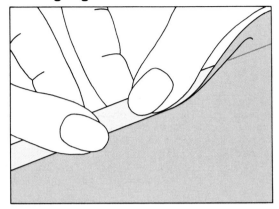

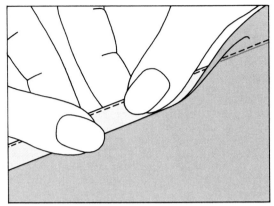

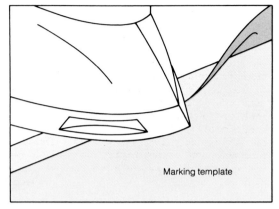

Marking template

Finger-pressing is one way of creasing a turned-under edge. Turn the edge under along its seamline, pressing the fold between your fingers as shown.

A row of staystitching placed just inside the seamline will make it easier to turn an edge under. While turning, use an iron or finger-pressing to crease the seamline.

A marking template can also be used as a guide for turning an edge under. Centre template on wrong side of piece and hold it in place. Then, using an iron, press edge back on to template.

Handling curves and corners

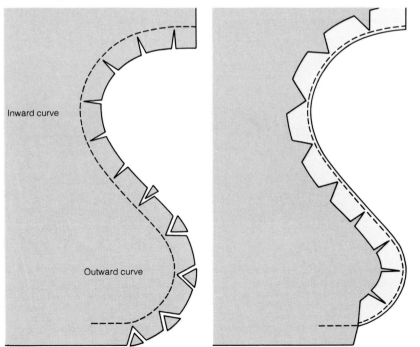

Inward curve

Outward curve

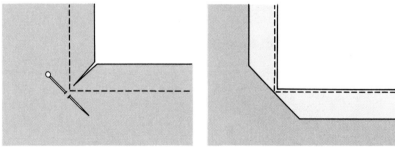

For an inward-cornered edge, first staystitch for at least 2 cm on each side of corner. Place a pin through stitches at corner, then clip up to the stitches. Pin keeps you from cutting into the stitches; clipping lets seam allowances spread so they can be turned under.

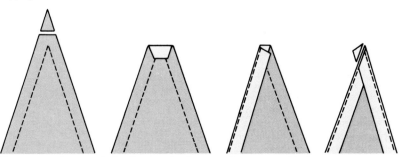

Curved edges will need to be either clipped or notched before they can be turned under; they should also be staystitched. If the edge has an *inward curve,* clip the seam allowance so it can be spread as the edge is turned. Notch an *outward curve* to reduce fullness and facilitate turning.

For an outward-cornered edge, first staystitch for at least 2 cm on each side of corner. Trim half of the seam allowance across the corner; then turn the remainder back across point of corner. Then, one at a time, turn back the seam allowance on each side of the corner; trim any excess seam allowances.

Preparing and sewing a block-unit patchwork

Single-layer appliqué block units

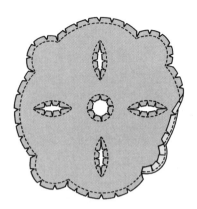

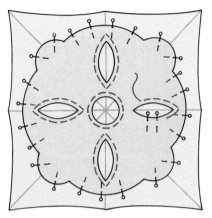

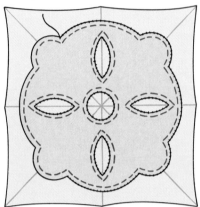

Appliqué block units involving a single-layer appliqué, such as the Snowflake above, are easy to construct. The only pieces called for are one fabric layer for the appliqué and one for the base block. All edges of such an appliqué will need to be turned under.

1. Using the methods described on p. 227, turn under all the edges of the appliqué. Since all the edges of this appliqué are curved, they should all be staystitched; then edges that have inward curves should be clipped and those with outward curves should be notched.

2. Fold base block of fabric in half, then into quarters. If parts of the appliqué must be centred diagonally, as do the four 'corners' of appliqué above, fold block into eighths as well. Lightly press all folded edges; open up block. Using foldlines as guides, centre the appliqué on the block. Pin and tack appliqué in place from centre out. Be sure to catch the turned-under edges in the tackings.

3. Working from the centre of the appliqué out, hand-sew the appliqué to the base block. If you want the stitches to be almost invisible, use either the slipstitch (p. 195) or blindstitch (p. 225) and a thread colour that matches the appliqué. For a more decorative finish, use an embroidery stitch; thread colour can match or contrast. Remove the tackings and press.

Multiple-layer appliqué block units

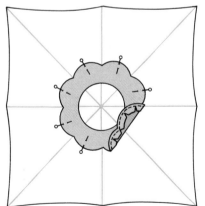

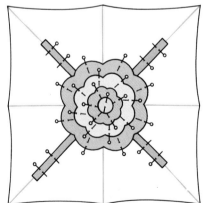

Before constructing a multiple-layer appliqué block unit, for example, the Rose above, plan a layering sequence for the appliqué pieces. When the sequence has been decided, identify the edges that can be lapped under other pieces and those that will need to be turned under.

1. Prepare all the pieces of the appliqué. Referring to its planned layering sequence (p. 226) and using the methods on p. 227, turn under only those edges that will be exposed. Form centring guidelines on the base block of fabric by folding it in quarters, and eighths if necessary (see Step 2 above). Begin to lay down and pin the pieces to the base block according to the planned sequence.

2. Continue to lay down the pieces of the appliqué according to the planned layering sequence, pinning each piece in place. If necessary, lift an edge so another can be lapped under it (as happens above with each stem at the edge of the centre rose).

3. When all the pieces have been pinned to the block, tack them in place. Remove pins as you tack, and work the tackings from the centre of the appliqué out to its edges. Then hand-sew the appliqué to the block as explained in Step 3 above.

Pieced appliqué block units

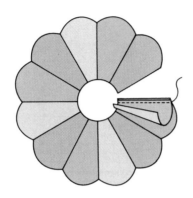

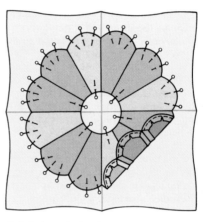

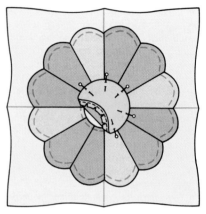

Some appliqué block units, such as the Dresden Plate, employ pieced block techniques to form all or part of the appliqué design. If more than one layer is involved, as is the case with the Dresden Plate, plan a layering sequence and determine which edges need turning.

1. Construct the pieced appliqué, using pieced block techniques (pp. 220–5). Choose those seaming techniques that are suited to the character of the pieces being joined; wherever possible, press seams open. The pieced portion of the Dresden Plate appliqué (above) is formed by means of plain straight seams; all of the seams are pressed open.

2. Referring to the layering sequence and using the techniques on p. 227, turn under the necessary edges of the appliqué. For Dresden Plate, the edge of the centre circle and outer edges of pieced portion need to be turned; before turning, each curved edge is staystitched, then clipped or notched. Form centring guides on the base block (Step 2, top of opposite page). Begin to lay down and pin pieces to block.

3. When all of the pieces have been pinned to the base block of fabric, tack them in place, removing the pins as you tack. When tacking, be sure that the turned-under edges are caught in the stitching. Then hand-sew the appliqué to the block as described in Step 3 at the top of the opposite page. Remove all tackings and press.

Appliqué-pieced block units

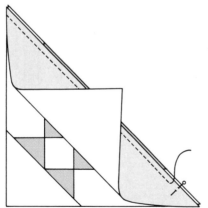

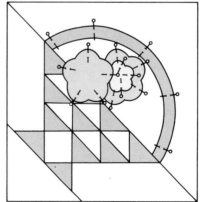

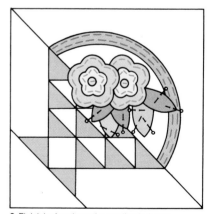

Certain appliqué block units combine a pieced block with a single or multiple-layer appliqué. Basket of Flowers is an example. Base block, including bottom of basket, is pieced; flowers and basket handle in the upper half of the block are a multiple-layer appliqué.

1. Construct the pieced base block, using the appropriate pieced block techniques (see pp. 220–5). Plain straight seams are used to join all the pieces in the block above; pairs of triangles are its smallest repeated unit. The lower half of the block is pieced first, and is then sewn to the upper half, which is a large triangle.

2. Refer to the planned layering sequence (p. 226) and turn under the appropriate edges of the appliqué, using the methods on p. 227. If necessary, fold the block to form centring guidelines (Step 2, top of opposite page). Begin to lay down the pieces of the appliqué; pin each in place. The basket handle is a bias fabric strip that has been shaped into a curve (p. 199).

3. Finish laying down the appliqué pieces, pinning each in place. When all are pinned to block, tack each in place. Remove pins as you tack; be sure to catch the turned-under edges in the tackings. Then hand-stitch the appliqué to the block (see Step 3, top of opposite page). Remove tackings and press.

Preparing and sewing a block-unit patchwork

Joining blocks, dividers and borders

In general, the best order for joining blocks, dividers and borders to form a patchwork fabric is as follows. Sew the units to form strips; sew the strips to each other; add the borders last. To determine how a particular patchwork should be formed, study its chart and mentally group the units into strips. In most designs, the strips go *across* the patchwork (see examples, immediate right). If vertical dividers are included, strips will be vertical (facing page, top left); in a diagonal setting (facing page, right), they will be diagonal.

The elements in a strip will depend on the units to be used and their arrangement in the design. If a patchwork is blocks only, the strips will be the same. If only vertical or only horizontal dividers are used, there will be, in addition to the strips of blocks, strips for the dividers. If *both* vertical and horizontal dividers are included (facing page, bottom left), there will be strips composed of blocks and vertical dividers and also strips for horizontal dividers.

Finishing techniques for any patchwork will depend on the item being made; refer to the Quilting chapter and the projects that follow Quilting.

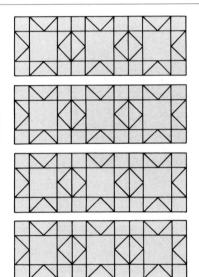
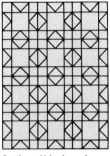

Setting of blocks only. Form strips of blocks to be set horizontally. Sew strips of blocks to each other. If setting contains *horizontal dividers* (not shown), sew block strips to divider strips – one divider between each pair of block strips.

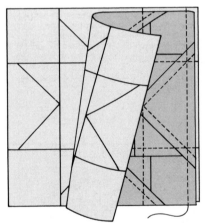

1. Join units to form strips. The number of units in a strip and the number of strips will depend on the planned patchwork. When joining units, use 5 mm seams; match cross seamlines.

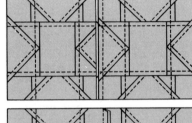
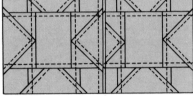

2. Press seam allowances between units to one side; alternate the direction from strip to strip. For example, press all in one strip to left, all in the next strip to the right.

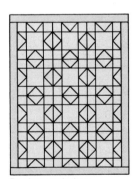

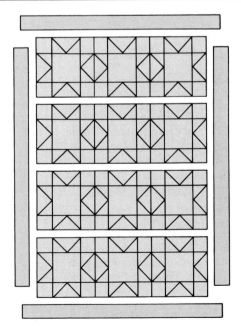

Borders are the last strips to be added to any patchwork. After all of the other units have been joined, sew a border strip to each edge of the patchwork – first to the right and left edges, then to the top and bottom.

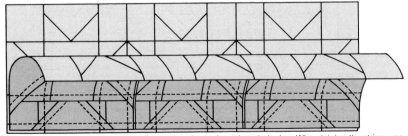

3. Join strips to each other according to the planned patchwork design. When joining the strips, use 5 mm seams and be sure to match cross seamlines. Press these seam allowances down.

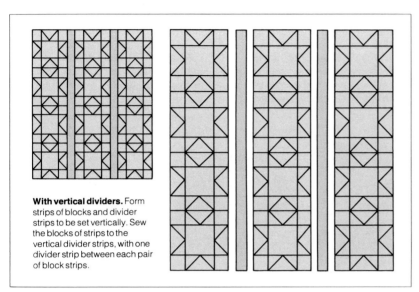

With vertical dividers. Form strips of blocks and divider strips to be set vertically. Sew the blocks of strips to the vertical divider strips, with one divider strip between each pair of block strips.

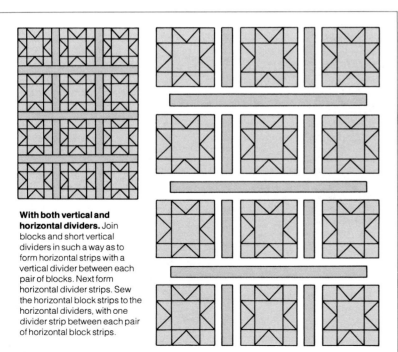

With both vertical and horizontal dividers. Join blocks and short vertical dividers in such a way as to form horizontal strips with a vertical divider between each pair of blocks. Next form horizontal divider strips. Sew the horizontal block strips to the horizontal dividers, with one divider strip between each pair of horizontal block strips.

Diagonal setting. Here units are joined to each other to form strips that will be set diagonally. The number of units in a strip will depend on the location of that strip in the patchwork. Parts of units (necessary to permit all edges of the patchwork to be straight when all the strips are joined) are usually required at the ends of strips; some strips only contain part of a unit. Shown below is the strip breakdown of the patchwork on the right. Notice that each strip is different from the others, and that the upper right corner is formed by a quarter of a block and the lower left corner by two diagonally halved blocks. The numbers next to the strips indicate a suggested sequence for joining the strips.

Strip 1 →
Strip 2 →
Strip 3 →
Strip 4 →
Strip 5 →
Strip 6 →
Strip 7 →

Preparing and sewing a one-shape patchwork

Preparatory steps
Shell
Baby Blocks
Grandmother's Flower Garden

Preparatory steps

The Shell, Baby Blocks and Grandmother's Flower Garden (hexagon) are three popular one-shape patchworks; for instructions on how to draw their necessary shapes, see p. 213. Many of the preparatory steps taken for a one-shape patchwork are the same as those taken for a block-unit patchwork. A one-shape patchwork should be charted and its colour arrangement planned (pp. 216–17). Once charting is complete, finished-size marking and cutting templates can be made and the pieces cut out of the appropriate colours of fabric (pp. 218–19). If you are making the **Shell** patchwork (below), use its marking template to mark the seamlines of each shell shape. For **Baby Blocks** or **Grandmother's Flower Garden,** use the marking template as a pattern for cutting out finished-size paper shapes.

Shell

Many different colour arrangements can be used with the Shell patchwork; the one above produces diagonal stripes. If you want the outer edges of the patchwork to be straight, place partial shell shapes at the edges. Make marking and cutting templates for them, and sew them as you would full shells. Turn under the seam allowances of the edges that form the patchwork's edges.

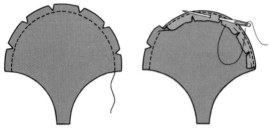

1. Staystitch and notch (p. 227) the upper seam of each shell shape. Turn each upper seam allowance to the wrong side and tack it in place.

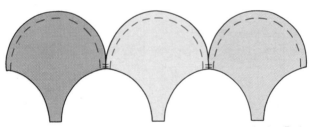

2. Referring to chart for colour, place top row of shells next to each other. Tack shells to each other, forming tacks within lower seam allowances.

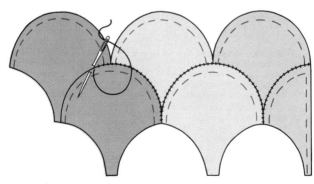

3. For each successive row, overlap appropriately coloured shells along lower curved seamlines of shells just positioned. Blindstitch (p. 225) in place.

Baby Blocks

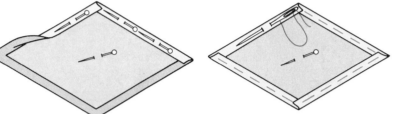

1. Using marking template as a pattern, cut out a paper diamond for each fabric diamond. Back each fabric diamond as follows. Centre a paper diamond on wrong side of fabric diamond. Turn seam allowances under and tack in place, through paper.

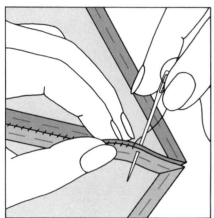

2. Form each Baby Block as follows. Position a set (3) of diamonds as shown in the far left illustration and sew them together, working from the centre of the Baby Block out. When sewing, hold the diamonds with their right sides together and oversew the matched edges neatly as shown in the illustration on the left.

When colours are appropriately chosen and placed, Baby Blocks patchwork produces the overall effect of three-dimensional blocks. The simplest way to achieve this effect is with three tones of one colour, placed in the same position in each block (Step 2). The Baby Blocks above combines three tones of brown, with the lightest at the top of the block, the darkest at the left, and the medium tone to the right. If you want the patchwork to have straight edges, use part shapes (see Shell, facing page).

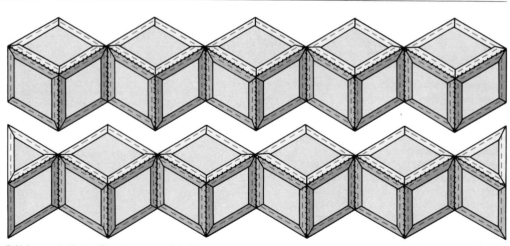

3. Using small stitches (Step 2), oversew Baby Blocks to each other to form strips. Check chart for number of strips and of blocks in a strip. Oversew the strips together to form the patchwork. When stitching is done, remove paper backing pieces.

233

Preparing and sewing a one-shape patchwork

Grandmother's Flower Garden

Patchwork made from hexagons is easy to work, as each 'flower' shape can be sewn separately and joined to the others to make a quilt. All quilts look better if the arrangement of the colours in the hexagons is planned and not developed haphazardly. In this example, the orange centres to the 'flowers' and the white 'paths' between draw the whole quilt together, even though the groups of hexagons are made up of different colours and prints. Cardboard templates last for a long time, and must be cut with a metal ruler and utility knife.

Cut the hexagons of fabric using a cutting template. Place the cardboard template hexagon centrally on the wrong side of the fabric.

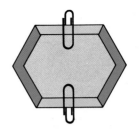

Fold the fabric over the template and use paper clips to keep the template in the centre of the fabric before sewing.

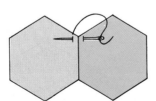

With needle and cotton begin to sew opposite sides together, pulling the thread tightly to 'lace' them together. Keep the stitches spaced evenly.

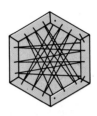

A completed hexagon showing the sides securely laced together. If the fabric is springy, take an extra stitch at corners. When sewn to six other hexagons, remove template.

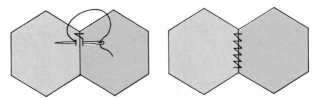

Sew the hexagons using farmer's shirt stitch, picking up the fabric with the needle but not piercing the cardboard templates. Make a backstitch and then insert the needle below.

Pull the thread through, making a slanting stitch, and make a backstitch from right to left. Repeat. The diagram on the right shows the finished seam, which is both strong and decorative.

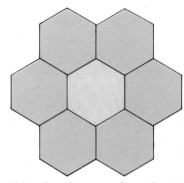

Make a 'flower' by surrounding one hexagon with six others of the same fabric. Sew each hexagon to the centre hexagon, and then to each other.

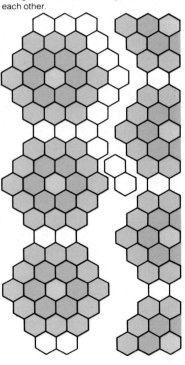

Make several 'flowers' of two circles of hexagons, combining colours and prints to make each attractive in itself. Then arrange them, to balance the colours and prints used, and join with a 'pathway' of white hexagons. The 'pathway' could alternatively be made of black fabric for a rich, dark effect.

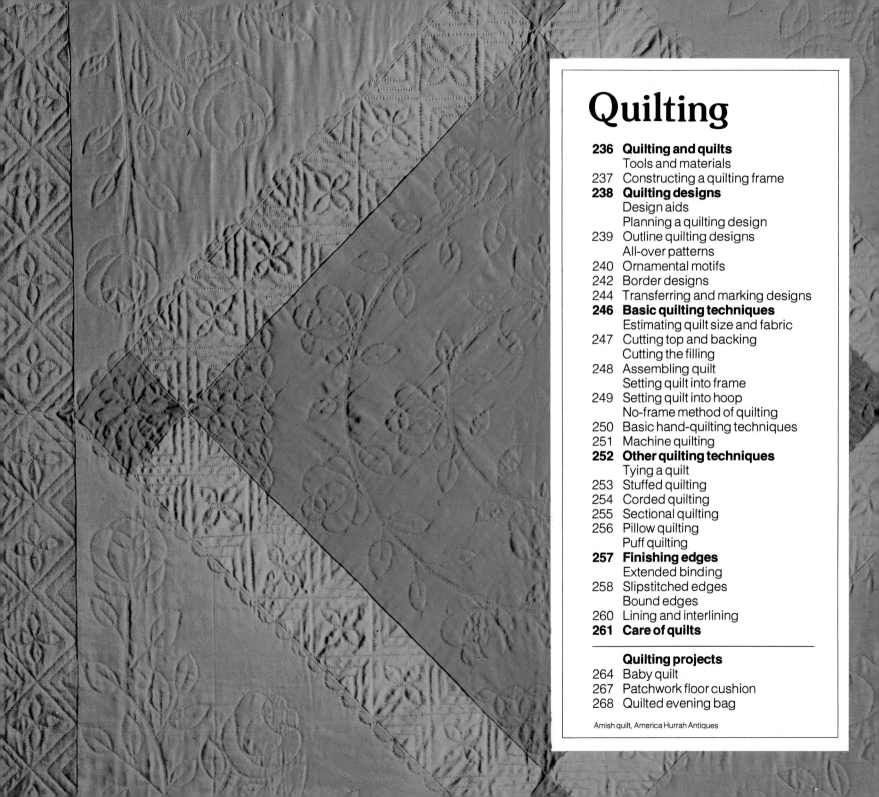

Quilting

Amish quilt, America Hurrah Antiques

Quilting and quilts

Introduction to quilting
Tools and materials
Constructing a quilting frame

Introduction

Quilting, like so many needlecraft techniques, is centuries old. Throughout history it has been valued as a source of warmth in such forms as clothing and bed quilts. The basic quilting technique involves simple running stitches used to anchor a soft filling between two layers of fabric. These stitches are usually worked in a systematic pattern to create a subtly textured fabric surface. The quilting patterns (see pp. 239–43) may be the primary or only source of decoration on a particular article, or they may be a secondary source that is introduced to enhance a completed design surface, such as patchwork or appliqué.

Although this basic quilting technique is usually associated with the making of a quilt (or bed covering), it is often decoratively applied today to sections of such garments as jackets, waistcoats and dressing-gowns. Quilting is also suitable for decorating such accessories for the home as cushions and wall hangings.

Ornamental motif quilted on plain fabric is quilt's primary design source.

Outline quilting merely enhances the main patchwork design of this quilt.

Tools and materials

Fabrics and filling. The top layer or decorative side of a quilted project can be a plain or patterned fabric, or it can be a completed piece of patchwork, appliqué or embroidery. Whatever it is, the fabrics used should be smooth, light to medium-weight and opaque. Cotton, poplin and polyester/cotton are popular choices, although fine linen-weave fabrics or flannels are also suitable. Rich fabrics such as velvet, satin and silk can also be used for special quilted projects. For a delicate effect, use sheer fabric (voile, organdy, organza) as a transparent overlay on an opaque top. Avoid heavy or stiff fabrics; they are not suitable. Bed sheets are convenient to use as they are made in a wide range of colours and prints, and in widths that make it possible to have a conveniently large seamless piece. Sheeting may also be bought by the metre.

The bottom layer, backing or lining, traditionally has been a utilitarian medium-weight fabric such as calico. Nowadays, it, too, is likely to be decorative, and made from fabrics as bright in pattern and colour, and similar in type and style to the top fabric layer. Avoid any slippery fabric, as the quilt will slide off the bed.

If the backing will also be the binding (see p. 257), you will need to cut it larger than the quilt top. Before quilting, pre-shrink all fabrics for both the top and the bottom.

The most common filling is synthetic wadding, manufactured in sheet form. It is washable, lightweight, warm and easy to quilt. It gives an attractive, plump quilted surface. It is available in a variety of thicknesses and widths. Good-quality synthetic wadding is uniformly thick and dense, which makes it easy to handle when assembling a project. Try to buy wadding that is large enough to be used as a single piece. If the wadding is too small, you can join two pieces to produce one of the desired size (see p. 247). Cotton wadding is available, but as it is not washable it is only suitable for items such as spectacle cases, which do not need laundering.

Old blankets may be used as wadding. Avoid using parts that have been worn thin, as the quilting will be uneven.

Traditionally, teased sheep's wool was used. This would make a very warm filling if used for a garment such as a child's waistcoat.

Needles, thread and hand-sewing aids. *Quilting needles,* which are also known as 'betweens', are the usual choice. As a rule, the sizes are 8 or 9, but a heavier size 7 can be used on heavier quilt fabrics, and a finer number 10 can be used on fabrics that are delicate.

Thread for quilting must be strong. Cotton thread coated with a 'glaze' is sometimes labelled *quilting thread* and does the job well. A good, all-purpose thread, number 50 or coarser number 40, can also be used; you may want to run each strand of thread through a cake of *beeswax* to help prevent tangles and fraying as you work. For a richer look, use a lustrous silk twist.

A *thimble* that fits your finger snugly is very helpful, as are small *embroidery scissors* for cutting thread.

Frames and hoops. When quilting is put in a frame or hoop the material is stretched taut, and the stitching done under tension. When removed, this produces a plump look which is most attractive. For quilting large expanses of fabric, a quilting frame is most convenient.

A simple but strong frame is shown below. If you decide to make many quilts, it is worth getting a frame made by a local handyman or carpenter. Traditional frames were rectangles made of end rails and stretchers, and were placed on the backs of kitchen chairs when being used. Pine is the most usual wood, although oak and mahogany frames may be seen in museums.

Although a frame is the most convenient method for a large piece, it takes up space. Many people prefer to use a

hoop. These are available up to 56 cm wide. This size will hold the quilting layers securely and can be adapted for any size quilting project. To use a hoop on a large quilt, shift it from area to area. The hoop should be at least 45 cm in diameter to provide a practical working area. You may like to look for a hoop with a stand which leaves both hands free. A hoop made for embroidery will not be suitable, as the two hoops will fit together too tightly to take the sandwich of fabric and wadding.

However, if you are a beginner, and wish to experiment with a fairly small piece of quilting, you can work the piece in your hands, without a hoop. If you do this, remember to tack the layers together very securely so that they will not slip while quilting.

Quilting hoops come in several diameter sizes; select one appropriate for your project. This model comes with a convenient stand, and frees both hands for work.

Constructing a quilting frame

A sturdy quilting frame can easily be constructed at home by following the instructions below. When not in use, it can be taken apart and stored.

Materials
To make the frame, you will need four lengths of 25 mm × 50 mm wood that have been sanded smooth to prevent any snagging of the quilt fabric. Two of the lengths will be used as *rails* around which the quilt will be rolled. Each rail should equal the width of the quilt, plus 30 cm to allow for clamping at corners. The two remaining lengths will act as side *stretchers*; a length of approximately 60 cm to 90 cm, plus another 30 cm to allow for clamping, should be adequate for most projects. You will also need about eight 15 cm *G-cramps,* and two strips of *webbing, ticking* or other sturdy fabric about 5 cm to 8 cm wide and as long as the cut rails. *Staples* or *drawing pins* are needed to hold the ticking or webbing to the rails. Support the frame with two *trestles.*

Assembly
To assemble the frame, first attach a strip of webbing or folded ticking to each rail as shown below. (Ends of quilt will be sewn to webbing when quilt is set into frame.) Position the four lengths at right-angles to each other with the rails resting on top of the stretchers. Secure lengths together with a G-cramp at each outside corner. Raise the frame on to the trestles, placing it so that the stretcher bars lie directly on the trestles. Hold the frame steady with additional G-cramps. Set the quilt into the frame, following the procedure described on pp. 248–9.

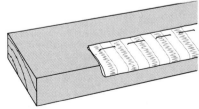

To attach fabric strip, fold and staple or tack to long edge of rail. Use webbing singly.

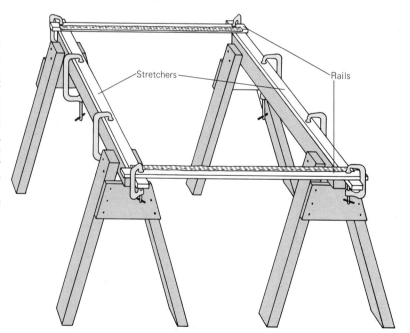

To assemble frame, clamp rails to stretchers at corners. Position frame so the stretchers rest on the trestles, then clamp trestles and stretchers together as shown.

Quilting designs

Design aids

A wide range of accessories exists to help with designing, or with the transfer of designs, but not all of them will be needed for any single project. What you select depends upon your design, and the transfer method it requires.

Patchwork templates or ready-made stencils, sold for interior decorating, can be used to make quick and easy quilt designs. You can make your own if you need or wish to (see p. 245).

Planning a quilting design

There are many different kinds of quilting designs, each offering a particular look or effect (see pp. 239–43). In deciding which one (or ones) to use, you must first consider the top fabric layer. Then, with that in mind, plan the quilting design so that it both enhances the piece and maintains its original character. In general, an already patterned top layer (such as patchwork or an appliquéd top) will be most appealing with simple, unobtrusive quilting. A common design practice is merely to quilt around the shapes that are already there. Elaborate quilting designs, on the other

There are several kinds of paper that will help with planning and transfer. *Graph paper* is useful for planning or sketching a design to scale. For full-size quilting designs and perforated patterns, *tracing paper* is the best choice. Use a stiff, *sturdy paper*, manila card or cardboard, to make durable templates and stencils. *Dressmaker's carbon* is handy for transferring markings.

A *ruler* or *metrestick* will double as a

hand, stand out most attractively against plain, solid colours. In fact, the most detailed quilting designs often appear on plain white quilts. A typical antique quilt of this sort may feature an ornate central motif surrounded closely by smaller motifs and an overall quilted background. Sometimes a single quilting project may combine both of these design approaches. For example, an intricately quilted solid-colour border may be used around a patchwork top quilted in a simple style.

The type of filling can also influence your quilting plans. Of the fillings previ-

straight-edge for marking straight-line designs and as a measuring device. A *compass* or a *round object* (such as a tea-cup) can be used for drawing curves. A single-edged *razor blade* or a *craft knife* will cut stencils and templates accurately. To mark directly on fabric, use a hard *pencil* or *dressmaker's chalk*. A special powder called *pounce* is used for temporary markings with perforated patterns (see p. 11).

ously mentioned (p. 236), cotton wadding is the least stable, and should be closely quilted to prevent the wadding from shifting and separating into unsightly lumps. Far less quilting is needed to anchor synthetic wadding, or any of the more stable fillings; with these, as much as a 25 cm square can be left unquilted. If you want a comparatively flat overall surface, plan on a closely quilted piece, whether the filling is cotton or polyester. Widely spaced quilting designs hold the filling down less, and so will result in a plumper surface.

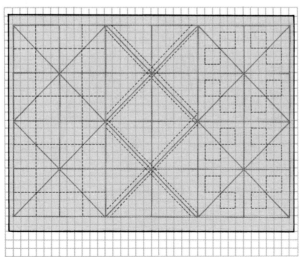

To plan a design for a quilt or any large expanse of fabric, sketch the proposed design on graph paper.

For patchwork, first draw the completed patchwork design on graph paper, then lay a sheet of tracing paper on top and sketch a quilting plan over the drawing as shown. Try several quilting plans in this way, and select the one you feel most enhances the patchwork.

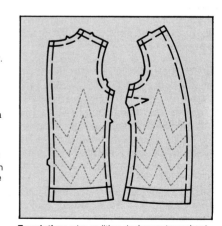

For clothes, plan quilting design on traced pattern pieces. Match quilting at seamlines. Remove wadding from darts before making up the garment.

Types of quilting designs/Outline quilting

Outline quilting follows the outlines of existing shapes. Patchwork, appliqué and patterned fabrics are suitable for this type of quilting. Position quilting lines about 5 mm from the seamed edges of stitched-down shapes or the outer edge of printed motifs.

Each shape can be outlined as in the first illustration; every patch in design is quilted.

Selected areas can be quilted to emphasise certain aspects of a design. In the second illustration the 8-sided star is accentuated by quilting around the patches that form the star.

In echo quilting, the outline of a shape is repeated in concentric quilting lines. This technique is often used for appliquéd tops.

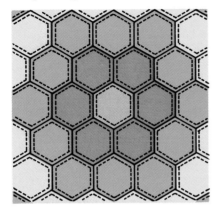
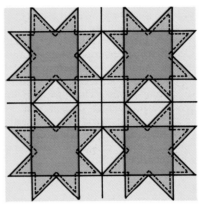

Types of quilting designs/All-over patterns

All-over quilting produces a regular pattern by consistent repetition of one or more shapes. Designs can be adapted to any space, and so are widely used. They can be used to cover an entire surface with a simple, unobtrusive quilted background, or to fill open areas around or within other quilted motifs.

Straight-line designs are the easiest patterns to use; they can be drawn using just a metrestick or ruler. A simple vertical pattern is shown in the first illustration.

Criss-crossed diagonals produce a pattern of diamond shapes in the second illustration.

Diamond shapes surround and emphasise a central motif in the third illustration.

All-over curved patterns make interesting background designs. Templates of stiff paper are used in repeat to create the patterns. Some patterns are formed by overlapping one or more templates; notches are cut along template curve to indicate overlapping points.

Shell pattern in first illustration calls for the simple repetition of a single template.

Overlapping circles in next illustration are marked with one round template, notched to indicate overlapping points of circles.

Crescent pattern is formed by using round templates in two sizes. A predetermined arc on each one is used to mark the top and bottom curves of the crescent shape.

Quilting designs

Types of quilting designs/Ornamental motifs

Another type of quilting design is the ornamental motif, which depicts traditional subjects in a somewhat formal fashion. These motifs usually contain intricate details (see illustrated examples) that can best be seen and appreciated when they are worked on plain fabric surfaces. In many of the most elegant quilts from earlier periods, the larger, more elaborate designs act as a central motif; smaller motifs may surround the centre design, perhaps deco-rate the corners as well. If you would prefer to combine two or more motifs in a single piece, work out your design ideas first on graph paper. A single ornamental motif is a satisfactory way of decorating individual patchwork blocks or cushion covers. These patterns for ornamental quilting designs can be used, or you can make your own perfo-rated patterns (p. 245). Quilt the tight curves that are typical of the designs with very fine stitches.

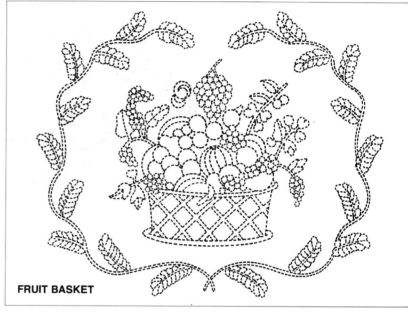

FRUIT BASKET

VASE OF FLOWERS

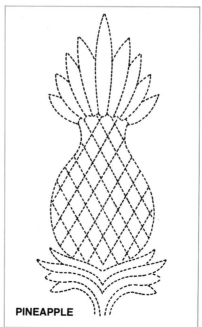

PINEAPPLE

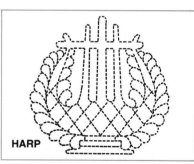

HARP

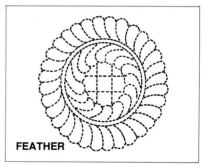

FEATHER

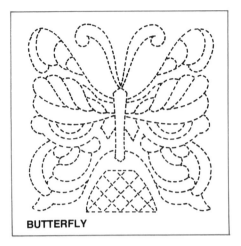

BUTTERFLY

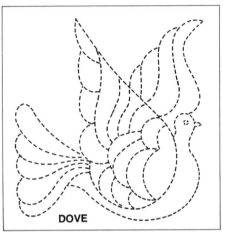

DOVE

EAGLE

TULIP

SNOWFLAKE

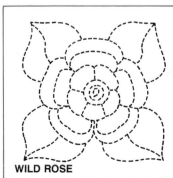

WILD ROSE

Quilting designs

Types of quilting designs/Borders

Border designs are made up of repeated patterns of motifs that frame and complement the main design on a quilt. To be effective, the border should relate to the overall character of the other quilt decorations. Traditionally, flowing motifs, such as undulating feathers and gracefully twined cables, were drawn. Now, almost any design suited to long and narrow spaces can be used; even simple geometric shapes and some all-over patterns are appropriate. Some designs are quite rigid in structure and require special planning (see opposite page). When a border turns corners, plan the design so that it flows smoothly around the corner, and is balanced on either side (see below).

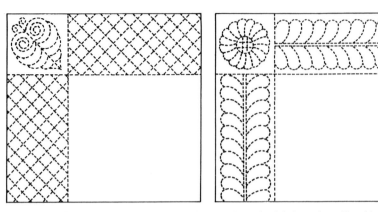

Corners can be filled with *unrelated motifs* provided border design is balanced on either side.

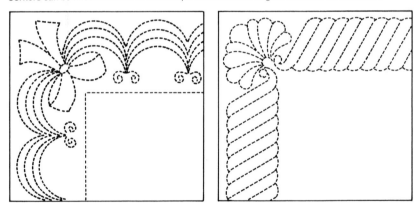

Or a *related motif can be introduced* at corners to bring the border to a conclusion.

Plan any border design on graph paper. Select the design and corner treatment, then work out from each corner to centres of sides, adjusting design repeats in between. In example above, tulip motif is placed in each corner and at centre of each side; graceful scroll design connects motifs.

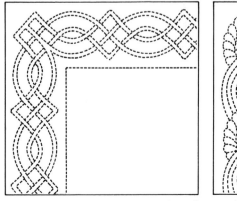

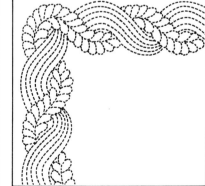

Or the *border design itself might be modified* to fit corners in one continuous line.

The patterns of rigidly structured designs develop basically from a square, and must be laid out according to the measurement of that square. For such a design to be successful, the border must be made long enough and wide enough to accommodate full repeats; partial repeats spoil the continuity. To be sure of full repeats, work out your border design on graph paper, then adjust quilt dimensions as needed. Because each border will consist entirely of full repeats, the corners will usually work out satisfactorily. When repeats have different motifs or internal patterns (see the top two designs on the far right), you will want particular motifs to fall at the corners and will have to plan for this.

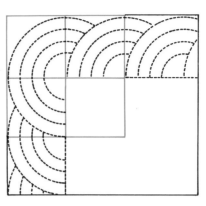

Design of concentric circles is like one on left, except overlaps are differently handled.

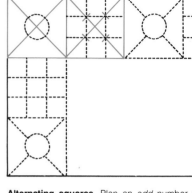

Alternating squares. Plan an *odd* number of squares placing crossed circle in corners.

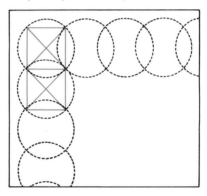

Wine-glass design stems from a circle drawn *around* basic square and made into template.

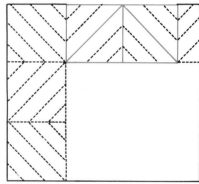

Squares of diagonals. Plan an *even* number of squares to have lines slanting towards centre.

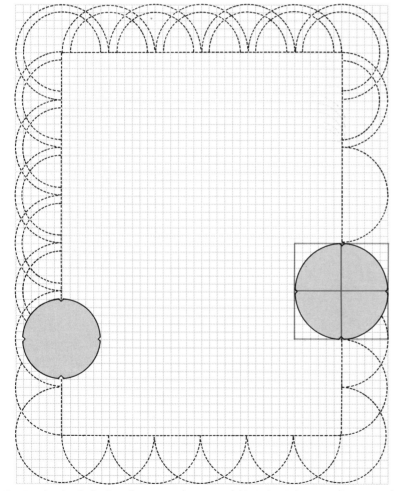

To plan a border design based on geometric repeats, divide the border into equal-size squares. The squares themselves may be the repeated shape (see top two designs, far right). In the design above, circles are developed from the square; templates are notched to show placing and intersecting points.

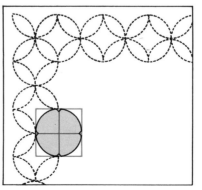

For petal-like motif, the template is made from a circle drawn *within* the square.

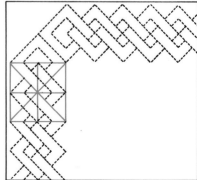

Interlocking links. Both their shape and placing evolve from a basic square as shown.

Quilting designs

Transferring and marking quilting designs

Quilt designs can be marked on fabric in a variety of ways. Which method you use will depend upon the type of design that is being marked and whether you will be marking it in or off the frame.

In-frame marking is done *after* the three quilting layers have been assembled and set into a frame or hoop. Designs must be marked a part at a time, as much as will fit within the exposed working area. In-frame markings are usually temporary, which allows the quilter to quilt each section after marking, thereby avoiding smudges and smears.

Off-frame methods (see far right and opposite page) are used more often. With these, the quilting design is marked on the top fabric layer *before* it is assembled with the other layers and set into a frame or hoop. Marking off the frame permits the entire design to be done at one time, a real advantage with highly complex designs.

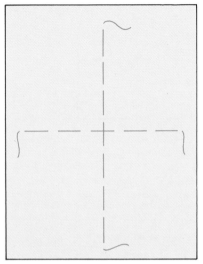

To prepare fabric for marking, press out any wrinkles or creases first. As a guide for proper placing of quilting designs, mark the centre of the piece by connecting side-to-side and top-to-bottom centre points with tacking threads.

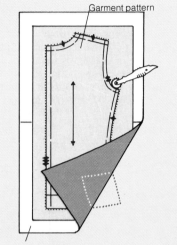

To mark odd shapes, such as parts of garments, lightly transfer the outline of each section on to the fabric, using dressmaker's carbon. Mark quilting design, but do not cut out garment sections until all quilting has been completed.

Off-frame methods

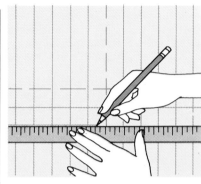

Straight-line designs begin with centring lines. *For a grid of squares,* use the tacked lines; space subsequent lines equally from these.

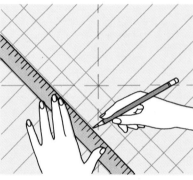

For a grid of diamonds, mark dividing lines from corner to corner; space the remaining lines evenly from these initial markings.

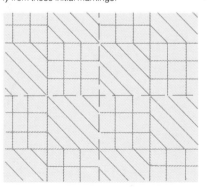

Design above combines both grid types. Notice the interesting pattern produced by having horizontal and vertical lines meet the diagonals.

In-frame methods

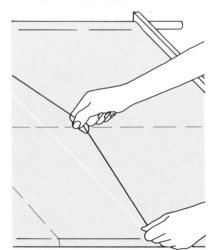

Chalking of straight-line designs such as squares, diagonals and channels is easily accomplished by snapping a taut chalk-coated string across a stretched quilt. Two people are needed to hold the ends of the string securely.

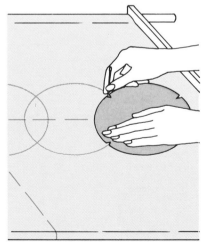

Needle marking, a useful though temporary method, usually follows a straight-edge or metre-stick, a template or a stencil. Holding needle like a pencil, draw it firmly across the fabric surface to produce an indentation of the design.

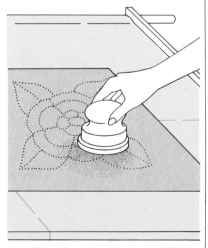

Perforated patterns are the usual choice for transferring intricate designs to top fabric. Make and use the perforated patterns as described for the off-frame method on the opposite page, but do not go over the dots with a pencil.

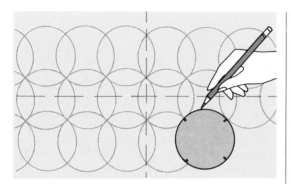

Templates are pattern shapes, usually cut from sturdy paper, that you simply trace around. Template for this design is notched on the edge to indicate where the shapes should overlap.

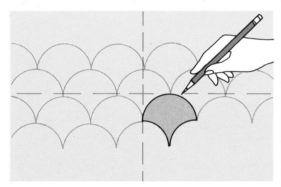

A frequent use of templates is repetition to produce an all-over pattern, such as this shell design. When you are using a template for such all-over marking, work from the centre.

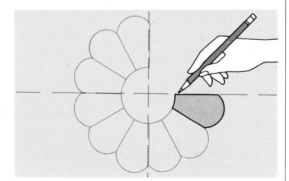

A template can also be the basis for forming a larger motif. The template used here is a wedge-shaped piece, called a *sector*, of a larger circle. Small centre circle is formed as well.

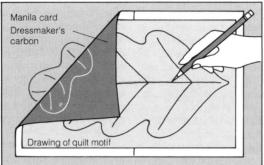

To make your own stencil, work out a line design on paper, keeping the details within the motif very simple. Using dressmaker's carbon, transfer the design to sturdy paper or manila card.

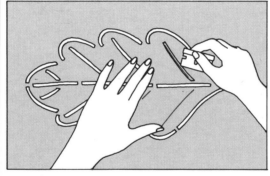

Cut out narrow channels along the drawn lines, using a single-edged razor blade or a craft knife. Be sure to leave connecting 'bridges' where lines intersect so that the stencil holds together.

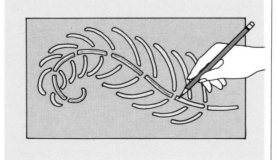

With stencil on fabric and fabric on firm surface, draw lines through slots with hard pencil, to mark simple quilting motifs. Do not use a soft pencil as the mark will be difficult to remove.

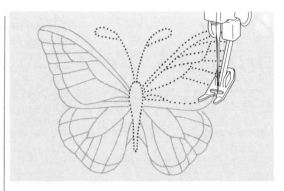

A perforated pattern is usually used to transfer intricate motifs. The design lines on the paper pattern may be pricked with a needle or stitched with an unthreaded sewing machine.

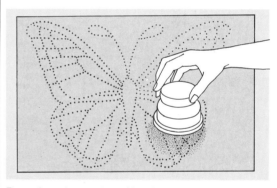

The perforated pattern is positioned on the fabric and a special powder called pounce is gently rubbed over the surface, leaving a dotted outline of the design on the fabric beneath.

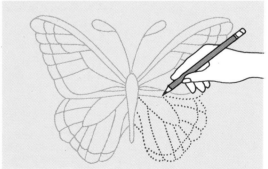

To reinforce the powder markings so that they do not disappear or smudge with handling, go over the dotted lines with a hard lead pencil or a dressmaker's chalk pencil.

Basic quilting techniques

Estimating quilt size and fabric amounts
Cutting top, backing and filling
Assembling quilt
Setting quilt into frame
Setting quilt into hoop
No-frame method of quilting
Basic hand-quilting techniques
Hand-quilting tips
Machine quilting

Estimating quilt size and fabric amounts

To determine the size of a quilt, first consider the size of the bed the quilt is intended for. Measure the bed when it is fully made up, with sheet, blankets and pillows in place (see below). Use a flexible tape measure. Next, consider the way the quilt will be used; this will determine how much extra length is needed for the drop at the sides and at the foot of the bed, and whether or not a tuck-in allowance is desired for the pillows. For example, a quilt used as a bedspread will need a drop that falls to the floor and an extra allowance (about 38 cm) to tuck under the pillow. A short coverlet, on the other hand, need only hang down as far as the valance, and may

or may not be tucked in at the pillows. Many times, the depth of the drop is a matter of personal preference. If you are in doubt about what you prefer, drape a sheet over the bed, then fold and pin it in place until you arrive at a size of suitable and pleasing proportion. Remove the sheet and measure it. The overall size of a quilt is calculated from these basic measurements – bed length plus depth of drop, plus tuck-in allowance (if any), equals finished quilt length; bed width plus depth of drop (times 2) equals finished quilt width.

To estimate the fabric needed for a quilt, first determine its overall cutting size (see opposite page) and work out

your estimates according to that. Fabric requirements for a pieced top will depend, of course, on the patch design you select (see Patchwork). For a plain top, the amount of fabric required will depend upon the fabric width and its relation to the cutting size of the quilt width. For example, if the quilt width is narrower than the fabric width, only one length of fabric (a length equal to the quilt cutting length) is needed. If the quilt width is wider than one fabric width and anywhere up to twice as wide as the fabric width, two lengths of fabric are needed. You will need to add an extra amount to your estimate if you plan to use the same fabric as binding.

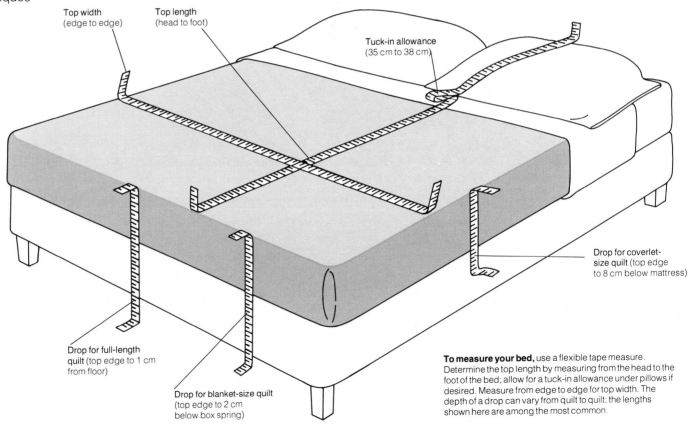

Top width (edge to edge)

Top length (head to foot)

Tuck-in allowance (35 cm to 38 cm)

Drop for coverlet-size quilt (top edge to 8 cm below mattress)

Drop for full-length quilt (top edge to 1 cm from floor)

Drop for blanket-size quilt (top edge to 2 cm below box spring)

To measure your bed, use a flexible tape measure. Determine the top length by measuring from the head to the foot of the bed; allow for a tuck-in allowance under pillows if desired. Measure from edge to edge for top width. The depth of a drop can vary from quilt to quilt; the lengths shown here are among the most common.

246

Cutting quilt top and backing

To calculate cutting dimensions of quilt top and backing, consider these variables along with your estimated quilt size. Depending on the edge finish that you select, you may only need an additional 1 cm seam allowance all round, or you might have to add several centimetres to your calculations. To compensate for the 'shrinkage' that usually results from quilting, add a few more centimetres to your overall figures as well. A quilt can be as much as 8 cm to 16 cm smaller after quilting; as a rule, the thicker the wadding and heavier the quilting, the greater the reduction in size. When proper sizes are determined, cut out the top and backing. Mark the centre points on each side of both pieces to simplify alignment when they are assembled.

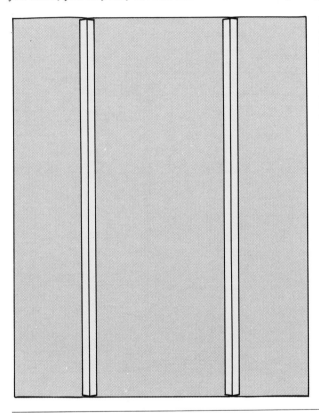

If the fabric is not wide enough for the top or backing, panels of appropriate widths can be joined to achieve the required measurement. When joining panels, avoid running a seam down the centre of the quilt; instead, use one central panel, usually a full fabric width, and add matching panels to each side. Press seams open. Any quilt top, whether patchwork, appliquéd or embroidered, can be enlarged in size if necessary by adding a border of the appropriate depth.

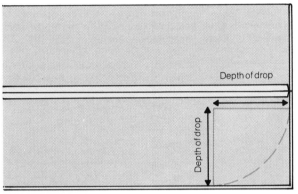

Depth of drop

Depth of drop

Rounding off corners for a quilted spread. On wrong side of quilt top, mark a square on corner of foot end; sides of square should equal depth of drop. Using a metrestick, measure from inner corner out, marking an arc as shown. Duplicate arc on opposite corner. Tack along arc to transfer curve to right side. Cut along arc after quilting has been completed.

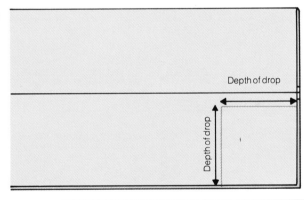

Depth of drop

Depth of drop

Cutting away corners to accommodate beds with foot posts. On right side of quilt top, mark a square on a corner of foot end; sides of square should equal depth of drop. Duplicate corner marking on opposite corner. Cut away corners along marked lines after quilting is completed.

Cutting quilt filling

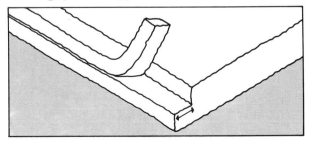

Cut wadding to same size as quilt top. If wadding must be pieced, separate it into two layers along one of the edges to be joined; cut a 1 cm strip from one layer. Separate and cut off a similar strip from the adjoining edge.

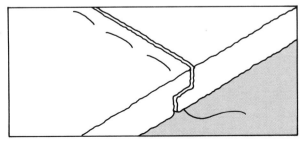

Overlap the cutaway edges as shown and tack the two together through both thicknesses. They are now joined with no tell-tale ridge.

Basic quilting techniques

Assembling quilt

When assembling any quilting project, stack the top, filling and backing carefully, then tack them together securely so they remain smooth and wrinkle-free throughout the quilting process. Proceed slowly when tacking; this can be the key to your quilting success. Even if you are using a frame or hoop, tacking is an important step, especially when working a large quilt; the stitches hold the layers together to prevent any shifting and bunching. For small projects, such as cushion covers, pin-tacking can be sufficient. If you are using the no-frame method (described lower right, on opposite page), or are quilting by machine (see p. 251), careful tacking is even more essential.

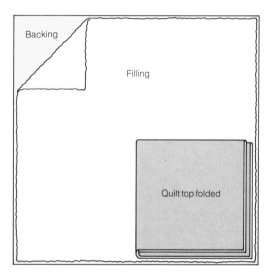

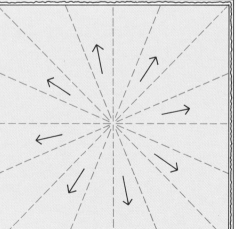

To assemble quilting layers, lay backing, wrong side up, on a hard, flat surface such as a table. Spread the wadding or other filling over the backing, then lay the top piece, right side up, over all.

For large quilts, lay backing on floor. Spread wadding over it, then stroke wadding with a metrestick to help remove any wrinkles. Do not stretch the wadding to fit, as it may tear. Fold quilt top into quarters with right side folded inside, and place it on one corner of the filling as shown; use the marked centre points on backing and top piece for accurate alignment. Carefully unfold the top, and again use the metrestick to smooth it in place. Do not kneel or stand on the fabric to reach the centre; this can cause hidden wrinkles in the filling and the backing.

Tack the three layers together in a sunburst pattern to avoid forming a lump of filling in the centre. Using large running stitches, start from the centre and work out towards the edges. Tack only from the top, being careful not to shift layers. As a general rule, there should be a tacked line about every 15 cm around the edges; tack more generously if the quilting will be done off a frame or hoop. Tacking stitches may be cut and released as needed during the quilting process.

Setting quilt into frame

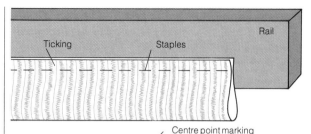

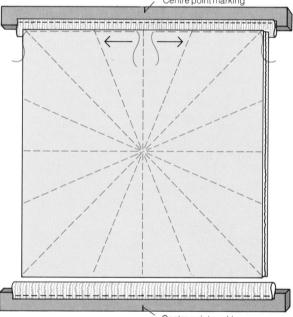

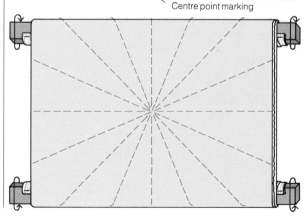

Staple ticking or other sturdy fabric to the rails as shown on p. 237. Mark the centre points of each rail for proper alignment when attaching the quilting project.

To attach quilt to rails, lay the tacked quilt on the floor and position the rails at each end, matching the centre points of rails and quilt top. Tack the quilt to the ticking along each rail, working from centre point out to each side.

Roll the quilt evenly and tightly on to each rail so a central area is exposed for quilting.

Attach the rails to the stretchers, adjusting them both so the quilt is held taut and straight, without sagging. Check for any wrinkles on the top and the backing of the exposed working area.

Secure the sides of the quilt by pinning cotton tape to the edges, and looping it around the stretchers as shown; pin at about 8 cm intervals. After completing the quilting within the exposed area, reveal a fresh section by unpinning the taped sides and rolling the completed part on to one of the rails. Secure the sides again as before.

Setting quilt into hoop

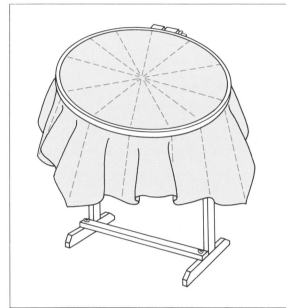

To set quilt or any other project into a hoop, place the centre of the tacked project over the inner hoop. Work out any fullness from the quilt by smoothing it over the edges of the hoop. Slide the outer ring in place and tighten the adjustment screw to keep the layers taut.

After quilting within this central area, remove the hoop and re-position the quilt to expose a fresh section; work from this central area out towards the edges. To quilt up to the edges, use a smaller hoop along the sides, or quilt without a hoop.

No-frame method

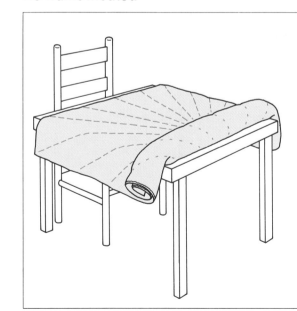

To quilt without a frame or hoop, place the tacked project over a table or ironing board so that its weight is fully supported. Do not allow large portions of the project to hang heavily over the sides of the table; this can cause pulling and some distortion. If necessary, roll or fold up the sides so they are properly supported. For small projects, you can simply spread the work over your lap.

Basic quilting techniques

Basic hand-quilting techniques

To quilt by hand, use an even *running stitch* that is short and closely spaced so as to give the illusion of an unbroken line (see below). Though a matching thread is the usual choice, a white thread or one which contrasts with the fabric can be used if you prefer. To avoid excessive tangling, use a single length of thread, no more than 50 cm long. Ideally, the quilting stitches should be fine (about 2 mm long), and even on both the top and backing. As you become more proficient with experience, you can increase your working speed by picking up several stitches on the needle before pushing it through; you will begin to develop a rhythm as your needle rocks back and forth, picking up the stitches. To facilitate this rhythmic motion, keep your quilting project slightly less than drum-tight when working in a frame or hoop.

You will also find stitching easier and more natural if you start an arm's length away, and quilt towards yourself, changing your position as the quilting dictates. Extra-thick fillings should be avoided, especially if you are working an intricate design.

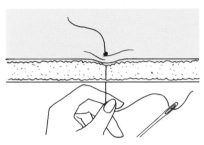

To start a line of quilting, knot end of thread and insert needle from the top through all three layers. Gently but firmly pull the thread from underneath so knot slips through the top layer and lodges in the filling. Cut off any thread end that may be visible on the surface.

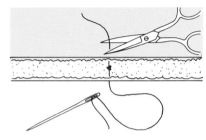

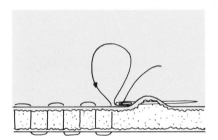

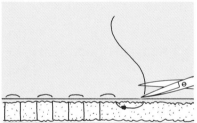

To end a line of quilting, make a knot on top of quilting surface. Insert needle a stitch length away and run needle through filling for a short distance; bring needle up, and gently pull the thread so knot slips through the top layer. Cut off thread end close to the surface.

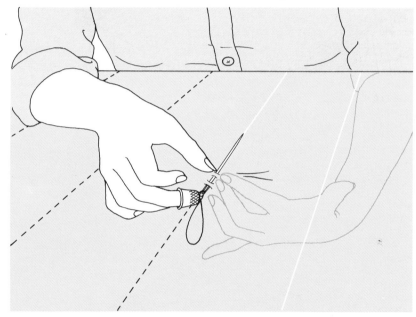

To quilt with running stitch, grasp needle with thumb and forefinger; take a few stitches, and push needle through with middle finger. To be sure needle penetrates all layers, hold other hand beneath the surface so tip of finger actually feels point each time a stitch is taken.

Hand-quilting tips

For curved or circular motifs, use a double length of thread and start quilting at the 2 o'clock position; quilt in each direction from this starting point so that you are able to quilt towards yourself at all times.

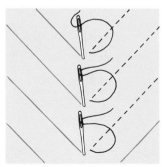

Keep several threaded needles in action. Quilt on a design line until it turns away from you or until you reach the end of an exposed quilting area. Leave needles on top layer and pick them up after you have shifted your position or have rolled a fresh area on to the frame.

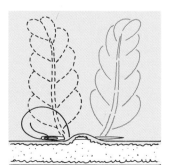

Avoid unnecessary starts and stops when quilting closely spaced motifs. Instead of knotting each time, simply run the needle from a completed motif through the filling and start again at next motif.

Machine quilting

Quilting with a sewing machine creates a durable and even stitching line that takes a fraction of the hand-quilting time. While it is possible to quilt almost any kind of project by machine, it is not always convenient to do so. Machine quilting is especially appropriate for small projects, such as cot quilts, garment sections and household articles, because they are easy to manoeuvre under the needle and can be made to fit under the arm of the machine when necessary. (It is also best for hard-to-quilt fabrics.) For such large projects as full-sized quilts and bedspreads, the sewing area must be modified and the sequence of quilting precisely planned to allow for the bulk as it passes through the sewing machine (see above right). If possible, avoid a single large piece by dividing the project into smaller sections – bedspread panels, for example, or quilt blocks. These can be quilted separately and joined later (see unit method of quilting on p. 255).

The sewing machine also limits the type of quilting design that is advisable. Avoid elaborate or curved designs that require cumbersome and frequent turning under the machine needle; they are both awkward and time-consuming. Simple quilting designs composed of straight lines are better choices and can be worked quickly and easily, especially if the lines of quilting extend from one edge of the project to the other. For this reason, all-over grid designs are highly suitable and frequently chosen (see lower right corner).

When preparing a project for machine quilting, be sure to tack generously so the layers do not shift as they are being fed through the machine. To avoid unsightly puckers, adjust the machine by loosening the tension and decreasing the pressure. Set the stitch length to medium-size stitches and test the setting on a complete sample of top, filling and backing tacked together.

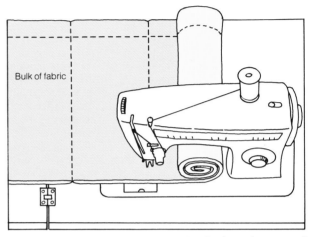

To modify the sewing area for large projects, move the sewing machine out into an open space. Raise a large piece of cardboard or wood on trestles or chairs to the level of the sewing machine and place alongside the machine. This extension will support a large, heavy project, and so make it easier to manoeuvre.

When quilting by machine, be sure to plan the direction and sequence of your stitching so that the bulk of the project always lies to the left of the needle. When working on a large project, such as a quilt, extend the working area as shown on left; roll the project up tightly enough to fit under the sewing machine arm as it becomes necessary.

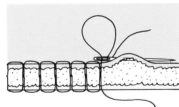

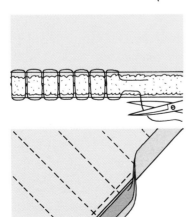

To secure thread ends that start or end away from raw edges, leave long thread ends on both top and bottom of quilted surface. Thread one of the ends through a needle and run needle through filling for a short distance.

Bring needle out, and cut off excess thread end close to the quilting surface. Run the other thread end through the filling in the same way.

If quilting line starts or ends at the edges, the thread ends need not be secured; the final edge finish (such as a binding) will keep the stitches from pulling out.

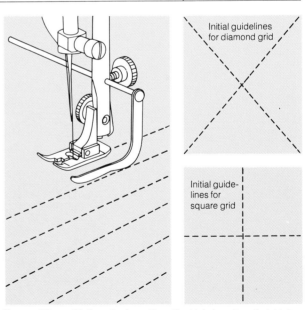

Initial guidelines for diamond grid

Initial guidelines for square grid

Use a quilting guide-bar attachment to quilt grid designs. Its adjustable bar extends out from the machine foot and falls along a guideline so that each quilting line can be equally spaced. Stitch initial guidelines as shown in the small drawings, then use the attachment to quilt lines on either side.

Other quilting techniques

Tying a quilt
Stuffed quilting
Corded quilting
Quilting in units
Sectional quilting
Pillow quilting
Puff quilting

Tying a quilt

Tying is a method of holding a quilt together without making lines of running stitches. To tie a quilt, take a single stitch at regular intervals through all layers, leaving thread ends long enough to tie in a knot on the quilt top. Tying is faster than quilting with a running stitch, and more practical when the filling is thick or otherwise difficult to handle. Also, crazy quilts, which have no filling, are usually tied. This technique is not suitable when the filling may shift with washing, and so needs the control of stitching. For tying, you will need a large-eyed crewel needle and a strong decorative thread, such as stranded cotton, pearl cotton, narrow ribbon or knitting yarn.

This quilt top is secured to the wadding and backing with knots tied at regular intervals.

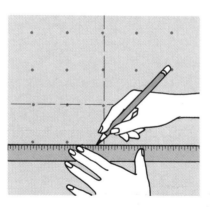

To prepare a quilt top for tying, mark its horizontal and vertical centres with tacking lines. Then, moving out from them with a ruler and a pencil or chalk, indicate the points for tying. Make sure the points are equally spaced and no more than 10 cm to 15 cm apart.

On a patchwork top, you can follow the design of the quilt to place the points for tying. Keep spacing as even as possible, and try not to leave large areas untied.

After marking, tack the top, filling and backing together as shown on p. 248.

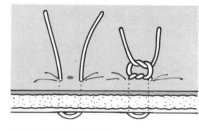

Make a tie at each of the marks on the top layer as follows. Take a stitch down through all three layers, then come up, leaving enough thread at ends to tie a reef knot, as shown. Trim ends to a uniform length, usually about 2 cm.

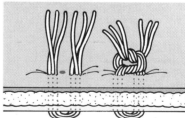

To make tufts, thread a needle with two or three lengths of thread. Take a stitch as above, and tie all of the ends in a reef knot. Trim ends evenly.

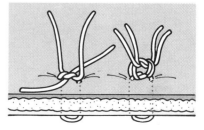

Another way of tufting, useful when a quilt is difficult to penetrate with multiple strands of thread, is to make the stitch with one length of thread and then add one or more lengths while tying the reef knot, as illustrated.

Stuffed quilting

Stuffed quilting is a type of quilting in which only certain sections of the stitch design are padded, bringing them into relief and giving dimension to the design. It is especially effective on a solid-colour fabric. To do this kind of quilting, you stitch the design through two layers of fabric (top and backing) and then insert the filling (synthetic or cotton wadding) between them by means of slits cut in the backing. The top layer is usually a tightly woven fabric, such as cotton or poplin. Because the filling is inserted through the backing, the best choice for this is a loosely woven fabric, such as lightweight muslin, voile or cheesecloth. To protect the back of the quilt and conceal the ragged edges left from the insertion of filling, the work should be lined with fabric of a type similar to that used for the top layer. For quilting stitches, use cotton quilting thread or a synthetic thread of a similar weight. Silk twist can be substituted for a richer look.

The designs best suited to this type of quilting include motifs and geometric shapes composed of many small sections, as shown in the photograph (right). It is difficult to stuff large areas uniformly. If you want to try a quick, modern approach to stuffed quilting, find a printed fabric with a distinct motif composed of small, enclosed areas, and use the techniques described below to put the motifs in relief.

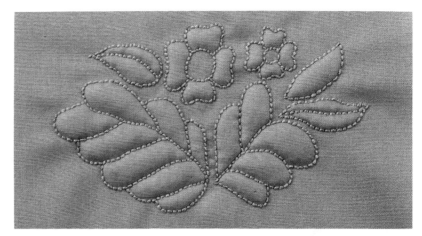

Leaves and flower petals above are stuffed with small pieces of wadding inserted through backing.

1. Transfer the quilt design to the fabric, using pounce, pricking or other invisible method. Then, with raw edges and grainlines aligned, tack fabric to backing through horizontal and vertical centres, and diagonally from corner to corner, as shown.

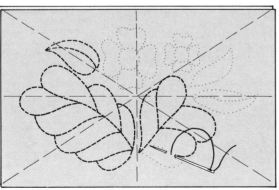

2. Hand-sew the fabric layers together along the design lines, using either a backstitch or an even running stitch. Or straight-stitch around the design by machine. Keep stitches as small as fabric thicknesses will permit. If you prefer a stronger marking line, transfer the design to the backing fabric, tracing the mirror image of the design. When stitching is complete, remove tacking.

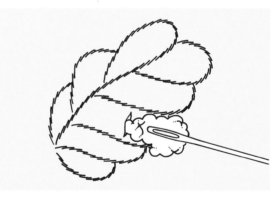

3. Cut a slit in centre of one small section of the muslin backing. Make the slit slightly off-grain to avoid weakening the fabric. Stuff the section lightly with filling so the area is raised but not so packed as to distort the fabric.

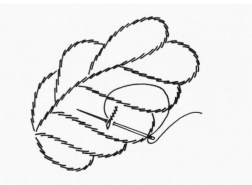

4. Close the slit with oversewing, as shown. Repeat the procedure of cutting a centre slit, stuffing the section and closing the slit for each of the design areas that you want to pad.

Other quilting techniques

Corded quilting

Italian or corded quilting is a type of quilting in which linear designs are raised from the background with a cord or wool filling. This kind of quilting is often combined with stuffed quilting to accentuate both the lines and shapes of the design. There are two ways to achieve the raised look. The first and most common method is to stitch the quilt design, in parallel lines, through two layers of fabric. The resulting channels are then threaded with wool or other rope-like filling. Pre-shrink the filling to avoid puckering after laundering. The top fabric should be tightly woven, the back fabric a loose weave.

Use cotton or synthetic quilting thread or, for a richer look, stitch with silk twist. The piece must be lined to protect and conceal the filling insertions.

The second method involves only one layer of fabric. The cord is laid under the fabric and stitched in place at the same time. Since only one layer of fabric is used, this method is suitable for projects where a backing or lining is undesirable. For either method, use a soft cotton cord or wool to fill the channels. Select the thickness according to the width between the parallel lines; the cord should fill the space so the channel is raised, but not so tightly that it distorts the fabric.

METHOD I

1. Transfer the quilt design to the fabric, using pounce, pricking or other invisible method. Then, with raw edges and grainlines aligned, tack fabric to backing through horizontal and vertical centres, and diagonally from corner to corner, as shown.

2. Sew the two fabric layers together along marked lines, using a small running stitch or backstitch, or the straight stitch on your machine. Keep stitches small and even.

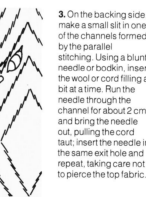

Backing

3. On the backing side, make a small slit in one of the channels formed by the parallel stitching. Using a blunt needle or bodkin, insert the wool or cord filling a bit at a time. Run the needle through the channel for about 2 cm and bring the needle out, pulling the cord taut; insert the needle in the same exit hole and repeat, taking care not to pierce the top fabric.

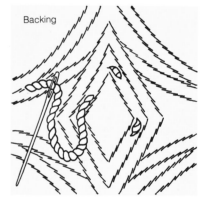

Backing

4. When filling a curve or corner, proceed as in Step 3, but do not pull the cord taut. Instead, leave a bit of slack at the turn to fill in the space, as shown. This will prevent puckering at these points on the top of the quilt.

METHOD II

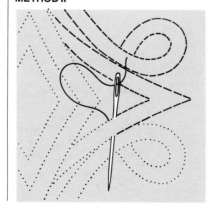

1. Transfer the quilt design to the right side of the fabric. Insert the fabric in a frame or hoop to leave both hands free for working. Use a sharp needle and buttonhole twist. Holding the cord in position underneath the fabric with one hand, backstitch along the parallel lines, alternating stitches from side to side.

2. The crossed threads on the underside of the fabric hold the cord within the design lines and keep it flat against the fabric. As you work, keep the stitches even and the tension consistent.

254

Quilting in units/Sectional quilting

Quilting in units simplifies the making of large quilts or other quilted items by dividing the work into small, manageable units. **Sectional quilting** enables you to quilt one block or panel at a time. This technique, adapted from traditional quilting, is especially appropriate when you want a portable project or when you want to stitch by machine. **Pillow quilting** and **puff patchwork** (described on the next page) are contemporary techniques that also enable you to stitch and stuff one block at a time before assembling several of them.

Although these methods are generally limited to simple quilting designs and simple patchwork, they do offer several advantages: they require little work space, they need no frame or hoop, and all or part of the stitching involved can be done by machine, which makes the work considerably faster.

Sectional quilting, or dividing a quilt into sections for quilting, makes it easier to handle. Although adaptable to any size project, this technique is particularly helpful when it would be awkward to quilt a big project by machine. No mat-

ter how large the finished quilt is to be, it can be divided for quilting purposes into sections no bigger than one of its blocks.

To divide a project into sections, use the existing seams in the item. For example, a patchwork or appliqué quilt top can be quilted so that each block constitutes a section, or the quilt can be divided into groups of blocks. A border for such a quilt would be another separate section for quilting. These parts would be joined together after the quilting of all of the parts is completed.

This seaming approach can also be used for quilting and assembling a garment. For example, the fronts and back of a waistcoat can be quilted separately and then stitched together at the side seams. When choosing fabric for backing, remember that in this technique of sectional quilting, the backing fabric functions as a kind of lining because all of the raw edges are enclosed. No extra lining need be added for a finished look.

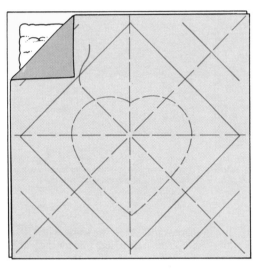

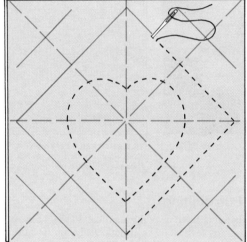

1. Cut the top and backing the same size for each section, allowing a 5 mm seam allowance on each side. Cut the filling for each section to the same size, but omit the seam allowances. Transfer the quilting design to the top fabric. Stack the layers and tack them together through the centre, as shown.

2. Quilt the section, being careful to start and stop the quilting 1.5 cm from the seamline so the seam allowances are left free for joining and turning back. Remove the tacking.

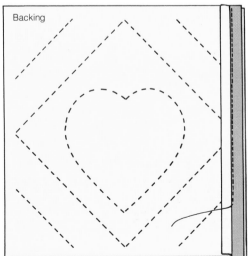

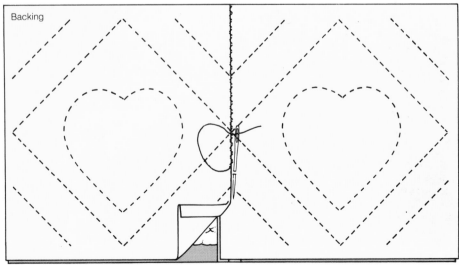

3. To assemble, place adjoining sections together, right sides facing, and join the *top fabrics only*, stitching the seam by hand or machine.

4. To finish the back, place the sections face down on a flat surface. Finger-press the seam open. The filling edges should meet; if they overlap, trim off excess. Turn under the seam allowance of one edge of the backing and slipstitch it securely to the backing of the adjoining section. Where necessary, go back and finish the quilting to the seamline.

255

Other quilting techniques

Making templates 218
Outline quilting 239

Quilting in units/Pillow quilting

In pillow quilting, each patchwork piece is backed, filled and finished on all sides before the pieces are assembled. The effect of the finished quilt is similar to outline quilting in that the shape of each individually stuffed piece stands out. Any patchwork block or one-patch design that is a straight-edged geometric shape can be used. If the backing and top fabric are the same, the quilt will be identical on both sides; to create a reversible quilt, use a contrasting fabric for the backing. Or you could use up remnants by cutting each patch from a different fabric. For stuffing, use synthetic wadding.

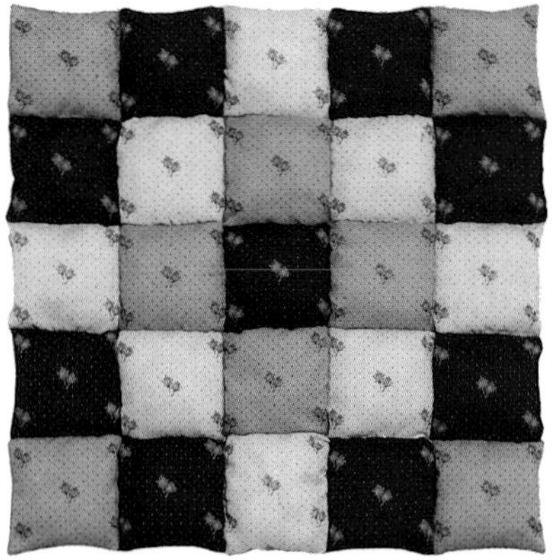

Pillows are sewn and stuffed before assembly.

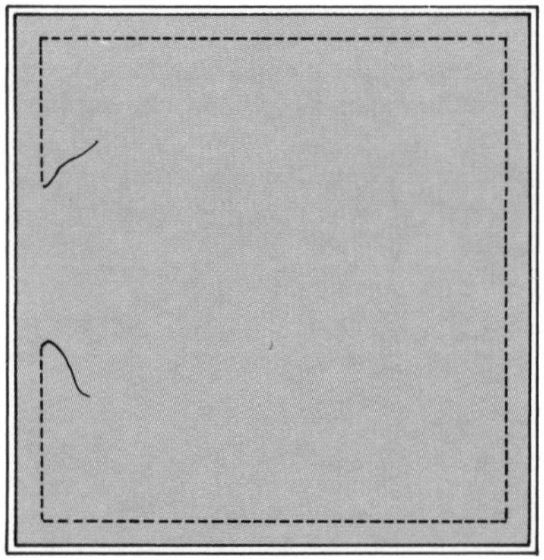

Cut a patch and a backing from the same template. Align them, right sides facing; stitch around edge, leaving an opening for turning.

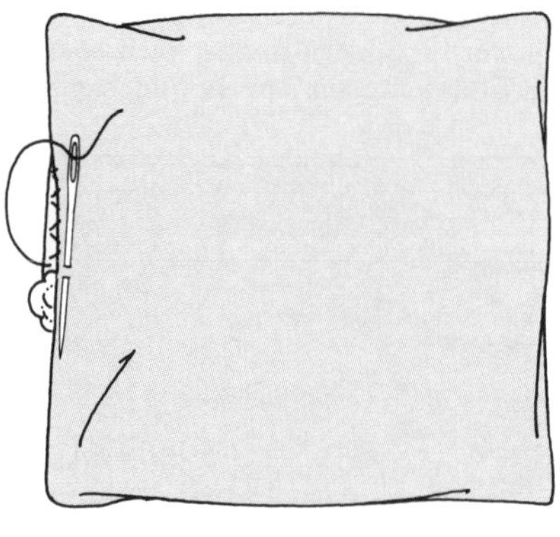

Carefully turn patch right side out. Add filling through the opening, stuffing lightly and evenly. Slipstitch the opening closed by hand.

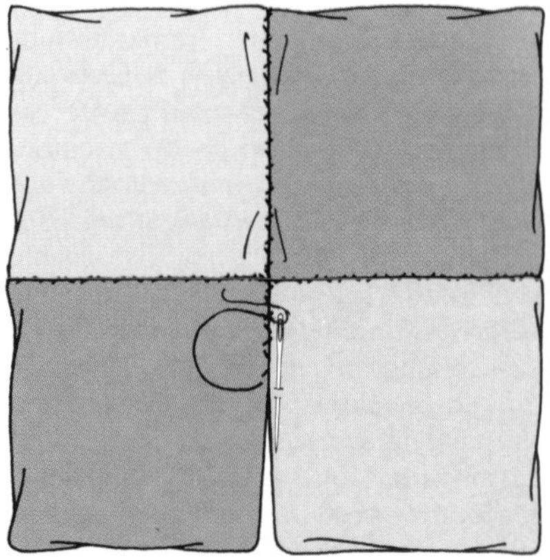

To assemble the finished patches, butt the edges and join them by hand with a slipstitch, or by machine with a fine zigzag stitch.

Quilting in units/Puff quilting

In puff quilting, a top patch is eased or tucked to fit a smaller backing so the top patch can be heavily stuffed to produce a puffy look. The edges are concealed after assembly with a lining, so the backing can be muslin. For stuffing, use synthetic wadding. Because of its puffiness, this style is confined to quilts and cushion covers. Although any one-patch design can be used, straight-sided shapes are easiest to work with. Two templates are needed: one for the patch, and another, which is the same basic shape but smaller, for the backing. The patch is usually one and a half times larger than the backing – for example, a 15 cm top fabric will be eased to fit a 10 cm backing. The greater the difference between the sizes, the puffier the finished unit will be.

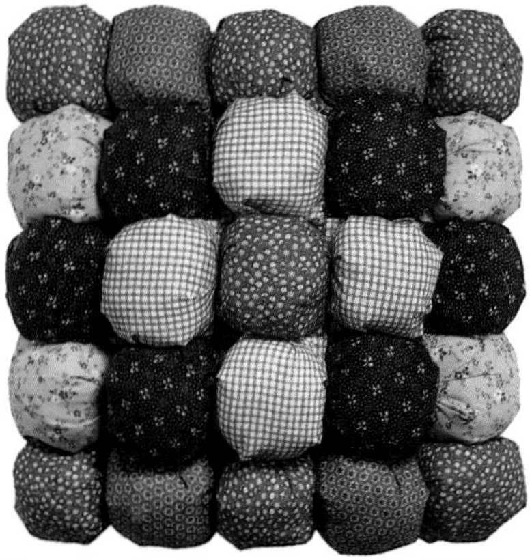

Pieces in puff quilting are more heavily stuffed.

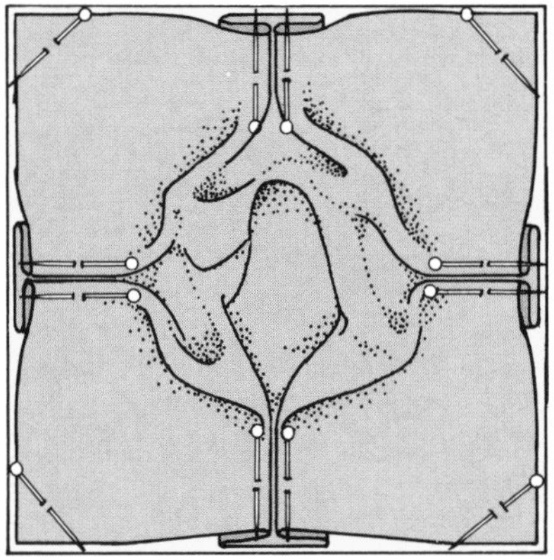

Wrong sides facing, pin patch to backing at corners. Match centre points at sides and pin. Fold excess fabric in centre into tucks as shown.

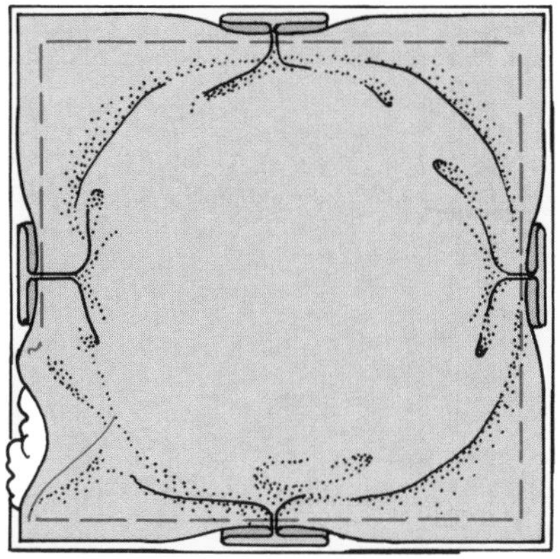

Tack around the edge by hand or machine, leaving an opening to one side of one tuck. Add filling, then tack the opening closed by hand.

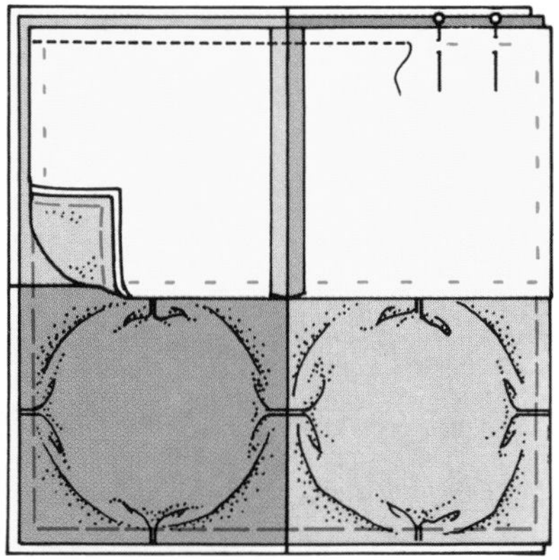

To assemble individual units, sew seams with right sides facing. To finish, line the entire piece or add a backing (for directions see p. 260).

Finishing edges

Self-finished edges/Extended binding

When the quilting part of a project is completed, it is still necessary to finish the edges. Several methods are available; the choice depends upon the type of quilt you are making and its design. The first, called the self-finished edge, utilises only the quilt top and backing.

There are two kinds of self-finish: the **extended binding**, which can be used only if the backing fabric is of the same quality as the top fabric; and the **slip-stitched edge** (explained on the next page). To make an extended binding, you must plan it before you cut the main

pieces; in order for the extra fabric to be folded up over the raw edges on to the quilt top, the backing must be cut larger than the top. This method can also be worked in reverse—that is, the top fabric can be cut larger and folded down over the backing.

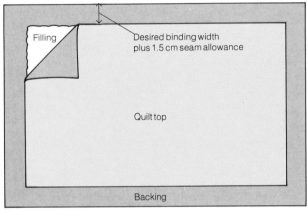

To prepare for self-finishing, you must cut the backing large enough to extend beyond the top piece by the desired binding width plus a 1.5 cm seam allowance on all four sides. Cut both top and filling to finished quilt size.

After quilting, press up the seam allowances of the backing. Then fold it over the edge to form the binding and slipstitch it to top fabric. Decide before you begin to stitch which corner treatment (below) you want to use.

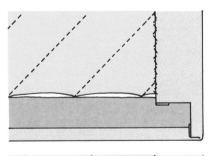

For a straight corner, slipstitch one side of the quilt. To reduce the bulk, trim away some of the corner fabric as shown.

Turn up the adjacent side and slipstitch it to the binding, then to the top fabric, as shown.

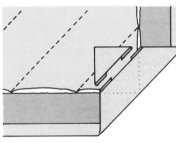

For a mitred corner, fold up the corner of the backing fabric so the diagonal fold lies at the corner point of the top fabric. Trim off the corner of the backing as shown.

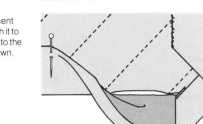

Fold up one side of the binding and slipstitch it in place. Then fold up the adjacent side and slipstitch it in place. Slipstitch the mitre – the diagonal line where the two edges of the binding meet – to close it.

Finishing edges

Self-finished edges/Slipstitched edges

The slipstitched method of finishing a quilt creates an inconspicuous finished edge, formed simply by folding under the seam allowances for both the top and backing fabrics, and slipstitching the folds together. This method requires no additional fabric, but trimmings, such as piping, ricrac, or ruffles, can be inserted between the folds if desired. When using the slipstitched method, be sure the quilting stitches stop about 1 cm from the edge so the seam allowances can be folded under. Do not stop the quilting too far from the edges, however, because this method does not secure the filling along the edges.

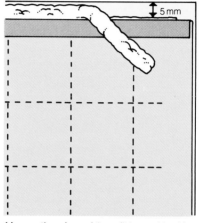

Line up the edges of the quilt top and backing. Trim the wadding so it is about 5 mm shorter than the top and backing fabrics.

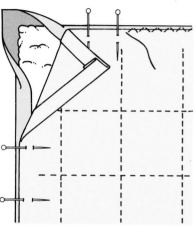

Fold the seam allowance from the top over the filling. Turn under the backing seam allowance. Align folds; pin, then slipstitch them together.

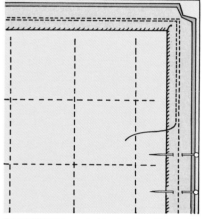

To add trimming, pin trimming to quilt top with raw edges of both trimming and quilt facing in the same direction; stitch along the quilt seamline.

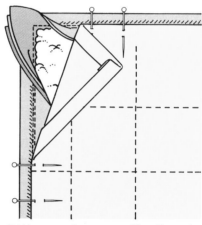

Fold top seam allowance over filling. Turn under backing seam allowance. Pin. Slipstitch backing to trimming along stitched line of trimming.

Bound edges

Binding is a type of edge finish that calls for a separate strip of fabric to cover the raw edges of the quilt. It is neat, durable, and especially practical if the raw edges are worn or uneven from having been stretched in the quilting frame. Binding is also recommended for finishing a quilted garment in order to avoid a bulky hem. This edge finish should be planned from the beginning so you can buy enough fabric. Finished bindings are traditionally narrow, about 5 mm to 1 cm wide. Cut from a contrasting fabric, binding becomes an attractive trimming. Binding can be cut either from the straight grain or on the bias of the fabric. Curved edges require bias binding; either will do for straight and angular edges. There are both single and double bindings. Single is used most often for quilts; for greater durability, however, you can use a double binding.

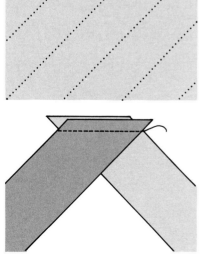

To make bias bindings, cut strips of fabric along the true bias of the fabric. For single binding, cut strips four times the desired finished width. For double binding, cut strips six times the desired finished width.

To join bias strips, place two together as shown and stitch on the straight grain of the fabric. Press the seam open.

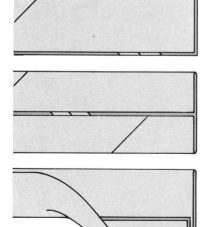

For a single binding, fold the strip in half lengthwise with wrong sides facing and press the fold lightly.

Open the pressed strip and fold the edges in so that they meet at the centre; press.

For a double binding, fold the strip in half lengthwise and press. Then fold this halved strip in thirds and press.

Applying binding

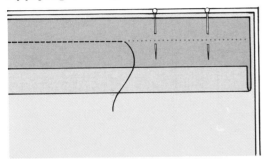

To apply single binding, open one folded edge. With right side of binding facing quilt top, pin binding to the edge of the quilt. Stitch along the foldline of the binding.

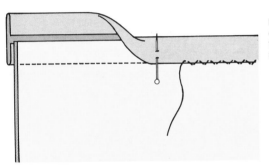

Press binding up. Turn it over raw edge so fold meets stitched line on the backing. Pin it in place and slipstitch to seamline by hand.

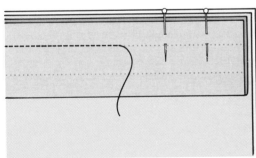

To apply double binding, open both folds. Pin binding to the quilt top with raw edges of binding and quilt aligned. Stitch binding to quilt along foldline nearest the edge.

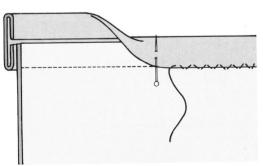

Press binding up, turning in second fold. Turn it over the raw edge so fold meets stitched line on backing. Pin it in place and slipstitch to seamline by hand.

Handling corners

Bound corners, whether curved or straight, are handled in different ways. If a corner is curved, binding can be eased to fit around it. To do this, binding must be bias. If a corner is square, the binding can be applied so that corners are straight, as below, or mitred (see next page). The techniques for all three remain the same whether the binding is single or double.

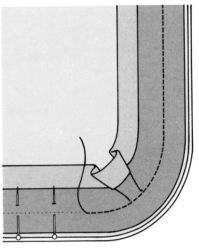

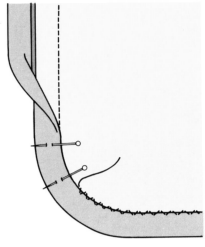

To bind a curved corner, pin bias binding to quilt edge as shown. Gently stretch the binding as you round the corner. Stitch along fold.

Press binding up and fold over to the backing. Binding will mould naturally over curved raw edge of quilt. Slipstitch to backing at stitch line.

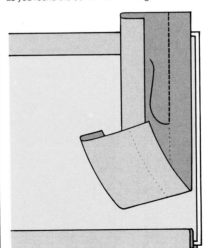

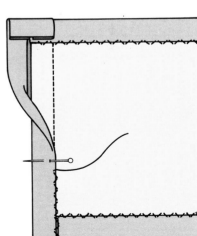

For straight corners, bind two opposite sides of the quilt. Then pin and stitch binding to one of the two remaining sides, letting the binding extend 1 cm at both ends.

Turn the extended portion of the binding over the bound edge, then finish binding the raw edge in the usual way. Repeat the same procedure to bind the remaining raw edge.

Finishing edges

Handling corners/Mitring

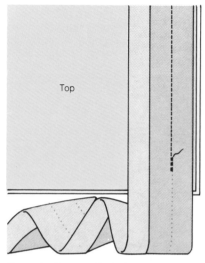

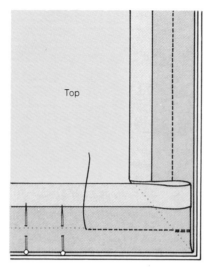

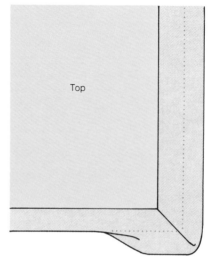

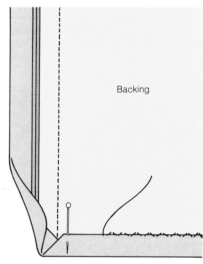

For a mitred corner, pin binding to one raw edge of quilt. Stitch along binding fold nearest raw edge, stopping and securing stitches at point where adjacent seam will cross this seamline.

Fold free binding to right, perpendicular to stitched edge, forming diagonal fold. Place binding parallel with lower edge and align right-hand fold with right edge. Stitch as shown.

Press the binding away from the quilt top, then fold it over raw edge to backing. A mitre will form on the quilt top. Another mitre will be formed by manipulating binding on back.

On backing side, bring folded edge to stitched line; pin. Fold excess binding under at corner, then bring adjacent binding together to form a mitre. Slipstitch binding along fold, and mitre.

Lining and interlining

Some quilting methods, the raised quilting techniques and puff patchwork in particular, require a lining or interlining to protect the stitching on the backing and to hide any raw edges. A lining is appropriate if you want to finish an item – such as a quilt, place-mat or tablecloth – to the edge. You will also want to use an interlining if you are working on a project, such as a garment, where the quilting will be seamed to adjoining sections, or where you want to finish the edge with a binding. A lining or interlining should be planned from the beginning so you can allow for the extra fabric that is needed.

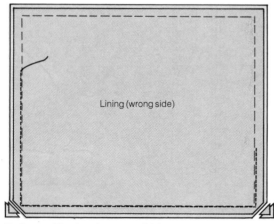

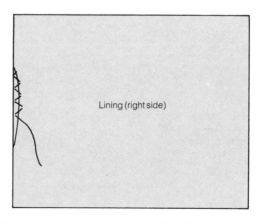

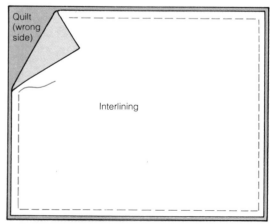

To line a quilt to the edge, cut the lining the same size as the quilt. Pin or tack the lining to the quilt with right sides facing. Stitch around the edge, leaving an opening for turning.

Remove the pins or tacking stitches. Trim off the corners to reduce bulk and turn the quilt right side out. Turn under the seam allowances of the opening and slipstitch it closed.

To interline. Cut interlining the same size as quilt. With wrong sides facing, tack interlining to quilt along edges. Treat quilt and interlining as one layer during subsequent construction.

Care of quilts

Washing, drying,
pressing and storing
Repairing damage

Careful laundering, proper storage and attention to repairs will prolong the life of quilts and quilted items.

To wash a quilt by machine, use a mild detergent and gentle agitation. Avoid bleach, harsh detergents or too much detergent, because these chemicals weaken textile fibres. Do not spin a quilt dry; this strains the quilting stitches and may break them. When washing by hand, use mild soap and do not twist or wring the quilt. Roll it in towels to remove as much moisture as possible.

To dry a quilt, tumble in a dryer or hang it on a clothes-line. Or, if you have the space, dry the quilt by spreading it out flat on a clean sheet.

If a quilt is made from fabrics such as wool, silk or velvet, which must be dry-cleaned, have this done as seldom as possible. Dry-cleaning chemicals wear out textile fabrics in time.

To press a quilt, pad the ironing board with a thick towel. Place the item quilted side down and steam-press lightly. Never press with the weight of the iron on the quilt.

Because textiles need to breathe, store a quilt by rolling it in a clean bed sheet. Do not use plastic because it prevents the air from circulating. Air a stored quilt at least once a year by hanging it on a clothes-line, preferably on a breezy day, and launder it approximately every five years to prevent the fabric from yellowing. If a quilt is folded for storage in a chest, re-fold it yearly to avoid permanent creases.

Quilts can easily be repaired if damaged. Re-binding will renew a worn edge. Remove the original binding before applying the new one. To blend new with faded colours, prepare the new binding fabric by washing it repeatedly or by bleaching it in the sun. To mend broken quilting stitches, insert the damaged area in a small hoop, carefully pull out the broken threads and re-stitch.

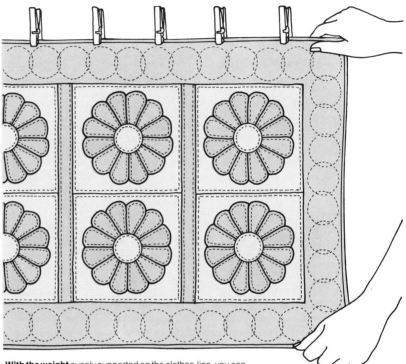

With the weight evenly supported on the clothes-line, you can straighten the edges of the wet quilt by pulling them.

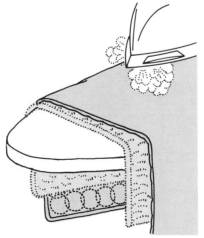

To press a quilt, steam-press lightly with the item quilted side down on a thick towel.

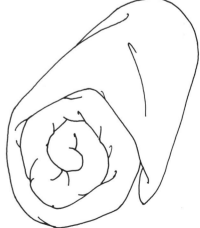

Store a quilt by rolling it up in a clean sheet. Do not use plastic.

261

Man's patchwork waistcoat

A patchwork waistcoat is a handsome addition to any man's wardrobe. A small one-shape design will work better than a block design.

Materials needed

1 m each of two different fabrics
Sewing thread
Fabric for waistcoat back and lining as indicated on pattern envelope

Making a template

To determine what size template to use, decide how many shells you want to fit across the front of the waistcoat and divide this number into the waistcoat width. For example, the waistcoat shown here measures 60 cm across. To fit 12 shells across the front, we used a 5 cm template. The template should not be smaller than 5 cm, but it may be larger. To make the template, see pp. 213 and 218.

Estimating fabric needs

To determine how large the pieced fabric must be, you need paper patterns for two waistcoat fronts. To make the sec-ond, place the front pattern piece, turned over, on a piece of paper, trace and cut it out, duplicating markings.

Position the two pieces on graph paper, leave 5 cm between them for matching. The pieced fabric should equal at least the length and width of the combined fronts. Draw the shell design over the graph paper, colour it in. Count the shells in each colour, you will need enough of each fabric for the shells in its colour. To calculate the actual amount, see p. 219. Here it was 1 m of each fabric.

Stitching

Cut out the shells (see p. 219) and sew them together (p. 232). Press the pieced fabric. Lay it on a flat surface; place the pattern pieces on top. To match the design down the centre front, place the markings for the centre front (which allow for an overlap for a button closure) at edge of one row of shells. Cut out pieces. Staystitch fronts 1 cm from the edge. Follow pattern directions.

The shell design used for the waistcoat was adapted from the one shown on p. 213.

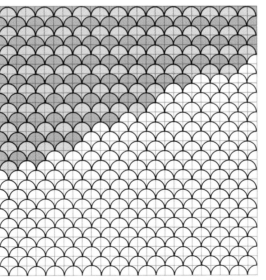

Place pattern piece and its mirror image on graph paper, leaving 5 cm between the two for matching the design. Pieced fabric should equal the length and width of combined pattern pieces.

To determine amount of fabric needed, draw shell design on graph paper and colour it in. Count number of shells in each colour; you will need enough of each fabric for each quantity of shells.

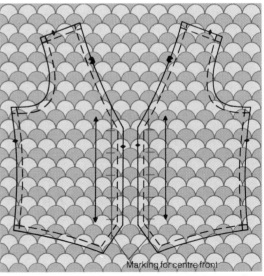

Marking for centre front

To match shell design down centre front of waistcoat, place marking for centre front (not seamline marking) at edge of one row of shells as if you were matching plaid or printed fabric.

Boy's dungarees/Machine appliqué

A child's name spelled out in printed cotton letters and a polka-dot tortoise are machine-appliquéd to boy's dungarees. A name or initials could also be appliquéd to a dress or skirt.

Materials needed
Paper and pencil for enlarging design
10 cm square pieces of various print or plain fabrics
Sewing thread

Enlarging the design
To enlarge the design, make a grid with 5 mm squares and copy the appropriate letters and the tortoise square for square (see p. 14). The enlarged letters measure 3 cm high by approximately 3 cm wide, depending on the width of the specific letter. To see if the name you want to appliqué will fit the available space, multiply the number of letters in the name by 3 cm. Allow 3 mm to 5 mm space between letters.

Cut out the letters and the separate parts of the tortoise. Pin these pieces to the appropriate fabrics and trace around each one with a pencil. Cut out each piece outside the marked lines, leaving an ample seam allowance.

Stitching
Position letters on the bib and pin them in place. Here the name is placed about 3 cm above top seam of waistband. The placing of both name and tortoise will vary, depending on type and size of garment used. To position the parts of the tortoise, pin the shell on the dungarees first. We placed it in the centre of the bib, 3 cm down from the top edge. Then pin head, legs and tail pieces in position, lifting edge of shell so it overlaps the other pieces. (The extra allowance outside the marked lines will overlap still more.) Straight-stitch around the shell on the marked line. Then, with sharp, pointed embroidery scissors, trim away extra fabric around shell, cutting as close to the straight stitching as possible. Straight-stitch around the head, legs and tail; straight-stitch also around each of the letters; trim the excess fabric from all these pieces. Use zigzag stitch to go round each letter and parts of tortoise to cover raw fabric edges and stitching (see p. 196). To zigzag around corners and curves, see p. 197. Pull thread ends to inside, knot them and trim excess.

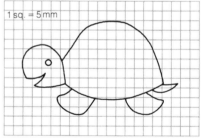

To enlarge tortoise, make grid with 5 mm squares; copy design by squares (see p. 14).

Machine appliqué, sturdy enough for children's clothing, is easy to do on a zigzag machine.

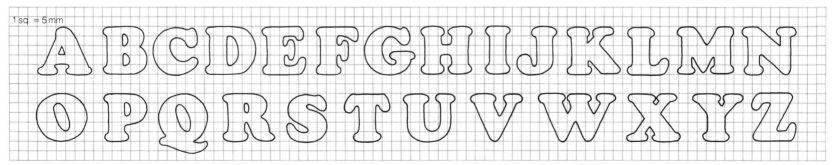

To enlarge the letters, make a grid with 5 mm squares and copy the desired letters square for square (see p. 14). Make sure the letters in the name you want to appliqué will fit the available space.

Baby quilt

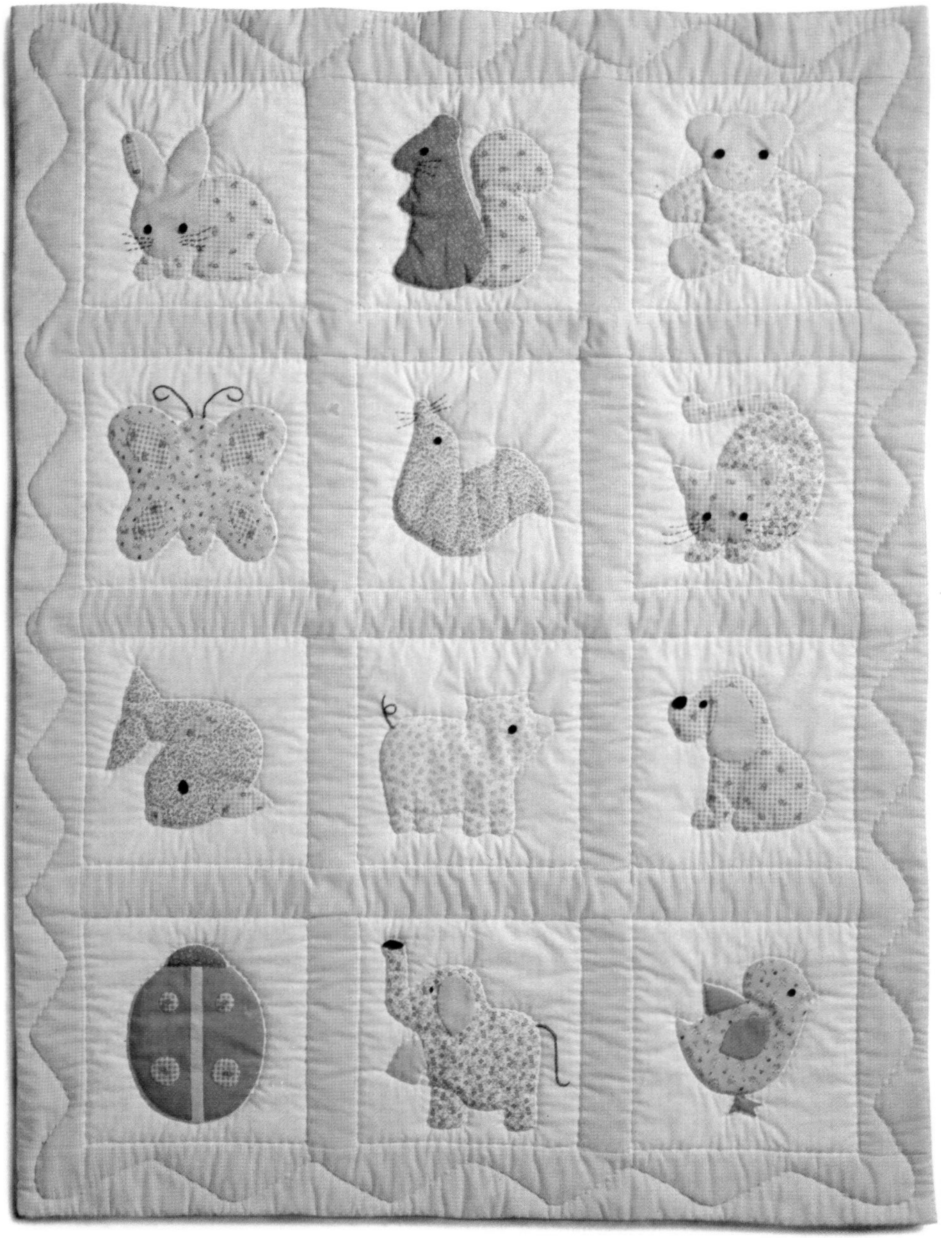

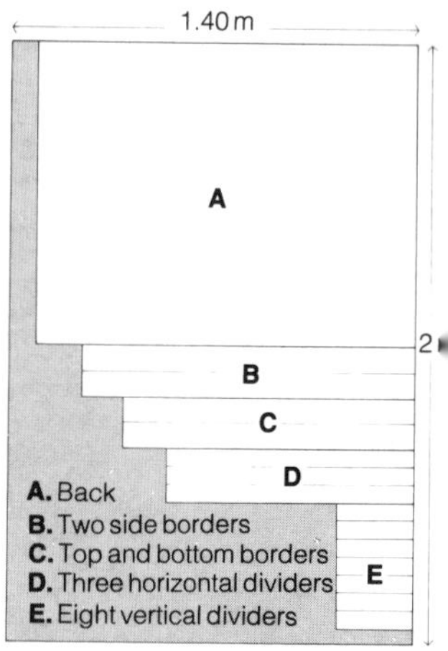

A quilt appliquéd with baby animals is a delightful addition to any child's room. The directions that follow are for making up the quilt exactly as pictured on the right. To change the quilt to suit your needs, you can choose one favourite animal and appliqué it twelve times. Or you could select three or four animals, arranging them any way that pleases you.

Materials needed

Paper and pencil for enlarging designs
Stiff paper for templates
25 cm each of ten different fabrics for animal appliqués
1 m × 1.40 m wide white fabric for base squares
2 m × 1.40 m wide fabric for strips, borders and quilt backing
1.01 m × 1.31 m piece of wadding
White quilting and sewing thread
1 skein black stranded cotton
Embroidery hoop
Sharps and crewel needles

The appliqué animals

To enlarge the animals, make a grid with 2.5 cm squares; copy the shapes square for square (see p. 14). Each animal appliqué is composed of two or more fabrics. The animal's body is made of one fabric; the head, tail, ear and other body parts indicated in grey on the drawing (see opposite page) are of a second fabric. You will need a template for each shape. Trace around each piece of each animal separately; follow the directions on pp. 193–4 for making templates and cutting out each shape. We used ten different printed and plain fabrics in pink, yellow, pale blue and pale green for the animals; you can use fabrics in colours of your choice.

On the white fabric, mark twelve 26 cm squares (a 25 cm square plus a 5 mm seam allowance on each side). Appliqué the animals to the squares by hand (see p. 195). To decide the layering order of the appliqué, see p. 198. For most of the animals, the body is appliquéd first,

with such separate parts as the head, tail or ear applied as the second layer. Exceptions are the squirrel's tail, the elephant's leg, the ladybird's head and the chick's back wing; these parts are appliquéd first. A third layer is used for the teddy bear's nose.

Embroidery

The animals' small features, those that are too small to be cut out of fabric, are embroidered. The eyes are satin stitched (see p. 48), the tails and antennae are backstitched (see p. 22), and the whiskers are worked in running stitch

(p. 46). When appliqué and embroidery are complete, cut out the squares.

The quilt top

To complete the quilt top, cut out, from the backing fabric, three 6 cm × 86 cm strips for the horizontal dividers and eight 6 cm × 26 cm strips for the vertical

The baby quilt combines the techniques of appliqué, patchwork and quilting. Animals are appliquéd; blocks, dividers and borders are pieced; and the layers are quilted together. Each appliquéd block is also embellished with embroidery stitches. You can make the quilt exactly as pictured on the left, or you can change it to suit your needs. One animal could be appliquéd in twelve different fabrics. Or you could use three or four favourite animals in a pleasing arrangement. Or you could use fabrics in colours that are bolder than the pink, yellow, light blue and light green used here.

Cutting layout for backing, strips and borders

A. Back
B. Two side borders
C. Top and bottom borders
D. Three horizontal dividers
E. Eight vertical dividers

dividers. For borders cut two 8.5 cm ×
1.01 m rectangles for the top and bottom, and two 8.5 cm × 1.15 m rectangles for the sides. These measurements
allow a 5 mm seam allowance on all
edges. To sew the blocks, dividers and
borders, see pp. 230 – 1. Join them in
this order. Join the blocks and the vertical dividers to form horizontal strips;
sew horizontal strips and horizontal
dividers together; add the borders last.
Follow the drawing (right) for the placing of the individual blocks. Then press
the seam allowances between blocks and
vertical dividers to one side; alternate
the direction from strip to strip. When
all blocks and dividers have been joined,
add the borders. Attach the side borders
first, then stitch top and bottom borders, overlapping the side borders.
Press seams, then entire top.

Assembling the quilt
Cut a 1.01 m × 1.31 m rectangle of
fabric for the backing, and a piece of
wadding the same size. Place the backing right side down on a flat surface; put
the wadding on top. Fold the quilt top in
quarters with right side inside (see
p. 248). Place folded top on bottom
quarter of wadding, then unfold it,
smoothing wrinkles. Pin and tack
layers through the centre.

Quilting
Each animal appliqué is outline quilted
(see p. 239). Quilt around each animal
and around the inside of each square. To
quilt the border, enlarge the border
quilting design (see p. 14) and transfer it
to the fabric (see p. 244), following the
drawing on the right. Remove the
tacking.

Finishing
The edges of the quilt are finished with a
technique called self-finishing (see
p. 258). Turn under 5 mm on all four
edges of both the quilt top and backing;
trim away 5 mm of wadding on all sides.
Slipstitch quilt top to backing, being
careful not to catch wadding in between.

To enlarge the animals,
make a grid with 2.5 cm
squares and copy the
shapes square for square
(see p. 14). The grey areas
represent changes of
appliqué fabric. The
drawing shows placing of
squares to make the quilt
pictured opposite; you can
place the animals in any
positions you wish.

The sewing of blocks,
dividers and borders is
done in a precise order.
The vertical dividers are
first sewn to the blocks;
strips of blocks are sewn to
horizontal dividers. Then
borders are attached: side
borders first, then top and
bottom borders.

To quilt, outline each
animal, then quilt around
the inside of each block. To
quilt the border, enlarge the
border design by making a
grid with 2.5 cm squares
and copy the quilting
design square for square.
Transfer the border design
to the quilt (see p. 244).

**Finished size
of quilt:**
1 m × 1.30 m

**Cut size of
quilt parts:**
Twelve base squares,
26 cm square

Eight vertical
dividers,
6 cm × 26 cm

Three horizontal
dividers,
6 cm × 86 cm

Top and bottom
borders,
8.5 cm × 1.01 m

Two side borders,
8.5 cm × 1.15 m

265

The motif for this wall hanging is adapted from the cut-through appliqué design shown on p. 201.

Cut-through appliqué wall hanging

Cut-through appliqué gets its striking effects for very little money. Fabrics are all simple cottons.

Materials needed
50 cm each of white, green, beige and yellow cotton fabrics
25 cm orange cotton fabric
Thread to match each fabric colour
50 cm fabric for backing
50 cm interfacing
Crewel needles
Embroidery scissors
Two 15 mm diameter brass curtain rods

Cut-through appliqué
To enlarge the design, make a grid with 1 cm squares and copy design square for square (see p. 14). Cut 40 cm × 48 cm rectangles from white, green, beige and yellow fabrics. Trace design centrally on the green fabric. To assemble fabrics, place the yellow right side up, followed by the beige, the white and the green. Tack layers together around the edges. Orange fabric is used to insert patches (see p. 205).

To work the appliqué, follow the directions on p. 205, using the diagram below to determine which shapes are cut from which layers.

Finishing
For the backing, cut a 40 cm × 48 cm rectangle of backing fabric and one of interfacing. Tack interfacing to wrong side of backing 5 mm from the edge. To make hanging loops, cut six 16 cm × 9 cm rectangles. Fold them in half crosswise with right sides facing; stitch 5 mm from the edge. Turn the resulting tube right side out; press tube with seam in centre back. Fold tube so that raw edges meet and seam is on the inside. To attach loops to backing fabric, pin one loop on each end and one in the centre of the two 48 cm sides, aligning raw edges of loops and backing. Stitch 1 cm from raw edge; remove pins. Place appliqué face down on top; stitch around all four sides, leaving a 15 cm opening. Trim corners, turn right side out, and press. Stitch opening up by hand.

To enlarge design, make a grid with 1 cm squares and copy the design square for square (see p. 14).

To cut out shapes for reverse appliqué, follow directions on p. 205, using the key above to determine which shapes are cut from which layers.

First layer
Second layer (white)
Third layer
Fourth layer
Patches

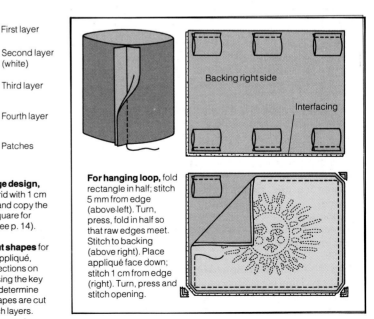

Backing right side

Interfacing

For hanging loop, fold rectangle in half; stitch 5 mm from edge (above left). Turn, press, fold in half so that raw edges meet. Stitch to backing (above right). Place appliqué face down; stitch 1 cm from edge (right). Turn, press and stitch opening.

Patchwork floor cushion

Floor cushion adapts Drunkard's Path, a traditional design, to a modern setting.

Materials needed

50 cm × 70 cm each of two contrasting cottons

2 m unbleached calico (50 cm for patches, 1.50 m for cushion shape)

1 m fabric for backing

63 cm square piece of wadding

Polystyrene beads or foam chips

Sewing and quilting thread

The patchwork

The cushion top consists of four Drunkard's Path patchwork blocks. Each block is made up of sixteen 8 cm squares, which in turn are composed of two curved pieces. The cut size of the squares is 9 cm; this allows for 5 mm seams. To make the templates for the two curved pieces, see p. 218. Use the drawing below, left, to decide how many pieces you will need to cut from each fabric. To stitch the pieces together for each block, see p. 223. To join the blocks, follow the directions on p. 230.

Quilting

Cut a 63 cm square of calico. Place calico on a flat surface; put the wadding on top, followed by the patchwork right side up. Pin and tack these three layers together. The quilting outlines the shape formed by the red patches; the quilting stitches are placed 5 mm inside the seamlines.

Assembling the cushion

To make a cushion form, cut two 64 cm squares of calico. With right sides facing, stitch 1 cm from the edge around all four sides, leaving a 25 cm opening. Trim the corners, turn right side out, and fill with polystyrene beads or foam chips. Sew the opening up by hand. To finish the cushion cover, cut a 63 cm square of backing fabric. With right sides together, stitch the quilted cushion top to the backing along three sides 5 mm from the edge. Trim the seams and turn cushion cover right side out. Insert the cushion form and stitch up the opening by hand.

The design for the floor cushion was adapted from the Drunkard's Path block shown on p. 213.

The cushion top is composed of four blocks in the Drunkard's Path pattern. The patches that form the design are red; the background patches are off-white in the centre and brown at the corners.

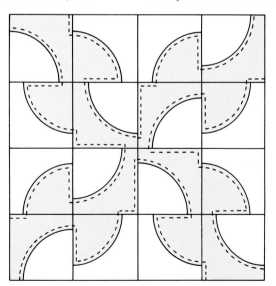

The quilting outlines the shape formed by the red patches. Place quilting stitches 5 mm inside the seamlines. The drawing shows stitching plan for one block; the others are quilted the same way.

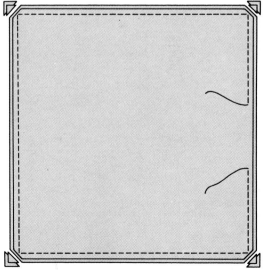

To make a cushion form, place two 64 cm squares of calico together. Stitch 1 cm from the edge, leaving a 25 cm opening. Clip corners, turn right side out and fill. Stitch opening by hand.

Quilted evening bag

Stuffed and all-over quilting decorate an attractive and original evening bag.

Materials needed

Paper and pencil for enlarging design
40 cm satin, 90 cm wide
40 cm muslin
Wadding
1 m cord
3 spools silk buttonhole twist
Sewing thread

The design

To enlarge the pattern for the bag, make a grid with 1 cm squares and copy the shape square by square (see p. 14). Put the pattern on the satin and trace around it; cut it out about 5 cm beyond the cutting lines. Transfer the oval and quilting lines to the fabric (see pp. 16–17). Enlarge the floral design by making a grid with 5 mm squares; transfer the design to the fabric. Back satin with muslin and using the silk buttonhole twist, work the padded quilting first (see p. 253).

Trace the bag pattern on the remaining muslin and the wadding. Cut out the shape about 5 cm beyond the cutting line. Place the bag face up on top of the wadding and muslin. Pin and tack the layers together. Quilt along marked lines with running stitch (see p. 250), using the silk buttonhole twist.

Assembling the bag

Trim the quilted bag along the cutting line. Use the pattern to cut the shape for the lining from the satin. Place lining and bag with right sides together. Stitch 1 cm from the edge, leaving a 15 cm opening. Trim corners; turn right side out. Stitch up opening by hand. For the handle, cut a 66 cm length of cord. To finish the ends, cut two 2.5 cm × 5 cm rectangles of satin. Fold under 5 mm on all sides, then fold the rectangles in half crosswise. Put one end of the cord inside each fold; stitch the top edges, catching the cord securely; sew satin pieces to bag lining. To assemble, fold the bag, following diagram below right, and stitch the sides.

The floral motif on the flap of the evening bag is the padded quilting design shown on p. 253.

1 sq. = 5 mm

To enlarge the design, make a grid of 5 mm squares and copy the design square for square (see p. 14). Transfer the design to the oval area on the bag. To work the padded quilting, follow the directions on p. 253.

To enlarge pattern for bag, make a grid with 1 cm squares and copy the shape square for square. Transfer oval motif and black quilting lines, starting with black lines, to bag (see pp. 16–17). Work padded quilting first. Assemble bag, wadding and muslin; stitch quilting lines.

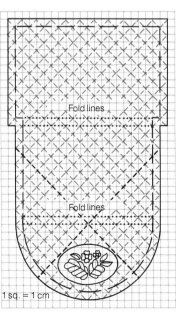

Fold lines

Fold lines

1 sq. = 1 cm

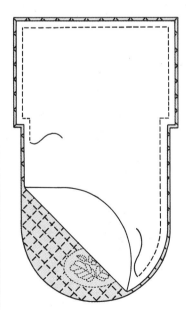

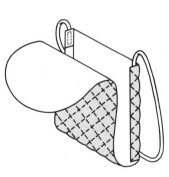

Place lining on bag with right sides facing. Stitch 1 cm from the edge, leaving a 15 cm opening for turning. Trim seam; turn right side out. Sew up opening.

To assemble bag, fold as shown. Stitch sides to body of bag along bottom and back. Sew one satin-covered cord end to lining at each side.

Crochet

Crochet basics

Yarns

Crocheting can be done with any stringy material from finest tatting cotton to raffia, leather cords or fabric strips. Your choice only has to suit the purpose and be worked with an appropriate hook (see opposite page for selection).

For convenience in comparing similar yarn types, a chart of wools and synthetic yarns appears on the opening page of the Knitting chapter; below is a chart of crochet yarns. A significant difference between these two groups: yarns in the first are sold by weight, those in the second by ball. Sometimes the length is shown in metres.

Most cotton yarns are *mercerised;* this means they have undergone a process that strengthens and gives them greater lustre. Most are *colourfast,* a term that signifies colours will not run or fade in hot water. Some of these terms appear on the label, along with other descriptive information, such as number of *plies* or *cords* – single units – that have been twisted together, and sometimes a number (usually between 10 and 60) that signifies thickness of the ply. The higher the number, the finer the yarn. If yarn comes in a skein, it is best to wind it in a ball to prevent it tangling in use.

VARIETIES OF YARNS

Coloured crochet cotton, No. 5. This is a 4-ply, firmly twisted thread, made in a large selection of colours. It is suitable for making shawls, blouses, dresses, bedspreads, curtains and trimmings.

Metallic synthetic yarn, No. 5. This is a 4-ply synthetic yarn, bound with metallic thread, available in white and some colours. It is suitable for making sweaters, blouses and fashion accessories.

Crochet cotton, No. 5. This is a 4-ply, firmly twisted thread, made by a different manufacturer and slightly finer than the thread shown at the top of this table. It is suitable for making the same items.

Crochet cotton, No. 3. This is a 2-ply firmly twisted thread, made in a large selection of colours, and can be used to make place mats, tablecloths and bedspreads.

Crochet cotton, No. 5. This is a thread more firmly twisted and slightly finer than the other No. 5 threads shown in this table. It is very suitable for bedspreads, tablecloths, place mats and trimmings.

Pearl cotton, No. 5. This 2-ply thread is very loosely twisted and has a high sheen. It is made in a large selection of colours and is suitable for clothes, trimmings and fashion accessories.

Tatting thread, No. 60. This is a 6-ply cotton thread, very firmly twisted, and is made in several colours. It is used for tatting, lacemaking and for crochet trimmings.

Bouclé yarn. This is made in various thicknesses, and is mostly 3-ply. It is a loosely twisted slubbed yarn suitable for sweaters, dresses and fashion accessories.

Crochet cotton, No. 20 and 30. This is a 6-ply, fine firmly twisted thread, mostly available in pale shades and suitable for lace, trimmings and delicate crochet tablecloths and mats.

Crochet cotton, No. 10, 20, 30 and 40. This is a 6-ply, fine firmly twisted thread available in many thicknesses and colours and suitable for trimmings, lace, place mats and tablecloths.

Hooks and supplementary equipment

Crochet hooks are made in many sizes and materials. Thickness of most hooks is indicated by a number (the number corresponds to the same size in a knitting needle); the larger the number, the larger the size. Steel hooks for fine crochet are usually 13 cm long, and made in a range of sizes from 60 mm to 1.75 mm. When selecting a hook, the thicker your yarn, the larger your hook should be to make the work easier.

Collect several sizes of crochet hook, so that if the tension of a sample is not right you can make another sample using a hook that is one size larger or smaller.

To prevent the hooks getting lost, keep them together with an elastic band in your work-basket, or if you prefer, make a felt bag with a narrow pocket for each hook, like a pencil case. Mark each section with the size of the hook and it will be easy to keep the hooks safe, and to find a hook quickly to use for any piece of crochet.

The illustration below shows two hooks – the fine steel hook and the normal hook that are available from most shops. The others are more unusual, but are included for general interest. Most hooks are made of aluminium, but wood or plastic hooks make a change to work with.

There are supplementary knitting aids that can be useful for crochet. Among these are row counters to keep track of the work completed, coiled ring markers, a ruler for measuring tension, and a gauge for measuring hook sizes (see Knitting, p. 413).

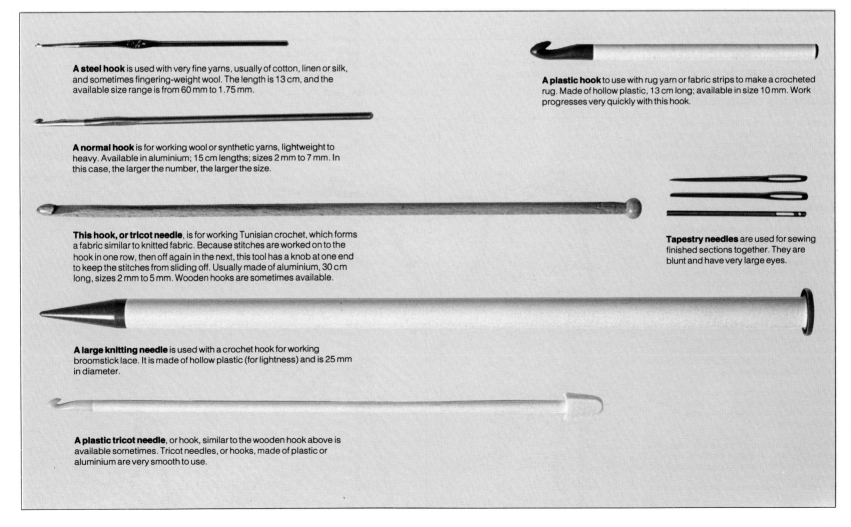

A steel hook is used with very fine yarns, usually of cotton, linen or silk, and sometimes fingering-weight wool. The length is 13 cm, and the available size range is from 60 mm to 1.75 mm.

A normal hook is for working wool or synthetic yarns, lightweight to heavy. Available in aluminium; 15 cm lengths; sizes 2 mm to 7 mm. In this case, the larger the number, the larger the size.

This hook, or tricot needle, is for working Tunisian crochet, which forms a fabric similar to knitted fabric. Because stitches are worked on to the hook in one row, then off again in the next, this tool has a knob at one end to keep the stitches from sliding off. Usually made of aluminium, 30 cm long, sizes 2 mm to 5 mm. Wooden hooks are sometimes available.

A large knitting needle is used with a crochet hook for working broomstick lace. It is made of hollow plastic (for lightness) and is 25 mm in diameter.

A plastic tricot needle, or hook, similar to the wooden hook above is available sometimes. Tricot needles, or hooks, made of plastic or aluminium are very smooth to use.

A plastic hook to use with rug yarn or fabric strips to make a crocheted rug. Made of hollow plastic, 13 cm long; available in size 10 mm. Work progresses very quickly with this hook.

Tapestry needles are used for sewing finished sections together. They are blunt and have very large eyes.

Crochet basics

Introduction to crocheting

All crochet stitches are formed by inter-locking loops. The basic stitch is the chain stitch, shown below. To work a chain, the hook is held in one hand and yarn is held taut in the other, while the hand holding the yarn also supports the work where the hook enters it.

Two common ways to hold a hook with the right hand are shown on the immediate right. Use whichever feels more comfortable. There are several correct methods of holding yarn; one is illustrated below. The basic idea is to keep the yarn taut over your index finger so you can manipulate it easily and with even tension around the hook.

Holding the hook/Right-handed

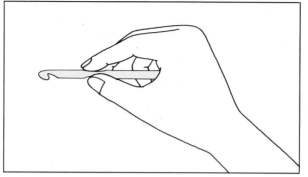

Method 1. With hook facing down, grasp tool in the right hand, holding it almost as you would a knife, with thumb and index finger on either side of the flat part, middle finger resting against the thumb.

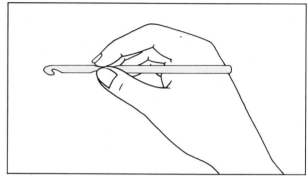

Method 2. With hook facing down, grasp tool in the right hand, holding it as you would a pencil, with thumb and index finger on either side of the flat part, middle finger resting against the thumb.

Making the chain stitch/Right-handed

The chain stitch (ch) is used to form the first row of crochet, and is an integral part of many pattern stitches as well. As the foundation, it should be formed loosely enough for the hook to enter each chain easily, without drawing in the edge of the work.

1. To start chain, make a slip knot about 15 cm from the yarn end; insert hook right to left.

2. Pulling both yarn ends, draw in the loop until it is close to hook, but not too tight.

3. Wrap ball end of yarn around little finger of left hand, take it under fourth and third fingers, then over top of index finger, leaving about 5 cm of yarn between finger and hook.

4. Holding the slip knot between thumb and middle finger of left hand, and keeping yarn taut over index finger, push hook forward, at the same time twisting it, so yarn passes over it back to front and is caught in the slot.

5. Draw yarn through the loop, thus forming a new loop on the hook. The newly formed loop should be loose enough for the next chain to be drawn through it easily.

6. Holding chain nearest the hook with thumb and middle finger, repeat Steps 4 and 5 until you have desired number of chains (loop on hook does not count as part of the total). All chains should be the same size. If they are not, it is best to pull them out and start again.

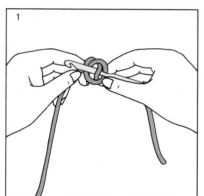

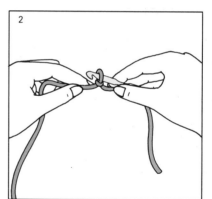

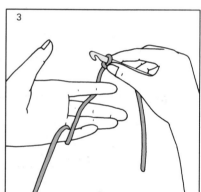

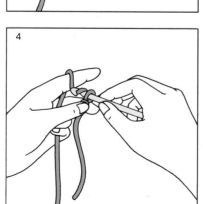

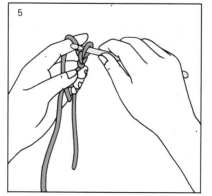

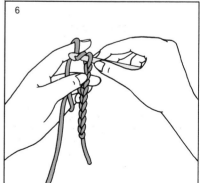

Holding the hook/Left-handed

Crocheting with the left hand is exactly the same as with the right hand, but with the hook and yarn position reversed. Because starting a new technique can be difficult if you have to mirror illustrations, instructions on this page are provided to help the left-handed person.

Two common ways to hold a hook with the left hand are shown on the immediate right. Use whichever feels more comfortable. There are several correct methods of holding yarn; one is illustrated below. The basic idea is to keep the yarn taut over your index finger so you can manipulate it easily and with even tension around the hook.

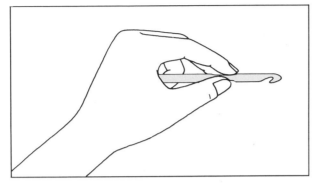

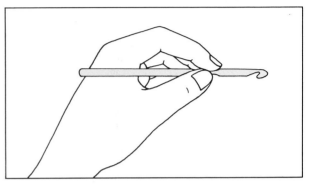

Method 1. With hook facing down, grasp tool in the left hand, holding it almost as you would a knife, with thumb and index finger on either side of the flat part, middle finger resting against the thumb.

Method 2. With hook facing down, grasp tool in the left hand, holding it as you would a pencil, with thumb and index finger on either side of the flat part, middle finger resting against the thumb.

Making the chain stitch/Left-handed

The chain stitch (ch) is used to form the first row of crochet, and is an integral part of many pattern stitches as well. As the foundation, it should be formed loosely enough for the hook to enter each chain easily, without drawing in the edge of the work.

1. To start chain, make a slip knot about 15 cm from the yarn end; insert hook left to right.

2. Pulling both yarn ends, draw in the loop until it is close to hook, but not too tight.

3. Wrap ball end of yarn around little finger of right hand, take it under fourth and third fingers, then over top of index finger, leaving about 5 cm of yarn between finger and hook.

4. Holding the slip knot between thumb and middle finger of right hand, and keeping yarn taut over the index finger, push hook forward, at the same time twisting it, so yarn passes over it back to front and is caught in the slot.

5. Draw yarn through the loop, thus forming a new loop on the hook. The newly formed loop should be loose enough for the next chain to be drawn through it easily.

6. Holding chain nearest the hook with thumb and middle finger, repeat Steps 4 and 5 until you have desired number of chains (loop on hook does not count as part of the total). All chains should be the same size. If they are not, it is best to pull them out and start again.

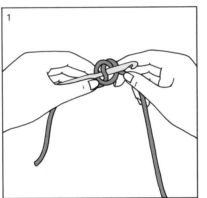

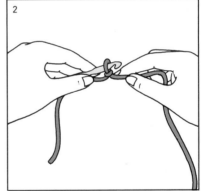

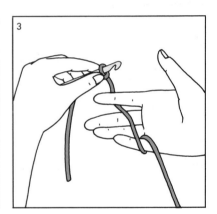

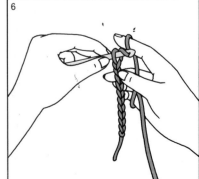

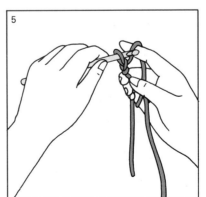

Crochet basics

Forming the elementary stitches

Double crochet (dc). Shortest of the basic stitches, it makes a firm, flat fabric. Often used to finish edges of other stitch patterns, and sometimes to join two finished sections.

Insert hook in 2nd chain from hook, catch yarn (A), and draw a loop through the chain (2 loops on hook), yarn round hook and draw through 2 loops to complete stitch (B). Work 1 double crochet in each chain across row. After last stitch, work 1 chain and turn; insert hook in 1st stitch to start next row (C).

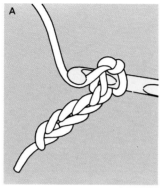

A

Insert hook in 2nd ch

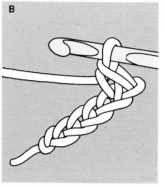

B

Double crochet stitch completed

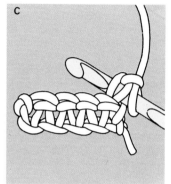

C

1 ch to turn, insert hook in 1st st

Half treble crochet (htr). Slightly taller than double crochet, this stitch has a pronounced ridge in its texture; makes a firm, attractive fabric.

Yarn round hook and insert hook in 3rd chain from hook, catch yarn (A) and draw a loop through the chain (3 loops on hook), yarn round hook, draw a loop through 3 loops to complete stitch (B). Work 1 half treble crochet in each chain across the row. After last stitch, work 2 chain and turn; yarn round hook, insert hook in 1st stitch to start next row (C).

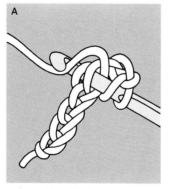

A

Insert hook in 3rd chain

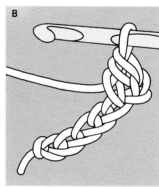

B

Half treble crochet stitch completed

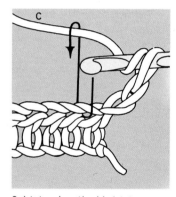

C

2 ch to turn, insert hook in 1st st

Treble crochet (tr). Twice as tall as double crochet and less compact. Forms the basis of many pattern stitches.

Yarn round hook and insert hook in 4th chain from hook, catch yarn (A), draw a loop through the chain (3 loops on hook), yarn round hook, draw through 2 loops, yarn round hook, draw through last 2 loops to complete stitch (B). Make 1 treble crochet in each chain across the row. After last stitch, work 3 chain and turn; yarn round hook, insert hook in 2nd stitch for next row (C).

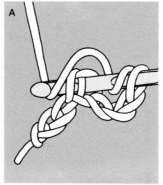

A

Yarn round hook, insert hook in 4th ch

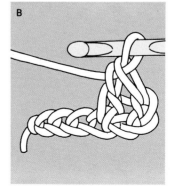

B

Treble crochet stitch completed

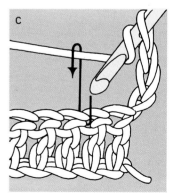

C

3 ch to turn, insert hook in 2nd st

Double treble crochet (dtr). A tall stitch, more open than treble crochet and used less frequently.

Yarn round hook twice, insert hook in 5th chain from hook, catch yarn (A), draw a loop through the chain (4 loops on hook), yarn round hook, draw through 2 loops, yarn round hook, draw through 2 loops, yarn round hook, draw through last 2 loops to complete stitch (B). Work 1 double treble crochet in each chain across row, 4 chain, turn, yarn round hook twice, insert hook in 2nd stitch to start next row (C).

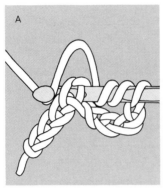

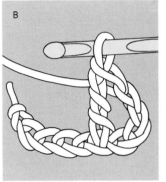

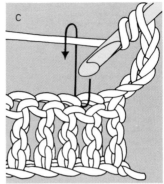

Yarn round hook twice, insert in 5th ch

Double treble crochet stitch completed

4 ch to turn, insert hook in 2nd st

Triple treble crochet (trtr). Essentially the same as double treble but taller. You can make an even taller stitch by adding yet another loop of yarn round the hook at the beginning.

Yarn round hook 3 times, insert hook in 6th ch from hook, catch yarn (A), draw a loop through chain (5 loops on hook), *yarn round hook, draw through 2 loops*, repeat the instructions between *3 more times to complete stitch (B). Make 1 triple treble crochet in each chain across row, 5 chain, turn; yarn round hook 3 times, insert hook in 2nd stitch to start next row (C).

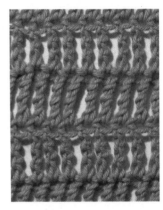

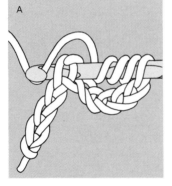

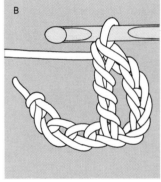

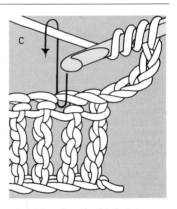

Yarn round hook 3 times, insert in 6th ch

Triple treble crochet stitch completed

5 ch to turn, insert hook in 2nd st

Slipstitch (ss). A very short stitch used primarily for joining, as in the closing of a ring or motif round, or the seaming of two finished pieces. Though not used to produce fabric, it is sometimes worked along an edge to strengthen it and to minimise stretching.

Insert hook in chain (or stitch), catch yarn (A), draw a loop through both the chain and the loop on the hook (B).

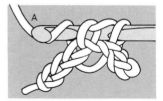

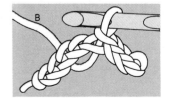

BASIC CROCHET RULES

1. The chain on the hook is never counted as part of a foundation row. For example, if directions say 18 chain, you should have 18 in addition to one on the hook.
2. Always insert hook into a chain or stitch from front to back.*
3. Always insert hook under the two top loops of a chain or stitch.*
4. There should be just one loop left on the hook at completion of a stitch or sequence.

*Unless directions say otherwise.

TURNING CHAINS

At the beginning of each row (including the first one) a certain number of chains are needed to bring work up to the level of the stitch that is to be formed. The exact number of chains depends on the height of the stitch (see below), and in the case of tall stitches – treble, double treble, and so on – this chain usually replaces the first stitch of each row. When instructions place the turning chain at the end of a row, you should turn work right to left to avoid twisting the chain, then insert hook in the stitch that is specified.

Double crochet .... 1 chain to turn, insert hook in 1st stitch
Half treble crochet................................2 chains to turn, insert hook in 1st stitch
Treble crochet...................................... 3 chains to turn, insert hook in 2nd stitch
Double treble crochet .... 4 chains to turn, insert hook in 2nd stitch
Triple treble crochet .... 5 chains to turn, insert hook in 2nd stitch

Crochet basics

Variations on elementary techniques

Working under one loop produces a ribbed effect and a more open pattern than is achieved with the usual technique (that is, inserting the hook under two loops).

To work the back loop only, insert hook front to back with a downward motion, catch the yarn (A), draw up a loop and complete the stitch.

To work the front loop only, insert hook front to back with an upward motion, catch the yarn (B), draw up a loop and complete the stitch.

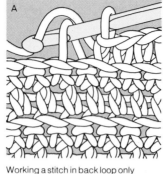

Working a stitch in back loop only

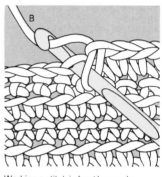

Working a stitch in front loop only

Working between stitches is a technique used in many patterns, meshes (p. 292), for example. One or more chains are made between stitches in one row; in the next row, you crochet into the *chain* or *chain space*. Always note which method is specified, because results are different for each.

To work into chain between stitches, insert hook under the 2 top loops; make stitch *through* the chain (A).

To work into a chain space between stitches, insert hook under the chain and make a stitch or group of stitches *over* the chain (B).

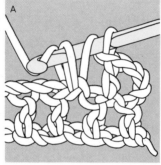

Working *into* chain between stitches

Working *over* chain between stitches

Raised stitches use a technique that creates a three-dimensional effect. Though it is shown here applied to treble crochet, the method is suitable also for double or double treble crochet. The raised stitches can be worked to either the front or the back, or alternately front and back, depending on the desired results. See p. 285 for patterns in which this technique is employed; p. 310 for ribbing that can be produced by it.

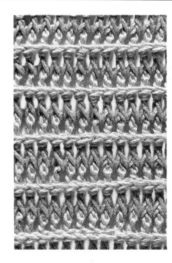
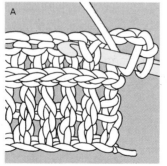

Raised treble round the front. Yarn round hook, insert hook front to back between next 2 stitches, then bring it forward between the stitch being worked and the one after it; hook is now positioned horizontally behind stitch. Complete the treble crochet.

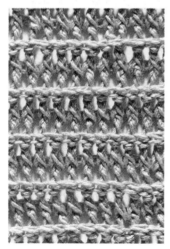
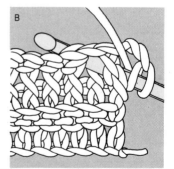

Raised treble round the back. Yarn round hook, insert hook back to front between next 2 stitches, then back again between the stitch being worked and the one after it; hook is now positioned horizontally in front of stitch. Complete the treble crochet.

A double chain stitch makes a sturdier foundation than a simple chain. It can also be used alone for a narrow trimming or cord.

Make a slip knot and 2 chain, work 1 double crochet in 2nd chain from hook, *insert hook under the left loop of the double crochet, catch yarn (A) and draw up a loop (B), yarn round hook, draw through 2 loops (C)*. Repeat instructions between asterisks until chain is the desired length.

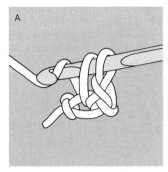

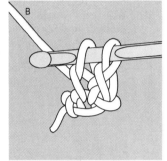

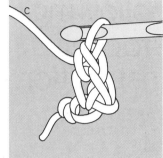

Working under left loop of the dc | Two loops on the hook | Loop drawn through the 2 loops

Double-faced treble crochet makes a sturdy, very thick fabric.
Multiple of any number of chains
Row 1: *1 treble crochet in each chain*, 3 chain, turn
Row 2: With fabric sideways, miss 1st stitch, *yarn round hook, insert hook in back loop of next stitch and back loop of foundation chain, catch yarn (A), draw a loop through 2 back loops, then complete treble crochet (B)*, repeat from asterisk to end of row, 3 chain, turn. Repeat Row 2, working into back of each treble crochet on this and previous row (C).

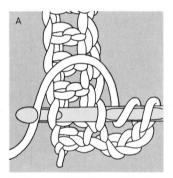

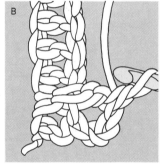

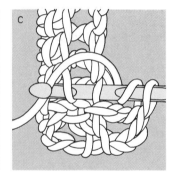

Working under 2 back loops of Row 1 | A treble crochet completed in Row 2 | Starting the 1st stitch of Row 3

Solomon's knot is a double knot stitch. The elongated loops are interlocked in such a way that they produce a mesh fabric similar to netting. Though 1.5 cm is the typical recommendation for loop length in many instructions, any length is suitable so long as it is consistent. A general rule is to make a longer loop for a thick yarn, a shorter loop for a fine one. As you follow the directions, right, for forming a single knot, pay close attention to where the hook is inserted after a chain is drawn through the long loop (illustration A); correct insertion of the hook in this step is important to obtain the desired result.

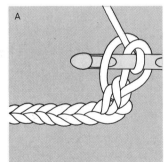

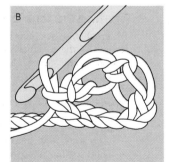

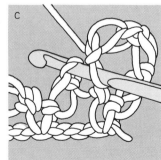

Work 1 double crochet in the 2nd chain from the hook, *lengthen loop on hook to 1.5 cm, draw up new loop, take hook across front of elongated loop and insert it under the yarn that was drawn up for the new loop (A), work 1 double crochet* to complete single knot.

Repeat instructions between asterisks and you will have made a *double knot*. *Miss 3 chains, work 1 double crochet in next chain (B), make 1 double knot.* Repeat instructions between these last 2 asterisks across the row, ending with 3 single knot stitches.

Turn, *work 1 double crochet in centre of next double knot (C), make 1 double knot.* Repeat instructions between the last 2 asterisks across the row, ending with 1 single knot. This row is repeated to form a pattern (see p. 293 for an example of the finished stitch).

Following crochet instructions

Crochet terminology

For written crochet instructions, there is a special vocabulary, much of it expressed in abbreviated or symbolic form. The forms used in this book are listed below with their definition. Also included are the numbers of pages on which techniques are illustrated. You may encounter slight variations of the terms given here, but these are common British forms. Before using new instructions, you should find out whether they are British or American, because American terms have different meanings. Our double crochet, for example, is the same as American single crochet.

An alternative to written instructions is a chart. For this purpose, different symbols are used (see pp. 302 and 304).

ch	chain pp. 272–3
ss	slipstitch p. 275
dc	double crochet p. 274
htr	half treble crochet p. 274
tr	treble crochet p. 274
dtr	double treble crochet p. 275
trtr	triple treble p. 275
alt	alternate
beg	begin, beginning
dec	decrease pp. 280–1
inc	increase p. 280
patt	pattern
rep	repeat
rnd	round p. 282
tog	together
st	stitch
sp	space
yrh	yarn round hook
* *	Instructions between asterisks should be repeated as many times as there are stitches to accommodate them
( )	A series of steps within parentheses should be worked according to instructions that follow the parentheses. Such a series is either worked into one stitch, or repeated a specified number of times
[ ]	Instructions within brackets explain the method for working a particular stitch or technique
tension	The number of stitches and rows per cm
mark stitch	Tie on contrasting yarn or slip a coil ring marker on the stitch indicated
unit	The number of stitches required to work one repeat of a pattern stitch
work straight	Continue to work pattern without increasing or decreasing

Testing the tension

All crochet instructions have a specified tension – the number of stitches that equals 5 cm. Some also include row tension – the number of rows to 5 cm. Because the size of a finished piece is based on these calculations, it is important to get the tension right before proceeding with any new project.

For a test sample, make a chain 10 cm in length, using the specified yarn and hook size. Work in pattern until the pattern measures 10 cm; fasten off. Measure the tension as shown on the right. If an adjustment is necessary, make a new sample using a hook either one size larger or smaller.

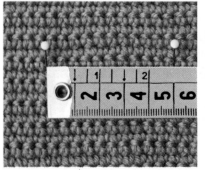

To measure stitch tension, place sample on flat surface; insert two pins, 5 cm apart; count stitches between them. If pin falls in centre of a stitch, tension may be measured over 10 cm.

To measure row tension, insert two pins, 5 cm apart (as shown) and count the number of rows between them. In measuring a sample, always take care to keep it flat and avoid stretching it.

Bag is approximately 38 cm wide by 36 cm deep and measures 15 cm across the bottom.

Bag to crochet

Backstitch 485
Oversewing 485

Useful bag, easy enough for a first attempt at following a crochet pattern.

Materials

Thick rug wool, 225 g red, 500 g grey, 500 g camel. Size 6.00 hook; 2 dowels, each 36 cm by 2 cm; sturdy cardboard 15 cm by 36 cm

Tension

5 dc = 5 cm, 2 rows = 2 cm.

1st handle: 11 ch with grey.

Row 1: miss 1 ch, 10 dc, 1 ch, turn.

Row 2: 1 dc in each st, 1 ch, turn.

Rep Row 2, 15 more times, fasten off. Make 2nd handle the same way.

Top edge: 8 ch, 10 dc across 1st handle, 17 ch, 10 dc across 2nd handle, 9 ch, turn.

Body: miss 1 ch, 1 dc in each ch and st across row (total of 53 dc), 1 ch, turn. Work 7 more rows in grey, attach red on last loop of last dc (see illustrations, top right), 1 ch, turn. Continue with red for 2 rows, then work 4 rows camel, 4 rows red, 8 rows grey, 2 rows red, 38 rows camel, 2 rows red, 8 rows grey, 4 rows red, 4 rows camel, 2 rows red, 8 rows grey, fasten off.

3rd handle: miss 8 dc, attach grey, work 10 dc, turn, work 17 rows, fasten off.

4th handle: miss 17 centre dc, attach grey, work 10 dc for 18 rows, fasten off. Sew as directed below. Slip dowels into handles. Place cardboard in bottom.

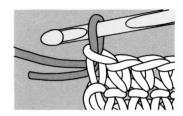

TO JOIN AND SECURE YARNS

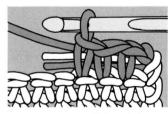

To join a new yarn at the end of a row, work last stitch with first yarn to final 2 loops; draw up last loop with new yarn.

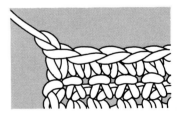

Cut first yarn to 5 cm. Make a chain; turn. Pull up 2 short yarns and lay over previous row; work over them for 4-5 stitches.

To secure yarn end on a finished piece, cut yarn to a 15 cm length; pull this end through the last loop and tighten it.

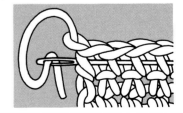

Thread yarn end in tapestry or rug needle; weave into back of work for 2 to 5 cm, below top row of stitches. Cut remainder.

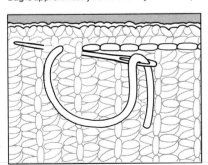

To join sides, fold bag with right sides together and top edges aligned. Working from bottom to top, backstitch each side seam 1 stitch in from edge (see Knitting for backstitch method).

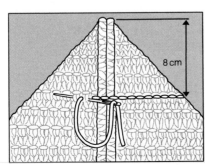

To sew bottom corners, lay bag flat with one side seam centred over the bottom, forming an angle. Measure 8 cm up from bottom of seam; backstitch across base of triangle at this point.

8 cm

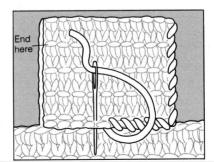

End here

To sew handles, fold in half, wrong sides together, top edge and top of bag aligned. Oversew side edges together, top edge to the bag, centre edges together, ending 2 rows from top.

Following crochet instructions

Shaping

Shaping in crochet is done by increasing and decreasing. Once mastered, these techniques permit you to crochet any shape or form. Three examples are shown opposite, more on pp. 282–3.

A single increase is made by working twice into the same stitch. If made within a row, and repeated over several rows, the increase positions move right or left. To keep the progression orderly, place a marker (contrasting yarn or a plastic coil ring) where increasing begins. For shaping to the right, increase before the marker; to the left, after the marker. On the next row, reverse this order to maintain consistency of the direction.

A single decrease is made by working two successive stitches into one final loop. Repeated over several rows, progression is the same as for increasing.

Increasing

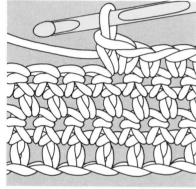

To make a single increase, work 2 stitches in 1 stitch. Double crochet is shown in the example; all other stitches are increased the same way.

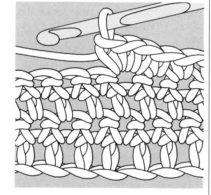

To make a double increase, work 3 stitches in 1 stitch. Double crochet is shown in the example; all other stitches are increased the same way.

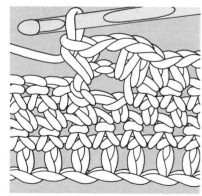

To make a decorative double increase (lacy chevron), work 2 chains at increase point. On next and subsequent rows, work (1 stitch, 2 chains, 1 stitch) in 2-chain space of previous row.

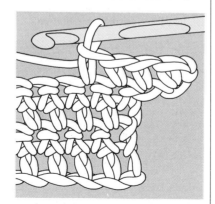

To increase several stitches at one edge, as when a sleeve is made in one piece with the garment, extend a chain from the side edge, then work back along the chain on the next row.

Decreasing

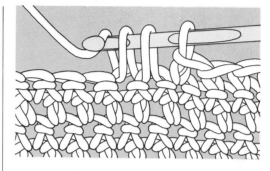

To decrease 1 stitch in double or half treble crochet, insert hook in stitch, draw up a loop, insert hook in next stitch, draw up a loop (3 loops on hook), yarn round hook, draw through the 3 loops.

If a decrease occurs at the beginning of a row, you can, if you prefer, miss the first stitch instead of working 2 stitches together. If a decrease is designated for the end of a row, miss the next to last stitch.

To decrease 2 stitches in double or half treble crochet, insert hook in stitch, draw up a loop, miss next stitch, insert hook in next stitch, draw up a loop (there are 3 loops on the hook, as shown), yarn round hook, draw through the 3 loops.

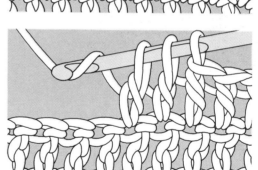

To decrease 1 stitch in treble crochet, yarn round hook, insert hook in stitch, draw up a loop, yarn round hook, draw through 2 loops, yarn round hook, insert hook in next stitch, draw up a loop, yarn round hook, draw through 2 loops (3 loops on hook), yarn round hook, draw through 3 loops.

If a decrease occurs at beginning of a row, you can miss the first stitch instead of working 2 stitches together; if at end of a row, miss next to last stitch.

To decrease 2 stitches in treble crochet, yarn round hook, insert hook in stitch, draw up a loop, yarn round hook, draw through 2 loops, miss next stitch, yarn round hook, insert hook in next stitch, draw up a loop, yarn round hook, draw through 2 loops (there are 3 loops on the hook, as shown), yarn round hook, draw through 3 loops.

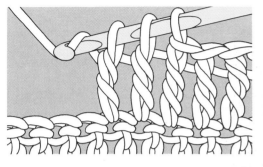

To decrease 1 stitch in double treble crochet, yarn round hook twice, insert hook in stitch, draw up a loop, yarn round hook, draw through 2 loops, yarn round hook, draw through 2 loops (2 loops remain on hook); yarn round hook twice, insert hook in next stitch, draw up a loop, yarn round hook, draw through 2 loops, yarn round hook, draw through 2 loops (there are 3 loops on the hook, as shown), yarn round hook, draw through last 3 loops.

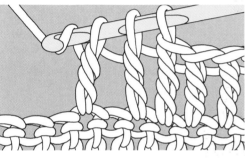

To decrease 2 stitches in double treble crochet, follow the method for decreasing 1 stitch, but miss a stitch between the 2 stitches that are worked together.

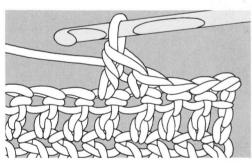

To decrease several stitches at the beginning of a row without an abrupt change in stitch heights, omit turning chain and work slipstitches for the number of decreases, make 1 double crochet in next stitch, then continue in pattern. Do not work the slipstitches on return row.

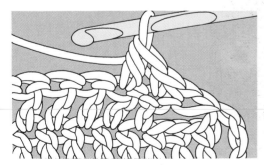

To decrease several stitches at the end of a row without an abrupt change in stitch heights, leave unworked the number of stitches to be decreased, work 1 slipstitch at end of row, 1 chain and turn. Miss the slipstitch, work 1 double crochet in the next stitch, then continue in pattern.

Geometric shapes/Worked in rows

Oval. Stitches worked around the chain instead of back and forth.
6 ch
Row 1: miss 1 ch, 1 dc in each of next 4 ch, 3 dc in last ch, turn work so bottom of ch is on top.
Row 2: 1 dc in each of next 5 ch (working into single loop that remains after working Row 1), 3 dc into ch that was missed in Row 1, continue around, working next row in sts of Row 1.
Row 3: *1 dc in each st*, 2 dc in last st, 2 dc in end st, 2 dc in st that begins row on opposite side. Continue as in Row 3, increasing stitches at ends as needed.

Triangle. Formed by increasing the first and last stitches every other row. The triangle becomes a diamond if, after reaching the desired width, you continue in pattern, decreasing the first and last stitches on alternate rows.
2 ch
Row 1: 1 dc, turn.
Row 2: 3 dc in the 1 dc, ch 1, turn.
Row 3: 2 dc in 1st dc, 1 in each of next 2 dc, 2 dc in last dc, 1 ch, turn.
Row 4: *1 dc in each dc*, ch 1, turn.
Row 5: 2 dc in 1st dc, *1 sc in next dc*, 2 dc in last dc, ch 1, turn. Continue increasing in this manner until desired size is reached; fasten off.

Square. Formed by working increases in the centre stitch of each row. An attractive variation on the usual approach, which is to work a square in straight rows.
2 ch
Row 1: 3 dc in 2nd ch from hook, 1 ch, turn.
Row 2: 1 dc in 1st st, 3 dc in next st, 1 dc in last st, 1 ch, turn.
Row 3: 1 dc in each of 1st 2 sts, 3 dc in next st, 1 dc in each of last 2 sts, 1 ch, turn.
Row 4: 1 dc in each of 1st 3 sts, 3 dc in next st, 1 dc in each of last 3 sts, 1 ch, turn.
Continue as in Row 4, working 1 dc in each st except the centre one, in which you work 3 dc.

Following crochet instructions

Geometric shapes/ Worked in rounds

Crocheting in rounds is an alternative to working in rows. Flat geometric shapes, also bowl and tube shapes, are formed in this way. Each is started with a ring (see method below), and is then developed in either concentric or spiral rounds, always working from the right side. For concentric shaping, each round is started with a chain, which acts as a substitute for the first stitch, and ends with a slipstitch into the starting chain (see illustration D, below). Examples of a concentric approach are the geometric shapes, right, and patchwork motifs, pp. 290–1. Angles on motifs are formed with increases of two or four stitches placed directly above one another.

In spiral shaping, each round continues out of the previous one, with no starting chain or closing slipstitch. For this method, you should place a marker at the end of Round 1, then move it up with each new round to keep track of the rounds completed. For smooth shaping, the position of increases or decreases is usually moved forward by one stitch on each round. The hats, opposite, are typical examples of this technique.

A tube is also made in spiral fashion. To form a tube, you start with a ring of the desired diameter, then keep working around it (usually with double crochet), neither increasing nor decreasing, until the tube is as long as you wish.

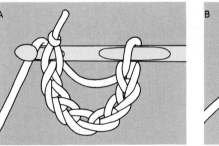

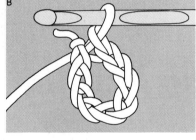

To form ring, make a chain; join last chain to first with a slipstitch (A and B). Depending on how large you want the centre space to be, allow 1 chain for every 2 to 4 stitches of first round.

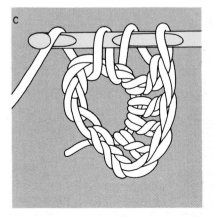

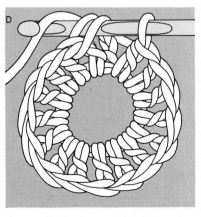

To work the first (centre) round, start with a chain or stitch, as directed, and work stitches over the ring (C); for concentric rounds, close with a slipstitch in top of first chain (D).

Circle. Concentric rounds worked with enough increases to keep edges from curling. The number and placing of increases may have to be adjusted for a particular yarn, hook size or stitch that is used, but a general formula is to increase each round by the number of sts that you started with.
6 ch and join in a ring with ss
Round 1: 3 ch, 11 tr in ring, ss in top of beg ch (total of 12 sts).
Round 2: 3 ch, 1 tr in ss, 2 tr in each tr of Round 1, ss in top of beg ch (24 sts).
Round 3: 3 ch, 2 tr in next tr, (1 tr in next tr, 2 tr in next tr) 11 times, ss in top of beg ch (36 sts).
To continue, increase in every 3rd st on **Round 4**, every 4th st on **Round 5**, and so on, increasing by 12 stitches on every round.

Square. Sample (left) is in treble crochet, but any stitch is suitable, as long as number of stitches in Round 1 is divisible by 4.
6 ch and join in a ring with ss
Round 1: 3 ch, 2 tr in ring, 1 ch, (3 tr in ring, 1 ch) 3 times, ss in top of beg ch (total of 12 sts).
Round 2: 3 ch, 1 tr in each of next 2 sts, *(2 tr, 1 ch, 2 tr) in ch sp, 1 tr in each of next 3 sts*, (2 tr, 1 ch, 2 tr) in last ch sp, ss in top of beg ch (28 sts).
Round 3: 3 ch, 1 tr in each of next 4 sts, *(2 tr, 1 ch, 2 tr) in ch sp, 1 tr in each of next 7 sts*, (2 tr, 1 ch, 2 tr) in last ch sp, 1 tr in each of next 2 sts, ss in top of beg ch (44 sts).
Continue evenly along each side, working (2 tr, 1 ch, 2 tr) in the ch sp at each corner, increasing 16 sts on each round.

Octagon. Structured same as a square, but with 2 increases in each angle instead of 4 (to keep it flat). Number of stitches in Round 1 is divisible by number of sides.
4 ch and join in a ring with ss
Round 1: 2 ch, 1 htr in ring, 1 ch, (2 htr in ring, 1 ch) 7 times, ss in top of beg ch (total of 16 sts).
Round 2: 2 ch, 1 htr in next st, *(1 htr, 1 ch, 1 htr) in ch sp, 1 htr in each of next 2 sts*, (1 htr, 1 ch, 1 htr) in last ch sp, ss in top of beg ch (32 sts).
Round 3: 2 ch, 1 htr in each of next 3 sts, *(1 htr, 1 ch, 1 htr) in ch sp, 1 htr in each of next 4 sts*, (1 htr, 1 ch, 1 htr) in last ch sp, ss in top of beg ch (48 sts).
Continue evenly along each side, working (1 htr, 1 ch, 1 htr) in each angle, increasing 16 sts on each round.

Hats to crochet

Three hats to crochet for yourself or a young child. The women's hats fit small to average head sizes.

BERET
A classic style for any season.
Materials
125 g double knitting yarn, size 4.00 hook
Tension: 7 htr = 5 cm
Crown: 4 ch, join in a ring with ss
Round 1: 8 htr in ring, attach marker; move it up with each new round
Round 2: 2 htr in each st
Round 3: *1 htr in next st, 2 htr in next st* (total of 24 htr)
Round 4: *1 htr in each of next 2 sts, 2 htr in next st* (32 htr)
Round 5: increase 8 htr, placing the increases every 4th st (40 htr)
Rounds 6 and 7: increase 10 htr in each round (60 htr at end of Round 7)
Rounds 8, 9, 10, 11, 12: increase 6 htr in each round (total of 90 htr)
Rounds 13 and 14: increase 10 htr in each round (110 htr at end of Round 14)
Rounds 15, 16, 17: work evenly
Rounds 18, 19, 20, 21: decrease 10 sts in each round (70 htr at end of **21**)
Band: work in dc for 6 rounds; join last round with ss to 1st dc; fasten off. Weave yarn end under edge for 2.5 cm.

HAT WITH BRIM
Using a flecked yarn: fits head 53 cm to 58 cm.
Materials
125 g double knitting yarn, size 4.00 hook. **Tension:** 9 dc = 5 cm
Crown: 3 ch, join in a ring with ss
Round 1: 1 ch, 9 dc in ring, mark end of round with spare yarn; continue to move marker with each new round
Round 2: 2 dc in each st of Round 1 (total of 18 dc)
Round 3: *1 dc in next dc, 2 dc in next dc*, (27 dc)
Round 4: *1 dc in each of next 2 dc, 2 dc in next dc* (36 dc)
Round 5: *1 dc in each of next 3 dc, 2 dc in next dc* (45 dc)
Round 6: 1 dc in each st (no increase)
Work 7 more rounds, increasing 9 dc on every other round. You will have 81 dc at end of Round 13. Increase 9 dc in both **Rounds 14 and 15** (99 dc); continue to work straight until hat measures 18 cm from centre of crown.
Brim: for the first round, increase in every 4th st (124 dc); work straight until brim measures 5 cm. Working from left to right on the right side, work 1 dc in each st, ss to 1st dc, fasten off. Weave yarn end under the edge on the right side for about 2.5 cm.

CHILD'S CAP
For ages four to eight.
Materials
125 g double knitting, size 4.00 hook
Tension: 9 dc = 5 cm
Crown: work 13 rounds, following the instructions for hat with brim. Work straight on 81 dc until cap measures 16.5 cm from centre of crown, ss to 1st dc in final round to close
Cuff: work in rows on the wrong side
Row 1: 1 dc in ss of last rnd, 1 dc in each of next 80 dc, 1 ch, turn
Row 2: 1 dc in each dc, 1 ch, turn
Row 3: 1 dc in each of 1st 2 dc, 1 raised tr round front of 3rd dc in Row 1 [yrh, insert hook across front of 3rd dc in Row 1, draw up a loop, yrh, draw through 2 loops, yrh, draw through remaining 2 loops], *miss 1 dc, 1 dc in each of next 2 dc, 1 raised tr round next dc in Row 1*, rep from * across row, 1 ch, turn
Rows 4–6: *1 dc in each st*, 1 ch, turn
Row 7: 1 dc in each of 1st 2 dc, 1 raised tr in raised tr 3 rows below, *miss 1 dc, 1 dc in each of next 2 dc, 1 raised tr in raised tr 3 rows below*, 1 ch, turn
Rep Rows 4–7 once more, fasten off.
Right side facing you, work 1 row of ss along edge, then oversew back seam together from wrong side. Fasten off; weave end into seam. Turn cuff back.

Crochet stitches

Selecting a pattern stitch
Textures
Shells
Clusters
Motifs
Motifs/Patchwork
Meshes
Shaping mesh ground
Filet crochet
Overlaid meshes
Irish crochet
Tunisian crochet
Loop stitches
Multicolour crochet
Charting a pattern stitch

Selecting a pattern stitch

A **pattern stitch** is a sequence of crochet techniques, repeated continuously to form a fabric. There are two ways of working a pattern – in *rows* or in *rounds*.

To work a pattern in rows, start with a number of chains which is a multiple of the stitches needed to complete one horizontal motif, plus any additional chains indicated. These extra chains include the ones that will be missed at the beginning of Row 1, and sometimes a few for balancing pattern motifs. (The chain on the hook is never counted.) After completing all rows in the pattern, begin again, usually at Row 2; the first row is usually a setting-up row. If a pattern is complex, use a row counter or markers to keep count.

To work a pattern in rounds, begin with a ring of chain stitches or yarn and work the first round into the ring (see p. 282 for the method). All subsequent rounds are worked with the right side facing you; the item is complete when you have obtained the desired size. It is not necessary to work all rounds.

Whether worked in rounds or rows, there is usually little difference between the two sides of a crochet pattern. Exceptions are some Tunisian stitches, also two-colour patterns in which yarn is carried up one side. Unless directions specify otherwise, Row 1 begins the right side.

Most pattern stitches can be classified according to structure. Familiarity with these basic structures will permit you to 'read' almost any pattern from a picture or sample. Patterns in this section are grouped according to type, though in some cases a stitch fits more than one category. The first group, *textures*, is a selection of compact patterns that are variations of basic crochet stitches. They are firmer and stiffer than the comparable knitted stitches. In selecting a pattern, consider its suitability for both yarn and purpose. Make a test sample to find out.

Textures

Alternate stitch. Two double crochets worked in every other stitch yield a firm fabric with leaf-like motif.
Unit of 2 ch plus 2
Row 1: miss 3 ch, 2 dc in next ch, *miss 1 ch, 2 dc in next ch*, 2 ch, turn
Row 2: *miss 1 st, 2 dc in next st*, 2 ch, turn
Rep from Row 2

Double stitch. Each stitch spans two.
Unit of 2 ch plus 2
Row 1: miss 2 ch, 1 double st [insert hook in next ch, yrh, draw through a loop, insert hook in next ch, yrh, draw through a loop, yrh, draw through 3 loops], *1 double st, inserting hook first in st where 2nd yrh was made for previous double st*, 2 ch, turn
Row 2: *1 double st in each pair of sts*, 1 double st inserting hook in last st and top of ch at beg, 2 ch, turn
Rep from Row 2

Up and down stitch. A varied texture produced by alternating double and treble crochet stitches.
Unit of 2 ch plus 2
Row 1: miss 2 ch, 1 dc in next ch, *1 tr, 1 dc*, 1 tr, 2 ch, turn
Row 2: miss 1st tr, *1 tr in dc of previous row, 1 dc in tr of previous row*, 1 tr in 2 ch of previous row, 2 ch, turn
Rep from Row 2

Chequerboard. Alternating bands of double and treble crochet stitches.
Unit of 10 ch plus 6
Row 1: miss 2 ch, 4 dc, *5 tr, 5 dc*, 3 ch, turn
Row 2: miss 1st st, 4 tr, *5 dc, 5 tr*, work last tr in top of ch at beginning of previous row, 2 ch, turn
Row 3: miss 1st st, 4 dc, *5 tr, 5 dc*, work last dc in top of turning ch, 3 ch, turn
Rep from Row 2

Woven stitch. Double crochet stitches worked in single chain spaces.
Unit of 3 ch plus 3
Row 1: miss 2 ch, 1 dc, *1 ch, miss 1 ch, 1 dc*, 2 ch, turn
Row 2: *1 dc in ch sp of previous row, 1 ch*, 1 dc in the turning ch sp, 2 ch, turn
Rep from Row 2

Crossed stitches. Treble crochet stitches worked in reverse order.
Unit of 3 ch plus 2
Row 1. miss 6 ch, 1 tr in next ch, 1 ch, 1 tr in 4th ch from beginning (crossing over the 1st tr), *miss 2 ch, 1 tr, 1 ch, 1 tr in 1st of missed ch*, 1 tr in last ch, 4 ch, turn
Row 2: miss 2 tr, 1 tr in next tr, 1 ch, 1 tr in last missed tr, *miss 1 tr, 1 tr in next tr, 1 ch, 1 tr in missed tr*, 1 tr in 3rd ch of turning ch, 4 ch, turn
Rep from Row 2

Diagonal stitch. Long stitch pulled diagonally across each group of three.
Unit of 4 ch plus 1
Row 1: miss 1 ch, *1 dc in each ch*, 2 ch, turn
Row 2: *miss 1 st, 1 tr in each of next 3 sts, insert hook in last missed st, yrh, draw through an elongated loop, yrh, draw through 2 loops*, 1 tr in last st, 1 ch, turn
Row 3: miss 1 st, *1 dc in each st*, 1 dc in turning ch, 2 ch, turn
Rep from Row 2

Open ridge stitch. A firm and heavy, yet airy pattern; especially suitable for a place mat or handbag.
Unit of 2 ch plus 1
Row 1: miss 1 ch, *1 dc in each ch*, 1 ch, turn
Row 2: 1 htr, *miss 1 st, 1 htr in next st, 1 htr between 2 preceding htr*, miss 1 st, 1 htr in ch at beg of row, 1 ch, turn
Row 3: *1 dc, inserting hook through back loop only of each st in previous row*, 1 ch; turn
Rep from Row 2

Basket weave. An unusual dimension is created by working raised stitches, first to the front, then the back. (See p. 276 for this technique.)
Unit of 6 ch
Row 1: miss 6 ch, *1 tr in next ch*, 2 ch, turn
Rows 2 and 3: miss 1 tr, *(1 raised tr round front) 3 times, (1 raised tr round back) 3 times*, (1 raised tr round front) 3 times, 1 tr in top of turning ch, 2 ch, turn
Rows 4 and 5: miss 1 tr, *(1 raised tr round back) 3 times, (1 raised tr round front) 3 times*, (1 raised tr round back) 3 times, 1 tr in top of turning ch, 2 ch, turn
Rep from Row 2

Relief stitches. A three-dimensional chunky pattern.
Unit of 2 ch
Row 1: miss 1 ch, *1 tr in each ch*, 1 ch, turn
Row 2: *1 dc in each tr*, 2 ch, turn
Row 3: *1 raised htr round front of 1 tr of Row 1, 1 tr in next dc*, 1 ch, turn
Row 4: *1 dc in top of raised htr, 1 dc between raised htr and the tr*, 1 dc in turning ch, 2 ch, turn
Row 5: *1 raised htr round front of raised htr of 2 rows below, 1 tr in next dc*, 1 ch, turn
Rep from Row 4

Steps. Pattern moves on the diagonal.
Unit of 8 ch plus 3
Row 1: miss 2 ch, *1 tr in each ch*, 2 ch, turn
Rows 2 and 3: miss 1 tr, *4 raised tr round front, 4 raised tr round back*, 1 tr in top ch at beg of Row 1, 2 ch, turn
Row 4: miss 1 tr, 1 raised tr round back, *4 raised tr round front, 4 raised tr round back*, 3 raised tr round back, 1 tr in turning ch, 2 ch, turn
Row 5: miss 1 tr, 3 raised tr round front, *4 raised tr round back, 4 raised tr round front*, 4 raised tr round back, 1 raised tr round front, 1 dc in turning ch, 2 ch, turn
Rep from Row 4, moving pattern one st to left on even rows

285

Crochet stitches

Shells

A **shell** is a group of stitches, usually three or more, worked into one stitch or chain space. Stitches come together in close formation at the base and spread out at the top so that they resemble seashells or fans. The width and depth of a shell depends on the number of stitches that are in it and the size of the space in which these are worked. The shape, too, can be varied. It is symmetrical when all stitches are the same size, asymmetrical when long and short stitches are combined (see far right, opposite page, for the latter).

The shell is a pretty stitch that has a lacy appearance even in a solid pattern.

Made up in medium-weight or heavy yarns, it is suitable and attractive for a blanket. Worked with fine yarns, it is appropriate for shawls, dressy garments and baby clothing. In any yarn type, the shell stitch makes a nice edging because of its curved shape. Examples can be seen on p. 313.

Because of the shell's comparatively elaborate structure, it is best suited to smooth yarns. It also requires more yarn than simpler stitch types (textures, for example), a factor that must be considered in estimating yarn for your own design. Guidelines for making yarn estimates are on p. 305.

Lacy scallops. Small shells worked in narrow chain spaces form a delicate, open pattern; suitable for a baby garment.
Unit of 6 ch plus 4
Row 1: *miss 5 ch, (2 tr, 3 ch, 2 tr) in next ch*, miss 3 ch, 1 tr in last ch, 3 ch, turn
Row 2: *(2 tr, 3 ch, 2 tr) in 3 ch sp*, 1 tr in top of turning ch, 3 ch, turn
Rep from Row 2

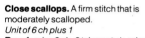

Close scallops. A firm stitch that is moderately scalloped.
Unit of 6 ch plus 1
Row 1: miss 3 ch, 2 tr in next ch, miss 2 ch, 1 dc, *miss 2 ch, 4 tr in next ch, miss 2 ch, 1 dc*, 3 ch, turn
Row 2: 2 tr in 1st dc, *1 dc between 2nd and 3rd tr of next 4 tr group, 4 tr in next dc*, 1 dc in 3 ch sp at beginning of row, 3 ch, turn
Rep from Row 2

Wide arches. A moderately large pattern in which the shells alternate with open areas.
Unit of 8 ch plus 3
Row 1: miss 2 ch, *1 tr, 3 ch, miss 3 ch, 1 dc, 3 ch, miss 3 ch, *1 tr, 3 ch, turn
Row 2: *1 dc in 2nd ch of 3 ch group, 3 ch, 1 dc in 2nd ch of next 3 ch group, 1 ch, 1 tr in tr, 1 ch*, 1 tr in the turning chain, 3 ch, turn
Row 3: *7 tr in 3 ch sp, 1 tr in tr*, 1 tr in turning chain, 3 ch, turn
Row 4: *3 ch, 1 dc in the centre of the shell, 3 ch, 1 tr in tr*, 1 tr in the turning chain, 3 ch, turn
Rep from Row 2

Simple shells. A moderately large motif.
Unit of 6 ch plus 5
Row 1: miss 3 ch, 1 tr in next ch, *(2 tr, 1 ch, 2 tr) in next ch, yrh, insert hook in next ch, draw up a loop, yrh, draw through 2 loops, miss 3 ch, yrh, insert hook in next ch, draw up a loop, (yrh, draw through 2 loops) 3 times*, 1 tr, 3 ch, turn
Row 2: 1 tr in tr before the ch sp, *(2 tr, 1 ch, 2 tr) in ch sp, yrh, insert hook in next tr, draw up a loop, yrh, draw through 2 loops, miss 3 sts, yrh, insert hook in next tr, draw up a loop, (yrh, draw through 2 loops) 3 times*, work last st in top of turning ch, 3 ch, turn
Rep from Row 2

Arcade stitch. Lacy but firm; the pattern repeats on the diagonal.
Unit of 6 ch plus 8
Row 1: miss 1 ch, 1 dc in each of next 2 ch, *3 ch, miss 3 ch, 1 dc in each of next 3 ch*, 3 ch, miss 3 ch, 1 dc in each of last 2 ch, 1 ch, turn
Row 2: 1 dc in 2nd dc, *5 tr in 3 ch sp, 1 dc in 2nd dc of 3 dc group*, turn
Row 3: *3 ch, 1 dc in each of 3 central tr*, 2 ch, 1 dc in turning chain, 3 ch, turn
Row 4: 2 tr in 2 ch sp, *1 dc in 2nd dc, 5 tr in 3 ch sp*, 1 dc in 2nd dc, 3 tr in 3 ch sp, 1 ch, turn
Row 5: 1 dc in each of first 2 dc, *3 ch, 1 dc in each of 3 central tr*, 3 ch, 1 dc in last tr, 1 dc in turning chain, 1 ch, turn

Wave stitch. A popular pattern for baby blankets and rugs. The crest of each wave is formed with one shell stitch; the distance between the crests can be varied, if you wish, by adjusting the multiple.
Unit of 13 ch
Row 1: miss 3 ch, 4 tr in next 4 ch, 3 tr in next ch, 5 tr in next 5 ch, *miss 2 ch, 5 tr in next 5 ch, 3 tr in next ch, 5 tr in next 5 ch*, 3 ch, turn
Row 2: miss 1 st, 4 tr in next 4 sts, 3 tr in next st, 5 tr in next 5 sts, *miss 2 sts, 5 tr in next 5 sts, 3 tr in next st, 5 tr in next 5 sts*, on the last multiple, end with 4 tr, miss 1 tr, 1 tr in turning ch, 3 ch, turn
Rep from Row 2

Bushy stitch. These shells are a combination of double and treble crochet stitches, and are asymmetrical in form.
Unit of 3 ch plus 1
Row 1: miss 3 ch, (1 tr, 2 ch, 1 dc) in next ch, *miss 2 ch, (2 tr, 2 ch, 1 dc) in next ch*, 2 ch, turn
Row 2: *(2 tr, 2 ch, 1 dc) in each 2 ch sp*, 2 ch, turn
Rep from Row 2

Fan stitch. Elegant large shells.
Unit of 14 ch plus 2
Row 1: miss 1 ch, 1 dc, *miss 6 ch, 1 long tr [yrh, insert hook, draw up a loop 1.5 cm long, yrh, draw through 2 loops, yrh, draw through 2 loops], 12 more long tr in the same ch, miss 6 ch, 1 dc*, 3 ch, turn
Row 2: 1 long tr in 1st dc, *5 ch, 1 dc in 7th of 13 long tr, 5 ch, 2 long tr in dc between the fans*, 2 long tr in last dc, 1 ch, turn
Row 3: 1 dc between the 1st 2 long tr, *13 long tr in the dc worked at the centre of fan in previous row, 1 dc between the 2 long tr of previous row*, 3 ch, turn
Rep from Row 2

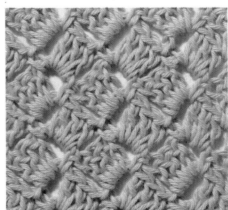

Brick stitch. Squares of asymmetrical shells with openwork between them.
Unit of 4 ch plus 6
Row 1: miss 3 ch, *2 tr in next 2 ch, (1 tr, 3 ch, 1 tr) in next ch, miss 1 ch*, 3 tr in last 3 ch, 3 ch, turn
Row 2: *(3 tr, 3 ch, 1 dc) in each 3 ch sp*, 1 tr between last group of 3 tr and turning ch, 3 ch, turn
Rep from Row 2

Starburst. Shells and clusters combined.
Unit of 8 ch plus 10
Row 1: miss 1 ch, 1 dc, *miss 3 ch, 9 tr in next ch, miss 3 ch, 1 dc*, 3 ch, turn
Row 2: miss 1 st, 4 tr cluster over next 4 sts [(yrh, insert hook, draw up a loop, yrh, draw through 2 loops) in each st, yrh, draw through 5 loops], *4 ch, 1 dc, 3 ch, 9 tr cluster over next 9 sts*, 4 ch, 1 dc, 3 ch, 5 tr cluster, 4 ch, turn
Row 3: 4 tr in top of 5 tr cluster, 1 dc in dc, *9 tr in top of 9 tr cluster, 1 dc in dc*, 5 tr in top of 4 tr cluster, 3 ch, turn
Row 4: miss 1 tr, *9 tr cluster, 4 ch, 1 dc, 3 ch*, 1 dc in turning ch, 1 ch, turn
Row 5: 1 dc, *9 tr in top of 9 tr cluster, 1 dc*, 1 dc in turning ch, 3 ch, turn
Rep from Row 2

Ripple stitch. Asymmetrical shell stitches in a compact pattern; also pretty worked in two or more colours.
Unit of 3 ch plus 1
Row 1: miss 2 ch, 2 tr in next ch, *(1 dc, 2 tr) in next ch, miss 2 ch*, 1 dc, 2 ch, turn
Row 2: 2 tr in 1st dc, *(1 dc, 2 tr) in each dc of previous row*, 1 dc in turning ch, 2 ch, turn
Rep from Row 2

Crochet stitches

Clusters

A **cluster** is a group of three or more stitches worked into one stitch or chain space, then drawn together at the top with one loop. Depending on how many stitches are in the group, results may be relatively flat, as in the soft cluster stitch directly below, or extremely chunky, as in the bobble stitch (lower right). Whatever the type, however, all clusters stand out from a flat surface, thus providing extra texture and dimension in the finished piece.

In an all-over pattern (examples below), the cluster makes a warm, somewhat bulky fabric that is suitable for a heavy sweater or a blanket. Used indi-vidually, or as one row in a plain crochet pattern, it is an attractive accent or trimming. It also works well in patchwork motifs (see pp. 290–1), where it contributes symmetry and textural interest.

Generally, clusters look best in heavy or medium-weight yarn. When estimating the yarn quantity, remember that each cluster is composed of several yarn loops, so half again or even twice as much yarn will be needed as for a simpler stitch, such as a mesh or texture.

In working a cluster, the yarn tension should be kept fairly loose to make the clusters soft, and to facilitate drawing the final loop through the top.

Soft clusters. Relatively flat stitch grouping; looks the same on both sides.
Unit of 2 ch plus 4
Row 1: miss 3 ch, *1 cluster [(yrh, insert hook, draw up a loop, yrn, draw through 2 loops) 3 times in the same ch, yrh, draw through 4 loops], 1 ch, miss 1 ch*, 1 cluster, 3 ch, turn
Row 2: *1 cluster in ch between clusters of previous row*, 1 cluster in top of turning ch, 3 ch, turn
Rep from Row 2

Large clusters. A thicker stitch than soft clusters above, but still fairly flat.
Unit of 2 ch plus 4
Row 1: miss 3 ch, *1 cluster [(yrh, insert hook, draw up a loop, yrh, draw through 2 loops) 4 times in the same ch, yrh, draw through 4 loops, yrh, draw through 2 loops], 1 ch, miss 1 ch*, 1 cluster, 3 ch, turn
Row 2: *1 cluster in each ch sp of previous row, 1 ch*, 1 cluster in top of turning ch, 3 ch, turn
Rep from Row 2

Lace clusters. A bubbly texture of thick puffs combined with openwork.
Unit of 6 ch plus 4
Row 1: miss 3 ch, *(1 tr, 2 ch, 1 tr) in next ch, miss 2 ch, 1 puff [(yrh, insert hook, draw up a loop) 4 times in the same ch, yrh, draw through 9 loops], 1 ch, miss 2 ch*, (1 tr, 2 ch, 1 tr) in last ch, 3 ch, turn
Row 2: *1 puff in 2 ch sp between 2 tr of previous row, 1 ch, (1 tr, 2 ch, 1 tr) under loop that closes the puff in previous row*, 1 puff, 1 tr in 3 ch sp at beg of previous row, 3 ch, turn
Row 3: (1 tr, 2 ch, 1 tr) in top of puff, *1 puff in 2 ch sp, 1 ch, (1 tr, 2 ch, 1 tr) in top of puff*, 1 tr in 3 ch sp at beg of previous row, 3 ch, turn
Rep from Row 2

Ball stitch. Soft rounded clusters combined with double crochet.
Unit of 4 ch plus 3
Row 1: miss 1 ch, *1 dc in each ch*, 1 ch, turn
Row 2: 3 dc, *1 ball [(yrh, insert hook, draw up a loop) 3 times in the same st, yrh, draw through 7 loops], 3 dc*, 1 ch, turn
Row 3: *1 dc in each st*, 1 ch, turn
Row 4: 1 dc, *1 ball, 3 dc*, 1 ball, 1 dc, 1 ch, turn
Row 5: *1 dc in each st*, 1 ch, turn
Rep from Row 2

Bobble stitch. Solid, three-dimensional pattern; be sure to allow ample yarn.
Unit of 3 ch plus 1
Row 1: miss 1 ch, *1 dc in each ch*, 1 ch, turn
Row 2: *1 bobble [(yrh, insert hook, draw up a loop, yrh, draw through 2 loops) 5 times in same st, yrh, draw through 6 loops], 2 dc*, 1 bobble, 1 ch, turn
Rows 3 and 5: *1 dc in each st*, 1 ch, turn
Row 4: *2 dc, 1 bobble*, 1 dc, 1 ch, turn
Row 6: 1 dc, *1 bobble, 2 dc*, 1 ch, turn
Rep from Row 2

Motifs

A motif is a self-contained design unit which may be symmetrical or asymmetrical. Motifs can be used singly or joined together in a patchwork.

The centre of a motif is usually a chain joined with a slipstitch to form a ring. The first row, called a *round*, is worked into this circle, with stitches taken over the chain, and adjusted to fit evenly around. Each subsequent round is worked from the right side and closed with a slipstitch at the starting point (unless the form is a spiral). The last round is fastened off.

Motifs can be used individually for appliqué, for example, or as coasters, place mats or potholders. Because there is no limit to their size, you can even fashion a rug. The most popular use for motifs, however, is patchwork. Square patterns, familiarly known as 'granny squares', are frequently used for this, but any symmetrical design will do. Larger items are easy to manage because motifs can be done one at a time, and joined at your leisure. Motifs are also ideal for using up yarn leftovers, as each round can be worked in a different colour (see p. 302 for how to change yarn colours). You can join motifs with an overcast stitch, or crochet them together with slipstitch or double crochet.

Posy. Use this for an appliqué or as the centre portion of a larger motif.
6 ch and join in a ring with ss
Round 1: 2 ch, 23 dc in ring, ss in 2nd ch at beg of rnd to close
Round 2: 4 ch, 1 tr in same st as last ss, 1 ch, (miss 2 st, 1 tr, 2 ch, 1 tr in next st, 1 ch) 7 times, ss in 2nd ch at beg of rnd to close
Round 3: 2 ch, (1 htr, 2 ch, 2 htr) in 2 ch sp at beg of Round 2, 1 dc in 1 ch sp, *(2 htr, 2 ch, 2 htr) in 2 ch sp, 1 dc in the 1 ch sp*, rep from 1st* 6 times, ss in 2nd ch at beg of rnd
Round 4: *(3 tr, 1 ch, 3 tr) in the 2 ch sp, 1 dc on each side of the dc*, rep from 1st* 7 times, ss to 1st tr, fasten off

Clover. The lucky kind with four leaves. For the traditional variety, turn to p. 296.
5 ch and join in a ring with ss
Round 1: 14 dc in ring
Round 2: 2 dc, 1 leaf [4 ch, (yrh twice, insert hook in next st, draw up a loop, yrh, draw through 2 loops, yrh, draw through 2 loops) 3 times in same st, yrh, draw through 4 loops, 3 ch], 1 dc in each of next 2 st, 3 more leaves as above, make stem [6 ch, work back along these 6 ch with 1 dc in each ch (or with a ss in each ch if yarn is thick)], ss in 1st dc to close, fasten off

Daisy. Chain stitches form the petals of this three-dimensional motif.
6 ch and join in a ring with ss
Round 1: 14 dc in ring, ss to 1st dc at beg of rnd to close
Round 2: (into front strand of each dc work 1 dc, 6 ch, 1 dc) 14 times, ss to 1st dc to close
Round 3: (into back strand of each dc work 1 dc, 8 ch, 1 dc) 14 times, ss to 1st dc, fasten off

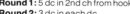

Star. The conventional five-pointed shape to use as an emblem or decoration.
2 ch
Round 1: 5 dc in 2nd ch from hook
Round 2: 3 dc in each dc
Round 3: (1 dc in next st, 6 ch, ss in 2nd ch from hook, 1 dc in next ch, 1 htr in next ch, 1 tr in next ch, 1 dtr in next ch, 1 dtr in base of starting dc, miss 2 dc) 5 times, ss in first dc to join, fasten off

Chrysanthemum. Broad petals that curl slightly towards the centre.
4 ch and join in a ring with ss
Round 1: 13 dc in ring, ss to 1st dc at beg of rnd to close, fasten off
Round 2: using 2nd colour, work 1 petal into the front strand of each dc of Round 1 [1 dc, 5 ch, 1 dc in 2nd ch from hook, 1 htr in each of next 2 ch, 1 dc in next ch, 1 dc in dc at beg], total of 13 petals
Round 3: work 1 petal into the back strand of each dc of Round 1 [1 ss, 6 ch, 1 dc in 5 of these 6 ch], total of 13 petals, fasten off

Crochet stitches

Motifs/Patchwork

Eyelet square. A simple centre motif surrounded by rows of double crochet; more interesting when worked in two or more colours. Round 1 is crocheted over a double yarn strand instead of the usual ring of chains.
Wind yarn twice around tip of index finger to form a ring
Round 1: 16 dc in ring
Round 2: (1 dc, 10 ch, miss 3 dc) 4 times, ss in 1st dc, fasten off
Round 3: using new colour, (11 dc in the 10 ch sp, 1 dc in next dc) 4 times, ss in 1st dc, fasten off
Round 4: using new colour, *1 dc in each of 6 sts, 2 dc in next st to form corner, 1 dc in each of 5 sts*, rep from *3 times, ss in 1st dc, fasten off
Round 5: 1 dc in each st and 2 dc at each corner, ss in 1st dc
Rep Round 5 as many times as desired for size, changing colours as it suits you, fasten off

Hawaiian square. Large clusters surround a small flower; a very simple motif.
8 ch and join in a ring with ss
Round 1: 1 large cluster in ring [(yrh, insert hook, draw up a loop) 4 times, yrh, draw through 9 loops], (2 ch, 1 large cluster) 7 times, 2 ch, ss in 1st st
Round 2: ss into next 2 ch sp, 1 large cluster in this sp, *2 ch, 1 large cluster in next sp, 2 ch, (1 tr, 2 ch, 1 tr) in next large cluster to form corner, 2 ch, 1 large cluster in next sp*, after tr group at end of rnd, 2 ch, ss into 1st large cluster
Round 3: ss into next 2 ch sp, 1 large cluster in this sp, *(2 ch, 1 large cluster) in each sp up to the corner, 2 ch, (1 tr, 2 ch, 1 tr) between tr groups at corner*, 2 ch, ss in 1st st
Rep from Round 3, working 1 more large cluster on each side for each rnd until there are 6 large clusters on each side, or until the square is the desired size, fasten off

Flower in a square. Long chains are the flower petals.
5 ch and join in a ring with ss
Round 1: 12 dc in ring, ss in 1st dc to close
Round 2: (11 ch, ss in next dc) 12 times
Round 3: ss in each of 1st 6 ch of 1st ch loop, *4 ch, 1 dc, in central st of next ch loop, 4 ch, 1 cluster in next ch loop [(yrh, insert hook, draw up a loop, yrh, draw through 2 loops) 3 times in same ch loop, yrh, draw through 4 loops], 4 ch, 1 cluster in same ch loop to form corner, 4 ch, 1 dc in next loop*, rep from *3 times
Round 4: 2 ss in 1st 4 ch sp, 3 ch, (yrh, insert hook in same sp, draw up a loop, yrh, draw through 2 loops) twice, yrh, draw through 3 loops, *4 ch, 1 dc in next 4 ch sp, 4 ch, (1 cluster, 4 ch, 1 cluster) in corner sp, 4 ch, 1 dc in next 4 ch sp, 4 ch, 1 cluster in next 4 ch sp*, rep from *3 times, 4 ch, ss in top of 1st cluster to close, fasten off

Old America square. This is a traditional type of granny square. It is usually worked in two or more colours.
6 ch and join in a ring with ss
Round 1: 3 ch, 2 tr in ring, 2 ch, (3 tr in ring, 2 ch) 3 times, ss in top of beg ch, fasten off
Round 2: join new colour with ss in 1st ch sp, 3 ch, (2 tr, 2 ch, 3 tr) in same sp to form corner, (1 ch, 3 tr, 2 ch, 3 tr in next 2 ch sp) 3 times for 3 more corners, ss in top of beg ch, fasten off
Round 3: join new colour with ss in 1st 2 ch sp, 3 ch, (2 tr, 2 ch, 3 tr) in the sp, *(1 ch, 3 tr) in each 1 ch sp (along the side), (1 ch, 3 tr, 2 ch, 3 tr) in each 2 ch sp (a corner)*, ss in top of beg ch, fasten off
Rep Round 3 as many times as desired for size

Hexagon. A simple, solid pattern.
6 ch and join in a ring with ss
Round 1: 2 ch, 2 tr in ring, 3 ch, (3 tr in ring, 3 ch) 5 times, ss in top of beg ch to close, fasten off
Round 2: using new colour, 4 ch, *(3 dtr, 2 ch, 3 dtr) in each 3 ch sp*, ss in top of beg ch to close, fasten off
Round 3: using new colour, 3 ch, *1 tr in each dtr, (2 tr, 2 ch, 2 tr) in each 2 ch sp*, ss in top of beg ch to close, fasten off
Round 4: using new colour, 3 ch, *miss 1 st, 1 tr in next st, 1 tr in the missed st*, 1 tr in last st, ss in top of beg ch to close, fasten off

Paddle wheel. The rounds are left open in this hexagonal spiral.
5 ch and join in a ring with ss
Round 1: (6 ch, 1 dc in ring) 6 times, do not close the round
Round 2: (4 ch, 1 dc in next sp) 6 times
Round 3: (4 ch, 1 dc in next sp, 1 dc in next dc) 6 times
Round 4: (4 ch, 1 dc in next sp, 1 dc in each of the 2 dc) 6 times
Round 5: (4 ch, 1 dc in next sp, 1 dc in each of the 3 dc) 6 times
Rep for as many rnds as desired, working 1 extra dc in each group on each rnd; beginning with the 10th rnd, work 5 ch for each sp instead of 4

Dogwood. Four large petals.
2 ch
Round 1: miss 1st ch, 8 dc in 2nd ch, ss in 1st dc to close
Round 2: 5 ch, miss 1 st, 1 dc in next st, (4 ch, miss 1 st, 1 dc in next st) twice, 4 ch, ss in 1st of 5 ch at beg of rnd
Round 3: ss in next ch sp, 3 ch, 6 tr in same sp as ss, (2 ch, 7 tr) in each of next 3 ch sp, 2 ch, ss in top of 4 ch at beg of rnd
Round 4: 2 ch, 1 dc in joining st, (1 dc in each of next 2 st, 2 dc in next st) twice, *(2 dc in next st, 1 dc in each of next 2 st) twice, 2 dc in next st*, rep from * twice, ss in top of beg ch
Round 5: 3 ch, 1 tr in joining st, 1 tr in next st, 2 tr in next st, 1 tr in next st, (2 tr in next st) twice, (1 tr in next st, 2 tr in next st) twice, 2 ch, turn
Round 6: (1 dc, 4 tr, 1 dc, 2 ch, miss 2 sts) twice, ss to bottom of turning ch, fasten off
Rep Rounds 5 and 6 for 3 other petals, each time starting with right side facing you

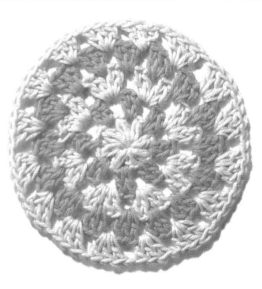

Wagon wheel. A versatile pattern; besides patchwork, it would be suitable for household items such as table mats or cushion covers.
4 ch and join in a ring with ss
Round 1: 3 ch, 1 petal in ring [(yrh, insert hook, draw up a loop) twice, yrh, draw through 5 loops, 1 ch], 7 more petals in ring, ss in top of beg ch, fasten off
Round 2: join new colour in 1st ch sp, 2 ch, 1 tr in 1st ch sp, 2 ch, (2 tr, 2 ch) in each of next 7 ch sp, ss in 2nd ch at beg, fasten off
Round 3: join new colour in 1st ch sp, 2 ch, (1 tr, 1 ch, 2 tr, 1 ch) in 1st ch sp, (2 tr, 1 ch, 2 tr, 1 ch) in each of next 7 ch sp, ss in 2nd ch at beg, fasten off
Round 4: join new colour in 1st ch sp, 2 ch, 2 tr in 1st ch sp, 1 ch, (3 tr, 1 ch) in each of next 15 ch sp, ss in 2nd ch at beg, fasten off
Rep Round 4 as many times as desired for size, but after Round 5, work 2 ch between tr groups

Crochet stitches

Meshes

A **mesh** consists of chain stitches and treble crochets combined in such a way that they form open spaces. By itself, or in conjunction with other techniques, it has a wide variety of uses.

Either of the square meshes below can serve as the basic element in **filet crochet** (see p. 294). To produce filet, selected meshes are filled with double crochet to form a pattern. (Or sometimes the reverse: the background is filled and open meshes form the pattern.) Once used extensively for doilies and antimacassars, filet is today used more for trimming and accessories. Square meshes also form the back-ground for **overlaid patterns** (see p. 295); in this technique, the spaces are filled with chain stitches, or yarns or ribbons are woven in. Diamond, honeycomb and diamond picot stitches, on the right, are used in the working of **Irish crochet** (see p. 296); as meshes, they form the lace background to flower and leaf motifs.

Used alone, any mesh pattern is ideal for a shawl, providing lightweight warmth. Mesh is also suitable for summer garments, evening wear and baby clothing. For the most lacy effect use lightweight yarns. Good choices are crochet cotton and fine knitting yarn.

Diamond mesh. A flexible stitch that is especially suitable for a flat round item such as a doily or tablecloth. It is also used in fringe-making and sometimes to join solid sections that have been knitted or crocheted.
Unit of 4 ch plus 2
Row 1: miss 1 ch, 1 dc in next ch, *5 ch, miss 3 ch, 1 dc in next ch*, 1 dc, 5 ch, turn
Row 2: *1 dc in next ch sp, 5 ch*, turn
Rep from Row 2

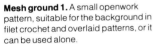

Mesh ground 1. A small openwork pattern, suitable for the background in filet crochet and overlaid patterns, or it can be used alone.
Fine yarns are most suitable.
Unit of 2 ch plus 6
Row 1: miss 5 ch, *1 tr in next ch, 1 ch, miss 1 ch*, 1 tr, 4 ch, turn
Row 2: miss 1st tr of previous row, *1 tr in next tr, 1 ch*, 1 tr in 3rd ch at beg of previous row, 4 ch, turn
Rep from Row 2

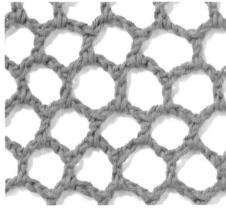

Honeycomb mesh. A popular pattern for backgrounds in Irish crochet (p. 296).
Unit of 4 ch plus 10
Row 1: miss 9 ch, *1 tr in next ch, 4 ch, miss 3 ch*, 1 tr, 8 ch, turn
Row 2: *1 tr in the 4 ch sp, 4 ch*, 1 tr, 8 ch, turn
Rep from Row 2

Mesh ground 2. An openwork pattern with larger spaces than the one above; can be worked with heavier yarns. Two treble crochet stitches are needed to fill a space, if this is used for filet crochet.
Unit of 3 ch plus 8
Row 1: miss 7 ch, *1 tr in next ch, 2 ch, miss 2 tr*, 1 tr, 5 ch, turn
Row 2: miss 1st tr of previous row, *1 tr in next tr, 2 ch, miss 2 tr*, 1 tr in 3rd ch at beg of previous row, 5 ch, turn
Rep from Row 2

Diamond picot mesh. Another favourite pattern for Irish crochet; this one has been used as a background for the cushion cover shown on p. 297.
Unit of 7 ch plus 2
Row 1: miss 1 ch, 1 dc in next ch, *2 ch, 1 picot [5 ch, ss in 1st of these 5 ch], 3 ch, 1 picot, 2 ch, miss 6 ch, 1 dc*, 2 ch, turn
Row 2: 1 picot, 3 ch, 1 picot, 2 ch, 1 dc in ch sp between picots of previous row, *2 ch, 1 picot, 3 ch, 1 picot, 2 ch, 1 dc in ch sp*, 2 ch, turn
Rep from Row 2

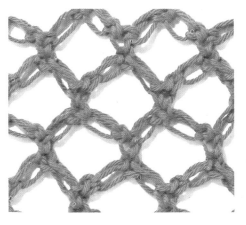

Solomon's knot. Lengthened chains form an open mesh that is similar in appearance to netting. The lengthened loop can be adjusted as desired. See p. 277 for the way to make the knots.
Unit of 4 ch plus 2
Row 1: miss 1 ch, 1 dc, 1 single knot [lengthen loop on hook to 1.5 cm, draw up a loop, take hook across front of lengthened loop and insert it under yarn of ch just completed, work 1 dc], make another single knot to complete the double knot, *miss 3 ch, 1 dc in next ch, 1 double knot*, 1 single knot, turn (total of 3 single knots for turning)
Row 2: *1 dc in centre of double knot in previous row, 1 double knot*, 1 single knot, turn
Rep from Row 2

Trestle stitch. A lacy pattern with alternating large and small spaces. Suitable for a shawl.
Unit of 4 ch plus 6
Row 1: miss 5 ch, *1 tr in next ch, 3 ch, miss 3 ch*, 1 tr, 4 ch, turn
Row 2: *1 dc in 2nd ch of 3 ch group, 2 ch, 1 tr in next tr, 2 ch*, 1 dc in turning ch of previous row, 5 ch, turn
Row 3: *1 tr in the tr, 3 ch*, 1 tr in turning ch of previous row, 4 ch, turn
Rep from Row 2

Open chequers. A large mesh ground with the alternate spaces filled in.
Unit of 6 ch plus 3
Row 1: miss 3 ch, 1 tr in each of next 2 ch, *3 ch, miss 3 ch, 1 tr in each of next 3 ch*, 3 ch, miss 3 ch, 1 tr in last ch, 3 ch, turn
Row 2: 2 tr in 1st ch sp, *3 ch, 3 tr in next 3 ch sp*, 3 ch, 1 tr in top of turning ch, 3 ch, turn
Rep from Row 2

Shaping mesh ground

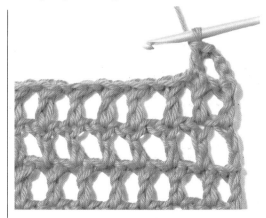

To decrease a space at the end of a row, do not work the last space (the one formed by the turning chain); instead, work 4 ch (for mesh ground 1) or 5 ch (for mesh ground 2) and turn; work 1 treble crochet in the next treble crochet. The resulting space will be triangular rather than square.

To decrease a space at the beginning of a row, do not work the usual turning chain; instead work 1 ch and turn; work 1 slipstitch in each chain stitch up to the next treble crochet, then 1 slipstitch in the treble crochet; work 4 ch (for mesh ground 1) or 5 ch (for mesh ground 2) and continue with the mesh pattern starting with 1 treble crochet in the next stitch. Use this method only when decreases must be paired on either side of the work.

To increase a space at the beginning of a row, do not work the usual turning chain; instead, work 5 ch (for mesh ground 1) or 7 ch (for mesh ground 2) and turn; work 1 treble crochet in the first stitch of the previous row.

Crochet stitches

Filet crochet

Filet crochet is a square mesh pattern with certain spaces filled to form a motif. Appropriate stitches for the openwork are mesh grounds 1 and 2 on p. 292. The filling is treble crochet, one stitch for a small space, two for a large one. Directions are usually charted, with background meshes represented by blank squares and motif stitches by filled ones. To follow a chart, read from right to left on the odd (right side) rows, from left to right on the even rows. Do the reverse, if you are left-handed. Suitable filet motifs are monograms, geometric shapes and flowers. Cotton is the traditional choice of thread.

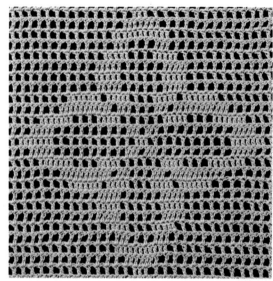

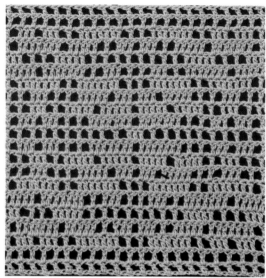

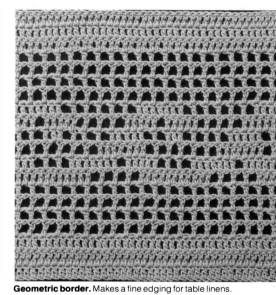

Flower motif. Suitable for an insertion or an all-over repeat.

Flower border. A kaleidoscope motif makes an attractive trimming.

Geometric border. Makes a fine edging for table linens.

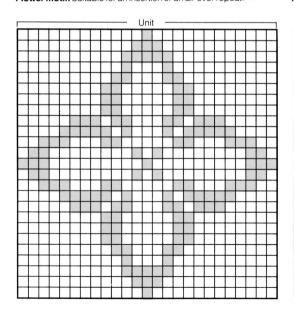

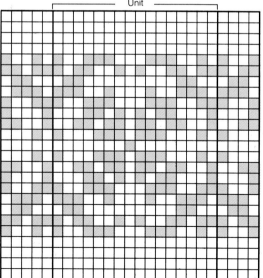

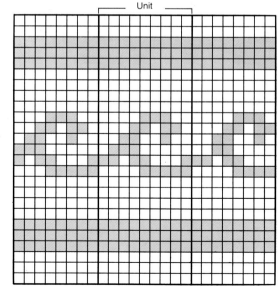

Overlaid meshes

Chained overlay. A mesh background with chain stitches worked in the spaces. An easy and effective way to create a crocheted stripe or plaid. Depending on the weight and type of yarn you choose, this technique can be used for a garment, a place mat, a cushion cover or a rug. The colour sequences should be planned before you begin.

To prepare the background,
use pattern for mesh ground I (p. 292).
To work the overlay chains,
use 2 strands of yarn; make a slip knot. With right side of mesh facing you, and yarn held behind the work, draw a loop through the first space in the lower right corner, insert hook in space directly above it, draw a loop through the space and the loop on the hook. Continue working this way to the top of the mesh, then begin again at bottom. In forming the chains, take care to maintain an even tension, or the background may be distorted.

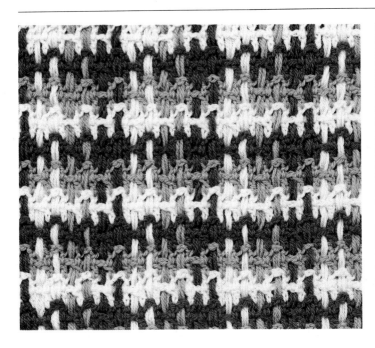

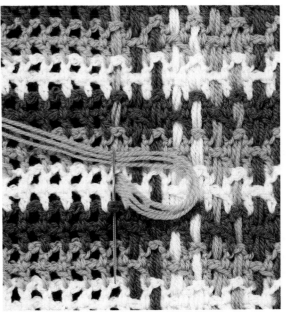

Woven overlay. Yarns intertwined with a mesh background. The fabric produced is thick and firm, usable for outerwear, a place mat or rug. Though any stitch might be used, a mesh (shown here) is the usual choice. The woven strands can be yarn, fabric strips or ribbon, and can be worked into the background vertically, horizontally or diagonally.

To prepare the background,
use pattern for mesh ground I (p. 292).
To weave the overlay,
use 3 strands of yarn threaded in a tapestry (blunt-ended) needle. Lace the yarns vertically under and over the chain bars, filling alternate spaces on each row. Yarn should be pulled firmly so that no loops remain, yet not too tightly, or the mesh may pucker.

Crochet stitches

Irish crochet

Irish crochet was developed in the mid-19th century, its style inspired by a popular Venetian lace. The lovely designs are most elegant worked in fine cotton or linen yarns. A typical pattern consists of floral motifs set in a mesh background. The mesh is usually worked around motifs, but in some modern adaptations it is crocheted separately and the motifs applied to it. A three-dimensional look can be given to the motifs by working certain portions over an additional yarn strand called a foundation cord. This cord, which is used also to control shaping, should be about twice the thickness of the working yarn.

Shamrock. Wind foundation cord twice around index finger and slip it off.
Round 1: 2 dc in ring, 1 picot [4 ch] (10 dc in ring, 4 ch) twice, 8 dc in ring, ss to 1st dc, pull cord so sts lie flat
Round 2: 15 dc over cord only, miss 1 picot and 1 dc; over cord and sts make 1 dc in each of next 7 dc, pull cord so sts lie flat, 18 dc over cord only, miss 1 picot and dc, 1 dc in each of next 7 dc, 15 dc on cord only, miss 1 picot and 1 dc, 1 dc in each of next 7 dc
Round 3: drop cord, round 1st leaf (1 ch, 1 dc) in each of next 2 sts, (1 ch, 1 tr) in each of next 3 sts, (1 ch, 1 dtr) in each of next 5 sts, (1 ch, 1 tr) in each of next 3 sts, (1 ch, 1 dc) in each of next 2 sts, ss in dc between leaves, work other 2 leaves as the 1st, but work 7 dtr in 2nd leaf, ss between leaves
Round 4: pick up foundation cord, miss 1st ch, *3 dc in each of next 2 ch, 4 ch*, rep from * round leaf, omitting last 4 ch, pull up cord, continue same way round other 2 leaves, ss to close
Short stem: 30 dc over cord, 1 ch, turn, leave loop of cord at end, work back up stem with 1 dc in each dc, ss to base
Long stem: same as short one but 160 dc

Loop for adjusting stem

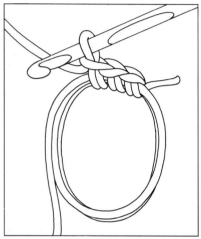

To form motif centre, wind foundation cord over index finger 1, 2, or 3 times (if number is not in directions, determine it by cord thickness). Slip ring off and work centre stitches over it. When ring is complete, pull cord gently to bring stitches close together. Work subsequent rounds over the cord where indicated in directions (stitches are

made over cord alone or over both cord and stitches). As work progresses, pull cord gently to keep stitches close together.
When motif is complete, cut the cord and working yarn, leaving ends at least 15 cm long. Using a rug or tapestry needle, weave each yarn end into the motif back for about 1.5 cm. Cut ends off.

Leaf. Worked over foundation cord and stitches, pulling up the cord periodically to make stitches lie flat. 15 ch, lay foundation cord over ch.
Row 1: miss 1 ch, *1 dc in each ch*, 5 dc in last ch (to form the tip), 1 dc in each loop along opposite side of ch, 3 dc over foundation cord only (to go around base), 1 dc in back loop of each dc on 1st side of ch, ending 4 dc from the centre dc in leaf tip, 1 ch, turn
Row 2: picking up front loop only, 1 dc in each dc down side, 3 dc in centre dc at base, 1 dc in each dc up other side, ending 3 dc from tip, 1 ch, turn
Row 3: picking up back loop, 1 dc in each dc down side, 3 dc in centre dc at base, 1 dc in each dc up other side, end 3 dc from tip of previous row, 1 ch, turn
Rows 4 and 6: as Row 3, working front loop only **Row 5:** as Row 3, working back loop only. Fasten off at end of Row 6

Rose. 8 ch and join in a ring with ss
Round 1: 6 ch, (1 tr, 3 ch) 7 times, ss in 3rd ch at beg or rnd
Round 2: (1 dc, 1 htr, 3 tr, 1 htr, 1 dc) over each 3 ch loop
Round 3: working behind Round 2, work 1 ss in ss of Round 1, 5 ch, (1 ss in next tr of Round 1, 5 ch) 7 times, ss in 1st ss to close
Round 4: (1 dc, 1htr, 5 tr, 1 htr, 1 dc) over each 5 ch loop
Round 5: working behind Round 4, work 1 ss in 1st ss of Round 3, 7 ch, (1 ss in next ss of Round 3, 7 ch) 7 times, ss in 1st ss to close
Round 6: (1dc, 1 htr, 7tr, 1 htr, 1 dc) over each 7 ch loop
Round 7: working behind Round 6, work 1 ss in 1st ss of Round 5, 9 ch, (1 ss in next ss of Round 5, 9 ch) 7 times, ss in 1st ss to close
Round 8: (1 dc, 1 htr, 9 tr, 1 htr, 1 dc) over each 9 ch loop, fasten off

Irish crochet cushion top

This lovely cushion is a fine way to display your talent for crochet. Approximate sizes are given, but the best result will be obtained if you crochet the top first, and then make or buy a cushion to fit.

Materials

200 g of No. 8 and 100 g No. 5 crochet cotton (for foundation cord); steel crochet hook 1.75 mm to obtain mesh tension; tapestry needle; 38 cm square of light-coloured muslin to work on; tacking thread and needle, 1 cushion of about 30 or 34 cm square, covered with plain, smooth fabric

Tension

For mesh, 16 chains to 5 cm
For motifs, no tension can be specified, but approximate sizes are: leaf, 5.5 cm from tip to base; shamrock, 5.5 cm from top to stem; rose 6.5 cm in diameter

Preparing the grid. Draw a 30 cm square on muslin. Mark off 2.5 cm segments along each side, then use the marks to draw lines diagonally (see illustration below). Work mesh over this.

Making motifs. Following the instructions on the opposite page, make one rose, eight leaves, two shamrocks with short stems facing in opposite directions, two shamrocks with long stems facing in opposite directions (to reverse a stem, turn it over just before slipstitching it to the base). Finish off all of the foundation cords except the ones extending from the long shamrock stems. Assemble the motifs and attach them to the grid as directed below.

Making the mesh. Work Rows 1 and 2, then tack the mesh to the grid, right side up, and follow instructions below.
98 ch and check your tension
Row 1 (wrong side): miss 1 ch, 1 dc, *2 ch, 1 picot [5 ch, ss in 1st of these 5 ch], 3 ch, 1 picot, 2 ch, miss 7 ch, 1 dc in next ch*, turn
Row 2: 10 ch, 1 picot, 2 ch, 1 dc in the 3 ch sp between picots of previous row, *2 ch, 1 picot, 3 ch, 1 picot, 2 ch, 1 dc in the 3 ch sp*, turn
Row 3: 2 ch, 1 picot, 3 ch, 1 picot, 3 ch, 1 picot, 2 ch, 1 dc in 3 ch sp, *2 ch, 1 picot, 3 ch, 1 picot, 2 ch, 1 dc in the 3 ch sp*, work last dc in the 10 ch sp of the previous row, turn
Repeat Rows 2 and 3 for pattern.
After mesh is attached to grid, each right-side row is worked with the grid facing you right-side up; for a wrong-side row, grid must be turned upside-down and the mesh pulled away from it slightly. Wherever mesh comes in contact with a motif, slipstitch it to one edge of the motif, then chain enough stitches to move up a row or to continue horizontally on the wrong side of the motif.

When mesh is complete, connect diamonds along top and left edges with *8 ch, 1 dc in each 3 ch sp*

Forming a border. Cut a length of foundation cord 152 cm long. Starting at one corner, work (5 dc, 5 ch) 3 times over cord and each 8 ch group. Pull up cord periodically to make stitches lie flat. Do not fasten off foundation cord until after cover has been mounted, as some adjustment may be necessary.

Finishing. Detach crocheted piece carefully from grid; remove tacking threads. Pin it to one side of cushion, adjusting fit either by stretching gently or pulling on the foundation cord. Sew the border with double thread, taking small stitches through back of border and under cushion fabric; weave foundation cord into back of border for 3 cm; cut remainder. Tack rose to prevent shifting. Steam-press lightly.

To assemble motifs, lay them out in the arrangement shown. Join seven leaves first, making small stitches at contact points. Next, attach rose and bottom leaf. Join shamrocks where picots touch, then draw up cords on stems, shaping them as shown. Sew each stem in position, cut its cord, weave end into the back. Centre motifs on grid; tack their centres to fabric, leaving edges free.

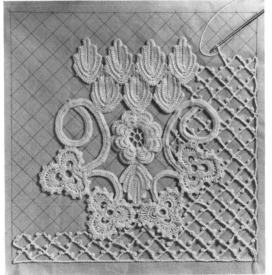

To crochet mesh around motifs, work first 2 rows, then tack foundation chain to bottom line of grid with the 10-ch group at right edge, mesh lines aligning with grid lines. Work 3rd row of mesh, taking it behind shamrocks as necessary. Continue up right side to top of motifs; fasten off; work left side, then top, tacking mesh to grid as work proceeds. Complete border as directed above.

Sew the completed piece by hand to one side of cushion, centring it between finished edges, as shown, or attaching it along the seams (if it fits precisely). Smooth fabric, in a dark or medium colour, sets off this lace to best advantage. For laundering, it would be wise to remove lace to avoid the risk of the colour running. Wash it gently by hand, wet-block on grid; re-sew to cushion when dry.

Crochet stitches

Tunisian crochet

Tunisian crochet (also called afghan stitch) is a cross between knitting and crochet methods. The fabric is similar to a knitted one, but firmer, especially suited to blankets, coats or suits.

To work these stitches, you need a special tool called a *tricot needle* or *hook*. This is longer than other types, uniform in diameter, and has a knob at one end to keep stitches from sliding off. The procedure is to work from right to left on one row, leaving all loops on the hook, then from left to right on the next row, never turning the work.

The foundation of most afghan stitches is two basic rows (see below); the finish can be one row of either slip-stitch or double crochet. Blocking is essential and must be done carefully, as this fabric tends to pull on the bias.

BASIC TECHNIQUE

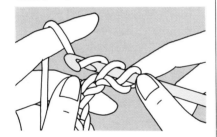

Work the desired number of ch plus 1.
Row 1: miss 1 ch, *insert hook in the next ch, draw up a loop and leave it on the hook*, do not turn work at the end of the row.

Row 2: yrh, draw yarn through 1st loop on hook, *yrh, draw through 2 loops*, do not turn work; 1 remaining loop counts as 1st st on next row.

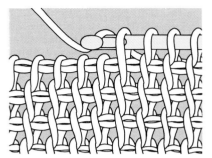

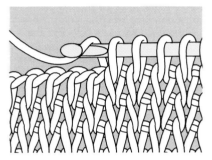

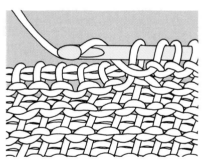

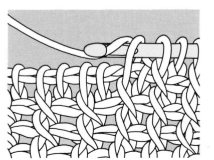

Basic Tunisian (knit stitch). The first two rows of this pattern are used for the foundation of most Tunisian stitches. Its texture, which resembles that of a woven fabric, is especially suitable for cross stitch embroidery.
Unit of any number of ch plus 1
Row 1: miss 1 ch, *insert hook in next ch, draw up a loop*
Row 2: yrh, draw through 1 loop, *yrh, draw through 2 loops*
Row 3: *insert hook right to left under next vertical stitch, draw up a loop*
Rep from Row 2

Tunisian stocking stitch. This pattern looks like the knitted version, except that it is thicker.
Unit of any number of ch plus 1
Rows 1 and 2: basic Tunisian
Row 3: *insert hook front to back in the centre of next vertical st loop (the centre can be seen more easily if you separate the 2 yarns using thumb and 3rd finger of left hand), draw up a loop*
Row 4: yrh, draw through 1 loop, *yrh, draw through 2 loops*
Rep from Row 3

Tunisian purl. Yarn is held in front of work as for purl stitch in knitting.
Unit of any number of ch plus 1
Rows 1 and 2: basic Tunisian
Row 3: *holding yarn to the front, insert hook right to left under next vertical st, draw up a loop*
Row 4: yrh, draw through 1 loop, *yrh, draw through 2 loops*
Rep from Row 3

Tunisian crossed stitch. Pairs of stitches are worked in reverse order.
Unit of 2 ch plus 1
Rows 1 and 2: basic Tunisian
Row 3: *miss 1 vertical st, insert hook right to left under next vertical st, draw up a loop, insert hook right to left under missed vertical st, draw up a loop*
Row 4: yrh, draw through 1 loop, *yrh, draw through 2 loops*
Rep from Row 3

Tunisian double stitch. Rows of diagonal stitches alternate with rows of the basic vertical pattern.
Unit of any number of ch plus 1
Rows 1 and 2: basic Tunisian
Row 3: *insert hook right to left under next vertical st, draw up a loop, yrh, draw through 1 loop*
Row 4: yrh, draw through 1 loop, *yrh, draw through 2 loops*
Rep from Row 3

Tunisian popcorn. The knobs are worked on a ground of basic Tunisian. If desired, popcorn size can be increased by lengthening the chain; also, spacing can be varied by adjusting the number of stitches between popcorns.
Unit of 4 ch plus 5
Rows 1 and 2: basic Tunisian
Row 3: draw a loop through each of next 4 vertical sts, *3 ch, draw a loop through each of next 4 vertical sts*
Rows 4, 5, 6: basic Tunisian
Row 7: draw a loop through each side of next 2 vertical sts, *3 ch, draw a loop through each of next 4 vertical sts*, 3 ch, draw a loop through each of next 2 vertical sts
Rows 8, 9, 10: basic Tunisian
Rep from Row 3

Tunisian rib. A combination of basic and purled Tunisian stitches.
Unit of 6 ch plus 4
Rows 1 and 2: basic Tunisian
Row 3: *3 sts basic Tunisian, 3 sts Tunisian purl*, 3 sts basic Tunisian
Row 4: yrh, draw through 1 loop, *yrh, draw through 2 loops*
Rep from Row 3

Tunisian honeycomb. Knit and purl stitches are alternated in the same way as for knitted moss stitch.
Unit of 2 ch plus 1
Rows 1 and 2: basic Tunisian
Row 3: *1 Tunisian purl under next vertical bar, 1 basic Tunisian under next vertical bar*
Rows 4 and 6: yrh, draw through 1 loop, *yrh, draw through 2 loops*
Row 5: *1 basic Tunisian under next vertical bar, 1 Tunisian purl under next vertical bar*
Rep from Row 3

Tunisian bias stitch. Worked in the same manner as Tunisian crossed stitch (opposite page), but pattern is moved one stitch to the left on alternate rows.
Unit of 2 ch plus 1
Rows 1 and 2: basic Tunisian
Rows 3 and 4: Tunisian crossed stitch
Row 5: draw a loop under next vertical stitch, *cross next pair of stitches*, draw a loop under last vertical stitch
Row 6: yrh, draw through 1 loop, *yrh, draw through 2 loops*
Rep from Row 3

Tunisian lace. An exceptionally pretty pattern that is very easy to work.
Unit of 4 ch plus 1
Row 1: basic Tunisian
Row 2: *3 ch, yrh, draw through 5 loops, yrh, draw through 1 loop*
Row 3: *draw up a loop through the top of each cluster, draw up a loop in each ch of the 3 ch group*
Rep from Row 2

Crochet stitches

Loops

Lattice loop. An airy pattern of elongated loops, especially suitable for a shawl, or one row might be used for a lacy insertion. See below for the way to work a lattice.
Unit of any number of ch
Row 1: miss 1 ch, *1 dc in each dc*, 1 ch, turn
Row 2: lengthen turning ch to height of strip, place strip between the loop and the yarn, draw a loop through the lengthened chain, *insert hook in next st, draw up a loop to top of strip, yrh, draw through the long loop, yrh, draw through 2 loops*, 1 ch, turn
Row 3: *1 dc in each st*
Rep from Row 2

Bouclé loop. Shaggy loops on one side of fabric, double crochet on reverse side. Loops can be worked in two different ways (see below). This stitch is suitable for a cushion cover, rug or garment; bouclé loop can also be knitted.
Unit of any number of ch
Row 1: miss 1 ch, *1 dc in each ch*, 1 ch, turn
Row 2: *1 loop st in each dc*, 1 ch, turn
Row 3: *1 dc in each st*, 1 ch, turn
Rep from Row 2

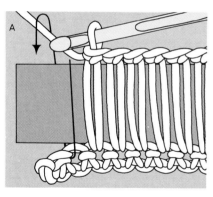

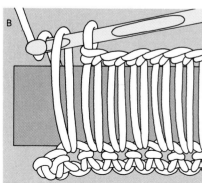

WORKING THE LATTICE LOOP

A lattice can be worked neatly over a ruler or a cardboard strip. If you do not have a ruler in a suitable size, cut a strip of sturdy card about 15 cm long and the desired depth of the stitch.
To begin lattice pattern, work a row of double crochet, 1 chain and turn. Lengthen the turning chain to the height of the strip, place strip between loop and yarn, draw a loop through the lengthened chain, *slide hook forward and down, and insert it in the next stitch, lower yarn behind the strip until it reaches the hook, draw up a long loop (hooking action is indicated by arrow, illustration A), yarn round hook (B), draw a loop through long loop, yarn round hook, draw through remaining 2 loops*. Repeat from asterisk across the row, removing strip and moving it forward as it becomes filled with stitches, 1 chain, turn.
To continue pattern, work a double crochet in each stitch, and on the last stitch, insert hook under the last long loop as well as the two top loops, 1 chain and turn. Repeat the lattice row next or, if preferred, work additional rows of double crochet, then a lattice.

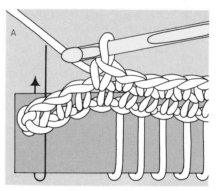

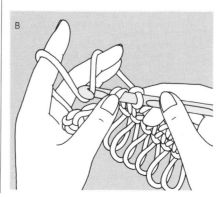

WORKING THE BOUCLÉ LOOP

A bouclé loop can be formed with the aid of an object such as a pencil, ruler or cardboard strip, or it can be worked over one or two fingers of the left hand. The first method is more precise; the second is faster once a rhythm is developed. Before you begin, work a sample to determine the length of the loops. Somewhere between 1 cm and 4 cm is usual. Once established, the loop length should be consistent throughout the pattern.
To form loops over a strip, first work a foundation row of double crochet, 1 chain and turn. *Bracing strip behind the work with left hand, insert hook in next stitch, transfer strip to right hand and take yarn round strip front to back (see arrow, illustration A), draw up a loop, yarn round hook, draw through 2 loops*. Repeat from asterisk to end of row, sliding loops off and moving strip forward as it becomes filled.
To form loops over the fingers, first make a foundation row of double crochet, 1 chain and turn. *Insert hook in next stitch, swing 3rd and 4th fingers on left hand forward under yarn then back against yarn so that a loop is formed over these fingers (B), draw a loop through the stitch, pulling it over top of 3rd finger, yarn round hook, draw through 2 loops, slip fingers out of the loop*. Repeat from asterisk across the row.

Chain loop stitch. Curly loops are worked on a background of double crochet. Different effects can be obtained by making longer chains, or by working the ground in treble crochet. This pattern has the same uses as bouclé loop (left).

Unit of any number of ch plus 2

Rows 1 and 2: double crochet

Row 3: working into front loop of each st *1 dc, 8 ch*, 1 dc, 1 ch, turn

Row 4: *1 dc, working into other loop of each st worked in previous row*, 1 ch, turn
Rep from Row 1

Broomstick lace. A soft and spongy texture; a useful stitch for shawls and baby blankets. The pattern is a combination of large loops, worked over a 'stick' (dowel or large knitting needle), and double crochet, worked over a group of 5 loops.

Unit of 5 ch

Row 1: transfer ch on hook to the stick, * insert hook in next ch, draw up a loop and place it on the stick*, do not turn

Row 2: *insert hook through 5 loops and slide them from stick, draw a loop through the 5 loops, yrh, draw through 1 loop, 4 dc over same 5 loops*, do not turn

Row 3: transfer ch on hook to the stick, *draw up a loop through next dc, place loop on stick*, do not turn
Rep from Row 2

WORKING THE CHAIN LOOP

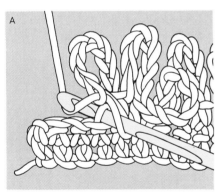

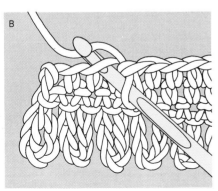

A chain loop is produced by making a long chain between 2 stitches. The crowding of these loops forces them to curl and form a thick, spongy texture on the fabric face.

To begin a chain loop pattern, work 2 rows of double crochet, 1 chain and turn. *Inserting hook into front loop of each stitch (A), work 1 double crochet, 8 chain*. Repeat from *, ending the row with 1 double crochet, 1 chain, turn.

To continue pattern, *insert hook into other loop of each stitch in the previous row (B), work 1 double crochet*, 1 chain, turn.

WORKING BROOMSTICK LACE

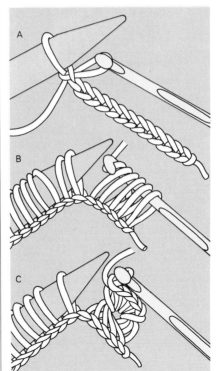

Broomstick loops are formed over a dowel or thick knitting needle, of a diameter between 1 cm and 2.5 cm, and of sufficient length to hold all stitches. To make a blanket, for example, a dowel 2.5 cm thick and 90 cm long might be used. If using a dowel, layers of tape or a few rubber bands should be wrapped round one end to keep stitches from sliding off.

To begin broomstick pattern, work a row of chain divisible by 5, counting the chain on hook. Transfer chain on hook to stick and brace the stick under your left arm. *Insert hook in next chain, draw up a loop (A) and place it on the stick*. Repeat from asterisk across the row; do not turn.

To continue pattern, *insert hook right to left through 5 loops, draw a loop through the 5 loops (B), yarn round hook, draw a loop through the 1 loop, 4 double crochet over the same 5 loops (C)*. Repeat from asterisk across the row; do not turn. All loops are worked from left to right, double crochet rows from right to left (the reverse if you are left-handed).

Crochet stitches/Multicolour

Introduction

Attractive effects are possible with the use of two or more colours in crochet. Because stitches are tall, however, results can never be as subtle or finely detailed as in multicoloured knitting. As a rule, simple designs, such as geometric shapes and stripes, work the best, and double crochet permits the greatest flexibility, with frequent colour changes.

There are three ways of working coloured patterns (also called jacquards), shown on the facing page. Each is suited to a particular situation. A colour change is always made the same way, whichever technique you use. Pick up the new colour as the final yarn round hook in the last stitch of the previous colour (second illustration on right).

WORKING WITH A COLOUR CHART

A chart is often used to give directions for colour patterns in crochet. This is a graph in which each square equals a stitch and each line equals a row. Usually, blank squares represent the main colour, symbols or coloured squares depict the contrasts and, where needed, an accompanying key interprets these usages. To follow a chart, start at the bottom and read from right to left for right-side rows, from left to right for wrong-side rows. It is possible to work crochet from other needlework charts, such as a cross stitch pattern, but a test sample must be made to decide if the proportions translate attractively, and the colour changes are workable.

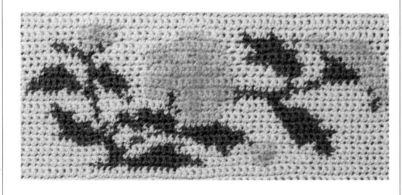

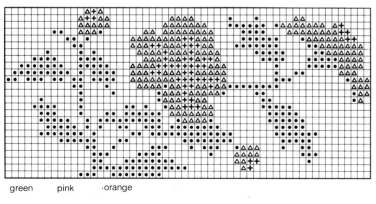

green   pink   orange

Jacquard techniques

To join in a new colour mid-row, lay the yarn end over the row below, introducing it a few stitches before you need it (A). Continue to work with the 1st colour, covering the end of the new yarn. Work the 1st colour to the final 2 loops of the last stitch, then draw the new colour through these last 2 loops (B).
The same technique can be used when changing colours at the beginning of a row by introducing the new colour on the last few stitches of the row below. Joining yarn by this method eliminates the need to weave in the yarn ends with a tapestry needle when the project is complete.

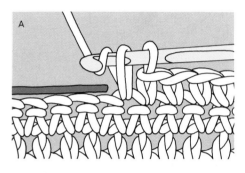

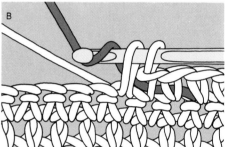

If unused yarn must be carried over more than 3 stitches, it is best to catch it into the work every other stitch. The yarn strands will be less likely to pull or be snagged, and tension will be more even. When using this technique, take care not to apply tension to the yarn being carried, as this will cause the work to pucker.
On a right-side row, insert hook into the stitch, then under the carried yarn at back of the work, catch working yarn with the hook (A), draw up a loop and complete the stitch.
On a wrong-side row, insert hook under the carried yarn, then into the stitch, catch working yarn with the hook (B), draw up a loop and complete the stitch.

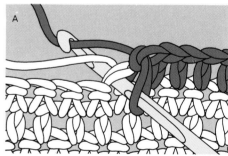

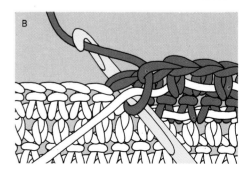

Carrying unused colours across the wrong side is suitable for any crocheted fabric that reveals just one finished surface – a pullover or a cushion cover, for example. If carried over more than 3 stitches, unused yarn should be caught into the work every other stitch (see lower right, opposite page).

To change colours on a right-side row, work the 1st colour to the final 2 loops of the last stitch, drop 1st colour back and to the left of 2nd colour, yrh and draw through 2 loops with 2nd colour.

To change colours on a wrong-side row, work 1st colour to the final 2 loops of the last stitch, drop 1st colour forward and to the right of 2nd colour, yrh and draw through 2 loops with 2nd colour.

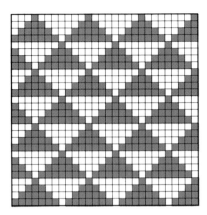  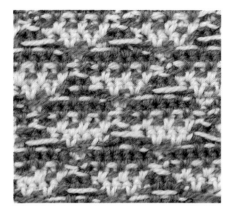

Working over colours not in use is one way to crochet a reversible fabric. This method is faster than cutting and weaving (below), but it consumes more yarn and produces a fabric that is quite heavy. The carried yarn, though covered by the stitches, *is* visible between stitches, and the fabric is attractive or not depending on the design and colours you are working with. Use a hook one size larger than usual to allow for the bulk of the unused yarn.

To carry the unused colour, lay it on top of the previous row as you work stitches in the contrasting colour.

To change colours, draw a loop of the 2nd colour through the final 2 loops of the last stitch in the 1st colour.

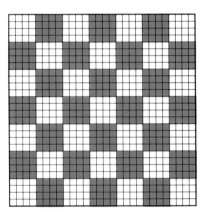  

Cutting and weaving the yarn ends is another way to manage colour changes on a reversible fabric. An alternative to working over yarn (above), this is a practical approach when unused yarn must be carried a great distance, when colours are changed at the end of a row, or when the pattern is an inset motif, as in the example on the right.

To discontinue a colour, work it to the final 2 loops of the last stitch, then draw up a loop with the new colour. Cut off the 1st colour, leaving a 15 cm end. When the work is complete, weave the yarn end through 4 to 6 stitches of the colour that matches it; cut off the remainder.

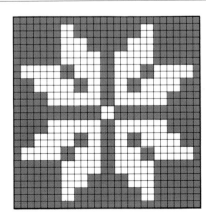  

Crochet stitches/Charted

Shorthand symbols

Crochet techniques can be represented by symbols and the symbols used to chart a pattern stitch, or an entire project, visually. Because a chart resembles the actual look of a pattern, it aids in visualising an unfamiliar stitch. It is especially suited to working in the round.

Listed on the right are symbols, their meanings and the numbers of pages on which illustrations of the techniques can be found. As a rule, no more than a few symbols are used in one pattern, so it is necessary to remember only the ones for which you have immediate use.

Though crochet symbols are used in many countries, they are not standardised. The ones given here are typical, but not universal, examples. If you need a symbol that is not shown here, you can invent your own.

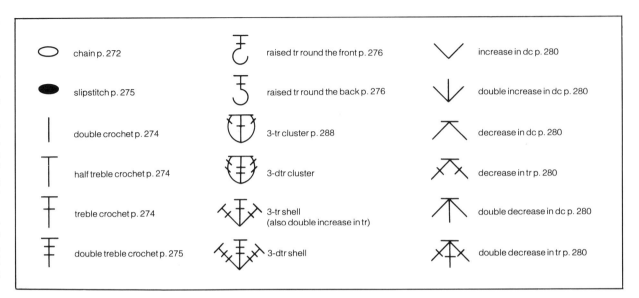

○	chain p. 272
●	slipstitch p. 275
│	double crochet p. 274
┬	half treble crochet p. 274
┼	treble crochet p. 274
╪	double treble crochet p. 275
	raised tr round the front p. 276
	raised tr round the back p. 276
	3-tr cluster p. 288
	3-dtr cluster
	3-tr shell (also double increase in tr)
	3-dtr shell
∨	increase in dc p. 280
	double increase in dc p. 280
∧	decrease in dc p. 280
	decrease in tr p. 280
	double decrease in dc p. 280
	double decrease in tr p. 280

Charted stitch

Clusters in a square. Directions below, charted form on the right.
6 ch and join in a ring with ss
Round 1: 3 ch, (yrh, insert hook in ring, draw up a loop, yrh, draw through 2 loops) twice, yrh, draw through 3 loops, 2 ch, *3 tr cluster in ring [(yrh, insert hook, draw up a loop, yrh, draw through 2 loops) 3 times, yrh, draw through 4 loops], 2 ch*, rep from *6 more times, ss in top of beg ch
Round 2: 3 ch, 2 tr in 2 ch sp, at end of Round 1 (in front of 3 ch) 2 ch, (3 tr in next 2 ch sp, 2 ch) 7 times, ss in top of beg ch
Round 3: 1 ch, *1 dc in 2nd tr, 2 ch, 3 dtr cluster in next 2 ch sp [(yrh twice, insert hook, draw up a loop, yrh, draw through 2 loops) 3 times, yrh, draw through 4 loops], 2 ch*, rep from *7 more times, ss in beg ch
Round 4: 1 ch, *3 dc in st at top of cluster, (3 tr, 2 ch, 3 tr) in next dc, 3 dc in top of next cluster, 1 ch, 1 dc in next dc, 1 ch*, rep from * 5 more times, ss in beg ch
Round 5: 1 ch, 1 dc in each st or ch, 3 dc in each 2 ch sp at corners, ss in beg ch, fasten off

Crocheting a garment

Introduction

This section contains the basic information necessary to help you understand how crochet patterns are constructed, and to help you plan and design crocheted garments. Before crocheting any garment, read through the instructions to make sure you understand them, and try out any new techniques.

Designing a crocheted garment

There are two ways to design a crocheted garment. One is to alter an existing pattern – making changes to fit your measurements – the other is to design your own. With either method you will need the following:
1. An accurate set of body or garment measurements (see Knitting, p. 464).
2. A sample square to decide which tension to use to calculate the amount of yarn needed.
3. Squared paper for the pattern.

Before you begin, read pp. 308–9 for information about shaping necklines, armholes and sleeves.

The first thing to do is write down the width and the length measurements for each section of the garment you are planning. If your plan is based on body measurements, you must add ease, using other patterns for guides and the general information on p. 464. You should also add 5 mm for seams, and plan the overall length, for example, from the underarm to the bottom edge of a sweater. Next, choose a yarn and stitch pattern, crochet a sample, or several if necessary, until you are satisfied with the appearance of the stitch, then measure the tension. To translate garment width dimensions into stitches, multiply the stitch tension by centimetres. For example, if you are planning a sweater that measures 45 cm at the bottom edge of the back, and the stitch tension is 8 stitches to 5 cm, you would need (45 ÷ 5 × 8 = 72) 72 stitches plus 2 stitches for seams for the

back section. To translate garment length measurements into rows, multiply row tension by centimetres. If a sweater measures 40 cm from bottom edge to underarm, and row tension is 6 rows to 5 cm, there would be (40 ÷ 5 × 6 = 48) 48 rows from bottom to underarm. To determine the number and placing of decreases for shaping armholes, sleeves and neckline, follow the guidelines on pp. 308–9. Prepare a chart or outline (see pp. 306–7 for the method), then calculate the quantity of yarn.

To estimate how much yarn you will need for your own design, there are several approaches; these are described below. One general rule to keep in mind is that pattern stitches with clusters, shells or bobbles usually require about 50 per cent more yarn than the basic stitches and textures (see p. 284).

One way to estimate yarn quantity is to use the amount specified for a similar pattern using similar yarn and stitch. (For this purpose, it is useful to keep a notebook of patterns.) This quantity may not be precisely what you need, so it is advisable to buy extra yarn to be sure of having enough from the same dye lot. Many shops will let you return unused yarn within a reasonable time; check with the shop at the time of purchase.

Another approach is to consult the sales assistant in a wool shop. The assistants usually have the experience from which to make an estimate.

If you cannot find either assistance or

Compare the measurements of the pattern with those of the person for whom the garment is intended. (Methods for taking measurements can be found in the Knitting section, p. 464.) If the measurements are not given, you can work them out by dividing the total of the row of stitches by the tension width (5 cm) and multiplying the answer by the number of stitches in the tension width. For example, if the shoulder has 20 stitches, and the tension is 8 stitches to 5 cm, you divide 20 by 8 which equals 2.5, and multiply this by 5. The answer is 12.5 cm and this is the shoulder measurement.

an appropriate pattern, here is a way to make your own estimate. Buy a ball of desired yarn and wind off a length of yarn that equals about one-eighth of the total length. Measure this length carefully. It might be, for example, 18 m. Make a tension sample and measure its area; if the sample is 10 cm by 7.5 cm, the area would be 75 sq. cm.

Next, calculate the approximate area for each garment section by multiplying widest measurement by overall length. Add these figures together, then divide the sum by the sample area and multiply this number by the length of yarn used for the sample. Here is an example:

Sweater

across the chest	45 cm
length, neck to bottom	50 cm
total area	2,250 sq. cm

Sweater front

area, same as back	2,250 sq. cm

Sweater sleeves

width at upper arm	30 cm
overall length	57.5 cm
total area, both sleeves	3,450 sq. cm

Total area for sweater 7,950 sq. cm

Sweater area divided by sample area (75) 106

106 is the approximate number of 10 cm by 7.5 cm samples needed to crochet the garment. Multiply 18 m (length of yarn used in sample) by 106 to determine total amount of yarn – 1,908 m. Deduct 10 per cent for shaping decreases – total of 1,717 m. Divide this by 144 (18 × 8) to get an estimate of balls required (12). See p. 465 for an alternative method.

Crocheting a garment

Charting a woman's cardigan

This tailored cardigan is shown in both written and charted form so you can compare the methods. Directions are for Misses' size 12 (86 cm bust).

Materials

400 g of double knitting yarn, sizes 3.50 and 4.00 hooks, 6 1.5 cm buttons

Tension

8 htr and 6 rows = 5 cm with 4.00 hook

BACK. Using 4.00 hook, 73 ch.

Row 1: miss 1 ch, *1 dc in each ch*, 1 ch, turn (you now have 72 sts).

Row 2: *1 htr in each dc*, 2 ch, turn.

Row 3: *1 htr in each htr*, 2 ch, turn. Rep Row 3 until piece measures 36 cm.

Armholes: 1 ss in each of 1st 4 sts, 1 htr in each st to last 4 sts, 2 ch, turn; dec 1 st at each end of next 4 rows. Work straight on 56 sts until the armholes measure 20 cm.

Shoulders: 8 ss in 1st 8 sts, 9 htr in next 9 sts, 2 ch, turn; dec 1 st at beg of next row, 1 htr in each of next 6 sts, 1 dc in next st, fasten off. Miss centre 22 sts, join yarn and work other shoulder to match.

LEFT FRONT. With 4.00 hook, 37 ch. **Row 1:** miss 1 ch, *1 dc in each ch*, 1 ch, turn (you now have 36 sts).

Row 2: *1 htr in each dc*, 2 ch, turn.

Row 3: 1 htr in each of 1st 14 htr, 4 raised tr round the front of next 4 dc in Row 1, 1 htr in each of next 18 htr, 2 ch, turn.

Row 4: *1 htr in each htr*, 2 ch, turn.

Row 5: 1 htr in each of 1st 14 htr, 4 raised tr round front of 4 raised tr 2 rows below, 18 htr in next 18 htr, 2 ch, turn.

Repeat Rows 4 and 5 until piece measures 36 cm, ending on wrong side.

Armhole: 1 ss in each of 1st 4 sts, work to end of row; dec 1 st at armhole edge 4 times. Work straight on rem 28 sts until armhole measures 10 cm, ending at front edge.

Shaping neck: 1 ss in each of 1st 8 sts, work to end; dec 1 st at neck edge 4 times. Work straight on rem 16 sts until armhole measures 20 cm, ending at armhole.

Shoulder: 1 ss in each of 1st 8 sts; work to end of row, fasten off.

RIGHT FRONT. Work as for left front reversing the pattern and shapings.

SLEEVES. With 4.00 hook, 33 ch. Work **Row 1** in dc and **Row 2** in htr as for left front, but on 32 sts.

Row 3: 1 htr in each of 1st 14 sts, 4 raised tr round the front of next 4 dc in Row 1, 1 htr in each of next 14 sts. Continue in pattern, increasing 1 st at each end on every 4th row, 8 times. Work straight on 48 sts until piece measures 40 cm.

Shaping cap: ss in each of 1st 4 sts, work to last 4 sts, turn; work 1 row, dec 1 st at each end of next and every other row 6 times; dec 1 st at each end of every row 5 times, 18 sts remain, fasten off.

FINISHING. Sew side, shoulder and sleeve seams. With right side facing you, using 3.50 hook, begin at right side seam, work 2 rows of dc along bottom, front and neck edges of sweater; work 3 dc in each corner st. Mark 6 buttonhole positions on right front, placing 1st one

A woman's tailored cardigan is worked in htr with a panel of 4 raised tr on each front and sleeve.

1 cm from neck, last one 1.5 cm from bottom; space others between.

Next round, work in dc, making a horizontal 1 ch buttonhole at each marking and 3 dc at each corner. Work 2 more rounds of dc, decreasing round curve of neck; fasten off. With right side facing you, using 3.50 hook, work 5 rnds of dc along bottom of each sleeve. Sew in sleeves. Attach buttons.

How to make a garment chart

A garment chart is a visual representation of written instructions. There are two different forms – **outline** and **graph**. Either can be used when designing a garment or adjusting an existing pattern.

An outline is a drawing of the exact dimensions of each main garment section, with shaping information written on it. This form gives you a realistic view of garment shape, and can be used later, if desired, for blocking. To make an outline, use sturdy wrapping paper and start by drawing a straight line on it equal to the widest dimension (usually the underarm) of the garment back, then draw a second line perpendicular to and through the centre of the first. Using these as reference points, measure the other areas. Draw the sleeve and any other garment sections in the same way.

A graph is worked out on paper marked off in squares. Each square represents a stitch, each line of squares a row. To chart this way, the tension must already have been determined. You can graph an entire garment section, or just those areas that are shaped (as shown opposite); only half need really be graphed. A graph is a less realistic view of garment shape than an outline, but it is easier to follow.

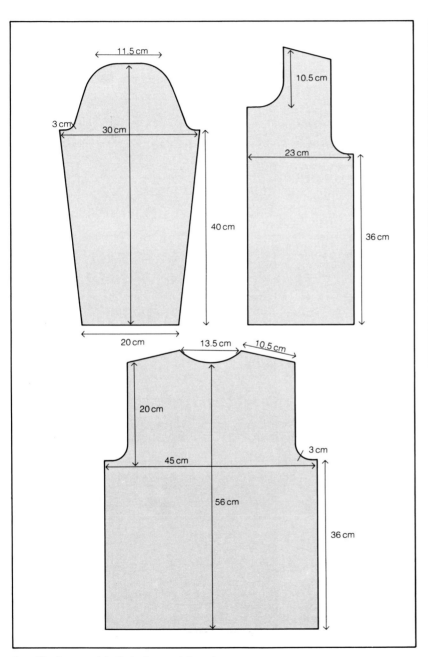

An outline is an exact duplicate of garment dimensions.

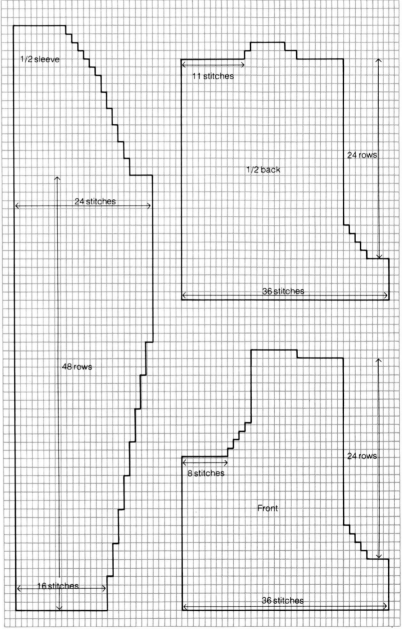

In a graph, each square represents a stitch, each line of squares a row.

Crocheting a garment

Shaping necklines

Special care should be taken in crocheting a neckline; this part of a garment is particularly noticeable. In general, the fit should be smooth, with no gaping or wrinkling. In the case of a high neck on a pullover, a slit opening must be provided so that the head can pass through. (There is not enough stretch in crochet for the neckline to expand.)

The neck width calculation is based on shoulder width and equals about one-third of it, or the number of stitches that remain after subtracting the two shoulder lengths. Front neck depth is calculated in relation to armhole depth, and varies according to style (see the directions on the right). Usually, a back neck is straight, formed by leaving the stitches unworked just below the last row of shoulder shaping. If a front is a deep scoop or square, the back may be shaped the same way, but would be less deep as a general rule.

In shaping a neckline, work is usually divided, each half crocheted separately, and all decreases made on the right side of the work. Distribution of decreases depends to some extent on stitch height. You can miss one or two rows between decreases for a short stitch (dc or htr), but should decrease every row for a tall one (tr and taller), or the edge will be jagged.

A crocheted neck edge may be naturally neat – a square neck is an example – but it will hold its shape better and have a more finished appearance if you work an edging. One or more rows of double crochet makes a firm edge. Ribbing is also suitable. It can be crocheted (see p. 310) or knitted by picking up stitches along the edge. Shoulder seams should be joined before the edging is added.

Guidelines for making three basic neck shapings are shown on the right. These are typical, but do not represent all possibilities. If you wish to use them for altering an existing pattern, or designing your own, chart the design first.

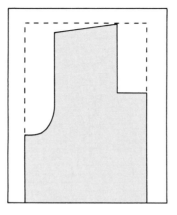

Square neckline shaping is begun 8 cm to 15 cm below the start of shoulder shaping by leaving unworked all stitches allotted for the neckline opening. (The number of stitches for the neck is what remains after subtracting stitches for each shoulder.) There is no decreasing for this style; you work straight up to the shoulder, completing one-half of the neckline at a time.
To make the edging shown here, work 2 rounds of double crochet along the neck edge, starting and ending at one shoulder seam, decreasing 1 stitch at each corner.

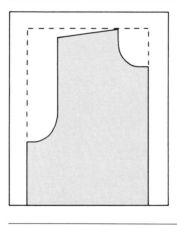

High round neckline shaping is begun about 5 cm below shoulder for an adult garment, 4 cm for a child's. One-third of stitches to be decreased are left unworked at the centre; another third are allotted to each half of the neck, decreasing at the neck edge 1 stitch every row, then working even to the top of the shoulder.
A slit opening must be provided for this style; usually it is worked at the back by dividing the work at the centre, 8 cm to 10 cm below the shoulder.
To make the edging shown here, work 3 rows of double crochet, starting and ending at the slit, decreasing where necessary (usually in the curved areas) to keep the edging flat.

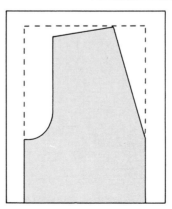

A V-neckline is usually started 15 cm to 23 cm below the shoulder, or just after the start of armhole shaping. Work is divided at the centre and each half is worked separately, decreasing gradually at the neck edge, always on the right side of the work. For a wide V, decrease 1 stitch every row; for a narrower one, every second or third row. If you have an odd number of stitches across the front, decrease centre stitch before dividing work.
To make the edging shown here, work 1 round of double crochet on the neck edge, then a second round of reverse double crochet, starting and ending at a shoulder seam, decreasing 2 stitches at the V on each round.

Shaping armholes and sleeves

Armhole and sleeve shapings are important to crocheting a well-fitted garment. Three basic styles are described below – **classic, raglan** and **semi-raglan.**

To chart an armhole with the methods given here, you need measurements for *shoulder width,* the *chest* (or underarm) across half the garment, plus the standard *shoulder length* and *armhole depth* for your garment size and *neck circumference* (for raglan only). To shape a sleeve, you should have the *wrist,* the *underarm* length and the *upper-arm* measurements.

The usual way of crocheting a sleeve is from the bottom edge up, increasing the underarm seam gradually and symmetrically between the wrist and the underarm. The armhole and sleeve cap are shaped with decreases. To avoid a jagged decrease underarm, follow the instructions on p. 281 for decreasing several stitches at the beginning and end of a row. These methods are appropriate also for shaping the shoulder seam.

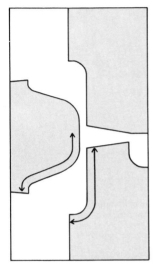

A classic armhole shape is formed by subtracting the stitches needed for shoulder width from the number at the underarm. Half this figure is the number of stitches to decrease for each armhole. At start of shaping, decrease at least 3 cm of stitches, then decrease remainder over next few rows. Work even until correct depth is reached.
For set-in sleeve cap, decrease the same number of stitches as at beginning of armhole. Continue decreasing symmetrically until cap length is the same as armhole length; work 1 more row and fasten off.

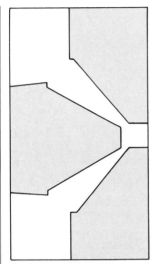

A raglan armhole ends at the neckline and must be planned in relation to it. It is shown here combined with a square neckline, a simple combination often used in crocheted garments. To determine the number of decreases, subtract the stitches for neck width from the number of stitches at the underarm. Start raglan with 1.5 cm of decreases on each side; distribute remaining decreases symmetrically and evenly over the number of rows needed to reach the neckline.
Shape top of sleeves the same way, having 8 cm to 15 cm at neck edge depending on neckline depth.

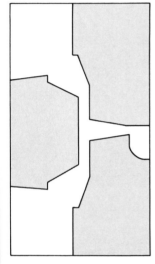

A semi-raglan armhole is shaped like a raglan on the lower half, like a classic armhole on the upper half and shoulder. Calculate the number of decreases as for a classic armhole, but instead of distributing them over the first 4 to 5 rows, space them in a sloped line over half the armhole depth; work evenly for the remaining depth.
For the sleeve cap, decrease symmetrically over the same number of rows as for the armhole; work 1 more row straight across and fasten off.

A set-in sleeve has a symmetrically curved cap.

A raglan sleeve is shaped in a continuous slope to neckline.

A semi-raglan sleeve has raglan slope combined with a wide cap.

Crocheting a garment

Knitted ribbing 420   Working a raised stitch 276
Picking up stitches 437 How to form a ring 282

Ribbing

Crocheted ribbing is used on the edges of a garment to provide a firm and somewhat elastic finish. Four variations are described below. The easiest of the four to produce is the ridge stitch, in which the ribs are worked horizontally, then turned and the garment pattern worked along one side edge to obtain the vertical effect. All the other rib patterns are worked vertically.

Crocheted ribbing is not as elastic as knitted ribbing and never fits as snugly. You can, if you prefer, knit the ribbed edging for a crocheted garment. The usual method is to work the garment, join the seams, then pick up stitches along the edge. As a general rule, one knitted stitch is picked up for each crocheted one. Make a sample to decide correct needle size.

Ridge stitch ribbing. Ridges are formed horizontally, then turned sideways for ribbing.
Unit of any number of ch that will form desired depth of ribbing
Row 1: miss 1 ch, *1 dc in each ch*, 1 ch, turn
Row 2: *1 dc in back loop of each st*, 1 ch, turn.
Repeat Row 2 for the pattern. When ribbing is long enough for the garment edge on which it is to be used, fasten off yarn; sew the ends together, then work the pattern stitches along one side of the ridge pattern.

Raised stitch ribbing 1. Vertical ridges are formed on two sides.
Unit of 2 ch plus 1
Row 1: miss 1 ch, *1 dc in each ch*, 1 ch, turn
Row 2: *1 raised dc round the front, 1 raised dc round the back*, 1 dc in last sp, 1 ch, turn
Row 3: *1 raised dc round the front, 1 dc under the 2 crossed strands of next raised st*, 1 dc in last sp, 1 ch, turn
Repeat Row 3 for pattern

Raised stitch ribbing 2. Vertical ridges are on one side only.
Unit of 2 ch
Row 1: miss 1 ch, *1 dc in each ch*, 1 ch, turn
Row 2: 1 dc, *1 raised tr round the front of next stitch, 1 dc in next st*, 1 ch, turn
Row 3: *1 dc in each st*, 1 ch, turn
Row 4: 1 dc, *1 raised tr round front of raised st 2 rows below, 1 dc in next st*, 1 ch, turn
Repeat Rows 3 and 4 for pattern

Tunisian crochet ribbing. Ridges are less pronounced than in other crocheted ribbings, but this is a neat pattern, particularly suited to a garment of Tunisian crochet.
Unit of 2 ch
Rows 1 and 2: basic Tunisian
Row 3: 1 Tunisian purl under 2nd bar, *1 Tunisian stocking st, 1 Tunisian purl*
Row 4: yrh, draw through 1 loop, *yrh, draw through 2 loops*
Repeat Rows 3 and 4 for pattern

Buttons

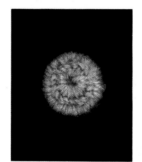 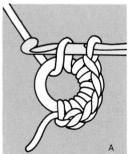 

Ring button. Yarn is worked over a plastic ring 3 mm smaller than button size. To start, make a slip knot. Inserting hook through ring to form each st, work round it in dc (A) until ring is completely covered; ss in 1st st to close, fasten off. Cut yarn leaving 30 cm; thread the end in tapestry needle. Oversew a st in each outside loop (B), then pull stitches towards centre. Tie beginning and end strands together, then sew an X across the button back for attaching it to the garment.

 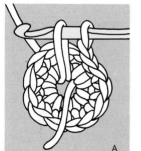 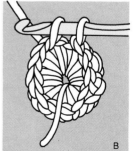

Ball button. Yarn is worked into a three-dimensional motif; size and thickness depend on yarn weight. 3 ch and join in ring with ss. **Round 1:** 1 ch, 8 dc in ring, ss to beg ch. **Round 2:** 1 ch, (1 dc in next st, 2 dc in next st) 4 times, ss to beg ch; pull the short yarn end up through centre hole. **Round 3:** 1 ch, (insert hook through centre hole, draw up a long loop (A), yrh, draw through 2 loops) 16 times, ss to beg ch. **Round 4:** 1 dc in every other st, fasten off; oversew and finish back as for ring button.

Buttonholes

Horizontal buttonhole, double crochet.
At the beginning of buttonhole position, work a number of chain stitches that will accommodate the diameter of the button (usually from 1 to 5). Miss the number of stitches for which you have chains, then continue in pattern (A).
Next row. Work over the buttonhole chain in double crochet, making the same number of stitches as there are chains (B).

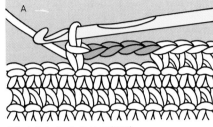

A 4-chain buttonhole completed

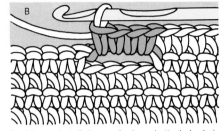

Double crochet stitches worked over buttonhole chain

Horizontal buttonhole, treble crochet.
Insert hook under diagonal strand halfway down last stitch (A), *draw up a loop, yarn round hook, draw through 2 loops, insert hook under left strand at front of last stitch*, repeat from * to * for desired length. To complete buttonhole, draw up loop, miss same number of stitches as made for buttonhole, insert hook in next stitch, draw up a loop, complete a treble crochet (B).

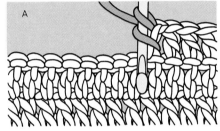

Inserting hook under the diagonal yarn

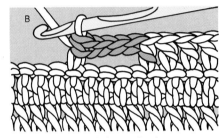

A double-chain buttonhole completed

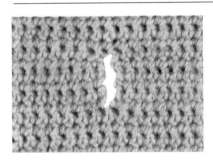

Vertical buttonhole, any stitch.
On right side of garment, work across the row to buttonhole position; turn and continue to work this half until depth of buttonhole has been obtained. If the number of buttonhole rows is uneven, fasten off yarn (A), weave into back of work later; if even, leave yarn at side of work. Starting at buttonhole edge, attach yarn, work second half to match the first. Next row, start at side edge and continue in pattern across both sections (B).

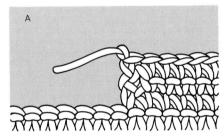

First half of vertical buttonhole completed

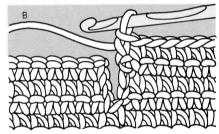

Second half of vertical buttonhole completed

Buttonhole loop of double crochet.
On a right-side row, work to end of buttonhole position. Work a chain the same length as buttonhole, join it to beginning of buttonhole thus: slip hook out of chain, insert it front to back through top of stitch, hook chain and pull it through; insert hook in next stitch to the right, yarn round hook (A), draw a loop through both stitch and chain. Work double crochet over chain, slipstitch in stitch where chain was started (B); continue in pattern.

Joining chain to beginning of buttonhole

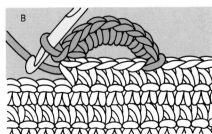

Working double crochet over buttonhole loop

311

Assembling and finishing

General information
Joining sections right sides together
Joining sections edge to edge
Crocheted edgings and insertions
Blanket in Tunisian crochet

General information

There are several ways to finish crochet; select methods that suit your needs and work patiently for professional results.

Blocking is generally the first step. This procedure shapes crocheted pieces to specific measurements and, at the same time, usually smooths slight stitch irregularities. There are two basic blocking methods – steam and wet. These and pressing techniques are fully described in Knitting, pp. 482–3. Before beginning, check the yarn label; some yarns should not be blocked.

Joining is the step after blocking for any project worked in sections. There are several methods (see below). Selection should be made according to, first, the needs of the situation, then personal preference. Joining with a seam allowance (right sides together) is necessary when edges are uneven; it is often preferred for its firm and neat appearance. Joining edge to edge is possible only when edges are even and have the same number of stitches. This method is especially suitable for ribbings and motifs.

Edging may be applied as a final step to provide extra firmness and a uniform appearance for a crocheted edge. Suggestions for finishes are given opposite.

JOINING SECTIONS RIGHT SIDES TOGETHER

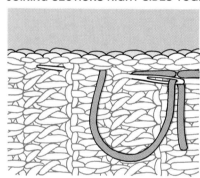

Backstitch. Worked any distance from edge; use for uneven edges or to alter garment.
Bring needle up through 2 corresponding stitches; *insert through 2 stitches behind thread (where thread emerges for last stitch); bring up through 2 stitches in front of the thread.*

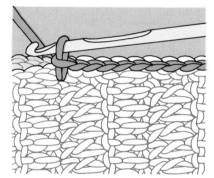

Slipstitch. A firm joining that is suitable for seams in which minimal stretch is required.
Draw up a loop through a corresponding stitch on each section; *insert hook through the next 2 stitches; draw a loop through both stitches and the loop on the hook.*

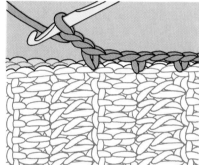

Slipstitch plus chain. A more flexible joining than plain slipstitch; use for bulky yarns or when a greater degree of stretch is desired.
Work slipstitch through 2 corresponding stitches at start of row; *make a chain equal to height of row; work slipstitch at point of next row.*

JOINING SECTIONS EDGE TO EDGE

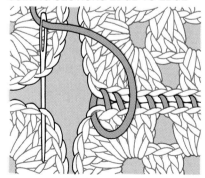

Overcasting. Used mainly to join patchwork motifs. *Insert needle at a right-angle under back loop of a corresponding stitch on each edge; draw yarn through.* When you reach the corners of 2 motifs, continue as shown above.

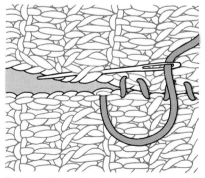

Mattress stitch. An invisible joining, especially suited to taller stitches and filet.
Lay sections right side up. *Take needle under lower half of edge stitch on one piece, then under upper half of edge stitch on adjacent piece.*

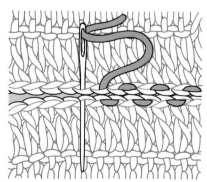

Weaving top or bottom edges. Invisible joining for straight edges with equal numbers of stitches.
Right sides up, *bring needle up through 1 loop, down through next loop on one edge; weave down and up through 2 loops on other edge.*

Crocheted edgings and insertions

Crochet lends itself so naturally to use as a trimming that pattern possibilities are nearly endless. Worked along the edge of crochet or knitting (see directly below), it serves to make an edge firm, give it a neat look, and reinforce its shape with a distinctive outline. When applied to a garment, seams should be joined first and the edge stitch begun at one seam. Worked separately, a trimming can be crocheted horizontally (examples in centre row) or vertically (bottom row), and sewn to crocheted, knitted or woven fabrics. Any yarn is suitable so long as it is compatible with the fabric to which it is applied.

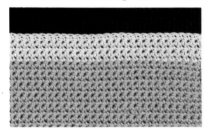

Double crochet edging. Use one to four rows for sleeveless armholes or a neckline, at least 2 to 3 cm for front or bottom edges of a garment.

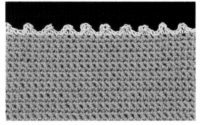

Corded edging. A very firm and neat trimming.
Row 1: double crochet, worked right to left
Row 2: slipstitch, worked left to right

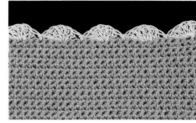

Little picot edging. For a child's dress.
Every row: *1 ss in each of next 2 sts, 1 dc in next st, 3 ch, 1 dc in same st as last dc*

Scalloped edging. Suitable for any lacy item.
Every row: 1 ss, *miss 2 sts, 5 tr in next st, miss 2 sts, 1 ss in next st*

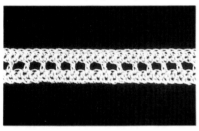

Eyelet insertion. Unit of 2 ch plus 2
Row 1: miss 1 ch, *1 dc in each ch*, 1 ch, turn
Row 2: *1 dc in each dc*, 4 ch, turn
Row 3: miss 2 dc, *1 tr in next dc, 1 ch, miss 1 dc*, 1 tr in last dc, 1 ch, turn
Row 4: *1 dc in each tr, 1 dc in each ch*, 1 ch, turn
Row 5: *1 dc in each dc*, fasten off

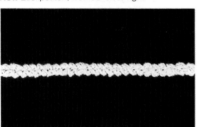

Twisted braid. Unit of any number of ch
Row 1: miss 1 ch, *insert hook in next ch, draw up a loop, twist hook horizontally and clockwise 1 full turn, yrh, draw through 2 loops*; at end of row, 1 ch and continue round opposite side of ch; repeat instructions between asterisks in each loop on that side; fasten off

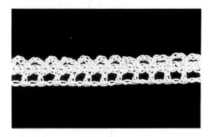

Filet and picot edging. Unit of 2 ch plus 4
Row 1: miss 5 ch, 1 tr in next ch, *1 ch, miss 1 ch, 1 tr in next ch*, 1 ch, turn
Row 2: 1 dc in each st and ch sp, 4 ch, turn
Row 3: miss 1 dc, *ss in next dc, 4 ch, miss 1 dc*, ss in 4th ch at beg of Row 1, fasten off

Fancy scalloped edging. Unit of 5 ch plus 3
Row 1: miss 1 ch, *1 dc in each ch*, turn
Row 2: ss in 1st dc, *3 ch, miss 3 dc, ss in next 2 dc*, turn
Row 3: ss in 1st 2 ss, *(1 tr, 1 ch) 4 times in next 3 ch sp, 1 tr in same sp, 2 ss*, turn
Row 4: *(1 dc, 3 ch in next 1 ch sp) 4 times, ss in next 2 ss*, fasten off

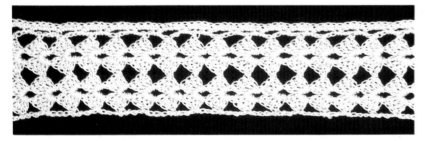

Double shell edging. 19 ch. **Row 1:** miss 9 ch, 1 shell [4 tr, 3 ch, 4 tr] in next ch, miss 5 ch, 1 shell in next ch, miss 2 ch, 1 trtr in last ch, 5 ch, turn. **Row 2:** 1 shell in each ch sp of shell below, 1 trtr in last tr of 2nd shell, 5 ch, turn. Repeat Row 2 for pattern, ending last row with 2 ch, 1 tr in last tr; do not turn. **Along one edge,** 1 ch, 1 dc in loop just formed, *3 ch, 1 dc in next loop* for entire length, 1 ch, turn. **Next row:** 1 dc in 1st dc, *3 ch in next 3 ch sp, 1 dc in next dc*, fasten off.

Looped edging. 13 ch. **Row 1:** miss 6 ch, 1 dtr in next ch, 9 ch, miss 5 ch, ss in last ch, 1 ch, turn. **Row 2:** in 9 ch sp (3 dc, 3 ch) 5 times, 2 dc in same sp, 1 dc in dtr, 2 dc in 6 ch sp, 5 ch, turn. **Row 3:** miss 2 dc, 1 dtr in next dc, 9 ch, miss 2 3 ch loops, ss in next 3 ch loop, 1 ch, turn. **Row 4:** in 9 ch sp (3 dc, 3 ch) 5 times, 2 dc in same sp, 1 dc in dtr, 1 dc in 4th ch of turning ch, 5 ch, turn. Repeat Rows 3 and 4 for desired length; fasten off.

Blanket in Tunisian crochet

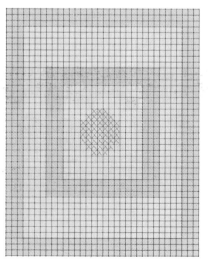

This wool blanket, approximately 122 cm by 160 cm, is worked in Tunisian crochet.

Twenty-five geometric blocks form the basis of this blanket. Each block is worked in the basic Tunisian stitch, bordered with double crochet, then embroidered with cross stitch to create the centre motif.

Materials

Double knitting wool, 900 g of beige, 800 g of blue, 6 mm tricot needle or hook, rug needle, knitting bobbins (optional)

Tension

8 sts and 7 rows = 5 cm

Preparation

Make several butterflies of each colour (see p. 358 for method), allowing 5 to 6 m of yarn for each one.

MAKING A BLOCK. With blue, 34 ch

Rows 1–6. Work in basic Tunisian stitch, and at the end of each row insert hook under both the last bar and the yarn directly behind it. This makes a firm edge on which to work the border.

Row 7. Pick up 3 loops in blue and then *change colours* as follows. Make a slip knot 10 cm from the end of the beige yarn; pull up this loop through the next stitch, leaving short yarn end at back to be woven in later. Pick up 27 more beige loops; fasten in a new blue yarn with a slip knot; pick up 3 blue loops.

Row 8. Work off 2 loops in blue, then pick up beige yarn from under the blue, thus *twisting* the yarns; draw it through the last blue loop and 1 beige loop. Continue with beige until 1 beige loop remains; pick up blue yarn from under the beige; work off last 4 loops in blue. Continue in pattern, adding new colours where needed (you will have 7 butterflies on Row 27), and twisting yarns when changing colours on the return rows. When the square is finished, do not fasten off, but continue with blue.

Border. Across the top work 2 dc under the 2nd bar, *1 dc under the next bar*, 2 dc in the last bar. Continue down the left side with 1 dc under the double loop of each bar; continue along bottom with 2 dc in the first ch, *1 dc in the next ch*, 2 dc in the last ch; work up the right side with 1 dc under both loops of each end st; join with a ss to the 1st dc; fasten off. Weave all yarn ends into the back.

CROSS STITCHING. Work an oval design in centre of each block, following diagram and directions below left.

BLOCKING AND ASSEMBLING. Carefully block each piece so that all are the same size (approximately 23.5 cm by 31 cm). Lay out 10 blocks in 2 rows of 5 each, one row above the other, with all tops facing away from you. Using 1 long strand of blue and working from right to left, overcast adjacent top and bottom edges, taking yarn through each back loop only (see example of this technique, p. 312). Add on 3 more rows of 5 squares each until all squares are joined horizontally. Turn blanket sideways and join all the rows vertically.

WORKING THE BLANKET BORDER. With blue, work 2 rows of dc round the outside edge of the blanket, working 1 stitch in each stitch, 2 stitches in each corner, missing the overcast joining. Fasten off. Gently press.

Each block is worked in basic Tunisian stitch, using this chart as a guide. A square in the chart equals 1 stitch and a row represents 2 rows of the pattern; there are 34 stitches and 84 rows. Though the cross stitch pattern in the centre appears to be off-balance, the motif, when finished, is actually centred because cross stitches are worked over the upright bars of the extra beige stitch.

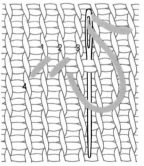

To make cross stitches, use a tapestry needle and one strand of blue yarn. Bring the needle up just below crossbars of stitch **1**; pull yarn through, leaving 10 cm at the back; take needle top to bottom behind both crossbars of stitch **2**, then behind crossbars of stitch **3**.

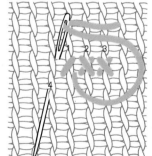

Work back across the same row, inserting the needle behind crossbars as before. To start the next row, weave needle down behind crossbars of stitch **4**; continue making rows of stitches until oval is complete; cut yarn; weave in ends. Stitches should not show on back.

Lacemaking

Nineteenth-century Belgian bobbin lace with needlepoint lace insertions, from the collection of Susanna E. Lewis, Brooklyn, New York.

Needlepoint lace

Introduction

Needlepoint lace is what its name suggests – lace made with a needle and thread. The techniques probably evolved from those used for openwork embroidery, but the structure is built entirely of thread, with fabric used only as an anchoring device. While there are several styles of needlepoint lace, just one, called **Renaissance lace**, is dealt with in this chapter; it is not difficult to do. To produce this lace, variations of buttonhole stitch are worked between sections of a narrow tape that has been tacked, along the lines of the design, to a backing. When work is completed, the backing is removed, leaving just the lace structure.

Renaissance lace was popular in the Victorian era.

Materials

First consideration is usually given to selecting a tape, because the thread is then chosen to match or blend with it. For best performance, the tape should be between 5 mm and 1.5 cm wide, flexible enough to mould to curves in a design, constructed loosely enough so that it offers little resistance to a thick needle, and woven in a way that will guide the spacing of stitches. Braids, eyelets, tape with picot edging, and two ricracs twisted together are suitable possibilities. See examples on the right.

For the thread, medium-weight crochet cotton is recommended because it has the firm twist needed for these techniques and enough body to give character to the stitches. The needle should have an eye large enough to accommodate the thread; a tapestry needle is preferable because it will not catch in the backing. You will also need an ordinary needle and sewing thread for tacking, sturdy paper for backing, and fabric that contrasts with thread colour to show it up. A transfer pencil is useful because it allows you to hot-iron a design on to backing fabric. A thimble and small scissors are also necessary.

Making a sampler

A sampler is an easy and practical way to learn needlepoint lace techniques.

Materials

3.60 m of tape (see opposite page for suitable choices), 1 ball medium-weight crochet cotton, tapestry needle, tacking thread and needle, medium-weight drawing paper 28 by 35 cm, plain, smooth fabric, 28 by 35 cm, in colour to contrast with the thread.

Preparation

Cut 4 strips of tape 20 cm long, 3 strips 30 cm long, and a 1 m piece for the border. Lay fabric on the paper and strips on the fabric, arranging them so that the large centre spaces measure about 6.5 by 4.5 cm. Tack strips to

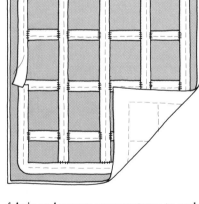

fabric and paper; oversew tapes to each other at intersections. Tack border over ends of strips, rounding the corners.

Working the stitches

Following key (above right), work stitches 1–37 in order. The number of rows to work is given with the stitch instructions on pp. 318–22. Where no number of rows is given, fill section as shown on right. Do not stitch into backing.

Sampler diagram:

	37				
27	21 · 19 · 20A-B	15 · 16 · 17A · 17B			27
32	22	1, 2, 3	4	23	32
33	30	6, 8 8, 7	9, 10, 11	5	33
34	31	12, 13, 14	18	29	34
28A	24	26 26	25	28B	
	35	36	35		

KEY TO SAMPLER DIAGRAM

1. Single net stitch
2. Double net stitch
3. Buttonholed net stitch
4. Brussels net stitch
5. Pea stitch
6. Cloth stitch
7. Eyelets in cloth stitch
8. Embroidered cloth stitch
9. Side stitch
10. Double side stitch
11. Shell stitch
12. Spanish point
13. Twisted Spanish point
14. Twisted Spanish point patterns
15. Twisted bar
16. Double twisted bar
17A, B Buttonholed bars
18. Branched bar filling
19. Bar with buttonholed picot
20A, B Bar with pinned picots
21. Bar with bullion picot
22. Woven leaves
23. Open leaves with wheels
24. Beaded insertion
25. Wheel filling
26. Rings
27. Rosettes
28A, B Spiders' webs
29. Buttonholed Russian stitch
30. Double Russian stitch
31. Half bars
32. Knotted edging
33. Side stitch edging
34. Pinned picot edging
35. Bullion picot edging
36. Buttonholed picot edging
37. Shell edging

Needlepoint lace stitches

General information

All the stitches for Renaissance lace are variations of just one, buttonhole stitch, illustrated below in both right and left forms because most of the patterns are worked back and forth in rows. To produce such variety, the buttonhole stitch

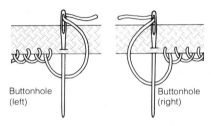

Buttonhole (left)   Buttonhole (right)

is worked three different ways: (1) loosely, referred to in directions as a loop; (2) tightly and closely spaced, called stitch or buttonholing; (3) to one side over another loop, known as sideways stitch. For more variety, buttonhole stitch may be combined with embroidery techniques, such as bullion knot or weaving. The page references for these are given where needed.

General rules for working

1. The stitches should be pulled firmly enough to prevent their sagging, but not so taut as to draw in the tape edges.

2. The tape edge is used as a guide in spacing the stitches and rows.

Oversewing

3. Oversewing stitch (illustration above) is used along tape edges between rows.

4. For a mesh stitch or filling, the number of loops remains constant for a regular space, is increased or decreased as needed for an irregular space, but stitch depth remains the same.

5. For most patterns with a one-row repeat, each row is started with a whole loop, and ended with a half-loop.

Meshes

Meshes are especially suitable for filling large or irregular spaces in a lace pattern. They are grouped here and opposite according to the basic way of working each stitch. *Net stitches* (this page) are openwork patterns, each a variation of the single net stitch (right). *Cloth stitches* (top row opposite) are closely spaced in a solid cloth effect; they can be embellished with eyelets or embroidery. *Side stitches* (centre row) are characterised by a second stitch that is made sideways over the first and locks it in place. *Spanish points* (bottom row) are similar to single net, but have an extra twist in the loop.

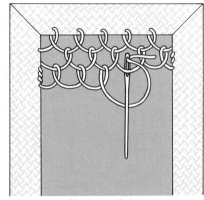

Single net stitch

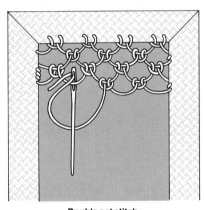

Double net stitch

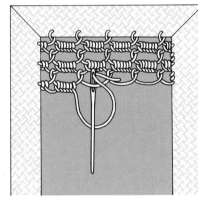

Buttonholed net stitch

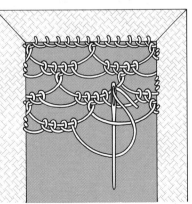

Brussels net stitch

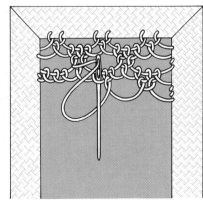

Pea stitch

Single net stitch (4 rows, No. 1). An open pattern, simplest and most basic of the meshes.
Row 1: work evenly spaced loops, making each loop about as deep as it is wide.
Row 2: repeat Row 1, working each stitch into the centre of the large loop above. Repeat this row for the pattern.

Double net stitch (5 rows, No. 2). This stitch looks better if you make the large loop a bit shallower than for the single net stitch (above).
Row 1: work 1 large loop and 1 small loop alternately.
Row 2: repeat Row 1, working large and small loops into each of the large loops above. Repeat this row for the pattern.

Buttonholed net stitch (8 rows, No. 3). This stitch is purposely started at the right edge because the second row, closely spaced buttonhole stitches, is easier to work from left to right. Also, it is evenly spaced, because it has a two-row repeat.
Row 1: working right to left, make widely spaced loops, beginning and ending with a half-loop.
Row 2: working left to right, fill each loop with closely spaced buttonhole stitches (about 6 for each full loop, 2 for each half-loop).
Row 3: working right to left, work large loops into the small spaces between buttonholed bars of the row above.
Repeat Rows 2 and 3 for pattern. For last row in sampler, catch tape between buttonholed bars.

Brussels net stitch (No. 4).
Row 1: make closely spaced loops in multiples of 6 (18 were made on the sampler).
Row 2: make 1 large loop into every sixth stitch above.
Row 3: make 4 stitches to form 3 loops on each large loop above.
Row 4: make 1 large loop into the centre of the 4-stitch group above.
Repeat Rows 3 and 4 for the pattern.

Pea stitch (No. 5).
Row 1: make 1 large loop and 1 small loop alternately, beginning and ending with half-loops.
Row 2: work 1 loop into the small loop above and 3 stitches forming 2 loops on each large loop, ending with 1 loop.
Row 3: make 2 stitches into the 3-loop group above (1 stitch between the first and second stitches, and 1 stitch between the second and third stitches).
Row 4: work 3 stitches on each large loop above and 1 stitch into the small loop.
Repeat Rows 3 and 4 for the pattern.

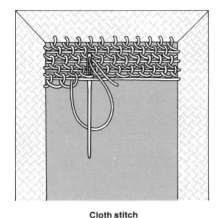

Cloth stitch

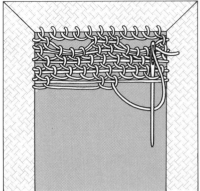

Eyelets in cloth stitch

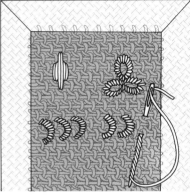

Embroidered cloth stitch

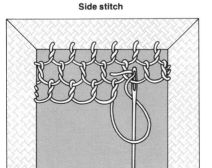

Side stitch

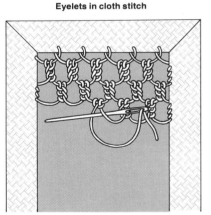

Double side stitch

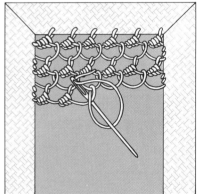

Shell stitch

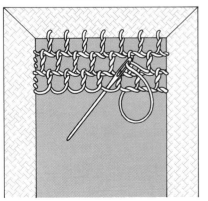

Spanish point

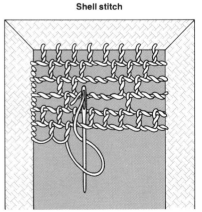

Twisted Spanish point

Twisted Spanish point patterns

Cloth stitch (12 rows, No. 6).
Row 1: working left to right, make closely spaced loops, then pull thread back across the space.
Row 2: again left to right, make a loop into each loop above, going over the loose thread as well. Pull thread back to left side and repeat this row.

Eyelets in cloth stitch (7 eyelets, No. 7).
Row 1: for each eyelet, miss 4 stitches, carrying thread straight across the empty space. At end of row, pull thread back to the left side.
Row 2: for each eyelet, work 3 buttonhole stitches over the 3 strands.

Embroidered cloth stitch (No. 8). Centre of the raised spot is 2 satin stitches worked over 1 cloth stitch and 4 rows; sides are 2 satin stitches over 1 cloth stitch and 2 rows. Leaves consist of 3 bullion knots; to hold it flat, each clover leaf is anchored with 1 stitch at centre of outside curve.

Side stitch (4 rows, No. 9).
Row 1: left to right, make 1 loose buttonhole stitch; make a second stitch sideways around both threads of first one; pull tightly in place.
Row 2: working right to left, and reversing position of thread, repeat Row 1.

Double side stitch (5 rows, No. 10).
Row 1: make single loops spaced widely apart.
Row 2: make 1 loose buttonhole stitch into loop above; make a second stitch in same loop; pull it tight. Make 2 sideways stitches below second buttonhole stitch. Repeat this row for pattern.

Shell stitch (6 rows, No. 11).
Row 1: working left to right, make 1 side stitch, pulling thread firmly so that the sideways stitch lies against the tape and the loop slants left. Make 3 more sideways stitches above first, each one slightly looser than preceding one. One shell is now completed; start next shell touching it.
Row 2: right to left, work 1 stitch between each shell, drawing loop thus formed closely under shell.

Spanish point (4 rows, No. 12).
Row 1: left to right, make a thread loop that faces right; holding loop with left thumb, take needle through the tape (or stitch above), then through the loop; adjust stitch to desired depth.
Row 2: repeat Row 1, facing each loop to left.

Twisted Spanish point (2 rows, No. 13).
Row 1: work as for Row 1 in Spanish point.
Row 2: work back along row above; pass needle once behind bottom of each loop. Pull thread firmly, but not so tight as to pull bars askew.

Twisted Spanish point patterns (5 rows, No. 14). Arrange stitches as shown.

Needlepoint lace stitches

Bars and picots

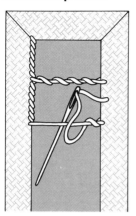

Twisted bar (No. 15). Fasten thread to tape at the left side, stretch it across the space, and take a stitch in tape on opposite side. (When laying the foundation of a bar, stretch the thread firmly across the opening, but not so taut that you draw the tape inwards.) Work back to the left side, winding the thread 4 times around the bar (for a wider space, you would wind more times to make bar firm).

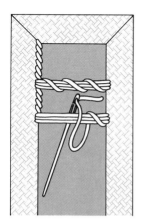

Double twisted bar (No. 16). Lay a foundation across the space as for twisted bar on left, but stretch thread across 3 times instead of once. Work back to the left side, going over the bar 3 times. (Fewer twists are needed for this stitch to make it firm.)

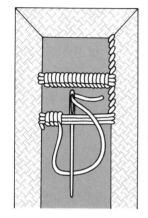

Buttonholed bar (No. 17A). Starting at the right edge, stretch thread across the space 3 times for foundation, then work closely spaced buttonhole stitches across it. Before starting the stitches, oversew 1 space down on the tape to secure the end of the bar and prevent it from curling. For a thicker bar (No. 17B), make buttonhole stitches over 5 threads.

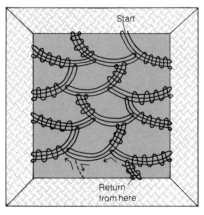

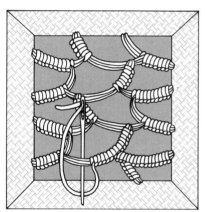

Branched bar filling (No. 18). Each bar should emerge from last one without having to cut and join the thread. Starting in the upper right corner (see diagram), make a foundation of 3 threads; work buttonhole stitches for half its length. Make a new foundation for the next bar, anchoring it through bottom of the last stitch; work buttonhole stitches for half its length. Begin the third and subsequent bars the same way. When all bars have been laid out and partially buttonholed, complete them by working back along each one in reverse order.

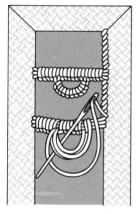

Bar with buttonholed picot (No. 19). Make a buttonholed bar, working stitches three-quarters of the way across, or 6 stitches beyond where the picot is to start. Take thread back to the left and pass needle between the sixth and seventh stitches, then back to the right and around the bar, then back to the left and between the same 2 stitches (there should be a 3-strand loop below the bar). Work closely spaced buttonhole stitches over the loop, then complete the bar.

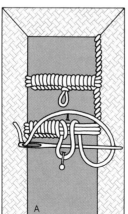

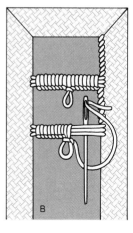

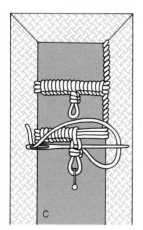

Bar with pinned picot (No. 20). Make a buttonholed bar, working stitches to the point where you want the picot; insert a pin into backing fabric to the desired depth of the picot. Pass thread around the pin, then behind the foundation threads to the outside of the loop. Make a side stitch around the loop and the working thread (as shown in illustration A). Complete the buttonholed bar (B). For a longer picot, make 2 or more side stitches, placing the first one down low enough for the additional stitches to fit between it and the bar (C). Take care not to sew backing.

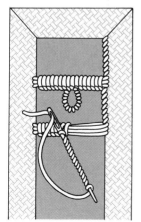

Bar with bullion picot (No. 21). Make a buttonholed bar, working stitches to the point where you want the picot; insert needle halfway through the last stitch that was made and wind thread around the needle point 15 times (not too tightly). Pull needle through and draw the bullion into a circle. Complete the buttonholed bar.

Insertions/Woven

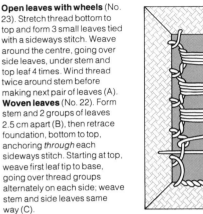

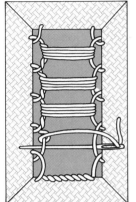

Open leaves with wheels (No. 23). Stretch thread bottom to top and form 3 small leaves tied with a sideways stitch. Weave around the centre, going over side leaves, under stem and top leaf 4 times. Wind thread twice around stem before making next pair of leaves (A).

Woven leaves (No. 22). Form stem and 2 groups of leaves 2.5 cm apart (B), then retrace foundation, bottom to top, anchoring *through* each sideways stitch. Starting at top, weave first leaf tip to base, going over thread groups alternately on each side; weave stem and side leaves same way (C).

Beaded insertion (No. 24). Make 1 row of large, evenly spaced loops along each long side of the space (7 loops were made in the sampler). Starting at the top left side, connect opposite loops by taking the thread 4 times through each pair; be sure the thread does not become crossed or twisted. Before moving from one group to the next, oversew once around the left loop.

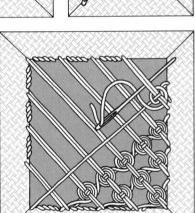

Wheel filling (No. 25). First fill the space with double strands laid diagonally in parallel rows (see diagram). Oversew along the tape between rows. Fasten off the thread and re-attach it where indicated. Stretch thread across the grid, take a stitch in tape at the opposite side, and return across the row. At each intersection, weave a wheel, going 3 times under the diagonals and over the single thread. Oversew once around single thread before starting next wheel. Alternate wheels are wound in the opposite direction.

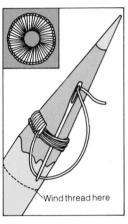

Wind thread here

Rings (No. 26). These are made separately, then sewn on to the work wherever desired. Wind thread around a rubber pencil 15 times, then buttonhole over all the strands. (The buttonholing is easier if you push the threads up towards the pencil point.) When ring is complete, remove from pencil, flatten, and sew in place.

Rosette (No. 27). This appears in the sampler as one filling for a small space. It can also be worked in multiples to fill a larger area. First prepare a grid as in the diagram, laying 2 pairs of parallel strands for each rosette. Notice that the intersecting areas for each rosette are spaced 1 stitch apart and interlaced. For each rosette, weave a wheel, going around the circle 4 times, then buttonhole closely over all threads, placing 2 stitches between the parallel strands and 3 stitches at the corners.

Spiders' webs (No. 28A, No. 28B). This stitch is good for filling a square space. First make 4 twisted bars, 2 across the centre and 2 diagonally. Twist the fourth bar only to the centre, work spider's web, then complete the bar.

Woven web (No. 28A). Working from the centre out, weave a wheel, missing 1 bar at the end of each round so threads will alternate on each row.

Ridged web (No. 28B). Starting at the centre, take thread under 2 bars, then weave in a circle, going back over 1 bar, forward under 2 bars (backstitch).

Needlepoint lace stitches

Insertions/Russian

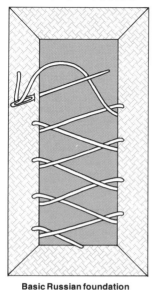

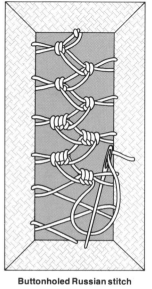

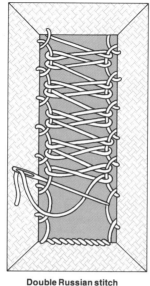

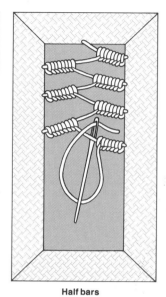

Basic Russian foundation   Buttonholed Russian stitch   Double Russian stitch   Half bars

Buttonholed Russian stitch (No. 29). Starting at bottom centre of the space, make a basic Russian foundation, looping thread from side to side as in first illustration, left (for sampler, there are 9 loops on each side). Take a small stitch at top centre to secure thread, then work down the centre of the foundation, making closely spaced buttonhole stitches over each pair of threads. Make 2 stitches over each of the first 4 pairs, 4 stitches over the next 5 pairs, 6 stitches over the next 4, and 8 stitches over the last 4 pairs.

Double Russian stitch (No. 30). Make 1 row of evenly spaced loops along the tape on each side of the space (for the sampler, 14 loops). Connect opposite pairs of loops with 2 Russian foundation stitches through each one. Density can be increased by taking 3 or 4 stitches in each loop.

Half bars (No. 31). Starting at the top centre, make 1 Russian foundation stitch on the right side and pull it up to a loose diagonal; take 1 stitch in the tape to secure the bar (not shown), then make 8 buttonhole stitches over the diagonal thread. Repeat this procedure on alternate sides.

Edgings

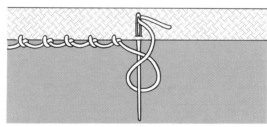

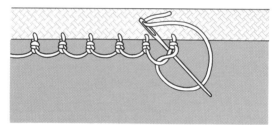

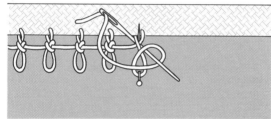

Knotted edging (No. 32). Make a loop as illustrated; take the needle through the tape edge, then through the loop, going behind the upper and over the lower thread. Work this and all the edgings on the sampler from left to right.

Side stitch edging (No. 33). Make a buttonhole loop on the tape; over this loop make 1 sideways stitch and pull it up close to the tape. Take the thread through the loop and then make another sideways stitch next to the first one.

Pinned picot edging (No. 34). Make a buttonhole loop on the tape. Insert a pin into backing to desired depth of picot; take thread around it right to left. Make a second loop in front of the pin; pass the needle through buttonhole and second loop; pull thread tight.

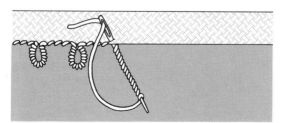

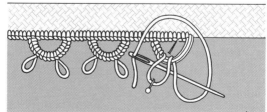

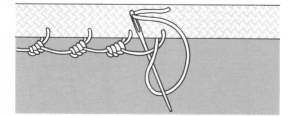

Bullion picot edging (No. 35). Oversew along the tape to desired place for picot. Insert needle halfway through tape; wind thread around needle point 15 times, draw bullion into a tight circle.

Buttonholed picot edging (No. 36). Work 7 buttonhole stitches along the tape edge. Make a buttonholed picot (see directions, p. 320), adding 1 pinned picot (p. 320) every 5 stitches, if desired.

Shell edging (No. 37). Make 1 loose buttonhole loop on the tape; make a second stitch sideways around both threads of the first one and pull it tight. Make 3 more sideways stitches above the first.

Needlepoint lace butterfly

Make this butterfly to adorn the front of a long dress, or mount it as a decorative motif – on the back of a simple evening jacket, for example. As shown here, the butterfly is sewn to a yoke, made from two layers of sheer fabric, and used on a dress made from a commercial pattern. You could apply it also to a ready-made garment; the style should be simple, and the colour one that complements all the thread colours used. If the backing colour matches any one thread, the section worked in that colour will blend into the background. For example, if this butterfly had been backed with black fabric, you would not see the black stitches.

Materials for the lace

5 mm tape for outlining the design, 1 m black, 1.50 m beige, 1.50 m white (in the project shown here, black and beige tapes are rayon Russian braid, white tape is a flexible polyester braid); pearl cotton, 1 ball each brown, black and white medium-weight crochet cotton, 1 ball ecru; tracing paper; transfer pencil; medium-weight drawing paper; 28 by 35 cm piece of plain, smooth fabric, in a colour to contrast with the threads; thread for tacking (any colour); black thread for sewing lace to garment; tapestry and sewing needles.

Preparation

Using transfer pencil and tracing paper, trace the half-butterfly pattern from p. 324. It is essential to trace the tape outlines and branched bar filling stitches (the black stitches at the bottom and just below the antennae); copying of the other stitches is optional. Turn the paper over and trace again, this time just the wing, placing it a few centimetres from the first tracing. Pin the paper to your fabric and lay these on an ironing board with a piece of aluminium foil beneath them. Using a dry iron at 'wool' setting, press firmly against the pattern area where pencil marks are against the fabric, avoiding contact with the area where they are face up; do not slide iron

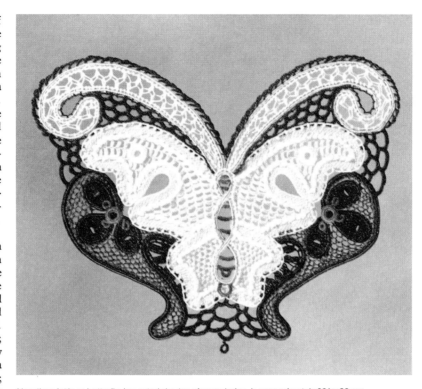

Needlepoint lace butterfly, in neutral shades of your choice, is approximately 23 by 30 cm.

The butterfly adds sophistication to a long dress.

back and forth. Turn paper over and fit second tracing with the design on the fabric, pinning pattern and fabric to the ironing board to prevent shifting; press this part, then remove pattern. Tack tapes in place using the pattern (p. 324) or the photograph (above) as a colour guide. When you cut tapes, leave 1.5 cm ends, and tuck each one under an adjacent tape layer. These ends are finished later (see below right). With tiny stitches, join tape edges that touch. Tack fabric to the drawing paper.

Working the stitches

Each stitch used in the butterfly appears in the sampler. The stitch names, also page numbers where directions for them can be found, are next to the pattern. As with the sampler, stitches are numbered

in the order in which they should be worked. In this case, each section is worked with filling stitches first, decorations next, and edgings last. To keep the appearance of your stitches the same, and to lessen the possibility of tangles, always thread the needle with the thread end that is coming off the ball, then cut the thread.

Finishing

Snip the tackings, then remove the backing; handle the butterfly gently to avoid stretching it out of shape. On the wrong side, trim each tape end and sew it with oversewing to the tape that it overlaps (see illustration on right). Attach lace to the yoke of the dress, with small stitches through the back of the tape; avoid sewing into the lace stitches.

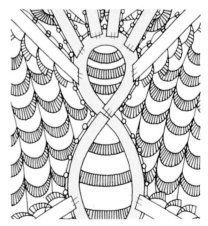

To oversew tape ends, insert needle at right-angle, picking up a few threads of the end and tape under it. Take care not to pierce right side.

Needlepoint lace butterfly

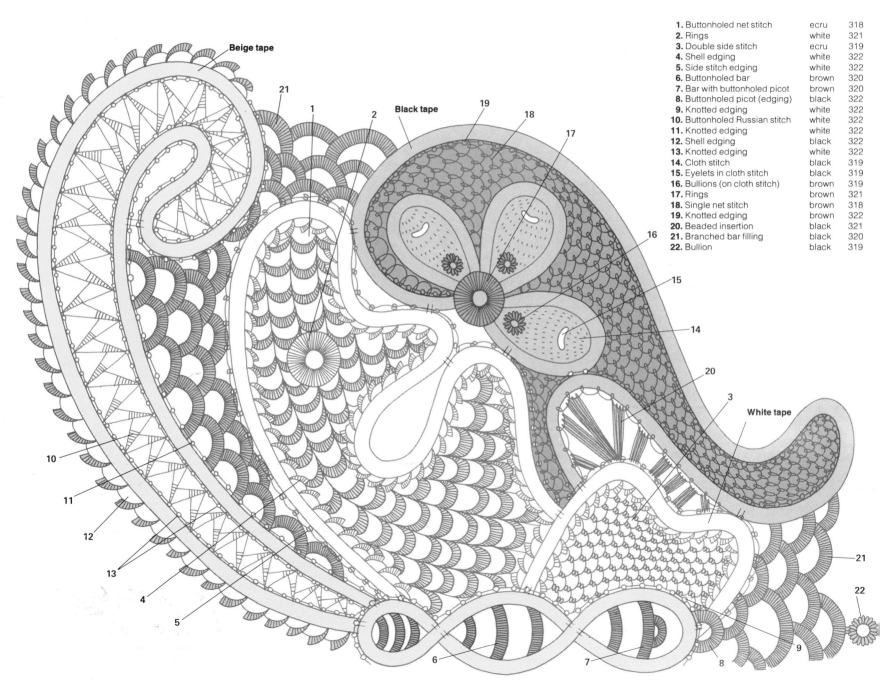

Beige tape

Black tape

White tape

1. Buttonholed net stitch — ecru 318
2. Rings — white 321
3. Double side stitch — ecru 319
4. Shell edging — white 322
5. Side stitch edging — white 322
6. Buttonholed bar — brown 320
7. Bar with buttonholed picot — brown 320
8. Buttonholed picot (edging) — black 322
9. Knotted edging — white 322
10. Buttonholed Russian stitch — white 322
11. Knotted edging — white 322
12. Shell edging — black 322
13. Knotted edging — white 322
14. Cloth stitch — black 319
15. Eyelets in cloth stitch — black 319
16. Bullions (on cloth stitch) — brown 319
17. Rings — brown 321
18. Single net stitch — brown 318
19. Knotted edging — brown 322
20. Beaded insertion — black 321
21. Branched bar filling — black 320
22. Bullion — black 319

Tatting

Introduction

Tatting is a form of lacework that consists of one knot, called double stitch, worked in groups over a single thread. This thread is pulled to draw stitches into rings and chains, and these in turn are joined in larger groupings or motifs. Traditionally, the technique has been used to make edgings and insertions, but a tatting enthusiast can produce items such as collars or a table centre piece. This lace is usually worked with fine cotton thread, so it is delicate looking but very strong.

In tatting, a continuous thread is used and it is wound on a small shuttle (see below). A loop of thread is held in the left hand while the shuttle, held by the right, is manoeuvred around it; double stitches (the same knots are known as lark's head in macramé) form over the shuttle thread. To use the instructions in this section effectively, you should practise a double stitch (p. 326) until you can do it smoothly – and rapidly. Then try each technique in the order presented: they are arranged in order of increasing complexity.

For tatting directions, there are special terms and abbreviations. Those used in this book are listed on the immediate right. These are in common use elsewhere, except for slip join and lock join. Most patterns make no distinction between the two, but simply say 'join'.

Materials

There are two types of tatting shuttles commonly available. One is metal with a removable bobbin and a hook for joining rings. This is best suited to fine crochet cotton in sizes No. 60 to 10. The other shuttle is plastic and has a centre post around which the thread is wound, and a tapered point to use in joining. It is more suitable for No. 5 or No. 3 (a thread thicker than No. 3 is impractical because you cannot wind enough on the bobbin). In addition, you might want a steel crochet hook to use instead of the shuttle point for joining, and needles for finishing thread ends (see p. 328).

The best thread for tatting is smooth cotton with a firm twist. Samples made with different thicknesses of thread are shown on the far right. For practice, No. 5 or 3 crochet cotton or thin string is best.

Terms and abbreviations

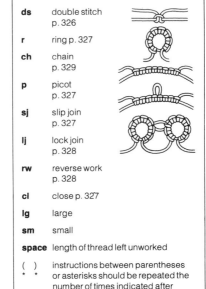

ds	double stitch p. 326	
r	ring p. 327	
ch	chain p. 329	
p	picot p. 327	
sj	slip join p. 327	
lj	lock join p. 328	
rw	reverse work p. 328	
cl	close p. 327	
lg	large	
sm	small	
space	length of thread left unworked	
( ) * *	instructions between parentheses or asterisks should be repeated the number of times indicated after parentheses or asterisks	

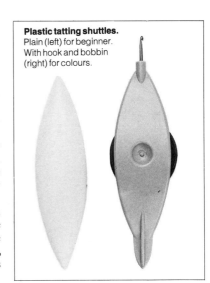

Plastic tatting shuttles.
Plain (left) for beginner.
With hook and bobbin (right) for colours.

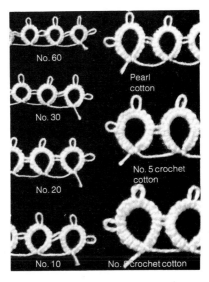

No. 60

Pearl cotton

No. 30

No. 20

No. 5 crochet cotton

No. 10   No. 5 crochet cotton

Tatting techniques

Forming the double stitch

Double stitch (ds) is the fundamental technique used in tatting. It is formed in two stages, with the right hand used to manoeuvre the shuttle around a loop of thread controlled by the left hand. It is this left-hand loop that forms the stitches over the shuttle thread. Once you grasp this principle, and master the forward and backward movement of the shuttle, co-ordination of the tatting movements is fairly easy and a steady rhythm can be established.

Preparing a bobbin. Wind thread firmly from centre to edge of bobbin; insert bobbin in the shuttle.

Holding the thread. Unwind 40 cm; hold the end firmly between thumb and index finger of left hand. Spread your fingers, wind thread around them, and grasp thread again after it comes full circle. Hold shuttle horizontally in right hand, with thread unwinding from the back, passing over the top of the hand and supported by raising the little finger (A).

First half of double stitch. Holding the thread as shown, pass shuttle *under* the top thread of loop held in left hand (B). Still holding shuttle horizontally, slide it backwards *over* the same thread (C). Allow thread to slide off the right hand and pull shuttle thread taut. At the same time, relax fingers of the left hand slightly, so that the *loop forms around the shuttle thread* (D).

Second half of double stitch. Hold the shuttle horizontally as before, but instead of passing thread over the right hand, push down on it with the fingers. Pass the shuttle *over* the top thread of the left-hand loop (E), then slide it backwards *under* this thread (F). Pull shuttle thread taut, allowing *loop to transfer to the shuttle thread* (G). If the stitch has been formed correctly, you should be able to slide the shuttle thread through it. Practise until actions are automatic.

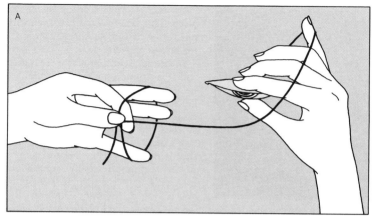

A

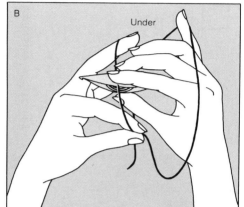

B

Under

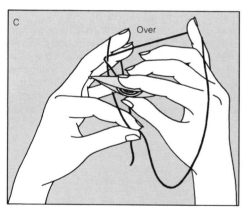

C

Over

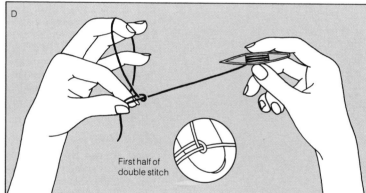

D

First half of double stitch

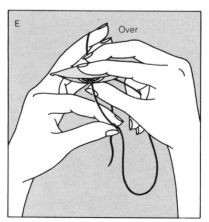

E

Over

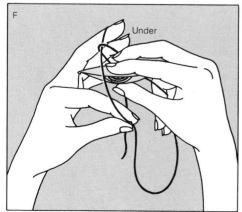

F

Under

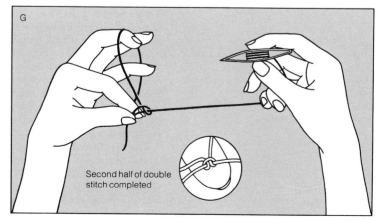

G

Second half of double stitch completed

Practice with one shuttle

Two of the basic elements in tatting are **rings** and **picots**. These should be mastered along with the **slip join** technique (bottom of page) before you proceed to the more complex methods that follow.

A 'ring' is a circle, semicircle or oval of double stitches formed by pulling on the shuttle thread. Its size and shape can vary depending on the number of stitches, the thickness of the thread and how tight the shuttle thread is pulled.

A picot is a thread loop set between two stitches. It is used for decoration and to join rings. Picot size, too, can be varied, but should be consistent in one pattern, unless picots of different sizes are called for in the directions. As a rule, small picots (3 to 5 mm long) are used for joining rings; large picots (5 mm or longer) are used to enhance a design.

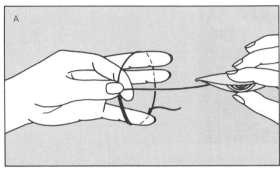

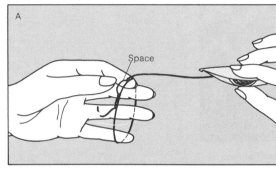

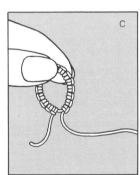

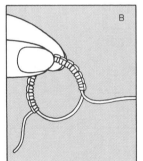

A ring (r) is formed by releasing left-hand loop with which double stitches are made, and pulling on the shuttle thread until stitches are drawn into a tight circle (see above) or semicircle. In instructions this is called *closing* (*cl*).
To practise making a ring, wind thread around left hand and work 20 ds (A), slide thread off left hand, and, holding the stitches between left thumb and index finger, pull shuttle thread gently so that stitches are drawn together. Keep pulling until stitches are as closely set as possible (C).

A picot (p) is formed by leaving a length of thread between two double stitches, then sliding the stitches together so that the thread length becomes a loop.
To practise making picots, start with 5 ds, work first half of the sixth stitch, leaving 5 mm space between it and the fifth ds (A), complete the sixth stitch, then slide it next to the fifth, thus pushing up the loop (B). Work (5 ds, p) 2 more times, 5 ds, cl. Remember, the stitch that closes a picot is counted as the first one in the next group of stitches.

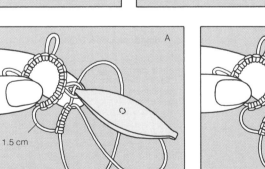

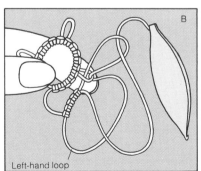

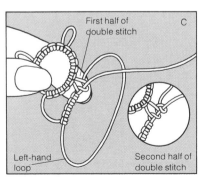

A slip join (sj), made by working a double stitch through an adjacent picot, is the conventional method of joining two rings. **For practice,** make r of 20 ds and 3 p, as explained above right.

Leave 1.5 cm space (length of thread) and start second r with 5 ds (A). Lay the third p of the first r over the left-hand loop. Using tip of shuttle or a crochet hook, draw up a loop through the p and

pass shuttle through this loop (B). Keeping shuttle thread taut, pull loop close to last ds, taking care not to pull shuttle thread back through the picot (C). The join counts as first half of a ds;

complete the second half (see inset) and count this as the first ds in the next group. Finish r with (5 ds, p) twice, 5 ds, cl. Repeat second r as many times as desired to produce a handsome edging.

Tatting techniques

Practice with one shuttle

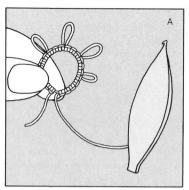

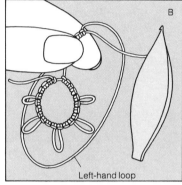

Reversing work (rw) is the turning of a completed ring downwards, so that the next ring is worked above the previous ring. This technique permits a greater variety in design, and also allows you to make wider patterns.

To practise reversing, make this tatted braid.
Make r of 5 ds, sm p, (3 ds, lg p) 3 times, 3 ds, sm p, 5 ds, cl (A); rw, 5 mm space, make second r like the first (B), rw, 5 mm space, make third r of 5 ds, sj to fifth p of first ring, 3 ds, lg p, (3 ds, lg p) twice, 3 ds, sm p, 5 ds, cl. Repeat instructions for the third ring until braid is the desired length, joining each ring to the fifth picot of the ring adjacent to it.

Left-hand loop

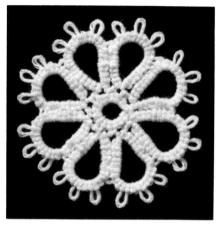

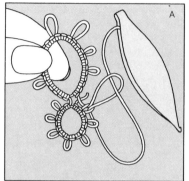

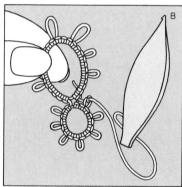

Locking join (lj) is the connecting of two parts with half a slip join. Once made, shuttle thread can no longer be pulled through stitches, so method is limited to completed rings or chains.

To practise locking join, make this medallion.
Make centre r of (2 ds, sm p) 7 times, 2 ds, cl; starting next to last ds of centre r, make petal of r of 5 ds, sm p, 3 ds, sm p, (3 ds, lg p) 3 times, (3 ds, sm p) twice, 5 ds, cl; lj to centre r by drawing up a loop through first p, passing shuttle through this loop (A), then pulling the loop tight (B). Do not count lj as a stitch. Make 7 more petals as follows: r of 5 ds, sj to last p of previous petal, 3 ds, sj to next p, (3 ds, lg p) 3 times, (3 ds, sm p) twice, 5 ds, cl; lj to next p in centre r. Join 8th ring to 2nd and 1st p of 1st r.

Points to remember

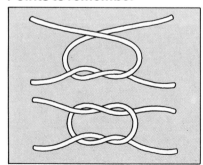

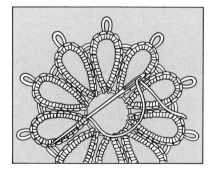

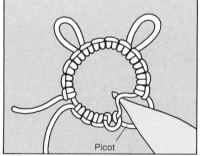

Picot

A new thread is joined only at the end of a ring or chain, before starting the next part of the design. A reef knot, illustrated, is an effective way to tie threads together. Leave enough length so that the thread ends can be woven into the back of the completed work.

A thread end is finished most neatly by weaving it under a few stitches, then cutting the remainder. The needle used must have an eye large enough for the thread but thin enough to pass under stitches. An alternative is to run the thread up and down along the edge and pull tight.

A mistake is corrected most easily while a ring is in progress. If it is necessary to open a ring, you have a better chance of success if you pry loose a thread between two stitches of a picot, as illustrated. Otherwise, thread must be cut, then rejoined after eliminating the error.

To avoid confusion, remember:

1. The thread in the left hand is the one to show itself in the stitches; if it is looped, the result will be a ring; if it is passed over the fingers, the result will be a chain.

2. Work progresses from left to right.

3. The knotted edge of the double stitches are facing to the left while a ring or chain is being formed.

4. The term *picot* refers only to a thread loop, not to the double stitch that encloses it. The closing stitch is counted as the first in the next group of stitches.

5. Never set work down in the middle of a ring or chain; it is difficult to resume the correct position and tension.

Working with two threads

Working with two threads considerably enlarges the scope of tatting. It permits introduction of a second colour, and allows you to work stitches over the connecting threads between rings – a form called **chain** (**ch**). To make a chain, one thread is passed over the left fingers and around the little finger to provide tension; the second is used to make double stitches. As with a ring, thread in the left hand forms the stitches.

For working two threads of one colour, use a shuttle plus ball of thread and work over the ball thread to form chains. Tatting with two colours usually requires two shuttles.

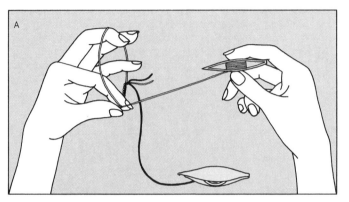

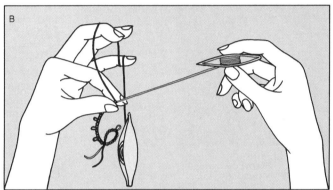

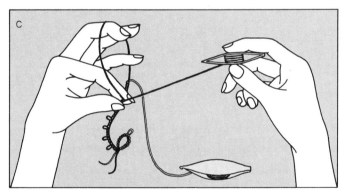

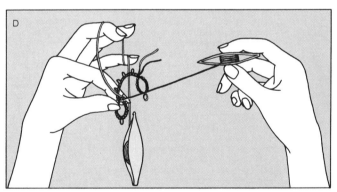

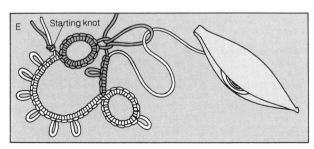

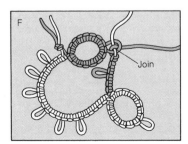

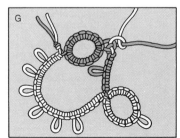

Two-colour edging. Composed of rings and chains in two colours, this is a good practice piece for mastering the use of two shuttles. Keep in mind that the shuttle not in use rests in the lap or on a table, and whatever colour is in the left hand will form the stitches. Wind one shuttle with blue, the other with white; knot the two ends loosely together. Starting close to knot, **with blue**, make r of 8 ds, p, 8 ds (A), cl, rw; **with white** tensioned over left hand and blue in right hand, make ch of (3 ds, p) 6 times, 6 ds (B), do not rw; **with white**, make r of 8 ds, p, 8 ds (C), rw; **with blue** tensioned over left hand and white in right hand, start ch with 3 ds, p, 3 ds (D), sj to p of 1st blue r as follows: pull up a loop of blue, insert white shuttle through it (E), pull loop close to the last ds (F), and complete sj (G), finish ch with (3 ds, p) 3 times, 3 ds, rw; **with white**, make r of 8 ds, sj to p of 1st white r, 8 ds, cl, rw; **with blue**, make ch of (3 ds, p) 5 times, 3 ds, rw; make 2 more sm white rings, connecting them to p of first white r and with a blue ch between them, do not rw; **with white**, make ch of 6 ds, sj to 1st p of opposite white ch, 3 ds, sj to next p, (3 ds, p) 4 times, 3 ds, rw; **with blue**, make r of 8 ds, sj to 2nd p of last blue ch, 8 ds, cl. First repeat is now complete. To begin the next one, do not rw, but make 1st blue r right next to last one, rw; begin 1st white ch with 3 ds, sj to 1st p on opposite ch, finish with (3 ds, p) 5 times, 6 ds. Continue as for first repeat.

329

Shawl with tatted border

The tatted border for the shawl consists of three motifs, made separately, then sewn in place. **Tatting** is done with No. 20 crochet cotton, one ball each of the colours specified in the instructions. **For beading**, you need 180 small glass beads in red-orange (for flowers) and 552 in green (for leaves); 252 4 mm silver-coloured beads for fringe. **Equipment** two tatting shuttles; beading needle (or twisted fuse wire) to transfer the beads to cord (see below right); 4 × 8 cm cardboard gauge for fringe; thread to match tatting.

For shawl: 1.5 m wool challis, at least 140 cm wide; 75 cm lightweight lining; thread to match challis; 1.25 m of wrapping paper to make shawl pattern.

To make the shawl: trim off selvedges, straighten each cut end by drawing out a horizontal thread and cutting along drawn line. Fold fabric on the true bias into a triangle; press fold gently. Tack layers together from centre of base to point opposite. Make paper pattern for curve (opposite page); use to mark both halves of fabric; cut along line.

To attach tatting: mark centre of edge and place motifs in position. Cut bias lining pieces (for backing) slightly larger than separate groupings; holding backing pieces behind challis, pin and sew pieces in place with matching thread; trim backing.

To hem the shawl: fold in half with right sides facing; stitch, leaving a 13 to 15 cm opening. Turn right side out; press edge well. Slipstitch opening.

Placing tatting on edge of fabric. *Grey-and-yellow edging sections (3):* centre one; put the other two at ends. *Flower-and-leaf clusters (12), each 1 flower, 2 leaves:* put group of 4 above centred edging; groups of 3 between the centre and end pieces; one cluster above the last full curve at both ends.

Flowers and leaves (above and below) are separately made and then joined, two leaves to each flower. Small glass beads are used in both: red-orange in flowers; green in leaves.

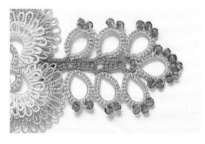

FLOWERS (make 12)
Materials (per flower). Crochet cotton, 4.50 m dk pink, 3.50 m lt pink (plus a little extra for beginning and end of shuttle); 15 red-orange beads. Wind dk pink on one shuttle, lt pink on the other. Put 15 beads on lt pink. Note: wind enough thread on shuttles to make several flowers; add beads just before making each flower.

With lt pink. Bring 5 beads into loop around hand; let hang at bottom of loop until needed. 4 ds, lg p (bring the 5 beads to top of loop and stretch the picot, not too tightly, across them), 4 ds, close. Place 2 more beads against base of ring (when beginning next ring, make sure these 2 beads remain loose on the thread). *Ring: 4 ds, sj into centre p between 1st and 2nd beads, 4 ds, close. Place 2 beads against base of ring* 4 times, putting one bead between each join in centre picot, lj to base of 1st ring, rw. Attach second shuttle (dk pink) to beginning thread of lt pink with a temporary knot.

With dk pink. Chain: *10 ds, lj with lt pink to base of next ring below* 5 times. Do **not** rw.

With lt pink. Chain: *3 ds, 8 p separated by 2 ds, 3 ds, lj with dk pink to next space between chains below* 5 times.

With dk pink. Chain: *3 ds, 10 p separated by 2 ds, 3 ds, lj with dk pink to next space between chains below* 5 times.

With dk pink. Chain: *3 ds, 12 p separated by 2 ds, 3 ds, lj with lt pink to next space between chains below* 5 times.

With dk pink. Chain: *3 ds, 14 p separated by 2 ds, 3 ds, lj with lt pink to next space between chains below* 5 times. Cut threads. Tie ends in tight reef knot on back; clip close.

LEAF MOTIF (make 24)
Materials. Crochet cotton, 2 m lt blue for **rings**, 50 cm green for **chains**; 23 green beads per leaf. One shuttle. Wind shuttle with blue; put on 23 beads; leave green on ball. All joins are sj.
1. Chain: 5 ds, sm p, 1 ds, rw (do not push stitches too close; they should lie in a straight line). **Ring:** (2 beads in loop) 10 ds, bead, 2 ds, bead, 2 ds, p, 10 ds, close, rw.
2. Chain: 5 ds, sm p, 1 ds, rw. **Ring:** (2 beads in loop) 5 ds, j to p of 1st r, 5 ds, bead, 2 ds, bead, 2 ds, p, 10 ds, close, rw.
3. Chain: 5 ds, sm p, 1 ds, rw. **Ring:** (3 beads in loop) 5 ds, j to p of 2nd r, 5 ds, bead, 2 ds, bead, 8 ds, p, 2 ds, close, rw.
4. Chain: 2 ds, rw. **Ring:** (9 beads in loop) 1 ds, j to p of 3rd r, 5 ds, bead, 2 ds, bead, 2 ds, bead, 2 ds, beads together, 2 ds, bead, 2 ds, bead, 5 ds, p, 1 ds, close, rw.
5. Chain: 2 ds, rw (to work ch more easily from here, fold 1st half of leaf towards you, making ds from behind, joins from front). **Ring:** (3 beads in loop) 2 ds, j to p of 4th r, 8 ds, bead, 2 ds, bead, 2 ds, bead, 5 ds, p, 5 ds, close, rw.
6. Chain: 1 ds, j to p of opposite ch by pulling up loop of green and inserting shuttle, 5 ds, rw. **Ring:** (2 beads in loop) 10 ds, j to p of 5th r, 2 ds, bead, 2 ds, bead, 5 ds, p, 5 ds, close, rw.
7. Chain: 1 ds, j to p of opposite ch, 5 ds, rw. **Ring:** (2 beads in loop) 10 ds, j to p of 6th r, 2 ds, bead, 2 ds, bead, 10 ds, close, rw.
8. Chain: 1 ds, j to p of opposite ch, 5 ds. Cut threads; leave ends for tying. To tie 2 leaves to flower, pull one set of threads through space between ch on last row of flower; tie in a tight reef knot on back. Leave 2 petals; join 2nd leaf.

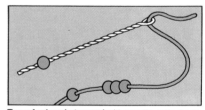

Transfer beads to cord with needle, or by knotting the working thread tightly to the thread on which the beads are sold. Beads can then be slipped over the knot on to the working thread.

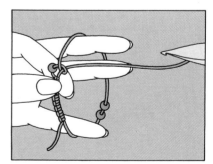

Beads for flowers and leaves are brought into loop around hand before ring is begun; moved into position as needed. Keep beads not in use wound three turns back in shuttle. *Silver beads for the fringe* are put on ball, enough for a section; moved up as fringe is wound, one to a picot.

Fringed swag is made in three sections. Do grey rings first, then yellow edging.

RINGS IN GREY

Materials. Crochet cotton, 31 m med. grey per section; one shuttle. Edging is designed in repeats of 8 large and 7 small rings – 11 repeats to a section.

Large ring: 6 ds, p, 6 ds, p, 6 ds, p, 6 ds, close, rw. Leave 5 mm space (thread length) between rings.

Small ring: 3 ds, p, 3 ds, p, 3 ds, p, 3 ds, close, rw. Leave space as before.

2nd lg r: 6 ds, sj to 3rd p of 1st lg r, 6 ds, p, 6 ds, p, 6 ds, close, rw. Leave space as before.

2nd sm r: 3 ds, sj to 3rd p of 1st sm r, 3 ds, p, 3 ds, close, rw.
Leave thread as before.
Continue with 2nd lg and sm r until you have 8 large and 7 small r (one repeat). Begin second repeat with a large r; it will be joined to last small r of first repeat.

Similarly, first small r of this repeat will be joined to last large r of the first repeat. Continue until 11 repeats are completed. Tie off threads close to stitches; clip close.

YELLOW EDGING AND FRINGE

Materials. Crochet cotton, 21 m lt yellow for chains, 4 m dk pink for rings; 84 silver beads per section. One shuttle; 4 by 8 cm cardboard gauge for fringe. Wind dk pink on shuttle; leave yellow on ball; thread 84 beads on yellow. Upper edge will be worked first. Turn grey edging so the first group of small rings at each end faces upwards. Attach both threads to the 1st p of the 1st small ring at the *left* end.

Chain: 6 ds, p, 6 ds, lj with dk pink to top of *next* sm r.

*Chain: 6 ds, p, 6 ds, rw.

Small ring: 3 ds, p, 3 ds, miss one sm r below and sj to top of *next* sm r, 3 ds, p, 3 ds, close, rw.

Chain: 6 ds, p, 6 ds, miss one sm r below and lj to top of next sm r. 6 ds, p, 6 ds, miss last sm r and lj to top of 1st lg r. (6 ds, p, 6 ds, lj to top of next lg r) 7 times. 6 ds, p, 6 ds, miss 1st sm r and lj to top of next sm r. Repeat from * across top. When next to last sm r has been joined, go around end as follows: 6 ds, p, 6 ds, lj to last p of last sm r, 6 ds, p, 6 ds, lj to 1st p of 1st sm r below, 6 ds, p, 6 ds, lj to top of same lg r. Begin fringe.

Fringes are just very large picots, each with one bead, made on a cardboard gauge for uniformity. Fringe picots (fr p) are made on chains joining lg r. Chains and ring joining sm r are same as above.

Chain: (4 ds, fr p, 4 ds, fr p, 4 ds, lj to top of next lg r) 7 times, then proceed across sm r as above.

To make fringe picot, see below right.

After bottom edge is completed, go around the end as before; tie ends in a tight reef knot and clip close.

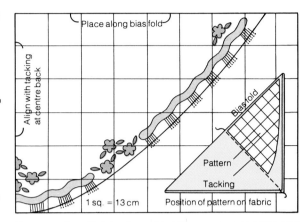

To curve edge of fabric, draw grid of 13 cm squares on paper; on it duplicate curve above, square for square. Align pattern with tacking on shawl; trace curve on fabric. Turn pattern over; trace other half.

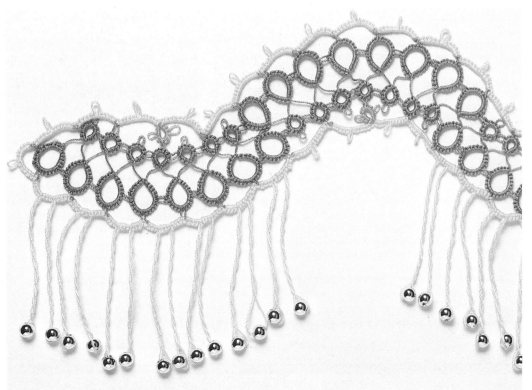

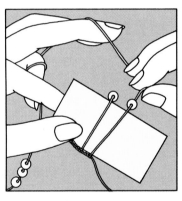

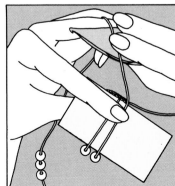

To make fringe picot, after 1st 4 ds in chain, hold cardboard in horizontal position above work. Wrap ball thread with one bead, once around cardboard, *from* side facing you, *over* top, *to* side away from you; twist thread as you wrap by rolling it between fingers (be sure to twist in the same direction as thread twists naturally). *Make 1st half of next ds* from behind the gauge, pushing it up underneath the gauge next to previous ds stitches (but not too tightly). Complete this ds and 3 more, then make another fr p, 4 ds, and lj to the top of next lg r. Proceed in this way across all the large rings (14 fr p in each group), then remove gauge and arrange the twists and beads to hang properly. Proceed across the small rings as for the top, then again place gauge for next group of fr p.

Filet lace netting

What is filet lace netting?
Materials and equipment
Making the basic knot
Basic mesh techniques
Plain square mesh/Filet lace sampler
Embroidering the sampler
Filet lace cushion cover

What is filet lace netting?

Filet lace netting is a type of netting used for many items, from tennis nets and hammocks to lace of the delicate kind shown on the right. No matter what form the netting takes, the basic technique remains the same and involves only one knot (see opposite page).

In lacemaking terms, filet netting is a mesh worked in diamond or square shape, with a design embroidered on it. (Actually, all mesh is diamond-shaped; it is squared as explained on p. 335.)

Netting reached its peak of popularity in 17th-century Europe, when it featured intricate embroidery in many colours and textures. It came back into favour during the Victorian era, but in a less ornate form characterised by geometric patterns in natural-coloured cotton and linen thread. Our example shows this more moderate style, the one associated most closely with the tradition. Today, tradition can be followed with fine crochet cottons. Bear in mind, however, that the knots should look crisp and be nearly invisible; this requires smooth, tightly twisted cord (but not so hard a twist that knots will be obvious). Embroidery thread can be crochet cotton or stranded cotton.

Example of filet lace netting in which both beginning mesh and embroidery are worked in natural colours.

Diamond mesh

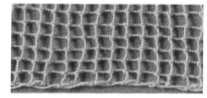
Square mesh

Materials and equipment

Besides knotting cord, you need heavier cord (about 30 cm) for a **foundation loop**, into which the starting meshes are made; a **shuttle** to hold knotting cord; and a **mesh stick** to establish mesh size. The number of starting meshes depends on the shape: several for diamond mesh, which starts at an edge (see facing page and p. 334); two for square mesh, which begins at a corner (p. 335). The ideal shuttle for lace is the netting needle below; an alternative, also shown, is two 15 cm upholsterer's needles placed in opposite directions and taped together below the eyes. A good mesh 'stick' for lace is a double-pointed knitting needle. The size of the needle will determine the size of the netting holes.

The best shuttle for lace is this special netting needle, made for the knotting of fine mesh.

An alternative shuttle can be made of two 15 cm upholsterer's needles, facing in opposite directions and taped together below the eyes.

Good mesh 'stick' for filet netting is a double-pointed knitting needle: slim enough to establish small openings, short enough to be manageable.

Making the basic knot

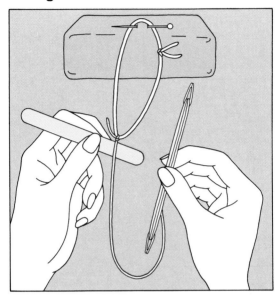

Knot foundation cord into loop; anchor to stable object so it will not move when pulled. Thread shuttle; be sure, when wound, it is not larger than mesh stick. Knot end of shuttle thread into foundation

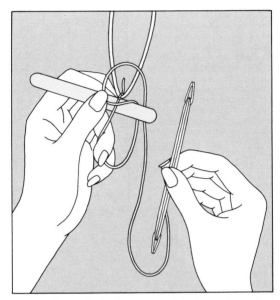

cord. Holding mesh stick between thumb and index finger of left hand and shuttle in right, as shown, pass shuttle thread over stick, around the third finger, and back up behind stick. Holding thread

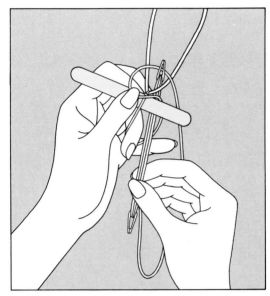

against stick with thumb, loop thread up and around figure-eight style. Pass shuttle through loop on finger, behind stick, through foundation loop, and over top of figure-eight loop.

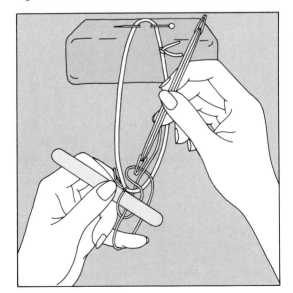

Draw shuttle through and away, *hooking trailing thread on little finger*. Release thumb, then loop on third finger; continue pulling until all slack tightens around stick, but *do not release thread on*

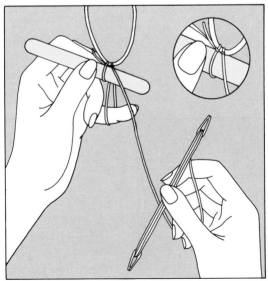

little finger. Place knot on top of and touching stick, then release little finger, drawing thread towards you and keeping foundation cord taut. This forms first knot. Make starting loops on stick and

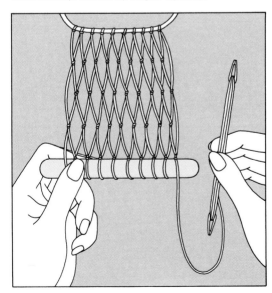

over foundation (about 10 for diamond mesh above; for square mesh, see p. 335). Remove stick; turn work (knotting always goes left to right). Continue knotting, except now into loop above.

333

Filet lace netting

Basic mesh techniques

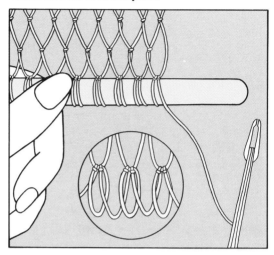

Shaping is accomplished by increasing (left) to widen the mesh, and decreasing (right) to narrow it. These drawings show the basic techniques; for the method used in making square mesh, refer to the opposite page. **To increase**, form two or more knots in one loop, widening that row, and also those that follow, since you will be knotting into an additional mesh wherever an increase was made.

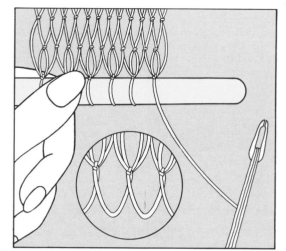

To decrease, work one knot in two or more loops, tying them together, and reducing the number of meshes to be worked in subsequent rows. Though shaping is the main use for both these techniques, especially by a beginner, decorative netting can be made by alternating decreases and increases from row to row, or at fixed intervals.

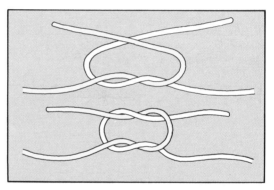

A new thread is best joined at the end of a row. Tie the end of the new thread very close to the last knot that was made, then join the two ends in a reef knot as shown. Clip the ends close to the joining knot.

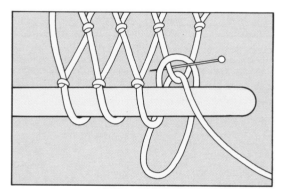

Try to correct mistakes before the knot is tightened. Use a pin to loosen it. If a knot cannot be untied, cut the thread close, untie it, and join a new thread. If you make very tight knots, whole sections of netting can be cut without knots coming undone.

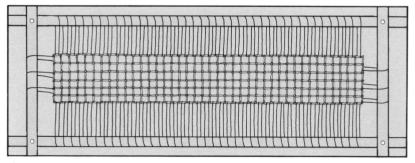

For embroidery, mesh must be stretched in a frame. Be sure to leave at least 3 cm allowance between mesh and inner edge of frame. Wind cord through each mesh and around the frame at top and bottom and through every other mesh at sides. Adjust tension so stretching is even and netting is taut. A mesh too long for a frame can be rolled up and the rolled part finished after the first is completed.

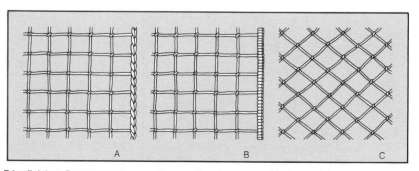

A   B   C

Edge finishes. For any technique, use the same thread as was used for the mesh. In square mesh, the shaping causes side meshes to come out double; to conceal this, and produce a straight, firm edge, good finishing choices are double crochet (A) or close buttonhole stitch (B). The edges of diamond mesh are often cut close to the knots (C). There is no danger of the knots coming undone.

Plain square mesh/Filet lace sampler

The square mesh being made at the bottom of the page is the beginning of the sampler-insertion below (the embroidery directions are on the next page). The directions produce a rectangular mesh approximately 5 by 40 cm, enough for the embroidery charted:

2 repeats, each 32 meshes (about 15 cm) long, *plus* an additional final triangular shape for balance, *plus* 6 extra meshes at each end – 83 meshes in all. To make a longer strip, add multiples of 32 meshes.

Though the quantities are specifically

for the sampler, the technique applies to any square mesh. The progression will be easier to grasp if you remember that the work is turned for each new row.

All work is done with size 20 crochet cotton: the mesh in ecru; embroidery in ecru or white as directed. You also need

a mesh stick (or knitting needle, size 2.75 or 2.25 mm); a steel netting needle (or a pair of 15 cm upholsterer's needles facing in opposite directions and taped together – see p. 332); a frame to stretch mesh for embroidery; tapestry needle for working embroidery.

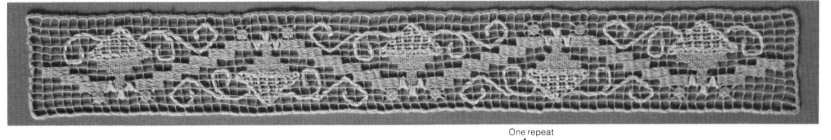

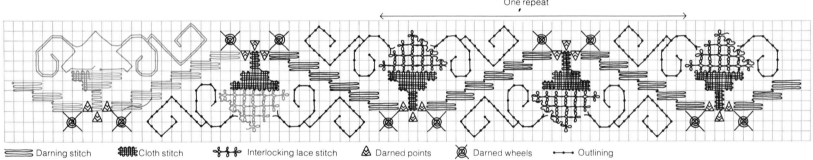

One repeat

〰️ Darning stitch   ▦ Cloth stitch   ⸙ Interlocking lace stitch   △ Darned points   ⊗ Darned wheels   •—•—• Outlining

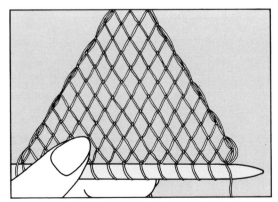

To begin a square mesh. Make two knots in foundation loop; turn work. Starting with second row, *increase one knot in each row* (put two knots in last loop) until you have enough knots for the width. The right-hand edge becomes sampler width (13 knots, 12 meshes).

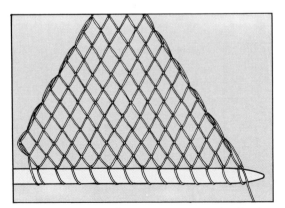

To make straight sides. On next row, *decrease one knot* (knot last two loops together); on following row, *increase one knot* (put two knots in last loop). *Alternate these rows* until long side of mesh is the desired length. In the sampler, this is 83 meshes.

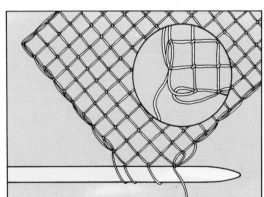

To square the last corner. Beginning with the next row after the length has been established, *decrease one knot at the end of each row* until two loops are left. Knot these two together and cut the threads close. Remove the foundation loop.

Filet lace stitches

Embroidering the sampler

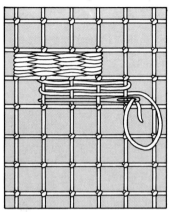

1. Darning stitch (ecru, single thread). In 1st group at left end, tie thread to top left corner of 1st mesh of design. Weave over and under meshes, from top to bottom, until space is filled – 10-12 threads will usually be enough. With next section, attach thread to left corner of 1st mesh, and proceed downwards.

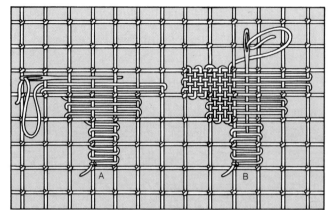

2. Cloth stitch (ecru, single thread). Done in two steps – first warp, then weft threads, in each pattern area. (A) Attach thread at bottom left. Weave single meshes first, over and under, bottom to top, 4 threads per mesh. Weave somewhat loosely; slack is taken up in second step. At next mesh, be sure to weave 1st thread as you did last thread on previous mesh; thread between will be included in next step. (B) Without breaking thread, begin at upper left and weave weft threads back and forth across warp threads. Include all intervening mesh threads in weaving; put in 4 threads per mesh. After each row, pull slightly on warp threads so that weaving is flat and even.

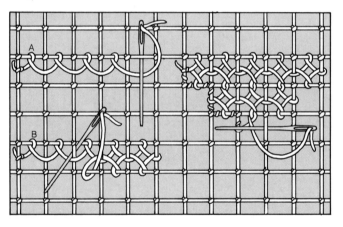

3. Interlocking lace stitch (white, single thread). Done in loop or buttonhole stitch; can be worked diagonally as well as back and forth. Each row takes two steps. (A) Begin with longest row on chart. Attach thread to centre of mesh on left side. Make one loop stitch in each mesh, large enough to cover half the mesh. At end of row, make a loop stitch in side of mesh. (B) Going right to left in same row, make loops as before, going over each loop in preceding row and under each vertical mesh. To move to second row, oversew around last mesh; begin again as in A, but pass needle through bottom loops of previous row to interlock.

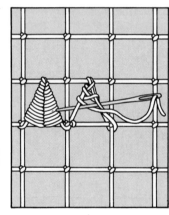

4. Darned points (white, single thread). Darn from top to base. Begin with left point. Attach thread at lower left corner of mesh. Loop around top, down to opposite corner, back up to top. This forms a scaffold for darning. Beginning at top, darn alternately from each side into centre – from right a buttonhole stitch, from left a plain stitch; catch in loose end from knot as part of scaffold. When working last stitch on each side, go around bottom of mesh to anchor base of point. Run thread behind mesh to centre top of next point and form scaffold as before.

5. Darned wheels (ecru, single thread). Attach thread at centre of 4 meshes. Make a bar from there to each corner of 4-mesh square by passing thread around corner, then passing needle twice around it to twist bar. When bars are made, weave thread spirally around centre, over bars and under mesh threads, until wheel is desired size (about four times). Fasten off on back by passing thread through twists of a bar or tying a reef knot with beginning thread.

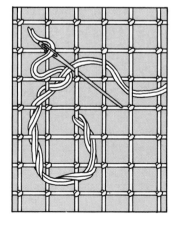

6. Outlining (white, double thread). Begin at bottom centre of interlocking lace stitch; weave over and under mesh threads as indicated by dots on chart. Following chart and photograph, weave first spiral. When centre is reached, begin weaving back alongside first thread, except pass thread *under* each mesh thread previously passed *over* and twisting once around previously laid thread. Continue around second spiral, then finish off top of first on way back to triangle. Continue around triangle, making other side the same. Fasten off thread with reef knot to beginning thread.

Filet lace cushion cover

Materials

Small netting shuttle; knitting needle, 2.25 mm, for mesh stick; tapestry needle; embroidery scissors; frame and cord to mount mesh (at least 30 cm square inside space); size 20 crochet cotton, 1 ball, ecru; size 8 pearl cotton, 1 ball each, 5 shades of blue; square cushion for the finished piece. It is 56 meshes (about 25.5 cm) square; for a larger size, use size 10 crochet cotton, size 2.75 or 3 mm knitting needle, size 5 pearl cotton.

Making the net (square mesh)

To begin, make two knots into foundation loop; turn. Starting with second row, *increase* one knot at end of each row until you have 57 knots. On next row, net plain (no increase). Next row, begin *decreasing* one knot at end of each row until two knots are left. Knot these together, cut thread, remove foundation loop. Stretch mesh in frame, winding the cord through every other mesh.

Embroidery

In five shades of blue, charted as A, B, C, D, E (lightest to darkest). Stitches are those in sampler, but worked as listed on this page. To secure thread ends during work, run thread back and forth a few times from back (do not make knots). Always thread needle with thread as it comes off the ball or skein, this enhances sheen of stitches and keeps thread from untwisting. Turn frame with stretched mesh so the raised mesh threads run vertically and face you; those on the back run horizontally. Direction of raised threads makes a difference in the darning stitches.

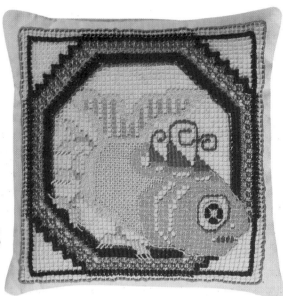

Cloth stitch (fish's outline and head). Numbers on diagram mark starting points for first threads. Follow lines to point where thread turns and second threads are woven in. Weave second threads in as far as possible, then begin at next number before completing first area. Lay in 4 threads per mesh; remember that first thread in each mesh is woven the same as last thread of previous mesh. Travelling threads, sometimes needed to get from one row to next, are incorporated into mesh threads during second stage of weaving. Work numbers 1–3 in colour A. Complete work in this colour before going further. Numbers 5–10 are worked in colour B, number 11 in colour C.

Darning stitch (fish's fins, tail bars and eye; all darkest areas in border). Lay in about 12 threads per mesh. Work bars in tail vertically in colour B (4). Raised vertical threads of mesh help 'outline' them. Go from bar to bar by passing thread through edge of cloth stitch from back. All other darning is worked horizontally. Fins on left side are worked in colours B and A in that order. Small bars are made after last row is completed by passing thread 3 times around mesh, then wrapping twice around threads and going to next small bar. Fins above head are worked, bottom to top, in colour D. When top mesh is completed, pull end of thread down so it is doubled, and proceed with outline at top of each fin. Work darning in eye, all border darning, in colour E.

Darned wheels (fish's eye; border). Worked somewhat differently from sampler. Thread is brought out from darned area adjacent at corner between first two wheels. Diagonal bars are laid from centre to each corner, but first corner will have only one thread. Its second thread is laid after wheel itself is darned, enabling you to begin second wheel from adjacent corner. After second wheel is completed, thread is concealed in darning and brought around between next two wheels to be worked. In these wheels, corner threads are laid under mesh; darning is done by passing needle over mesh threads and under corner about 3 times. Work fish's eye in colour A, border wheels in D.

Interlocking lace stitch (fish's body; border). Work fish's body in colour A. Begin in upper left corner and work down. Conceal travelling threads in edge stitches at left side. Work outside border areas in colour E; begin and end at point indicated. Work inside border area in colour C; begin above fish's head and work first row all the way around, putting in diagonal stitches as indicated. Diagram shows how to lay in return row on diagonal (pass needle under mesh knot in same way that you pass it under mesh thread when doing a straight row).

Darned points (fish's teeth). Work in colour D, left to right. Scaffold for each point will have one thread on left, two on right.

Outlining (fish's eye, around head; inside border). Use double thread. Outline fish's eye in colour A, eye socket in D; top of head, from last tooth to first fin, in colour B; bottom of head, from tooth to halfway around back of head, in colour A; inside border in colour D.

Edging. With double thread in colour C, work 4 buttonhole stitches into each mesh all around (one extra at each corner).

A □ B □ C □ D □ E □

Bobbin lace

Introduction

This section shows the continental method for making bobbin lace, simplified for beginners. Bobbin lace is a lace woven of pairs of threads wound on bobbins. Only two basic stitches are involved, half stitch and whole stitch (see pp. 340–2), but from these many designs can be woven. The weaving is done over an actual-size paper pattern mounted on a pillow or padded board (see below). Pins are inserted through the pattern into the pillow to hold threads in place; the pattern is called a *pricking* because the design lines are perforated.

Bobbin lace is an old technique, dating back to the 15th century. As its popularity spread, local styles developed with patterns and stitches whose names reflected their place of origin. As a result, old pieces of bobbin lace exhibit a wide range of styles, from geometric patterns made with a few pairs of bobbins, to complex floral and pictorial designs requiring hundreds.

Russian braid

Cluny

Honiton

Examples of torchon

Scandinavian (free-form)

Tools and materials

Though their forms may be different, the elements required for bobbin lace have stayed the same for centuries: appropriate thread, bobbins, a pattern to follow, a pillow on which to mount the pattern. Traditional threads were silk, metallic or linen, spun very smooth and incredibly fine; for most modern bobbin lace, the choice is a smooth cotton. Bobbins were wood, bone or ivory, often weighted ('spangled') with glass beads to help hold thread taut. These bobbins can still be found in antique shops, but modern plastic and turned wooden bobbins are available. There are many satisfactory alternatives: slotted clothes pegs; dowelling or pencils cut to 15 cm lengths and grooved at one end; swizzle sticks; tapestry or fly shuttle bobbins used in weaving. Traditional prickings were of parchment so they could be re-used; for present purposes, use graph paper. The pillow or board must support the work firmly and take pins easily. A sawdust-filled cushion is ideal.

Lace pillow showing pocket (see p. 344) being made. Traditional antique and modern bobbins are being used. A pincushion is attached at the side to provide pins as the knots are made.

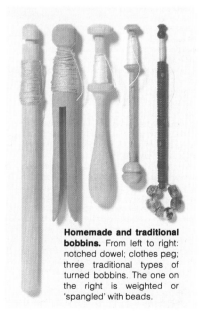

Homemade and traditional bobbins. From left to right: notched dowel; clothes peg; three traditional types of turned bobbins. The one on the right is weighted or 'spangled' with beads.

Preparing the pricking/Bobbin lace sampler

The sampler is designed to introduce you to the half stitch and whole stitch, and several of the patterns that can be made from them; and to the pattern, or pricking, that you follow to produce bobbin lace designs. On your graph paper (see equipment list on right), using waterproof ink, copy the diagram below square for square, putting in all dots, lines and numbers precisely as shown. One colour is sufficient; three are used here to make the diagram easier to follow. The right side of the braid-tape that edges the sampler is exactly the reverse of the pattern for the left side.

Pin your pricking at the corners, in the centre and as near the top of the pillow or board as possible. Using a pricker (a pin vice with a No. 8 needle), or a large needle fitted with a dowel or penholder handle, punch holes through all dots into the board.

The diagram is labelled with the names of the stitches in the order in which they are worked in the sampler, and the numbers of the pages on which instructions for them appear. You may find it helpful to indicate these stitch names on your diagram, perhaps also the page numbers. Listed below are abbreviations used in the instructions, and some working suggestions.

Abbreviations used in instructions

h st (or **t,c**)	half stitch	**c**	cross
w st (or **c,t,c**)	whole stitch	**pr,**	pair,
t	twist	**prs**	pairs

Points to remember

1. Pairs of bobbins are numbered left to right; numbers refer to their position on the board, not to actual bobbins.

2. In twisting, the right partner crosses over the left partner.

3. In crossing, the right bobbin of the left pair crosses over the left bobbin of the right pair.

4. Pins are placed perpendicular to the pillow or board, except at the edges where they are slanted outwards.

5. Place pins in their holes *between* the last two pairs of bobbins worked.

6. Always keep bobbins hanging evenly.

7. Do not roll bobbins on the board; this makes thread unwind. Instead, push them back and forth in pairs.

8. Join a new thread by working both new and old ends into the weaving together; clip when lace is completed.

Equipment specifically for sampler:

Board or 'pillow' approximately 65 cm square (usable also for project, p. 344). You can make your own with two or more pieces of corrugated cardboard taped together and padded with layers of felt, cotton or wool fabric. Acoustic tile or similar soft board will also work well, provided the surface is smooth. Insert a few pins in 'pillow' to be sure they go in easily and hold firmly. If they protrude at the bottom when pushed in all the way, place thick towelling or some similar padding underneath, or change to a shorter type of pin.

Dressmaker's straight pins (or shorter pins if they are more suitable) to use in weaving. Long T-pins are helpful for pinning bobbins not in use out of the way.

Bobbins, 24, either the traditional style (available in some shops) or one of the alternatives described in the list of materials on the opposite page.

Thread of almost any kind can be used in contemporary work. For learning, a smooth medium-weight crochet cotton is best. Sampler calls for one ball of size 10 in white or ecru.

Pricker, or a needle-like equivalent that will make satisfactory pinholes, for perforating the pricking at all the dots in the design. These are the points at which pins will be inserted, and piercing makes insertion far easier.

Pricking requires two 22 by 28 cm sheets of centimetre graph paper.

Crochet hook, size 4, 3.75 or 3.50 mm, which is used in making sewing joins (see p. 343).

Cloth cover, a 40 to 50 cm square of smooth fabric to protect lace that has been woven as you work on another section, or to cover your project when you put it aside or away.

Dowel, 3 mm in diameter and about 18 cm long, for mounting bobbins so that the sampler is ready for hanging when it is completed.

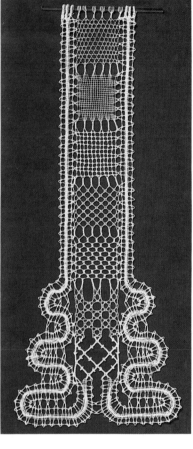

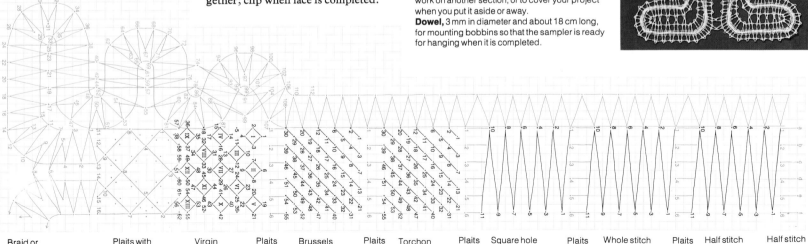

| Braid or tape 343 | Plaits with picots 343 | Virgin ground 342 | Plaits | Brussels ground 342 | Plaits | Torchon ground 342 | Plaits | Square hole ground 342 | Plaits | Whole stitch ground 342 | Plaits | Half stitch ground 342 | Half stitch plaits 340 |

Bobbin lace techniques

Winding bobbin pairs

Measure off enough thread to fill the bobbins but not overload them. For the sampler, this is about 6 metres – 3 m per bobbin. Wind bobbins from each end towards centre, leaving about 45 cm

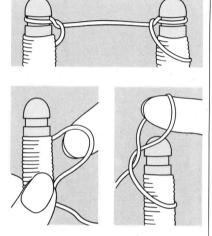

unwound for mounting. Secure thread with noose, made by looping thread as

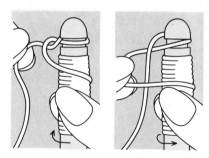

shown, twisting bobbin away from you, then slipping noose over head of bobbin. Pull thread to tighten. Noose lets you unwind thread as needed (above left) or wind up excess thread (right) without undoing the knot. Mount two pairs of bobbins together with a lark's head knot (p. 359). Place a pin between each two pairs, just under dowel – points a to f on pricking.

Working the basic (half and whole) stitches

The illustrations below show two bobbin pairs mounted as described on the left. Work is done on the side shown; the reverse side becomes the right side when lace is finished. Two adjacent pairs are woven together, the left pair held in the left hand and the right pair in the right. In directions, pairs are numbered left to right. Numbers indicate board position, not actual bobbins. The first row of drawings shows the steps to a half stitch plait. These occur in the sampler in series of six, made by plaiting all the pairs as you did prs 1-2 (prs 3-4, pin at No. 2, prs 5-6, pin at No. 3, and so on).

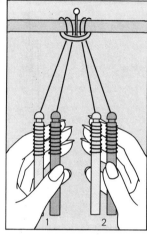

Start weaving, as illustrated above, with pair 1 held in the left hand and pair 2 in the right; pin the other bobbins out of the way.

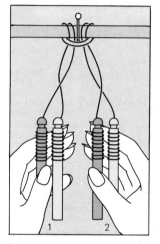

Begin the **half stitch** (written t,c) with a *twist*, worked as follows: push right member of each pair over left with thumb of each hand.

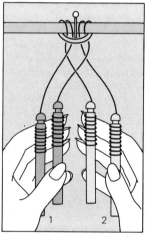

In the *cross*, inside members exchange places, the one on the left crossing over the one on the right. This completes one half stitch.

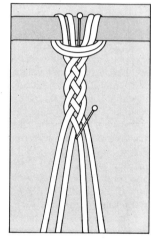

To produce a plait, make half stitches as described down the pricking to the first hole. Place a pin at No. 1 between the two pairs.

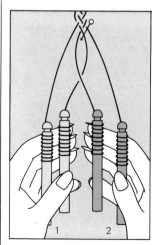

In whole (or cloth) stitch (written c,t,c), pairs are crossed, twisted, then crossed again. The illustration above shows the first *cross*.

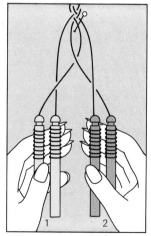

All crosses and twists are worked exactly the same for whole stitch as for half stitch. The *twist* is being worked in the drawing above.

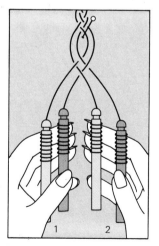

The step illustrated here is the second *cross*, which completes the whole stitch. A plait cannot be made with a whole stitch. When it

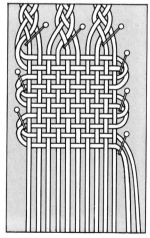

is repeated, the result is **whole stitch ground**, (fourth stitch area in sampler). For whole stitch ground instructions, see p. 342.

Weaving a design

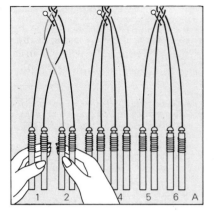

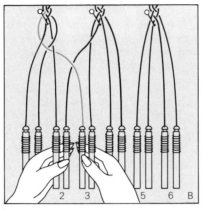

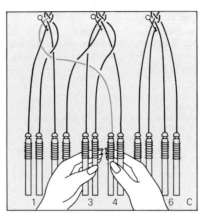

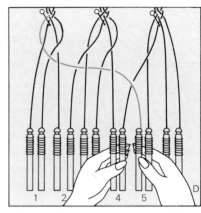

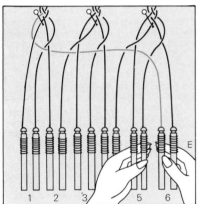

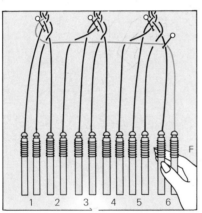

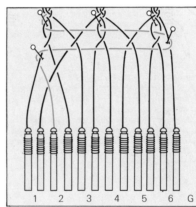

This sequence, of basic steps to half stitch ground, is designed to give a general sense of the interaction of pairs of bobbins. The drawings also clarify what is meant by numbers signifying positions of bobbins on board, not actual bobbins. Space limitations permit showing only 6 pairs of bobbins instead of the 12 used in the sampler, but the principles are the same. In A, the half stitch (t,c) has been completed with prs 1-2; B, C, D and E show half stitches made with prs 2-3, 3-4, 4-5 and 5-6 respectively; in illustration F, the left-to-right sequence has been pinned. (Unless otherwise indicated, pins are always placed between the two pairs of bobbins involved in the just-completed stitch.) In illustration G, half stitches have been worked in reverse (prs 6-5, 5-4, 4-3, 3-2, 2-1). Stitch is worked the same way regardless of direction. This sequence, repeated, produces the ground.

Pinning within a design

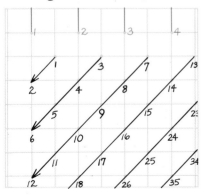

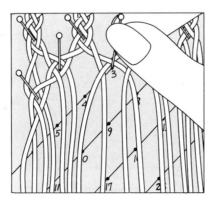

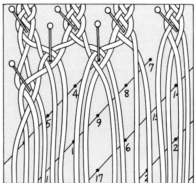

Another pinning principle is demonstrated by torchon ground, a mesh form of the whole stitch ground. It is worked diagonally, making it necessary to place a pin in the centre of each whole stitch to hold it in place. The mesh is created by twisting both pairs of bobbins before each whole stitch; the twists force the stitches apart, producing diamond-shaped holes. Edge bobbins are also given an extra twist for added firmness. The drawings show only the start of the procedure; for full instructions, see next page. To begin the stitch, t,c prs 3-2, pin at No. 1, t,c. This makes a whole stitch with a pin at its centre, both pairs having been twisted first. Then t,c prs 2-1, pin at No. 2, t,c, extra twist to pr 1 (the edge pair). t,c prs 5-4, pin at No. 3, t,c, and so on down the second diagonal row.

Bobbin lace techniques

Ground patterns

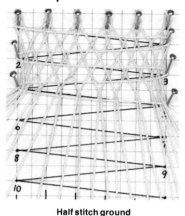

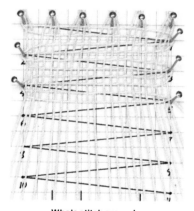

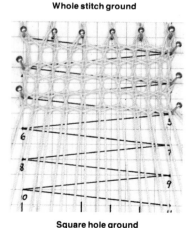

Plaits are worked at start and between sections. See p. 339 for positions, p. 340 for technique.

Half stitch ground (also net or lattice ground).

1. t,c prs 1-2 (lay down pr 1, shift pr 2 to left hand and take up pr 3 in right); t,c prs 2-3 (shift prs again); t,c prs 3-4, 4-5, etc., to prs 11-12; pin at No. 1 between 11-12. Twist pr 12 once more (extra twist makes edge firmer); pull slightly on all bobbins to make threads lie even. *Remember numbers signify board position, not actual bobbins.*

2. Work back across row the same way: t,c prs 12-11, 11-10, 10-9, 9-8, etc., to prs 2-1. Pin at No. 2 between prs 2 and 1, extra twist to pr 1.

3. Repeat these two rows until space is filled, ending with pin No. 11.

Half stitch ground

Whole stitch ground (also cloth stitch) worked over an area looks like a woven fabric. In this stitch (written c,t,c), pairs are crossed, then twisted, then crossed again.

1. c,t,c prs 1-2, 2-3, 3-4, etc., to prs 11-12. Pin at No. 1 between prs 11-12, twist pr 12 once more.

2. Work back across row the same way: c,t,c prs 12-11, 11-10, 10-9, etc., to prs 2-1. Pin at No. 2, extra twist to pr 1.

3. Repeat rows 1 and 2 to pin No. 11. Occasionally pull down on threads to keep tension even. *In this stitch*, an 'active' pair passes back and forth through the other 'passive' pairs. Variations can be achieved by twisting active, or passive, or both, between stitches or groups of stitches.

Whole stitch ground

Square hole ground (or whole stitch and twist), a variation of the whole stitch ground, is worked exactly as above, except both pairs of bobbins are twisted once before each whole stitch is made. The twists force the whole stitches apart, making 'square holes'.

1. t,c,t,c prs 1-2, 2-3, 3-4, etc., to prs 11-12. Put a pin between prs 11-12 at No. 1. Edge bobbins do not get extra twists in this pattern.

2. Work back across row the same way: t,c,t,c prs 12-11, 11-10, 10-9, etc., to prs 2-1. Put a pin between prs 2-1 at No. 2.

3. Repeat rows 1 and 2 to pin No. 11. Pull threads into position carefully after every row. Do this by pulling down on the bobbins, not by pulling the threads themselves.

Square hole ground

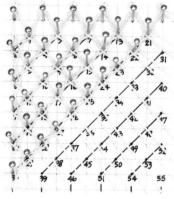

Torchon ground

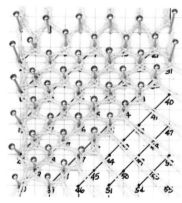

Brussels ground

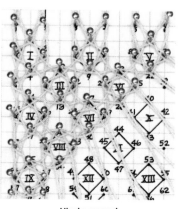

Virgin ground

Torchon ground is like square hole ground, except worked diagonally, making it necessary to put a pin in the centre of each w st to hold it in place.

1. t,c prs 3-2, pin at No. 1, t,c (makes a w st with a pin in its centre, both prs having been twisted first). t,c prs 2-1, pin at No. 2, t,c. Extra twist to pr 1.

2. t,c prs 5-4, pin at No. 3, t,c. t,c prs 4-3, pin at No. 4, t,c; t,c prs 3-2, pin at No. 5, t,c; t,c prs 2-1, pin at No. 6, t,c. Extra twist to pr 1.

3. t,c prs 7-6, pin at No. 7, t,c; t,c prs 6-5, pin at No. 8, t,c; t,c prs 5-4, pin at No. 9, t,c; t,c prs 4-3, pin at No. 10, t,c; t,c prs 3-2, pin at No. 11, t,c; t,c prs 2-1, pin at No. 12, t,c. Extra twist to pr 1.

4. Continue, always picking up the two prs of bobbins on either side of 1st hole for each new diagonal row. Remember to give pr 12 an extra twist before making stitch at No. 31, etc., so each edge has 2 twists.

Brussels ground sequence is the same as for torchon ground, except Brussels ground has two whole stitches at each pin, with pin placed between them.

1. t,c,t,c prs 3-2, pin at No. 1, t,c,t,c (extra twist made after the pin because you cannot cross the same prs twice without twisting them first); t,c,t,c prs 2-1, pin at No. 2, t,c,t,c. No extra twist needed to prs 1 and 12 in this pattern.

2. t,c,t,c prs 5-4, pin at No. 3, t,c,t,c; t,c,t,c prs 4-3, pin at No. 4, t,c,t,c; t,c,t,c prs 3-2, pin at No. 5, t,c,t,c; t,c,t,c prs 2-1, pin at No. 6, t,c,t,c.

3. Continue in this way, always starting each new diagonal row by picking up the prs of bobbins on either side of 1st hole.

Virgin ground (or Rose ground) is worked in a series of large diamonds, each in a 'box'. Whole stitches with a twist between are worked in each corner of diamond and pinned in centre. Corners of boxes are completed with one half stitch (no pins).

1. t,c prs 2-3, pin at No. 1, t,c; extra twist pr 1, t,c prs 1-2, pin at No. 2, t,c; t,c prs 3-4, pin at No. 3, t,c; t,c prs 2-3, pin at No. 4, t,c; Diamond I complete. Extra twist pr 1, t,c prs 1-2, pin at No. 5, t,c; t,c prs 3-4. Lower corners of box around Diamond I are now complete. Begin Diamond II.

2. t,c prs 6-7, pin at No. 6, t,c; t,c prs 5-6, pin at No. 7, t,c; t,c prs 7-8, pin at No. 8, t,c; t,c prs 6-7, pin at No. 9, t,c; t,c prs 7-8 and prs 5-6 to complete lower corners of box around Diamond II.

3. t,c prs 4-5, pin at No. 10, t,c; t,c prs 3-4, pin at No. 11, t,c; t,c prs 5-6, pin at No. 12, t,c; t,c prs 4-5, pin at No. 13, t,c; t,c prs 3-4 and prs 5-6.

4. t,c prs 2-3, pin at No. 14, t,c; extra twist pr 1, t,c prs 1-2, pin at No. 15, t,c; t,c prs 3-4, pin at No. 16, t,c; t,c prs 2-3, pin at No. 17, t,c; extra twist pr 1, t,c prs 1-2, pin at No. 18, t,c; t,c prs 3-4.

5. Continue same way with Diamond V, giving pr 12 an extra twist for a firmer edge. Each diamond begins with prs on either side of its 1st (top) hole – prs 10 and 11 for Diamond V. As Diamond IX, XII, XIII are completed, put pins under half stitches at holes No. 57-62 to hold them in place for next section.

Other lace techniques

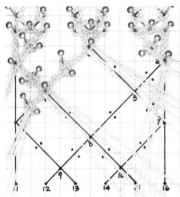

Plaited lace

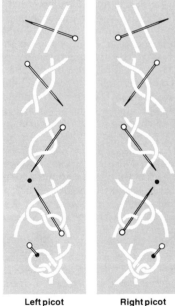

Left picot   **Right picot**

Windmill join

Plaited lace is simply half stitch plaits enhanced with tiny picots and joined. Begin by making a plait with prs 1-2 long enough to reach pin No. 1. Do not put in a pin yet, but lay the plait aside, and make a plait with prs 3-4 halfway to pin No. 1. The two holes at this point mark the positions for the picots.

Left and right picots are made with the left and right pairs of bobbins – see diagram. Use a pin to help pull up the loop as shown; then insert pin in the loop and pull down carefully on the two bobbins to lock the picot in place. Continue making the plait to pin No. 1 and then join this plait to the first by means of a 'windmill join' (below).

The windmill join is just a whole stitch, with a pin in its centre, made with each pair of bobbins functioning as a single bobbin. Cross pr 2 over pr 3; cross pr 4 over pr 3 and pr 2 over pr 1 (this is the twist). Put pin in No. 1. Cross pr 2 over pr 3. Join is now completed. Repeat this procedure with prs 9 to 12, putting another join at No. 2. With prs 5 to 8, make plaits and join at No. 3. Continue making plaits, picots and joins where indicated on the pricking. At pins No. 11 to No. 16, place pins between the pairs of bobbins in each plait to hold them in position for the next section.

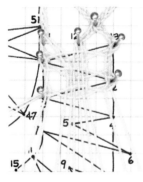

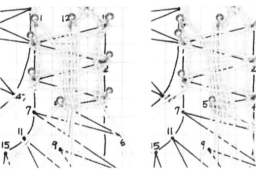

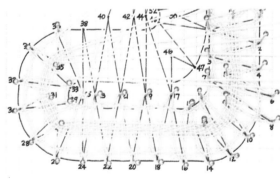

Braid or tape lace, a style popular in Russia and Eastern Europe, is characterised by curving lines and free forms. Although apparently complex, designs require only a few pairs of bobbins, just enough for the width of the tape, which turns, curves and joins to itself by means of 'sewings' (below). The tape is made like whole stitch ground, varied by twisting the pairs to make openings. Before starting, remove all centre pins from the ground patterns, and push the pins right in along both edges. Cover the completed lace, but leave the pricking exposed where you will be working the tape. You will be making two sections, one at each side, with six pairs of bobbins for each; 6th pair is active for left side, 1st pair for right. Pin the right-side bobbins out of the way – left side is made first. When thread runs out on active weavers, turn into passive, then join a new thread and work old and new together for a few rows. Cut off old ends.

Making the tape:
1. t,c,t,c prs 6-5, t pr 5; c,t,c prs 5-4, 4-3, 3-2; t,c,t,c prs 2-1; pin at No. 1.
2. t,c,t,c prs 1-2, t pr 2; c,t,c prs 2-3, 3-4, 4-5; t,c,t,c prs 5-6; pin at No. 2.

Blind pin (pins No. 5, 9, 13, 27, 31, 35, etc.). To make a smooth curve in the tape, there must be more threads at the outer edge and fewer at the inner edge. To achieve this, the active pair is woven from the outer edge halfway to the inner edge, then woven back out again. For example, after pin No. 4 has been placed: t,c,t,c prs 6-5; t pr 5; c,t,c prs 5-4; c,t,c prs 4-3; c,t,c prs 3-2; pin at No. 5; c,t,c prs 2-3; c,t,c prs 3-4; c,t,c prs 4-5; t,c,t,c prs 5-6, etc.

Sewings. As the tape curves, it must be joined to itself at intervals with 'sewings', made by joining the active pair of bobbins to previously made portion of tape at a pin. Sewings are made here at pins No. 6, 8, 17, 19, 21, 23, 25, etc. These pins are placed further than usual from the edge of the tape, and best given one or two extra twists for added firmness. Pins No. 6 and 8 are joined on the other side, so the first sewing comes after pin No. 36. When it has been placed, weave through tape as usual towards pin No. 25; extra twist to active pr. Remove pin at No. 25; with crochet hook, reach down through loop at No. 25 and pull up thread of nearest bobbin. Insert other bobbin through pulled-up thread, then gently pull both threads back in position. Replace pin at No. 25, and continue weaving as usual. Sewings are sometimes made without an extra twist on the pair: e.g., at No. 49, where a sewing is made to No. 1; at No. 51, where one is made into the plait; along edges of ground patterns, where tape is joined to sampler edges. After completing tape, finish off dowel by making a plait with each group of 4 bobbins long enough to go around it. End with sewing made through base of plait with each pair acting as a single bobbin. Tie prs in tight reef knot; clip close.

343

Apron trimmed with bobbin lace

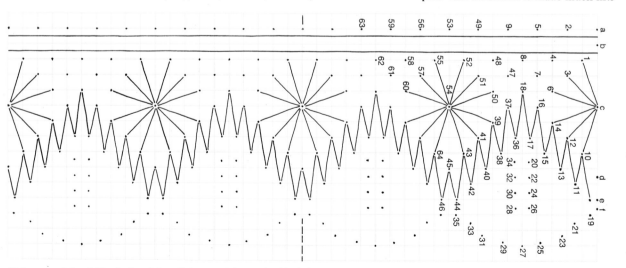

Lace edging and medallion, worked in pretty pastels, enhance a plain linen apron.

The lace consists of an edging in torchon patterns and a medallion in a combination of styles. The patterns are worked in three thread colours to make the lace construction easier to understand. For information about prickings, and other details about the patterns, read each set of instructions.

Materials needed to make the lace

Board or 'pillow', at least 65 cm long (the sampler board is suitable)

Dressmaker's pins

Paper for prickings: graph paper for the edging pattern, 4 squares to 2.5 cm, enough to make a pricking 61 cm long; medium-weight drawing paper for the medallion pattern, shown actual size

Bobbins: 14 pairs for edging; 8 pairs for medallion

Heavy crochet cotton (approximate equivalent of pearl cotton No. 5), one ball each of white, ecru and light blue

Crochet hook, 3.75 mm, for sewings (in medallion only)

Pricker, drawing ink, metrestick

The edging motifs are all torchon patterns; see pp. 341–2 for general principles. The medallion is made much like the braid in the sampler (p. 343): a few pairs of bobbins to make a tape in several variations, here both whole and half stitch tapes with occasional picots, joined at various points by sewings. After tapes are completed, fillings are added: Brussels ground in flower petals, half stitch plaits in the background.

To make the apron, you need 1 m of 90 cm or 114 cm wide dress-weight linen or cotton, and sewing thread to match.

From fabric, cut an *apron front* 63 cm wide by 60 cm long; a *pocket lining* the shape of the medallion, plus 1.5 cm seam allowance all around; *waistband* 11 cm wide by 44 cm long; two 6.5 cm by 69 cm *ties*.

To finish side edges of apron, stitch 5 mm from edge, turn, topstitch in place. Turn 5 mm again and topstitch. Finish both long edges and one end of ties the same way. To hem apron, turn cut edge under and topstitch; turn up an 8.5 cm hem and topstitch in place. Place the scalloped edge of the edging on hemline; stitch lace in place along top and sides. Stay-stitch along seamline of pocket lining. Turn back seam allowance; clip and notch as needed. Stitch in place with two rows of straight stitch or one of zigzag; trim excess. Centre pocket lining, seam allowance up, on right half of apron, bottom edge 14 cm up from top of lace. Topstitch in place; hand-sew lace to pocket.

Divide top edge of apron into three 20 cm sections; place gathering stitches along seamline of first and last parts. Turn under seam allowance at each end of the waistband; place a pin 10 cm in from fold. With right sides together, pin waistband to apron front, gathering fullness to fit 10 cm spaces at ends of the waistband. Stitch; trim seam allowances. Turn waistband to right side, turn under second seam allowance, slipstitch band in place. Slip unfinished end of a tie into each end of waistband; topstitch in place.

Make a complete pricking for the edging with ten complete repeats of the fan, putting in all dots, lines and numbers exactly as shown.

EDGING (9 cm by 61 cm)

This pattern introduces three traditional torchon motifs: spider (white), made with 6 pairs of bobbins; zigzag (ecru), often worked in half stitch but here in whole stitch; fan (blue), also in whole stitch, with twists between stitches. The straight edge is the **footing**; the opposite side, which hangs freely, is the **heading**; ground pattern is torchon.

Prepare pricking, using graph paper as specified, with ten complete repeats of fan. Spider begins and ends at its centre pin. Broken line indicates last row. Pin prepared pricking as near as possible to top of board and a place or two on the sides. Prick through all dots.

Prepare 14 pairs of bobbins as follows: 2 prs white, 1.5 m each bobbin; hang both pairs at b. 10 prs white, 2 m each bobbin; hang 2 prs at a, 6 prs at c, 1 pr each at d and f. 1 pr ecru, 4.5 m each bobbin; hang at e, 1 pr blue, 5.5 m each bobbin; hang at e. To secure bobbins around pins, w st prs 1-2. At e, place ecru pr left, blue pr right. Make w st and place pin between two prs at first hole below e (has no number), t both prs and make another w st. Ecru should be left, blue right. With prs 5 to 10 at c, work as follows: w st prs 8-7, 7-6, 6-5. w st prs 9-8, 8-7, 7-6. w st prs 10-9, 9-8, 8-7. Draw up around pin carefully, making sts lie flat and tight. Then twist prs 5, 6, 7 twice, prs 8, 9, 10 three times.

Torchon ground and footing:
t pr 2 twice, w st prs 2-3, w st prs 3-4, t,c prs 5-4, pin No. 1, t,c.
Footing: t pr 4, w st prs 4-3, w st prs 3-2, t prs 2-1 twice, c, pin at No. 2, t,c. t pr 2 twice, w st prs 2-3, w st prs 3-4. (Hint: pull down on both passive prs and up on the active pr before placing pin.)
t,c prs 6-5, pin No. 3, t,c. t,c prs 5-4, pin No. 4, t,c. Rep footing, pin No. 5, t,c prs 7-6, pin No. 6, t,c. t,c prs 6-5, pin No. 7, t,c. t,c prs 5-4, pin No. 8, t,c. Rep footing, pin No. 9.
Zigzag, 1st half: w st prs 12-11, w st prs 11-10, pin No. 10.
*Pattern repeat begins here
t pr 10, w st prs 10-11, w st prs 11-12, pin No. 11. t pr 12, w st prs 12-11, 11-10, 10-9, pin No. 12. t pr

9, w st prs 9-10, 10-11, pin No. 13. t pr 11, w st prs 11-10, 10-9, 9-8, pin No. 14. t pr 8, w st prs 8-9, 9-10, pin No. 15. t pr 10, w st prs 10-9, 9-8, t pr 7, w st prs 8-7, pin No. 16. t pr 7, w st prs 7-8, 8-9, pin No. 17. t pr 9, w st prs 9-8, 8-7, t pr 6, w st prs 7-6, pin No. 18.
Fan, bobbin prs 9 to 14 (draw up sts carefully after each row): t,c,t,c prs 13-14, pin No. 19. t,c,t,c prs 14-13, 13-12, 12-11, 11-10, 10-9, pin No. 20. t,c,t,c prs 9-10, 10-11, 11-12, 12-13, 13-14, pin No. 21. t,c,t,c prs 14-13, 13-12, 12-11, 11-10, 10-9, pin No. 22. t,c,t,c prs 10-11, 11-12, 12-13, 13-14, pin No. 23. t,c,t,c prs 14-13, 13-12, 12-11, pin No. 24. t,c,t,c prs 11-12, 12-13, 13-14, pin No. 25. t,c,t,c prs 14-13, 13-12, pin No. 26. t,c,t,c prs 12-13, 13-14, pin No. 27. t,c,t,c prs 14-13, 13-12, pin No. 28. t,c,t,c prs 12-13, 13-14, pin No. 29. t,c,t,c prs 14 to 11, pin No. 30. t,c,t,c prs 11 to 14, pin No. 31. t,c,t,c prs 14 to 10, pin No. 32. t,c,t,c prs 10 to 14, pin No. 33. t,c,t,c prs 14 to 9, pin No. 34. t,c,t,c prs 9 to 14, pin No. 35. t,c,t,c prs 13-14.

Zigzag, 2nd half, prs 6 to 13:
t pr 6, w st prs 6-7, 7-8, t pr 9, w st prs 8-9, pin No. 36. t pr 9, w st prs 9-8, 8-7, pin No. 37. t pr 7, w st prs 7-8, 8-9, t pr 10, w st prs 9-10, pin No. 38. t pr 10, w st prs 10-9, 9-8, pin No. 39. t pr 8, w st prs 8-9, 9-10, t pr 11, w st prs 10-11, pin No. 40. t pr 11, w st prs 11-10, 10-9, pin No. 41. t pr 9, w st prs 9-10, 10-11, t pr 12, w st prs 11-12, pin No. 42. t pr 12, w st prs 12-11, 11-10, pin No. 43. t pr 10, w st prs 10-11, 11-12, t pr 13, w st prs 12-13, pin No. 44. t pr 13, w st prs 13-12, 12-11, pin No. 45. t pr 11, w st prs 11-12, 12-13, pin No. 46.

Torchon ground and footing, 2nd part, prs 1 to 7: t,c prs 6-5, pin No. 47. t,c. t,c prs 5-4, pin No. 48, t,c. Rep footing, pin No. 49. t,c prs 7-6, pin No. 50, t,c. t,c prs 6-5, pin No. 51, t,c. t,c prs 5-4, pin No. 52, t,c. Rep footing, pin No. 53.

Spider, prs 5 to 10: t prs 5 to 10 three times each pr. *w st prs 8-7, 7-6, 6-5. w st prs 9-8, 8-7, 7-6. w st prs 10-9, 9-8, 8-7*, pin No. 54 (between 8 and 7). Draw up carefully around pin. Rep * to *. Draw up carefully again. Twist prs 5, 6, 7 twice, prs 8, 9, 10 three times.

Torchon ground and footing, 1st part, prs 1 to 7: t,c prs 5-4, pin No. 55, t,c. Rep footing, pin No. 56. t,c prs 6-5, pin No. 57, t,c. t,c prs 5-4, pin No. 58, t,c. Rep footing, pin No. 59. t,c prs 7-6, pin No. 60, t,c. t,c prs 6-5, pin No. 61, t,c. t,c prs 5-4, pin No. 62, t,c. Rep footing, pin No. 63.

Zigzag, 1st half, prs 6-13: t pr 13. w st prs 13-12, 12-11, 11-10, pin No. 64.
Repeat from
To finish off, tie bobbin prs together in tight reef knot around last pin. Clip close to knot or weave ends back with tapestry needle. Steam lace if desired (footing especially may need it if it has pulled in slightly).

MEDALLION (about 19 cm wide, 20 cm deep at widest and deepest points)
Pricking (p. 346) is half the total pattern (a bit more for correct placing) shown actual size. Flower (worked first) is in red; vine, stems and leaves are black; fillings are black. Dots are pinholes; second rows of dots mark picots. Circled dots are sewings; two circles signify two sewings at the same place. Tie off bobbin pairs with sewings to start of tape; touch knots with glue if necessary.

Trace half given, reverse paper, trace again, matching carefully in centre. Second half mirrors first, except for working direction of flower fillings – left to right on both sides. Trim paper about 5 mm around design; pin to centre of board.

FLOWER
Centre. 6 prs bobbins. 4 prs blue and 1 pr white, 50 cm each bobbin; 1 pr white, 1.25 m each bobbin (active pr). Hang 2 prs blue each at a and b; 2 prs white at c with the active pr outside. *t,c,t,c prs 6-5, t pr 5. w st prs 5-4, 4-3, 3-2, 2-1, pin No. 1. t pr 1. w st prs 1-2, 2-3, 3-4, 4-5, t,c,t,c prs 5-6, pin No. 2, repeat from *. After pin No. 3, place a pin at No. 4. Twist active 3 times, go around pin, t twice and continue as usual. Do this each time where indicated; the last time, t 3 times, make a sewing through all loops at No. 4, t twice. Tie off threads at beginning.

Petals. Large portion of petal done in h st with one white pr at each side in w st to form an outline. Small area at inner curve between crosshatchings is done in w st with a blind pinhole. 6 prs bobbins. 2 prs white, 1.50 m each; 4 prs blue, 2.5 m each. Hang 1 pr white and 1 pr blue at a with white at outside, 2 prs blue at b, 1 pr blue and 1 pr white at c with blue at outside. *Begin w st area:* t pr 6, w st through pr 2, t pr 1, w st prs 2-1, pin No. 1. t pr 1. w st through pr 6, pin No. 2. t pr 6. w st through pr 2, t pr 1. w st prs 2-1, sewing at No. 3. *Blind pinhole:* t pr 1, w st through pr 4, pin No. 4. w st back through pr 1, pin No. 5. Remove pin No. 4 and pull on actives gently, do not replace pin No. 4. Repeat this procedure for pin No. 6 and sewing at No. 7. Continue with w st through all prs until pin No. 11 is reached. *Change to h st ground:* *t,c,t,c prs 1-2. h st prs 2-3, 3-4, 4-5, t,c,t,c prs 5-6, pin No. 12. t,c,t,c prs 6-5, h st through pr 2, t,c,t,c prs 2-1, pin No. 13. Repeat these two rows until crosshatched bar indicates change to w st. First picot occurs after pin No. 20. These are made exactly as in the

sampler (directions, p. 343). After placing the pin for the picot, work the knot so that it lies snugly against pin No. 20, then continue as before. Work all around the 5 petals, fastening off thread to the beginning of the tape.

VINE, STEM, LEAF
These are worked all in one braid, beginning with the scroll on the right and ending with the scroll on the left. The tape works down the right side, across the bottom centre to the left side of the loop. The left stem and leaf are worked next, then the top of the bottom loop, then the right stem and leaf. The bottom loop is then completed with the tape passing over the completed tape at bottom centre and continuing up the left side.

Before starting, remove the pins of petal picots, which will be covered by subsequent work. 6 prs bobbins. 3 prs ecru, 2.5 m each bobbin; 1 pr white, 1.25 m each bobbin; 2 prs white, 4 m each bobbin. Hang the two large prs of white bobbins, one at a and one at c. Hang 2 prs ecru at b. The last 2 prs of bobbins will be added after completion of the scroll. The scroll is worked with these 4 prs in w st ground (refer to sampler if necessary). Blind pins are made through two prs of passives. Two sewings are made along the way, with a third at a, when the work is stopped at A. At this point, the last two prs of bobbins are added: the ecru pr to the two ecru prs at b, and the white prs to the white pr at c, all with sewings.

Vine. Now begin the vine down the right side, which is worked exactly like the Russian braid in the sampler (refer if necessary), with sewings where indicated; be careful not to undo the knot on the picot when tightening the sewing. Continue across the bottom centre and up the left side of the bottom loop to point B. Pin the active and the first passive pr (both white) out of the way. The stem and leaf are made with the remaining 4 prs with the remaining white pr as active.

Stem, lower half. Made with 4 prs in w st ground exactly as for the scroll with the white pr as active. The bottom half of the stem is made first, with the upper half being made after the leaf is completed and attached with sewings all the way down the centre. Begin by taking up pr 4 (white pr) at C, t, and w st across, pin No. 1, then continue up the bottom half of the stem. The blind pin near the top is taken through two prs. Stem ends at point D.

Leaf. The upper half is made first, in w st, then the lower half in h st, with sewings down the centre, and picots at the edge. To begin: continue w st ground for pins No. 1 and 2. After pin No. 2 and through pin No. 14, t the active pr once between each st to separate the sts. Then continue around the tip in plain w st ground, going through 2 prs for the blind pins, and pulling down sts very

Apron trimmed with bobbin lace

carefully to make the tip firm and even. Stop work when pin is placed at E. Begin h st: take up pr 1, which is hanging from pin No. 14, and h st prs 1-2, 2-3, t,c,t,c prs 3-4, pin F, make picot. t,c,t,c prs 4-3, h st through pr 1, make sewing. Continue to point D.

Stem, upper half. At G, remove pin and replace between prs 4 and 3. Begin w st ground with pr 4, making a sewing at centre of stem. Continue down stem, with a sewing at the leaf tip, ending at point H.

Continue vine. Take up the first two prs at B and continue with the Russian braid pattern, starting with prs 1 and 2. Remove the pin at H and re-use it as the first pinhole for the continuation of the vine.

Second stem and leaf. These are worked like the first except that the upper half of the stem and lower half of the leaf are worked first. Continue

vine to point B. At H, begin stem as before, with the white pr as active. Work stem to point G. Place pin between prs 1 and 2 at D, and begin h st with prs 1 and 2 with w st through the white pr as before, using hole at G as first pinhole (replace pin). Then continue to pin No. 2, remembering the extra twist around the centre pins. Work to pin No. 14, then: t pr 1, h st prs 1-2, 2-3. Place pin at E between prs 3 and 4. t pr 4, w st prs 4-3, 3-2, blind pin. Continue around tip with w st as before, making a sewing at the tip and another at pin No. 14. Continue with w st ground as before, twisting actives once between each st, to pin No. 2. Continue in plain w st ground, making a sewing at D, and work down stem to C. Pick up bobbins at B and continue vine, using pinhole at C twice.

Rest of vine and scroll. Remove pins that will be covered, and continue working the vine right over the first part at bottom centre, making sewings in

the four corners. At A, pin prs 1 and 2 aside and work around scroll as before. Make sewing with active pr at a and tie off. Make sewings with remaining bobbins, one or two prs together, and tie off.

Fillings. 8 prs bobbins, each wound with 2 m white. All fillings are made with these pairs, without re-winding, which means that the ends of each pair are knotted together at the beginning of each section, then attached to the work with a sewing so that the knot is placed against the sewing the same as when finishing off.

Brussels ground (filling for petals of flower). Attach one pr each at a,c,d,f and 2 prs knotted together at b and e. Make Brussels ground (see sampler) with sewings at sides where indicated (t pr once before making sewing).

prs 2-1 No. 1, sewing pr 1 at g. prs 4-3 No. 2, prs 3-2 No. 3, prs 2-1 No. 4, sewing pr 1 at h. prs 6-5 No. 5, prs 5-4 No. 6, prs 4-3 No. 7, prs 3-2 No. 8, sewing pr 2 at i. prs 8-7 No. 9, sewing pr 8 at j. prs 7-6 No. 10, prs 6-5 No. 11, prs 5-4 No. 12, prs 4-3

No. 13, sewing pr 3 at k. prs 8-7 No. 14, sewing pr 8 at l. prs 7-6 No. 15, sewing pr 7 at m. prs 6-5 No. 16, sewing pr 6 at n. prs 5-4 No. 17, prs 4-3 No. 18, sewing pr 3 at o. prs 6-5 No. 19, sewing pr 6 at p. sewing prs 5-4 together at q. Tie off all prs and move to next petal.

Plaits (continue with same bobbins, 4 pairs). Attach with sewings two prs together at A and B. Make two plaits with windmill joins at crossings (see p. 343) and sewings where indicated (sewings may be made with one pr or both prs together, as you prefer). At C, knot and cut off bobbins and re-attach at F. With other plait, make sewing at D, continue plait to E, making sewing, and start next section with bobbins hanging at F. Plaits are continued across the stems to bottom section (will not show from front) – from blue H to blue C and from leaf tip to G. Tie off at H and I and re-attach at J for centre section. Tie off at K and complete plaits on other side. Making sure that all knots are secure, remove all pins, turn lace over, and sew to pocket of apron.

Pricking for medallion is actual size, but only gives half the design, plus a bit more for correct placing. The broken line near the bottom shows exact halfway point.

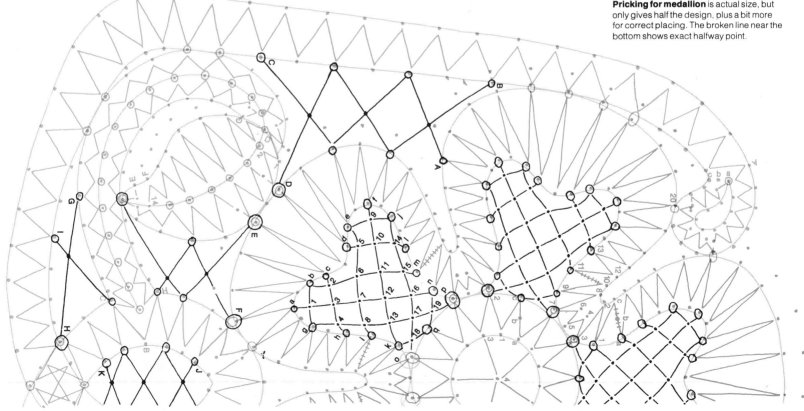

Lace
weaves

Introduction

Lace can be created by the technique of weaving, which is the interlacing of two sets of threads, the warp and the weft, to produce a textile. In most forms of weaving, all warp threads are parallel to each other and all weft threads are parallel to each other, with the warp and the weft at right-angles to one another. In lace weaving, warp and weft are diverted somewhat from their parallel course to form spaces in the weave. The resulting textile is an openwork form of lace.

Lace weaving can be worked on a simple frame loom or a complex mechanical one. Whichever loom is used, lace weaving is manoeuvred by the weaver. The technique, in fact, is called weaver-controlled or finger-controlled because, to manipulate warp or weft threads, the weaver uses her fingers or a stick-like instrument rather than the mechanism of the loom.

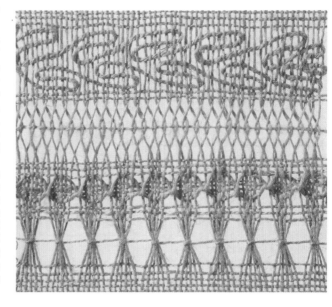

The woven lace sampler, left, incorporates a variety of the lace weaves shown on pp. 349–50. They are, from top to bottom: Spanish lace, Mexican lace, Danish medallion and Brook's bouquet.

Materials

Lace weaves can be worked on any loom. The purpose of the loom is to keep the warp threads evenly spaced and under tension while the weft is passed over and under them. We chose to work on a frame loom because it is simple to use and inexpensive. The weaves shown on pp. 349–50, however, can be woven on almost any loom you may have.

To make a frame loom, you will need canvas stretcher bars, available at art shops in different sizes. You will need one set of two bars for the width of the frame, and one set of two bars for the length of the frame. To decide what size frame you need for the size weaving you want to make, see p. 348. To assemble the stretcher bars into a frame loom, see p. 348.

For the weaving process, you will also need a shuttle, a tool used for carrying the weft; a shed sword or shed stick, a tool used to help in manipulating the warp threads; and appropriate thread.

Canvas stretchers, sold at artists' suppliers, can be used to make a frame loom.

A shuttle is a flat wooden stick with a deep indentation at each end; the weft thread is wrapped on the shuttle (see p. 348).

Yarns for lace weaving include fine, strong linen thread in sizes 10/1, 10/2 or 10/5. For an explanation of the sizes, see p. 371.

A shed sword or pick-up stick is a flat stick pointed at one end. It is slightly longer than width of weaving.

Lace weaves

Setting up the loom

On a frame loom, the maximum size of the textile you can weave is slightly less than the dimensions of *the frame opening*. Maximum width is 2 to 5 cm less; maximum length is about 15 cm less because warp threads become too tight to work with as a consequence of what is called *take up*. Take up is the small amount of warp that is used up as the warp threads curve over and under the weft. Since stretcher bars, which are 4 cm wide, are sold by their outside length measurement, you must use a frame that is larger than the size weaving you want. If, for example, you want to weave a 25 by 40 cm textile, you will need a 40 by 65 cm stretcher frame.

To estimate the amount of warp thread needed, multiply warp threads per centimetre (see Step 2, below) by width of weaving by *length of loom*. To estimate the amount of weft, multiply weft threads per centimetre by width of weaving by *length of weaving*.

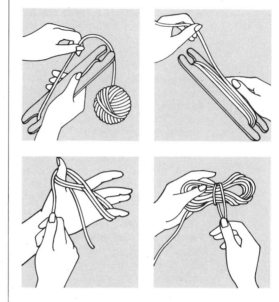

Weaving is the interlacing of weft threads and warp threads. On a frame loom, warp threads are first wrapped around the loom so they are held taut. Weft is woven over and under the warp.

Preparing the weft

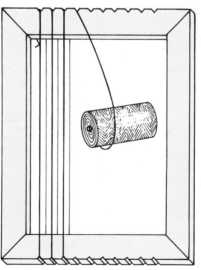

To wind thread on to a shuttle, hold thread end against shuttle with your thumb (left). Wind thread around shuttle so thread end is secured (right). Continue winding thread, making sure you do not pull it as you wind. Do not wind too much thread on shuttle or it will not pass easily through the warp.

To make a butterfly, wind thread in a figure-eight around your thumb and little finger (left). Slip the bundle off your fingers and secure it in the centre with a rubber band (right).

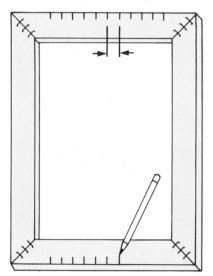

1. Assemble the stretcher bars by fitting the corners together. Be sure corners make a true square; staple them to secure the joins. With a pencil, mark off centimetres along top and bottom of the frame on the outer edge.

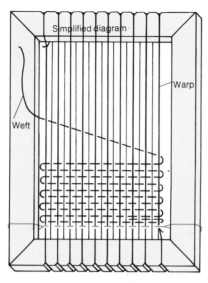

2. To determine number of warp threads per centimetre, wind thread around ruler. Count wraps; multiply by width to be woven. Divide amount in half to give numbers of threads for front and back of loom.

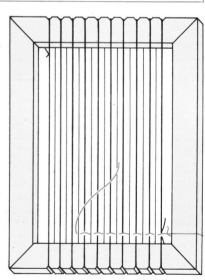

3. Mark threads per centimetre along frame top. With small saw, make a notch at each mark; sand frame. Tie warp to frame at top left. Bring warp down the front, around bottom edge, and up the back, keeping thread in the notches.

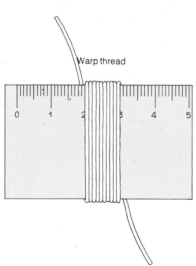

4. As you warp the loom, keep the tension slack but not loose. Threads are now in two layers – in front of and behind loom. To make them one layer, weave a piece of string, called a heading, over top and under bottom threads. Tie at sides.

The weaves

Plain weave is the simplest weave; the weft goes over one warp thread and under the next across the row. On a frame loom, one shed or space between warp threads is already created by the loom. The first weft shot (term for passage of weft) goes in this shed; pass the shuttle through this space (A), leaving an 8 cm tail. Pack the weft in with a fork. For the next row, weft goes in the *countershed*, created by weaving shed stick *over* threads on top of loom and *under* threads behind it. Turn stick on its side and pass the shuttle through the space made by it (B). Put tail in this shed. Repeat these rows.

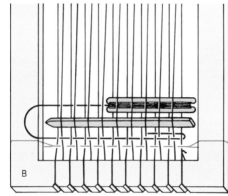

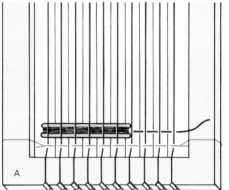

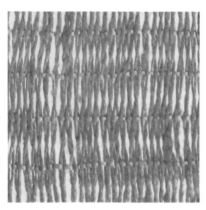

Gauze or leno weave is created by manipulating warp threads so they change places with one another. If *one* warp thread changes places with one other, the lace is 1/1 gauze; if *pairs* of threads change places, the lace is called 2/2. Starting at the right side, pick up the far right thread and bring it to the left over the second thread. Pick up the second thread with the shed stick, letting the first thread fall beneath it. Work across the row in this way (A). Turn stick on its side and insert the weft. Then work a row of plain weave left to right (B). Continue alternating these two rows.

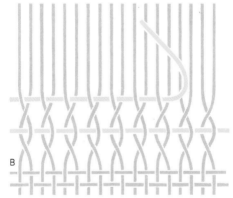

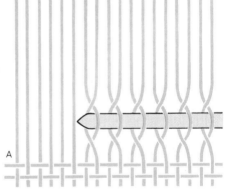

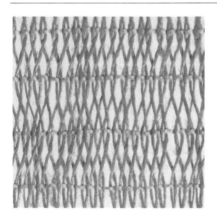

Mexican lace is a variation of the gauze weave. Starting at the right, twist first thread over third, pick up third. To begin pattern, twist second thread over fifth, pick up fifth. Twist fourth thread over seventh, pick up seventh. Continue across the row in this way, twisting the next untwisted even-numbered thread with the next odd-numbered one three threads away (A). Turn the shed stick on its side and insert the weft. Then work a row of plain weave to maintain the twists (B). Repeat these two rows.

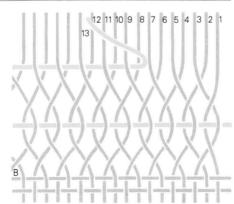

13 12 11 10 9 8 7 6 5 4 3 2 1

12 11 10 9 8 7 6 5 4 3 2 1
13

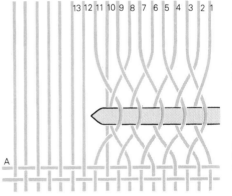

Lace weaves

The weaves

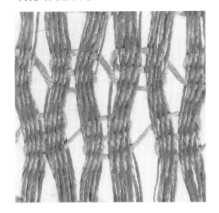

Spanish lace is worked with a butterfly rather than a shuttle. Starting on the right, weave a small group of warp threads in plain weave, going back and forth as many times as you like. Here, it is three times (A). Carry the weft to the next group of warp threads and weave this group the same number of times as the first. Continue across the row this way. Many variations in this pattern can be made with the second row of weaving (B) by changing the groups of threads, varying the number of warp threads in each group, and alternating and splitting groups.

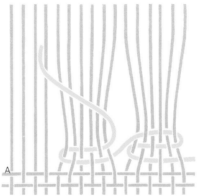 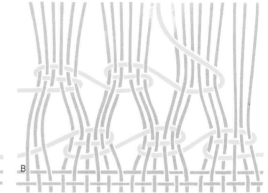

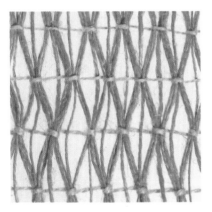

Brook's bouquet is a lace pattern that uses the same technique as backstitch in embroidery. The weft is carried over warp threads and then back under them. Begin this weave after several rows of plain weave. Bring the weft under a group of warp threads, up over the threads, and back under them. Pull the weft to gather the warp threads (A). Continue gathering groups, leaving one warp thread between them as shown here, or no threads between groups. For second row, alternate the placing of groups, centring them between two groups in the previous row (B).

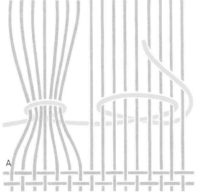 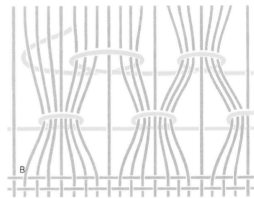

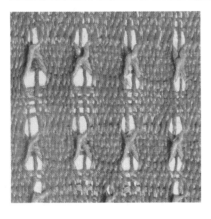

Danish medallion consists mostly of plain weave using two different weft threads. Primary weft thread is usually the same as the warp; secondary weft contrasts in colour, weight or texture. To begin, weave a row of secondary weft from left to right. Change to primary weft and weave several rows of plain weave. Determine where you want the medallions to be; use a crochet hook to pull up a loop of secondary weft half as high as the plain weave (A). Weave secondary weft from right to first loop; pull weft through loop with crochet hook (B). Weave to next loop and pull weft through it. Repeat.

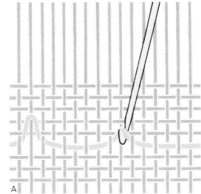 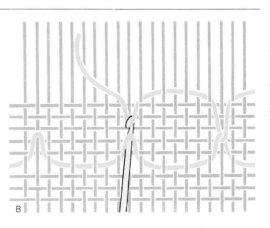

Woven lace place mat

Lace bands on place mat are 2/2 gauze or leno, a variation of 1/1 gauze shown on p. 349.

The 30 by 45 cm linen place mat has a red warp and pale blue weft. A 5 cm wide area of lace, called 2/2 leno or gauze (see below), is woven on either side of the centre area.

Materials needed

100 m of 2/10 linen thread (for an explanation of thread size, see p. 371) for the warp for one place mat
60 m of 2/10 linen thread for the weft for one place mat
45 by 75 cm wood stretcher frame
Pencil
Ruler
Small saw
Sandpaper
50 cm string
Shuttle
Shed stick

The mat

The place mat is worked from side edge to side edge. The width of the weaving in this case is the height of the place mat; the height of the weaving is the width of the place mat. The place mat is mainly plain weave (see p. 349), with a lace inset on either side of 2/2 leno or gauze weave, a variation of the 1/1 gauze weave shown on p. 349. In 2/2 gauze, pairs of warp threads are twisted around each other so they change places and create a space in the weave.

Setting up a frame loom

To make the loom and to attach the warp threads, see. p. 348. There are 10 warp threads per 2.5 cm (see p. 348). Make 10 marks along each 2.5 cm marked on the frame loom. Saw a small notch at each mark; sand the edge to eliminate any splinters. Wind the warp on to the loom, keeping the tension of the threads even as you wind. Weave a heading (a piece of string) over the top threads and under the bottom ones (see p. 348).

Weaving

With the weft thread, weave 5 cm of plain weave (see p. 349). End the plain weave with the weft going from left to right; then start the lace weave. On the

right, use your fingers to pull the two threads on the far right towards the left and over the next two threads to the left to create a twist. Pick up the second two threads with the shed stick, letting the first two threads fall under the stick (see A, below). With these two threads still on the stick, pull threads 5 and 6 to the left over threads 7 and 8. Pick up threads 7 and 8. Continue this way across the row, each time picking up the two threads on the right after the twist is made. When you finish the row, turn the stick on its side to create a shed or space for the weft and put the weft through the shed from right to left. For the next row, work a row of plain weave but go over and under *pairs* of threads rather than single ones; this will retain the twist (see B, below). Continue alternating these two rows until the lace measures 5 cm. Then work the plain weave for 25.5 cm and the lace weave for 5 cm; finish with 5 cm of plain weave. To end the weft, cut off the excess, leaving a 5 cm tail. Wrap tail round end warp thread and put it back in the shed.

Fringing

At top and bottom of loom, cut pairs of warp threads; tie in overhand knot (see below). Knot as you cut; do not cut all threads at once. Trim the ends.

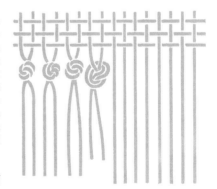

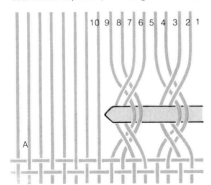

For 2/2 gauze weave, bring two end warps to the left over the next two threads. Pick up second pair on shed stick. Continue to end of row.

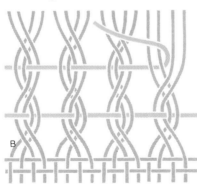

For second row, work row of plain weave, going over and under *pairs of threads* to keep twist created in first row. Alternate these two rows.

To keep the ends of the place mat from unravelling, knot each pair of warp threads with an overhand knot as shown. Trim ends even.

Hairpin crochet lace

Making strips
Joining strips
Finishing edges
Variations
Hairpin crochet lace shawl

Making strips

Hairpin crochet lace is a type of crochet worked with a two-pronged fork, or hairpin, and a crochet hook. Yarn is wound round the prongs of the hairpin to form a series of large loops held together by a row of crochet stitches worked in the centre, called the spine. The strips produced by this process are then joined together. (See opposite page for methods of joining.) The width of the strips is determined by the distance between the prongs. The hairpins are U-shaped, and available in a wide range of sizes from 10 mm to 100 mm. They may or may not incorporate detachable clips for use at the end of the prongs. (See diagrams below for placing.) The lacy strips can be made from any type of yarn from thin cotton to thick knitting yarn. Directions for the basic crochet stitches are on pp. 273–5.

1. To begin, hold the hairpin in the left hand with prongs pointing downwards. Use the metal clip if it is provided with the hairpin. Make a slip knot in the yarn and slide the loop that it forms on to the left prong. Adjust the knot so that it is in the centre between the prongs.

Metal clip

2. Wind the yarn around the right prong, front to back, and hold it taut with your left hand. Insert the crochet hook under the front strand of the loop. Pick up the yarn at the back and bring it through the loop to form a loop on the hook.

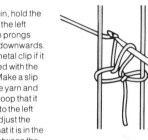

3. With the crochet hook, pick up the yarn at the back again. This is called yarn round hook.

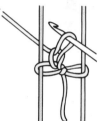

4. Draw the yarn through the loop on the hook; you will have one loop on the hook. This completes the joining of the first loop on the right of the hairpin.

5. Remove the hook from the loop. From the back, insert the hook in the dropped loop. Turn the hairpin from right to left in front of you.

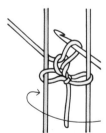

6. Turning the hairpin causes the yarn to wrap round what is now the right prong to form another loop. The crochet hook is now at the front of the hairpin.

7. This new loop is secured in the centre with a double crochet stitch. To do this, insert hook under front strand of left loop, yarn round hook and draw through the left loop so you have two loops on the hook.

8. Yarn round hook and draw through both loops on the hook. Continue making the strip by repeating steps 5, 6, 7 and 8. Each new loop is formed by turning the hairpin at the completion of double crochet stitch in the centre.

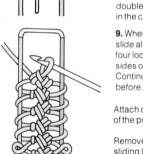

9. When hairpin is full, slide all but the top four loops on both sides off the prongs. Continue working as before.

Attach clip at the end of the prongs.

Remove clip before sliding loops off prongs, then replace.

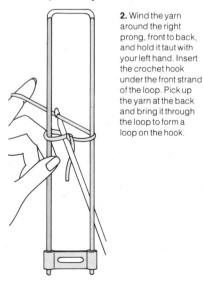

Metal clip

Joining strips

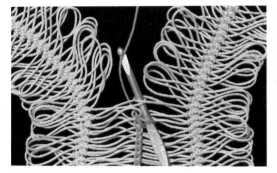

Slipstitch. With a crochet hook and extra yarn held underneath the work, join the strips by inserting the hook into one loop from left and one loop from right strip. Slipstitch them together by catching yarn on hook and drawing it through the three loops.

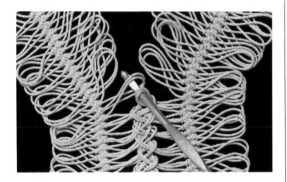

Weaving. This method requires no extra yarn. Insert the crochet hook into one, two or three loops of one strip, then into the same number of loops of the other strip. Draw the second group through the first. Continue along the length of the strips.

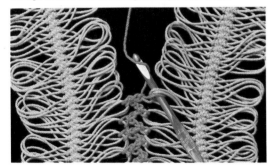

Chain stitch. With a crochet hook and extra yarn, pick up two loops from one strip and work a double crochet stitch (p. 274) in the space. Work 2 chain (p. 273), pick up two loops from the other strip and work a double crochet in the space, 2 chain. Repeat.

Finishing edges

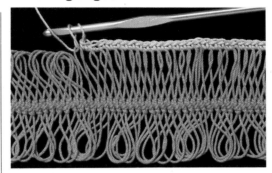

A double crochet stitch along the edge is the simplest way to finish the outside loops of a strip. To do this, make a loop on the hook with a separate length of yarn. Work a double crochet stitch into each loop along the length of the strip.

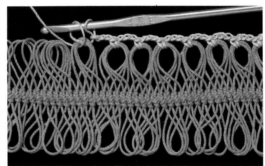

To group the loops, pick up several loops, keeping the twist in them. Work a double crochet stitch in the centre space of the groups of loops. Make a chain between groups of loops that has one stitch less than the number of loops you picked up.

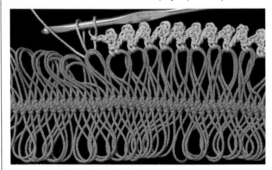

To make a picot edging, work a double crochet stitch into first two loops held together. 4 chain, work a double crochet stitch into third chain from hook, 2 chain, work a double crochet stitch into next two loops held together. Repeat from the 4 chain.

Variations

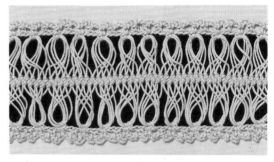

An insertion. Make a strip of the appropriate length. To edge each side, work 1 dc (for abbreviations, see p. 366) in first 4 loops, keeping the twist in them, 3 ch. Repeat for the length of the strip. For second row, work 1 dc in dc of previous row, 3 ch, 1 dc in centre stitch of 3 ch loop, 3 ch. Repeat across row.

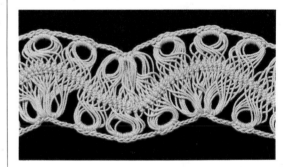

A wavy band. Make a strip of the appropriate length. To edge one side, work (4 dc in 6 loops held together, 4 ch) 3 times, then work (1 dc in 6 loops held together) 3 times, 4 ch. On the other side, start with second group of stitches – double crochet without chain stitches – so groups are opposite each other.

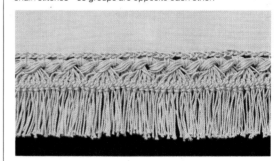

Fringe. Make two strips of the appropriate length. Join the two strips by weaving them together. Fold the resulting band in half so that the weaving is on top. To finish this edge, work 1 dc in the first space, 2 ch, work 1 dc in the next space, 2 ch. Repeat along the strip. For fringe, cut loops along other side of strip.

353

Hairpin crochet lace shawl

For added glamour, make this shawl in chenille.

This shawl is made of one long strip of hairpin crochet laid out in an oval shape and joined together with chain stitches. The fringe is a wider strip.

Materials needed
Double double knitting wool in 50 g balls: 15 light colour; 9 dark colour
80 mm and 100 mm hairpins
Crochet hook size 5.00

Making the strip
Directions for making the basic hairpin crochet strip are on p. 352. To begin the shawl, with light coloured yarn on the 80 mm hairpin, *make a strip with 15 dc (8 loops on one side, 7 on the other). Turn hairpin, then make a bobble: 1 tr in front thread of last loop, 1 ch, (yrh, insert hook between tr and last dc, draw up a loop, yrh, draw through 2 loops) 4 times. Yrh, draw through all 5 loops on hook, 1 ch*. (Total of 8 loops on each side of hairpin.) Repeat from * to * until you have 151 bobbles; end strip with 16 dc. During work, as loops are dropped from the hairpin, tie 8 loops together

with spare yarn on the right side, then next 8 loops on the left side; leave 8 loops between yarn markers free.

Edging the loops
With dark colour, attach yarn to first dc at the beginning of strip, 2 ch, *insert hook through 8 loops grouped together, remove spare yarn, work 4 dc through all 8 loops at once. This will automatically put a twist in the group of loops. 1 ch, (1 dc, 1 ch in next single loop, keeping twist) 8 times*. Repeat from * to * along the length of the strip. To work round end of strip: 2 ch, dc in last dc of strip, 3 ch. Continue pattern from * to * down opposite side of strip. End with 2 ch; fasten off yarn in first dc of strip.

Joining the strip
On a clean, flat surface, coil strip in an oval (see diagram, below left). Begin joining at outside edge and work inwards. Pattern for joining straight edges is shown in red; pattern for joining curves is shown in blue. All joining is done with light coloured yarn.
Straight joining: *1 ch, 1 dc in centre (4th) space between single loops in strip below; 4 ch, miss 2 loops, 1 dc in next space above; 4 ch, miss 2 loops, 1 dc in next space below; 8 ch, miss last 2 loops, 1 dc in space between last loop and the 4 dc in strip above; 8 ch, miss last 2 loops, 1 dc in space between last loop and 4 dc below; 1 dc in centre of 4 dc below, 1 ch, make a bobble, 1 ch; 1 dc in space between 4 dc and 1st single loop of next group below; 8 ch, 1 dc in space between 4 dc and 1st single loop of next group above; 8 ch, miss 2 loops, 1 dc in next space below; 4 ch, miss 2 loops, 1 dc in next space above; 4 ch, miss 2 loops, 1 dc in next space (centre) below; 1 ch, miss 2 loops, 1 dc in next space (centre) above*. Repeat from * to *. Centre space below will have 2 dc in it.
Curved joining: *1 ch, 1 dc in 4th (centre) space between single loops below; 4 ch, miss 2 loops, 1 dc in next

space above; 8 ch, miss 4 loops, 1 dc in space between last loop and 4 dc below; 1 dc in centre of 4 dc below; 1 ch, make a bobble, 1 ch; 1 dc in space between 4 dc and 1st single loop of next group below; 8 ch, 1 dc in same space as previous dc above; 4 ch, miss 4 loops, 1 dc in centre space between loops below; 1 ch, 1 dc in centre of 4 dc above; 1 ch, 1 dc in same space below as previous dc; 4 ch, miss 2 loops, 1 dc in next space above; 8 ch, miss 4 loops, 1 dc in space between last loop and 4 dc below; 1 dc in centre of 4 dc below, 1 ch, make a bobble, 1 ch; 1 dc in space between 4 dc and first single loop of next group below; 8 ch, 1 dc in same space as previous dc above; 4 ch, miss 4 loops, 1 dc in centre space between loops below; 1 ch, miss 2 loops, 1 dc in centre space above*. Repeat from * to *. Note three exceptions to the above: to taper strip end, at the beginning fasten yarn to centre space of single loops above and put 1st dc at beginning of single loops below. When working next dc below, miss 4 loops instead of 2. The very end of the joining ends with 2 extra dc with 1 ch between and a bobble. On the last curved repeat, the 2 centre dc with 1 ch between are omitted.

Fringe
With dark coloured yarn and 100 mm hairpin, make a strip with 480 loops on each side or 960 dc. Put markers at convenient intervals on one side to aid in counting. To join the fringe to the shawl, insert hook in space between single loops and the 4 dc, draw up 1st 2 loops of fringe, keeping twist in loops. Retain on hook. Insert hook in next space (to the left of the 4 dc), draw up next 2 loops of fringe, keeping twist in loops, and bring them through the 1st 2 loops on hook. Repeat. In every 4th (centre) space between single loops, draw up 4 fringe loops instead of 2. Continue round the edge this way; fasten last loops to first loops with a separate piece of yarn.

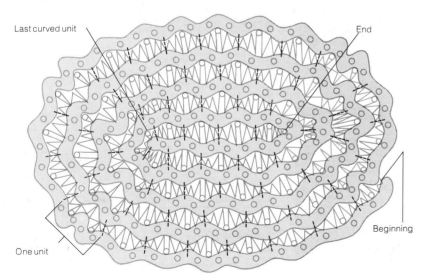

Last curved unit

End

One unit

Beginning

To join strip, lay it in an oval shape. Begin joining at outside edge and work in towards centre. Straight joining is shown in red, curved joining in blue. Pattern repeats are marked with dotted lines; joining begins with seven units of straight pattern, then one unit of curved.

Macramé

Macramé © 1978 Marion T. Leyds

Introduction to macramé

History

Macramé, the art of ornamental knotting, originated as a decorative way of securing the ends of a piece of woven fabric, creating a lacy edge. Later macramé was worked separately and attached to both household items and garments as a trimming. By the Victorian era, entire items, such as tablecloths, were made of macramé.

The word macramé is derived from the Arabic word *migramah*, which translates as towel or shawl or the fringe on either one. It now means the process itself, regardless of the finished item.

There is some evidence that macramé fringes were used in Arabia as early as the 13th century. From there, the art of macramé spread very quickly. The Spanish learned it from the Moors; from Spain the technique spread to Italy and to France. The use of macramé for clothing decoration in these countries is documented in paintings. In England, Queen Mary, wife of William of Orange, taught macramé to her ladies-in-waiting.

British and American sailors are credited with perpetuating the craft. It was known as McNamara's Lace or Square Knotting because of the predominance of square knots in the work. The sailors knotted to while away the long hours at sea, and then used the things they had made for barter when they went ashore.

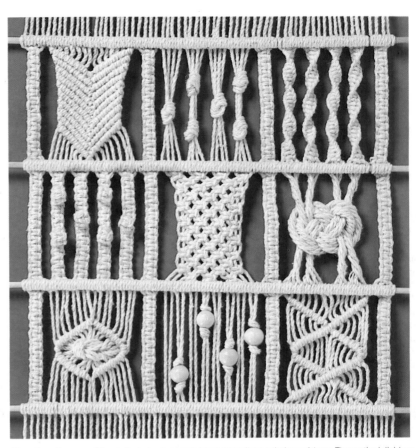

Sampler of macramé knots includes the basic knots as well as variations of them. The vertical dividers are sennits of square knots; the horizontal dividers are rows of double half hitches, worked on dowels.

Cords

It is possible to buy cords specially made for macramé, but suitable material may be found in the home. The knots use up the cords quickly, so large quantities are needed. The cords should be strong enough to withstand the abrasion of repeated knotting and should not have excessive give or elasticity. Household string, piping cord, garden twine or venetian-blind cord are types that work well; most knitting yarns are not suitable because they are too elastic.

Natural-fibre cords are used most often in macramé. *Cotton, linen* and *jute* are some of the most popular natural materials because they are readily available, knot easily, have the requisite strength, come in a variety of weights and colours and can be dyed. Jute is not colourfast, so it should not be made into a project that will be used outdoors. Certain *wool* yarns can be used if they are fairly regular in texture and are not too elastic; weaving wools are better

than knitting wools. *Silk* cord produces a beautiful knot, but it is expensive and not always easy to obtain.

Synthetic-fibre cords include acrylic and polyester, which knot easily and are weather-resistant. They are usually available in bright colours, and can also be dyed. Nylon and rayon are silky, shiny fibres that tend to slip during knotting unless damp. Synthetics combined with natural fibres give added strength to a cord.

Construction of the cord is another way to group macramé cords. Most cords are constructed of several lengths of fibres tightly twisted together. Each length is called a *ply*. A three-ply cord is composed of three separate lengths twisted together. The number of plies is not the same as the size measurement. A five-ply cord made of thin fibres can be smaller than a three-ply cord of thicker fibres. The size of a cord is given by its diameter measurement. Some cords are composed of lengths of fibres that are plaited rather than twisted together. Venetian-blind cord is an example of a plaited cord.

Cords with regular texture are best suited for macramé. They can be thick or thin, smooth or rough, but their thickness should not vary and they should not be knobbly. However, cords not suitable for whole projects, such as knobbly or elastic yarns, can often be introduced in small quantities.

Suppliers for cords are almost as diverse as the cords themselves. Besides local craft shops, try such outlets as hardware stores, stationers, ships' chandlers, garden centres, theatrical wholesalers, weaving shops and the haberdashery departments of big stores.

Cords for macramé are sold either by length in pre-packaged balls or skeins, or by weight, with the cord unwound from a large ball or tube and weighed on a scale. When buying by weight, do not assume that a bulkier cord will cost less than a thinner one in the long run. Thick cords are used up more rapidly, and weigh more per comparable length.

Before you buy a large amount of cord for an entire project, you may want to buy a small amount and test it. Knot an 8–10 cm square sample to see how the cord handles and what the knot pattern looks like worked in that particular cord. If the knotted item is going to be laundered or used outdoors, wash a piece of cord to test it for shrinkage and colour-fastness. When making a garment of a certain size, use sample to estimate length of cord needed.

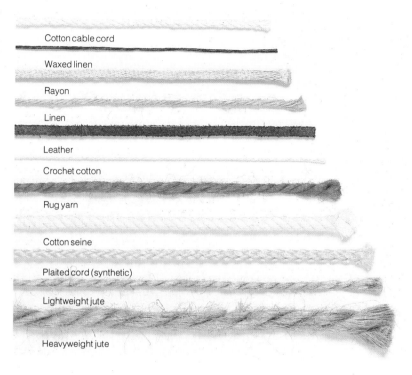

Cotton cable cord

Waxed linen

Rayon

Linen

Leather

Crochet cotton

Rug yarn

Cotton seine

Plaited cord (synthetic)

Lightweight jute

Heavyweight jute

Equipment

Macramé is one craft that requires very few tools. There are a few items, however, most of which can be found around the house, that will make the process of knotting easier and the end result more uniform.

Macramé is usually worked, especially by a beginner, on a flat surface called a *knotting board.* The board has to be thick enough to support the work, but soft enough to have pins inserted in it. Some suitable boards are insulating material, fibreboard, a clipboard, or a thick slab of foam rubber. To keep the cords and the knots even, the board may be covered with paper marked off in squares. A *G-cramp* attached to a table makes a good anchor for working lengths of macramé, such as a belt.

Cords to be knotted are mounted on a support so they can be tied under tension. A support can be another length of cord, a dowel, a ring or a belt buckle. A stretcher frame can also be used as a support. The finished macramé can be removed or, if you wish, left on, with the stretcher forming a frame.

Pins that can be used to hold cords to the board include glass-headed pins, millinery pins (which are extra long), and T-pins. You will also need a sturdy pair of scissors for cutting the cords, a tape measure or metrestick for measuring off lengths of cord, rubber bands to hold bundles of cord called *butterflies* (see next page), and Bulldog clips to hold the cords that are not being used out of the way of the working area.

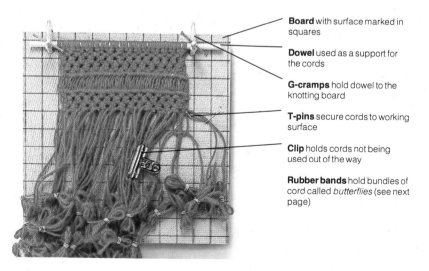

Board with surface marked in squares

Dowel used as a support for the cords

G-cramps hold dowel to the knotting board

T-pins secure cords to working surface

Clip holds cords not being used out of the way

Rubber bands hold bundles of cord called *butterflies* (see next page)

Introduction to macramé

Setting up

Estimating cord length. There is no exact formula for estimating the length of cords necessary for a particular macramé project, but a good way to start is with individual cords that are seven to eight times the length of the finished piece. This means that when the strands are folded over and mounted, each working cord will be three and a half to four times longer than the finished piece. As a beginner, add a little extra to your estimate because there are many factors that determine how much cord is needed. If a design is predominantly vertical, as a belt or plant holder would be, less cord will be required than for a design with many horizontal areas. If a design has lots of knots, it will take more cord than a design with areas of floating cords (cords without knots). Tightly tied knots require more cord than loosely tied knots. Thick cords are used up more rapidly than thin cords. As you gain experience, you will become better at estimating how much cord is needed for a particular project. It is ideal to start with cords that are long enough to finish the project, but if you should happen to run short in the middle of a project, there are several ways to add to cords (see p. 366).

Estimating the number of cords. To determine how many cords you will need, you must first decide how wide the piece is to be. A belt may be 5 cm wide; a wall hanging may be 38 cm wide. Take the cord you have chosen and lay strands side by side until they equal 1 cm. Multiply the number in 1 cm by the number of centimetres in your piece to get the total number of cords needed. For example, if you are making a 38 cm wide wall hanging, and there are two cords to the centimetre, you will need 76 cords; since each length of cord is folded over when mounted, you will need 38 lengths of cord.

Measuring and cutting cords. Measuring and cutting long cords can be cumbersome, but there are several ways to accomplish it efficiently. The simplest method is to measure one length with a ruler or metrestick, cut it, and use that length to measure all subsequent cords. If you have many cords to cut, you can attach two G-cramps to the edge of a table, setting them a distance apart equal to half the length of your cord. Tie the end of the cord to one G-cramp, wrap the cord around the other, and bring it back to the first. This span is equal to the length of one cord. Continue wrapping until you have the appropriate number of cords, then cut the cords at the first G-cramp. The cords are already halved and ready for mounting.

You can also measure cords using the backs of two chairs that are set a certain distance apart. Or you can wind the cord around two doorknobs or between the handles of kitchen cabinets. A weaver's warping board, a flat board that has pegs projecting at certain distances, is handy to use if one is available.

Anchoring cords. Macramé knots must be tied with the cords held under tension. The way this is accomplished varies with the particular project, the working materials and the amount of working space available. If you have never worked macramé knots before, it is advisable to do the work on a board (described on the previous page) so that you can pin cords to the board and follow the path of the cords. As you become more adept at tying the knots, you may want to dispense with the knotting board. There are several alternatives for anchoring the cords. If the cords are attached to a dowel, you can slip the dowel between the handles of two kitchen cabinets. If a mounting cord is used, tie the ends to the posts of an upright chair weighted down with a stack of books. Articles that are long and narrow, such as belts and plant holders, can be kept under tension by tying one end to a doorknob or the handle of a dresser drawer.

Terms and abbreviations

Terms used in macramé have evolved so that cords can be identified by their function as a piece is being worked. *A mounting cord* is the support on which the other cords are tied. This does not always have to be a cord; a dowel, a ring or a belt buckle can function as a mounting cord. *Knotting cords* are the cords that are actually tied in any given knot. *Anchor cords* are those cords within a knot that are not tied, as in the centre of a square knot (see p. 362). *A holding cord* or *knot-bearing cord* is a cord on which other cords are tied, as in the double half hitch knot (see p. 360). *Floating cords* are any cords within a design that are not knotted; areas of floating cords contrast nicely with knotted areas. *A sennit* is a chain made up of a series of one kind of knot.

Abbreviations are used in macramé directions so that the names of the individual knots (which are discussed on the pages that follow) do not have to be repeated. Where abbreviations are used, a key is provided; this is especially helpful because some knots are known by more than one name. These are the abbreviations of the knots used here:

ask	alternating square knot	**jk**	Josephine knot
ddhh	diagonal double half hitch	**lh**	lark's head knot
dhh	double half hitch	**ok**	overhand knot
hdhh	horizontal double half hitch	**rlh**	reverse lark's head knot
hk	half knot	**sk**	square knot
hc	holding cord	**vdhh**	vertical double half hitch

Making a butterfly

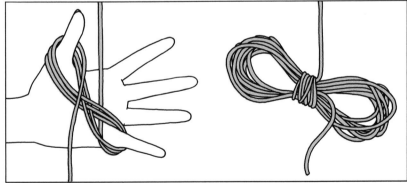

Handling long cords during knotting can be unwieldy. One way to avoid this awkwardness is to make a butterfly. Leave a length of cord below the mounting knot. Wind the remainder of the cord in a figure-eight shape around your thumb and little finger (above left). Slip the bundle off your hand and wrap the cord round the middle to secure it (above right). Do not start winding at the bottom end of the cord, or the excess cord will not pull out from the bundle as it should. If you are working with two cords together, wind both cords into the same butterfly. Otherwise, wind each cord separately so you can release as much of each cord as you need. Another method of handling long cords is to wind them around lace-bobbins, or small pieces of cardboard.

Basic macramé knots

Lark's head knot
Lark's head sennit
Double half hitch
Shaping with double half hitches
Square knot
Square knot sennits
Alternating square knots
The bobble
Gathering square knot

Lark's head knot

The lark's head knot is a mounting knot. Because macramé knots must be tied under tension, the cords are mounted on a support, such as a length of cord, a dowel or a ring. The lark's head knot is used to mount the knotting cords on that support. A series of lark's head knots forms a definite horizontal ridge along the bottom of the dowel or other support. If you do not want this ridge, use *the reverse lark's head knot.* When the cords have been mounted, each half is considered a separate cord.

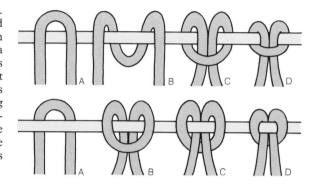

To tie a lark's head knot, fold a cord in half; place loop *in front of dowel* (A). Take loop back and bring forward under dowel (B). Put two ends through loop (C); pull it tight (D).

For reverse lark's head knot, place loop *behind dowel* (A). Bring loop down in front of dowel (B). Pull ends through loop (C) and tighten the knot (D).

Lark's head sennit

A chain of lark's head knots worked vertically is called a *lark's head sennit.* The anchor cord (the cord around which knots are tied) can be made up of more than one strand. A sennit can be worked with the left cord tied around the right cord as shown (right), or the right cord can be tied around the left cord. An attractive way to vary sennits of three or more cords is to alternate a knot with the left cord and a knot with the right cord around a centre cord.

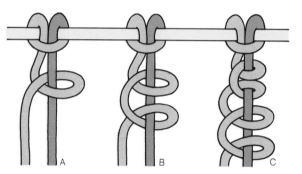

To tie a lark's head knot vertically, bring knotting cord *over* anchor cord, around *behind* it, and through space between the two (A). Then take knotting cord *under* the anchor cord, around *in front* of it, and down through space between knotting and anchor cords (B). Tighten knot and repeat (C).

Variations

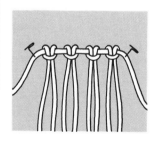

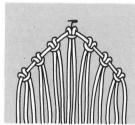

A holding cord can be used as a support in place of a dowel. Mount the cords with lark's head knots; the holding cord becomes two additional knotting cords, one on each side.

To begin a tie belt, mount an odd number of cords on a holding cord. Pin the centre knot to hold it, then angle the sides down. The holding cord becomes knotting cords at the sides.

To attach cords to a ring, use lark's head knots for each cord. To cover the ring completely, work lark's head knots around the ring with one long cord (see vertical knotting above).

For a loop, make a circle with mounting cord, overlapping ends. Place first knots at joining to secure. Add other cords. Mounting cord can become knotting cord, or trim ends.

Basic macramé knots

Double half hitch

The double half hitch (also called the clove hitch) and the square knot (see p. 362) are the two basic knots used in macramé. The double half hitch is two half hitches knotted in succession. The half hitch is rarely used by itself, although it can be added to the double half hitch to make a triple half hitch.

The double half hitch requires two cords: one is the knotting cord; the other is the holding cord, which is held taut during the knotting process. The double half hitch is tied in multiples. A series of knots is used most often to make straight lines; the position of the holding cord, horizontal or diagonal, determines the direction of the lines. Rows of double half hitches can be combined to form a great number of designs, such as diamonds or crosses, that involve diagonal lines (see sampler, p. 356).

The vertical double half hitch is a variation of this knot; it can be tied in horizontal rows or it can be worked vertically to form a chain or sennit.

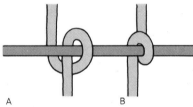

To make a half hitch, start the knotting cord behind the holding cord. Bring it under the holding cord, then up and over it. Put the end through the loop (A). Tighten the knot (B).

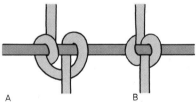

To form a double half hitch, follow the steps given above for the half hitch. Then bring the knotting cord up and over the holding cord, putting the end through the loop formed by the knotting cord (A). Pull the knot tight (B).

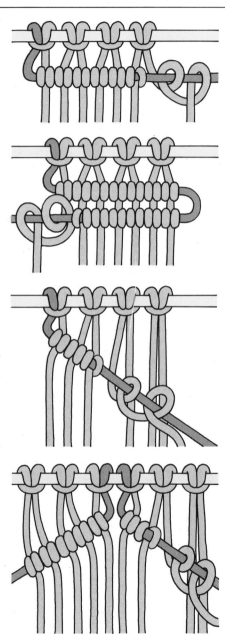

Horizontal double half hitches. Place the left cord in a horizontal position across the other cords in the row. Tie a double half hitch with the second cord on the left. Then tie a similar knot with each of the cords across the row.

When the last cord is knotted, turn the holding cord in the opposite direction and tie a reversed double half hitch with each cord, working from right to left.

To make a diagonal line of double half hitches going from upper left to lower right (shown), place first cord on left diagonally across the knotting cords. Make a double half hitch with each cord. To make a diagonal line from upper right to lower left, place the last cord on the right diagonally across the cords and knot from right to left.

Diagonal lines do not have to start at the edges; any cord can be used as a holding cord. Shown on left are diagonal lines worked from the two centre cords out to the sides.

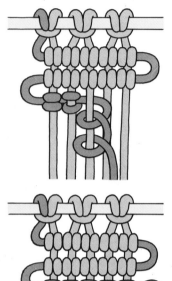

Vertical double half hitch knot is a variation of the double half hitch; the way it is made differs from the basic knot technique in that the holding cord becomes the knotting cord and each of the knotting cords becomes a holding cord. To work vertical double half hitches in a row from left to right, use the holding cord to tie a double half hitch vertically around the first knotting cord. Then tie a knot on each knotting cord in row.

To work a row from right to left, tie a double half hitch with the holding cord around the first cord on the right. Continue tying a knot on each cord from right to left across the row.

A sennit of double half hitches makes a chain that twists around itself (see drawing A).

One variation of a double half hitch sennit using four cords (see drawing B) is to tie left and right cords in a double half hitch alternately around two centre cords. This sennit lies flat.

Shaping with double half hitches

To make angled edges, the double half hitch is worked in solid blocks consisting of horizontal and vertical rows. The angled edges that result are a departure from the straight parallel edges usually associated with macramé. The angle can protrude from either side of the piece. To make the angle extend to the right, you use the first cord on the left as the holding cord and work double half hitches from left to right. You then use each cord in turn as the holding cord. To make the angle extend to the left, you start with the right cord and work the knots from right to left.

Narrow zigzag shapes, which can be made in the centre of a piece, are achieved with four angled cords as described on the left. Two shapes, knotted separately, can be overlapped.

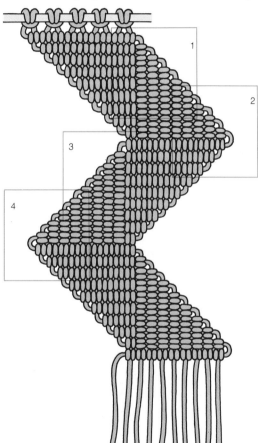

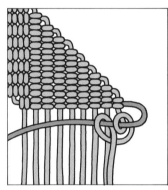

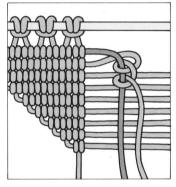

To angle the right edge to the right (1), work an area of vertical double half hitches. To begin, lay the top cord vertically across the other cords and tie a vertical double half hitch with each cord in turn. Then use the second cord, which is now on top, as the holding cord and tie a knot with each cord in turn. Using each of the cords in turn as a holding cord, work a row of knots with the other cords.

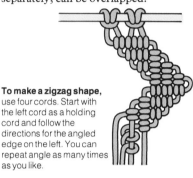

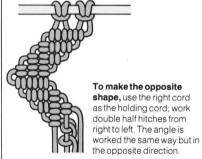

To angle the right edge back towards the left (2), knot an area of horizontal double half hitches, working each row from right to left. To begin this area, place the first cord on the right horizontally across the other cords and make a knot with each cord, working from right to left. Using each of the cords in turn as a holding cord, work a row of horizontal double half hitches with each cord.

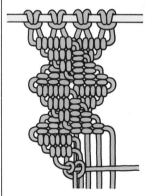

To make a zigzag shape, use four cords. Start with the left cord as a holding cord and follow the directions for the angled edge on the left. You can repeat angle as many times as you like.

To make the opposite shape, use the right cord as the holding cord; work double half hitches from right to left. The angle is worked the same way but in the opposite direction.

Sharply angled edges are created by alternating areas of horizontal with areas of vertical double half hitches. To begin, the left edge is angled towards the right with an area of horizontal double half hitches. Each cord, starting with the first cord on the left, is used as a holding cord for a row of knots. The cords are left hanging on the right side. The details above show the directional changes (horizontal to vertical double half hitches and vice versa) on either edge.

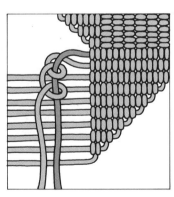

To angle the left edge to the left (3), work an area of vertical double half hitches. To begin this area, lay the top cord vertically across the other cords and tie a vertical double half hitch with each cord in turn. Using each of the cords in turn as a holding cord, tie a row of vertical double half hitches with the other cords.

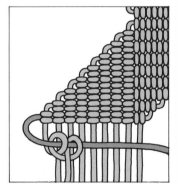

To angle the left edge back towards the right (4), work an area of horizontal double half hitches. To begin, place the first cord on the left horizontally across the others and tie a knot with each one in turn. Then use each cord in turn as a holding cord. Repeat design from here; area is the same as the beginning.

Intertwine the zigzag shapes by overlapping the angles as shown.

Basic macramé knots

The square knot

The square knot is one of the two fundamental macramé knots; the other is the double half hitch (p. 360). The basic square knot is tied with four cords; the two inside cords are anchor cords, the two outside cords are knotting cords. A square knot lies flat. When only half a square knot (a half knot) is tied in a sennit or chain, it will twist around itself. The square knot and the half knot can be tied with the left cord going over the centre cords and the right cord under them for a left-hand knot. Or the left cord can go under centre cords and the right cord over them for a right-hand knot. Either is correct; you can make whichever is more comfortable for you. We show the left-hand knot in the detail (right) and use it for all the variations (below and on the facing page).

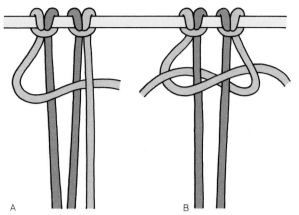

A   B

Working with four cords, put the left cord over the two centre cords and under the right cord (A). Then bring the right cord under the centre cords and up through the loop formed on the left (B). This completes the **half knot** and is the first half of the square knot. Make the opposite knot (right hand) by placing left cord under centre cords, right cord over them.

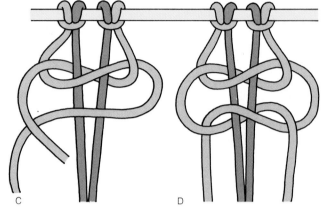

C   D

To continue the square knot, bring what is now the right cord over the two centre cords and under the left cord (C). Then bring the left cord under the two centre cords and up through the loop formed by the right cord (D). Tie the opposite knot by putting the right cord under and the left cord over the centre cords after initial half knot has been tied.

Square knot sennits

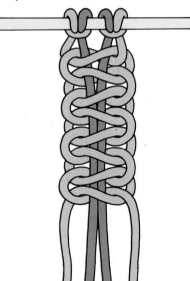

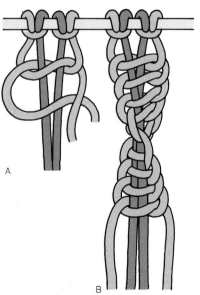

A

B

A square knot sennit or chain uses four cords and is formed by tying a series of square knots in a row. The result is a flat, braid-like chain that, by itself, can be used as a belt, a bracelet, a handle or a dog lead. The sennit can also be incorporated into larger designs.

A half knot sennit is formed by repeating the half knot (A). After about four knots are tied, the chain will twist around itself (B). As it turns, be sure to continue using the cord that is on the left. If knots are tied with the right cord, the chain will twist in the opposite direction.

A multiple-strand sennit is a series of square knots that uses two or more knotting cords on each side and two or more anchoring cords in the centre. Hold each set of knotting cords together and tie a basic square knot around the centre cords. Do not twist the cords as you tie the knot.

Inside-out square knot sennit is formed by interchanging knotting and anchor cords. To begin, tie a square knot. Bring knotting cords into centre to be anchor cords and tie another knot with former anchor cords as knotting cords. For the next knot, return cords to original positions.

Alternating square knots

The alternating square knot pattern is formed by exchanging the knotting cords and anchor cords in succeeding rows of square knots. The first row is made up of square knots tied with groups of four cords; the second row makes use of cords from two adjacent knots in the first row. The pattern alternates the two rows. Alternating square knots can have a lace-like appearance if the knots are widely spaced, a solid texture if the knots are tied close together.

For the first row, make a basic square knot with each group of four cords. The total number of cords in the row will vary with the design, but must of course be multiples of four.

For the second row, put aside the first two cords. Tie a square knot with two cords from the first knot and two cords from the second knot. For the next square knot, use two cords from the second knot and two cords from the third knot. Continue this way across the row. Leave last two cords untied.

To make a circular article, take the two spare cords at each end and knot together to form a square knot. This completes the circle.

The third row repeats the first row; square knots are tied with the original groups of four cords. The pattern is formed by repeating the two rows.

The bobble

The bobble is a three-dimensional knot formed by pulling a square knot chain up and through itself. The knot can be used for additional surface texture on a flat macramé piece, or as a button closure on a waistcoat or belt.

To make a bobble, leave a space in the knotting where you want the bobble to be. Then tie three square knots close together. The bobble is made with at least three square knots; use more knots if you want the bobble to be larger.

Bring the anchor cords up over the knots and between anchor cords in the space which you have left. Pull the cords through so that knots roll into a ball.

Tie a square knot directly below the bobble to hold it securely. You can tie just one bobble or make several of them in a row.

Gathering square knot

A gathering square knot is one that uses multiple cords; it is worked at a point in a design where it is desirable to have many cords meet. This knot is tied in the same way as the square knot described on the opposite page.

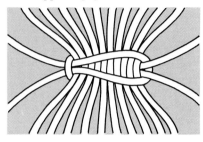

Multiple anchor cords tied into a square knot with one knotting cord on either side form a type of gathering square knot that brings many cords together in one thick knot.

Four knotting cords, two on either side, make the square knot more visible against the many anchor cords. This type of gathering square knot can be used with any number of anchor cords.

Another variation of the gathering square knot is possible only if total number of cords is divisible by four. Divide cords into four groups; make a square knot using each group as one cord.

Additional techniques

The overhand knot

The overhand knot is the simplest of the additional knots used in macramé; it is the same knot that is tied at the end of a length of sewing thread. The knot itself requires only one cord, which is unusual in macramé. However, there are several variations of the overhand knot, some of which require more than one cord. The variations are an overhand knot tied with an anchor cord, intertwining overhand knots and the barrel knot, which is an overhand knot that is made with the working end of the cord wrapped around the loop several times.

Both overhand knots with anchor cords (left) and intertwining overhand knots (right) can be worked into a mesh-like pattern by alternating the position of the knots in alternate rows.

To tie an overhand knot (A), make a loop and bring the end of the cord through the loop. Pull to tighten the knot.

To tie an overhand knot with an anchor cord (B), make a loop around the anchor cord and tie the knot. Pull the end to tighten the knot.

To tie intertwining overhand knots, tie an overhand knot with one cord. Before you pull it tight, slip the second cord through the loop and tie an overhand knot with it. Pull both knots tight.

To tie a barrel knot, make a loop with the cord and wrap the end around the loop several times; pull it tight. The more wraps you make, the longer the knot will be.

Picots

Picots are decorative elements added to macramé either along the top edge or at the sides. If they are added to the top edge, picots are worked before the cords are mounted or as they are being mounted. This is done by pinning the centre point of the cord above the dowel and working a decorative knot above the dowel. Cord ends are then mounted to the dowel with double half hitches (p. 360). Picots added to the sides are made during the knotting process.

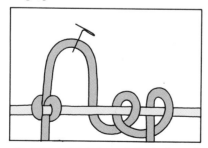

To make a simple loop picot, pin the centre point of the cord above the mounting cord or dowel; the higher it is above the cord, the larger the loop will be. Attach each of the cord ends to the mounting cord with a double half hitch.

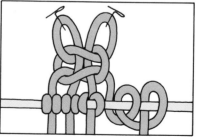

To make a square knot picot, pin the centre points of two cords next to each other above the dowel. Using centre cords as anchor cords and outside cords as knotting cords, tie a square knot. Mount cord ends with a double half hitch.

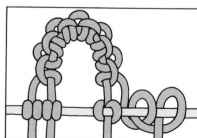

To make a lark's head picot, mount one end of each of two cords on to a dowel. With the left cord, tie lark's head knots over right cord. The more knots you make, the larger the loop will be. Mount cord ends with double half hitches.

Cavandoli work

Josephine knot

Berry knot

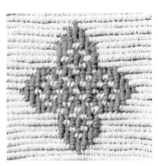

Cavandoli work is a technique that consists of closely worked horizontal and vertical double half hitches in two colours; horizontal knots are used for the background and vertical knots form the motif. The technique originated in Italy where it was taught to young school children.

The Josephine knot is also known as the Carrick bend. It can be made small or large depending on the number of cords used. It is often tied with two cords held together as shown, but four or six can be used. The knot can be left loose or pulled tight.

The berry knot, also known as the hobnail, is another knot that adds surface texture to a macramé piece. The berry knot is a variation of the double half hitch. To make the knot, several double half hitches are puffed up and kept in place with square knots. This knot requires eight cords.

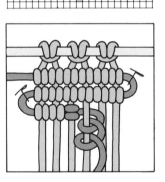

A design to be knotted in Cavandoli work can be planned. Each square represents one double half hitch knot. The white squares are the background worked in horizontal knots; the coloured squares represent the motif and are worked in vertical knots.

Mount two cords at their centre points so you have four working cords. Make a loop with the left cords, placing the working end under the beginning end, as shown.

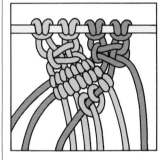

Tie a square knot with each group of four cords. Place the fifth cord diagonally across the first four cords and tie a double half hitch with each of the first cords. Use the sixth, seventh and eighth cords in turn as holding cords, and tie double half hitches with the first four cords.

To work Cavandoli, mount cords in the background colour on to a dowel; there should be as many cords as there are squares in the graph. Use a separate cord in a second colour as a holding cord. Using the graph as a guide, tie a horizontal double half hitch for each white square on the graph. For a coloured square, tie a vertical double half hitch, using the holding cord as a tying cord.

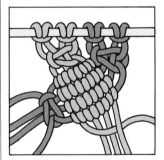

Place the right cords on top of the loop that was formed with the left cords. Bring the ends of the right cords under the ends of the left cords.

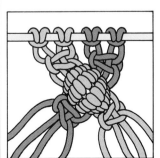

When the second four cords have all been used as holding cords, tie a square knot with these four cords (they are now on the left). As you make the knot, put one finger behind the berry and push it up until it is rounded.

Tie a horizontal double half hitch where there is a white square on the graph. The tying cord in the background colour will cover the holding cord. Tie knots across each row, following the graph for position.

The right cords are woven over and under the other cords, going from upper left to lower right. To do this, bring the right cords around and over the first pair of cords, under the second pair, over the third pair, and under the last pair. Pull cord ends to make loops even, and tighten knot as much as you wish.

To hold the rounded, puffy shape of the berry knot, make another square knot with the first four cords (they are now on the right). Tie this knot tightly to keep the shape of the berry.

365

Additional techniques

Adding beads

Adding beads to a macramé piece creates textural variety. Beads can be bought from craft shops, handmade or taken from pieces of old jewellery. A bead can be attached to one or more cords depending on the size of the bead, the size of the hole in the bead and the particular knotting pattern. When choosing beads, make sure the hole in the bead is large enough to accommodate the thickness of the cord you are using. Small beads can be added to almost any design. Large beads look best if the knotting pattern is designed to accommodate their size.

With an overhand knot. Tie an overhand knot above point where you want bead. Slip the bead on to the cord; tie another knot below to secure it.

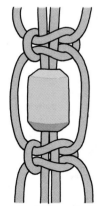

With a square knot. Tie a square knot above point where you want bead. Slip bead on to anchor cords. Tie a square knot below bead.

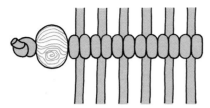

With horizontal double half hitches. If separate holding cord is used, ends can be secured with a bead. To do this, tie overhand knot in end of cord, slip bead on, and use cord as holding cord.

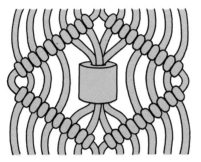

With double half hitches in diamond shape. Bead can be emphasised by being placed inside a configuration of knots. Here, upper knots are worked, bead slipped on, then lower ones worked.

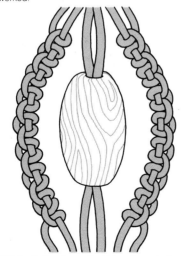

With lark's head sennits. Using six cords, bead is slipped on centre two. Outside cords are knotted into sennits that echo curve of the bead.

Replacing short cords

Regardless of how carefully you plan and how accurately you measure the cords, it will occasionally be necessary to replace a cord that is too short. There are several ways to do this, and three are shown below. Another quick way is to tie in a new cord with a reef knot (or weaver's knot). Tie the knot tightly and pull the ends to the back of the work. Trim ends when work is finished.

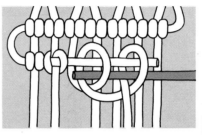

To add to a holding cord in horizontal double half hitches, place the new cord next to the old one and tie several knots over both cords.

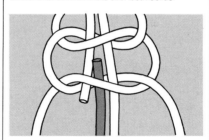

To add to an anchor cord in a square knot, place the new cord so that it overlaps the old one and continue tying square knots over both cords.

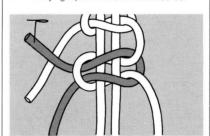

To add new knotting cord, pin new cord to board. Drop old cord and use new one. When piece is completed, tie ends together and trim.

Adding new cords

Additional cords can be required in macramé for different reasons. The dimensions of some projects will have to be changed as the piece is being worked; an example is a narrow piece that becomes wider. In other projects, colour may be added as work progresses. There are several ways to add cords to available spaces so the addition looks natural and is not immediately visible.

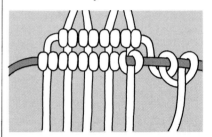

A new holding cord can be introduced in a row of horizontal double half hitches. The cord ends can become knotting cords in subsequent rows.

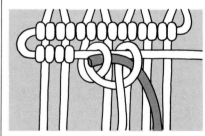

A new cord can be added as a knotting cord in a row of horizontal double half hitches. Make several knots over the end of the cord to secure it.

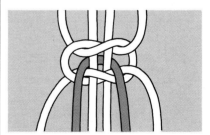

Two new cords can be added by slipping one long cord through the anchor cords of a square knot. Pull it through to make two equal cords.

Subtracting cords

Cords will sometimes need to be eliminated, either gradually or suddenly. The simplest way to drop a cord is to knot over it, leaving it hanging at the back of the piece where later it can be cut off. Of the other methods of eliminating cords shown below, the one to be chosen depends on whether the cord in question is in the centre of the work or at the edge, and on the knotting pattern used.

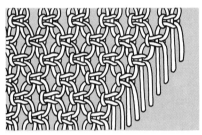

Cords at the edges can be eliminated simply by not knotting them. The cord ends can be woven into the back when the piece is finished.

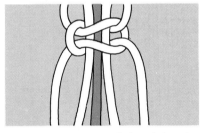

You can knot over unwanted cords by using them as anchor cords in a square knot. The ends can be trimmed off later.

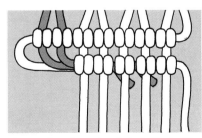

Unwanted cords can be eliminated by knotting over several of them with horizontal double half hitches; trim off ends on back of piece.

Finishing edges

The method used to finish the edge of a macramé piece contributes to the overall look of the work. The most common way is to let the cord ends hang loose to form a fringe (see pp. 368–70). If the fringe is not suitable to your particular piece, you can weave the ends into the back of the work, finish the edge with bias tape, or wrap groups of cords together.

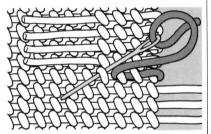

To weave cord ends into the work, thread each cord end into a large rug needle and bring the needle under several knots on back of work.

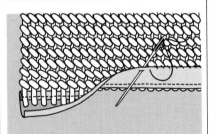

To face edge with bias tape, trim cord ends to 1 cm. Machine-stitch tape to right side of macramé. Fold tape to back; stitch by hand.

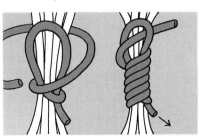

To wrap ends, place loop over bundle; wrap from bottom up. Put working end in loop; pull starting end so loop and working end are hidden.

Designing macramé

The overall design of a macramé piece is composed of several elements: the size of the piece, the type of cord or yarn, the colour or colours, and the knotting pattern. If you will be designing for the first time, keep the size of the piece and the complexity of the design in line with your ability and the time that you want to spend working on it.

You will want to decide if the piece is going to be **functional** or **decorative**. A functional piece will have to conform to its intended purpose in terms of size, texture and finishing techniques; a purely decorative piece permits great freedom in all of these areas.

The size of a piece is determined by its outer dimensions and the size of the cord that is used. A thick cord can be worked quickly and will give the impression of the piece being larger.

Texture is a product of both the cord and the knotting pattern. A smooth cord shows off the configuration of the knots better than a knobbly one. Usually the fibre content of a cord determines the texture of the cord. For example, jute makes a rough, scratchy cord while linen makes a smooth one; both of these cords hold knots securely. Nylon makes a smooth and shiny cord that is difficult to work with because it is slippery. An interesting texture can be introduced into a macramé piece by using a variety of materials in the same colour family – cords smooth and rough, thick and thin, dull and shiny. How knots are tied also contributes to the texture of a piece. Knots tied tightly and close together create a compact, dense texture while knots tied loosely or spaced far apart create a lacy look.

The knotting pattern is the result of both the particular knots used and the way in which the knots are combined with each other. The most frequent design elements in macramé are horizontal, vertical and diagonal lines and areas featuring small patterns. Circles, curves and flowing lines are possible, but they do require some knotting experience.

Colour can be used in macramé in a variety of ways. The usual way, except in Cavandoli, is to work in one colour only, with the colour merely enhancing the pattern. Or a knotted piece can be mostly one colour, with just a few cords in a contrasting colour to highlight a certain area of the piece. Using several tones of a single colour can add depth to a work. A bold colour contrast looks best when it is used with a simple knotting pattern.

Whether to add such ornaments as beads, feathers or shells is a matter of personal taste. These additions can enhance a macramé piece if their size and colour are in harmony.

A bold colour contrast of black, brown and beige cords is used with a simple knotting pattern of double half hitches and square knots.

Fringing

Introduction

Any kind of fringe, whether used to complete a macramé project or added to a fabric garment, utilises macramé knots. The purpose of a fringe is to gather individual thread ends or cords into a decorative pattern. With a coarse fabric, such as heavy linen, canvas and some wools, a fringe can be made from the fabric's own threads. This is done by drawing out horizontal threads, then knotting the remaining vertical threads. For fabrics that lack the requisite coarseness, you can add yarn or cord to the edge of the fabric after it has been hemmed. The fringe on a macramé piece does not have to be limited to the number of cords used in the piece itself; others can be added in several different ways, the choice depending on the knotting pattern that is used.

To form a fringe, cords can be attached to the hemmed edge of fabric and tied in a variety of knots. Here, linen cord was attached to printed fabric with lark's head knots. The cords were then tied to form two rows of diamonds; the first row of diamonds is formed by rows of diagonal double half hitches and the second row is square knot sennits woven over and under each other. Cord ends are gathered into groups and wrapped.

Determining fringe measurements

Adding a fringe to an item requires some planning. You must first decide how many cords you want to use and how far apart they will be; cords can be added individually or in groups. On fabric, cords can be mounted 1–2 cm apart, depending on the thickness of the cords. Fringes made from fabric threads will be a fixed distance apart. The number and spacing of macramé fringes can be adjusted by adding cords. Decide on the thickness of cord you will use according to the effect required. On a macramé piece, you will add more of the same cord that was used to knot the piece. When adding a fringe to fabric, you can use many thin cords in each group or a few thick ones, depending on the knotting pattern. Cords are mounted at their centre point, so cut length must be twice the mounted length. To allow for knotting, cut each cord four times as long as you want the finished fringe to be; this will assure that mounted length is twice as long. Trim off any excess cord when knotting is complete.

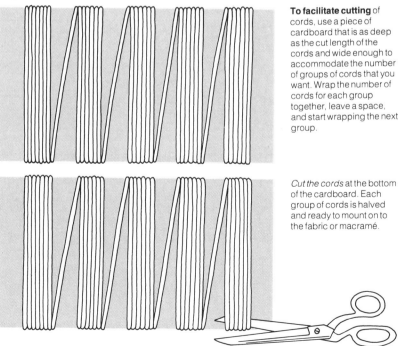

To facilitate cutting of cords, use a piece of cardboard that is as deep as the cut length of the cords and wide enough to accommodate the number of groups of cords that you want. Wrap the number of cords for each group together, leave a space, and start wrapping the next group.

Cut the cords at the bottom of the cardboard. Each group of cords is halved and ready to mount on to the fabric or macramé.

Fringing fabric

If the fabric you are working with is coarse enough, which means the individual fabric threads are thick enough to manipulate, a fringe can be created with the fabric threads. A fringe that is made from fabric threads will be much finer than a fringe made of added cords, and will look like an integral part of the fabric rather than a separate entity. To fringe fabric, gently draw out the horizontal threads and knot the remaining vertical threads. A fabric fringe looks best when the fabric is a plain colour.

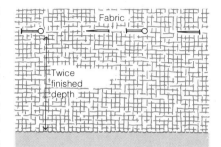

To make a fabric fringe, pin-tack a line on fabric at twice the depth finished fringe will be.

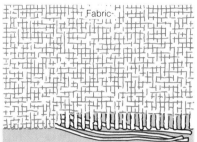

With pin, push each horizontal thread down. Remove each separately or the threads will knot.

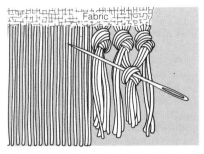

Knot groups of vertical threads, adjusting height of knots with a tapestry needle. Trim ends.

Attaching cords to fabric

To attach extra cords to fabric, allow at least 1 cm beyond the edge of the fabric for a hem. (Make the hem deeper if this is necessary for the item you are making.) Fold hem allowance under 5 mm twice, and stitch the fold to the fabric. Besides finishing the raw edge of the fabric, the hem creates a firm base on which to mount the extra cords. Take care that the cord chosen for the fringe is not too thick for the fabric. If you are using groups of cords, make sure the groups are not so thick that they tear the fabric as they are being mounted.

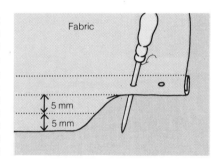

Use a stiletto or a sharp knitting needle to make holes in the fabric at predetermined distances. Keep the holes within the hem.

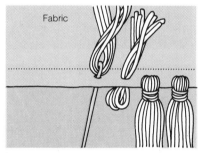

To attach cords, insert a crochet hook through the hole from the back. Catch the centre of a cord or group of cords and pull through the hole.

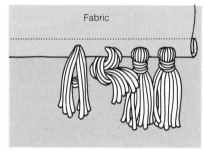

Put ends of cord or bundle through the loop and pull it tight. Repeat with each cord or group of cords. This forms a lark's head knot (see p. 359).

Adding to a macramé fringe

If the cord ends on a piece of macramé are left hanging, they will act as a natural fringe at the end of the work. If you want to make an elaborate fringe that requires more cords than are in the piece, you can add cords at the bottom of the work; the appropriate way depends on the particular knotting pattern used and the configuration of knots that occurs at the end of the work. Shown on the right are several ways to add cords to a macramé piece that ends with either a row of horizontal double half hitches or a row of alternating square knots.

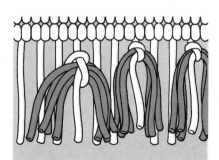

To add groups of cords, tie each group on to the macramé, using one cord from the existing fringe. Leave several cords between groups.

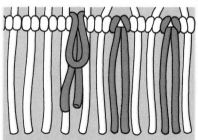

If the macramé ends with a row of horizontal double half hitches, add new cords to the holding cord with a reverse lark's head knot (see p. 359).

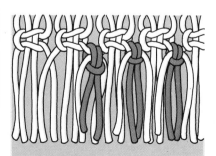

If the macramé ends with square knots, add new cords with a lark's head knot tied over the knotting cords from two adjacent square knots.

Fringing

Turning a corner

If a fringe is to be put on two adjacent sides of a piece of fabric, on two edges of a shawl for example, cords must be added to the corner area as it is being worked so that the design of the knots can continue around the corner. Begin by inserting extra cords into the corner hole in the fabric. Then, as the work progresses, you can add more cords (see p. 366) so that the macramé will turn the corner without drawing up.

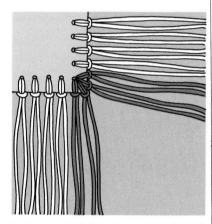

In the corner hole, insert three extra cords. With groups of cords, insert one group that contains four times as many cords as the other groups.

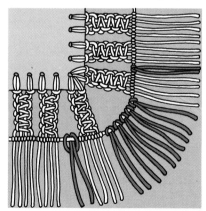

As the work progresses, add more cords both to the corner area and to the space on either side of the corner – enough to fill any gaps.

Finishing the fringe ends

Although fringing is the customary technique for finishing the cord ends on a macramé piece, a fringe can begin to look worn and frayed very easily. There are a number of ways to prevent or compensate for this; several are shown below. Choose the one that is most suitable for your macramé.

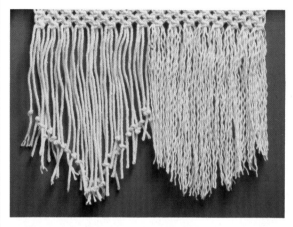

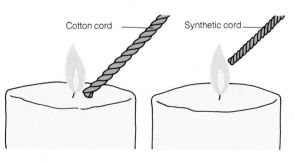

Cotton cord   Synthetic cord

If each individual cord end is going to hang separately, tie an overhand knot where you want the fringe to end, then trim the fringe off right below the knot (far left).

Another way to finish a fringe is to unravel the individual plies that comprise each cord (near left). Before you unravel the fringe, unravel a small piece of leftover cord to see if you like the separated effect with the cord you are using.

Another method with individual cord ends is to divide them into groups of two or four cords and tie them into sennits. The sennits illustrated are, from left to right, overhand knots tied with two cords (see p. 364), alternating half hitches tied with two cords, and alternating lark's head knots tied with two cords around two anchor cords (see p. 359).

If you prefer to let the individual cord ends hang free, there is a simple way to protect ends and keep them from unravelling. If the cord is cotton or linen, dip the end into melted candle wax (far left). With nylon cord, melt the plies together by placing the cord end in a candle flame (near left).

Making a tassel

A separate tassel can be made from extra lengths of the same cord that is used to make the fringe. Tassels add bulk and weight to a fringe; this may be desirable if the fringe is on the end of a wall hanging where the added weight will make the piece hang nicely. To determine how much extra cord you will need, decide how long you want the tassels to be. Cut a piece of cardboard that is as high as the tassel is long. Wrap cord around the cardboard until you have the thickness of tassel that you want. Unwind the cord and measure it; multiply this amount by the number of tassels you want to make.

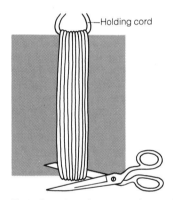

Holding cord

To make a tassel, wrap cord around cardboard. Tie a holding cord around the cords at the top; cut the cords at bottom.

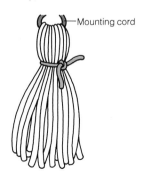

Mounting cord

Tie separate cord a quarter of distance from top. To mount, put mounting cord in space at top; remove holding cord.

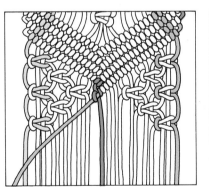

Woman's macramé belt

Linen belt uses only two basic knots – square knot and double half hitch – and their variations.

This macramé belt, tied with sturdy but soft linen cord, has a repeat design of diamonds composed of diagonal double half hitches with a bobble in the centre.

Materials needed
Ten 10 m lengths of 6/10 linen cord
Belt buckle with 4 cm centre bar
Knotting board
T-pins
Rubber bands

Introduction
Finished belt fits a 65 cm waist. It has 12 motifs and measures 73 cm; the length can be changed in 4.5 cm increments (the length of one motif). To do this, you lengthen or shorten the cut length of each strand by 62 cm for each motif you want to add or subtract. Size of linen cord is indicated by two numbers, such as 6/10. The first stands for the number of plies in the cord; the higher the number, the more plies, so the thicker the cord. The second refers to the thickness of each ply; the higher the number, the thinner the ply. Linen cord comes in skeins or cones from weaving suppliers.

Knotting
To begin belt, fold each 10 m strand in half; mount on centre bar of buckle with a lark's head knot (p. 359). Wind cord ends into butterflies and secure with rubber bands (p. 358). Tie alternating square knots (p. 363) for 6.5 cm. To shape square knots to conform to point of first motif, continue knotting each side separately, decreasing one knot each row until there is only one knot on each side (see Step 1).

The motif
To work the motif, tie cord 10 in a double half hitch (see p. 360) over cord 11 in centre of belt. Bring cord 11 diagonally across first nine cords and cord 10 diagonally across the last nine cords. Using these cords as holding cords, tie diagonal double half hitches (referred to as ddhh) with each of the other cords. Tie three more rows of ddhh (see Step 2) to form top half of diamond. Holding cords from previous rows are not used as knotting cords so the number of knots in each row decreases. Leave the holding cords hanging at the sides; they will also be holding cords for the bottom half of the diamond. Make a bobble (see p. 363) with centre four cords, placing it 5 mm below inner point of upper half of diamond. Use five square knots and secure with a sixth knot.

To make bottom half of diamond, bring cord 11 diagonally across first nine cords so it is 5 mm below bobble. Tie ddhh with next nine cords, working from left to right. Place cord 10 diagonally across cords on the right; tie ddhh from right to left, using the holding cord from the left side (cord 11) as the last knotting cord. Tie three more rows of ddhh in the same way to complete bottom half of diamond.

Between motifs
To fill triangular shapes between motifs, work alternating square knots as shown in Step 3. Do not use centre four cords. Repeat motif, using the last holding cord on the right as first holding cord placed diagonally from centre to left.

Finishing
After twelfth motif (or last motif for your size), work 15 cm of alternating square knots from lower point of last motif to point of shaped end (see Step 4). Using last cord at left edge, tie ddhh from left to centre, following shape of point. Repeat with last cord on right side, using holding cord from left side as last knotting cord. Work three more rows of ddhh in same way as bottom half of diamond. With a needle, work cord ends into macramé on the back.

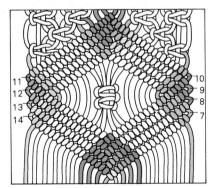

1. For first motif, work square knots as shown. Tie cord 10 in a double half hitch over cord 11; use cord 11 as holding cord for row of knots on left side, cord 10 as holding cord on right side.

2. Motif that is repeated along length of belt consists of a diamond shape formed by four rows of diagonal double half hitches. Bobble is worked in centre when top half of diamond is complete.

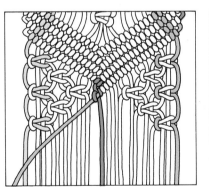

3. To fill triangular shapes between motifs, work alternating square knots as shown. Do not use centre four cords. Last holding cord on right from previous motif becomes first holding cord on left.

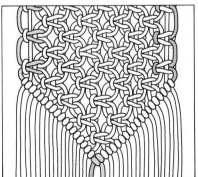

4. After last motif, work 15 cm of alternating square knots. To shape point continue tying knots, decreasing one knot on each side in successive rows until there is one knot in centre.

Window screen

A window screen, worked in natural-colour jute, uses variations of two basic knots.

Materials needed

3 kilos of heavyweight, 3-ply, natural-colour jute
1.5 cm dowel, 90 cm long
1 m × 1 m knotting board
T-pins
Rubber bands
G-cramps
Paper and pencil
Wide felt-tipped pen

Setting up

To enlarge design, make a grid with 2.5 cm squares and copy design square for square (see p. 14). Go over design lines with felt-tipped pen so you will be able to see them under the jute. Secure enlarged design to knotting board with tape or T-pins. Attach dowel to knotting board with G-cramps. Cut 22 cords that are 8.25 m long; 42 cords 11 m long. Mount the cords at their centre point with lark's head knot (p. 359) in this order: 11 short cords, 42 long, 11 short. You will have 128 working lengths. Wrap each cord end into a butterfly (p. 358).

Knotting

Work alternating square knots in Section A. Line 1, a row of double half hitches, is worked from top of three points down; arrows indicate knotting direction. For holding cords, use cords indicated on diagram below. Always tie left cord over right cord first. For example, tie cord 36 in double half hitch over cord 37, then use these two cords as holding cords. Work Line 2 the same as

Window screen, 75 cm × 1 m without tassels, is made with heavy 3-ply jute.

Line 1; hold floating cords (cords without knots) taut. Work Line 3, then the top diamond. Make half knot sennits to just below middle of diamond; work alternating square knot bobbles in bottom half. Bobbles are made with four square knots, secured with a fifth. Work Line 4, knot centres of the two large diamonds, then work Line 5. There are 6 floating cords between the side of each large diamond and side edge of piece. Work centre of bottom diamond, then knot Line 6. Knot Lines 7 and 8, keeping floating cords taut, then make alternating square knots in Section H. Knot Line 9.

To finish, weave cord ends into back of work (p. 367); glue them if you wish, and trim ends. Make five 30 cm long tassels with 36 cords in each (p. 370). To secure tassel, wrap a separate length (p. 367) around cords for 3 cm. Tie tassels to the five points at bottom edge. Hang piece at window. Trim ends.

Diagram labels

Cords 64 and 65 (centre)
Cords 44 and 45
Cords 84 and 85
Cords 36 and 37
Cords 92 and 93

A
B
C
D
E
F
G
H

Line 1
Line 2
Line 3
Line 4
Line 5
Line 6
Line 7
Line 8
Line 9

1 sq. = 2.5 cm

To enlarge design, make a grid with 2.5 cm squares and copy design square for square (see p. 14).

Key

A. Alternating square knots (p. 363)
B and C. Floating cords (p. 358)
D. Half knot sennits (p. 362)
E. Alternating square-knot bobbles (p. 363)
F and G. Floating cords
H. Alternating square knots
Lines 1 and 2. One row of double half hitch (p. 360)
Lines 3, 4, 5, 6. Two rows of double half hitch
Lines 7, 8, 9. One row of double half hitch

Rug-making

Hooked rug with plaited circles, Shelburne Museum, Vermont, USA.

Hooking and knotting

Types of hooked and knotted rugs

A hooked or a knotted rug consists of a pile surface attached to a rug base. The primary difference between the two types of rugs is the way that the pile is attached to the base. With a hooked rug, the pile is 'threaded' through the rug base; with a knotted rug, the pile is 'tied' on to the rug base. There are two ways of forming a hooked rug – with a hand hook or with a punch needle. There are also two ways of forming a knotted rug – with a latchet hook or with a rug needle

and Rya stitches (also known as Ghiordes knots). Examples of all four types of rugs are shown below. Notice that the quality of the pile differs from sample to sample. These differences are a result of both the method and the materials most commonly used for each rug type. In general, the pile of a hooked rug is short and, in most cases, its loops are uncut (as shown below). The pile of a knotted rug is long and shaggy. If a knotted rug is made with a latchet hook,

it will have a cut pile; if it is made with Rya stitches, the pile can be cut or uncut (uncut pile is shown in the example). As with any other needlework technique, variations can be introduced once you become familiar with the basics of the craft. Materials for the four rug methods and tips about designing them are given on the next five pages. For instructions on the two hooked rug methods, see pp. 382–7; for the two knotted rug techniques, see pp. 388–91.

HOOKED RUGS

Hand hook method

Punch needle method

KNOTTED RUGS

Latchet hook method

Rya stitch method

Equipment for hooked rugs

Different equipment is needed for each of the hooked rug methods. For a hand hooked rug, you need a base fabric (usually hessian), fabric strips and a hand hook to pull small loops of the strip up through the base fabric, thus forming the pile surface. The texture of the pile depends on the width of the strip and the fabric used to make it. Medium-weight, finely woven wools, such as flannel, work best. Wool resists dirt and wears better than other fibres. Flannel can be cut into strips 5 mm or 1 cm wide. Strips should be cut carefully with scissors

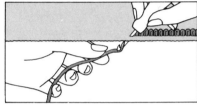

Hand hook method

along the grain of the fabric. Hooks set in wooden handles are available from specialist suppliers.

To make a rug by the punch needle method, you need a base fabric, yarn and a punch needle. The pile is formed by bringing the threaded needle in and out of the base fabric. Evenweave fabric, jute embroidery cloth or hessian can be used. Rug wool and thrums are best, though heavy knitting yarn is sometimes suitable. Be sure the yarn can pass easily through the eye of the needle. The handle of the punch needle can be moved to alter the length of the pile.

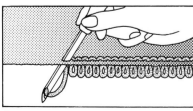

Punch needle method

HAND HOOK METHOD

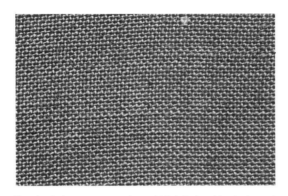

Hessian is the most commonly used fabric for hand-hooked rugs. It is made of jute, is fairly closely woven and comes in a number of weights. If hooking narrow strips, use a heavier weight. The fabrics on the right can also be used.

Rug hook. Metal hook held in a turned wooden handle, available in sizes suitable for narrow strips.

Handmade rug hook. Sharp metal hook mounted in wood shaped to fit the palm of the hand. Suitable for wider strips.

Wool flannel or suiting is the best fabric to use for strips. It is closely woven, medium weight and does not fray easily.

PUNCH NEEDLE METHOD

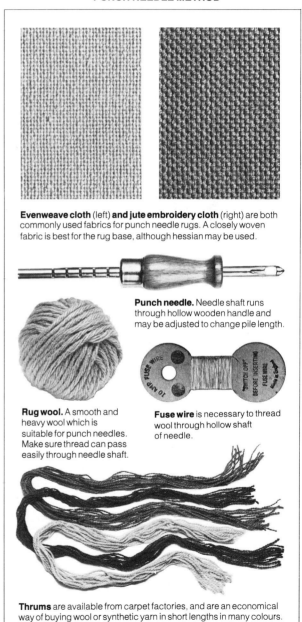

Evenweave cloth (left) **and jute embroidery cloth** (right) are both commonly used fabrics for punch needle rugs. A closely woven fabric is best for the rug base, although hessian may be used.

Punch needle. Needle shaft runs through hollow wooden handle and may be adjusted to change pile length.

Rug wool. A smooth and heavy wool which is suitable for punch needles. Make sure thread can pass easily through needle shaft.

Fuse wire is necessary to thread wool through hollow shaft of needle.

Thrums are available from carpet factories, and are an economical way of buying wool or synthetic yarn in short lengths in many colours.

Hooking and knotting

Equipment for knotted rugs

A knotted rug made with a latchet hook is one in which cut yarns are 'tied' on to the horizontal threads of a rug canvas with the aid of a latchet hook. The character of the pile is determined by the type of yarn used and its length before knotting. Rug and Rya yarns are the most popular types for the purpose. Rug yarn is heavy and smooth; Rya is lighter and has a rope-like twist. Both types are available in packages of cut pieces. Rug yarns in packs are 7 cm long (to produce a 2.5 cm pile) and Rya yarns are 17 cm long (for an 8 cm pile). If other yarns are

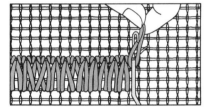

Latchet hook method

used, they must be cut into pieces that are twice the desired pile length plus 1.5–2 cm for the knot.

The pile of a true Rya rug is formed by making Rya stitches (also known as Ghiordes knots) on the exposed vertical threads of Rya canvas. The stitches are made with a large tapestry needle (size 14) and thrums or rug wool cut to a convenient length. Loop length can be judged by eye or worked round gauge stick. Rya stitches can also be worked on rug canvas, with two or three holes to the centimetre. See pp. 389–90 for both variations.

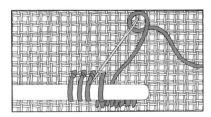

Rya stitch method using gauge stick

LATCHET HOOK METHOD

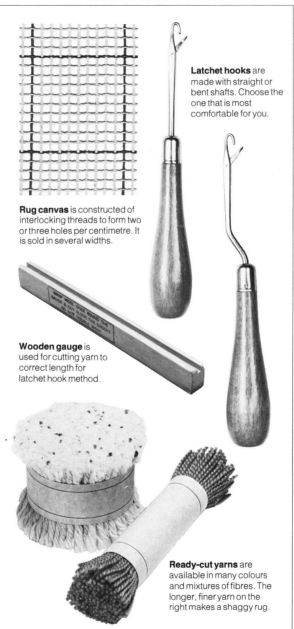

Rug canvas is constructed of interlocking threads to form two or three holes per centimetre. It is sold in several widths.

Latchet hooks are made with straight or bent shafts. Choose the one that is most comfortable for you.

Wooden gauge is used for cutting yarn to correct length for latchet hook method.

Ready-cut yarns are available in many colours and mixtures of fibres. The longer, finer yarn on the right makes a shaggy rug.

RYA STITCH METHOD

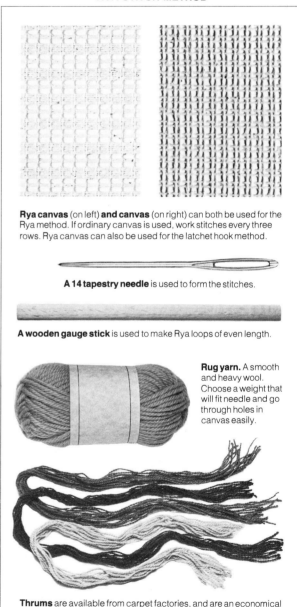

Rya canvas (on left) **and canvas** (on right) can both be used for the Rya method. If ordinary canvas is used, work stitches every three rows. Rya canvas can also be used for the latchet hook method.

A 14 tapestry needle is used to form the stitches.

A wooden gauge stick is used to make Rya loops of even length.

Rug yarn. A smooth and heavy wool. Choose a weight that will fit needle and go through holes in canvas easily.

Thrums are available from carpet factories, and are an economical way of buying wool or synthetic yarn in short lengths in many colours. A few strands of finer yarn can also be used together.

Frames

For the best results, hooked rugs should be worked on a frame. The frame below is strong and capable of holding many different sizes of rugs, from very small to quite large.

A canvas work frame or a quilting hoop could also be used for a small rug.

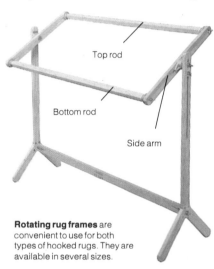

Rotating rug frames are convenient to use for both types of hooked rugs. They are available in several sizes.

Do-it-yourself rug frame. An improvised rug frame can be cheaply and easily made by screwing two large, strong cup-hooks firmly into a plank of wood, long enough to take the rug base fabric. Tack or pin base fabric to plank. Use strong string to tie the frame round table legs, and tighten as the work progresses.

Design transfer equipment

If you are designing your own rug, you will have to transfer the design to the rug base. There are four ways of transferring a design; the method used will depend mainly on whether the rug base is fabric or canvas. If it is a *fabric base* – hessian or evenweave cloth – there is a choice of three transfer methods. One is to re-draw the lines of the design with a **special transfer pencil** and apply heat to the re-drawn lines so they will transfer to the fabric. Second is the pricking transfer method, in which **pounce** (a powder) is used with a **dressmaker's pencil**. The lines of the design are perforated, and pounce is patted through the holes on to the fabric; the pencil is used to connect the dots. The third fabric method is to trace the design with dressmaker's **carbon paper** and a **tracing wheel**. If rug base is *canvas*, transfer the design by slipping the drawing under the canvas and using a waterproof **felt marker** to draw the design on to the canvas. For instructions on all four of these methods, see pp. 380–1.

Finishing equipment

Some pieces of equipment needed to finish rugs (pp. 392–6) are unique to rug-making; others, like heavy needles and threads or a thimble, are common to many other types of needlework. The equipment shown on the right is exclusively for rug-making. **Rug binding**, a strong woven tape, is used to finish the edges of some rugs. It is 3.5 or 5 cm wide and is available by the metre. **Latex** is useful in two ways. Applied to the back of a hooked rug, it 'glues' the pile to the rug base. Its other purpose is to form a non-slip surface on the back of any rug, hooked or knotted. A pair of strong sharp scissors is needed to trim the pile of the rug when finished. Special rug scissors are available with angled handles, so that the blades are held parallel to the pile while cutting.

Felt-tip marker (waterproof) can be used to draw design on canvas.

Pounce and a dressmaker's pencil are used to transfer designs by the pricking method.

Dressmaker's carbon and tracing wheel are used together to transfer design on to fabric.

Special transfer pencil changes a drawing into a hot-iron transfer.

Scissors should be sharp to cut pile neatly.

Rug binding is strong cloth tape, made in different widths, used to finish edges of some rugs.

Latex is applied to the back of a rug to secure the pile or to make the rug slip-proof.

Hooking and knotting

Designing principles

While working on the design of a hooking or knotting project, you should consider several things. First, decide what the finished project will be – a rug, a cushion or a seat cover. Once its purpose is established, you can think about its finished size and shape, and what type of design will look best in that shape. Should the design be extremely detailed and realistic, or undetailed and abstract? Will it be best if the design fills the entire shape, or should it be a central motif surrounded by a plain background?

Very often it is the design that determines what rug method should be selected for a project. In general, both of the hooked methods (hand hook and punch needle) are better suited to executing a detailed or realistic design than are the two knotted methods (latchet hook and Rya stitch). The knotted techniques are better for carrying out abstract designs. These differences stem from the base fabrics and the pile that each method forms.

Two rug bases, hessian and evenweave fabric, are used interchangeably for the hooked rug methods. Each of these is a fairly closely woven fabric. The fineness of the weave allows the loops of the pile to be set close to each other and thus to follow any drawn line fairly accurately. The worked pile stands up from the drawn line and tends to reinforce it. The first sample below was done on evenweave with the hand hook method and fabric strips. It shows a row of loops forming a line with opposite curves. The drawn line above the row of loops is identical to the marked guideline on which the loops were formed. Notice that the row of loops is almost an exact duplicate of the drawn line. If the sample had been worked with a punch needle and rug yarn, the resulting row would have looked almost the same. There would have been fewer loops because the rug yarn used with a punch needle tends to be thicker than the fabric strips used for hand hooking.

Bases used for the knotted rug methods are rug canvas and Rya canvas. The canvas can be used for either latchet hook or Rya (or Ghiordes) knots. With rug canvas, three or four knots per centimetre can be formed across and up and down. With Rya canvas, about three knots for 2 cm can be formed across, but only two rows of knots up and down. Because knots can be formed only in certain places, many drawn lines, especially those that are curved or diagonal, have to be adapted to follow the holes in the canvas. The second sample below was done on rug canvas with the latchet hook method. The drawn line above the row of knots, an adaptation of the curved line used for the first sample, is the same as the guideline used for placing the knots. Notice how the curves had to be 'stepped' to conform to the places where knots are possible on rug canvas. If the sample had been done on Rya canvas, there would have been only two knots up and down. With either of these two methods, the line on which the row is based becomes feathered and almost lost. This is because a knotted pile, being shaggy and long, has a tendency to fall to one side of the line. This falling tendency decreases, however, after several rows of knots have been worked; the thickness of the wool helps the rows to stand up.

It should not be concluded from these precautionary comments that a detailed design cannot be done with a knotted rug method, or an undetailed design with a hooked method. Detail can be achieved with a knotted rug method if the areas are large enough to permit the number of knots needed to execute the design. Also the pile should not be too long; a short (about 2–3 cm) pile will stand up and reinforce the lines of the details better than a longer pile would. If you should want to work an abstract design with a hooked method, the areas

for the elements would not have to be changed. There would be a noticeably different effect – a greater crispness in the overall design would be produced because of the crisper pile.

At the top of the opposite page there are four samples, each worked with a different rug method and illustrating the primary textural effects achievable with that method. What these samples do not show is how to produce a pile variegated in colour, a technique that can be useful in producing a rich and interesting design. With the hand hook method, variegation in colour is achieved by cutting the fabric strips for the pile from a multicoloured fabric, such as a plaid. A similar effect can be produced with the punch needle by threading the needle with multiple strands of a finer-than-usual yarn, each one a different colour (p. 387). With the latchet hook method, colour can be accomplished in two ways. One way is to alternate colours from knot to knot; the other is to use several strands and colours of a finer yarn for each knot (p. 389). The multicolour effect is produced with the Rya stitch method by using yarns of several colours to form stitches (p. 390).

As you formulate your design, keep the drawing of it to a manageable size within the intended finished shape. For help in drawing circular, semicircular and oval shapes, see the bottom of the facing page. Colour your drawing, but bear in mind that the actual shades will depend on the colour range of the yarn or fabric that will be used to work the design. Before transferring the design to the rug base (p. 380), enlarge the design to finished size (p. 14), then mark its centre. The dimensions of your rug base must be at least the finished size, plus any necessary margins for finishing edges (pp. 392–6). For guidance in estimating the amount of fabric or yarn for a hooked rug, see p. 382; for a knotted rug, see p. 388.

The bases for hooked rugs are fairly closely woven fabrics. Because of their weave, the loops can be formed at almost any point on the base and can with practice be made to follow almost any kind of drawn line in a design.

The bases for knotted rugs determine the possible points where knots can be placed. Because of this, many lines, especially curved and diagonal lines, have to be adapted. The stepped line used above is an adaptation of curved line on left.

Hand hook method

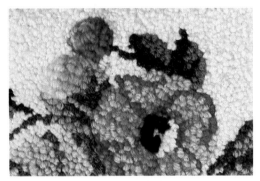

Punch needle method

Hooked rug methods were used to make the two samples on the left. The top sample was worked with the **hand hook method,** the lower sample with the **punch needle method.** Although the two samples look slightly different from each other, each was based on the same design in the same amount of space. The differences are due to the technique and the materials used to form the pile in each sample. The sample done with the hand hook method has finer line and colour detail than the one done with the punch needle method. This is because it is possible to form more loops per centimetre with narrow fabric strips than with the rug yarn used in the punch needle method. With the hand hook method, it is even possible to work several tones of a colour to show the shading that occurs when light hits a three-dimensional object – its high points become lighter in tone than its lower points. With the punch needle method, dimensional detail can be achieved by altering the height of the pile. A fuzzy texture can be produced by cutting some of the loops. For more information on the hand hook and punch needle methods, see pp. 382–7.

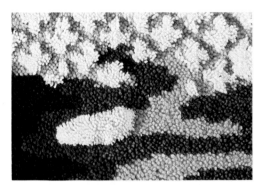

Latchet hook method

Rya stitch method

Knotted rug methods were used to make the two samples on the left. The **latchet hook method** was used to form the top sample, the **Rya stitch method** was used for the lower sample. Both were based on the same design within the same amount of space. The differences in texture between the samples are due to differences in the character of the pile. With the latchet hook method, the pile is always cut because pre-cut lengths of yarn are used to form the knots. With the Rya stitch method, the loops that connect the stitches and form the pile can be cut or uncut. Both methods allow for variations in pile length. The pile formed with each method can even be sculpted to produce a definite dimensional contour. A cut pile is sculpted by trimming it to the shape of the contour; an uncut pile is sculpted by forming the loops between stitches to the lengths required to form the contour. For more information on the two knotted rug methods, see pp. 388–91.

How to draw circles, semicircles and ovals

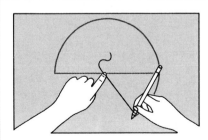

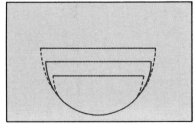

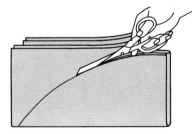

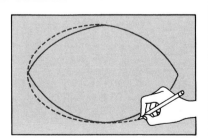

Circle. Draw a line equal to desired width of circle; mark centre of line. Tie a string to the end of a pencil. Place pencil point at end of drawn line; hold in place. Stretch string taut and hold at centre of line, then swing pencil around to draw the circle.

Semicircle. Draw the bottom half of a circle. To make the shape *shallower,* draw a new line below straight edge of semicircle; adjust curved ends to meet new line. For a *deeper* shape, draw a new line above the straight edge and adjust curved ends.

Oval. Cut out a rectangle the same height and width as the intended oval. Fold the rectangle in half, then into quarters. On the top quarter, draw a gently curved line to connect the top and the outer cut edges. Cut through all layers along the curved line.

Unfold the paper; place it on a larger piece of paper. Holding the cut paper in place, trace around its outer edge. Remove the cut shape. It may be necessary to refine the curves of the traced outline to round the ends or make the oval less pointed.

Hooking and knotting

Preparing the rug base

The rug base should measure the same as the finished rug, plus turnings at each edge if necessary. For a hooked rug, add a minimum 8 cm turning at each edge so the base can be set into a frame. Turnings will be used later when the rug is being finished. For a knotted rug, add turnings equal to the amount needed to finish each edge (pp. 394–6). Before working any rug, finish all raw edges so they will not unravel as you work. If masking tape is used for edge, cut back when rug is made and cover with binding. To transfer the design, you must first mark the exact centre of the base and the centre of each edge.

If necessary, join lengths to produce the required width. *If using a fabric base* (hessian or evenweave cloth), cut the lengths to be joined to the rug base length required (see above). Place them side by side and trim selvedges. Overlap the raw edges 2 cm, and stitch through both layers. When working, form pile through both layers.

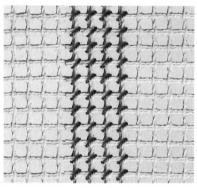

If using a canvas base, cut the lengths to be joined and trim their selvedges as explained for fabric rug bases (see left). Overlap the cut edges by four vertical threads; match all the vertical and horizontal threads. Then, working down each row of matched vertical threads, oversew each matched mesh. When working the rug, form the pile through both layers.

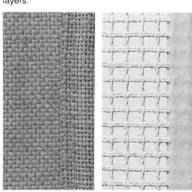

Finish the raw edges of the rug base so they will not unravel while the rug is being worked. If the rug base is *fabric*, turn under each raw edge 1 cm and machine-stitch in place (A). If the rug base is *canvas*, finish the raw edges by wrapping them with 2.5 cm wide masking tape (B).

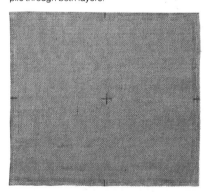

Mark the exact centre of the rug base as well as the centre of each of its edges. Use a dressmaker's pencil to mark a *fabric* base; use a waterproof felt-tipped pen to mark a *canvas* base. These markings will be used as guides when the design is transferred to the rug base.

Methods of design transfer

To transfer a design to a fabric rug base (hessian or evenweave fabric), use either the **pounce method**, a **hot-iron transfer pencil**, or **dressmaker's carbon paper and tracing wheel**. If the rug base is canvas, use the **canvas method**. With any of these methods, only the lines of the design are transferred. The design can be coloured in on a canvas base using oil paint or acrylic. This is not usually

POUNCE METHOD

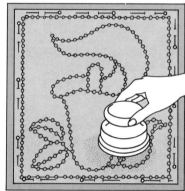

Hand hook or Rya stitch method 1. Using a heavy darning needle (set in a cork for comfort if preferred), form holes along the lines of the design. A quicker way to do this is to 'sew' along the lines with an unthreaded sewing machine set for a long straight stitch.

2. With its *wrong side down*, centre the perforated drawing on the rug base; pin it in place. Sprinkle some pounce over the holes; then, using a felt pad or a thick wad of fabric, rub the pounce through the holes of the drawing and on to the rug base.

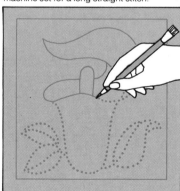

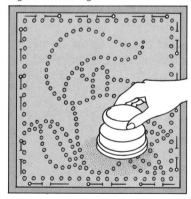

3. Remove the drawing from rug base, being careful not to smudge the dots of pounce. Using a dressmaker's pencil, connect the dots to produce the lines of the design. When all the lines have been drawn, shake the base to remove the excess pounce.

Punch needle method Perforate the drawing as in Step 1. With its *right side* facing the base, centre the drawing on the rug base and pin it in place. Sprinkle pounce and rub through holes as in Step 2. Remove drawing and connect dots (Step 3).

necessary on a rug base made of fabric.

It is when the design is transferred that the face and back sides of a rug are determined. (The face side is the pile side of the finished rug.) If the rug will be made with the *hand hook, Rya stitch or latchet hook method,* the side to which the design is transferred becomes the face side because it is the side where the pile will be. If the *punch needle method* will be used, the side to which the design is transferred becomes the back side of the rug; the pile will be on the opposite, or face side. To ensure that the design takes the proper direction on the face side of the rug, the design is transferred to the back side of the rug base in the direction opposite to what it will be on the face side. See below for specific instructions.

HOT-IRON TRANSFER PENCIL METHOD

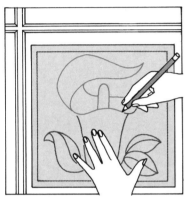

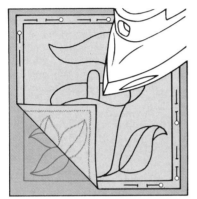

Hand hook or Rya stitch method 1. Turn the drawing of the design to its *wrong side* and hold it up to a window. Using the hot-iron transfer pencil, re-draw the lines of the design on the wrong side of the drawing.

2. With *wrong side* of drawing down, centre it on base; pin it in place along the edges. Working an area at a time, press hot iron down on the drawing and lift up after a few seconds. Repeat if lines have not transferred. Be careful not to scorch rug base.

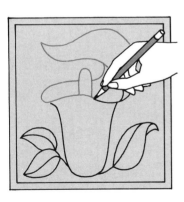

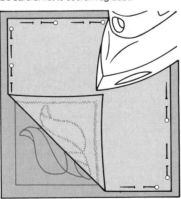

Punch needle method 1. Transfer the design in the following manner. Using a special hot-iron transfer pencil and working on the *right side* of the drawing of the design, carefully re-draw all the lines of the design.

2. With *right side* of drawing down, centre on rug base and pin in place along outer edges. Working an area at a time, press the hot iron down on the drawing and lift up after a few seconds. Repeat if lines have not transferred. Be careful not to scorch rug base.

DRESSMAKER'S CARBON PAPER AND TRACING WHEEL METHOD

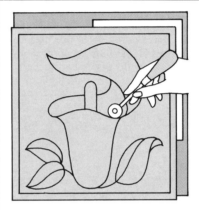

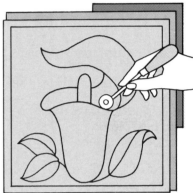

Hand hook or Rya stitch methods. *Wrong side* down, centre drawing on base. *Carbon side down,* slip carbon paper under drawing. Trace lines with wheel. Re-position carbon to mark various areas of design.

Punch needle method. Place drawing, *wrong side* down, on base. Slip carbon paper, *carbon side up,* under the rug base. Trace lines with wheel; re-position carbon to mark various areas of design.

CANVAS METHOD

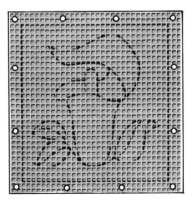

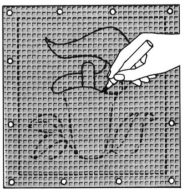

1. Slip drawing of design under the canvas and centre it. Tack layers together.

2. Using a wide felt-tipped waterproof marker, draw the design on to the canvas.

Preparing for and working a hooked rug

Estimating and preparing fabric for hand hook method
Estimating and preparing yarn for punch needle method
Setting a rug base into a frame
Hand hook method
Punch needle method

Estimating and preparing fabric for hand hook method

Fabric, cut into strips, is used to form the pile of a rug that is made with the hand hook method. The amount of fabric necessary for strips is roughly equal to the combined measurements of four layers of fabric, each layer the same size as the finished rug. This total should be shared among the colours in the design and, as a precaution, 15 per cent added to each colour's total. If you are using finer strips or a higher pile than usual, increase the amount proportionally; if strips are wider or pile is lower, decrease the amounts. The soundness of your estimate can be tested if you are careful as you work the first few areas of the rug.

Before the fabric is cut, it should be washed and pre-shrunk. Shrinking tightens the weave so the cut strips will be less likely to unravel. To make large pieces of fabric easier to cut into neat and even strips, first cut the material into pieces about 10 cm by 30 cm. Use sharp scissors and cut fabric vertically or horizontally using a warp or weft thread as a guide. Fabric can also be cut on the bias, or in a circular fashion to give a long strip, but it may fray. Different fabrics can be used in one rug, and can be most effective for a wall hanging, but beginners will find it best to use all wool or all cotton at first. Old material or scraps can also be used, but springy fabric is not suitable. If the fabrics are mixed, the strips will need to be cut to different widths, as thin fabric needs to be cut wider than thick.

It is sometimes helpful to dye a group of fabrics with one colour. The fabrics will take up the colour in different amounts, but will be in tones of one colour.

Some rug-makers like to collect fabric, cut it into strips and store it until they have enough to make a rug.

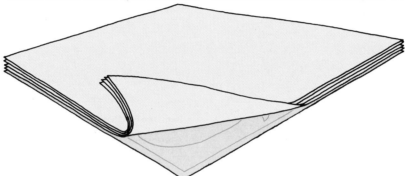

The amount of fabric needed for the pile strips is roughly equal to the combined measurement of four layers of fabric, each layer the same size as the finished rug.

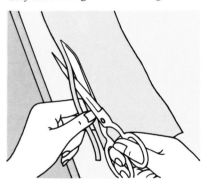

To cut the strips, use a fabric thread as a guide to a uniform strip width.

Estimating and preparing yarn for punch needle method

Yarn, usually in rug-weight, is used to form the pile of a rug that is made with the punch needle method. The basic formula for estimating the required amount of rug yarn is: allow 100 m of yarn for every 30 cm square of design area; calculate the total by multiplying the number of square centimetres in the design by 100. Then divide the total among the colours used in the design. As a precaution, add 15 per cent to the amount of each colour. This formula is based on the rug being worked with a 2 cm pile, the height that is achieved by using a punch needle set in the correct position. If you intend to use a higher pile, or a thinner yarn, increase the amounts proportionally. For example, you will need about twice as much tapestry yarn as rug yarn because about twice as many rows of loops will be formed with tapestry yarn as with rug yarn. Test the accuracy of any estimate by recording how much yarn was actually used in the first few areas worked. Before working the rug, wind the yarn into balls (p. 411) so that it will feed easily through the punch needle. Winding will be easier if you open the skein of yarn and place it over the back of a chair.

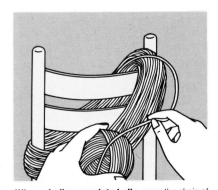

When winding yarn into balls, open the skein of yarn and place it over the back of a chair.

Setting a rug base into a frame

A hooked rug should be worked while it is stretched taut in a frame. The loops will be easier to form and they are less likely to slip out of the rug base.

A strong rotating slate frame, as shown below, would be a good choice, or a frame made with side stretchers, slots and pegs can be used.

If the rug is small, an embroidery frame or hoops made for quilting or embroidery will be suitable. All these frames are suitable for making rugs by hand hook or punch needle.

For instructions on setting a base into an embroidery frame, see p. 184; to set a base into a quilting hoop, see p. 249. When you set any type of rug base into any type of frame, be sure that its design side is facing up as the pile of the rug will be formed on top.

ROTATING FRAME

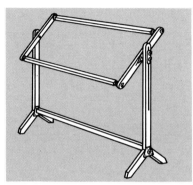 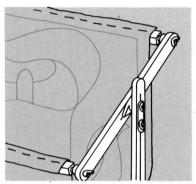 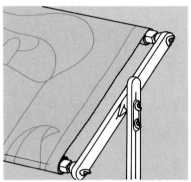 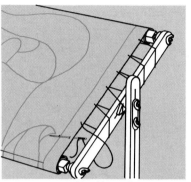

1. Assemble stand and attach side arms. Insert the ends of the top and bottom rods into the top and bottom ends of each side arm. If necessary, refer to the instructions that accompany the frame and stand.

2. Lap the top edge of the rug base over the top rod of the frame. Centre the rug base on the rod and nail or staple it in place. Attach the bottom edge of the rug base to the bottom rod of the frame in the same way.

3. Loosen the screws that hold the top and bottom rods in the side arms. Turn rods to take up the excess rug base. As you take up the excess, centre the area to be worked. When it is properly centred, tighten the screws.

4. Oversew each side of the rug base to an arm, using a heavy needle and thread. Begin stitching with a knot; end it with a few backstitches in the rug base. To re-position base, remove stitches and repeat Steps 3 and 4.

TO ATTACH THE SIDES OF RUG BASE WITH TAPE

During the work of hooking a rug, you will find that the pressure of pushing a hook through the base, or punching a needle through, will cause the base fabric to stretch and thus loosen the tension. It is essential to keep the base fabric taut for good work, and this can be done by lacing the sides of the base fabric to the frame with tape and pinning the tape to the base fabric (as shown). To tighten the tension in one place only, remove the pin, pull the tape loop over the base fabric and insert the pin again. Some rug-makers prefer this method for convenience when moving the rug along.

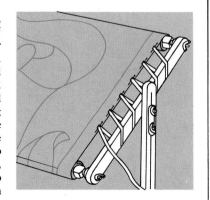

Lace the sides of the base fabric to the frame with tape, attaching the loops with pins. To move on the rug, follow Steps 3 and 4 above.

TO CENTRE THE FABRIC BACKING ON A SLATE FRAME

Fold the fabric backing in half and mark the centre with a pin. Measure the centre of the webbing attached to the rod with a tape measure, or by eye if you have experience in this. Mark the centre with a pin. Align the pins, make sure the fabric is straight, and begin to sew the backing fabric firmly to the webbing from the centre outwards, first on the left, then on the right, with back stitches. Use strong thread such as linen, or fine twine with a large needle. Finish off the ends securely so that the fabric backing will not pull away from the frame when the rug is under tension.

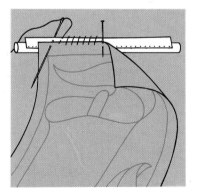

Pin fabric to webbing on end rod of frame at centre point. Sew firmly with strong thread from centre outwards to left edge (as shown).

Preparing for and working a hooked rug

Hand hook method

Strips of fabric are used to produce the pile of a rug that is made with the hand hook method. The strips can be cut to a number of different widths; which width to use depends on the amount of detail in the design and the amount of space allowed for the detail. In general, the greater the quantity of detail and the smaller the space given to it, the narrower the strips should be. A medium strip width is 3 mm; a strip this wide can achieve an average amount of detail within an average space. (The project on p. 406 was carried out with 3 mm wide strips.) For instructions on cutting strips, see p. 382. Hand hooks are available in two sizes in this country. The hand-made hook is used for larger strips about 1 cm wide, and the commercially made hook is used for narrower strips from 3 mm to 5 mm wide. Hooks in other sizes are available in the USA. The loops, as a rule, should be about as high as the strip is wide. For example, if the strips are 3 mm wide, make the loops 3 mm high. The basic techniques are explained below; for more specialised information refer to the opposite page.

Basic techniques

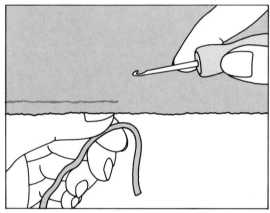

Position hands so that your left hand is below the rug base holding the fabric strip and your right hand above the base holding the hook. Work rows from right to left. (If you are left-handed, reverse the position of hands and the working direction of rows.)

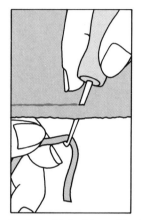

To start a fabric strip, push hook down through the rug base and place one end of the fabric strip over the hook. Then pull the hook and the end of the strip up through the rug base. Ends of strips will be cut even with pile when the rug is finished.

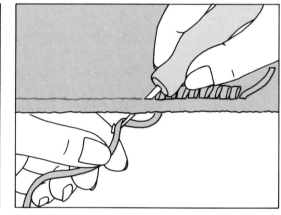

To form loops, push hook down through base, catch fabric strip, and bring it up in the form of a loop. If you have trouble pulling the loop up, push back on hook to enlarge the hole. The space between loops will depend on the strip width (see facing page).

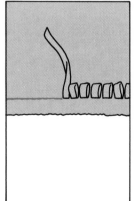
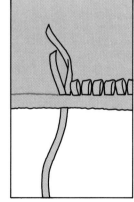

To end a fabric strip, bring its cut end up through the rug base. If the strip is still quite long, pull up a large loop, cut it, and pull the excess out through the back. Begin next strip in the hole where the last strip ended. Ends will be evened off later.

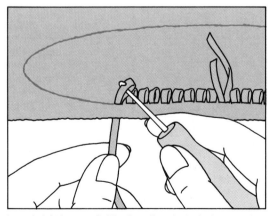

Loop height is controlled by the pull on the hook. As you pull up loops, keep each one even with the others. If you should pull up too large a loop, keep the hook in the loop and pull down on the strip until the loop is the correct height.

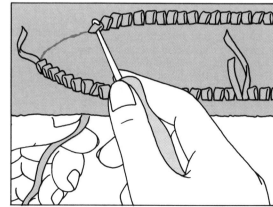

Work rows, especially long rows, from right to left as much as possible. If row starts to swing in opposite direction, end it, and work rest of row from right to left to meet it (as above). Work short rows continuously, in any direction necessary.

Working a design

To make a rug with the hand hook method, work the details of the design first and then the background area. Unless the detail will be shaded (see below), first form rows of loops to outline the shape of the detail, then work additional rows to fill in the area (see right). As was explained with Basic techniques (facing page), work the rows from right to left, stopping and starting the rows whenever necessary to maintain the proper row-working direction. The amount of space between loops and rows of loops will depend on the strip width. In general, if the strips being used are 3 mm wide, leave two of the base fabric's threads between loops and rows of loops; if the strips are 5 mm wide, leave two to three threads. If the rug starts to buckle, increase the amount of space between loops and rows; if the rug base can be seen between loops from the pile side of the rug, decrease the intervening space. As you work, do not carry the strip from one section to another; this causes a bulge that will wear out quickly when the rug is in use. If the design calls for pile of variegated colours, cut the strips for the pile from a multicoloured fabric, such as striped or herringbone.

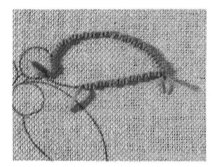

Outline a detail first. Work the rows from right to left. Start and stop rows as necessary to maintain the proper row-working direction.

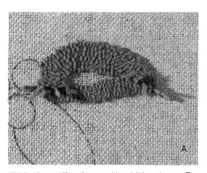

Fill in the outlined area with additional rows. The rows can be made to follow the contours of the outlined shape (A), or they can be worked across

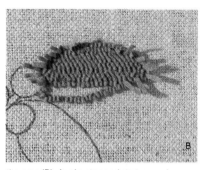

the area (B). Again, stop and start rows whenever necessary to maintain the proper row-working direction (see Basic techniques opposite).

The amount of space between loops and rows of loops depends on the strip width. The wider the strip, the more space between loops and rows.

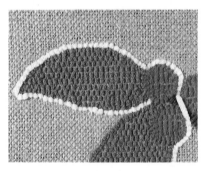

Do not carry a fabric strip from one area to another. Instead, end the strip in the one area and start it again in the other.

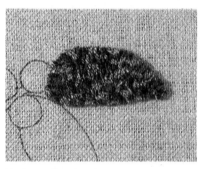

To form pile of variegated colours, cut the fabric strips from a multicoloured fabric that contains the colours you want or need for the pile.

Shading

Shading is the hooking of a detail with several tones of colour to portray the way a real, three-dimensional object changes in tone with the angle at which light hits its contoured surface. An example of a shaded detail is shown on the right. When planning how to shade a detail, imagine how its colour will vary when it is exposed to a hypothetical light source. The number of tones worked will depend on the real-life shape of the object, the amount of space allowed for the detail on the rug base, and the width of the strips being used. The larger the space for the detail and the narrower the

strips, the greater the possible number of tones. Assign the lightest tone to the area that receives the most light, the darkest tone to the area that receives the least. Then, depending on the amount of space you have left, assign intermediate tones to the remaining areas according to the relative amount of light each receives. When working the detail, work its inner areas and outer edges simultaneously. This differs from the approach to a simple detail (top of page). If there is enough space to allow it, work the rows in a slight zigzag; the colours will blend together better.

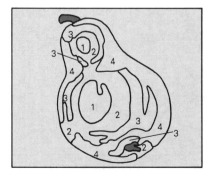

Indicate the tones on drawing of detail. Give the lightest tone to area nearest you (1), the darkest tone to the furthest away (4).

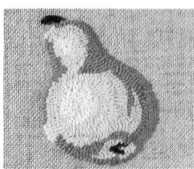

Work rows of loops within each tonal area. If the space allows, work rows in a slight zigzag; the tones will blend better.

385

Preparing for and working a hooked rug

Punch needle method

The punch needle method uses a hollow needle to 'thread' yarn in and out of a fabric base. This type of needle is available in one size only, but can be used with rug wool or several strands of finer wool. The wooden handle can be moved up and down the needle shaft by twisting to produce loops of between 2 and 5 cm long. Continental or American rug hooks are sometimes available, and are made in different sizes with an adjustable wire gauge to alter the loop height. This can produce a very small loop of only 5 mm in height.

The punch needle rug method is easy and quick to carry out. The basic techniques of the method are shown below, more specific techniques on the facing page. In forming the pile, it is very important not to lift the needle too far above the surface of the rug base. When the needle is lifted too high, excess yarn is pulled through it and sometimes loops already formed are pulled out. If either of these situations should occur, place the point of the needle where the next loop is to be, pull the excess yarn back through the needle, and continue.

Basic techniques

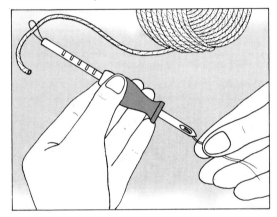

To thread a punch needle. Take a piece of fuse wire 35 cm long. Double it and twist the strands together. Push the loop end through the shaft. Insert end of yarn through the loop and pull through. Remove threader, and push end of yarn through eye of needle.

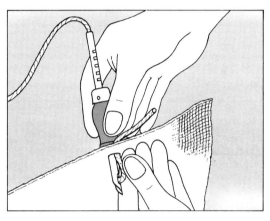

To begin. With back or grooved side of needle facing the way the row will be worked, plunge needle into fabric up to wooden handle. Pull cut yarn end all the way down through the rug base. Withdraw needle until point touches surface of base.

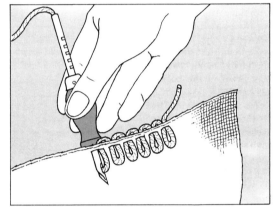

To form loops. Slide the point of the needle along fabric for a few threads. Then plunge needle into fabric up to wooden handle and bring it out to form the next loop. Spacing between the loops will depend on the weight of the yarn (see facing page).

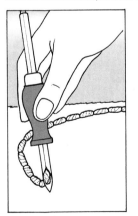

To change row-working direction. Turn the needle so its grooved side is facing in the new direction. If the grooved side of the needle is not facing in the same direction as the row to be worked, the yarn will not feed through the needle properly.

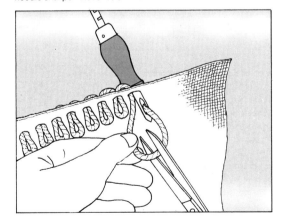

To end a yarn. Plunge the needle into the fabric. Tug on yarn supply, then cut the yarn behind the eye at the point of the needle. Bring the needle out. The starting and ending yarn ends should be trimmed even with the pile when the rug is finished.

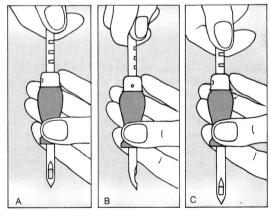

To alter the size of the loop. Hold the punch needle in the left hand, and twist the shaft with the right until it disengages (A). Pull until the exposed shaft is the right length (B), and twist until the internal wire in the handle catches the slot (C).

Working a design

When working a rug, work the details of the design first, then its background. Begin each detail by forming a row of loops to outline its shape, then work rows to fill the shape. Fill-in rows can be worked in two ways (see right); each way has a different effect on the clustering of the pile. These same two row-working directions can be applied to the filling-in of the background area. The amount of space that is left between loops and rows will vary according to the weight of the yarn being used. For heavy rug yarn, leave about three base-fabric threads between loops and rows; for a lightweight yarn, leave about a two-thread space. Since thread counts will vary slightly among rug bases, alter the spacing if necessary. Generally, if the rug starts to buckle, the loops and rows are too close together; if you can see base fabric between loops on the pile side of the rug, they are too far apart. As you work the areas, do not take the yarn over one area to get to another (see right). From time to time, check the pile side of the rug. If you discover that some loops are uneven, lift them with a knitting needle until they are even with the rest of the pile (see far right).

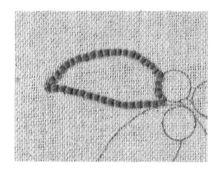

Outline the shape of each detail with a row of loops that follows the line on the rug base. Alter direction of row as many times as necessary.

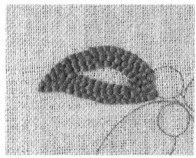

Fill in the outlined area with additional rows. The fill-in rows can be worked in two different directions – to follow the contour of the outlined shape

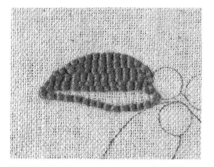

(A), or in straight rows across the outlined shape (B). Each way has a slightly different effect on the way the pile looks.

Spacing between loops and rows varies with the yarn weight. For a heavy rug yarn, leave about three threads; for lightweight yarn, two threads.

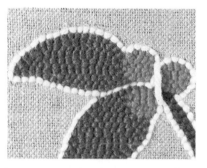

Do not take yarn from one area to another. Instead, cut and end the yarn in the first area, then start it again in the next.

If some loops are uneven, slip a knitting needle through several and pull up on them to make them even with the rest of the pile.

Special techniques

Pile made with the punch needle method can be varied in several ways. A multicoloured pile can be produced by threading the needle with several strands of a lightweight yarn, each a different colour. Dimensional detail can be added to a design by forming the pile to different heights and by cutting only the higher loops (those about 2 cm high). Differences in pile height are achieved by altering the length of the loops by moving the wooden handle along the needle shaft, or by using the pile gauge on a continental or American needle.

For a multicoloured pile, thread the needle with several strands and colours of a lightweight yarn. Experiment with different colour combinations and work the loops in the usual way.

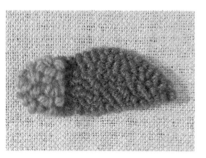

To vary pile heights to produce an interesting texture, work loops of different lengths by moving the handle along the needle shaft, or moving the pile gauge if your needle has one.

To cut loops, remove rug from frame. Working several loops at a time, insert scissor blade through loops and cut. Rug can be held flat, or curved over your hand for cutting.

387

Preparing for and working a knotted rug

Estimating and preparing yarn for latchet hook method
Estimating and preparing yarn for Rya stitch method
Latchet hook method
Rya stitch method
Working a charted design
Trimming and sculpting pile

Estimating and preparing yarn for latchet hook method

The amount of yarn needed to make a rug with the latchet hook method will depend on the number of knots needed to form the design, and the number and length of the strands used in the knots (see facing page). The cut length of a yarn strand used in any knot should be twice the desired pile length plus 1.5 cm. The length is double because the strand becomes halved when knotted; the 1.5 cm is taken up in the knot. Yarn for the knots can be purchased in packs of cut strands or in skein form (p. 376).

To calculate yarn amounts, first estimate the number of knots in the design (the number of knots in a square centimetre of canvas times the number of square centimetres in the design). Then decide the number of yarn strands required for the knots (knot count times the number of strands needed for each knot). Divide the resulting strand count among the colours and yarn types in the design and add 15 per cent to each total. If you are buying packs of pre-cut yarns,

divide the total strand count of the rug by the count of one pack; the result is the number of packs needed. If the yarn will be purchased in skeins, you must translate the total strand count into metres (multiply the strand count by the cut length of the strands, then divide by 100). Yarn to be cut is wrapped around a cutting gauge, then cut along the groove with scissors, taking care to cut down the middle. You can make your own gauge of cardboard, cut to the length of the strand and wide enough to accommodate several turns of yarn.

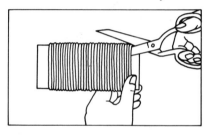
Yarns being cut on a cardboard gauge

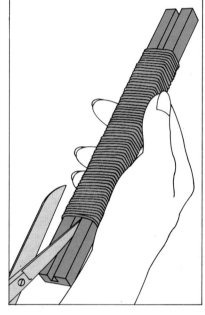
Yarns being cut on a wooden gauge

Estimating and preparing yarn for Rya stitch method

The Rya stitch method is the formation of Rya stitches (Ghiordes knots), and is made with three or more strands of yarn (usually Rya). The pile formed by the knots is usually 5 cm long, but can be as short as 2 cm or as long as desired. To calculate the amount of yarn needed for a Rya stitch rug, first determine how much yarn is needed for each knot, then multiply this amount by the total number of knots in the design. The quantity of yarn needed for one knot made with a single strand of yarn is twice the desired pile length plus 1.5 cm. This

much is required because the yarn is halved when knotted; the 1.5 cm is absorbed in the knot. If the knot will be made with several strands, the amount of yarn needed is the length needed for a single-strand knot multiplied by the number of strands that will be used to form the knot. To determine the total amount of yarn needed for the rug, multiply the length needed for one knot by the number of knots in the rug. (If the pile length varies, make a calculation for each pile length.) Divide these totals among the colours and yarn types used

in the design, add 15 per cent to each total, then divide by 100 to arrive at number of metres. To prepare the yarn for work, cut it to equal lengths of about 140 cm. Skeins of Rya yarn can usually be opened up and cut at one end to produce many equal lengths, each about 140 cm long. The skein structure of other yarns, however, may necessitate pulling the yarn out as a single strand and cutting the working lengths individually. Thrums come in ready-cut lengths. If you find 140 cm too long, cut a length convenient for yourself.

An open skein of yarn being cut into equal working lengths

Individual lengths being cut from a wound skein

Latchet hook method

With the latchet hook method, cut yarns are knotted on to horizontal threads of a rug canvas with the aid of a latchet hook. The knots are worked row by row across the canvas and from the bottom edge of the design up. This direction of working ensures that the latchet hook can slip easily through the canvas while the knots are being formed. As a rule, single strands of rug yarn, 6.5 cm in length, are used to form the individual knots (see right); the pile length produced is 2.5 cm. When using this type of yarn, form a row of knots across every set of horizontal threads of the canvas. Quite often, however, three or four strands of Rya yarn, 17 cm long, are used to make the knots (see below); the pile length produced with these is about 7 cm. When forming a knot with several strands of yarn, treat the multiple strands as a single unit. To produce a thick pile with *multiple-strand knots*, form a row of knots across every set of horizontal threads; for a less dense pile, and one that will fall, form a row across every other set of horizontal threads. A *multicoloured pile* can be formed with either single or multiple-strand knots; the method differs with each type of knot (see below).

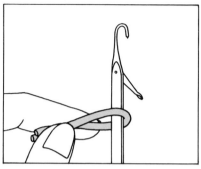

1. Fold the yarn in half around the shank of the latchet hook; hold both of the cut yarn ends between your thumb and index finger.

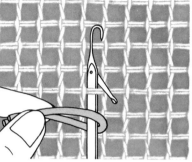

2. Holding the yarn around the shank, slip tip of hook under a set of horizontal threads and push it through until the bar of the hook falls open.

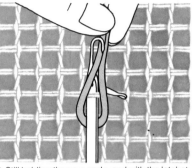

3. Still holding the yarn ends, and with the latchet hook remaining open, bring the yarn up and around into the open latchet hook as shown.

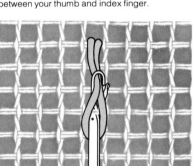

4. Carefully pull the hook down under the horizontal threads. When the bar of the hook closes, release both of the cut yarn ends.

5. Continue to pull the hook down and under the horizontal threads. The yarn ends will be pulled with the hook to form the knot.

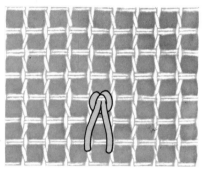

6. Pull on the cut yarn ends to tighten the knot around the horizontal threads and to bring both cut yarn ends even with each other.

Additional techniques

To form a multiple-strand knot, treat strands as a single unit. Fold all yarns around hook and form knot as described at top of page.

Rows of multiple-strand knots can be worked on every set of horizontal threads, or on every other set of threads as shown above.

To form a multicoloured pile with *single-strand knots*, alternate the colours of knots across each row; stagger position of colours from row to row.

If using multiple-strand knots, use strands of different colours to form the knots. Form rows on each set or every other set of horizontal threads.

Preparing for and working a knotted rug

Rya stitch method

A Rya stitch rug is produced by working Rya stitches (Ghiordes knots) row by row across Rya or ordinary canvas from the bottom of the design up. A size 14 tapestry needle is used to work the stitches (knots); the loops that connect the stitches form the pile of the rug. The quality of the pile depends on the type and amount of yarn used for the stitches,

the length of the loops, and whether or not the loops are cut. Rya stitches are generally made with three or four strands of Rya yarn, the loops are 2–5 cm long, and they are cut after all the stitching is done. Loop length is controlled as you work the stitches, or can be worked over a gauge stick. The rows of exposed vertical threads on Rya canvas

(p. 376) are spaced 5 mm apart. The loops can be as long as desired; they must be at least long enough to cover the tops of knots worked in the row immediately below. The loop length and yarn colour or type can be changed as they occur in the design across a row. If the design calls for a multicoloured pile, use yarn strands of different colours to

make the knots. Rya stitches can be done on rug canvas, as shown. Work every third row of canvas for a Rya effect, or for a rug nearer to traditional carpet techniques work each row with a close pile. If you are left-handed, work the stitches and the rows from the right to the left and with the needle pointing to the right.

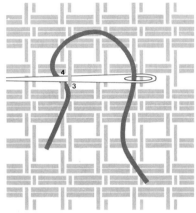

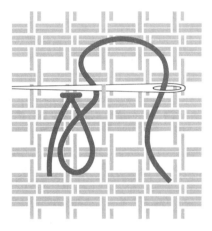

1. Begin at left. Slip needle between double vertical threads (1 to 2) and pull yarn through to desired length.

2. With yarn above needle, slip needle under next vertical thread (3 to 4). Tug yarn downwards to complete stitch.

3. Work across row to the right, forming a loop of the desired length and holding it in place as you form the next and each successive stitch.

4. Work each new row from left to right, above row just done. When stitching is finished, trim yarn ends even with pile; cut loops (below) if desired.

Additional techniques

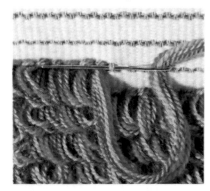

To form a multicoloured pile, thread the needle with strands of yarns in the colours needed for the pile. Form stitches in the usual way.

To cut loops, slip blade of scissors through a few loops, tug on them slightly and cut. Proceed to next group of loops and cut them the same way.

To form a Rya stitch on rug canvas, separate a double vertical thread; slip needle under one thread (1 to 2), then the other (3 to 4). You can

work stitches across every row of vertical threads, or miss one or more between stitch rows. Loops must cover tops of knots in row below.

Working a charted design

Sometimes a design intended for use with one of the knotted rug methods will be presented in chart form. In chart form, each stitch (knot) in the design is represented by one square on graph paper. In addition to the location of the stitches (knots), a chart will usually specify the colour and type of yarn and the length and number of strands to use in each stitch (knot). If these elements are not described, it is up to you to decide. Colours are represented by filled squares on the chart, filled either with the colours intended for the knots or with symbols to represent them. The yarn type, length and number of strands can also be denoted by symbols, but are usually explained in a written statement.

If symbols are used, their meanings are defined in a list known as a key. A row of blank squares on a chart usually signifies an unworked row on the rug base.

The amount of rug base needed to work a charted design is equal to the number of threads required to form the stitches called for by the chart across and up and down. To this amount should be added any turnings necessary along each edge of the rug base (p. 380). When you calculate the amount of rug base, also decide the amount of yarn needed to work the design (p. 388). Read and follow the chart to work the design on to the rug base. Work and read from left to right and from the bottom edge of the design upwards.

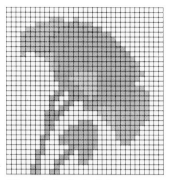

When a design is charted, each square on the chart means a stitch or knot on the rug base. Shown above is a charted design; on the right, the same design worked on rug canvas with latchet hook method. Sample shows reverse side.

Trimming and sculpting pile

The last step in working a latchet hook or Rya stitch rug is to trim any stray yarn ends even with the rest of the pile. Do this with a pair of specially angled rug scissors if available: these can be held parallel to the pile as you cut the yarn ends (see p. 394). With knotted rugs in which certain areas of the design have been worked with longer cut pile than others, trimming can mean something more explicit. It can mean cutting the pile in an area to a shorter, more suitable length (as in the first sample below) or the sculpting of the pile to produce a specifically shaped, three-dimensional contour (second and third samples). All three samples are parts of the rug on p. 407. Trimming to shorten pile length or to form a contoured shape is not applicable to a Rya stitch rug worked with uncut loops. Here the loops must be formed, as the rug is being worked, to the length or lengths that will produce the desired pile or contoured shape.

To cut pile to a shorter length, hold several of the strands straight up and cut them straight across to the desired length. Proceed to the next group and cut them the same way.

To sculpt an area, cut the pile to the lengths needed to form the desired shape. The area above is being cut so that the strands at one edge are shorter than those at the opposite edge.

This area is being sculpted to form a mound. The strands at the edges are being cut shorter than those in the centre. If a mistake is made, re-work the knots and cut them again.

Finishing techniques

Finishing hooked rugs
Finishing knotted rugs/Canvas
Finishing knotted rugs/Rya
canvas

Finishing hooked rugs

Before you begin a finishing process for a rug made with either the hand hook method or the punch needle method, check the front of the rug to make sure that all the fabric and yarn ends have been cut to the same length as the pile. Check the back of a rug made with either of these methods to see if there are any long cross-over stitches. If there are, cut them in the centre and pull the ends to the front; trim the ends even with the pile. The finishing techniques shown below and opposite include applying latex; hemming and binding; making a lining for a rug; and making a cushion.

APPLYING LATEX

Latex, a viscous rubber available in liquid form, is used to anchor the pile firmly to the base fabric. It is essential to use latex on a rug made with the punch needle method or the pile will pull out when the rug is used. Latex makes a rug more durable and also makes it slip-proof. Traditionally, latex is not used on a rug made with the hand hook method; however, you may use it if you wish, although dirt and grit will be easier to remove without a latex backing, and the rug cannot be dry cleaned. When using latex, let the rug dry thoroughly, following package directions. When the rug is dry, you can proceed with a finishing technique such as binding the edges with tape. You will have to use a sharp needle, and a thimble to help push the needle through the coated fabric.

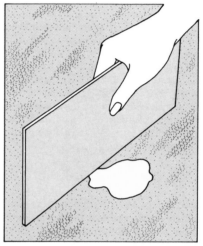

To apply liquid latex, pour a small amount in the centre of the base fabric. Use a piece of stiff cardboard or an old spatula to spread it.

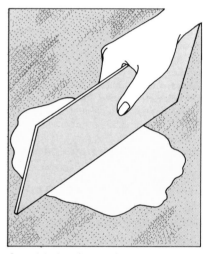

Spread the latex into as thin a layer as possible. Continue applying a small amount at a time until the entire back of the rug is coated.

HEMMING

It is possible to hem the edges of a rug made with the hand hook or the punch needle method if the base fabric is even-weave linen and if the rug is not too large. The fibres in evenweave are pliable, so the excess fabric can be turned under and hemmed; the fibres in hessian, being stiff, crease when folded and are likely to crack in time. If you have used hessian as a rug base, you should bind the edges (see opposite page). In general, use binding on any rug that is large and will get a lot of use – bound edges are far more durable. Binding also makes a neater edge for a round or oval rug. For hemming, you will need button thread or any heavy-duty linen thread, a sharp needle and a thimble.

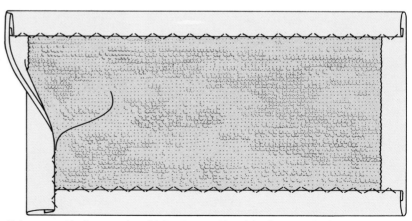

To hem a rug, trim the excess base fabric to 5 cm on all four sides. Fold under (towards the back) 5 mm on all edges; then fold the excess fabric to the back, making this fold as close as possible to the last row of pile. Stitch the hem first on two opposite sides, then turn up the remaining sides. On the last two sides, stitch the fold to the hemmed edge and then to the rug back as shown.

BINDING

Binding is the best finishing technique if you want to create a strong edge for a rug. It is essential to use binding if the edges of the base fabric have become frayed from being stretched in a frame. It is also necessary to use binding if you have used hessian as the base fabric, because exposed hessian threads tend to crack and wear out in time.

Rug binding is a woven cotton tape 2.5 or 5 cm wide; it comes in tan and other neutral colours. Since the binding does not show, it is not necessary for the binding to match the colours in the rug, but you can dye rug tape if you wish. When buying rug binding, be generous. You will need enough to go around the outside measurement of your rug, plus a 5 cm overlap. You will also need a heavy linen or cotton thread, such as button thread, and a needle. If latex has been applied to the back of the rug, you will also need a thimble to push the needle through the fabric.

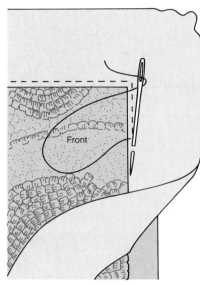

To bind a square or rectangle, trim base fabric to 2 cm from edge of last row of loops. Lay rug tape on right side of rug with edge of tape even with last row of loops. With heavy thread, stitch tape to rug about 3 mm from edge of tape.

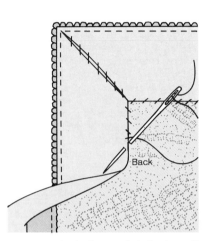

Fold tape to back of rug and pin in place. At corners, form mitre by folding excess tape under as shown. Sew tape to rug with an overcast stitch; sew mitre line closed at corners. Stitch loosely so edges do not gather up and pucker.

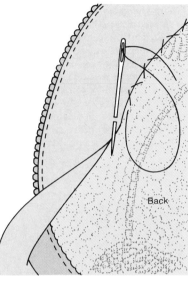

To bind a round or oval rug, you will have to make bias tape (see p. 258) because it is not available in widths for rugs. Apply tape by stretching outer edge of tape slightly as you stitch it to rug; ease inner edge to fit rug shape.

LINING

Rugs are not usually lined, as it is best if dirt and grit fall through the yarn and canvas to the floor underneath, rather than remain trapped in a lining. If you wish to do so, there are two main ways to make a lining. The first method requires turning the rug inside out; it is limited to small rugs and cushions. If a rug is too large to turn, you can make a lining by folding under the edges of lining fabric and base fabric and stitching the two together, as shown far right.

For a lining fabric, choose a sturdy, firmly woven cotton, such as twill or duck. If you are making a cushion top, you can select a less durable and more decorative fabric for the backing. To make the cushion, follow the directions on the right, and insert a cushion form or loose polyester wadding through the opening before you stitch it.

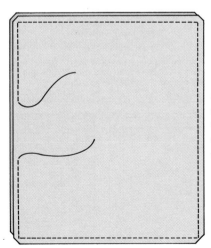

To make a lining, cut lining fabric 2.5 cm larger than rug. Trim excess base fabric to 1.5 cm. With right sides facing, stitch lining to rug 1.5 cm from edge. Leave opening for turning. Trim corners, turn right side out; stitch opening closed.

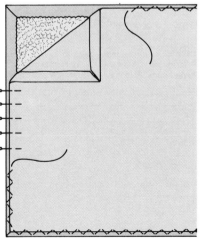

If rug is too large to turn, cut lining fabric 5 cm larger than rug; press under 2.5 cm on all sides. Trim excess base fabric to 2.5 cm, then fold to back of rug. Pin lining to rug back so that the folds meet, then stitch them together.

PRESSING

A hooked rug should be steam-pressed. If you are going to apply latex, press the rug first. If not, press after hemming or other finishing technique is completed. Press the rug with a steam iron and a pressing cloth; this sets the loops and gives a finished look to the rug. To do this, place the rug face down on an ironing board. If the rug is too big for this, place it face down on any clean, flat, firm surface. For a pressing cloth, wet a towel or a piece of heavy cotton fabric and wring it out; cloth should be damp but not wet. Spread the cloth on the rug and iron over it. As the pressing cloth dries, dampen it again. Continue until the entire back of the rug has been pressed. You can turn the rug face up and repeat the entire procedure on the right side of the rug. Let the rug dry thoroughly before you use it.

Finishing techniques

Finishing knotted rugs/Canvas

Before you begin a finishing process for a rug knotted on a canvas base, examine the back of the canvas to see whether you have missed any areas; missed areas are more easily seen from the back. Knot any such areas. The cut ends of a knotted pile can be somewhat uneven. To trim the ends evenly, use a pair of specially angled rug scissors as shown below. To sculpt pile by cutting ends to different lengths, see p. 391.

BINDING

To apply binding to a rug that has been knotted on a canvas backing, you will require 4 cm wide rug binding, a heavy-duty needle and strong cotton or linen thread. When the knotting is completed, trim excess canvas to 3 cm on edges; trim corners diagonally. On a square or rectangular rug, it is not necessary to fold this excess canvas to the back of the rug and stitch it down; however, you can stitch it down first if you find it easier. On a round or oval rug, stitch excess canvas to the back of the rug first; this makes it easier to apply binding as shown below.

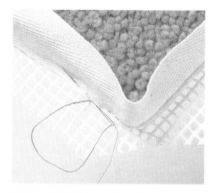

With rug right side up, place tape face down along edge. Overlap ends 5 cm. Stitch from wrong side, keeping tape close to knots.

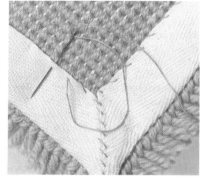

Fold tape to back of rug, covering excess canvas, and stitch. At corners, fold tape to form mitre. Stitch diagonal mitre line to close it.

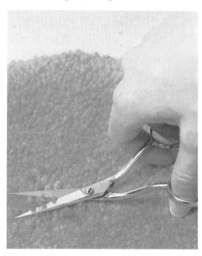

To trim yarn ends on cut knotted pile, use angled rug scissors if available. They allow space for fingers yet keep blade flat against pile.

On oval or circle, trim canvas to 3 cm. Cut out notches so canvas will not fold on itself when turned back. Do not cut up to last row of knots.

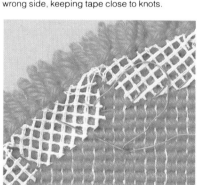

Fold excess canvas to back of rug, making sure sections of canvas lie next to each other but do not overlap. Stitch canvas to back of rug.

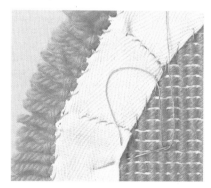

Stitch tape to back of rug along outer edge. Sew inner edge of tape to rug back, folding excess tape into darts as needed; stitch darts closed.

LINING

To add a lining to a rug or make a cushion, follow the directions for hooked rugs on p. 393, taking note of two exceptions. If you are making a cushion or lining a small rug, make sure that the longer yarn ends are pushed towards the centre of the work; stitch carefully so the yarn ends do not get caught in the seam. If you are lining a large rug, fold back the excess canvas and stitch it to the back of the rug. It is easier to attach the lining to the rug if the excess canvas has been secured first.

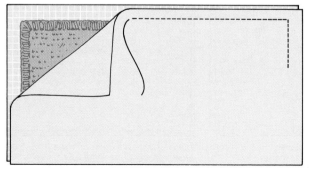

When backing a small rug or making a cushion, push yarn ends to the centre so they do not get caught in the stitching.

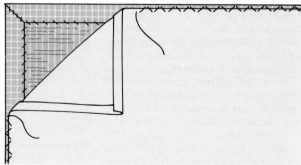

When lining a large rug, fold excess canvas to back of rug and stitch in place. Press under 3 cm on lining fabric; stitch fold to edge of canvas.

STITCHED BORDERS

Another way to finish the edges of a canvas rug base is to stitch a border with yarn that matches or co-ordinates with colours used in the rug. If you want to add a stitched border, this must be decided before you start the rug because the canvas must be turned under around all edges and secured by working knots at the outer edges through two layers of canvas. If you have used pre-cut yarn, buy a skein of the same type of yarn for the border. If you have used Rya or lightweight yarn, use at least two strands for the border stitches so the border will be thick enough to cover the canvas.

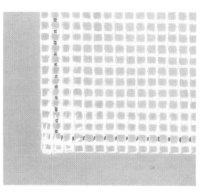

Before you begin, fold back excess canvas, leaving row of holes beyond design. Secure canvas with knots at edges through both layers.

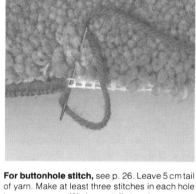

For buttonhole stitch, see p. 26. Leave 5 cm tail of yarn. Make at least three stitches in each hole to cover canvas. Work over tail at end.

To overcast, take needle from back to front, over canvas, then back to front again. Work enough stitches in each hole to cover canvas.

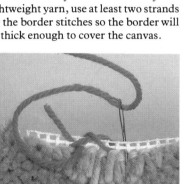

To work braided or plaited stitch, bring needle from back through first hole; go over edge and put needle through fifth hole. Go over edge and

bring needle through second hole; go over edge and bring needle through sixth hole. Continue from next hole on left to fourth hole from it.

To combine plaited border with binding, a technique used on round and oval rugs, sew excess canvas to rug back, leaving one row of

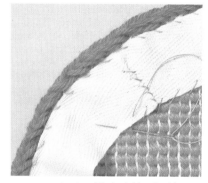

holes around edge. Work plaiting in this row. Place binding so edge meets plaited stitch; sew binding in place (see opposite page).

FRINGE

To add a fringe to a rug that has been worked on canvas, you can use long strands of the same yarn that was used for the knotting. Or, to simulate the look of a fringe on an Oriental carpet, you can use strong string or cotton crochet yarn in beige or ecru. Oriental carpets have a fringe on two ends only; other rugs can have a fringe on all edges. Cut the yarn into strands that are slightly more than twice as long as the finished fringe length. You can add binding after you have knotted the fringe if you wish.

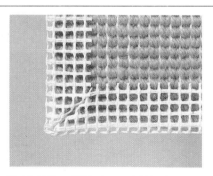

To fringe four sides of a rug, fold back excess canvas so that one hole is exposed on all edges. Stitch canvas to back of rug (see facing page).

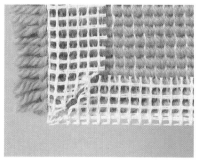

To fringe ends only, fold back excess canvas so no canvas shows on two long sides; one row of holes is exposed on ends. Stitch canvas to back.

To attach a fringe, fold yarn in half and pull through canvas hole from the back with a crochet hook. Put ends through loop, pull to tighten.

Finishing techniques

Finishing knotted rugs/Rya canvas

The special canvas used for Rya rugs is specially woven so that it provides evenly spaced areas of exposed vertical threads. Rya and ordinary canvas are available in a variety of widths with selvedge edges on both sides. The knotting is worked right up to the selvedge edges; they do not have to be turned under and hemmed. You will need to finish only the top and bottom edges, unless you made a stitched border (see p. 395).

If you are making a small cushion, you may have raw edges on all four of the sides. These edges will be enclosed when the cushion backing is sewn to the base fabric, as shown on the right.

The finishing techniques shown below include applying binding to the top and bottom edges and adding a fringe. It is a matter of choice whether to add a fringe or not. If a rug is made with a long shaggy pile, a fringe is unnecessary. As fringes tend to wear more quickly than the rest of a rug, make them very firm and neat.

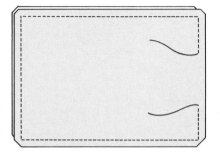

To make cushion, trim excess fabric. Sew to backing 1.5 cm from edge, leaving opening.

Trim corners; turn right side out. Insert cushion form or loose polyester fibre. Sew up opening.

BINDING

Because Rya canvas has selvedge edges on the sides, you only have to apply binding to the top and bottom. Binding is sewn along the row of spaces (exposed vertical threads) above the first row of knots and below the last row. When the binding is folded to the back of the rug, there will be a small area (less than 3 mm) of backing fabric showing. The loops will cover this when the rug is placed on the floor. In addition to the binding, you will need a heavy-duty needle and a strong thread, such as carpet or linen thread.

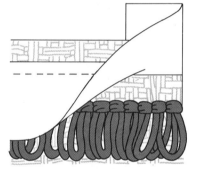

Cut rug binding to rug size plus 5 cm. Place binding on rug, leaving 2.5 cm on either side. Stitch binding to rug along row of spaces.

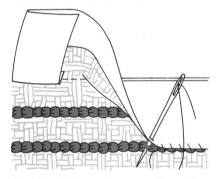

Before you fold the binding to the back of the rug, fold the 2.5 cm extensions on both sides to the back to create a clean side edge.

Stitch the binding to the rug as shown. Then slipstitch the fold of the binding to the rug base fabric along the side edge.

FRINGE

Traditionally, a fringe is added only to the top and bottom edges of a Rya rug stitched on Rya canvas. Make the fringe with the same Rya yarn used for the rug. To add a fringe, you stitch a row of the same knots used in the rug, placing them in the row of spaces (exposed vertical threads) immediately below the last row of knots and immediately above the first row of knots. Make the loops of the fringe at least twice as long as the loops in the rug; you can make them longer if you like. You can cut the fringe or leave the long loops. Apply rug binding to the edges of the canvas after the fringe is attached.

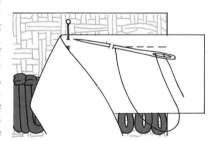

To add a fringe, make a row of the same knots as in the rug, placing them in the row of canvas above first row and below last row of knots.

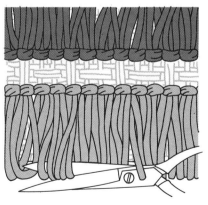

Make the loops of the fringe at least twice as long as the loops in the rug. You can cut the fringe or leave it in long loops, as you prefer.

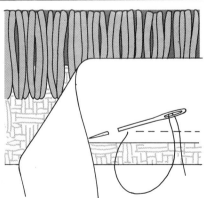

Apply rug binding (above) after the fringe has been worked. Sew binding along canvas just above top row of fringe and below bottom row.

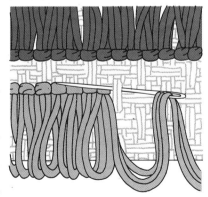

Care of handmade rugs

Slip-proofing, padding, vacuuming, removing spots, dry cleaning, washing, repair and storage

A handmade rug will look better and last longer if certain precautions are taken with its care and handling.

To stop rugs slipping. A small rug should be anchored by placing a non-slip pad underneath it. This can be a thin mat that is all rubber or rubberised on one side only. If a small rug is in an area where it does not get much wear, you can simply sew small pieces of rubber mat at each corner of the rug. If you have used latex on the back of the rug to secure the pile, the latex will help prevent slipping also.

Padding. Small handmade rugs are often used on top of carpeting, which acts as a cushion for the rug. If a rug is used on a bare floor, it will wear better with carpet underlay beneath. Without underlay, the pile surface will become flattened and will wear out sooner.

Vacuuming. Handmade rugs can and should be vacuumed regularly. Wool has great resistance to dirt; a vacuum will pick up loose dirt on the surface. Small rugs can be turned over and vacuumed on the back as well. Rya and latchet hook rugs, if they are small enough, can be picked up and shaken to dislodge loose dirt. Since the pile is higher on these rugs, it is easier for dirt to get caught. Shaking before vacuuming will loosen the dirt so the vacuum can pick it up; it will also make cleaning easier because you will not have to run the vacuum over the rug repeatedly.

Removing spots. A spot that occurs on a rug is much easier to remove if steps are taken immediately. Use a reliable spot remover, following package directions. A spot that is not removed immediately tends to stain the rug and is difficult to remove later.

Dry cleaning. Knotted rugs can be dry cleaned successfully, although the canvas will lose its stiffness and the rug will look limp. Hooked rugs cannot be dry cleaned as the loops may pull out. Rugs with latex backing cannot be dry cleaned as the spirit dissolves the latex.

Washing. Rugs should never be washed in such a way that they become saturated. There are several commercial rug cleaners available in both dry and liquid forms. A dry rug cleaner is sprinkled on the rug, allowed to remain for a while, then vacuumed off. Liquid rug cleaners are applied with a damp cloth. Before you use either type of rug cleaner, vacuum the rug thoroughly to remove loose dirt. Some rug cleaners are toxic; read directions carefully and make sure the room is properly ventilated.

Repairing. If you save a few pieces of yarn or fabric strips in the colours used in your rug, you can use these to repair a small area that has been damaged by a burn, a tear, or a stain that will not come out. To repair a damaged spot, outline the area with a row of pins (see below). Turn the rug over and carefully cut the damaged yarn or fabric from the back. Hook or knot the area with your leftover material. Trim any ends. If a stitched border becomes damaged, pull out the yarn in that area, and work ends under adjacent stitches. With matching yarn, re-work the border stitches.

Storing a rug. To store or transport a rug, roll it with the loops on the outside. This keeps the loops from getting wrinkled and does not put unnecessary strain on the backing fabric. Never fold a handmade rug. If you are going to store the rug, wrap it in an old sheet to keep it clean. Do not use plastic because it is not porous. Some wool yarns intended for rug use are moth-proofed; you may want to use mothballs as an extra precaution.

Repairing hooked rugs

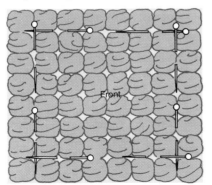

To repair a damaged area, outline it on the front of the rug with straight pins. Push the pile aside, if necessary, to insert the pins.

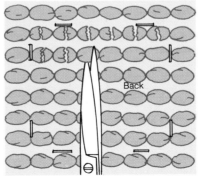

Turn the rug over. Cut the yarn or fabric strips within the pinned area. Carefully remove yarn or fabric strips, bringing ends to the front.

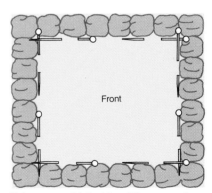

Using yarn or fabric strips of the same colour, hook the area. Bring ends to front and trim them even with the pile. Remove the pins.

Plaiting

Materials

Plaited rugs probably originated as mats of straw or grass used to cover earth floors. Plaited rugs as we know them started out as a way to utilise fabric scraps. Many plaited rugs are still made from left-over fabric or worn clothing that is cut into strips. Whether you plait with new or used fabric, there are certain guidelines to follow.

The fabric. Heavy or medium-weight wool is the best fabric for a plaited rug because it wears so well. The wool should be heavy and closely woven, soft but firm. Loosely woven fabrics wear out more quickly than those that are tightly woven; stiff wools, such as gabardine, are difficult to work with. Avoid using cotton, linen or silk; fabrics of these fibres do not wear well. Synthetics attract static and will not stand up to the wear that a rug is given. Do not use fabrics made of different materials in the same rug.

Assembling the fabric. If you use new fabric, buy manufacturer's remnants by the kilo to keep the cost down. Making a rug uses a great deal of fabric. Inquire in your area for woollen mills; most of them sell wholesale only, but some will probably be glad to sell offcuts.

The most economical way to make a rug is with fabric from old coats, suits, skirts and blankets. If you do this, make sure that all the wool is approximately the same weight. With old clothes, first remove any zips, linings, collars and pockets. Open darts and cut along seamlines. Cut out any worn areas, such as elbows, knees and seats. Also remove any areas damaged by moths. Wash the fabric in a machine or by hand, using a mild detergent and cold water. Hang it up to dry; do not put wool in a tumble dryer. You may also want to wash new wool remnants before using them.

Amount. If you are buying fabric by the metre, allow about 1 m of 140 cm wide fabric for a 30 cm square of plaiting. A rug 1 m by 75 cm would need approxi-

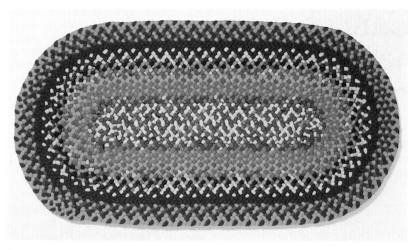

Oval plaited rug, worked in shades of brown and gold, is started with a straight centre plait.

mately 9 m of fabric. If you are buying or collecting wool by the kilo, allow about 500 g for 30 cm square of plaiting. The amount will vary, depending on how wide you cut your strips and how tightly you plait. Weigh garments after the lining, zip and collar have been removed. When buying wool by the kilo, allow from 10 to 30 per cent for waste. If you use material already cut into strips, allow extra length for plaiting; it takes up approximately one-third of the strip. Each plait ought to be about 20 cm longer than the plait in the previous row. If you have planned a colour scheme, buy or collect the maximum amount of fabric suggested before you start, so that you will not run out of a particular colour.

Using colour. There are several ways to use colour in a plaited rug. The easiest, especially for a beginner or for anyone using old fabrics, is to combine any colours that you have. A plaited rug will look more effective if you plan stripes or bands of certain colours. When planning a colour scheme, there are several design guidelines to bear in mind. Lighter shades look better in the centre

than dark ones; a dark centre tends to look like a bull's eye. Dark colours on the edge of a rug, however, have the effect of a frame. Keep the size of the centre of the rug in proportion to the size of the whole rug. To decide what the size should be, make a sketch of the rug and colour the rows. With this to guide you, you can decide how many rows to use in the centre. Plaits need not be made of one colour only. Since they consist of three strips, there can be three colours in them. Plain fabrics can be plaited with check, tweed or speckled material for an interesting texture. Bright colours look best combined with beige, tan or another neutral colour. Remember that the appearance of a colour can change according to the colour surrounding it.

Change colours gradually in a rug as you work. Add a new colour to the rug by first adding one strip of the new colour in the first plait, two strips in the second, and three strips in the third and subsequent plaits for a solid band of the new colour. Always change colours of plaits on a curve near the end of a round, in approximately the same place each time, to make the change less obvious.

Equipment

A plaited rug is made of plaited strips of fabric either sewn or laced together. In addition to the fabric strips, you will need a *sewing needle and button thread* to stitch the first bend of the braid to itself. The remainder of the rug is laced together with a *blunt-edged lacing needle and heavy thread,* such as upholsterer's twine or carpet thread. You will need a clip *clothes-peg* to keep the end of the plait from unravelling when you stop plaiting.

You will need some form of clamp to hold the ends of the fabric strips firmly under tension while you plait. Or you can improvise by nailing the strips to a board, or by tying the ends together with string and fastening the end to a door handle or drawer knob. The strips must be firmly fixed so that you can plait tightly. Prepare the plaits as you work, and lace them when you have plaited a suitable length as shown on the left, or plait approximately enough for the whole rug and lace the plaits together, and make more plaits if necessary.

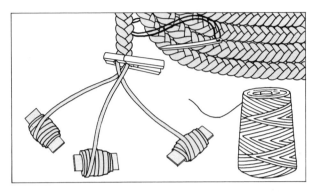

Making a plait. Each fabric strip has been wound on a bobbin to prevent tangling. A clothes-peg is used to stop the plait from coming undone and to keep the tension tight. A blunt-edged lacer, or bodkin, is used with heavy thread to lace the plaits together.

Making fabric strips

Fabric strips for plaiting are folded and sewn together by hand. With either method, you must first cut the fabric into strips 3 to 6 cm wide, the width depending on the weight of your wool and the width you want the plait to be. Always cut the strips with the grain of the fabric; cut either vertically or horizontally, whichever will give the longest strips. To determine the most desirable plait width, cut sets of three strips to various widths; fold and plait them, then use strips in the width that produces the plait width you prefer. It is also helpful to make experimental plaits of combinations of colours.

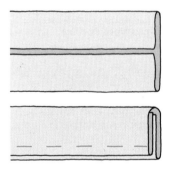

Fold fabric strip by bringing each raw edge to the centre (top). Then bring folded sides together (bottom). To keep the folded edges together, you can sew a long tacking stitch along the open edge.

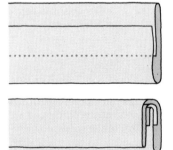

You can add bulk to the strips of lightweight fabric by folding the raw edges beyond the centre (top). Then bring folded edges together (bottom) as usual and tack open edges together if you wish.

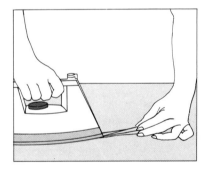

Iron the strips to prevent them from unfolding. With practice, you can fold the strips with one hand while you run the iron along with the other to set the crease.

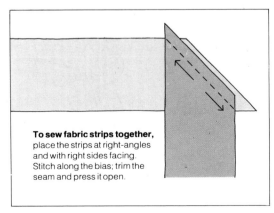

To sew fabric strips together, place the strips at right-angles and with right sides facing. Stitch along the bias; trim the seam and press it open.

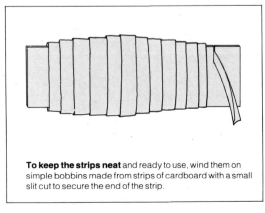

To keep the strips neat and ready to use, wind them on simple bobbins made from strips of cardboard with a small slit cut to secure the end of the strip.

Two skeins of finely cut strips ready to wind on to bobbins.

Plaiting

Making a three-strand plait

The simplest type of plait is made of three strips of fabric. It is possible to plait with four or more strips (see pp. 404–5) but larger multiples do not conform as well to the shaping of a rug. When plaiting, anchor the strip ends by tacking them to a board or using a table clamp so that the ends are under tension. Always keep the open edges of strips to the right. To make a tight plait, pull each strip to the side, not down, as you plait. When you stop plaiting for any reason, clip a clothes-peg to the plait end to hold it. The length of the plait you make to start will depend on the shape you want the rug to be.

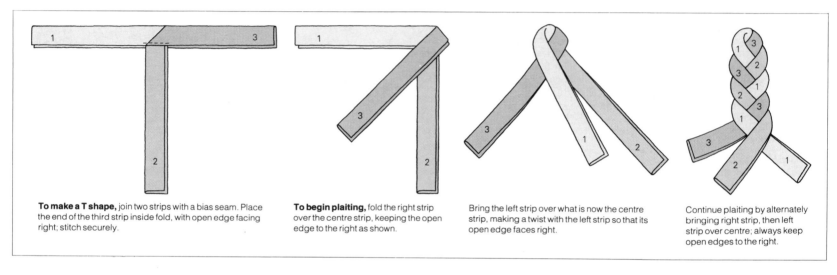

To make a T shape, join two strips with a bias seam. Place the end of the third strip inside fold, with open edge facing right; stitch securely.

To begin plaiting, fold the right strip over the centre strip, keeping the open edge to the right as shown.

Bring the left strip over what is now the centre strip, making a twist with the left strip so that its open edge faces right.

Continue plaiting by alternately bringing right strip, then left strip over centre; always keep open edges to the right.

Round rug

For a round rug to lie flat, it must be started correctly in the centre. To do this, you make a variation in the plaiting that is called either a *round turn* or a *modified square corner;* this variation makes it easier to coil the plait around itself. The turn is repeated from six to 12 times to form the centre circle, then normal plaiting is continued. How many times you repeat the turn depends on the weight of the fabric you are using, the width of the strips, and how tightly you plait. When the centre of the rug is formed so the plait coils around itself and lies flat, the rest is worked in normal plaiting.

Plait coiled around itself forms a round rug.

To begin, plait in the usual way with right over centre, left over centre, right over centre.

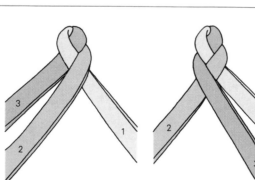

Start round corner turn by bringing the left strip over the centre strip.

Bring new left strip over new centre strip again, ignoring right strip.

Bring right strip over centre tightly to make plait curve towards the right.

Oval rug

An oval rug is made by coiling a plait around a length of straight plait. The length of the centre plait is determined by the overall size of the rug: length of rug minus width equals length of centre plait. For example, a 1 m by 1.5 m oval rug has a 50 cm long centre plait. To start the rug, make a plait of the appropriate length; then make three round turns as described for a round rug (see facing page) so that the plait turns the opposite way. Continue normal plaiting until you reach the starting end of the plait; make three round turns around the starting end. Continue normal plaiting for the remainder of the rug.

In oval rug, plait coils around straight centre.

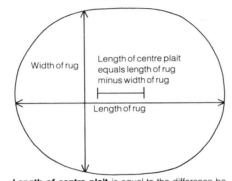

Length of centre plait is equal to the difference between the length and the width of the finished rug.

For oval centre, make plait of appropriate length; work three round turns. Straight plait to the next turn; make three round turns so plait wraps around starting end.

Rectangular rug

A plait can be made into a rectangular rug, although this shape is not as traditional as a round or an oval. To shape the plait into a rectangle, you make the variation in the plaiting that is called a *square turn*. This produces a right-angle in the plait so that it can turn a corner. The length of the centre plait of a rectangular rug is determined in the same way as with an oval rug: the length of the centre plait is equal to the length minus the width of the rug. The rectangular rug is made with normal plaiting along the sides and a square turn at each of the four corners of the rug in each row of the plaiting.

Rectangular rug has square turn at each corner.

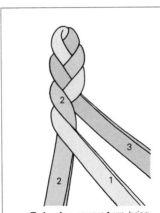

To begin a square turn, bring left strip over centre, then left strip over centre again.

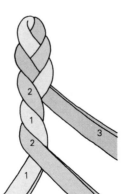

Bring left strip over centre again for total of three times. (Right strip is not yet plaited.)

Bring right strip over centre and pull it tight. The plait will turn towards the right.

Continue plaiting in the normal way with left strip, then right strip over centre.

Plaiting

Lacing

The centre of a plaited rug, where the plait first turns on itself, is sewn together; the rest of the rug is laced. Lacing is faster than sewing and makes a sturdier rug. For sewing, use any button thread and a sharp needle. For lacing, use a blunt-edged needle, called a lacer, and a heavy waxed thread, such as upholsterer's twine or carpet thread. Always use a double length of thread. Lace with one continuous strand; when a length of thread is used up, tie another length to it with a reef knot. Work on a table or other flat surface so the rug lies flat; do not let it hang over the side or it will be distorted. Pull the lacing thread tight as you work, so that it is hidden in the loops of the plait; if it does not show on either the top or the bottom of the rug, the rug will be reversible.

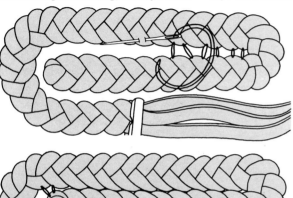

1. To sew first loops of plait together, start at first bend of plait (start of oval rug is shown). Knot thread; hide knot inside plait. Stitch through the folds of the inside loops of plaits, working from one plait to the other. Keep thread concealed as you stitch.

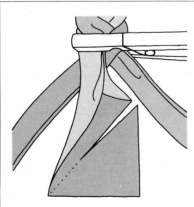

2. Continue stitching loops together until you are just beyond the second bend. Thread lacer with waxed thread; attach this to the end of the sewing thread with a reef knot.

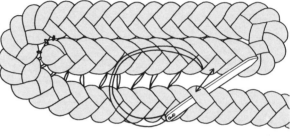

3. To lace, position plaits so they are not side by side but at an angle. Lacing cord goes between loops; it does not penetrate fabric. Bring lacer diagonally under inside loop of each plait; pull thread tight so it does not show. Lace all straight edges this way.

4. To lace curves of round or oval rug, loops must be missed (on plait, never on rug) so rug will lie flat and not buckle. Decide when to miss a loop after thread is through loop on rug. If next loop on plait is even with or behind the thread, miss it and lace the next loop.

Joining fabric strips

As you plait, you will need to add to the fabric strips because it is too cumbersome to start with strips that are long enough to make an entire rug. This is done by splicing a new strip on to the working strip. To avoid a bump in the plait, begin with fabric strips of uneven lengths so the splicing of each one will fall in a different place. If you want to change colours, you can splice a strip of the new colour on to the old strip. Plan your colour changes so they will occur at the same place on each round (see p. 398); planned colour changes give a more uniform look to a rug.

Always splice a strip when it is in the centre after it has been in an *over* position, so the seam you make will be hidden by another strip going over it.

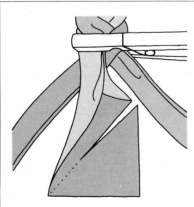

Before you begin splicing, secure the plait against unravelling with a clothes-peg. Unfold short strip and cut it on the bias.

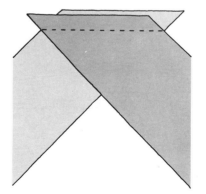

Place the old and new strips together, with right sides facing, and stitch along the bias. Trim the seam allowance to 3 mm.

Re-fold the spliced strip and continue plaiting; make sure the seam is hidden when the next strip is placed on top of it.

402

Tapering off

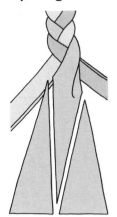

When the rug has reached the desired size, taper each strip into a long, thin point that extends for about 13 to 18 cm. Cut strips to slightly different lengths so they do not end in the same place.

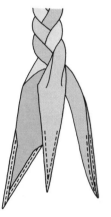

Fold edges under on both sides of each point; stitch fold by hand for about 4 cm. Re-fold each strip and continue plaiting and lacing as far as you can.

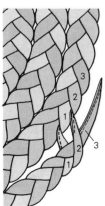

Insert strip ends into adjacent loops in the plait with a bodkin or pointed implement. If strip end and loop are of the same fabric, the end will be less visible. With sharp needle and sewing thread to match each of the fabrics, stitch the points to the loops; make stitches as invisible as possible. Clip thread ends close to the loops.

Butting

Butting – joining the beginning and end of a plait to form a complete circle – is an advanced technique that permits distinct colour changes. Although an entire rug can be made by this method, it is most often used on the final rows of a rug for a finished look. To prepare a plait for the final row of a rug, attach a safety pin 3 cm from the ends of three folded strips. Make a plait long enough to go around the rug, and place it so its ends will not be butted at the same point where the previous row was tapered. Leaving four loops of plait free at the beginning, lace the plait to the rug; leave about four loops of plait free at the end. Remove safety pin. To butt the ends, follow directions below.

Finishing end

Starting end

1. Put starting end of plait in front of you, finishing end above it. If your three strips are not identifiable by different colours, put a piece of coloured thread on corresponding strip ends to identify them. Start butting with strips in the position shown.

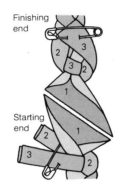

Finishing end

Starting end

2. Pin Strips 2 and 3 out of the way. Unfold both ends of Strip 1 and cut the ends along the bias.

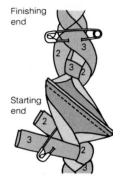

Finishing end

Starting end

3. Place the ends of Strip 1 together, with right sides facing, and stitch them together 3 mm from the edge.

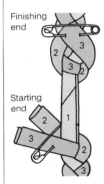

Finishing end

Starting end

4. Fold Strip 1 back into a tube; the seam allowance will be on the inside.

Finishing end

Starting end

5. At finishing end, plait Strip 3 over Strip 1, concealing the seam. Plait Strip 2 over Strip 3 and bring Strip 2 under Strip 1. At starting end, bring Strip 2 out from under Strip 1. Both ends of Strip 2 should be on the right side of the plait.

Finishing end

Starting end

6. Pull both ends of Strip 2 out of the plait slightly so that you can butt the ends together. If you do not pull the ends out slightly, the butted strip will be too long to fit in the plait and will bulge. The plait will be somewhat distorted now, but will be put back in shape later.

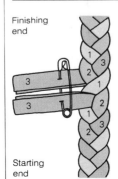

Finishing end

Starting end

7. Butt the ends of Strip 2 and fold the strip back into a tube, following the directions given for Strip 1. Pull both ends of the plait so it is smooth again.

Finishing end

Starting end

8. At starting end, bring Strip 3 under Strip 2. At finishing end, pull Strip 3 out from under Strip 2.

Finishing end

Starting end

9. Butt the ends of Strip 3 together, using directions given above for Strip 1.

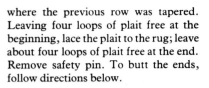

Plaiting

Multiple plaiting

The previous pages have dealt only with three-strand plaiting not because more strands cannot be used, but because the result would not be flexible enough to be formed into the oval, round and rectangular rugs being described. Plaits of more than three strands can be formed into an oblong rug, but only by running them lengthwise, then lacing the plaits together along the length of the rug and hemming the raw edges under at the strip ends. Other uses for multiple plaits include handbag handles and luggage straps, belts and headbands.

To start a multiple plait, secure the ends of the folded fabric strips with a large safety pin, or sew across them so they lie flat. Multiple plaiting can be somewhat confusing at the beginning. It will help to use fabric of a different colour for each strip, so you can follow its individual path to understand the configuration of the plait. All multiple plaits should be worked under tension.

Multiple plaits can be made into an oblong rug.

4-STRAND PLAIT

To begin four-strand plait, bring first strip on left over the second, under the third, and over the fourth.

Bring what is now first strip on the left (it was second strip) over the next strip, under the next, over the last.

Continue plaiting by repeating the motion of over, under, over, always using strip on the left.

4-STRAND VARIATION

For a variation on a four-strand plait, plait the four strips as if they were three (see p. 400) by holding the first two strips together as you plait.

5-STRAND PLAIT

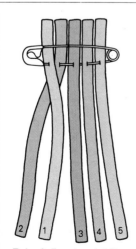

To begin five-strand plait, bring the left strip over the strip to its right.

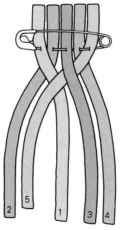

Bring the right strip over the strip to its left, under the next strip, and over the one after that.

Continue plaiting by repeating these two steps, always using the outer left and right strips.

5-STRAND VARIATION

For a variation, plait five strips as if they were three (see p. 400); hold the first two strips together and the last two strips together as you plait.

6-STRAND PLAIT

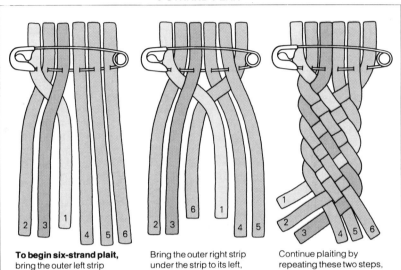

To begin six-strand plait, bring the outer left strip over the second strip and under the third.

Bring the outer right strip under the strip to its left, over the next strip, under what was the first strip.

Continue plaiting by repeating these two steps, always using outer left and outer right strips.

6-STRAND VARIATION

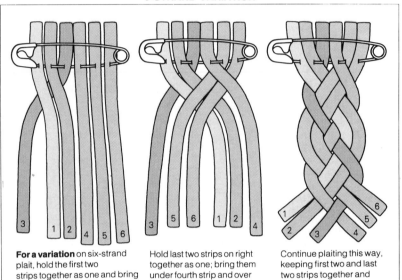

For a variation on six-strand plait, hold the first two strips together as one and bring them over the third strip.

Hold last two strips on right together as one; bring them under fourth strip and over what were first two strips.

Continue plaiting this way, keeping first two and last two strips together and using them as one.

7-STRAND PLAIT

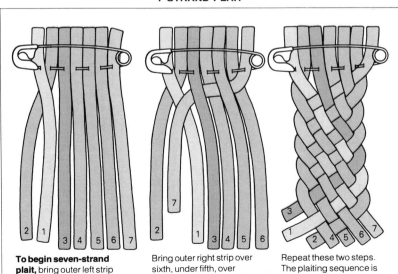

To begin seven-strand plait, bring outer left strip over the strip to its right.

Bring outer right strip over sixth, under fifth, over fourth, under third, and over what was the first strip.

Repeat these two steps. The plaiting sequence is the same for any odd number of strips.

7-STRAND VARIATION

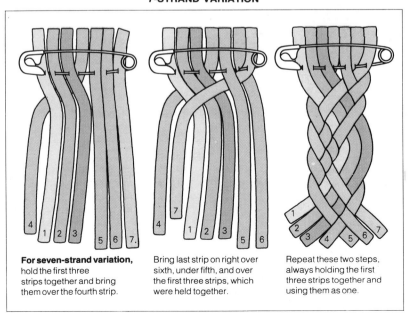

For seven-strand variation, hold the first three strips together and bring them over the fourth strip.

Bring last strip on right over sixth, under fifth, and over the first three strips, which were held together.

Repeat these two steps, always holding the first three strips together and using them as one.

405

Chair cushion

This intricate floral design is worked with the hand hook method.

Chair seat
The floral design chair seat is worked with a hand hook because of the intricate shading and detail possible.

Materials
50 cm square of hessian
Hand hook (small size)
1 m rug binding
1 m of 5 mm ribbon
Heavy-duty needle and thread
Rug frame
Wool flannel in the following colours and approximate amounts:

10×13 cm of four shades of grey
10×15 cm of four shades of blue
10×28 cm of light red
10×18 cm of three darker reds
10×8 cm of three shades of yellow
10×5 cm of medium olive-green
10×18 cm of light and dark olive
10×20 cm of three shades of leaf-green
10×5 cm of black
25×46 cm of white

Preparation
To enlarge the design, make a grid with 1 cm squares and copy the design square by square (see p. 14). Finish the edges of the hessian and mark the centres (see p. 380). Transfer the design to the base fabric (pp. 380–1). Put the hessian in a rug frame (see p. 383). Cut the flannel into 3 mm strips (see p. 382). To hook rug refer to pp. 384 and 385.

Shading
Guidelines for shading with different colours of fabric strips can be found on p. 385. This piece was shaded as follows: each flower is worked in four different tones of one colour. To simplify references, the lightest tone was chosen as the first shade, and the darkest as the fourth. The spokes are worked in the third tone, the shadows behind the spokes are in the second tone, and the petals are filled in with the first tone. The fourth or darkest tone is used round the outline of part of the flowers and for the individual petals to make them stand out. The flower buds are worked in three tones of one colour. The yellow buds start with the darkest tone near the enveloping leaf, and work out to the lightest shade at the upper tip. In the red buds, the three tones are used to make the bud appear round; the lightest where the light would strike, and the darkest where the bud would be in shadow. The leaves are worked in three tones of green, some in an olive-green combination and the others in leaf-greens. Stems and leaf veins are worked in the darkest tone, and two lighter tones are used to fill in the shapes.

Finishing
Cut away the excess hessian and attach the rug binding (see p. 393). To insert the chair ties, place the chair seat on the chair and mark the place on the seat nearest the part of the chair back you want to use to anchor it. Cut ribbon in half. Fold each piece in half; slip the fold between the chair seat and binding. Sew the binding and the ribbon.

To enlarge design, make a grid with 1 cm squares and copy the design square for square (see p. 14).

Key
A	White
B	Red
C	Blue
D	Grey
E	Yellow
F	Olive-green
G	Leaf-green
H	Black

Wall hanging

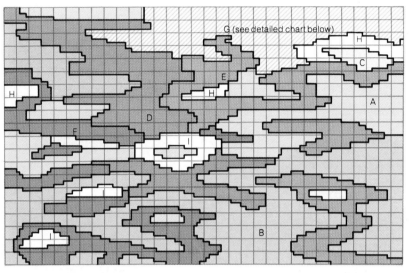

G (see detailed chart below)

Wall hanging is mainly one pile height, with areas of white Rya yarn in a higher pile.

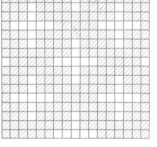

To enlarge design, make a grid with 2·5 cm squares and copy design square for square (see p. 14). To transfer the design to canvas, see p. 381.

A	Light blue	**G**	Charted design on left
B	Mottled light and		(see p. 391), light blue
	medium blue		background with white
C	Pink		crosses
D	Brown	**H**	White to be trimmed
E	Olive-green		shorter than I
F	Blue-green	**I**	White (see *Finishing* for
			details of trimming)

The 50 × 80 cm wall hanging is made with a combination of pre-cut rug yarn and Rya yarn. When the rug is finished the Rya yarn is trimmed to different lengths.

Materials
Paper and pencil
Waterproof felt-tip marker
1 m × 66 cm rug canvas with four holes per 2.5 cm
20 packets of white Rya yarn (168 pieces in each)
Packs of pre-cut rug yarn (320 pieces in each):
   12 light blue
   4 medium blue

   1 pale pink
   4 brown
   5 olive-green
   4 blue-green
Masking tape
4 m of rug binding
Latchet hook
Five 1.5 cm plastic rings
75 cm of 1.5 cm dowel rod

Knotting
To enlarge the design, make a grid with 2.5 cm squares; copy the design square by square (see p. 14). Bind the edges of the canvas with masking tape and mark the centre (see p. 380). Transfer the design to the canvas (see p. 381). You

can fill in the areas with coloured felt-tipped markers, or you can simply tie a piece of yarn in that area so that you know which colour yarn to hook.

With pre-cut rug yarns, use one length for each knot. Use four lengths of Rya yarn for each knot. Knot the rug, following the chart above and the directions on pp. 389 and 391.

Finishing
When the knotting is complete, sculpt the long white areas. Trim the crosses at the top to 3 mm above the level of the blue pile. Cut them straight across by holding the scissors parallel to the rug. Trim the two white areas in the lower

left corner so that each one is shorter on the right side and longer on the left side. The four white areas above these are rounded so they are shorter on the inner and outer edges, longer on top. Trim the parts marked H shorter than those marked I.

To finish the wall hanging, trim excess canvas to 3 cm. Attach rug binding to the edges, following the directions on p. 394. To hang the rug, sew the five rings to the rug binding at the top of the rug, spacing them evenly across the top. Slip the dowel through the rings and balance the dowel on nails or hooks that have been put in the wall.

Another view of this oval plaited rug, worked in shades of brown and gold, is shown on p. 398.

Plaited rug

Plaited rug

Fabrics in the rug illustrated are mainly plain shades of brown, gold and white. A striped fabric was used in some plaits to create a mottled effect.

Materials

Fabric – the following amounts of heavy-weight wool 140 cm wide:

1.30 m each of gold and brown
1 m tarnished gold
70 cm brown and white striped
50 cm off-white
30 cm each of dull gold and light brown
10 cm dark brown

Button thread
Sewing needle
Lacing thread
Lacer

Preparation

Prepare the fabric by cutting it into 5 cm wide strips, cutting along the grain. Begin to prepare the strips by making a T-shape (see p. 400). Anchor the strip ends by tacking them to a board or use a table clamp. Begin with the centre strip of off-white, tarnished gold and striped fabrics.

Beginning an oval rug

Anchor ends and make a plait 60 cm long (the length of the rug minus width).

Once the centre plait is 60 cm long, work three round turns (see p. 400) so that the plait will turn and go in the opposite direction. Continue plaiting until you reach the starting end of the plait. Make three round turns so that the plait will turn around the starting end (see p. 401). Continue forming a straight plait for the remainder of the rug. To lace the rug together, see p. 402.

Colour changes

To duplicate the colour changes in the rug illustrated, follow the drawing and chart below. The chart shows, for each row, the approximate length of plait necessary for that row and the three fabrics used to make the plait.

The drawing shows where the colour changes are made – on the curve in the same place in each round. To join fabric strips of a new colour, see p. 402.

Finishing

When the rug reaches the size you want, taper the ends of the three fabric strips and insert into adjacent loops as illustrated on p. 403. Stitch the ends to loops of plait, using sewing thread to match each fabric colour.

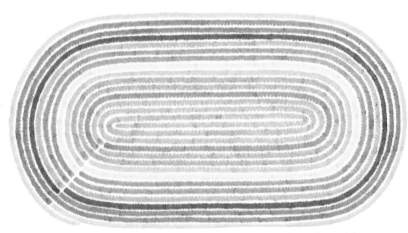

Centre plait is equal to length minus width of rug. 1.20 m minus 60 cm gives a 60 cm plait.

	Row	Plait length	Colours of strips
	1–3	4.26 m	Off-white, tarnished gold, striped
	4	1.82 m	Dull gold, tarnished gold, striped
	5–6	3.65 m	Dull gold, tarnished gold, gold
	7	2.13 m	Gold, tarnished gold, gold
	8	2.30 m	Gold, tarnished gold, striped
	9	2.58 m	Gold, dark brown, striped
	10	2.74 m	Off-white, brown, striped
	11	2.86 m	Off-white, brown, brown
	12	3.04 m	Brown, brown, brown
	13–14	6.70 m	Brown, light brown, gold
	15	3.65 m	Brown, gold, gold

Knitting

Detail of hand-knitted sweater, Icelandic Fashions Corporation

Knitting materials

Yarn descriptions
Yarn selection
Tips for buying yarn
Winding yarn
Knitting needles
Knitting accessories

Yarns

Many yarns are suitable for use in knitting. Choices differ in fibre content, texture, weight and ply. The chart below gives characteristics and uses of some wools and synthetic yarns that are widely available and frequently chosen for knitting. (Cotton yarns are also used for knitting, but more often for crochet, and so are described in that chapter.) In addition to basic types included in the chart, most yarn manufacturers produce synthetic and blended yarns of their own design, labelled with their trade names. These will become familiar to you after a few visits to local wool shops.

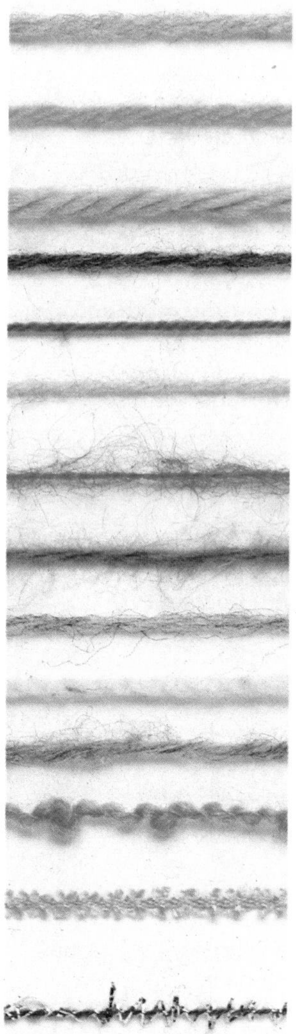

VARIETIES OF KNITTING YARNS

Double knitting	The most versatile of knitting wools, this is usually made in 4-ply and is suitable for warm garments such as sweaters, jackets, suits and hats.
Synthetic double knitting	This synthetic yarn is similar to double knitting wool, but is made of synthetic fibres. It is used for the same articles, is not so warm but washes easily.
Rug wool	A very heavy wool, this is sometimes mixed with synthetic fibres, and can be used to make rugs, cushion covers and bags.
Sock wool	This is a finer variety of double knitting, less heavy than those at the top of the list made in colour mixtures. It is used for socks, sweaters, waistcoats, hats and gloves.
Fingering	Made from wool or synthetics, this fine 3-ply yarn is used for lightweight garments such as baby clothes, bedjackets and shawls.
Baby wool	Another lightweight yarn suitable for baby clothes, this is slightly bulkier than the fingering shown above, but is made in pastel colours only.
Mohair	Spun from the fluffy hair of the Angora goat, this wool is sometimes combined with other fibres of wool or synthetics. It is used for sweaters, shawls and rugs.
Angora	This wool is used for the same garments as mohair, but is softer. It is made from the hair of the Angora rabbit.
Shetland	Usually made in soft gentle colours, this is a loosely spun wool made from Shetland sheep. It makes warm and hardwearing sweaters, gloves, mittens and hats.
Aran	This is natural, unbleached wool, ideal for thick sweaters and other garments knitted with the traditional stitches of Aran designs.
Icelandic	Made from the sheep of Iceland, this heavy homespun wool is suitable for bulky sweaters, ponchos or blankets.
Bouclé	Bouclé yarn is made from one thin and one thick strand twisted together. It may be wool or a mixture of wool and synthetics. It is used for sweaters, dresses and cardigans.
Chenille	This is a velvet-like yarn usually made of cotton mixed with synthetic fibres, with short tufts twisted round long strands. It is used for shawls, sweaters, jackets and other garments.
Metallic	Blended with wool or synthetic fibres, this yarn is ideal for evening garments.

Selecting yarn

A knitting yarn should be appropriate for both style and intended purpose. To reach a satisfactory decision, consider the differences in yarn characteristics and weigh the advantages and disadvantages for each situation.

The most significant factor in yarn performance is fibre content. *Wool* and *acrylic* are warm yarns, and the most versatile because they can be spun in many weights and types. Their resilience makes them especially desirable for garments. Most experts agree that wool gives the best results for warmth and appearance, but synthetics are chosen by some for their ease in washing. *Linen* and *cotton* are cool yarns, used mostly for summer garments and household items. *Orlon* and *nylon* are incorporated into some blends, mostly for strength.

A yarn's construction is crucial to its suitability for a purpose. Highly twisted yarns are smooth, easy to work with, generally durable, and suitable for any stitch pattern. Loosely twisted or homespun yarns are less durable, but

have an appealing texture and give great warmth due to their high loft (fluffiness). Novelty yarns, in which plies of different thicknesses or fibres are twisted together, are exciting in texture, but less durable than smooth yarns and suited only to simple stitch patterns.

The number of yarn plies (units twisted together) is not a significant factor in yarn selection, though the information is usually included on the label. It can indicate strength (four plies might be tougher than two), but never thickness, as plies can vary in diameter.

Yarn thickness can be expressed as a weight – light, medium or heavy. Suggestions for suitable articles in each weight are in the chart, opposite.

In selecting a garment yarn, good elasticity (stretch capacity) and recovery (return to original size) are desirable qualities. Both comfort and fit retention depend on them. In a yarn for household articles, ability to withstand many washings may be more important. Check yarn labels for the care requirements.

Tips for buying yarn

Most knitting projects represent a substantial investment in time and money. It pays to be an informed consumer when purchasing yarns.

1. Check yarn labels for the dye lot number and purchase all yarn of one colour from the same dye lot. Each number represents a different dye bath and may differ slightly from another.

2. Buy enough yarn of the same dye lot to complete the article. This is an instance where too much is better than not enough. Some shops will accept the return of unused balls within a reasonable time. You can check this possibility at the time of purchase.

3. Check the yarn label for washability and other care information. If none is given, you should wash and block your tension sample to see how the yarn responds to these procedures.

4. If a yarn label gives tension information, the needle size mentioned is the one recommended for that particular yarn. It is wise to stay within two sizes of the recommendation.

5. To duplicate the appearance and fit of your chosen pattern, you should always buy the yarn recommended for it, though you can of course choose a colour other than the one shown.

6. If you choose to substitute another yarn for the one recommended, select yarn as close as possible to the original in weight and type. It is a good idea to buy a single ball first and knit a sample to see how the tension and appearance compare with those of the pattern.

7. To calculate yarn needs for a substitution or your own design, see Designing a garment.

8. Should you need to convert grams to ounces or vice versa, use this formula: 100 grams = 3.52 ounces. For example, if 16 ounces of yarn are required, and you are substituting a yarn weighed in grams, divide 16 by 3.52 and multiply times 100. The quantity is 454 grams.

9. Before each purchase, check a yarn's recovery. Stretch and release a 15 cm length. If it does not return to its original size, you cannot expect the knitted article to hold its shape.

Winding yarn

The most convenient way to use yarn is from a ball or skein that can be pulled out from the centre. In this form it is less likely to tangle or to unwind too quickly. Yarn is often sold this way; if yours is not, it should be re-wound before you use it. Directions are given below for re-winding a skein. Before you begin, slip it over the back of a chair and cut the anchoring string. Take care to wind the ball loosely. If yarn is pulled too tight, it will stretch and may lose some elasticity.

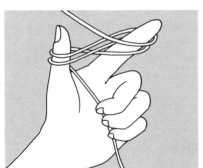 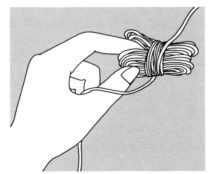 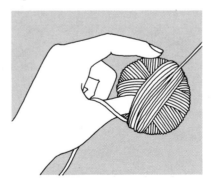 

Grasp a loose end of yarn firmly between fingers and palm of left hand, about 30 cm from the end. Wind yarn 6 or 8 times around thumb and index finger in figure-eight fashion.

Slip yarn off fingers and fold it in half, end to end. Holding the folded bunch between thumb and index finger, wind the yarn loosely around both yarn and fingers about a dozen times.

Keeping thumb in centre, continue to wind yarn, turning the ball constantly so it will be round. When it is 8 cm across, remove your thumb, but be careful not to wind over the centre yarn.

Continue winding *loosely* until all the yarn is taken up, then tuck the final end into the ball. Use the ball by drawing yarn out from the centre, as shown in the illustration.

Knitting materials

Needles

There are three basic types of knitting needles – *single-pointed, double-pointed* and *circular.* Examples are shown below; the chart on the right describes available materials, lengths and sizes.

Needle thickness is signified by sizes in millimetres. The higher a number, the thicker the needle and the larger the stitch. While there are no precise rules for needle and yarn relationship, generally, thicker yarns should be worked with large needles, thinner yarns with small ones. If a needle is too large for the yarn, the structure will be flimsy; if too small, texture will be too compact and inelastic. Yarn labels often suggest a needle size; a safe approach is to stay within two sizes of this number.

Needle length should be chosen according to a project's measurements, and only has to be sufficient to hold all stitches comfortably. In general, shorter ones are easier to manipulate unless you like to knit with one needle tucked under your arm. A circular needle should be at least 5 cm less than the circumference of the knitting.

Choice of needle material – plastic, metal or wood – is largely a matter of personal preference and availability. Plastic is quieter and somewhat easier for a beginner to manage. Metal is noisier, but stitches slide more readily, an advantage for the fast knitter. Wood is aesthetically pleasing, but wooden needles are scarce.

In caring for needles, it is best to store them flat with their points protected.

Needle types and sizes

Single and double-point knitting needles are made in aluminium, plastic and wood; they vary in length from 17.5 to 35 cm. Circular needles are made of nylon or nylon and aluminium, in lengths ranging from 40 to 90 cm.

The chart below compares needle thickness in the three standard sizing systems – metric (or 'international'), British and American. These latter two systems use arbitrary numbers to size needles, whereas metric size numbers give actual needle diameter in millimetres. Metric sizes for knitting needles are sometimes expressed with fractions, rather than decimals, so remember that metric size 4½, for example, is the same as metric size 4.50. In this book, needle sizes are always specified in metric.

Metric (mm)	British	American	Metric (mm)	British	American
2.00	14	0	5.50	5	9
2.25	13	1	6.00	4	10
2.75	12	2	6.50	3	10½
3.00	11	3	7.00	2	–
3.25	10	4	7.50	1	–
3.75	9	5	8.00	0	11
4.00	8	6	9.00	00	13
4.50	7	7	10.00	000	15
5.00	6	8			

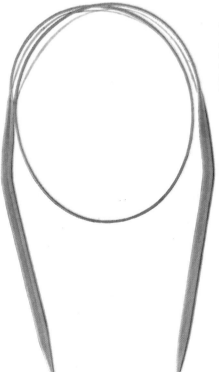

A circular needle is used to knit round, seamless garments and also large, flat pieces for which straight needles might not be long enough. It consists of two aluminium or nylon tips connected by a flexible nylon cord.

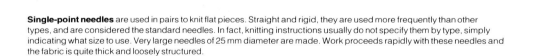

Single-point needles are used in pairs to knit flat pieces. Straight and rigid, they are used more frequently than other types, and are considered the standard needles. In fact, knitting instructions usually do not specify them by type, simply indicating what size to use. Very large needles of 25 mm diameter are made. Work proceeds rapidly with these needles and the fabric is quite thick and loosely structured.

Double-point needles are used in sets of four or more to knit seamless, circular items, such as socks or mittens.

Knitting accessories

There are many knitting accessories available, each one designed to make a certain task easier. Some of these are shown below. Besides those items specifically meant for knitting, other craft equipment is indispensable. Examples are the crochet hook and tapestry needle shown below, also scissors for cutting yarn, and straight pins and tape measure for blocking. In addition, graph paper and a notebook are useful for charting and keeping track of patterns, and a basket or bag will help to keep your work organised, free from dust and close at hand. The type with a folding stand is particularly useful and convenient.

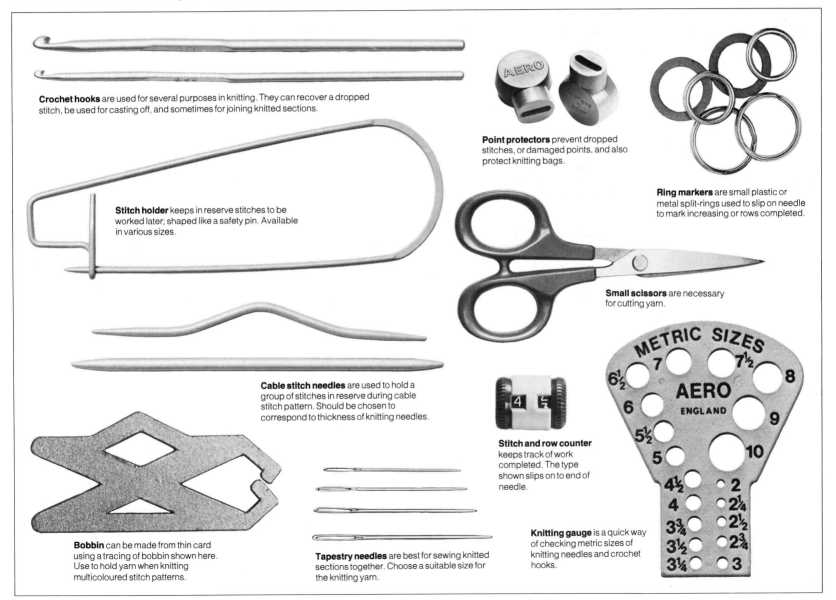

Crochet hooks are used for several purposes in knitting. They can recover a dropped stitch, be used for casting off, and sometimes for joining knitted sections.

Point protectors prevent dropped stitches, or damaged points, and also protect knitting bags.

Ring markers are small plastic or metal split-rings used to slip on needle to mark increasing or rows completed.

Stitch holder keeps in reserve stitches to be worked later; shaped like a safety pin. Available in various sizes.

Small scissors are necessary for cutting yarn.

Cable stitch needles are used to hold a group of stitches in reserve during cable stitch pattern. Should be chosen to correspond to thickness of knitting needles.

Stitch and row counter keeps track of work completed. The type shown slips on to end of needle.

Bobbin can be made from thin card using a tracing of bobbin shown here. Use to hold yarn when knitting multicoloured stitch patterns.

Tapestry needles are best for sewing knitted sections together. Choose a suitable size for the knitting yarn.

Knitting gauge is a quick way of checking metric sizes of knitting needles and crochet hooks.

METRIC SIZES

AERO
ENGLAND

6½ 7 7½ 8
6   9
5½   10
5
4½   2
4   2¼
3¾   2½
3½   2¾
3¼   3

Knitting basics

Casting on
Forming the knit stitch
Forming the purl stitch
Elementary stitch patterns
Variations on elementary stitches
Yarn tension
Casting off
Side selvedges

Casting on

Casting on is the first step in knitting. It forms the first row of stitches and one selvedge of the finished article, usually the bottom, or hem edge.

There are many methods for casting on; five of the most representative are shown here. Each is best suited to a particular type of knitting, depending on the elasticity or firmness required, and the simplicity or intricacy of the appearance desired.

The character of a cast-on edge is determined not only by the way in which stitches are put on the needle, but also by the way they are worked off. Knitting into the stitch fronts produces a looser edge, into the backs, a firmer edge.

Stitches of the cast-on row should be uniform in size or the edge will be untidy. It is worth doing them again if the first attempt is unsatisfactory. The cast-on stitches should also be moderately loose, so that they will be easy to work off. If yours tend to be too tight, try working over two needles, using one of the methods on the opposite page.

When casting on a large number of stitches, keeping count is easier if you slip a coil ring marker or yarn loop on the needle every 10 or 20 stitches.

To form slip knot for first stitch, make a loop 15 cm from yarn end; insert needle under short length, draw through a loop and tighten it.

Two-needle methods of casting on

KNITTING ON

Knitting on employs two needles and one yarn length. Each new stitch is formed as in knitting, then transferred to the left needle. A versatile selvedge, it is soft when worked through loop fronts, firm if worked through loop backs. Suitable also for increasing at one side or completing a buttonhole.

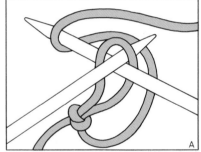

Hold needle with slip knot in left hand. Insert right needle and take yarn around it as for knitting (**A**); draw yarn through to form a new stitch, but do not

drop first loop from left needle (**B**). Instead, transfer new stitch to left needle and knit into it to form the next new stitch.

CABLE CASTING ON

Cable casting on is produced in the same way as knitting on, but for each new stitch the needle is inserted between the two previous stitches. The resulting edge is decorative and elastic, nicely suited to ribbing and attractive for the edges of socks. Stitches should be knitted off through the loop fronts only.

Make slip knot and first stitch as in knitting on (above). For each new stitch after that, insert the right needle between 2 stitches; take yarn around

needle as for knitting (**A**). Draw through a new stitch, then transfer it to left needle (**B**). Continue forming new stitches between 2 loops.

One-needle methods of casting on

SINGLE CASTING ON

Single casting on is done with one needle and one length of yarn. It forms a delicate selvedge that is particularly good for a hem edge or for lace. This is a very easy casting-on method, but somewhat difficult to work off the needle evenly in the first row. For a beginner, double casting on is easier to control.

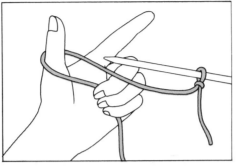

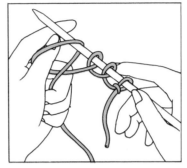

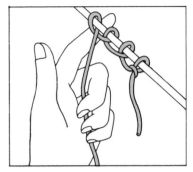

1. Make slip knot on needle held in the right hand. Wrap yarn from the ball around left thumb, as shown, then grasp yarn firmly between the palm and fingers.

2. Turn thumb so the back of it is facing you; insert needle front to back through the loop that is formed by twisting the thumb.

3. Slip thumb out of loop, at same time pulling yarn downwards to close the loop around the needle. Repeat Steps 2 and 3.

DOUBLE CASTING ON

Double casting on employs one needle and a double length of yarn; it is started a measured distance from the yarn end, allowing 2.5 cm per stitch. Firm, yet elastic, this method is suitable for any pattern that does not require a delicate edge. It is especially recommended for beginners.

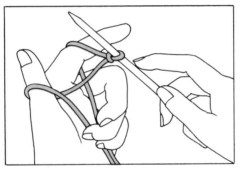

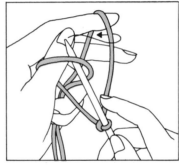

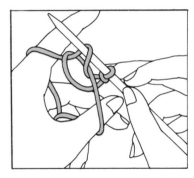

1. Make slip knot a measured distance from yarn end. Wrap short end over left thumb, yarn from ball over left index finger; hold both ends between palm and fingers.

2. Slip needle up through the thumb loop, then scoop yarn from the index finger (see arrow) and draw a loop on to the needle.

3. Release thumb loop; tighten loop on the needle by drawing the short yarn forwards with the thumb. Repeat Steps 2 and 3.

LOOPED CASTING ON

Looped casting on employs one needle and two yarn lengths; one yarn forms a foundation, the other is wrapped around it. Left intact, the edge is very flexible, especially suited to cotton yarns, which have limited elasticity. If the foundation yarn is removed, stitches can be picked up for knitting or grafting.

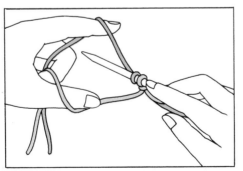

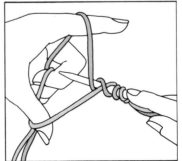

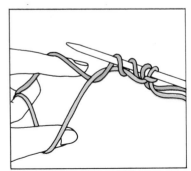

1. Make slip knot in foundation yarn (green), then casting yarn (red). Take foundation yarn over thumb, and casting yarn over index finger; grasp both yarn ends against palm.

2. Wrap casting yarn around needle, front to back; foundation yarn around needle, back to front (yarns cross as shown).

3. Wrap casting yarn around needle again, front to back. Pull downwards so that yarns are under needle. Repeat Steps 2 and 3.

Knitting basics

Forming the knit stitch/English (right-handed) method

The **knit stitch** is one of two fundamental movements in knitting; it forms a flat vertical loop on the fabric face.

Knitting methods vary from one place to another; two widely used ones are shown below and opposite. In both, the stitches are worked off the left needle on to the right, but in one, yarn is controlled with the right hand, in the other, with the left. Whatever your natural hand preference you should be able to master either method, because knitting is of course basically ambidextrous.

The right-handed technique prevails in English-speaking countries. In this approach, yarn is drawn around the right needle with the right index finger. Tension (control of yarn released with each stitch) is maintained between the two end fingers by wrapping yarn around the last, as shown. There are other correct ways to wrap yarn. The main thing is to feel comfortable and to achieve even tension and speed.

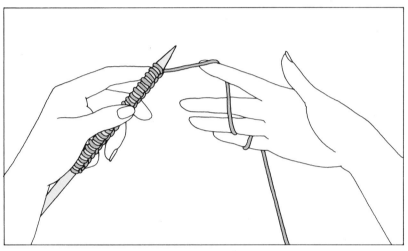

1. Grasp the needle with cast-on stitches in the left hand. The first stitch should be about 2 cm from the tip. Take yarn around little finger of right hand, under the next two fingers, and over the top of the index finger, extending it about 5 cm from the first stitch on the needle.

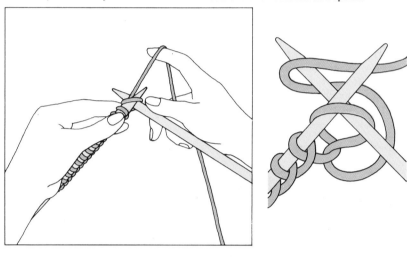

2. Holding yarn behind the work, *insert right needle into front of first stitch from left to right (needle tip points towards the back). With the right index finger, bring yarn forwards *under* the right needle, then backwards *over* the top (see detail above right).

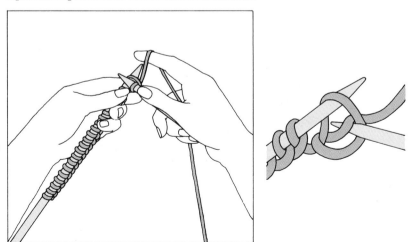

3. Draw the loop on the right needle forwards through the stitch, at the same time pushing the stitch on the left needle towards the tip. (With the deftness that comes with practice, these two movements will become smoothly co-ordinated. When they do, your speed will increase.)

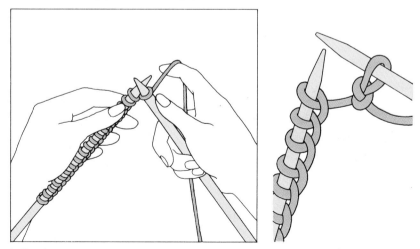

4. Allow first stitch to slide off left needle. New stitch (the loop just made) remains on right needle.* Repeat steps between asterisks, pushing stitches forwards on left needle with thumb, index and middle fingers, moving stitches back on right needle with the thumb.

Forming the knit stitch/Continental (left-handed) method

Controlling yarn with the left hand is the customary knitting practice in many European and Eastern countries. In this method, known as Continental, the fundamental action is to scoop yarn from the left index finger on to the right needle. There are several popular ways to hold yarn. In the one shown, tension is controlled partly with the index finger, extending it to tighten yarn after the needle passes underneath.

Many experts feel that greater speed can be attained with the Continental than with the English method. Whatever your own choice, you will find that speed is developed by holding the needles lightly and minimising all movements. For the right-handed method, nimble finger action is required; for the left-handed, the key is flexible wrist movement. If you learn both methods, you will be able to knit certain two-colour patterns more quickly and smoothly.

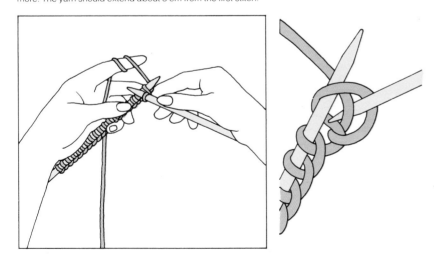

1. Hold the needle with cast-on stitches in the right hand and wrap yarn over the left, taking it between the 3rd and 4th fingers, under the next two fingers, over the top of the index finger, then around it once more. The yarn should extend about 5 cm from the first stitch.

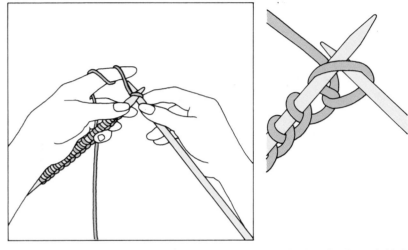

2. Transfer needle with stitches to the left hand and extend index finger slightly, pulling the yarn behind the needle. Push the first stitch up near the tip. *Insert right needle into front of first stitch from left to right (needle tip points towards the back).

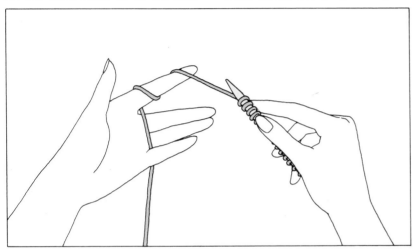

3. Twist the right needle and pull the tip *under* the yarn to draw a loop through the stitch. At the same time, push the stitch on the left needle towards the tip. (With the deftness that comes with practice, these two movements will become smoothly co-ordinated.)

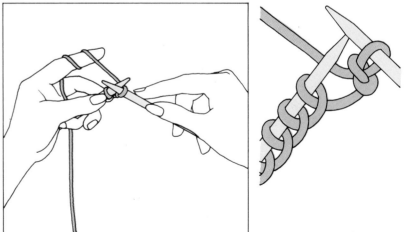

4. Allow first stitch to slide off left needle. New stitch (the loop just made) remains on the right needle. Repeat steps between asterisks, pushing stitches forwards on the left needle with thumb and middle finger, moving stitches back on right needle with the thumb.

Knitting basics

Forming the purl stitch/English (right-handed) method

A **purl stitch** is the reverse side of a knit stitch. Its loop structure is a horizontal semicircle, whereas the knit loop is vertical and flat (see preceding page).

In forming a purl stitch, the movements are the reverse of those used for knitting. The needle enters the front of the stitch from right to left, and the yarn, held in front of the work, is cast over the needle back to front.

When yarn is controlled with the right hand (as shown below), purl stitches tend to be looser than the knitted ones. This is because the yarn must be cast further to form a purl stitch than is required for the knit movements. With experience, a natural compensation is usually developed, especially if the index finger is kept close to the work. Should the difficulty persist, a good practice exercise is to work a 1 × 1 rib (see p. 420) until an even tension is established and the stitches appear the same on both sides of the fabric.

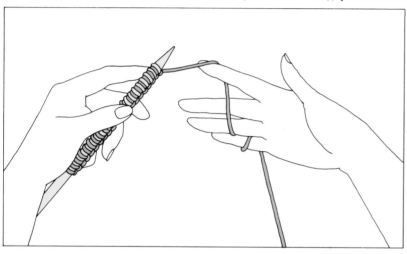

1. Grasp the needle with cast-on stitches in the left hand. First stitch should be about 2 cm from tip. Take yarn around little finger of the right hand, under the next two fingers, and over the top of the index finger, extending it about 5 cm from first stitch on needle.

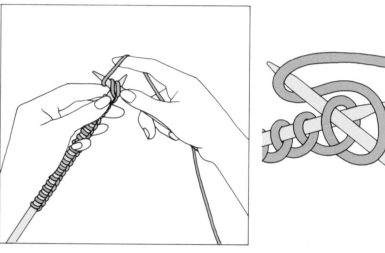

2. Holding yarn in front of the work, *insert right needle into front of first stitch from right to left (needle tip points upwards slightly). With the right index finger, take yarn backwards *over* the right needle, then forwards and *under* it (see detail above right).

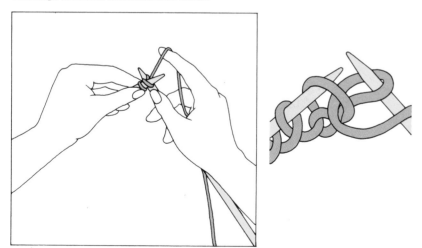

3. Draw the loop on the right needle backwards through the stitch, at the same time pushing the stitch on the left needle towards the tip. (With the deftness that comes with practice, these two movements will become smoothly co-ordinated.)

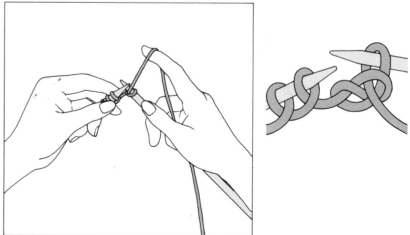

4. Allow first stitch to slide off left needle. New stitch (the loop just made) remains on the right needle.* Repeat steps between asterisks, pushing stitches forwards on left needle with thumb, index and middle fingers, moving stitches back on right needle with thumb.

Forming the purl stitch/Continental (left-handed) method

To form a purl stitch in the Continental style, yarn is held taut with the left index finger while a new loop is scooped up with the right needle. This action is facilitated by a forward twist of the wrist to release yarn, and by anchoring the working stitch with the thumb as the new stitch is drawn through it.

Shifting yarn from knit to purl position, and vice versa, can slow your working speed unless the manoeuvre is part of the working rhythm, and minimal effort is required for it. With yarn held in the left hand, a shift is made by swinging yarn forwards between needle tips to the purl position, and back again, the same way, to resume the knit position. Yarn in the right hand must be wrapped around the right needle, back to front, to work a purl stitch, then front to back again for the knit stitch. Less speed will be lost if you keep the index finger close to the work and working stitches close to the needle tips.

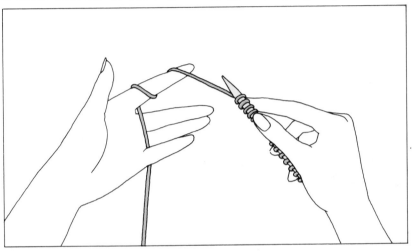

1. Hold the needle with cast-on stitches in the right hand and wrap yarn over the left, taking it between the 3rd and 4th fingers, under the next two fingers, over the top of the index finger, then around it once more. Yarn should extend about 5 cm from the first stitch.

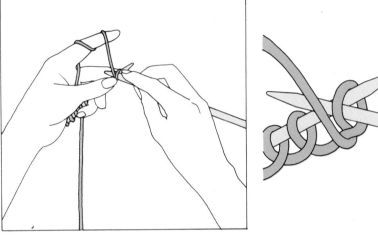

2. Transfer needle with stitches to left hand and extend index finger, pulling yarn in front of needle. Using thumb and middle finger, push first stitch up near tip. *Insert right needle into front of first stitch, right to left (tip points upwards slightly).

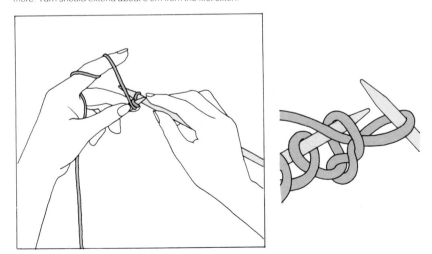

3. Turn left wrist so that yarn on index finger comes towards you, then push back and down with right needle to draw a loop back through the stitch. At the same time, push stitch on left needle towards tip. (With practice, these movements become smoothly co-ordinated.)

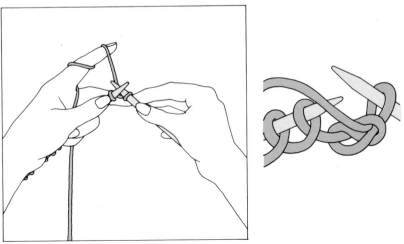

4. Allow first stitch to slide off left needle and straighten left index finger to tighten new stitch on right needle.* Repeat steps between asterisks, pushing stitches forwards on left needle with thumb and middle finger, moving stitches back on right needle with the thumb.

419

Knitting basics

Elementary stitch patterns

The elementary stitch patterns, shown below, are the most versatile and the easiest patterns to produce, ideal for a beginner. To practise these patterns, use double knitting and a 4 mm needle, and cast on 20 to 24 stitches. (**Note:** Each pattern has a *basic unit,* which is the least number of stitches needed to complete one pattern. If the unit is four,

for example, the number of stitches cast on must be divisible by four.) Work the first pattern row, then turn the needle and work the next row. As you knit, pay special attention to developing moderate and even tension (see opposite page for clarification), and always complete a row before putting the work down. Each time you try a new pattern or check

tension, you can proceed in this way. Eventually, if you like, squares can be joined to make something useful such as a cushion cover or child's blanket.

Each elementary pattern is produced with plain knit and/or purl stitches. The techniques are shown on pp. 416–19. These are all drawn to show the front of the stitch on the right side of the needle,

and the back of the stitch on the left.

The methods using plain stitches can be modified to produce the twisted variations illustrated opposite. If you are aware of these distinctions, you can avoid twisting stitches accidentally, a not unusual occurrence when a dropped stitch has been retrieved or work put down with a row in progress.

Garter stitch is normally produced by knitting every stitch of every row, though purling every stitch will give the same results. The simplest of all stitch patterns, it has a pebbly surface that is identical on both sides, and a somewhat loose structure that stretches equally in both directions. Use for sweaters, blankets and accessories.
Unit is any number of stitches
Every row: K

Moss stitch is produced by alternating one knit and one purl stitch within a row, then knitting the knit stitches and purling the purl stitches on the return row. This pattern makes a firmer fabric than garter stitch. Use it for blankets and garments, also as a contrasting texture for another pattern stitch.
Unit of 2 sts plus 1
Every row: *K 1, P 1*, K 1

Stocking stitch

Reverse stocking stitch

Stocking stitch is produced by knitting one row and purling the next. The most versatile of the basic stitch patterns, it is smooth on one (the knitted) side and pebbly on the other (the purled) side. The knitted side is usually considered to be the right side, but the purled side can be used for this purpose if desired; it is then referred to as **reverse stocking stitch** (below left). This fabric stretches more in the horizontal than the vertical direction. Use it for sweaters and dresses, also for knitted accessories such as hats, gloves and socks. See pp. 458–61 for the way stocking stitch is used in jacquard patterns.
Unit is any number of stitches
Row 1: K
Row 2: P

1 × 1 rib

2 × 2 rib

Rib stitch is produced by alternating knit and purl stitches on one row, then purling the knit stitches and knitting the purl stitches on the return row. The result is a pattern of vertical ridges that is identical on both sides when knit and purl stitches are interchanged in equal numbers, with no variations in technique. The ratio of knit to purl stitches may be even or uneven. It is frequently indicated by numbers. Examples are 1 × 1 and 2 × 2, shown left. These are the classic rib patterns often referred to as ribbing. They have considerable elasticity in the horizontal direction and are especially suitable for garment edges, where they provide a snug fit. For this purpose, ribbing is usually worked with needles a size or two smaller than those that are used for the garment.
For 1 × 1 rib, unit of 2 sts
Every row: *K 1, P 1*
For 2 × 2 rib, unit of 4 sts
Every row: *K 2, P 2*

Variations on elementary stitch patterns

The performance and appearance of basic stitch patterns can be altered by entering the stitch or wrapping yarn contrary to the usual way. These variations were common in the past; some are familiar practice today in certain parts of the world. The resulting fabrics (examples shown below) are somewhat firmer and more elastic than those shown on the opposite page. You can knit samples and compare the difference.

One variation is **twisted stitch,** formed by entering the back instead of the front of a loop. This action twists the loop a half turn at the base so that it does not lie as flat as the normal stitch. Either knit or purl stitches can be twisted in a pattern, but rarely both. For *twisted stocking* stitch, you work into the back loop of all stitches on the knit row and work all purl stitches normally. For a *1 × 1 twisted rib*, work into the back loop

of all knit stitches and work all purl stitches normally.

Another variation is **plaited stitch,** produced by wrapping yarn the reverse of the usual way, that is, *over* the needle for a knit stitch, *under* the needle for a purl stitch. Stitches formed this way are continually twisted and the resulting fabric is exceptionally firm. In *plaited stocking* stitch, both knit and purl stitches are worked with the techniques shown below right. On the right side, vertical rows resemble 3-ply plait. For *1 × 1 plaited rib*, plaited knit stitch is alternated with plaited purl.

The plaited methods are convenient for working with beads or sequins. They are also practical for knitting with large needles and heavy yarns because the fabric is firmer. Tension for these stitches must be kept looser than normal because of the twist in the stitch.

Twisted stocking stitch

1 × 1 twisted rib

Plaited stocking stitch

Plaited rib

To form a twisted knit stitch, enter *back* of loop, take yarn under needle as for normal knit stitch. On the return row, purl normally.

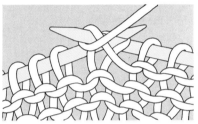

To form a twisted purl stitch, enter *back* of loop, take yarn over needle as for normal purl stitch. On the return row, knit normally.

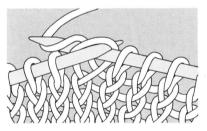

To form a plaited knit stitch, enter front of loop as for normal knit stitch, then take yarn *over* the needle to produce the new stitch.

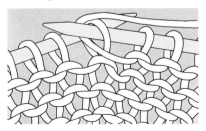

To form a plaited purl stitch, enter front of loop as for normal purl stitch, then take yarn *under* the needle to produce the new stitch.

Yarn tension

Tension is resistance on the yarn as it passes through the fingers that are controlling it. Moderate, consistent, correct and exact tension are the accomplishments of the expert knitter. They should be among the skills for which a beginner is striving.

Moderate tension is evident when stitches can be worked easily, yet no space is visible between the loops and the needle. If stitches are too tight, inserting the right needle is difficult and knitting speed will probably be slowed down; also, the yarn can become weakened by being overworked. If loops are too loose, they tend to slip off the left needle too soon; also, the knitted fabric holds its shape poorly.

Consistent tension results in an even fabric, that is, one in which stitches are the same size throughout. Achieving this requires practice, but the suggestions that follow may help. If your purl stitches tend to be looser than your knit stitches, or vice versa, work a practice sample of 1 × 1 rib stitch until you see a balance. If your tension varies from one day to the next, keep a practice sample handy and work a few rows on it before proceeding with your work. This warm-up period should bring your knitting to your usual tension.

Correct tension is exhibited in a fabric that is supple but not flimsy, firm but not stiff. It is the result of using a tension that suits both the yarn and the pattern stitch, and working with the proper needle size. Some understanding of yarn characteristics and experience with different pattern stitches help to achieve proper tension.

Here are some general guidelines: loosely spun or thick yarns should have an easy tension; firmly spun and inelastic yarns (cotton is an example of the latter) require a firm tension; twisted stitches (examples on the left), also crossed and cable stitches, need a little looseness in the tension, or they are difficult to work; open and lacy stitches need to be tensioned more firmly.

The correct tension is that specified at the beginning of a knitting pattern. Change the needle size to larger or smaller if necessary to produce the correct tension. It is not wise, however, to move more than two sizes away from that suggested in a pattern.

Knitting basics

Shaping: armholes, shoulders 472–3
Horizontal buttonhole 481

Casting off

Casting off is the removal of stitches from a needle in such a way that they will not come undone. It forms the last row of finished work and sometimes is used to begin the shaping of an armhole, or to produce one side of a horizontal buttonhole. As in casting on, this procedure forms a selvedge, and should be suitable for the type of knitting and the purpose it must serve.

Of several casting-off methods, the most versatile are plain and suspended, shown below. Unless instructions say otherwise, these stitches are worked from the right side and in the same sequence in which they were formed (that it, knitting the knit and purling the purl stitch). On the cast-off row, stitches should be moderately loose and uniform, or the edge may draw in or look distorted. If your stitches tend to be tight, cast off on a needle one size larger than the size that was used for knitting.

The three techniques illustrated on the opposite page have limited uses. One should know them, however, to obtain the best results in those situations for which they are suitable.

To secure yarn end after casting off, slip it through last stitch, pull to tighten loop.

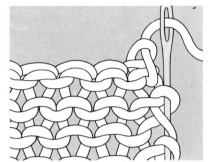

Thread yarn end in a tapestry needle and weave it into a seam edge for 5–6 cm. Cut remainder.

Casting-off techniques

PLAIN CASTING OFF

Plain casting off is the simplest, most frequently used method. It is suitable for any situation where an unadorned, firm selvedge is required, for example a shoulder seam or buttonhole.

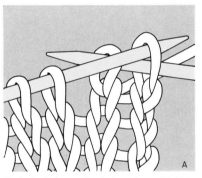

Work 2 stitches at beginning of row. *Holding yarn behind work, insert left needle in first stitch

(**A**). Pull the first stitch over the second one (**B**), and off the needle (**C**). Work the next stitch.*

Repeat instructions between the asterisks until desired number of stitches are cast off.

SUSPENDED CASTING OFF

Suspended casting off is similar to plain casting off (above), but more flexible. Use this method to finish ribbing, or as a substitute for the plain technique if your selvedges tend to be tight.

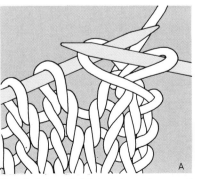

Work 2 stitches. *Pull first stitch over the second as for plain casting off, but keep pulled stitch on

left needle (**A**). Work the next stitch (**B**); drop both stitches off the left needle at the same time (**C**).*

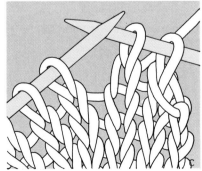

Repeat instructions between asterisks until 2 stitches remain; knit these together.

INVISIBLE CASTING OFF

Invisible casting off makes an inconspicuous finish for 1 × 1 ribbing, ideal for a cuff. To begin, cut yarn, leaving an end four times as long as the knitting width; thread yarn in a tapestry needle.

*Insert tapestry needle knitwise in knit stitch at end of needle; drop stitch off (**A**). Miss next purl stitch; insert needle purlwise in the next knit

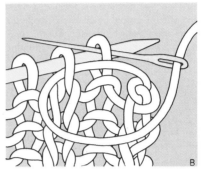

stitch; draw yarn through. Insert needle purlwise in purl stitch at end of needle (**B**); draw yarn through; drop stitch off. Take needle behind the

knit stitch and insert it knitwise in next purl stitch (bring yarn forwards between stitches first) (**C**); draw yarn through.* Repeat from first asterisk.

CROCHETED CASTING OFF

In **crocheted casting off**, the stitches are worked off in a chain stitch. The result is a firm and decorative edging appropriate for a blanket or rug, also a pretty finish for a hat or booties.

*Holding crochet hook in your hand as if it were a needle, insert it knitwise in first stitch; take yarn

around hook (**A**). Draw through a loop and let first stitch drop off needle. Draw a loop through next

stitch in same way (**B**). Draw a loop through 2 loops on hook (**C**).* Repeat from first asterisk.

PLAIN CASTING OFF OF TWO PIECES

Plain casting off of two pieces forms a neat, seamless join. It can be used for two straight edges having an equal number of stitches, or for shoulder edges that have been shaped by turning.

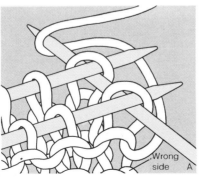

*With right sides together and both pieces held in the left hand, work the first stitch on both needles

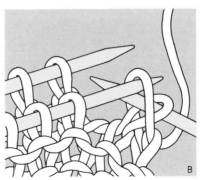

simultaneously (**A**). Work next 2 stitches together the same way. Slip first stitch over second one

(**B**).* Repeat from first asterisk. Ridge produced will be wrong side of seam (**C**).

Knitting basics

Slipping a stitch 428

Working two stitches together 433
Picking up stitches 437

Side selvedges

A side edge, whether it is exposed or in a seam, should be neat and suited to its purpose. Usually, greater precision is attained by working a narrow border, called a *selvedge*, in addition to the pattern stitches. Six ways to form selvedges are shown below. For each one, you must add two or four stitches to the total when casting on; instructions do not normally include selvedge stitches.

One-stitch methods are used for edges to be seamed, or along which stitches will be picked up. Two-stitch methods are more decorative, and also prevent curling. They are especially suitable where no other finish will be applied, for example, the edge of a facing. If appropriate, different selvedges might be used on the same piece – one type for the left side, another for the right.

Single chain edge 1. Use for stocking stitch and pattern stitches when seams are to be joined edge to edge or stitches are to be picked up later.

On *right side*, slip first stitch knitwise; knit the last stitch. On *wrong side*, slip first stitch purlwise; purl the last stitch.

Double picot edge. A decorative and delicate edging; very pretty for baby clothes. See p. 429 for the way to take yarn round needle at the beginning of a row.

On the *right* side, bring yarn in front of right needle (yarn round needle), insert needle knitwise in first stitch and slip it, knit the next stitch, pass the slipped stitch over the knitted one. On the *wrong* side, take yarn behind right needle (yarn round needle), purl first two stitches together.

Single chain edge 2. Forms a neat and flat edge for garter stitch.

Holding yarn at the front of the work, slip the first stitch of each row purlwise, then take yarn behind the work for knitting.

Double chain edge. Use when a decorative as well as firm edging is required.

On the *right* side, slip first stitch knitwise, purl the second stitch. At the end of the row, purl 1, slip the last stitch knitwise. On the *wrong* side, purl the first two and the last two stitches.

Single garter edge. A firm border, especially good for a stocking stitch or a pattern stitch where edges tend to be loose. Use also for seam edges that are to be backstitched or overcast.

Knit the first and last stitches of every row.

Double garter edge. A firm and even edge; will not curl.

On every row, slip the first stitch knitwise and knit the second stitch; knit the last two stitches.

Scarf to knit

Mohair scarf measures approximately 16 cm by 1.50 m plus 18 cm of tassels at each end.

A beginner can knit this warm, fringed mohair scarf.

It is worked in simple garter stitch, progressing rapidly on 4 mm needles. If tension is accurate, the scarf should measure 16 cm wide. Because of mohair's softness, and the natural stretchiness of garter stitch, your finished scarf may be slightly wider.

The scarf can also be knitted using a different wool or synthetic yarn. If this is your first attempt at knitting, you may find it difficult to keep the sides of the scarf straight as uneven tension will tend to pull in the sides giving a wavy edge. If your first rows are like this it is best to undo them and begin again, otherwise you will be dissatisfied with your scarf when finished as the two ends will not match.

Materials

120 g of mohair wool, 1 pair 4 mm needles, 1 crochet hook, medium to large, for fringe

Gauge

8 sts = 5 cm

Pattern stitch

Garter stitch

Selvedge stitch

Single chain edge 2

Instructions

Cast on 26 stitches loosely. Continue knitting in garter stitch until scarf measures 1.50 m; cast off loosely. When you finish one ball of wool, attach a new one at the beginning of a row (see explanation below). Weave in the wool ends later with a needle.

Finishing

Prepare fringe as directed below. Insert yarn groups in first and last stitches at each end of scarf, then every fifth stitch in between.

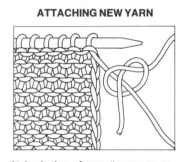

ATTACHING NEW YARN

At beginning of row, tie yarn on as shown, then slide it close to the needle. Weave the end into the edge later.

Making a fringe

A fringe with tassels is a handsome edge for a scarf or stole, and easy to make. On the scarf above, the tassels of 10 strands are spaced 5 stitches apart. For another project, you can experiment with dimensions to see what looks best.

To make this wool, wind wool 60 times around cardboard strip 20 cm long. Cut through the wool at one end, and divide it into groups of 5 strands each. Fold each group in half and, with a crochet hook, draw the folded end through one stitch in the scarf edge. Draw wool ends through the loop and pull to tighten it. The finished length is 18 cm because the knot uses 2–3 cm.

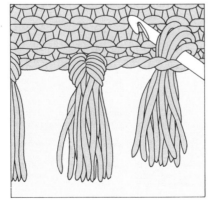

Draw folded end of tassel into a stitch.

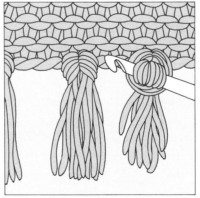

Draw the ends through the loop and tighten it.

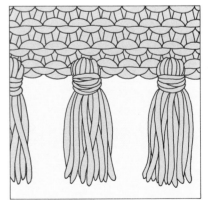

The tassels look like this on the reverse side.

Following knitting instructions

Knitting terminology

For written knitting instructions there is a special vocabulary, much of it expressed in abbreviated or symbolic form. Listed below are abbreviations, symbols and terms used in this book, with their definitions alongside. Also included are the numbers of pages on which illustrations of techniques can be found. These abbreviations are in common use elsewhere. You may encounter terms that are expressed differently, or which are not included here, but an explanatory key for them will usually be provided.

An alternative to written instructions is a chart. For this purpose, different symbols are used. Examples of chart symbols can be found on p. 462.

K	knit
P	purl
K-wise	insert needle as though to knit
P-wise	insert needle as though to purl
KP, KPK, etc.	knit and purl, or knit, purl, knit into same stitch as many times as there are letters
K 2 (3) tog	knit 2 (or 3) stitches together *p.433*
P 2 (3) tog	purl 2 (or 3) stitches together *p.433*
tbl	into back of loop (enter stitch from the back instead of the front) *p.421*
blw	below (work into the loop below the next stitch) *p.428*
alt	alternate
beg	beginning
dec	decrease *pp.432–3*
inc	increase *pp.429–30*
patt	pattern
rep	repeat
rnd	round
sl	slip a stitch, without working it, from the left needle to the right one *p.428*
st	stitch
psso	pass the slipped stitch over *p.432*
sl 1, K 1, psso	slip 1 stitch, knit 1 stitch, pass the slipped stitch over the knitted one *p.432*
dp	double-pointed (needles) *p.412*
ybk	yarn back (take yarn to back of work)
yfwd	yarn forward (bring yarn to front of work)

yrn	yarn round needle *p.429*
R	right
L	left
cm	centimetres
cross 2 RK	cross 2 stitches to the right, knitting *p.434*
cross 2 LK	cross 2 stitches to the left, knitting *p.434*
cross 2 RP	cross 2 stitches to the right, purling *p.434*
cross 2 LP	cross 2 stitches to the left, purling *p.434*
C4F	cable 4 front *pp.434, 450–1*
C4B	cable 4 back *pp.434, 451*
CC	contrasting colour
MC	main colour
* *	instructions between asterisks should be repeated as many times as there are stitches to accommodate them
( )	instructions enclosed by parentheses should be repeated the number of times indicated after the parentheses
[ ]	*for stitch patterns*, instructions within brackets explain the method of working a particular stitch or technique. *In garment directions*, numbers between brackets are for additional sizes
00, 000	wind yarn around the needle as many times as there are noughts *p.428*
tension	number of stitches and rows per centimetre to be obtained using suggested yarn and needles
place marker on needle	slip ring marker or a loop of contrasting yarn on the needle
selvedge	a finished edge, *pp.414–15, 422–4*
unit	the number of stitches required to work one motif horizontally in a pattern stitch
work straight	continue work without increasing or decreasing

Units and repeats

In knitting terminology, a **unit** is the number of stitches needed to complete one segment of a pattern stitch horizontally; it appears as a sequence of stitches between two asterisks. Here is a typical example of how it works:

Unit of 6 sts plus 3
Row 1: *K 3, P 3*, K 3
Row 2: P 3, *K 3, P 3*

The six stitches between asterisks comprise the unit. The three stitches following or preceding an asterisk are added to balance the pattern, or permit moving it left or right for a diagonal.

The number of stitches on the needle should be divisible by the unit. For instance, if a unit is 8 sts (plus 3), the number to be cast on would be 16 (plus 3), or 64 (plus 3), or 128 (plus 3), and so on. In following a pattern, the unit is then repeated as many times as there are stitches to be worked.

As a rule, a unit remains constant throughout a pattern. If a change does occur, as happens in some lace stitches, it is always temporary, and the count is restored eventually to the original.

If you should want to substitute one pattern for another, the relation of the unit to cast-on stitches must be considered. For instance, if instructions are to cast on 126 stitches and the pattern unit is 6, you could substitute a stitch with a unit of 7, because it divides evenly into 126. If you chose one with a unit of 8, which does not divide evenly into 126, you would have to adjust the stitch total and probably the tension too (see tension information below).

The term **repeat** is sometimes used as a synonym for unit. It can also denote the number of rows needed to complete one pattern motif vertically; the second meaning is used in this book.

Checking the tension

Knitting instructions always specify tension – the number of stitches and rows per centimetre that should be obtained using the recommended yarn and needles. The size of a finished article is based on the tension, so to achieve the correct size you must duplicate the tension precisely. Before beginning each new project, try the tension by working a sample 10 cm square, using the recommended yarn and needles. For example, if the instructions specified a tension of 10 stitches and 14 rows to 5 cm, you would cast on 20 stitches and work in the pattern for 28 rows. Place the completed sample right side up on a flat surface (such as an ironing board) and pin the corners, taking care not to stretch it. Using a tape measure, count the stitches and rows that fall within a 5 cm span (see below). If you count more stitches and rows than your pattern specifies, knit another sample using needles a size larger; if you have fewer stitches and rows, try needles a size smaller. Even half a stitch per 5 cm multiplies to a big size difference over a wide area, and results could be very disappointing. The horizontal tension is the most important to get right, as vertical tension can be corrected by adding or subtracting rows.

To measure the tension vertically (on right), place 2 pins 5 cm apart and count the rows between them. It is easier to count rows on the purl side of stocking stitch, where every two ridges equal one row; tension in the sample shows that 16 rows = 5 cm. In counting rows for garter stitch, every ridge equals one row and every furrow equals another.

To measure the tension horizontally (on left), place 2 pins 5 cm apart and count the stitches between them. It is easier to count stitches on the knit side of stocking stitch, where each loop represents one stitch; tension in the photo, left, shows that 10 stitches = 5 cm. In counting stitches for garter stitch, count the loops in one row only.

Following knitting instructions

Elongating stitches

Unusual textures can be produced by making certain stitches longer than others. Three methods are shown below.

A **slipped stitch** is a lengthened loop made by moving a stitch from the left needle to the right one without working it. Slipping forms a long vertical loop on one side of the work, a loose horizontal ridge on the reverse side. Unless the instructions say otherwise, stitches are slipped *purlwise* when working a pattern stitch, and the yarn is held in the working position of the preceding stitch. In making a decrease, the stitch is usually slipped *knitwise* (see p. 432).

A double stitch is a knit stitch that is twice as long as a normal one. It is produced by knitting into the loop below the stitch on the needle. This should not be confused with lifted increase, for which you knit into the loop below, then the one above. A double stitch is knitted just once, the upper and lower loops dropped off simultaneously. This method is limited to every other stitch in a row.

A **simple elongated stitch** is made by wrapping yarn more than once around the needle, then dropping the extra loop(s) on the next row. When used for a row, it makes an openwork band.

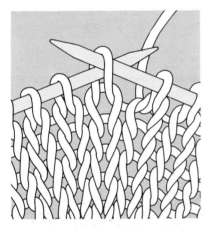

To slip one purlwise (sl 1 P-wise) in a knit row, hold yarn behind the work; insert needle into front of next stitch from right to left and slide the stitch on to the right needle.

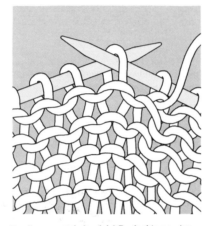

To slip one purlwise (sl 1 P-wise) in a purl row, hold yarn in front of work; insert needle into front of next stitch from right to left and slide the stitch on to the right needle.

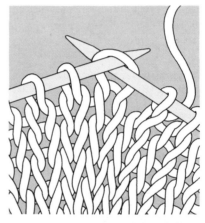

To slip one knitwise (sl 1 K-wise) in a knit row, hold yarn behind the work; insert needle into front of next stitch from left to right and slide the stitch on to the right needle.

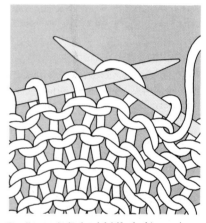

To slip one knitwise (sl 1 K-wise) in a purl row, hold yarn in front of work; insert needle into front of next stitch from left to right and slide the stitch on to the right needle.

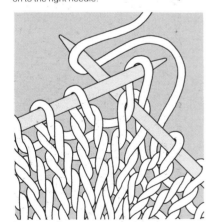

To knit one below (K 1 blw), also called double stitch, insert right needle front to back in centre of the loop just below next stitch. Take yarn around needle to make a knit stitch.

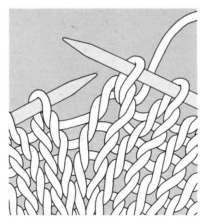

Pull the knit loop through the stitch, then slide stitch off the needle, at the same time pulling gently upwards to elongate the stitch. Always work a normal stitch between 2 double stitches.

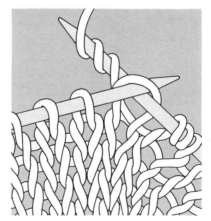

For a simple elongated stitch (K 00 or K 000), take yarn two or three times around the needle as you work the stitch. The number of wraps is indicated by the number of noughts.

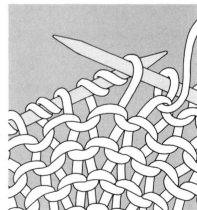

On the next row, let the extra loop(s) drop off the needle as you work each elongated stitch. Long stitches formed in this way are generally used as lacy bands between solid areas (see p. 447).

428

Increasing

Increasing (inc) in knitting means making additional stitches. Sometimes these are referred to as made stitches. Increasing is used to shape work by enlarging certain areas, but it is also used to produce fancy stitch patterns such as lace and bobbles. For pattern purposes it is combined with decreasing, in the same or a subsequent row, so the stitch total remains constant.

There are four basic methods of increasing: **yarn round** needle (right), **raised** (p. 430), **lifted** (p. 430) and **bar** (p. 431). Casting on (pp. 414–15) is also used for increasing, usually to add three or more stitches to either side of the work. Knitting instructions do not always say what type of increasing to use. If you familiarise yourself with all these methods, then you can choose the most appropriate in each case.

Choice of an increasing method is based largely on the appearance desired, and sometimes on its position. The yarn round needle method, which forms a hole in the fabric, is used only for a decorative effect, most often in fact to form lace stitches. Bar increasing is also decorative. It is a good choice when increasing must be made in steps, because it is readily seen and easily counted. Lifted increasing is nearly invisible. It is used when gentle shaping is required. Raised increasing can be decorative or inconspicuous, depending on how it is made. It is the most versatile of all the methods.

When increasing gradually, to shape a sleeve, for example, the seam edge will be smoother if you place the additions two or three stitches in from the edge. With a complicated stitch, however, it is better to increase at the edges so as not to disrupt the pattern sequence.

When increasing rapidly, or shaping a chevron, double increasing (p. 431) is used. In this method, paired additions are made on either side of a centre stitch, and can usually be seen.

YARN ROUND NEEDLE

A yarn round needle increase (yrn) is made by taking yarn around the needle between two stitches. Because a hole is formed, this method is used for knitting lace and for shaping work when a lacy effect is desired. The basic technique is to wind yarn once around the needle, making a loop to be knitted or purled on the next row. The direction in which the yarn is wound depends on the type of stitch that precedes and follows.

Occasionally directions specify a multiple yarn round needle. This is wound as for an elongated stitch, but all loops are worked on the return row.

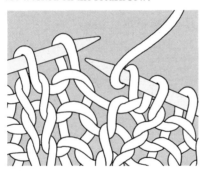

yrn – after knit stitch, before purl stitch (for rib patterns). Bring yarn forwards between needles, then back over right needle and forwards under it into position for next purl stitch.

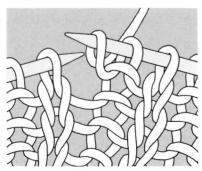

yrn – after purl stitch, before a knit stitch (for rib patterns). Take yarn over right needle from front to back. The made stitch can be seen after the next knit stitch is completed.

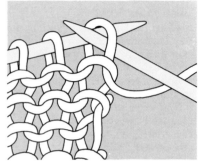

yrn – before first knit stitch (for picot selvedge, some lace). Holding yarn *in front of* right needle, insert needle knitwise in first stitch and knit it. The made stitch can then be seen.

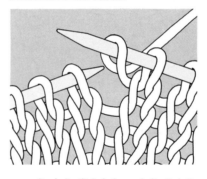

yrn – after knit stitch, before a knit stitch (for stocking and lace stitches). Bring yarn forwards *under* the right needle, then back *over* it into position for the next knit stitch.

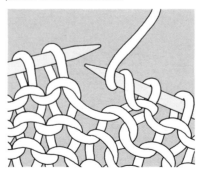

yrn – after purl stitch, before a purl stitch (for reverse stocking and lace stitches). Take yarn back *over* right needle, then forwards *under* it into position for the next purl stitch.

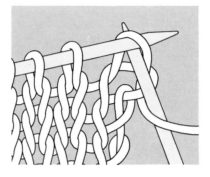

yrn – before first purl stitch (for picot selvedge, some lace). Holding yarn *behind* right needle, insert needle purlwise in first stitch and pull it. The made stitch can then be seen.

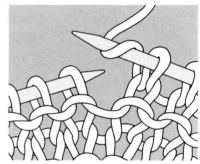

yrn – after knit stitch, before a knit stitch (for garter stitch). Bring yarn forwards *over* the right needle, then back *under* it again, into position for the next knit stitch.

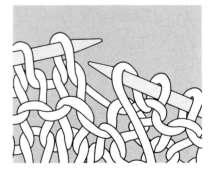

yrn – after purl stitch, before a purl stitch (for garter stitch). Take yarn back *under* right needle, then forwards *over* it. The made stitch can be seen after purl stitch is completed.

Following knitting instructions

Increasing

RAISED INCREASING

Raised increasing is made by picking up a horizontal strand between two stitches and working it as if it were a stitch. There are two ways to work the strand; each gives a very different result. If you knit or purl into the front of it, a hole is left beneath, a suitable approach for a lace stitch or wherever a decorative effect is desired. If you work into the back of the strand, the stitch thus made is twisted and the increasing is nearly invisible. This method of increasing can be used effectively where you want the shaping to be inconspicuous, for instance, when shaping a dart.

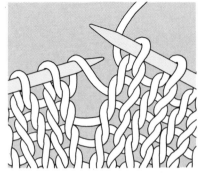

First step for raised increasing is to insert left needle front to back under the horizontal strand that lies between 2 stitches.

LIFTED INCREASING

Lifted increasing is made by working into the loop below a stitch as well as into the stitch itself. The result is basically inconspicuous, but there is a definite slant to the stitches, which makes them particularly suitable for paired increasing each side of a centre area (see illustration on the immediate right).

Because lifted increasing is not clearly visible, it can be used where several stitches must be made at intervals along one row, as above ribbing on a sleeve. It should be worked with a loose tension when repeated vertically, as it tends to draw in the fabric.

To pair lifted increasing on either side of a centre area, work *left* increasing as you approach the centre; work *right* increasing after it.

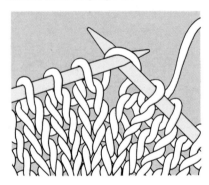

For decorative raised increasing on a knit row, knit into the front of the strand (a hole is formed under the stitch).

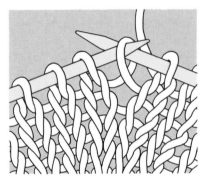

For invisible raised increasing on a knit row, knit into the back of the strand (the stitch is thus twisted; the result is almost invisible).

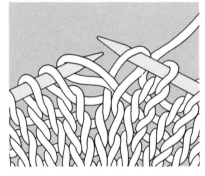

For lifted knit increasing, right, insert *right* needle in top of loop just below next stitch; knit the loop, then knit stitch on needle.

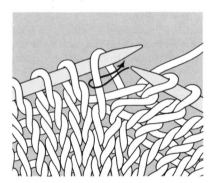

For lifted knit increasing, left, insert *left* needle in top of loop below last completed stitch; pull back gently; knit into front of the loop.

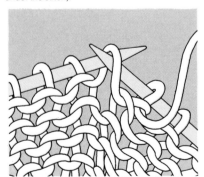

For decorative raised increasing on a purl row, purl into the front of the strand (a hole is formed under the stitch).

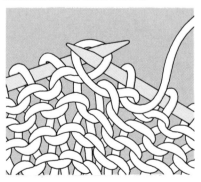

For an invisible raised increasing on a purl row, purl into the back of the strand (the stitch is thus twisted; the result is almost invisible).

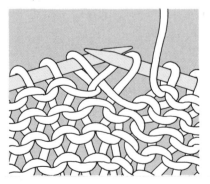

For lifted purl increasing, right, insert *right* needle under loop just below next stitch; purl the loop, then purl the stitch on the needle.

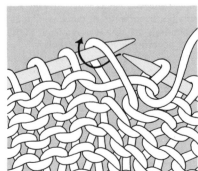

For lifted purl increasing, left, insert *left* needle under loop below last completed stitch; pull back gently; purl into front of the loop.

BAR AND MOSS INCREASING METHODS

Bar and moss increasing methods are produced by working into the same stitch twice. For bar increasing, you knit into the front and back of a stitch; for moss increasing, you knit and purl into the front. In both cases, the result is decorative, either a bar or knob, and it is easy to keep track of the increasing over several rows. The bar always follows the stitch on which an increase is made, a fact that must be allowed for in paired increasing. For example, when increasing is worked three stitches from the end on the right edge, it must be made four stitches from the end on the left edge.

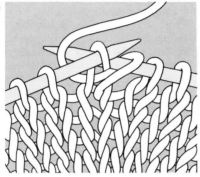

For bar increasing on a knit row, knit a stitch, but do not drop it off the needle; instead, knit again into the back of the same stitch.

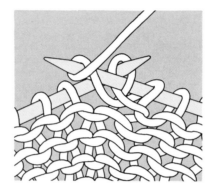

For bar increasing on a purl row, purl a stitch, but do not drop it off the needle; instead, purl again into the back of the same stitch.

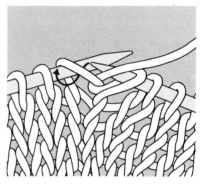

For moss increasing on a knit row, knit a stitch, but do not drop it off the needle; instead, purl into the front of the same stitch.

Double increasing

Double raised increasing. Knit into back of horizontal strand before centre; knit centre stitch; knit into back of the next strand.

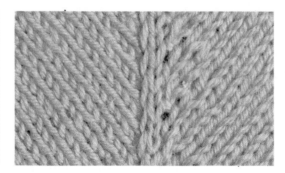

Double lifted increasing. In stitch before centre, make lifted increasing left; knit centre stitch; make a lifted increasing right.

Double lifted increasing into 1 stitch. Knit loop below centre st; knit into back of centre st; knit again into loop below centre.

Double bar increasing. Knit into front and back of stitch before centre stitch; knit into front and back of centre stitch.

Double moss increasing. Knit and purl the stitch before centre stitch; knit centre stitch; knit and purl the next stitch.

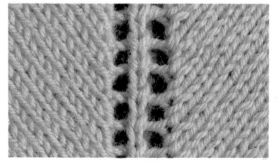

Double lace increasing. Pass yarn round needle just before the centre stitch; pass yarn round needle again immediately after.

431

Following knitting instructions

Decreasing

Decreasing (dec) in knitting is the reduction of one or more stitches to shape work by making it narrower or to form lace stitch patterns and bobbles.

Two basic methods are shown below and at the top of the opposite page. There is little difference in the way they look, but the slip stitch method (below) draws in less than two stitches worked together (above opposite), and is easier to work when tension is tight.

Each decreasing method pulls stitches on a diagonal to the right or the left. If decreasing is worked randomly, or at the edge of a garment, the direction of this slant is not significant. It *is* important for symmetrical shaping, such as a raglan or a V-neck where a line will be seen. The rule for this situation is to slant decreasing to the right at the left side of the centre, slant them to the left at the right of it. With stocking stitch, for

instance, you would sl 1, K 1, psso to decrease at the beginning of a row, K 2 tog at the end.

To use decreasing for gradual shaping, stitches are reduced one at a time on the right side, which means that you work them every other row. If stitches must be reduced every row, then decreasing can be worked on the wrong side, but care must be taken to keep direction of slant (as viewed from right

side) consistent for the best result.

To shape a chevron or mitred corner, **double decreasing** is used. This is paired decreasing, worked on each side of a stitch. It forms a rather thick knob or ridge.

When decreasing three or more stitches in succession, plain casting off is preferable (see p. 422). This would be used, for example, at the beginning of an armhole, or the centre of a neckline.

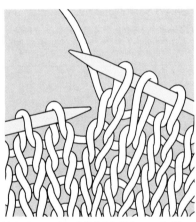

Knit decreasing, left (sl 1, K 1, psso). Slip a stitch knitwise; knit the next stitch.

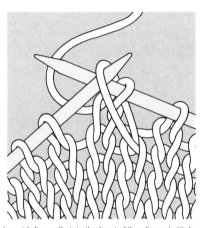

Insert left needle into the front of the slipped stitch and pull it over the knitted one.

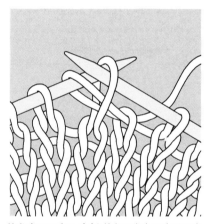

Knit decreasing, right. Knit a stitch and return it to the left needle. Pass the next stitch over it.

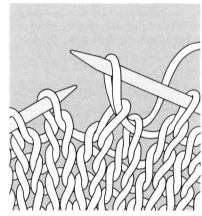

Replace the knitted stitch on the right needle by slipping it purlwise.

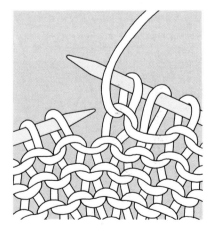

Purl decreasing, right (sl 1, P 1, psso). Slip a stitch knitwise; purl the next stitch.

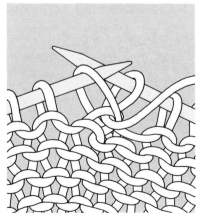

Insert left needle into the front of the slipped stitch and pass it over the purled one.

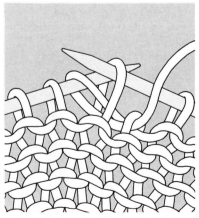

Purl decreasing, left. Purl a stitch and return it to the left needle. Pass the next stitch over it.

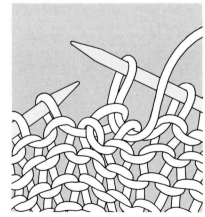

Replace the purled stitch on the right needle by slipping it purlwise.

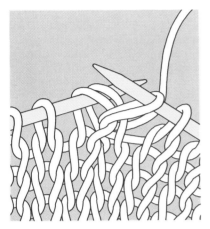

Knit decreasing, right (K 2 tog). Knit 2 stitches together through the front of both loops.

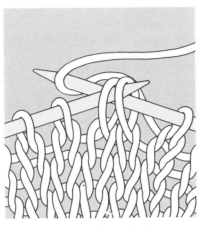

Knit decreasing, left (K 2 tog tbl). Knit 2 stitches together through the back of both loops.

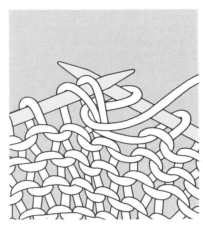

Purl decreasing, right (P 2 tog). Purl 2 stitches together through the front of both loops.

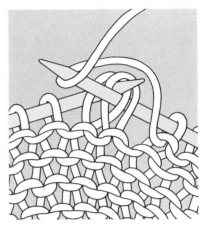

Purl decreasing, left (P 2 tog tbl). Purl 2 stitches together through the back of both loops.

Double decreasing

Double decreasing, left (K 3 tog tbl). Knit 3 stitches together through the back of all 3 loops. The result is a thick ridge with sharply slanted stitches on either side.

Double decreasing, right (K 3 tog). Knit 3 stitches together through the front of all 3 loops. The result is a rather thick ridge with sharply slanted stitches on either side.

Double decreasing, left (sl 1, K 2 tog, psso). Slip a stitch knitwise, knit the next 2 stitches together, pass the slipped stitch over the knitted ones. This method of decreasing is similar in appearance to the one above, but draws in a little less tightly. It is also a bit easier to work.

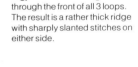

Double decreasing, vertical. Slip 2 stitches knitwise, inserting the needle into the second stitch, then the first one; knit the next stitch, then pass the 2 slipped stitches over the knitted one. This is an attractive method of decreasing, especially suitable for a V-neckline.

Following knitting instructions

Crossing stitches

Crossing stitches is a way to produce certain decorative effects, such as a plait, basket weave or honeycomb pattern. The crossed stitches appear to be twisted because they are pulled diagonally right or left. The twist direction is determined by the way stitches are worked – to the front or the back.

To cross two stitches, you work the second stitch on the left needle, then the first. Three stitches can also be exchanged this way, working the third stitch, then the first stitch, and finally the second one. The crossovers are easier to manipulate and yarn is less strained if you keep tension loose.

A variation of the above method is crossing through two stitches, as illustrated at the top of the opposite page. The results are slightly different from crossing two stitches, but close enough in appearance that you could substitute the variation for the normal crossing technique, if you preferred.

Crossing more than three stitches is called **cabling**. This technique requires a double-pointed or cable needle to hold the first stitches out of the way until needed. The holding needle should be the same size or smaller than the working needle; a larger one might stretch the stitches. It is correct to work cable stitches from the holding needle, as illustrated opposite, but some people find it easier to slip them back on to the left needle and then work them.

The appearance of a cable is varied by the number of stitches exchanged, the number of rows worked between twists, and the direction of the twist itself. If stitches are held to the front, a cable twists to the left; if held to the back, the twist is to the right. Because of the complexities, most cable instructions are written out rather than abbreviated. An exception is the common cable exchange of two pairs, abbreviated C4F and C4B.

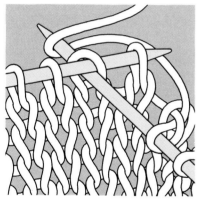

Cross 2 stitches right, knitting (cross 2 RK). Knit into the front of second stitch on the left needle, but do not drop the stitch off.

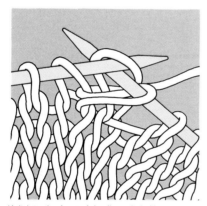

Knit into the front of the first stitch (the one that was missed); allow both first and second stitches to drop off the needle together.

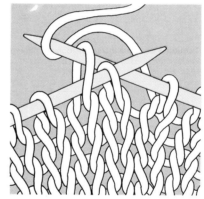

Cross 2 stitches left, knitting (cross 2 LK). Knit into the back of second stitch on the left needle, but do not drop the stitch off.

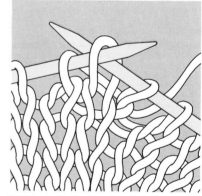

Knit into the back of the first stitch (the one that was missed); allow both first and second stitches to drop off the needle together.

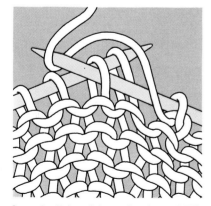

Cross 2 stitches right, purling (cross 2 RP). Purl into the front of second stitch on the left needle, but do not drop the stitch off.

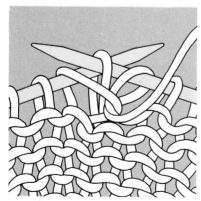

Purl into the front of the first stitch (the one that was missed); allow both first and second stitches to drop off the needle together.

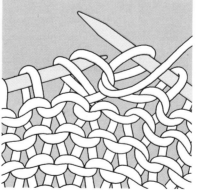

Cross 2 stitches left, purling (cross 2 LP). Purl into the front of second stitch on the left needle; pass it over the first stitch and off the needle.

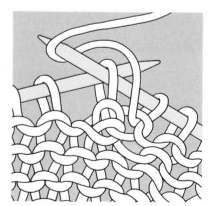

Purl into the front of the first stitch (the one that was missed), then allow this first stitch to drop off the left needle.

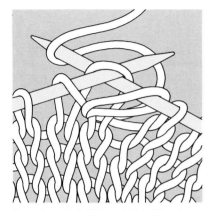

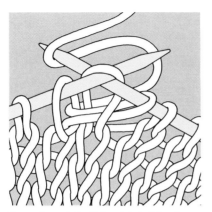

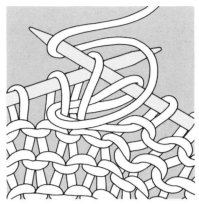

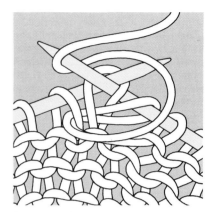

Cross through 2 stitches right, knitting (cross through 2 RK). Knit 2 stitches together through the *front*; knit the first stitch again, then drop both stitches off the left needle together.

Cross through 2 stitches left, knitting (cross through 2 LK). Knit 2 stitches together through the *back*; knit the first stitch again, but through the *front*; drop both stitches off together.

Cross through 2 stitches right, purling (cross through 2 RP). Purl 2 stitches together through the *front*; purl the first stitch again, then drop both stitches off the left needle together.

Cross through 2 stitches left, purling (cross through 2 LP). Purl 2 stitches together through the *front*; purl the first stitch again, but through the *back*; drop both stitches off together.

Crossing stitches with a cable needle

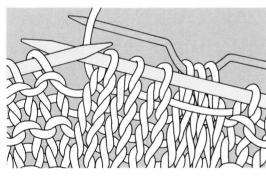

For a cable twisted right, slip the cable stitches on to a cable needle, or any double-pointed needle, and hold these at the back of the work while you knit the remaining stitches of the cable section.

Knit the stitches from the cable needle, as shown, or if you prefer, slip them back on to the left needle and knit them from there. Continue with the rest of the pattern according to instructions.

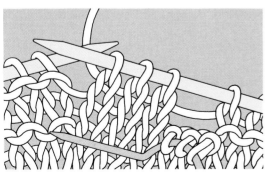

For a cable twisted left, slip the cable stitches on to a cable needle, or any double-pointed needle, and hold these at the front of the work while you knit the remaining stitches of the cable section.

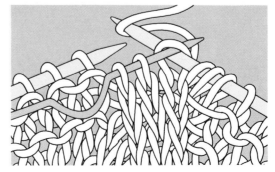

Knit the stitches from the cable needle, as shown, or if you prefer, slip them back on to the left needle and knit them from there. Continue with the rest of the pattern according to instructions.

Following knitting instructions

Ring markers 413
Pattern units 427

Correcting errors

Sometimes it is necessary to correct a mistake in your knitting. The methods given here will help you to correct in the easiest and most suitable way. If an error is one row down, drop the stitch off the needle directly above it, then retrieve it by the appropriate method of the two shown below. When it is a few rows down, let that stitch run, and pick it up with a crochet hook, as shown right. Use these same methods to pick up a stitch that has dropped or run accidentally. When the error is several rows down, or if for any reason you wish to unravel a portion of work, follow the directions at the top of the opposite page.

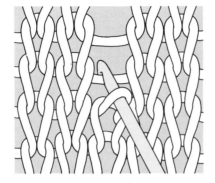

To retrieve a run in stocking stitch, insert a crochet hook front to back, hook it *over* the horizontal thread and draw through loop on hook.

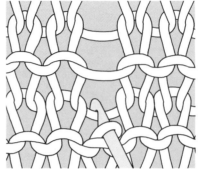

To retrieve a run in garter stitch, insert crochet hook front to back in each knit loop; pull through the loop on the hook.

For a purl loop in garter stitch, insert the crochet hook back to front, hooking it *under* the horizontal thread; draw through loop on hook.

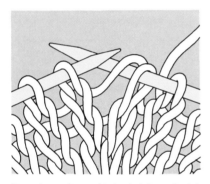

To retrieve a dropped knit stitch, insert the right needle through the loop and under the strand, as shown in the illustration.

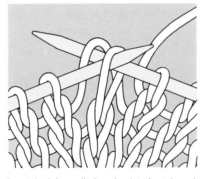

Insert the left needle from back to front through the top of the loop only, then pull gently upwards and forwards on it.

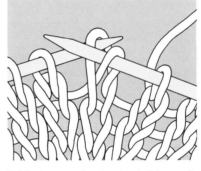

Pull the loop over the strand and off the needle. The stitch (which was the strand) remains on the right needle and is facing the wrong way.

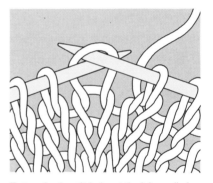

To transfer the stitch, insert the left needle from front to back and slip the stitch on to it. It will be in the correct position to knit.

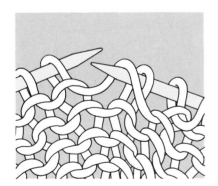

To retrieve a dropped purl stitch, insert the right needle through the loop and under the strand, as shown in the illustration.

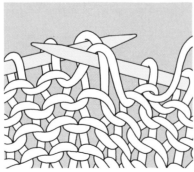

Insert the left needle from front to back through the top of the loop only, then pull gently upwards and forwards on it.

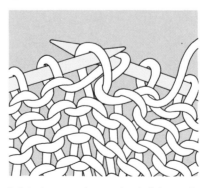

Pull the loop over the strand and off the needle. The stitch (which was the strand) remains on the right needle and must be transferred.

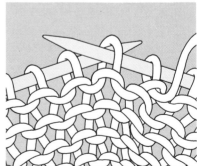

To transfer the stitch, insert the left needle from front to back and slip the stitch on to it. It will be in the correct position to purl.

To correct an error several rows down, mark the row in which the error occurs, using a yarn loop or a coil ring marker.

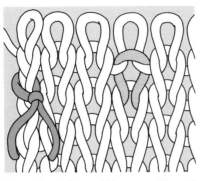

Unravel the stitches to within one row of the mark. Position the knitting so that the working yarn is on the left side (right side of the work faces you).

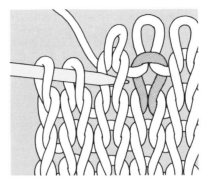

For each knit stitch, hold the yarn behind the work; insert the *left* needle front to back, then pull out the stitch.

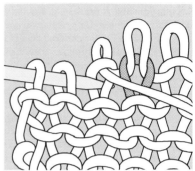

For each purl stitch, hold the yarn in front of the work, insert the *left* needle front to back, then pull out the stitch.

Picking up new stitches

By picking up stitches along a finished edge (usually written pick up and K in instructions), you can add a collar cuff, trimming, even sleeves, without sewing sections together. Two methods for picking up stitches are shown here. Results are the same with both, but Method 2 is easier to manage when the shape is a deep curve. Ideally, one loop should be picked up in each stitch, but this is not always possible. Before beginning, divide the edge in sections, marking with pins or yarn, calculate how many stitches will fit in each section, and decide how they should be spaced.

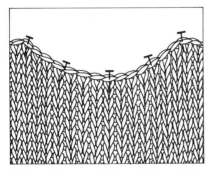

Before picking up stitches, divide work into equal sections, using pins or scraps of yarn. Tie on working yarn where stitches will begin.

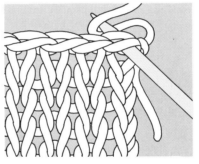

Method 1. Hold work in left hand, right side facing you. *Insert right needle under the edge stitch; take yarn around needle as for knitting.

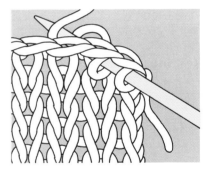

Bring stitch through to the right side.* Repeat from asterisk. Work proceeds from right to left; first row is knitted on the wrong side.

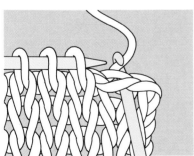

Method 2 (right-handed). Hold yarn, needle and work in left hand, right side facing you, needle just above edge. *Insert hook under stitch.

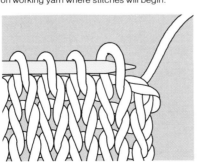

Pull through a loop, place on needle, pull it tight.* Repeat from asterisk. Work proceeds left to right; first row is knitted on the right side.

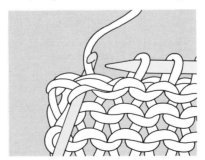

Method 2 (left-handed). Hold yarn, needle and work in right hand, wrong side facing you, needle just above edge. *Insert hook under stitch.

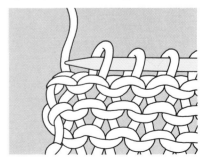

Pull through a loop, place on needle, pull it tight.* Repeat from asterisk, proceeding right to left; first row is knitted on the right side.

Following knitting instructions

Circular knitting

Circular knitting is the way of making a seamless tube or a flat piece worked from the centre out. There are two ways of working, with a circular needle or with a set of double-pointed needles.

The **circular needle** is practical for any large item, tubular or flat. It holds a great many stitches and permits most of the weight to be supported in the lap, thus lessening strain on the arms. To knit a tube or flat circle, the circumference of the knitted piece must be at least 5 cm larger than that of the needle for stitches to fit comfortably and without stretching. Available needle lengths are from 40 to 100 cm, so the smallest tube possible would be 45 cm. Anything smaller must be knitted on double-pointed needles.

A circular needle can also be used to knit a large, flat item that would other-wise be made on straight needles, a blanket, for instance. For this purpose, the stitches are worked back and forth as in normal knitting (see below right).

Double-pointed needles are used most often for small items, such as mittens, socks, or a polo neck. A large piece of work is possible, however, if the needles are long enough, and there are enough of them, that stitches will not slide off. As a rule, double-pointed needles are sold in sets of four. You will have to buy an extra set when five or more needles are required (the knitted square, opposite page, is an example).

When casting on for double-pointed needles, the stitches are divided evenly among the total number of needles in use. (One needle is always left free for working.) Some adjustment may be necessary to allow for the pattern unit.

For example, to knit a 2 × 2 rib, each needle would have to carry a multiple of 4 stitch units. The casting-on method at the top of the opposite page is best for most purposes. The casting-on method below it is more convenient to use when the centre area is very small.

Almost any stitch can be knitted in the round, but an adjustment must be made in the row sequence because the right side always faces you. Knitting every row, for example, produces stocking stitch; alternating knit and purl rows produces a garter stitch. Certain lace and jacquard patterns are easier to knit in the round because the pattern sequence becomes less complicated.

While there are some differences in using double-pointed and circular needles, the fundamental approach for knitting is the same with both.

Important points to remember:
1. As you start the first round, the bottom edge of all stitches must face the *middle;* twisted stitches cannot be adjusted without unravelling the work.
2. A marker should be placed after the last cast-on stitch, and slipped before the first stitch of each round. Pattern changes, for example, a switch from knit to purl stitches, will occur at this point, and progression will be uneven if the rounds are not clearly marked. (To mark other key points, such as increasing places, without confusion, use markers of a different colour.)
3. Every joining stitch (the first one on a needle or round) must be pulled extra firmly to avoid a ladder effect.
4. The right side of a tube or flat motif always faces you, and the stitch pattern must be adjusted accordingly.

Knitting with a circular needle

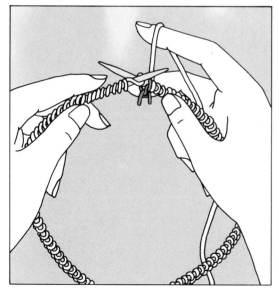

To knit a tubular fabric, hold needle tip with the *last* cast-on stitch (the one attached to ball of yarn) in your *right* hand, the tip with *first* cast-on stitch in your *left*. Knit the first stitch, pulling yarn firmly to avoid a gap where the tube is joined.

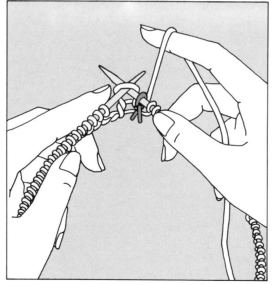

Knit around the circle until you reach the marker, then slip the marker and start the next round. At this point, check for twisted stitches; if you find any, unravel the work and start again. A twisted edge cannot be corrected in any other way.

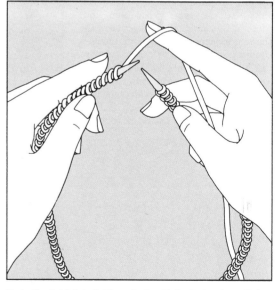

To knit a flat fabric, hold needle tip with the *last* cast-on stitch your *left* hand, the tip with *first* cast-on stitch in your *right*. Knit to the last stitch, then turn needle around so that wrong side faces you. Continue to turn work with each round.

Knitting with double-pointed needles

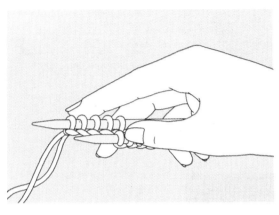

1. To knit a tube with 4 dp needles, cast one-third the total number of stitches on each of 3 needles. As you complete one needle, place the next one parallel and directly above it, with the point a little bit in front of the lower one. (To knit with 5 or more needles, use the same approach, dividing stitches evenly among the total, minus 1 needle for working.)

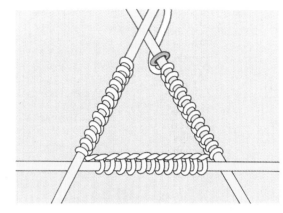

2. Lay the 3 needles in a triangle, with the bottom edges of all stitches facing the centre. Place a ring marker after the last stitch (where the ball end of the yarn is).

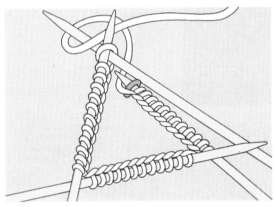

3. Using the fourth needle, knit into the first cast-on stitch, thus closing the triangle. Pull extra firmly on the yarn for this stitch, so there will not be a gap. When you have knitted all stitches off the first needle, use that one for the working needle, placing it behind the others as you knit the first stitch in the next group.

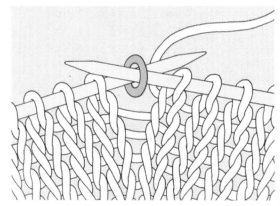

4. Knit each section of the circle until you reach the marker, then slip it and start the next round. Continue to slip the marker with each round; it marks regular progression of rows.

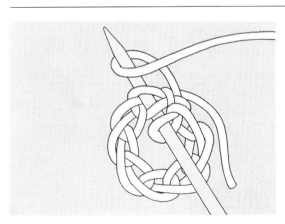

To knit a flat item, started at the centre (a tablecloth, for example, or a patchwork motif), cast on the stitches by this method: crochet a chain, having one loop for each stitch that is needed; join it in a ring. Transfer the loop that remains on the hook to one dp needle, then pick up stitches around the ring, setting the correct number on each needle. For a small centre area, this method is easier to manage than the one shown above, left.

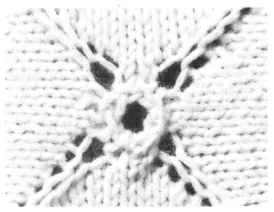

To knit a square from the centre out, crochet 8 chains, join in a ring, and pick up 2 stitches on each of 4 needles. On first round, increase 1 stitch between each 2-stitch group. On the next and subsequent rounds, increase 2 stitches at the centre of each section. A triangle is worked in the same way, but with 6 stitches in 3 sections. A circle is made similarly, but started with 10 stitches on 5 needles; increase by 1 stitch in each section every round, moving position 1 stitch forward each round.

Knitting stitches

Using a pattern stitch
Textures
Ribs
Diagonals
Lace stitches
Crossed stitches
Cables
Ornamental stitches
Knotted stitches
Aran knitting
Directions for Aran sweater
Multicolour knitting
Changing colours at the end
of a row
Twisting yarns to change colour
Stranding method
Jacquard patterns using
stranding
Weaving method
Jacquard patterns using weaving
Charting a pattern stitch

Using a pattern stitch

A **pattern stitch** (often called pattern for short) is the sequence of knitting techniques, repeated continuously, that forms knitted fabric. It consists of a *unit*, the stitches needed for one horizontal motif, and a *repeat*, the rows required to form one vertical unit (see p. 427).

Knitters are highly inventive, so there are more pattern stitches than anyone can count. Most have fanciful names that often suggest what the stitches look like. These names vary, however, from one region to another, so do not be surprised if you encounter a familiar stitch with an unfamiliar name.

Most pattern stitches can be classified according to structure. Familiarity with basic structures will permit you to knit almost anything as your skill increases, even to invent your own stitch if you do not find one to suit your needs.

Patterns in this section are grouped according to type, though in a few cases a stitch may fit more than one category. The first group, *Textures*, comprises those compact knits that are sometimes called fabric stitches. The first eight stitches in this group are ideal for beginners, as they are not difficult.

In choosing a pattern stitch, you will naturally be influenced by its appearance, but other things should be considered, too. Is it suitable for the yarn? A highly textured yarn and a busy pattern, for instance, do not mix. Is it appropriate for the intended use? Few lace stitches would make a warm winter garment.

To knit a pattern, cast on a multiple of the stitches that form the pattern unit; add any additional stitches indicated, plus selvedge stitches. Follow instructions to the last row, then begin again at Row 1. Unless stated otherwise, the first row is the right side. The word *reversible* appears whenever a pattern is identical on both sides, a desirable quality if both sides will be seen, as in a blanket. For a list of abbreviations, see p. 426.

Textures

Simple moss. A stocking stitch interspersed with purl stitches; a nice pattern for baby garments.
Unit of 4 sts
Row 1: *K 3, P 1*
Row 2 and alt rows: purl
Rows 3 and 7: knit
Row 5: K 1, *P 1, K 3*, P 1, K 2

Tracks. Streaks of purl stitches on a face of stocking stitch pattern.
Unit of 10 sts
Row 1: *K 4, P 6*
Row 2 and alt rows: purl
Rows 3 and 7: knit
Row 5: *P 5, K 4, P 1*

Chevron moss. Zigzags of purl stitches on stocking stitch background.
Unit of 8 sts
Row 1: *P 1, K 3*
Row 2: *K 1, P 5, K 1, P 1*
Row 3: *K 2, P 1, K 3, P 1, K 1*
Row 4: *P 2, K 1, P 1, K 1, P 3*

Diamond moss. Purl stitches making diamonds on a stocking stitch face.
Unit of 8 sts
Row 1: *P 1, K 7*
Rows 2 and 8: *K 1, P 5, K 1, P 1*
Rows 3 and 7: *K 2, P 1, K 3, P 1, K 1*
Rows 4 and 6: *P 2, K 1, P 1, K 1, P 3*
Row 5: *K 4, P 1, K 3*

Basket stitch (reversible).
Chequerboard squares of stocking stitch and reverse stocking stitches.
Unit of 10 sts
Rows 1 to 6: *K 5, P 5*
Rows 7 to 12: *P 5, K 5*

Gathered stitch. The gathered sections are created by doubling stitches, working even, then decreasing stitches to the original number. The section depths can be varied, also stocking stitch substituted for garter stitch if desired.
Unit is any number of sts
Rows 1 to 6: knit
Row 7: K into front and back of each st
Rows 8, 10, 12: purl
Rows 9 and 11: knit
Row 13: K 2 tog all along the row
Rep from Row 2

Quilted diamonds (reversible). The diamonds of reverse stocking stitch appear to be embossed on a background of stocking stitch. This pattern pulls inwards slightly in much the same manner as a rib (see p. 442 for rib characteristics).
Unit of 10 sts
Row 1: *K 9, P 1*
Rows 2 and 8: K 2, *P 7, K 3*, P 7, K 1
Rows 3 and 7: P 2, *K 5, P 5*, K 5, P 3
Rows 4 and 6: K 4, *P 3, K 7*, P 3, K 3
Row 5: P 4, *K 1, P 9*, K 1, P 5

Linen stitch. The appearance and firmness of a woven fabric; especially well suited to tailored garments.
Unit of 2 sts
Row 1: *K 1, yfwd, sl 1, ybk*
Row 2: *P 1, ybk, sl 1, yfwd*

Ridge stitch. Horizontal ridges stand out in strong relief against stocking stitch.
Unit of 2 sts
Row 1: knit
Row 2: *K 2 tog all across the row*
Row 3: K into front and back of each st
Row 4: purl

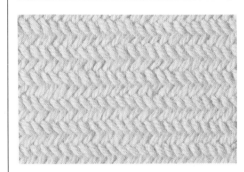

Herringbone. Very firm stitch, similar to a weave in appearance and elasticity. Tension must be kept fairly loose.
Unit of 2 sts
Row 1: K 2 tog tbl dropping only first loop off left needle, *K 2 tog tbl (the remaining stitch and next stitch), again dropping only the first loop off the needle*, K 1 tbl
Row 2: P 2 tog dropping only the first loop off left needle, *P 2 tog (the remaining stitch and next stitch), again dropping only first loop off needle*, P 1

Waved welt (reversible). Undulating rows of stocking stitch and reverse stocking stitch. The horizontal lines give a strong feeling of width to the fabric.
Unit of 8 sts plus 1
Row 1: *P 1, K 7*, P 1
Row 2: K 2, *P 5, K 3*, P 5, K 2
Row 3: P 3, *K 3, P 5*, K 3, P 3
Row 4: K 4, *P 1, K 7*, P 1, K 4
Row 5: *K 1, P 7*, K 1
Row 6: P 2, *K 5, P 3*, K 5, P 2
Row 7: K 3, *P 3, K 5*, P 3, K 3
Row 8: P 4, *K 1, P 7*, K 1, P 4

Waffle. A heavy, three-dimensional stitch; done in double knitting, it is suitable for a jacket, coat or blanket.
Unit of 2 sts
Rows 1 and 2: knit
Row 3: *K 1, K 1 blw* (see p. 428)
Row 4: *pick up the long (top) yarn produced by the K 1 blw and K it along with the st on the needle, K 1*
Row 5: *K 1 blw, K 1*
Row 6: *K 1, K the next st tog with the long yarn as for Row 4*
Rep Rows 3 to 6 for the pattern

Knitting stitches

Introduction to rib stitches

Rib stitches are characterised by vertical ridges and great elasticity in the horizontal direction. The classical rib patterns are 1 × 1 and 2 × 2 ribs, shown on p. 420; the examples here are meant to give you an idea of the many interesting variations that are possible.

A typical rib is formed by alternating knit and purl stitches in the same row. The ratio of knit to purl stitches may be even or uneven. The larger the numbers, the less elastic the fabric.

Because of its exceptional elasticity, a rib stitch is often used at garment edges. In this use, it is called *ribbing*. To assure a good fit, ribbing is usually worked with needles a size or two smaller than those used for the garment body. In selecting a ribbing, take care that it complements the fabric stitch.

Tweed stitch rib. A knobbly texture produced by slipping stitches on the knit portions; best suited to plain yarns.
Unit of 6 sts
Row 1: *P 3, sl 1 P-wise, ybk, K 1, yfwd, sl 1 P-wise*
Rows 2 and 4: *P 3, K 3*
Row 3: *P 3, K 1, yfwd, sl 1 P-wise, ybk, K 1*

Ribs

7 x 3 flat rib. Less elastic than narrower rib patterns; can be used successfully for a garment fabric.
Unit of 10 sts
Row 1: *K 7, P 3*
Row 2: *K 3, P 7*

Stocking heel stitch. Not a true rib structure, but has appearance and nearly the elasticity of one; often used for sock heels, as it withstands heavy wear.
Unit of 2 sts plus 1
Row 1: *K 1, sl 1*, K 1
Row 2: purl

Moss stitch rib. An attractive variation on a 5 × 6 rib pattern.
Unit of 11 sts plus 5
Row 1: K 5, *(K 1, P 1) 3 times, K 5*
Row 2: *P 5, (P 1, K 1) 3 times*, P 5

Changing rib. A pretty variation on a 1 x 3 rib; suitable for an all-over pattern as well as a rib trimming.
Unit of 8 sts
Rows 1 and 3 (wrong side): *K 3, yfwd, sl 1 P-wise, K 3, P 1*
Row 2: *K 1, P 3, ybk, sl 1 P-wise tbl, P 3*
Row 4: *K 1, P 3, K 1, P 3*

Broken ribbing. An interesting texture produced by fragmenting the rib stitches; especially suitable as a fabric stitch for sweaters.
Unit of 12 sts
Rows 1 and 3: K 2, *P 2, K 4*, P 2, K 2
Rows 2 and 4: P 2, * K 2, P 4*, K 2, P 2
Rows 5 and 7: K 1, *P 4, K 2*, P 4, K 1
Rows 6 and 8: P 1, *K 4, P 2*, K 4, P 1

Ribbed cables. Not a true cable rib but similar in appearance.
Unit of 5 sts plus 4
Row 1: *P 4, K into the front, back, and front again of next st*, P 4
Row 2: K 4, *P 3, K 4*
Row 3: *P 4, K 3 tog*, P 4
Row 4: K 4, *P 1, K 4*

Precautions in the use of diagonal stitches

Diagonals are patterns in which the stitch progression slants to the right, the left, or alternately right and left, produced by moving the unit one stitch left or right on successive rows.

Although attractive, one-way diagonal patterns have limited uses because they tend to stretch on the bias. This can be overcome to some degree by taking these precautions: (1) Choose firmly twisted yarns; avoid soft ones. (2) Use needles one size smaller than is normally recommended for the yarn choice. (3) Take special care in blocking and washing; do not wring, twist or tug.

The two-way diagonals (herringbone twill, for example) resemble their woven counterparts in both looks and performance. They have limited stretch and are suitable for tailored garments.

Diagonals

Oblique moss stitch. An interesting texture, and a very simple technique.
Unit of 5 sts
Row 1: *K 4, P 1*
Row 2: *P 1, K 1, P 3*
Row 3: *K 2, P 1, K 2*
Row 4: *P 3, K 1, P 1*
Row 5: *P 1, K 4*
Row 6: *K 1, P 4*
Row 7: *K 3, P 1, K 1*
Row 8: *P 2, K 1, P 2*
Row 9: *K 1, P 1, K 3*
Row 10: *P 4, K 1*

Ripple. A very subtle diagonal with the knit stitches twisted to the right on a stocking stitch face.
Unit of 3 sts
Row 1: *K 2 tog, then K the first st again before slipping both sts off left needle, K 1*
Rows 2 and 4: purl
Row 3: *K 1, K 2 tog, K the first st again*

Diagonal rib. Typical of diagonals produced by moving the pattern one stitch to the right on alternate rows.
Unit of 4 sts
Row 1: *K 2, P 2*
Row 2 and alt rows: knit the purl sts and purl the knit sts of previous row
Row 3: *K 1, P 2, K 1*
Row 5: *P 2, K 2*
Row 7: *P 1, K 2, P 1*

Steps. Small knots on stocking stitch face.
Unit of 5 sts
Row 1 (wrong side): *P 2, (K front and back) 3 times*
Row 2: *(K 2 tog tbl) 3 times, K 2*
Row 3: *P 1, (K front and back) 3 times, P 1*
Row 4: *K 1, (K 2 tog tbl) 3 times, K 1*
Row 5: *(K front and back) 3 times, P 2*
Row 6: *K 2 (K 2 tog tbl) 3 times*
Continue moving pattern 1 stitch to the right every odd-numbered row. After 10 rows, pattern repeats from Row 1.

Herringbone twill. Side-to-side zigzag.
Unit of 4 sts
Rows 1 and 5: *K 2, yfwd, sl 2, ybk*
Rows 2 and 6: sl 1, *yfwd, P 2, ybk, sl 2*, P 3
Rows 3 and 7: *yfwd, sl 2, ybk, K 2*
Rows 4 and 8: P 1, *ybk, sl 2, yfwd, P 2*, ybk, sl 2, yfwd, P 1
Rows 9 and 13: *yfwd, sl 2, ybk, K 2*
Rows 10 and 14: sl 1, *yfwd, P 2, ybk, sl 2*, yfwd, P 2, sl 1
Rows 11 and 15: *ybk, K 2, yfwd, sl 2*
Rows 12 and 16: P 1, *ybk, sl 2, yfwd, P 2*, ybk, sl 2, yfwd, P 1

Chevron rib. An up-and-down pattern to the zigzag, rather than side-to-side as in the herringbone twill above.
Unit of 12 sts
Row 1: *P 2, K 2, P 2, K 1, P 2, K 2, P 1*
Rows 2, 4, 6, 8: knit the purl sts and purl the knit sts of previous row
Row 3: *P 1, K 2, P 2, K 3, P 2, K 2*
Row 5: *K 2, P 2, K 2, P 1, K 2, P 2, K 1*
Row 7: *K 1, P 2, K 2, P 3, K 2, P 2*

Diagonal couching stitch. The slant is produced by pulling an extra knit loop across two stitches on the knit row. Each increase is compensated for by a decrease in the purl row.
Unit of 2 sts plus 1
Row 1: K 1, *insert right needle between next 2 sts, draw through a loop; keeping this loop on right needle, sl the first st K-wise, K the second st*
Row 2: P 1, *P 1, P 2 tog*
Row 3: K 2, *proceed as for Row 1*, K 1
Row 4: P 2, *P 1, P 2 tog*, P 1

443

Knitting stitches

Introduction to lace stitches

A **lace stitch** is basically any pattern with openwork. Its forms are numerous, ranging from eyelet bands in stocking stitch background to the most delicate lace and net. The structure also varies, and includes some of the simplest and some of the most complex of patterns. Those shown here and on the next three pages are some of the possibilities.

You can usually recognise a lace pattern by the frequent appearance of a yarn round needle increase. This technique creates a hole. Elsewhere in the sequence, each increase is offset by a decrease to keep the stitch total constant. Another lace technique is the elongated stitch (see drop stitch lace, p. 447), which forms more of a slit than a hole.

The casting on is important in lace knitting; it should be flexible and inconspicuous. Either the single or looped method is appropriate (p. 415).

Lace stitches, especially the airy ones, look best knitted with fine yarns and needles. Medium-weight yarns give a more solid appearance. For this, choose stitches with fewer openings.

Lace stitches

Oblique openwork. A stitch formation typical of many lace stitches, it is a combination of yrn increase (which forms a hole) and K 2 tog decrease (which keeps the number of stitches constant). Has a tendency to slant on the bias.
Unit of 2 sts
Row 1: K 1, *yrn, K 2 tog*, K 1
Rows 2 and 4: purl
Row 3: K 2, *yrn, K 2 tog*

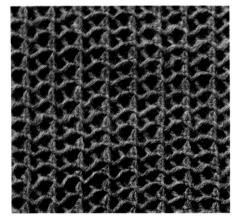

Turkish stitch. Openwork similar to that in stitch above, but more delicate. Here the yrn increase is combined with a decrease of sl 1, K 1, psso. (See p. 432 to review this last method.)
Unit of 2 sts
All rows: *yrn, sl 1, K 1, psso*

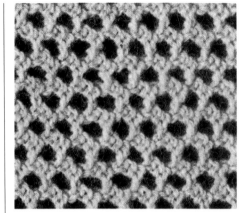

Eyelet stitch. Large holes formed by taking yarn twice around the needle for the increases. Yarn round needle at the beginning and end of Row 3 produces a delicate selvedge. For a firmer edge, add one selvedge stitch at each end.
Unit of 4 sts
Row 1: *K 2, yrn 00 (wind yarn twice around the needle), K 2*
Row 2: *P 2 tog, K 1, P 1, P 2 tog*
Row 3: *yrn 00, K 4, yrn 00*
Row 4: *P 1, (P 2 tog) twice, K 1*

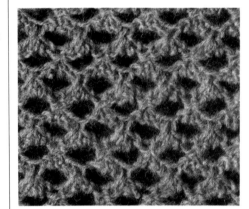

Net (reversible). Chunky texture interspersed with large holes. Worked with fine yarn and medium needles, this is a very good stitch for a shawl. Tension should be kept fairly loose, in order to work the P 4 together.
Unit of 4 sts
Row 1: P 2, *yrn, P 4 tog*, P 2
Row 2: K 2, *K 1, KPK into the yrn of the previous row*, K 2
Row 3: knit

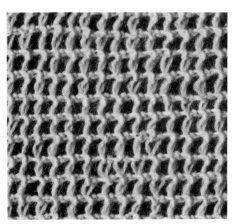

Cellular stitch. An airy pattern resembling a type of crochet; very light and easy to work; suitable for a baby blanket or shawl. For best results, work this stitch with medium or large needles and block carefully, as it has a tendency to stretch on the bias.
Unit is any number of sts
Row 1 (wrong side): purl
Row 2: K 1, *K under the horizontal strand before the next st, K 1, pass the made st over the K 1*

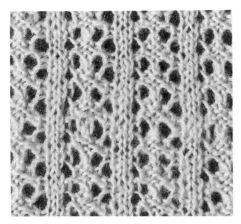

Lace rib. A combination of openwork and stocking stitch. The right side is shown, but the reverse side is just as pretty.
Unit of 7 sts plus 2
Row 1 (wrong side): P 2, *yrn, sl 1, K 1, psso, K 1, K 2 tog, yrn, P 2*
Rows 2 and 4: *K 2, P 5*, K 2
Row 3: P 2, *K 1, yrn, sl 1, K 2 tog, psso, yrn, K 1, P 2*

Bluebells. A delicate pattern suitable for a shawl or baby garments.
Unit of 8 sts plus 5
Rows 1 and 3: K 1, *yrn, 1 double dec [K 2 tog tbl, return st obtained to left needle, pass the next st over it, then put st back on right needle], yrn, K 5*, yrn, 1 double dec, yrn, K 1
Row 2 and alt rows: purl
Row 5: K 1, *K 3, yrn, sl 1, K 1, psso; K 1, K 2 tog, yrn*, K 4
Row 7: K 1, *yrn, 1 double dec, yrn, K 1*, yrn, 1 double dec, yrn, K 1

Travelling vine. Left edge is scalloped.
Unit of 8 sts
Row 1: *yrn, K 1 tbl, yrn, sl 1, K 1, psso, K 5*
Row 2: *P 4, P 2 tog tbl, P 3*
Row 3: *yrn, K 1 tbl, yrn, K 2, sl 1, K 1, psso, K 3*
Row 4: *P 2, P 2 tog tbl, P 5*
Row 5: *K 1 tbl, yrn, K 4, sl 1, K 1, psso, K 1, yrn*
Row 6: *P 1, P 2 tog tbl, P 6*
Row 7: *K 5, K 2 tog, yrn, K 1 tbl, yrn*
Row 8: *P 3, P 2 tog, P 4*
Row 9: *K 3, K 2 tog, K 2, yrn, K 1 tbl, yrn*
Row 10: *P 5, P 2 tog, P 2*
Row 11: *yrn, K 1, K 2 tog, K 4, yrn, K 1 tbl*
Row 12: *P 6, P 2 tog, P 1*

Horseshoes. One of many beautiful stitches that originated in the Shetland Islands in the 19th century, when gossamer lace was a favourite form of knitting.
Unit of 10 sts plus 1
Row 1: K 1, *yrn, K 3, sl 1, K 2 tog, psso, K 3, yrn, K 1*
Row 2 and alt rows: purl
Row 3: K 1, *K 1, yrn, K 2, sl 1, K 2 tog, psso, K 2, yrn, K 2*
Row 5: K 1, *K 2, yrn, K 1, sl 1, K 2 tog, psso, K 1, yrn, K 3*
Row 7: K 1, *K 3, yrn, sl 1, K 2 tog, psso, yrn, K 4*

Lace zigzag. Both side edges are scalloped. Suitable for a shawl or blanket.
Unit of 2 sts
Row 1: K 1, P 1, *yrn, K 1, P 1*
Rows 2, 4, 6, 8, 10: *K 1, P 2 tog, yrn*, K 1, P 1
Rows 3, 5, 7, 9: K 1, P 1, *yrn, K 2 tog, P 1*
Rows 11, 13, 15, 17, 19: K 1, P 1, *sl 1, K 1, psso, yrn, P 1*
Rows 12, 14, 16, 18, 20: *K 1, yrn, P 2 tog tbl*, K 1, P 1
Row 21: K 1, P 1, *yrn, sl 1, K 1, psso, P 1*
Rep pattern from Row 2
For openwork effect, knit loosely.

Hyacinths. Soft, bell-like clusters in an openwork background. This is a delicate stitch, especially suitable for a shawl. For best results, keep the tension fairly loose when working.
Unit of 6 sts plus 2
Row 1 (wrong side): K 1, *P 5 tog, KPKPK into next st*, K 1
Rows 2 and 4: purl
Row 3: K 1, *KPKPK into next st, P 5 tog*, K 1
Row 5: K 000 (winding thread 3 times around the needle for each st)
Row 6: purl, letting extra loops drop off the needle

Knitting stitches

Yarn tension 421
Yarn round needle increasing 429
Knitting front and back of loop 431
Decreasing methods 432–433

Lace stitches

Chevron lace. Horizontal zigzags. Unit is increased one stitch in Row 9, reduced one stitch in Row 2.
Unit of 8 sts plus 1
Row 1: *K 5, yrn, K 2 tog, K 1*, K 1
Row 2 and alt rows: purl
Row 3: *K 3, K 2 tog tbl, yrn, K 1, yrn, K 2 tog*, K 1
Row 5: K 1, *K 1, K 2 tog tbl, yrn, K 3, yrn, K 2 tog*
Row 7: *yrn, K 2 tog tbl, return st to left needle, pass next st over it and put st back on right needle, yrn, K 5*, K 1
Row 9: *K 1, K into front and back of next st, K 6*, K 1
Row 11: *K 2 tog, K 4, yrn, K 2 tog, K 1*, K 1
Rep from Row 3

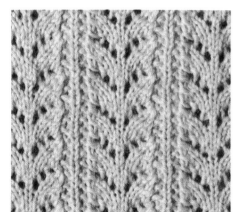

Baby fern. A very elegant lace pattern with the cast-on edge slightly scalloped. Suitable for baby clothing, a dress or a blanket; use medium-weight yarn.
Unit of 12 sts
Row 1 and alt rows (wrong side): purl
Row 2: *K 2 tog, K 2, yrn, K 1, yrn, K 2, sl 1, K 1, psso, P 1, K 1, P 1*
Row 4: *K 2 tog, K 1, yrn, K 3, yrn, K 1, sl 1, K 1, psso, P 1, K 1, P 1*
Row 6: *K 2 tog, yrn, K 5, yrn, sl 1, K 1, psso, P 1, K 1, P 1*

Fern stitch. Like baby fern but larger.
Unit of 29 sts
Row 1: *K 1, sl 1, K 2 tog, psso, K 9, yrn, K 1, yrn, P 2, yrn, K 1, yrn, K 9, sl 1, K 2 tog, psso*
Row 2 and alt rows: *P 13, K 2, P 14*
Row 3: *K 1, sl 1, K 2 tog, psso, K 8, (yrn, K 1) twice, P 2, (K 1, yrn) twice, K 8, sl 1, K 2 tog, psso*
Row 5: *K 1, sl 1, K 2 tog, psso, K 7, yrn, K 1, yrn, K 2, P 2, K 2, yrn, K 1, yrn, K 7, sl 1, K 2 tog, psso*
Row 7: *K 1, sl 1, K 2 tog, psso, K 6, yrn, K 1, yrn, K 3, P 2, K 3, yrn, K 1, yrn, K 6, sl 1, K 2 tog, psso*
Row 9: *K 1, sl 1, K 2 tog, psso, K 5, yrn, K 1, yrn, K 4, P 2, K 4, yrn, K 1, yrn, K 5, sl 1, K 2 tog, psso*

Diagonal lace stripe. A rib stitch pattern with diagonal bands of openwork.
Unit of 10 sts plus 3
Row 1: *P 3, yrn, sl 1, K 1, psso, K 5*, P 3
Row 2: *K 3, P 4, P 2 tog tbl, yrn, P 1*, K 3
Row 3: *P 3, K 2, yrn, sl 1, K 1, psso, K 3*, P 3
Row 4: *K 3, P 2, P 2 tog tbl, yrn, P 3*, K 3
Row 5: *P 3, K 4, yrn, sl 1, K 1, psso, K 1*, P 3
Row 6: *K 3, P 2 tog tbl, yrn, P 5*, K 3
Row 7: *P 3, K 7*, P 3
Row 8: *K 3, P 7*, K 3

Fancy trellis. Crossbars in relief; suitable for a pullover or cardigan.
Unit of 7 sts
Row 1: *K 2, K 2 tog, yrn, K 3*
Row 2: *P 1, P 2 tog tbl, yrn, P 1, yrn, P 2 tog, P 1*
Row 3: *K 2 tog, yrn, K 3, yrn, sl 1, K 1, psso*
Rows 4 and 8: purl
Row 5: *yrn, sl 1, K 1, psso, K 5*
Row 6: *yrn, P 2 tog, P 2, P 2 tog tbl, yrn, P 1*
Row 7: *K 2, yrn, sl 1, K 1, psso, K 2 tog, yrn, K 1*

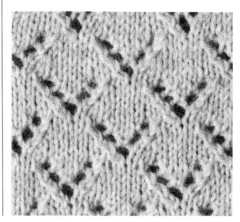

Vandyke stitch. V-shaped openwork on a stocking stitch background. An attractive stitch for a sweater.
Unit of 10 sts
Row 1: *yrn, sl 1, K 1, psso, K 8*
Row 2 and alt rows: purl
Row 3: *K 1, yrn, sl 1, K 1, psso, K 5, K 2 tog, yrn*
Row 5: *K 2, yrn, sl 1, K 1, psso, K 3, K 2 tog, yrn, K 1*
Row 7: *K 5, yrn, sl 1, K 1, psso, K 3*
Row 9: *K 3, K 2 tog, yrn, K 1, yrn, sl 1, K 1, psso, K 2*
Row 11: *K 2, K 2 tog, yrn, K 3, yrn, sl 1, K 1, psso, K 1*

Horizontal openwork. Lacy bands set at intervals in a stocking stitch. In the example, lace stitches occur every ten rows; they could be set closer together or further apart, or just one band used for decoration.
Unit of 2 sts
Rows 1, 3, 5, 7, 9, 10: knit
Rows 2, 4, 6, 8: purl
Row 11: *yrn, P 2 tog*
Row 12: knit

Lace insertion. A double band of openwork alternating with strips of garter stitch (or moss or stocking stitch). Can be used effectively for trimming or an entire fabric.
Unit of 2 sts
Rows 1 to 6: knit
Rows 7 and 9: *yrn, K 2 tog*
Rows 8 and 10: *yrn, P 2 tog*

Striped faggoting. Openwork ribs combined with reverse stocking stitch. This stitch can be worked as shown, or one unit of the lace might be used for a lacy insertion.
Unit of 8 sts plus 4
Row 1: *P 4, K 2 tog, yrn, K 2*, P 4
Row 2: *K 4, P 2 tog, yrn, P 2*, K 4

Drop stitch lace. Bands of elongated stitches alternating with bands of garter (or moss or stocking stitch). The open bands can be set close together or far apart, depending on the effect desired.
Unit is any number of sts
Rows 1 to 4: knit
Row 5: K 00 (winding thread twice around the needle)
Row 6: K, letting extra loop drop

Butterfly. A very pretty stitch for a child's sweater.
Unit of 10 sts plus 5
Rows 1 and 3: K 5, *K 2 tog, yrn, K 1, yrn, sl 1, K 1, psso, K 5*
Rows 2 and 4: *P 7, sl 1 P-wise, P 2*, P 5
Rows 5 and 11: knit
Rows 6 and 12: purl
Rows 7 and 9: *K 2 tog, yrn, K 1, yrn, sl 1, K 1, psso, K 5*, K 2 tog, yrn, K 1, yrn, sl 1, K 1, psso
Rows 8 and 10: *P 2, sl 1 P-wise, P 7*, P 2, sl 1 P-wise, P 2

Double drop stitch. Two rows of elongated stitches, back to back, make an attractive lacy insertion.
Use one row as trimming, or several for an airy fabric, as shown here.
Unit is any number of sts
Rows 1, 3, 5, 7: knit
Rows 2, 4, 6: purl
Row 8 (wrong side): K 00 (winding thread twice around the needle)
Row 9: rep Row 8, letting the extra loop drop
Row 10: K, letting extra loop drop

Knitting stitches

Introduction to crossed stitches

Richly embossed **crossed-stitch patterns** are produced by changing the working order of two or three stitches, which pulls knitted loops on a diagonal. Some of these patterns are actually cables in miniature (see pp. 450–1 for cable stitches), but are easier and faster to work because there are fewer steps. Other crossed-stitch patterns resemble woven fabrics, in both appearance and performance. Basket weave, right, is an example. In this case, crossing locks the stitches, limiting the elasticity.

To cross two stitches, you work the second stitch on the left needle, then the first one, slipping both stitches off the needle together. To do this comfortably and without stretching the yarn, tension should be kept fairly loose.

After stitches are crossed, they slant either to the left or right. The direction depends on the way in which loops are worked – to the front or back. A review of crossed-stitch methods may be advisable before starting (pp. 434–5).

Because the techniques produce unusual textures, these patterns are best carried out with smooth yarns.

Basket weave. Stitches crossed left and right to form a sturdy fabric that is similar to a woven structure.
Unit of 2 sts
Row 1: *cross 2 LK*
Row 2: P 1, *cross 2 RP*, P 1

Crossed stitches

Wasps' nest. A three-dimensional texture produced by crossing knit stitches alternately to the right and the left. It looks very much like smocking.
Unit of 4 sts
Row 1: *cross 2 RK, cross 2 LK*
Row 2 and alt rows: purl
Row 3: *cross 2 LK, cross 2 RK*

Basket weave rib. A very wide decorative pattern, more suitable for a fabric than for ribbing, or one panel of the rib might be used as a decorative insertion on a garment worked in stocking stitch or reverse stocking stitch.
Unit of 12 sts plus 5
Row 1: *P 5, K 1, (cross 2 LK) 3 times*, P 5
Row 2: K 5, *P 1, (cross 2 RP) 3 times, K 5*

Knotted cross stitch. The crossed stitches slipped over two increases form a moderate-sized knob on a stocking stitch background.
Unit of 4 sts plus 2
Rows 1 and 3: knit
Row 2 and alt rows: purl
Row 5: *K 2, cross 2 LK, (yrn, pass the second st on right needle over the first st and the yrn) twice*, K 2

Crossed-stitch ribbing. Forms a very elastic fabric that retains its springiness through many washings.
Unit of 3 sts plus 1
Row 1: P 1, *cross 2 RK, P 1*
Row 2: K 1, *P 2, K1*

Chain stitch. Resembles a cable rib, but is much easier to knit.
Unit of 8 sts plus 4
Row 1: *P 4, cross 2 LK, cross 2 RK*, P 4
Row 2: *K 4, P 4*, K 4
Rows 3 and 5: *P 4, K 1, P 2, K 1*, P 4
Rows 4 and 6: *K 4, P 1, K 2, P 1*, K 4

Small diamonds. A lattice pattern in a scale small enough for a child's sweater.
Unit of 6 sts plus 2
Row 1: K 3, *cross 2 RK, K 4*, cross 2 RK, K 3
Row 2 and alt rows: purl
Row 3: *K 2, cross 2 RK, cross 2 LK*, K 2
Row 5: K 1, *cross 2 RK, K 2, cross 2 LK*, K 1
Row 7: *cross 2 RK, K 4*, cross 2 RK
Row 9: K 1, *cross 2 LK, K 2, cross 2 RK*, K 1
Row 11: *K 2, cross 2 LK, cross 2 RK*, K 2

Double ricrac. Can be used effectively as an all-over pattern (shown), or one ricrac panel would make an interesting accent or trimming.
Unit of 9 sts plus 5
Row 1: *P 5, cross 2 RK, cross 2 LK*, P 5
Rows 2 and 4: K the K sts and P the P sts as they appear when this (wrong) side of knitting is facing you
Row 3: *P 5, cross 2 LK, cross 2 RK*, P 5

Twigs. Delicate branches traced on a stocking stitch background.
Unit of 13 sts plus 2
Row 1: *K 1, cross 2 RK, K 2, cross 2 RK, K 1, cross 2 LK, K 3*, K 2
Row 2 and alt rows: purl
Row 3: *K 4, cross 2 RK, K 3, cross 2 LK, K 2*, K 2
Row 5: *K 3, cross 2 RK, K 1, cross 2 LK, K 2, cross 2 LK, K 1*, K 2
Row 7: *K 2, cross 2 RK, K 3, cross 2 LK, K 4*, K 2

Twill rib. A very elastic as well as an attractive stitch, produced by crossing through two stitches (p. 435).
Unit of 9 sts plus 3
Row 1: *P 3, (cross through 2 RK) 3 times*, P 3
Row 2 and alt rows: *K 3, P 6*, K 3
Row 3: *P 3, K 1, (cross through 2 RK) twice, K 1*, P 3

Palm fronds. Leaves appear to be embossed on the stocking stitch background.
Unit of 14 sts plus 6
Rows 1 and 5: K 6, *K 2, cross 2 RK, cross 2 LK, K 8*
Row 2 and alt rows: purl
Row 3: K 6, *K 1, cross 2 RK, K 2, cross 2 LK, K 7*
Row 7: K 6, *K 3, sl 1, K 1, psso and K it before dropping off the needle, K 9*
Row 9: knit
Rows 11 and 15: *K 1, cross 2 RK, cross 2 LK, K 9*, cross 2 RK, cross LK, K 1
Row 13: *cross 2 RK, K 2, cross 2 LK, K 8*, cross 2 RK, K 2, cross 2 LK
Row 17: K 2, *sl 1, K 1, psso and K, K 12*, sl 1, K 1, psso and K, K 2
Row 19: knit

Knitting stitches

Introduction to cables

A **cable** is one of the handsomest of the pattern stitches. Learning the technique requires some knitting experience, but once it is mastered the applications are numerous and fascinating.

Like a crossed stitch, a cable results from an exchange of stitch positions, usually four or more. A double-pointed or cable needle is used to hold the first stitches while working the next group.

Holding stitches to the front produces a cable twist left; to the back, a cable twist right. To make a stronger contrast, the raised portion of a cable is usually knitted, the stitches on each side of it purled. Exceptions are the pattern types, shown below, in which cables are continuous.

Though cables can be worked successfully in fine yarns, their main use is for sportswear in heavier yarns.

Cable

Lattice stitch. Embossed crisscrosses, produced by cabling right and left on alternate rows.
Unit of 4 sts
Row 1: knit
Row 2 and alt rows: purl
Row 3: K 2, *sl 2 sts on cable needle and leave at back of work, K 2, K 2 sts from cable needle*, K 2
Row 5: *sl 2 sts on cable needle and leave at front of work, K 2, K 2 sts from cable needle*
Rep from Row 2

Sand tracks. Continuous cables form a deeply waved all-over pattern.
Unit of 12 sts
Rows 1, 5, 9: knit
Row 2 and alt rows: purl
Row 3: *sl next 3 sts on cable needle and leave at front of work, K 3, K 3 sts from cable needle, K 6*
Row 7: *K 6, sl next 3 sts on cable needle and leave at back of work, K 3, K 3 sts from cable needle*
.Rep from Row 3

Wild oats. A softly contoured pattern in low relief.
Unit of 4 sts plus 1
Rows 1 and 5: *K 2, sl 1 P-wise, K 1*, K 1
Rows 2 and 6: P 1, *P 1, sl 1 P-wise, P 2*
Row 3: *sl 2 sts on cable needle and leave at back of work, K the sl st of 2 rows previous, K 2 sts from cable needle, K 1*, K 1
Rows 4 and 8: purl
Row 7: K 1, *K 1, put the sl st on cable needle and leave at front of work, K 2, K st from cable needle*

Simple cable rib. The classic cable on a background of reverse stocking stitch.
Unit of 7 sts plus 3
Rows 1 and 3: *P 3, K 4*, P 3
Rows 2, 4, 6: *K 3, P 4*, K 3
Row 5: *P 3, C 4F [sl 2 sts on cable needle and leave at front of work, K 2 sts, K 2 sts from cable needle]*, P 3

Coiled rope. A spiral, the result of twisting the cable continuously to the right.
Unit of 9 sts plus 3
Rows 1 and 3: *P 3, K 6*, P 3
Rows 2, 4, 6: *K 3, P 6*, K 3
Row 5: *P 3, sl 3 sts on cable needle and leave at back of work, K 3, K 3 sts from cable needle*, P 3

Minaret stitch. Slender cabled columns.
Unit of 12 sts plus 4
Rows 1, 3, 5: P 4, *K 2, P 4*
Rows 2 and 4: K 4, *P 2, K 4*
Row 6: K 4, *yfwd, sl 2 P-wise, ybk, K 4*
Row 7: P 4, *sl 2 sts on cable needle and leave at front of work, P 2, yrn, K 2 tog tbl from cable needle, put 2 sts on cable needle and leave at back of work, K 2 tog, yrn, P 2 from cable needle, P 4*
Row 8: K 4, *P 2, K 1 tbl, P 2, K 1 tbl, P 2, K 4*

Plaited cable. A very wide pattern, suitable where a bold accent is desired.
Unit of 23 sts plus 5
Rows 1 and 5: *P 5, K 18*, P 5
Row 2 and alt rows: *K 5, P 18*, K 5
Row 3: *P 5, (sl 3 sts on cable needle and leave at back of work, K 3, K 3 sts from cable needle) 3 times*, P 5
Row 7: *P 5, K 3, (sl 3 sts on cable needle and leave at front of work, K 3, K 3 sts from cable needle) twice, K 3*, P 5

Crossed ribs. A bold, rather large pattern.
Unit of 16 sts plus 2
Row 1 and alt rows (wrong side): *K 2, P 2*, K 2
Rows 2, 4, 6, 8: *P 2, K 2*, P 2
Row 10: P 2, *sl 4 sts on cable needle and leave at front of work, K 2, slip the 2 P sts from cable needle to left needle and purl them, K last 2 sts from cable needle, (P 2, K 2) twice, P 2*
Rows 12, 14, 16, 18: *P 2, K 2*, P 2
Row 20: *(P 2, K 2) twice, P 2, sl 4 sts on cable needle and leave at back of work, K 2, slip the 2 P sts from cable needle to left needle and purl them, K last 2 sts from cable needle*, P 2

Honeycomb. A popular stitch for Aran knitting.
Unit of 8 sts
Row 1: *C 4B (sl 2 sts on cable needle and leave at back of work, K 2, K 2 sts from cable needle), C 4F (sl 2 sts on cable needle and leave at front of work, K 2, K 2 sts from cable needle)*
Rows 2, 4, 6, 8: purl
Rows 3 and 7: knit
Row 5: *C 4F, C 4B (see above)*

Crossed ribs with faggoting. Cable combined with openwork: suitable for lightweight or medium-weight yarns.
Unit of 6 sts plus 2
Rows 1, 3, 5, 7, 9, 11 (wrong side): K 2, *P 2 tog, yrn, P 1 tbl, P 1, K 2*
Rows 2, 4, 6, 8, 10: P 2, *sl 1, K 1, psso, yrn, K 2, P 2*
Row 12: P 2, *sl 2 sts on cable needle and leave at front of work, sl 1, K 1, psso, yrn, K 2 sts from cable needle, P 2*

Trellis stitch. Example of a cable worked with an uneven number of stitches.
Unit of 6 sts
Rows 1 and 3: *P 2, K 2, P 2*
Row 2 and alt rows: K the P sts and P the K sts of previous row
Row 5: *sl 2 sts on cable needle and leave at back of work, K 1, P 2 sts from cable needle, sl 1 st on cable needle and leave at front of work, P 2, K 1 st from cable needle*
Rows 7 and 9: *K 1, P 4, K 1*
Row 11: *sl 1 st on cable needle and leave at front of work, P 2, K 1 st from cable needle, sl 2 sts on cable needle and leave at back of work, K 1, P 2 from cable needle*

Crossed cables. Elongated cable ribs in an all-over pattern.
Unit of 8 sts plus 6
Row 1 and alt rows (wrong side): *K 2, P 2*, K 2
Rows 2, 4, 6: *P 2, K 2*, P 2
Row 8: *P 2, sl 3 sts on cable needle and leave at front of work, K 3, K 3 sts from cable needle*, P 2, K 2, P 2
Rows 10, 12, 14: *P 2, K 2*, P 2
Row 16: P 2, K 2, P 2, *sl 3 sts on cable needle and leave at back of work, K 3, K 3 sts from cable needle, P 2*

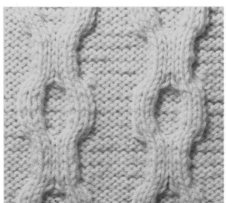

Chain cable. A bold stitch.
Unit of 18 sts plus 6
Rows 1, 3, 5, 7 (wrong side): *K 6, P 3* twice, K 6
Rows 2, 4, 6: *P 6, K 3* twice, P 6
Row 8: *P 6, sl 3 sts on cable needle and leave at front of work, P 3, K 3 sts from cable needle, sl 3 sts on cable needle and leave at back of work, K 3, P 3 sts from cable needle*, P 6
Rows 9, 11, 13, 15: *K 9, P 6*, K 9
Rows 10, 12, 14: *P 9, K 6*, P 9
Row 16: *P 6, sl 3 sts on cable needle and leave at back of work, K 3, P 3 sts from cable needle, sl 3 sts on cable needle and leave at front of work, P 3, K 3 sts from cable needle*, P 6

Knitting stitches

Slipping a stitch 428
Crocheted loop stitch (bouclé) 300

Ornamental stitches

Daisy stitch. Elongated petal loops.
Unit of 10 sts plus 8
Rows 1, 3, 5: knit
Rows 2, 4, 6: purl
Row 7: K 2, make daisy [insert needle in loop 3 rows below the 2nd st on left needle, draw up a loop, K 2, draw 2nd loop through same st, K 2, draw 3rd loop through same st], *K 6, make daisy*, K 2
Row 8: P 2, *(P 2 tog, P 1) twice, P 2 tog, P 5*, (P 2 tog, P 1) twice, P 2 tog, P 1
Rows 9, 11, 13: knit
Rows 10, 12, 14: purl
Row 15: K 7, *make daisy, K 6*, K 1
Row 16: P 2, *P 5, (P 2 tog, P 1) twice, P 2 tog*, P 6

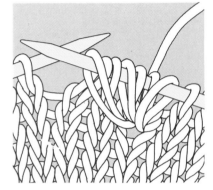

Drawing through the first loop

Three loops drawn through the same stitch

Bowknot. Yarn strands carried *loosely* across the knitted face, caught together at a designated point to form a bow.
Unit of 10 sts plus 7
Rows 1 and 3 (wrong side): purl
Rows 2, 4, 6, 8: knit
Rows 5, 7, 9: P 6, *ybk, sl 5 sts, yfwd, P 5*, P 1
Row 10: K 8, *make bowknot [slip right needle under 3 strands, knit next st, pulling the loop through under the strands], K 8
Rows 11 and 13: purl
Rows 12, 14, 16, 18: knit
Rows 15, 17, 19: P 1, *ybk, sl 5 sts, yfwd, P 5*, ybk, sl 5 sts, P 1
Row 20: K 3, *bowknot, K 9*, bowknot, K 3

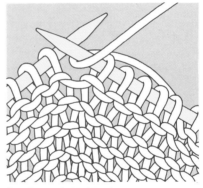

Carrying yarn behind the slipped stitches

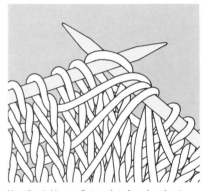

Needle picking up 3 strands to form bowknot

Loop stitch. Shaggy texture suitable for a rug, cushion cover, or trimming. The right-handed method is given here since it yields the firmest stitch. If desired, loop length can be adjusted by winding yarn over 1 or 3 fingers instead of 2. A loop stitch can also be crocheted.
Unit of 2 sts plus 1
Rows 1 and 3: knit
Row 2: K 1, *make 1 loop [insert needle in next st, wind yarn over needle point, then over 2 fingers of left hand, then over needle point again; draw 2 loops through the st and place them back on left needle; knit the 2 loops together through the back], K 1*
Row 4: K 2, *make 1 loop, K 1*, K 1

Winding yarn over 2 fingers of left hand

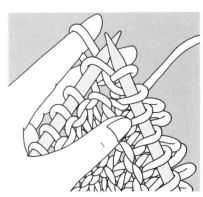

The 2 loops drawn through the stitch

Smocking

Smocked ribbing 1. A 2 × 2 rib pattern with groups of stitches tied together at intervals to form honeycomb smocking. One double-pointed needle or a cable needle is required.
Unit of 8 sts plus 10
Row 1 and alt rows (wrong side): *K 2, P 2*, K 2
Rows 2 and 4: *P 2, K 2*, P 2
Row 6: *P 2, tie 6 sts [sl 6 sts on dp needle and hold at front of work, wind the working yarn around the 6 sts twice, then K 2, P 2, K 2 off the dp needle]*, P 2, tie 6 sts, P 2
Rows 8 and 10: *P 2, K 2*, P 2
Row 12: P 2, tie 2 K sts, P 2, *tie 6 sts, P 2*, tie 2 K sts, P 2

Winding yarn around stitches on the dp needle

Knitting the stitches off the dp needle

Smocked ribbing 2. Knitted ribbing sewn together at intervals to form honeycomb smocking. Fabric should be twice the finished width that is desired.
Unit of 4 sts plus 1
Row 1: *K 1, P 3*, K 1
Row 2: *P 1, K 3*, P 1
Thread a tapestry needle with matching or contrasting yarn. Starting at upper right corner, sew first 2 ribs together. Taking yarn behind work, bring needle out 3 rows down, next to 2nd rib; sew 2nd and 3rd ribs together. Taking yarn behind work, return to upper row and join the 3rd and 4th ribs. Continue to join alternate pairs of ribs on each row. Repeat these 2 rows for desired depth.

The rib pattern ready to be embroidered

Working 2 rows of honeycomb smocking

Smocked stocking stitch. Honeycomb smocking on stocking stitch. Other smocking stitches would be suitable, too.
Unit is 4, 5 or 6 sts depending on the spacing of smocking sts
Work stocking stitch twice the finished width that is desired. Thread tapestry needle with heavy-duty thread. Starting at upper right corner, tack parallel lines across fabric, picking up same vertical stitches on each row. Space tacking 4 (5 or 6) stitches and 4 (5 or 6) rows apart (closer on heavy knitting, wider on fine). Draw up threads, gathering fabric to desired width; fasten. Make honeycomb stitches on the raised ribs; remove tacking.

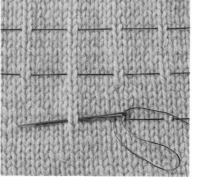

Tacking rows over which smocking will be worked

Working 2 rows of honeycomb smocking

Knitting stitches

Knotted stitches

Popcorn. A medium-size knot made by knitting several times into the same stitch, then slipping all extra loops over the first one. Knot size can be varied by working fewer or more times into a stitch. To keep popcorn in place, knit stitch after popcorn firmly, after pushing popcorn to front of work.
Unit of 6 sts plus 3
Rows 1 and 5: knit
Row 2 and alt rows: purl
Row 3: K 1, *make popcorn in next st [(K front and back of loop) twice, then slip the 2nd, 3rd and 4th sts over the 1st], K 5*, make popcorn, K 1
Row 7: K 4, *make popcorn, K 5*, make popcorn, K 4

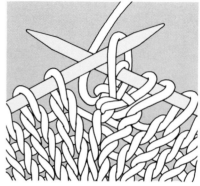

Pulling the second stitch over the first

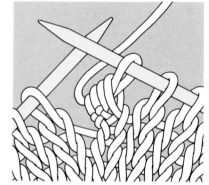

Three stitches slipped over one

Bobble. A dramatic-looking knot made by working several times into the same stitch, knitting back and forth on the increases, and finally slipping the extra stitches off the needle in the same way as for a popcorn (above). The bobble size can be varied, but it is essentially a large knot, suitable for a trimming, or to be used sparingly in an all-over pattern.
Unit is any number of stitches
On stocking stitch or other background, work bobble as follows: (K front and back of same st) twice, (turn work and P these 4 sts, turn work and K them) twice, slip the 2nd, 3rd and 4th sts over the 1st. Space bobbles as shown or as desired.

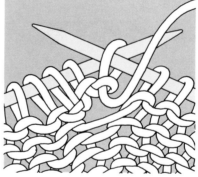

Purling the made stitches

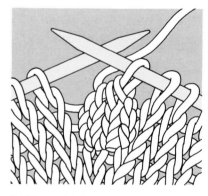

Bobble completed

Trinity stitch. A smaller, less complicated knot than either a popcorn or bobble. It is formed by making a double increase in one stitch followed by a double decrease in the next. Trinity (also called blackberry) is a popular choice for one panel in an Aran motif. Note that at the end of Row 2 there are 2 stitches fewer than you started with. At the end of Row 4, the pattern comes back to the starting number.
Unit of 4 sts plus 3
Rows 1 and 3: purl
Row 2: *P 3 tog, KPK into next st*, P 3 tog
Row 4: *KPK into first st, P 3 tog*, KPK into last st

Hazelnut stitch. A flatter and broader knot than either a popcorn or a bobble; it looks embossed. The knot is produced by making a double increase and working it even for two more rows.
Units of 4 sts
Row 1: *P 3, (K 1, yrn, K 1) in next st*
Rows 2 and 3: *P 3, K 3*
Row 4: *P 3 tog, K 3*
Rows 5 and 11: purl
Rows 6 and 12: knit
Row 7: *P, (K 1, yrn, K 1) in next st, P 2*
Row 8: K 2, *P 3, K 3*, P 3, K 1
Row 9: P 1, *K 3, P 3*, K 3, P 2
Row 10: K 2, *P 3 tog, K 3*, P 3 tog, K 1

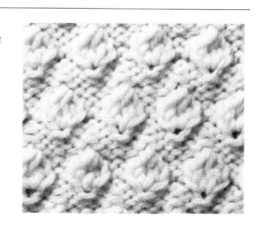

Aran-pattern sweater

Aran knitting is the combining of several stitches to form a richly patterned surface. This style, which originated in the Aran Isles, is traditionally worked in natural-coloured wool, using stitches that, to the islanders, symbolise married life and a fisherman's trade.

Cables are always included in Aran knits. Other popular patterns are popcorns or bobbles, travelling stitches, such as tree of life (see panel below), and knobbly textures like moss stitch.

A typical Aran sweater has a wide centre panel flanked by narrower bands repeated identically on both sides. Three or four motifs are used, each set on a background of reverse stocking stitch and separated by two crossed stitches or one slipped stitch. Sleeves repeat two or three motifs.

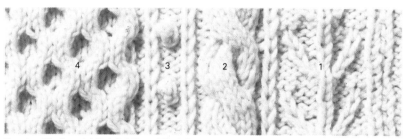

Panel motifs, from right to left. **1.** Tree of life. **2.** Coiled cable. **3.** Popcorn. **4.** Honeycomb.

Directions for Aran sweater

An Aran sweater in chest sizes 81, 86, 92 and 97. The style is suitable for a woman, or a teenager.

Materials 600 (700: 700: 800) g of Aran wool or Sirdar Majestic, 1 pair 4 mm needles, 1 pair 4.5 mm needles, 1 set 4 mm dp needles, 1 cable needle (optional)
Tension 12 sts and 12 rows = 5 cm

PANEL MOTIFS

PATTERN 1. Tree of life
Unit of 11 sts
Row 1: P 5, K 1, P 5
Row 2: K 5, P 1, K 5
Row 3: P 3, C 2B (sl 1 st on cable needle and leave at back of work, K 1, P 1 st from cable needle), K 1, C 2F (sl 1 st on cable needle and leave at front of work, P 1, K 1 st from cable needle), P 3
Row 4: K 3, yfwd, sl 1, ybk, K 1, P 1, K 1, yfwd, sl 1, ybk, K 3
Row 5: P 2, C 2B, P 1, K 1, P 1, C 2F, P 2
Row 6: K 2, yfwd, sl 1, ybk, K 2, P 1, K 2, yfwd, sl 1, ybk, K 2
Row 7: P 1, C 2B, P 2, K 1, P 2, C 2F, P 1
Row 8: K 1, yfwd, sl 1, ybk, K 3, P 1, K 3, yfwd, sl 1, ybk, K 1

PATTERN 2. Coiled cable
Unit of 14 sts

Row 1: ybk, sl 1, yfwd, P 2, sl 4 sts on cable needle and leave at front of work, K 4, K 4 sts from dp needle, P 2, ybk, sl 1
Rows 2, 4, 6, 8: P 1, K 2, P 8, K 2, P 1
Rows 3, 5, 7: ybk, sl 1, yfwd, P 2, K 8, P 2, ybk, sl 1

PATTERN 3. Popcorn variation
Unit of 3 sts
Row 1: P 1, K into front and back of next st 5 times, then slip the 2nd, 3rd, 4th and 5th sts over the 1st one, P 1
Rows 2, 4, 6, 8: knit
Rows 3, 5, 7: purl

PATTERN 4. Honeycomb (centre panel)
Unit of 38 sts
Row 1: ybk, sl 1, yfwd, P 2, *C 4B [sl 2 sts on dp needle and leave at back of work, K 2, K 2 sts from dp needle], C 4F [sl 2 sts on dp needle and leave at front of work, K 2, K 2 sts from dp needle]*, rep from * 3 times, P 2, ybk, sl 1
Rows 2, 4, 6, 8: P 1, K 2, P 32, K 2, P 1
Rows 3 and 7: ybk, sl 1, yfwd, P 2, K 32, P 2, ybk, sl 1
Row 5: ybk, sl 1, yfwd, P 2, *C 4F, C 4B*, rep from * 3 times, P 2, ybk, sl 1

SWEATER BACK. Using 4 mm needles, cast on 98 (104:110:116) sts. Work 1 × 1 ribbing for 8 cm, ending with a right-side row.
Purl across the wrong side.

Change to 4.5 mm needles.
Patt row 1: K 2 (5:8:11), over next 94 sts establish Patterns 1, 2, 3, 4, 3, 2 and 1, K 2 (5:8:11)
Patt row 2: P 2 (5:8:11), over next 94 sts work in patt, P 2 (5:8:11). Continue working in patt until piece measures 40.5 (42:43:43) cm.
Shaping raglan: Cast off 5 (6:7:8) sts at beg of next 2 rows.
Next row: K 2, K 2 tog tbl, work in patt to last 4 sts, K 2 tog, K 2.
Following row: P 3, work in patt to last 3 sts, P 3. Rep last 2 rows 19 (21:23:25) times.
Next row: K 2, K 3 tog tbl, work in patt to last 5 sts, K 3 tog, K 2. Dec same way every other row twice more. Place remaining 36 sts on holder. Armhole measures 19 (21:23:24) cm.
Front. Work as for back until 62 (64:66:68) sts remain, ending with a wrong-side row.
Shaping neck: K 2, K 2 tog tbl, work in patt for next 17 (18:19:20) sts; turn. Cast off 2 sts, work to end. Dec 1 st at neck edge every other row 4 times; at same time, dec 1 st at armhole every other row 6 (7:8:9) times, ending with a wrong-side row; turn. K 2, K 2 tog tbl, work to end. Dec same way every other row twice more. Cast off rem 2 sts. Put centre 20 sts on holder. Join yarn to next st; work left front to correspond.
SLEEVES. Using 4 mm needles, cast on 44 (46:48:50) sts; work in ribbing for 8 cm, ending with right-side row. Purl across wrong side

increasing 4 (6:8:8) sts evenly across the row. You should have 48 (52:56:58) sts. Change to 4.5 mm needles.
Patt row 1: K 1 (3:1:2), P 2, cable 8 sts as in Pattern 2, P 2, ybk, sl 1, yfwd, P 2, cable 16 (16:24:24) sts as in Pattern 4, P 2, ybk, sl 1, yfwd, P 2, cable 8, P 2, K 1 (3:1:2). Continue in patt, increasing 1 st (in stocking stitch) at both ends every 4 cm until you have 62 (68:74:80) sts. Work these sts until piece measures 44.5 (46:46:47) cm, ending with wrong-side row.
Shaping raglan: Cast off 5 (6:7:8) sts at beg of next 2 rows.
Next row: K 2, K 2 tog tbl, work in patt to last 4 sts, K 2 tog, K 2. Dec the same way every other row 21 (23:25:27) more times.
Place rem 8 sts on holder.
NECKBAND. Sew raglans together. Right side facing you, using dp needles, K the 36 sts from back holder, decreasing 6 (6:4:4) sts evenly across; 30 (30:32:32) sts remain. K 8 sts of one sleeve, decreasing 1 st at beg and end; 6 sts remain. Pick up and K 11 (12:13:14) sts along one neck edge, K the 20 centre sts, pick up and K 11 (12:13:14) sts along other side of neck; you should have 42 (44:46:48) sts for the front neck, K 8 sts of other sleeve, decreasing 1 st at beg and end; total of 84 (86:90:92) sts for neck. Work in 1 × 1 ribbing for 6.5 cm. Cast off.
FINISHING. Sew side and sleeve seams. Fold neckband in half and sew to inside of neck.

455

Knitting stitches/multicolour

Selvedge stitches 424   Lifted increasing 430
Joining in a new yarn 425   Duplicate stitching 488

Introduction

There are several methods for knitting with colours. The choice of any one depends on its suitability to the pattern and to the use of the finished article.

When knitting horizontal or chevron stripes and certain all-over patterns (examples below), you change colours at the end of a row. If a colour is repeated after two or four rows, yarns not in use can be carried loosely up the side.

Otherwise, the yarn is cut and joined with the new colour, with enough length left to weave into the edge later.

In wide vertical stripes, an inset motif or a tartan, colour changes occur within a row. Such patterns are usually worked in stocking stitch with the changeovers made on the purl side. One colour is dropped, the next one picked up, and the yarns *twisted* to prevent gaps.

For patterns in which two colours must be interchanged often, the yarn not in use is usually carried across the back by either *stranding* (p. 458) or *weaving* (p. 460). The advantage of these methods is that knitting progresses quickly and evenly, especially if work is done with both hands, as recommended. More yarn is used, however, which adds both thickness and warmth.

Typical uses for stranding and weaving are the Fair Isle and similar designs in which a motif (also called a jacquard pattern) is repeated to form a larger design or band.

An alternative to multicoloured knitting is embroidery, in which contrasts are worked on stocking stitch with duplicate stitches. The stitches stand out slightly, giving a different effect.

Changing colours at the end of a row

Horizontal stripes. Bands of colour in stocking stitch. Any number of rows can be worked in each colour, but the minimum, usually, is two rows. The example shown here has a sequence of 10 rows dark green, 2 rows rust, and 4 rows light green. Each colour change is made at the end of a row; a yarn not in use is carried loosely up the side, and caught periodically in the selvedge stitch on very long spans.

Chevron stripes. Zigzag bands of colour alternating in any proportions that suit. In the example, 4 rows of rust colour are inserted between 8 rows each of green. The cast-on edge of a chevron pattern is scalloped.
Unit of 13 sts
Row 1: *K 1, make 1 lifted inc L, K 4, sl 1, K 2 tog, psso, K 4, make 1 lifted inc R*
Row 2: purl

Sand stitch. A striped effect that is vertical, though colour changes occur at the end of a row.
Unit of 2 sts plus 1
Row 1: Light, knit
Row 2: Light, purl
Row 3: Dark, K 1, *sl 1 P-wise, K 1*
Row 4: Dark, *K 1, yfwd, sl 1 P-wise, ybk*, K 1

Star stitch. Chunky texture like that of certain crochet stitches. Produced by knitting 3 times into a group of 3 stitches. Tension must be kept loose.
Unit of 4 sts plus 3
Row 1: Light, purl
Row 2: Light, *make 1 star [insert needle into group of 3 sts as if to K 3 tog but instead K into front, back, and front again of all 3 sts], K 1*, make 1 star
Row 3: Dark, purl
Row 4: Dark, K 2, *make 1 star, K 1*, K 1

Woven stitch. Slipped stitches appear to be interlaced with knitted ones. Double-pointed needles are used to work two rows on the same side before turning.
Unit of 2 sts
Row 1: Dark, purl, return to beg of row
Row 2: Light, *P 1, sl 1 P-wise*
Row 3: Dark, knit, return to beg of row
Row 4: Light, *K 1, sl 1 P-wise*

Ladders. A very simple pattern with a distinctive optical effect.
Unit of 6 sts plus 5
Row 1: Light, K 2, *sl 1 P-wise, K 5*, sl 1 P-wise, K 2
Row 2: Light, P 2, sl 1 P-wise, *P 5, sl 1 P-wise*, P 2
Row 3: Dark, *K 5, sl 1 P-wise*, K 5
Row 4: Dark, *K 5, yfwd, sl 1 P-wise, ybk*, K 5

Twisting yarns to change colour

Working from a chart

Wide vertical stripes. Broad bands or similar large colour areas in which colours are changed in mid-row. A separate ball of yarn is used for each stripe, and with each colour change one yarn is dropped and the next one picked up from underneath it, thus crossing the yarns. This technique, called *twisting,* prevents a gap in the work. The near right illustration shows how twisting works on a knit row; illustration on far right shows twisting on purl side.

Inset design. A motif, in one or more colours, set into a plain background. The working method is similar to that used for wide stripes (above). A separate ball of yarn is introduced for each colour change, and yarns are twisted at each changeover. When a motif is complete, you cut the contrast yarns, also the extra strands of main colour, leaving enough length to weave into the back later. If you prefer, the motif can be embroidered on the background once the knitting is finished. For this method, see Duplicate stitching, p. 488.

Tartan pattern. Diamond blocks overlaid with stripes in two or more colours. This and similar multicoloured patterns are worked more easily using yarn bobbins as shown. Each bobbin holds a different colour, keeping yarn firmly wound until you release the quantity needed. As with the patterns above, yarns should be twisted with each colour change. Instructions for multicoloured patterns are usually given in charted form. See box, far right, for the way to read such a chart (and, incidentally, the chart for working this particular tartan pattern).

Often a chart is substituted for written instructions when a pattern is to be worked in two or more colours. This is usually the case for tartans, jacquards and inset motifs, as such patterns are easier to follow in visual form.

The chart is a graph with each square equal to one stitch, each line equal to a row. Plain squares usually represent the background colour, filled-in squares the contrast. If a design has more than two colours, each one is depicted by a symbol, such as a dot, and its equivalent noted in a colour key (example below).

A chart is easy to follow; starting at the bottom, you read from right to left for a knit row, from left to right for a purl row. A ruler placed below the working row is a helpful guide.

Still easier to follow is a chart coloured to match yarn colours to be used; the squares, however, must still be discernible. A coloured chart also gives you an idea of the pattern on the finished article.

Charts for multicoloured knitting are similar to those used for cross stitch, canvas work, and some other needle crafts. Following the guiding principles above, you can convert another chart for knitting. The success of such a project will depend on how well the design proportions adapt to the knitted scale. A sample will show this very quickly.

Colour key

△ = rust   ● = dark green

Knitting stitches/multicolour

Stranding technique

When two colours are interchanged often in the same row, it is practical to carry each colour that is not in use across the back (purl side). Fabric will be thick, but work will progress more smoothly than with separate balls of yarn. One method for doing this is **stranding,** as shown on the right.

Stranding is best accomplished by working one colour with the right hand (English style), the second colour with the left (Continental style), as shown below. One hand can do the work, if you switch with each colour, but progress will be slower and tension less even. With either method, carry the unused yarn *loosely,* or the fabric will pucker.

Stranding is suitable for colour changes that occur over one to five stitches. For a broader pattern, use twisting (p. 457) or weaving (p. 460).

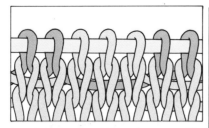

Stranded yarns are carried loosely on wrong side

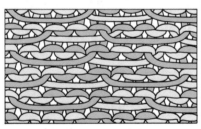

Back of knitted fabric with stranded yarns

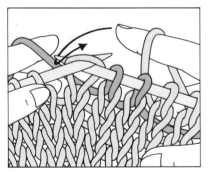

Knitting with right hand, stranding with left

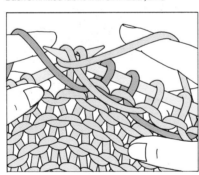

Purling with right hand, stranding with left

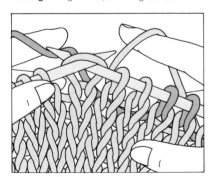

Knitting with left hand, stranding with right

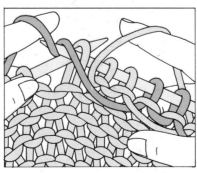

Purling with left hand, stranding with right

Two-colour stitches worked with stranding

Striped ribbing. A classic rib pattern in two colours. To maintain the natural rib elasticity, carry yarn very loosely across the back of the work.
Unit of 4 sts
Row 1: *P 1 light, K 2 dark*
Row 2: *P 2 dark, K 2 light*

Chequerboard. A simple pattern in which colours alternate in two stitches and two rows. For larger squares, you can change the colours every three, four or five stitches and increase the number of rows to match.
Unit of 4 sts plus 2
Row 1: K 2 light, *2 dark, 2 light*
Row 2: P 2 light, *2 dark, 2 light*
Row 3: K 2 dark, *2 light, 2 dark*
Row 4: P 2 dark, *2 light, 2 dark*

Houndstooth. A traditional pattern stitch that is easy to knit.
Unit of 4 sts
Row 1: K 2 light, *1 dark, 3 light*, 1 dark, 1 light
Row 2: purl *1 light, 3 dark*
Row 3: knit *1 light, 3 dark*
Row 4: P 2 light, *1 dark, 3 light*, 1 dark, 1 light

Fleur-de-lis. Charming small lilies. Their size is just right for a hat or small garment.
Unit of 6 sts plus 3
Rows 1 and 3: K 3 dark, *1 light, 5 dark*
Row 2: P 1 light, *3 dark, 3 light*, 2 dark
Rows 4 and 6: P 2 dark, *1 light, 5 dark*, 1 light
Row 5: K 2 light, *3 dark, 3 light*, 1 dark

Jacquard patterns worked with stranding

Abstract diamond. A lively pattern which can be equally attractive in subtle or bold colour combinations.

Flower border. Traditional motif in the Fair Isle style; typical use would be along the bottom of a plain sweater.

Geometric border. Fascinating theme of triangles and diamonds; suitable for a man's or a woman's garment.

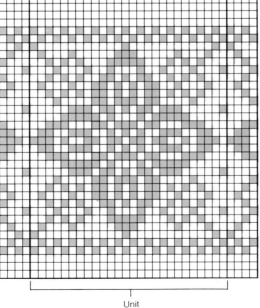

Unit

Unit

Unit

459

Knitting stitches/multicolour

Weaving technique

Weaving is a way of working unused yarn into the fabric back when colours must be carried over more than a five-stitch span. The procedure is similar to stranding (p. 458), but the carried yarn is brought alternately above and below each stitch, in effect, weaving it in. The result is a thick fabric, sturdy on both right and wrong sides. (The carried yarns cannot be snagged as they might with stranding.) Weaving is practical for a heavy outer garment or blanket.

This method, like stranding, is easier to work using two hands simultaneously. The movements may seem awkward at first, but work will go more smoothly as rhythm is established. If a pattern has a mixture of long spans and shorter ones (as in the Greek key, opposite), you can weave the longer yarns and carry the short ones by stranding.

Weaving is a Fair Isle technique, traditionally worked in the round. With this approach, only the *knit* weaving movements must be learned, because the knit side will always be facing you.

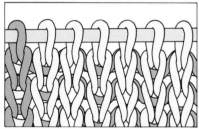

Woven yarns carried above and below stitches

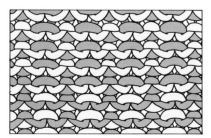

The back of a fabric with woven yarns

WITH KNIT STITCHES

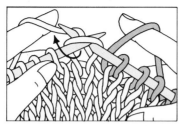

To weave right yarn above a knit stitch, simply hold yarn away from the work with the right index finger, then knit with the left yarn.

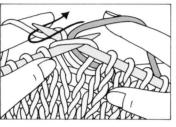

To weave right yarn below a knit stitch, two movements are necessary. (1) Make a knit movement with the right yarn, followed by a knit movement with the left yarn (top illustration). (2) Reverse the right yarn, taking it back around and beneath the right needle, at the same time drawing the left knit stitch through the loop (result shown in lower illustration).

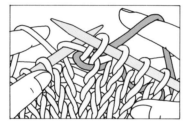

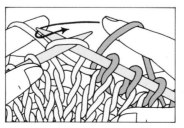

To weave left yarn above a knit stitch, bring it over (but not around) the right needle, as shown, then make your knit stitch with the right yarn.

To weave left yarn below a knit stitch, hold it away from the work with the left index finger, then make the knit stitch with the right yarn.

WITH PURL STITCHES

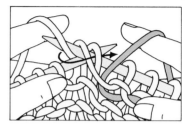

To weave right yarn above a purl stitch, pull it up with the right index finger, then make the purl stitch with the left yarn.

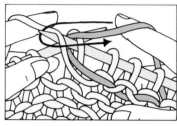

To weave right yarn below a purl stitch, two movements are necessary. (1) Make a purl movement with the right yarn, followed by a purl movement with the left yarn (top illustration). (2) Reverse the right yarn, taking it back around and beneath the stitch made with the left yarn (bottom illustration), then draw the purl stitch through the loop.

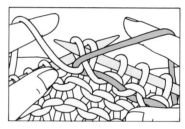

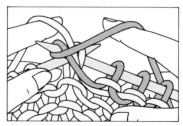

To weave left yarn above a purl stitch, bring it over (but not around) the right needle, as shown, then make your purl stitch with the right yarn.

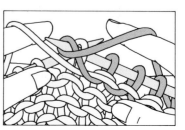

To weave left yarn below a purl stitch, hold it taut with the left index finger, as you make the purl stitch with the right yarn.

Jacquard patterns worked with weaving

Greek key. Perfect accent for a classic sweater; adaptable also for a blanket, cushion cover or other household item.

Diamond jacquard. Pleasing choice for a boy's or man's sweater; could be used effectively for just the front.

Norwegian tile. Elaborate yet delicate, this design is suitable for a border or an all-over pattern.

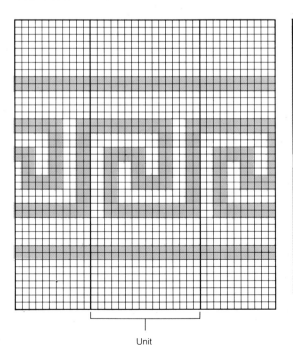

Unit

Unit

Unit

Knitting stitches/charted

Shorthand symbols

Knitting techniques can be represented by symbols, the symbols used to chart a pattern stitch visually. Because a chart resembles the actual appearance of a pattern, it helps you to visualise an unfamiliar stitch and keep track of a complicated pattern. No adjustment is needed for circular knitting because a chart represents each technique as viewed from the right side.

Though they are used in many countries, knitting symbols are not standardised. The ones given here are typical, but not universal, examples. If different pictures would have more meaning for you, or if you should need a symbol not included here, you can invent your own.

Listed on the right are symbols, their definitions, and the numbers of the pages on which illustrations of the techniques can be found. As a rule, no more than a few symbols are used in one pattern, so it is only necessary to remember those in use.

A comparison of charted and written directions is given below. For the stitches opposite, written forms can be found elsewhere (see top of page).

Reminders about charted patterns

1. Each row is represented as it appears on the right side. For example, a blob (●), which stands for a purl stitch, would be purled on a right-side row, but knitted on a wrong-side row.
2. A chart is read from bottom to top, starting at the lower right corner.
3. To keep track of rows worked, it is helpful to place a ruler on the chart, and move it upwards as work progresses.
4. The unit in a chart is enclosed by heavy parallel lines, the equivalent of asterisks in written directions.
5. Rows are numbered to either side of a chart; when the odd numbers appear to the left, they represent wrong-side rows, to the right, right-side rows.
6. A chart can show as many units or repeats as necessary for giving an accurate picture of the pattern stitch.

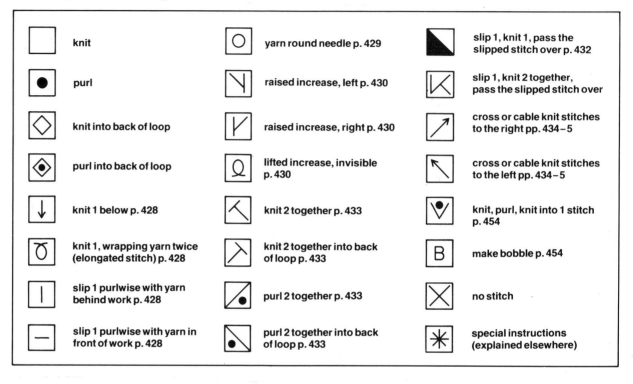

□	knit	○ yarn round needle p. 429	◥ slip 1, knit 1, pass the slipped stitch over p. 432
●	purl	⅄ raised increase, left p. 430	⊠ slip 1, knit 2 together, pass the slipped stitch over
◇	knit into back of loop	Ⅴ raised increase, right p. 430	⟋ cross or cable knit stitches to the right pp. 434–5
◈	purl into back of loop	Ω lifted increase, invisible p. 430	⟍ cross or cable knit stitches to the left pp. 434–5
↓	knit 1 below p. 428	⟋ knit 2 together p. 433	▾ knit, purl, knit into 1 stitch p. 454
⊙	knit 1, wrapping yarn twice (elongated stitch) p. 428	⟋ knit 2 together into back of loop p. 433	B make bobble p. 454
Ⅰ	slip 1 purlwise with yarn behind work p. 428	⟋ purl 2 together p. 433	⊠ no stitch
—	slip 1 purlwise with yarn in front of work p. 428	◣ purl 2 together into back of loop p. 433	✳ special instructions (explained elsewhere)

Charted patterns

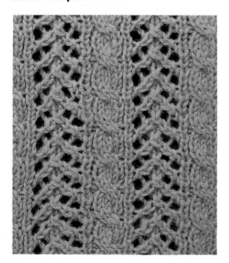

Lace and cable pattern. A richly textured surface that makes an interesting sweater fabric. The directions are given here in both written and charted form.
Unit of 13 sts

Rows 1 and 5: *K 1, yrn, sl 1, K 1, psso, K 1, K 2 tog, yrn, K 1, P 1, K 4, P 1*

Row 2 and alt rows: *K 1, P 4, K 1, P 7*

Row 3: *K 2, yrn, sl 1, K 2 tog, psso, yrn, K 2, P 1, C 4F [slip 2 sts on cable needle and leave at front of work, K 2, K 2 from cable needle], P 1*

Rows 7 and 11: *K 2, yrn, sl 1, K 2 tog, psso, yrn, K 2, P 1, K 4, P 1*

Row 9: *K 1, yrn, sl 1, K 1, psso, K 1, K 2 tog, yrn, K 1, P 1, C 4F, P 1*

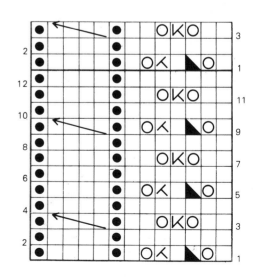

WAVED WELT

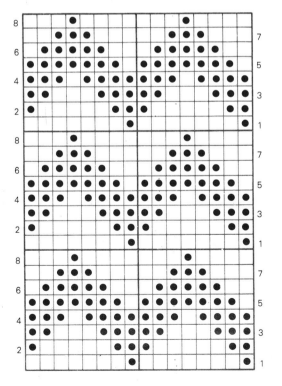

The pattern of purl stitches, as viewed from the right side, is easy to see on this charted version of waved welt stitch.

TRAVELLING VINE

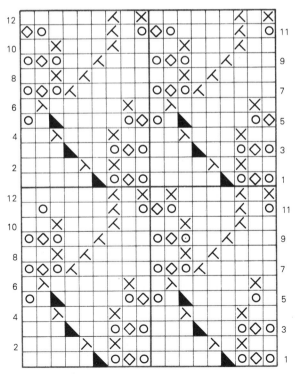

The basic unit here is 8, but increases to 9 on odd rows because of an extra yarn round needle. An X balances chart on even rows.

SMALL DIAMONDS

The number of stitches to cross, also their direction and position, can be followed readily on a chart.

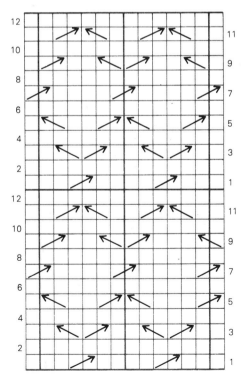

Knitting a garment

Introduction

This section contains the basic information necessary to help you understand how knitting patterns are constructed, and to help you plan and design knitted garments.

Before knitting a garment you should always do the following: (1) Compare its measurements with those of the person for whom it is intended. If measurements are not specified, you can calculate them by dividing the number of stitches in a pattern unit or a row by the tension. If the tension is 10 stitches per 5 cm, a shoulder with 20 stitches should measure 10 cm. (2) Check the tension. Planned garment dimensions can be obtained only by duplicating the one specified.

Taking and using measurements

Garment dimensions are based on body measurements plus ease. To achieve good fit, you should know what these are. The body measurements described on the right are all the ones you might need, but not, of course, for every garment. Waist and hip measurements, for example, are used only for a fitted style, usually a woman's; head circumference is needed only for a hat. To be accurate, measurements should be taken over undergarments and with someone's help.

Ease must be added to measurements of circumference, chest and upper arm for example. Ease allowances range from 1.5 to 10 cm and are determined by: **the garment's purpose** – a cardigan, for instance, would have more ease than a pullover; **garment style** – a dolman sleeve is a looser shape than a set-in sleeve; **the garment area** – more ease is needed for the bust than the wrist; **yarn type** – a garment of bulky yarn requires more ease than one of fine yarn; **personal preference** – a closer or a looser fit.

If you do not have body measurements to work with, there are two other alternatives for sizing a garment. One way is to measure a similar garment (see below right), bearing in mind that ease is included. The other is to work from measurement charts, like the ones opposite, which designers use to plan a garment in a certain size. Such charts are useful as guidelines, especially for determining proportions of a sweater. Remember, though, that these are merely average measurements. A person's measurements are always more reliable for obtaining perfect fit.

Chest or bust. Straight across back, under the arms, and across fullest part of chest or bust.
Shoulder width. Across back between outside edges of shoulder blades (about 7.5 to 10 cm below neck base on a child, 12.5 cm on a woman, 15 cm on a man).
Shoulder length. From base of neck to tip of shoulder.
Neck. Around the neck just above the collarbone.
Armhole depth. From top of shoulder blade, straight down to 2.5 cm below the armpit.
Underarm to waist. From 2.5 cm below armpit to waist indentation.
Sleeve upper arm. Around the top portion of the arm, just below the armpit.
Sleeve seam length. From 2.5 cm below armpit, straight down inside of arm to wristbone.
Wrist. Just above wristbone.
Waist. At natural indentation.
Hip. Around the fullest part (about 10 to 15 cm below waist for a child, 18 to 23 cm for an adult).
Head. Around the crown at mid-forehead level.

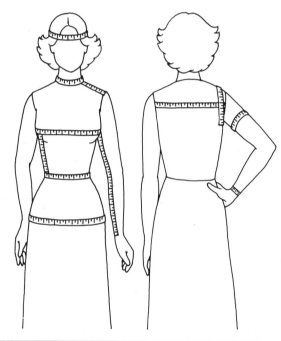

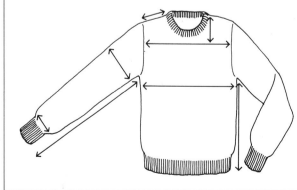

When taking measurements from a garment, lay it flat, and as you measure, pull each seam or area comfortably (that is, without distortion) to its fullest dimension. Take all measurements as indicated by arrows: double the upper arm and wrist measurements for the sleeve width.

BABIES/TODDLERS

Size	6 months	12 months	18 months	2	4
Chest	48	50.5	53	55.5	58
Shoulder width	19.5	20	21.5	23.5	24.5
Shoulder length	5.5	5.5	6	7	7.5
Back of neck*	8	9	9	9.5	9.5
Armhole depth	9.5	10	11	11.5	12
Bottom to underarm*	16.5	18	19	20	21.5
Sleeve upper arm	15	16.5	18	19	20
Sleeve seam length	16.5	19	21.5	24	26.5
Crotch length*	16.5	18	19	20	21.5

CHILDREN

Size	4	6	8	10	12
Chest	61	63.5	66	71	76
Shoulder width	24.5	26.5	28	29.5	31
Shoulder length	7.5	8	9	9.5	10
Back of neck*	9.5	10	10	11	11
Armhole depth	12.5	13.5	14	15	16.5
Bottom to underarm*	24	25.5	26.5	28	29
Sleeve upper arm	21.5	23	24	26.5	28
Sleeve seam length	29	30.5	33	35.5	38

TEENAGE GIRLS/MISSES

Size	6	8	10	12	14	16
Bust	77.5	80	82.5	86	91	96.5
Shoulder width	31	31.5	33	34	35.5	37.5
Shoulder length	10	10.5	11	11	11.5	12
Back of neck*	11	11	11.5	12	12.5	13.5
Armhole depth	16.5	17	18	18.5	19	19.5
Underarm to waist	18	18.5	19	19.5	20	21
Sleeve upper arm	28.5	29	30.5	31.5	33	34.5
Sleeve seam length	42	42.5	43	44	44.5	45.5

WOMEN

Size	18	20	40	42	44	46
Bust	101.5	106.5	112	117	122	127
Shoulder width	39	40.5	42.5	44	46.5	47
Shoulder length	12.5	13	13.5	13.5	14	14
Back of neck*	14	14.5	16	17	18.5	19
Armhole depth	20	21	21.5	23	23.5	24
Underarm to waist	21	21.5	21.5	22	32	23
Sleeve upper arm	35.5	37	38	39	40.5	42
Sleeve seam length	45.5	46.5	46.5	47	47	47

TEENAGE BOYS/MEN

Size	30-32	32-34	36-38	40-42	44-46	48-50
Chest	79	84	94	104	114	124.5
Shoulder width	33	35.5	40.5	43	46.5	49
Shoulder length	11	11.5	13.5	14	15	16
Back of neck*	11.5	12.5	14	15	16	17
Armhole depth	19	20	21.5	23	24	25.5
Bottom to underarm*	34.5	35.5	39	40.5	42	43
Sleeve upper arm	31.5	33	37	39	42	44.5
Sleeve seam length	40.5	44.5	48	49.5	50.5	52

*This is a garment, not a body measurement.   Note: All measurements are in centimetres.

Designing a knitted garment

There are two ways of designing a knitted garment. One is to alter an existing pattern to suit your needs; the other is to design a pattern. With either approach, you need to make a plan, for which you must have the following:

1. An accurate list of body or garment measurements (see facing page).
2. A test sample to determine tension and, if necessary, to calculate yarn needs.
3. Familiarity with the way to construct each garment piece (see pp. 468–81).
4. Paper to outline or chart a pattern.

The first step is to write down width and length measurements for each section of the garment you are planning. If your plan is based on body measurements, you must add ease, using for guidance other patterns and the average measurements given opposite. You must also add 5 mm for seams and plan the overall length – for example, from the underarm to the bottom edge of a sweater.

Next choose a yarn and a stitch pattern, knit a sample or several, if necessary, until you like the appearance of the stitch, then measure tension.

To translate garment width measurements into stitches, multiply the number of stitches per centimetre by the desired width. If a jacket back should be 45 cm at the bottom edge, and the tension is 10 stitches per 5 cm, cast on 90 stitches plus 2 for seams.

To translate garment length into rows, multiply the rows per centimetre by the desired length. If the jacket is 38 cm from bottom edge to underarm, and tension is 14 rows per 5 cm, you would knit about 105 or 106 rows.

To determine the number and distribution of increasing or decreasing for shaping, follow the guidelines on pp. 468–73. To plan garment details, see pp. 474–81. Prepare a chart or outline (see pp. 466–7), and estimate the quantity of yarn needed.

Estimating yarn needs

To work out how much yarn you need for your own design, you can use the amount specified for a similar pattern with the same yarn and stitch. (For this purpose, it is useful to keep a notebook of patterns you like.) This quantity may not be precisely what you need, so it is wise to buy extra yarn.

Another approach is to consult an assistant in a wool shop. The assistant will usually have the experience and access to pattern books from which to make an estimate of the amount of yarn your project will need.

If you cannot find either an appropriate pattern or a helpful assistant, here is a way to make your own estimate. Buy a skein and make a tension sample. Weigh it on a postal or kitchen scale. Record the weight: it might be 14.5 g. Also record the area: if your swatch is 10 cm square, its area is 100 *square centimetres*.

Next, calculate the approximate area for each garment section by multiplying widest dimension times overall length. Add these figures together, then divide the result by the sample weight. Here is an example of such a calculation:

Sweater back
across the chest	45 cm
length, neck to bottom	50 cm
total area (roughly)	2,250 cm^2

Sweater front
area (same as the back)	2,250 cm^2

Sweater sleeve
width at upper arm	30 cm
overall length	58 cm
total area, both sleeves	3,480 cm^2

Total area for sweater 7,980 cm^2
Divided by sample area (100) 80

The figure 80 represents the number of your samples needed to knit the sweater. Sample weight of 14.5 g multiplied by 80 gives 1,160 g; from this deduct 10 per cent to allow for shaping decreases. The resulting 1,044 g is the estimate of yarn needed. You can confidently buy 1,050 g.

465

Knitting a garment

Charting a man's sweater

This sweater is given in both written and charted methods. It is a man's size medium 40–42. Front and back work out to the same width, but the front has 6 extra stitches to allow for the pulling-in of the cable.

Materials

570 g double knitting, such as Sirdar Majestic; 1 pair 3.75 mm needles, 1 pair 4.50 mm needles, 1 cable or dp needle

Tension

10 sts and 14 rows = 5 cm

Cable pattern

Rows 1, 3, 5, 7 (wrong side): K 2, P 8, K 2

Rows 2, 4, 8: P 2, K 8, P 2

Row 6: P 2, C 8F [sl 4 sts on cable needle and leave at front of work, K 4, K 4 sts from cable needle], P 2

SWEATER BACK. Using 3.75 mm needles, cast on 105 sts. Work 1 × 1 ribbing for 7.5 cm, ending with a right-side row. Change to 4.50 mm needles and work in stocking st until piece measures 39 cm.

Armholes: Cast off 6 sts at beg of next 2 rows; dec 1 st at each end every other row 4 times. Work straight on rem 85 sts until armholes measure 22.5 cm.

Shoulders: Cast off 9 sts at beg of next 6 rows; place rem 31 sts on a holder.

FRONT. Using 3.75 mm needles, cast on 111 sts. Work 1 × 1 ribbing for 7.5 cm, ending with a right-side row. On 4.50 mm needles, work as follows:

Wrong side, P 18, K 2, P 8, K 2, P 51, K 2, P 8, K 2, P 18. **Right side,** K 18, P 2, C 8F, P 2, K 51, P 2, C 8F, P 2, K 18. Continue in stocking st; insert cable patt, over 12 sts and 8 rows.

Armholes: Shape as for back; on rem 91 sts work even until armholes measure 12.5 cm; end with a wrong-side row.

Shaping neck: Work across 34 sts, turn. Cast off 2 sts at beg of next row; thereafter dec 1 st at neck edge every other row 5 times. Continue on 27 sts until armhole measures 22.5 cm, end at armhole edge; cast off for shoulder 9 sts at beg of every other row; fasten off. Place centre 23 sts on holder; attach yarn to next st; work other neck half to correspond.

SLEEVES. Using 3.75 mm needles, cast on 47 sts. Work 1 × 1 ribbing for 7.5 cm. Change to 4.50 mm needles and stocking st; inc 1 st at each end every 6th row until piece measures 47.5 cm. Cast off 6 sts at beg of next 2 rows; dec 1 st at each end every other row 15 times. Cast off 2 sts beg of next 4 rows. Cast off rem 27 sts.

NECKBAND. Sew right shoulder seam. Starting at left shoulder, right side of front facing you, use 3.75 mm needles to pick up and K 26 sts at neck edge; K 23 sts from holder. Pick up and K 26 sts on right half of front; K 31 sts from back holder. Work 1 × 1 ribbing on 106 sts for 15 rows; cast off.

FINISHING. Sew left shoulder, neckband, side and sleeve seams; sew in the sleeves. Fold neckband in half and oversew loosely to inside of neck.

A man's handsome sweater has crew neck and one cable pattern inserted on each side of the front.

How to make a garment chart

A garment chart is a visual representation of written instructions. There are two different chart forms – **outline** and **graph**. Either can be used when designing or adjusting a pattern.

An outline is a drawing of the exact dimensions of each main garment section, with shaping information written on it. This form gives you a realistic view of garment shape, and can be used later, if desired, for blocking. To make an outline, use sturdy wrapping paper and start by drawing a straight line on it equal to the widest dimension (usually the underarm) of the garment back. Then draw a second line perpendicular to and through the centre of the first. Using these as reference points, measure other areas. Draw the sleeve and any other garment sections in the same way. (Note: if the front differs from the back only in neck shaping, you can superimpose an alternate line for the front neck on your back pattern.)

A graph is worked on paper that is marked off into squares. Each square represents a stitch, each line of squares a row. To chart this way, the tension must already have been decided. You can draw out an entire garment section or just the areas that are shaped (as shown opposite); only half need to be drawn. A graph gives a less realistic view of garment shape than an outline, but it is easier to follow, especially if you use a ruler to keep track of progress.

Taking and using measurements 464   **Blocking 482–483**
Designing a knitted garment 465   **Charting a crocheted sweater 306**

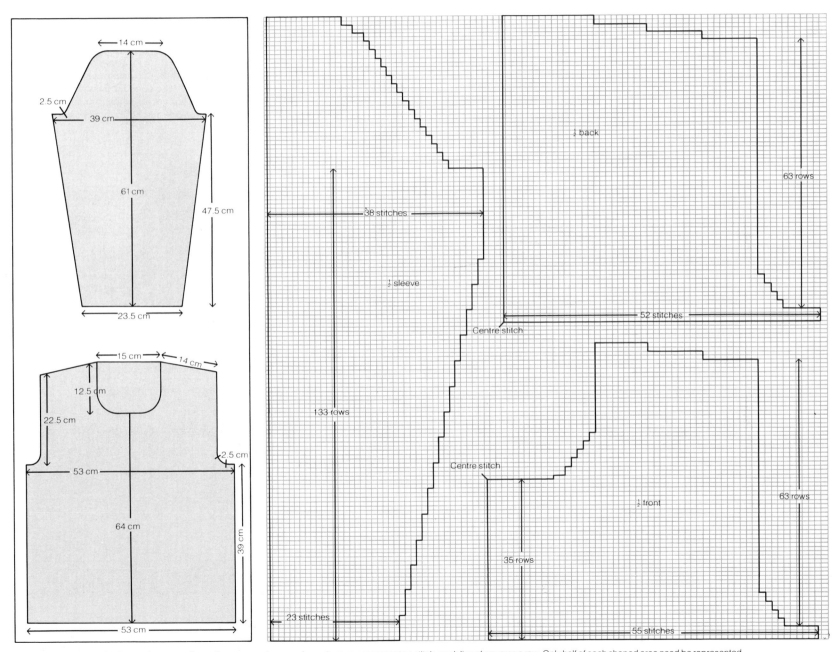

14 cm

2.5 cm

39 cm

61 cm

47.5 cm

23.5 cm

15 cm   14 cm

12.5 cm

22.5 cm

2.5 cm

53 cm

64 cm

39 cm

53 cm

½ back

38 stitches

½ sleeve

Centre stitch

52 stitches

133 rows

63 rows

Centre stitch

½ front

63 rows

35 rows

23 stitches

55 stitches

An **outline** is an exact duplicate of garment dimensions.

In a **graph,** each square represents a stitch, each line of squares a row. Only half of each shaped area need be represented.

Knitting a garment

Shaping

Shaping a knitted garment is a matter of increasing and decreasing where the fabric is to conform to body contours.

There are several methods for shaping major garment areas. In this section we have dealt with those for flat pieces (knitted on two needles) and, for simplicity, have presented all the examples in stocking stitch. Most flat pieces are shaped along outside edges only. Certain dress or skirt styles may require darts for a closer fit, but such shaping is suited mainly to garments worked in fine yarns and smooth textures.

If this is your first experience with shaping a garment, it may help to think of each piece initially as a rectangle, as wide and long as the widest and longest dimensions of that garment section. From the wide points, you subtract stitches gradually to obtain the narrower and shorter measurements.

These shaping guidelines can be used to design your own garment or alter an existing pattern to suit your needs, keeping these points in mind:

1. After making calculations, chart your design before knitting.
2. Except for necklines, shapings are usually the same for front and back.
3. Changes in shape are made on the right side and as gradually as possible.

Shaping diagonals

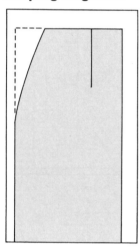

Forming a diagonal by decreasing is the way to shape an A-line; contour a skirt from hipline to waist, a sleeve cap, or a hat crown worked from the bottom up.
Side seam decreasing is calculated by subtracting the number of stitches required at the waist from the number at the starting point (skirt bottom or hipline), allotting half to each side and distributing them evenly over the rows to be knitted.
Skirt darts are calculated the same way and should end 10 to 15 cm from the side seam at the waist. Average depth is 2 to 2.5 cm, length 12 cm.
Hat darts are distributed evenly around the crown.

To shape side seams on a skirt, first calculate amount and distribution of decreasing, then work symmetrically. For example, if you decrease 30 stitches (15 on each side) over 90 rows, you decrease at the beginning and end of every sixth row.

To make paired darts on a skirt, place a marker at the beginning of each dart (approximately 12 to 18 cm from each side). For the first dart, knit to the marked stitch and decrease left (sl 1, K 1, psso); for the second dart, decrease right (K 2 tog).

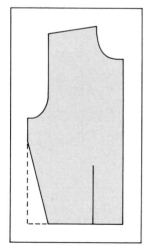

Forming a diagonal by increasing is the way to shape a bodice from waist to armhole, or a hat that is started at the crown. It is also the way to shape the sleeve underarm.
Side seam increasing is calculated by subtracting the stitches at the waist from the number required at the bustline, then allotting half the increasing to each side and distributing it evenly over the rows to be knitted.
Bodice darts are calculated the same way and increasing begun 10 to 15 cm from side seam. Average depth 2 to 2.5 cm, length 12 to 18 cm.
Hat darts are distributed evenly around the crown.

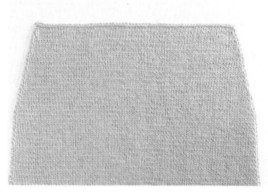

To shape side seams on a bodice, first calculate the number and distribution of the increasing, then work symmetrically. For example, if you increase 20 stitches (10 on each side) over 40 rows, you increase at the beginning and end of every fourth row.

To make paired vertical darts on a bodice, place a marker at beginning of each dart. For the first dart, increase right (lifted increasing is especially suitable); for the second dart, increase left, using the same type of increasing as for the first dart

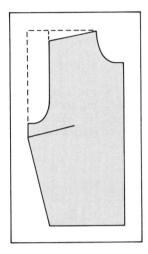

Forming a diagonal by turning is a way to shape a shoulder seam, horizontal dart or sock heel. *Turning* is the working of short rows in graduated lengths, with the steepness of the angle controlled by the number of stitches worked in each stage.

A shoulder is usually worked in 2, 3 or 4 steps.

A bustline dart averages 7.5 to 10 cm long, 2 to 2.5 cm deep; its shaping ends 2.5 cm below armhole. To estimate the number of stitches left unworked in each step, divide the stitch total (dart length) by half the number of rows (dart depth).

To turn a right shoulder, for example, in 3 steps on 24 stitches, *work to within 6 stitches of end of the knit row, turn, slip 1 stitch, purl to neck edge, turn.* Repeat from * twice, leaving 6 more stitches unworked each time; cast off. **To turn left shoulder,** work as for right shoulder, but start with a purl row.

To make paired horizontal darts, for example, on 20 stitches over 10 rows, *work to within 4 stitches of end of the purl row, turn, slip 1 stitch, work to within 4 stitches at end of knit row, turn, slip 1 stitch.* Repeat from * 3 times, each time leaving 4 more stitches unworked, then knit across all stitches in the row.

Pleats

Pleats add fullness to the bottom of a skirt and, in some instances, additional thickness at the waist. There are two basic pleat types, **real** and **mock**; examples of each are shown below. Both look best in finer yarns and are most suited to slender figures.

Real pleats have a *face, turn-back* and *underside.* When knitting is complete, pleat tops can be knitted together by putting the turn-back and underside on spare needles and working three stitches together across pleat width; they can also be sewn. Finished dimensions should equal waist size.

Mock pleats do not have true folds but the effect of them is created by knitting in a broad rib pattern, such as K 7, P 4, or in a textured stitch with one stocking stitch rib to suggest a fold.

Knife pleats. All folds face in the same direction; face, turn-back, and underside are the same width. This pattern has a unit of 26 and is knitted so that the seam can be placed at a backfold. **Right side,** *K 16, sl 1, K 8, P 1.* **Wrong side,** *K 1, P 25.*

Box pleats. The two outer folds face away from each other and the backfolds meet at the centre. Pattern shown has a unit of 58 and is worked as follows: **Right side,** *K 9, sl 1, K 18, sl 1, K 9, P 1, K 18, P 1.* **Wrong side,** *K 1, P 18, K 1, P 38.*

Mock pleats. The impression of folds is created by regular insertions of stocking stitch rib on the face of garter stitch. This pattern has a unit of 8 and is knitted as follows: **Right side,** *K 7, P 1* **Wrong side,** K 3, *P 1, K 7,* P 1, K 4

Knitting a garment

Shaping necklines and collars

Special care should be taken in knitting a neckline, as this part of a garment is particularly noticeable. In general, the fit should be smooth, with no gaping or wrinkling; in the case of a sweater, the opening must be large enough for the head to pass through comfortably. For a child's sweater, you may have to provide an additional opening, along one shoulder for instance, because a child's head is large in proportion to his neck size.

The neck width calculation is based on shoulder width and equals about one-third of it, or the number of stitches that remain after subtracting the two shoulder lengths. Front neck depth is figured in relation to armhole depth, and varies according to style (see below and opposite). With few exceptions, a back neck is cast off straight across. If a front is oval or square, the back may be shaped the same way, but would be less deep.

In shaping a neckline, work is usually divided, each half knitted separately, and all decreasing made on the right side.

A neckline is finished with a band, a facing or a collar that is knitted by picking up stitches along the neck edge, or worked as a separate piece and sewn in place. For the first method, a general rule is to pick up 1 stitch for each stitch and 3 stitches for every 4 rows. A more precise approach is to pick up a number of stitches that will yield the required measurement in the tension of your finishing stitch (a sample of the border stitch may be needed to determine this).

Basic neck shapings and suitable finishes for them are given here.

Square neckline

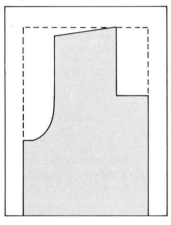

Square neckline shaping is begun 10 to 15 cm below the start of shoulder shaping with the casting off of all stitches allotted for the neckline. (Reminder: the number of stitches for the neck is what remains after subtracting stitches for each shoulder.) There is no decreasing for this style: after casting off the centre, you work straight up the sides. When adding a border, as shown right, you can cast off 2.5 cm more of stitches on each side to maintain the full width after a band is added.

Ribbed band. Pick up stitches across front; work 1 × 1 ribbing for 2.5 cm, decreasing 1 stitch at beginning and end of every right-side row. Repeat for other sections; sew corners.

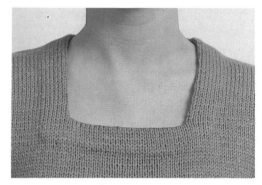

Facing. Pick up and knit each section separately as for a ribbed band, but work in stocking stitch and increase at each corner; fold facing to wrong side, oversew it to garment.

V-neckline

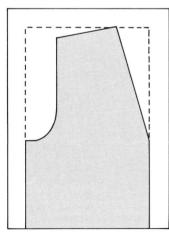

A V-neckline is usually started 18 to 23 cm below the shoulder, or just after casting off to begin armhole shaping. Work is divided at the centre and each side is knitted separately, with decreasing evenly spaced over the number of rows to be worked to the top of the shoulder. Decreasing can be made either at the neck edge, or 3 to 4 stitches from the edge. If you have an odd number of stitches across the front, decrease the centre stitch before dividing the work.

Ribbed band. Pick up stitches on 3 dp needles; knit 1 × 1 ribbing, making double decrease at the point every round; or use circular needle, decreasing at each end; sew V edges.

Overlapping band. Work a strip of 1 × 1 ribbing, 2.5 cm wide and long enough to fit around neckline. Sew strip to neck edge with oversewing, overlapping two ends at front, as shown.

Round necklines

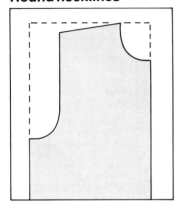

A high round neckline is the classic shaping in the same sense as the set-in sleeve. Shaping is begun 5 cm below the shoulder tip for an adult garment, 4 cm for a child's. Half the total of stitches to be decreased are either placed on a holder or cast off; the remaining stitches are decreased at each neck edge every other row. The rest of the neckline is then worked straight until the shoulder shaping is complete.

Polo neck. Pick up stitches on 3 dp needles; work 1 × 1 ribbing (or another rib pattern if preferred) for 15 to 23 cm. Cast off loosely. Fold collar to the right side.

Collar. Pick up stitches on straight or circular needle and work 1 × 1 ribbing in rows, increasing just inside each edge every other row; work chain selvedge on both edges for a neat finish.

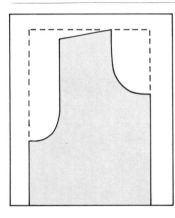

A lower round neckline can vary in depth from 7.5 to 10 cm below the shoulder tip. The 8 cm depth is ideal for a crew neck (right); the 10 cm depth is suitable for a summer blouse or evening wear. To shape the 8 cm neckline, cast off and decrease just as for a high round neck. To shape a lower neckline, subtract a few stitches from each shoulder and work them into the neckline so that the neck is proportionately wider as well as deeper.

Crew neck. Pick up stitches on 3 dp needles; work 1 × 1 ribbing for 5 to 8 cm. Cast off (invisible method, p. 423). Fold ribbing in half and sew loosely to wrong side of neck edge.

Crocheted edging. Using a hook 1 or 2 sizes smaller than knitting needles, work 1.5 cm of double crochet around neck edge, decreasing as necessary to keep the edge flat.

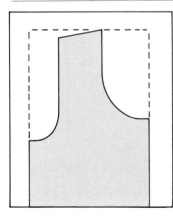

A low oval or U-shaped neckline is begun 15 to 18 cm below the shoulder tip; its overall depth is usually greater than its width. When calculating the division for shoulders and neck opening, be sure to include the width of the band, if you are using one. For example, if the finished neckline width is to be 18 cm, and the band will measure 2.5 cm, the neck opening should be 23 cm when you shape it.

Ribbed band. Pick up stitches on 3 dp needles; work 1 × 1 ribbing for 2.5 cm. When casting off, decrease several times along the deep part of the curve at the centre front.

Bias border. Knit a bias strip in stocking stitch, long enough to go around neck (p. 475). Sew one edge to garment; fold in half; sew other edge to inside of neck edge.

471

Knitting a garment

Decreasing in pairs 432
Turning 469

Shaping armholes and sleeves

The armhole and sleeve shapings are an important part of knitting a well-fitted garment. Five basic styles are described here. The **classic** armhole with a set-in sleeve is the type used most often, and is suited to any garment style. A **saddle yoke** is generally chosen for a casual style. It is especially attractive with a pattern insertion, such as a cable plait, running the length of sleeve and yoke. The **raglan** is comfortable and can become a decorative part of the garment design if the decreasing is worked two or three stitches in from the selvedge. A **semi-raglan** combines the comfort and decorative possibilities of a raglan with the classic look of a set-in sleeve. A **dolman** is an extension of the garment body, and with its deep armhole is the most comfortable of all the sleeve styles.

To chart an armhole with the methods given here, you need the measurements for *shoulder width* (distance across the back between the armholes), the *chest* or underarm across half the garment, plus standard *shoulder length* and *armhole depth* for your garment size, and for a raglan only, the *neck circumference*. To chart a sleeve, you need *wrist, underarm length* and *upper-arm* measurements.

The usual way of knitting a sleeve is from the bottom edge up, shaping the underarm seam as a diagonal, increasing symmetrically between wrist and underarm. For comfort, you may want to add 2 to 3 cm of ease at the wrist, 5 cm at the upper-arm area. Armhole and sleeve caps are shaped by decreasing; if you wish the decreasing to be decorative, it must be symmetrical, slanting to the left at the beginning of a row and slanting to the right at the end of a row.

There are two ways to shape a standard shoulder seam. One method is to cast off in steps (see pp. 466–7), which produces a slightly jagged edge. The other is to shape by turning (p. 469), for a smooth line that can be grafted.

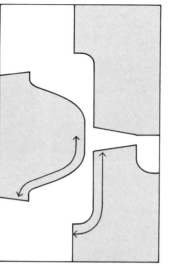

A classic armhole shape is made by subtracting the number of stitches for shoulder width from the number at underarm. This figure is then halved and the result is the number of stitches to decrease for each armhole. At start of shaping, cast off half these stitches (the equivalent usually of 2.5 to 4 cm); decrease the remainder over the next few rows, then work straight until correct depth is reached. To start sleeve cap, cast off the same number of stitches as at the beginning of the armhole. Decrease symmetrically until curve of cap matches that of armhole and measures 5 to 12.5 cm across. Cast off the remaining stitches.

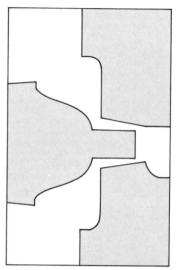

A saddle yoke armhole is shaped just like the classic style but is 2.5 to 4 cm shorter to accommodate the yoke width. The set-in sleeve cap is also shaped the same, but instead of casting off the shoulder stitches, you continue to work on them until the yoke section equals the shoulder length. To fit well, the top of the sleeve cap and the yoke should be no less than 5 cm and no more than 8 cm across. Keep in mind that the cast-off edge of yoke becomes part of the neckline.

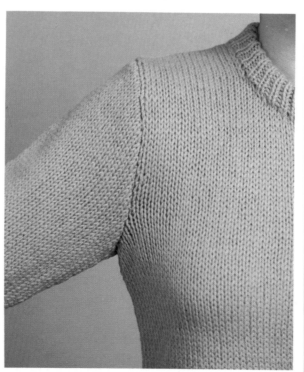

A set-in sleeve has a symmetrically curved cap that fits a classic armhole.

A saddle yoke sleeve combines a classic sleeve with yoke extension.

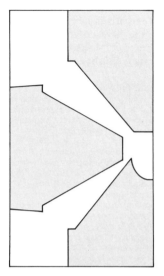

A raglan armhole ends at the neckline and must be planned in relation to it. To calculate decreasing, subtract stitches for half the neck circumference from the number of stitches at the underarm. Take off another 5 cm of stitches (these will go at the top of sleeves); this figure is the total decreasing for two armholes. Start raglan shaping with casting off 1.5 to 2 cm on each side; distribute the remaining decreasing symmetrically and evenly over rows to be knitted (armhole depth plus 2.5 cm). Work sleeves with the same number of rows and a 5 cm width at neckline.

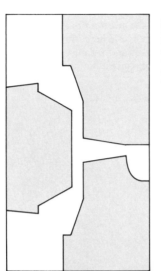

A semi-raglan armhole is shaped like a raglan on the lower half, like a classic armhole on the upper half and shoulder. Calculate decreasing as for a classic armhole, but instead of distributing it in the first 4 to 5 rows, space it in a sloped line over half the armhole depth; work straight for remaining depth and shape the shoulder by the standard method. For the sleeve, decrease symmetrically for the same number of rows as for the armhole, cast off remaining stitches straight across.

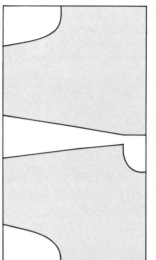

A dolman sleeve is formed by adding stitches to the garment body. Begin shaping 5 to 8 cm below normal armhole depth, increasing 2 stitches at each side over several rows to form an underarm curve. For the sleeve, cast on 2.5 to 5 cm of stitches at beginning and end of each right side row until you have the total sleeve length. Continue to work straight until sleeve depth is half the wrist measurement plus 2.5 to 5 cm for ease. Shape the top edge by casting off in the same stitch sequence as when casting on. Shape shoulder standard way.

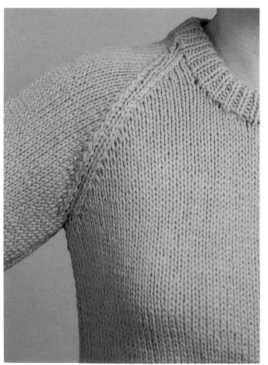

A raglan sleeve is shaped in a continuous slope to the neckline.

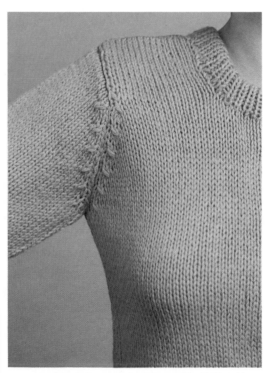

A semi-raglan sleeve has raglan slope combined with a wide cap.

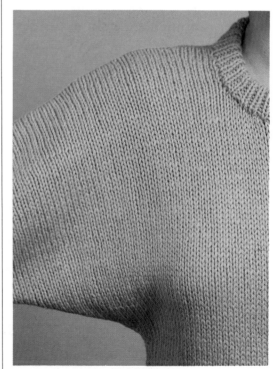

A dolman sleeve is wide at the armhole, narrow at the wrist.

Knitting a garment

Moss, garter, rib stitches 420
Picking up stitches 437

Horizontal buttonholes 481
Seam joining techniques 484–485

Long-sleeve finishes

A *ribbed cuff* is the typical finish for a long sweater sleeve. It is usually knitted to the wrist size plus 2 or 3 cm, so that the hand can pass through easily, and is worked on needles a size or two smaller than those used for the sleeve so it will fit comfortably. The usual stitch choices are 1 × 1 or 2 × 2 ribbing because these have good elasticity and trim appearance. A *bracelet cuff* is the type of sleeve finish that might be used for a blouse, sweater or jacket. It is usually worked in a firmer stitch, such as moss or garter, and so must be combined with a sleeve opening and some kind of closure. (Typical examples are shown below.)

A *border or hem* is a suitable finish for a full sleeve that is wide at the wrist (a kimono sleeve, for instance). See pp. 475–7 for these finishes.

Cuff in single ribbing. This neat and inconspicuous style is used more often than any other. Average depth is 5 to 10 cm; the fuller the sleeve, the longer the cuff should be.

Cast on an even number of stitches and work in 1 × 1 ribbing for the desired length. When sewing the cuff, use a backstitch, taking in one stitch (1 knit and 1 purl) from each side. The join should be nearly invisible.

Cuff in double ribbing. A bolder style than single ribbing, more suitable for casual than for tailored garments.

Cast on a multiple of 4 stitches plus 2; work in 2 × 2 ribbing, beginning and ending each right side row with K 2. Sew the cuff seam with a backstitch, taking in one knit stitch from each side. The finished cuff will appear to have continuous ribbing.

Turn-back cuff in ribbing. Either single or double ribbing can be used; overall length is 10 to 12 cm. This cuff is a particularly good choice for a child's sweater, as it can be adjusted to arm length.

Following the directions above for either single or double ribbing, knit to within 4 rows of half the cuff length; cast off 1 stitch at beginning of next 2 rows, then cast on 1 stitch at beginning of next 2 rows (there will be a notch at each edge). Complete the cuff. When joining the cuff seam, sew the lower half with wrong sides together; reverse seam edges at the notch; sew the upper half with right sides together.

Bracelet cuff with slit opening. Especially suitable for a knitted blouse with full sleeve. The opening should be 5 to 8 cm long and the cuff 2 to 2.5 cm deep in a stitch that does not curl.

To make the opening, divide the bottom of the sleeve into two parts – one-third for the back, two-thirds for the front. Work the parts separately, casting on 2 extra stitches at each opening edge for a facing, casting off these stitches again before joining the sections. When the sleeve is finished, sew the seam, turn the facings to the inside and oversew them in place. *To knit the cuff,* pick up stitches along the sleeve bottom equal to the wrist measurement plus 1.5 cm for ease. If the sleeve is exceptionally full, pick up more stitches than you need and decrease along the first row to obtain the wrist measurement. When cuff is finished, make a crocheted button loop on the edge that faces the sleeve back; sew a button on opposite edge.

Bracelet cuff with banded opening. This is appropriate for a sweater, jacket, or coat sleeve fitted at the wrist. It could also be used for decorative styling on a wider sleeve; in this use you would not need buttonholes. Opening should be 8 to 10 cm long, the cuff 2 to 2.5 cm deep.

To make the opening, divide and work the sleeve as directed above for a slit, but do not add facing stitches. Instead, make a double selvedge along the back edge of the opening; leave the front edge plain. Complete the sleeve and sew the underarm seam. *To knit the band and cuff,* pick up stitches along the bottom edge of the sleeve and front edge of the slit. Mark the corner stitch and work a double increase at this point every other row. Make two horizontal buttonholes in the band. When completed, sew top edge of band to sleeve; attach buttons.

Borders

A border or band is an extension of a knitted edge that makes a decorative finish and helps to retain shape. There are two basic types – single, which should be worked in a non-curling pattern, such as moss, garter, or ribbing; and double, which is usually done in stocking stitch. Finished width ranges from 5 mm to 4 cm. If necessary, work a border with needles of a size different from size used for garment so tensions match.

Border knitted with garment body. Direction of the garment and border stitch are the same.
For horizontal border, work bottom of garment in border stitch, then change to garment pattern.
For vertical border, knit the border stitches alongside the garment pattern.
Combine horizontal and vertical borders to edge a cardigan. The effect is similar to a mitred border (bottom right) but easier to work.

Horizontal border

Vertical border

Combined borders

Border knitted on picked-up stitches. This type needs no seam if you sew garment sections together before picking up the stitches.
For a single straight border, pick up the number of stitches needed to match the garment edge. For example, if edge measures 50 cm, and border stitch tension is 10 stitches per 5 cm, pick up 100 stitches, spacing them evenly along the edge. The finished border should lie flat.
For a single curved border, follow the same procedure as for straight border, but decrease or increase as needed to shape the curve.
For a double border, work in stocking stitch for 3 to 5 cm; purl 1 row on the right side for a turning ridge; continue in stocking stitch for another 3 to 5 cm; cast off loosely. Fold border in half and oversew free edge to inside of garment.

Single straight border

Single curved border

Double border

Border knitted separately and sewn on. This method takes more time than either of the two above, but size and shape are easier to control.
For a straight border, cast on stitches needed for length of garment edge; knit desired width; cast off loosely. Lay garment and border edge side by side; oversew together on wrong side.
For a bias border, cast on stitches needed; work in stocking stitch for twice the desired width, decreasing 1 stitch at beginning of every knit row, increasing 1 stitch at end. With right sides together, backstitch one edge of band to garment; fold strip in half; oversew free edge to garment edge on the wrong side.
For a mitred border, cast on stitches needed and mark corner stitch; work a double increase at the marked stitch every other row; cast off and oversew in place as for straight border.

Straight border, sewn on

Bias border

Mitred border

Knitting a garment

Slipping a stitch 428
Picot edging 478

Hems and facings

A hem is a turned-up finish for the lower edge of a garment; a facing is a turned-in finish for any other edge, such as an armhole. In general, these are functional rather than decorative finishes that help keep an edge from curling or stretching.

To make a flat edge where a facing or hem is to be folded, a turning ridge is usually worked into the pattern. Depending on the desired effect, this can be a slipped stitch, purl ridge on a knit face, or lacy picot ridge (see examples below). The picot ridge is particularly attractive on baby clothes.

To prevent buckling, a hem or facing allowance is knitted in stocking stitch on needles one to three sizes smaller than needles used for the garment. Average hem allowance is usually 2 to 3 cm.

To keep the stitch line inconspicuous, the hem or facing should be sewn with matching yarn, the stitches pulled firmly but not too tight. If yarn is thick, separate one or two plies for sewing.

Making a hem foldline

Purl ridge. Suitable for tailored garments in stocking stitch.

On smaller needles (one to three sizes smaller) than those used for the garment, cast on the stitches needed for the bottom edge. Work in stocking stitch until the hem is the desired length, ending with a wrong-side row. On the next (right-side) row, purl to form a ridge. Change to larger needles and continue in stocking stitch. When garment is completed, fold up hem along the purled ridge.

Slipstitch ridge. The best choice for a textured pattern stitch or a bulky yarn.

On smaller needles, work hem in stocking stitch for desired length, ending with a wrong-side row. On the next (right-side) row, *K 1, yfwd, sl 1, ybk, K 1.* At end of this row, change to larger needles and pattern stitch.

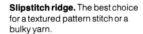

Picot ridge. Attractive for babies' and children's clothing and for dressy garments.

With smaller needles, cast on a multiple of 2 stitches plus 1. Work in stocking stitch until the hem is the desired length, ending with a wrong-side row. On the next (right-side) row, *K 2 tog, yrn*, K 1. At end of this row, change to larger needles and pattern stitch.

Sewing the hem edge

Oversewing is a neat and firm way to sew the hem on medium or lightweight knitting.

Using matching yarn, insert needle at a right-angle, taking it through the back of one stitch on the garment and a corresponding stitch on the hem edge. Pull stitches firmly but not too tight; otherwise the sewing line may pucker.

The stitch-by-stitch sewing method is a better choice for thick knitting because the ridge on the edge is eliminated. This technique can be used either when a hem is formed at the end of work or is started with the looped cast-on (see p. 415).

For hem at end of work, sew each stitch directly from the needle to a corresponding one on the wrong side (as shown). *For looped cast-on*, sew stitches in place; remove foundation yarn.

A blind-hemming stitch is the best choice for a heavy or bulky knit that has a cast-off edge, because the hem edge is not pressed against the garment. Stitches are taken inside between hem and garment.

Turn hem edge back 5 mm to 1.5 cm. Working from right to left, take 1 stitch in the garment, then 1 stitch in the hem, placing each stitch just to the left of the previous one. Do not pull yarn too tight.

Knitting a hem edge to the garment

Knitted-in hem on stocking stitch. A neat finish for a jacket or sweater for which limited stretch but a moderate fit is desired at the bottom edge. Usually worked without a turning ridge, but you could add one if you prefer. It is very important to use smaller needles for the hem allowance, or the edge will fan outwards at the bottom.

On smaller needles (two or three sizes smaller) than those used for the garment, make a looped cast-on with contrasting yarn for the foundation. Work in stocking stitch until you have twice the desired hem depth, ending with a purl row. Slip a spare needle through the stitches of the cast-on row and remove the foundation yarn. Fold hem in half, purl sides together. Knit together 1 stitch from each needle across the row. Change to larger needles and continue in stocking stitch.

Knitted-in hem on ribbing. A firm edge that can be used when a hem is desired on a ribbed border, or for a garment worked entirely in ribbing.

On larger needles (one size larger) than those used for the ribbing, cast on half the required stitches, using the looped cast-on method with contrasting foundation yarn. Work in 1 × 1 rib for 2.5 cm. Slip the cast-on edge on to a spare needle and remove foundation yarn. Fold hem in half, change to smaller needles working stitches alternately from front and back needles. Continue in ribbing.

Hemming corners and curves

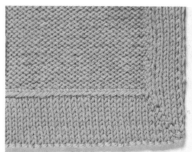

Hem and facing for mitred corner. Cast on stitches for hem, less 2.5 cm; work in stocking stitch for 2.5 cm, adding 1 stitch at front edge every 2nd row. Work turning ridge. For facing,

Facing for inside curve. Edge is enlarged because it is an outside curve when folded to wrong side. Using needles one or two sizes smaller than for garment, pick up stitches with right side fac-

Hem and facing for outside curve. Curve is formed at the lower front edge by working turned rows on about a quarter of the garment stitches and for about 2½ times the hem depth. Cast on stitches required for the hem and knit 2.5 cm. Next, work the curve, decreasing the turning

continue stocking stitch for 2.5 cm, increasing 1 stitch at front edge every 2nd row. For facing foldline, slip a stitch purlwise, where garment and facing meet, every knit row.

ing you, then *knit* a row (for turning ridge) on wrong side. Continue in stocking stitch for 2.5 cm, making several increases along the deep part of the curve. Cast off loosely.

stages gradually. For example, if garment has 78 stitches, you might leave 20 stitches unworked to start, then add on 4 stitches once, 3 stitches twice, 2 stitches 3 times, and 1 stitch 4 times, every other row; adjust numbers to keep work flat. After curve is shaped, cast on for front facing.

477

Knitting a garment

Pockets

Pockets are both decorative and functional additions to a knitted garment. The basic types are inside and patch.

Patch pockets (p. 480) are easier to produce. Any stitch is suitable for them, including crochet patterns. If stocking stitch is used, facings or a border must be added to make edges neat.

Inside pockets vary in style, but all are basically worked the same way, and each must be lined. A knitted lining is best, but a fabric lining plus knitted extension may be preferable for bulky yarns. Directions opposite are for a right pocket; reverse shaping for a left one.

A general rule for positioning a pocket is to set the centre of it about one-third of the distance from the side seam. Average pocket size is 10 to 12 cm square; 2 to 4 cm is allowed for a border.

Horizontal inside pockets

Horizontal pocket with ribbed border.
Knit the garment front to within 2.5 cm of the pocket opening. Place a marker at the beginning of the opening and another at the end. Continue up the front, working the stitches between markers in a rib pattern (1 × 1 ribbing shown here). When you have 2.5 cm of ribbing, cast off the pocket stitches loosely on a right-side row and complete the row (A).
To knit a lining, cast on to a spare needle the same number of stitches as for the pocket opening plus 4 stitches for selvedges. Work in stocking stitch for 10 to 12 cm, ending with a knit row, casting off 2 stitches at the beginning and end of it; cut yarn. Work purl stitches across the garment to the pocket opening, purl across the lining (B), then continue with garment on the other side of the opening. The pocket lining is now part of the garment front. Continue to work on all stitches until garment front is complete. Oversew the 3 sides of the pocket lining to the wrong side of the garment.

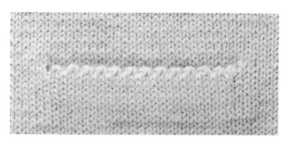

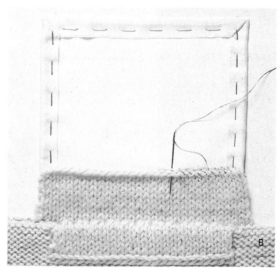

Horizontal pocket with picot edging.
Knit the garment front up to the pocket opening, ending with a purl row. Count off an odd number of stitches for the pocket opening and place markers at each end of it. On the knit row, work to the first marker, then work the pocket edge and facing as follows: slip first marker, K 1, *yrn, K 2 tog*, repeat instructions between asterisks to the second marker, turn; change to smaller needles and work 2 cm in stocking stitch; cast off and fasten off yarn (A), leaving a 30 cm end. Thread yarn end in a tapestry needle; fold facing to wrong side and oversew it to the garment.
To knit a lining extension, follow the directions for knitting a lining (far left), but work in stocking stitch for only 4 cm; cut yarn; join extension to garment front as directed.
To make a fabric lining, cut a rectangle of lightweight fabric 2.5 cm wider than the pocket opening and 8 to 10 cm deep. Press edges under 1.5 cm all around and tack them. With wrong side of garment facing you, fold back edge of pocket extension and oversew it to pocket lining along one edge (B). Lay the lining against the garment and slipstitch it all around (see photograph, upper right corner opposite). *If you prefer a pouch lining,* cut 2 pieces of fabric, sew them together on 3 sides, then attach 1 open edge to the pocket extension and the other to the pocket facing.

Vertical inside pockets

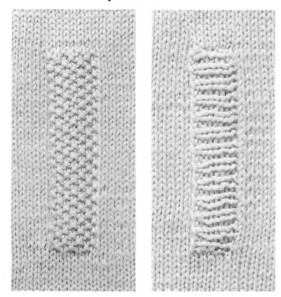

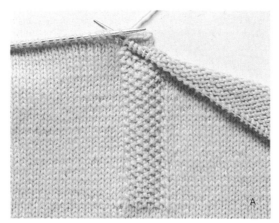

Moss stitch border is knitted on; ribbed border is picked up.

Vertical pocket with knitted-on border. Knit from centre front to pocket position; place remaining stitches on a holder. Work front stitch group with 3 cm of stitches at the pocket edge in border pattern. At top of pocket opening, end with a knit row; fasten off; place these stitches on a spare needle. Attach yarn to second stitch group and cast on 2.5 cm of stitches for lining extension. Work until this side is the same length as the first, ending with a purl row. On the next (knit) row, cast off extension stitches, then re-join the two (A), and complete the front. Cut lining fabric 10 cm wide and length of pocket opening plus 4 cm; sew to pocket extension (see facing page, lower right) and garment (B).

Vertical pocket with picked-up border. Knit two sides of pocket opening as a plain slit, without border stitches or pocket extension. When completed, pick up stitches along the front pocket edge and work in border stitch (ribbing shown left) for 4 cm; cast off. Attach lining. Sew top and bottom edges of border to garment.

Slanted inside pockets

Moss stitch border is knitted as an extension of pocket opening.

Ribbed border is knitted separately, then sewn to pocket edge.

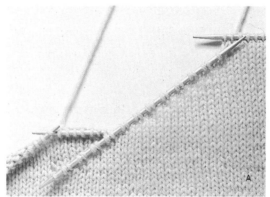

Slanted pocket with knitted-on border. Work to lower end of pocket opening; place remaining stitches (those close to side seam) on a holder. Working on first group, knit 2 to 3 stitches less at lower end of pocket every other row until 1 stitch of pocket opening remains; fasten off yarn; place pocket stitches on spare needle, leave front stitches on another. Knit a lining extension as for picot pocket (opposite), ending with a purl row. Next row, knit across both extension and side group of stitches (A); continue until this portion is the same length as front section, then join these two groups and complete the garment front. *For the border,* work pocket edge in a non-curling pattern, increasing 1 stitch at the top (front) end, decreasing 1 stitch at the lower (side) end, every other row. Attach lining as for horizontal pocket.

Slanted pocket with separate border. Work pocket opening in steps as directed on left, but cast off stitches with each turning instead of leaving them unworked (B). *For border,* cast on 1 stitch and place marker in it. Increase 1 stitch every other row until border is 3 cm wide; continue in pattern until border measures 1.5 cm less than pocket opening. Decrease 1 stitch every other row at marked edge until 1 stitch remains. Fasten off. Sew in place.

479

Knitting a garment

Patch pockets

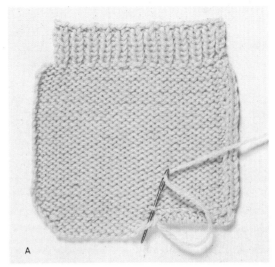

Patch pocket in garter stitch. Cast on the number of stitches for width, less 4. Work in garter stitch (or other non-curling pattern such as moss stitch), increasing 1 stitch at each end of rows 2 and 4. When pocket is desired depth, cast off. Mark position lines on garment with contrasting yarn; sew pocket with oversewing.

Patch pocket in stocking stitch with ribbed border. Cast on the number of stitches for the width, less 2. Purl the first row; continue in stocking stitch, increasing 1 stitch at each end of first 3 knit rows. You now have pocket width plus a 3-row facing at bottom and a 2-stitch facing at each side. Work to within 3 cm of finished depth,

then cast off 2 stitches at beginning of next 2 rows. Change to needles one size larger; work 1 × 1 ribbing for 2.5 cm, cast off. Fold facings to wrong side; oversew to pocket (A). Slipstitch pocket to garment. To make sewing easier, insert a needle through stitches along the position line; sew through the raised loops (B).

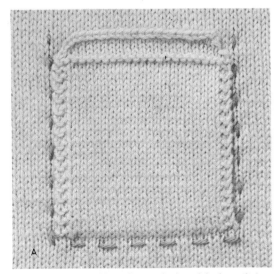

Patch pocket in stocking stitch worked on picked-up stitches. Mark pocket position with contrasting yarn. With right side of work facing you and yarn behind it, pick up stitches along bottom position line, taking up 1 stitch through each garment stitch; fasten off yarn and secure. Turn work, fasten on new yarn and work in

stocking stitch with a double garter selvedge until pocket is desired depth; work a purl ridge for a foldline. To knit a facing, change to smaller needles and work 4 rows of stocking stitch, decreasing 1 stitch at each end of knit row; cast off (A). Fold facing to wrong side; oversew in place. Oversew pocket sides to garment (B).

To add a flap, mark a row 1.5 cm above top edge of pocket. Pick up stitches along marked row to equal pocket width. Work towards the pocket in stocking stitch, with 2 cm of garter stitch each side, until flap is a quarter of pocket depth; change to garter stitch and work for 2 cm, decreasing 1 stitch at each end, every other row.

Buttonholes

There are three basic buttonhole types – *round*, used for baby garments and eyelets; *vertical*, usually centred on a vertical band; and *horizontal*, suitable for jackets, coats and cardigans.

Buttonholes are always placed in relation to button position. A round hole aligns with the button exactly; the top of a vertical style extends 1 row above it; the front end of a horizontal type extends 1 stitch beyond it. Three key position points are the neck, the fullest part of the bust, and the bottom just above the hem or border. All others are evenly spaced between these points.

Buttonhole finish is optional; you can leave it as formed, or hand-work the edges as shown below. A ply or two of matching yarn is most attractive, but buttonhole twist is suitable, too.

Round buttonhole (also used for eyelet). *Right side row,* for each buttonhole, make a yarn round needle, then knit 2 together. *Wrong side row,* work all stitches in pattern, including the yarn round needle.

Vertical buttonhole. Divide work at base of buttonhole and knit each part separately for the desired depth, then re-join the sections. The last row for both sections must be worked in the same direction. That is, if the first section ends with a right-side row, so must the second.

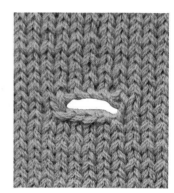

Horizontal buttonhole. *Right side row,* cast off the number of stitches that equals the button diameter. *Wrong side row,* work to within 1 stitch of buttonhole opening; increase by working into front and back of this stitch. Using the single casting-on method, cast on to right needle the same number of stitches that were cast off, less 1; continue in pattern

---

Finishing a buttonhole

Oversewing is the simplest finish for a buttonhole. It reinforces the edge without diminishing its flexibility. *To oversew,* take diagonal stitches over the edge, spacing them an even distance apart and at a uniform depth.

Buttonhole stitch is a firm finish. It is the better stitch to use if you have a tape or ribbon facing, as it covers a cut edge more effectively than oversewing.
To buttonhole, work right to left with needle pointed away from the opening, thread looped as shown. Space stitches close together.

Cut-in buttonhole

Cut-in buttonhole technique can be used if you want to add a buttonhole after work is finished.
To make the buttonhole, mark its position by tacking above and below the row where it is to be made and at each end of opening. With small scissors, snip a stitch at the centre and carefully pick out the

yarn to each end (A), then tie knots on the wrong side to prevent further unravelling.
For a simple finish, draw matching yarn through each loop of the opening (B); fasten off.
For a crocheted finish, make a slip knot and place on hook. Working on wrong side, insert hook in loop of

2nd stitch at right of buttonhole, make 1 slipstitch, then another in next loop; make 1 slipstitch in each open loop of buttonhole, inserting hook from right to wrong side, then 2 more slipstitches at top left of opening. Turn work; repeat along opposite edge (C); fasten off. Remove tacking carefully.

Assembling and finishing

Blocking and pressing

Blocking is the shaping of knitted pieces to specific dimensions. It can be used, at the same time, to smooth stitch irregularities and flatten curling edges.

Knitting directions usually mention blocking or pressing dimensions. If they do not, or if only some measurements are given, you can calculate the ones you need using the tension specified. For example, if there are 28 stitches on the shoulder, and the tension is 14 stitches per 5 cm, the shoulder should be blocked to measure 10 cm.

There are two basic blocking methods – *steam* and *wet* – illustrated below and opposite. The first employs moisture plus heat, and is most suitable for wool and other natural yarns. The second relies on moisture only and is preferred for some synthetic yarns and highly textured stitches in any yarn type.

Yarn manufacturers sometimes recommend the proper blocking method. If there are no instructions with your yarn, or if you have doubts about which procedure to follow, use the wet method. It takes more time, but the yarn will not be subjected unsuitably to heat.

Some yarn labels say 'do not block'. Always heed this recommendation, as certain yarns do not respond well to blocking and may, in fact, be altered unfavourably by it. Most acrylic yarns and some blends are in this category.

Because blocking works on the principle that damp yarn can be moulded, it can be used, if necessary, to alter garment size. The amount of adjustment possible will depend on fibre type, how tightly spun the yarn is, and how close or open the pattern. Natural yarns – wool, linen, cotton and silk – are more responsive to this process than most synthetics; an open stitch expands more than a closed one. Whatever the yarn or stitch type, alteration is usually limited to enlarging a garment one size; it is difficult to block to smaller dimensions.

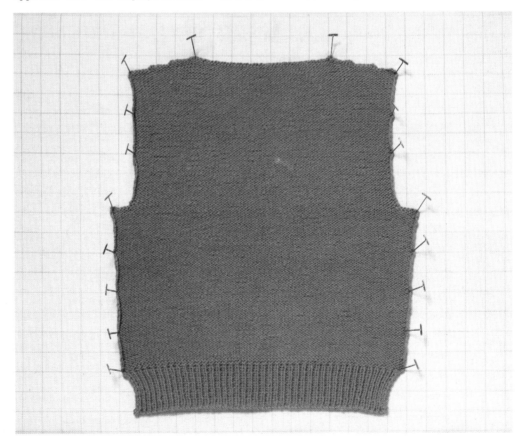

In steam blocking, a combination of moisture and heat is used to mould the knitting to desired shape and dimensions. A steam iron is the best source of steam for this purpose; if unavailable, a dry iron and damp cloth can be substituted. To produce steam, the dry iron should be held lightly against the cloth without applying pressure.
To block a section as shown here, lay it wrong side up on a padded surface (as described above); adjust measurements. Pin the corners, then pin along the edges. Fewer pins are usually better, but not if the edges become scalloped. Apply steam until the knitting is uniformly damp. Leave it pinned until thoroughly dry. Remove the pins and press the piece lightly, if necessary.

Blocking requires a flat surface large enough to lay out items to their full dimensions. A padded board is ideal for this purpose. There are directions on p. 55 for making a blocking board for embroidery. This would serve nicely for knitting and crochet, too, but a larger size, about 60 by 90 cm, would be more versatile. A suitable substitute is a dressmaker's cutting board, or a carpeted floor area. With either of these, a sheet of plastic should be used to protect the surface from moisture. In addition to a padded surface, you will need a towel and a large cloth for wet blocking, an iron for steam blocking, and rustproof pins (the rustproof pins are optional).

A garment is usually blocked before sections are joined; they are more easily adjusted in this state, and assembling is easier to do after blocking. To prepare the pieces, weave in all loose yarn ends, as illustrated on the far right. Block the back first, then the front, matching the armholes, and the shoulder and side seams. Next, do the sleeves, matching one to the other so that the dimensions are the same. Do not block ribbing, as it may lose its elasticity.

Pressing is sometimes done after blocking to remove wrinkles or smooth the surface of the knitting, or to open seams. The decision to press or not depends on yarn type, pattern stitch and personal preference. Most synthetic yarns should not be pressed – heat and pressure have an adverse effect on them. Stocking stitch and similarly smooth stitches can be pressed and are often improved by this, but a deeply textured pattern, such as an Aran knit, would be spoiled if flattened. Pressing tends to even out the natural irregularities of hand knitting, and some people do not press because they prefer to keep this look. If you choose to press, use a damp cloth and apply the iron lightly. Press seams with just the tip of the iron.

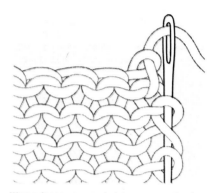

Weave loose yarn ends into a seam edge for about 5 cm, using a tapestry needle; cut excess.

Washing hand knitting

HAND WASHING
Suitable for any yarn type, but especially recommended for wool.
Wash in lukewarm to cool water, using soap flakes or a mild detergent. Work lather through the fabric by pressing the article up and down; do not twist it. If using liquid detergent, you can pour a little of it directly on to a soiled area, such as a cuff, then rub gently until dirt is removed.
Rinse several times, using the same water temperature as for washing. After final rinse, drain water, then lift the article and, supporting it with both hands, gently squeeze out excess water. Roll it in a towel and squeeze again to remove as much moisture as possible.
Dry article on a flat surface, moulding it into shape (see method, left); allow to dry completely before moving it.

MACHINE WASHING
Use only for synthetics when indicated by yarn label. Turn garment inside out.
Wash with setting on 'delicate synthetic' or 'gentle' cycle and warm or cold water.
Rinse with cold water, adding fabric softener to the final rinse if possible.
Dry in automatic dryer with low setting (50°C or 120°F), removing article when it is just dry. Check its condition every few minutes during the drying process, as the required time will probably be less than a full machine cycle.

In wet blocking, moisture alone is used to mould knitting. *To block a section* (as shown opposite), lay it on a wet towel and adjust measurements, pinning if necessary. Lay a damp cloth over the knitting; leave knitting undisturbed until dry. *To block a finished piece* (one that is wet from washing), squeeze out excess moisture, then lay knitting on a dry towel. Push or 'bunch' knitting into shape; check measurements if necessary; let dry thoroughly before moving.

Assembling and finishing

Joining sections edge to edge

The joining of knitted sections edge to edge makes a smooth seam that is nearly invisible. There are two ways to do this: **weaving** finished edges (see directly below); and **grafting** stitches (bottom of page). Both methods are especially recommended for heavy yarns.

Four weaving methods are illustrated below. All are worked basically the same way, that is, yarn is woven under alternate loops on each edge so that a row of stitches is formed between the sections. One strand of the knitting yarn is best for this purpose, unless it is knobbly; then a matching smooth yarn might be substituted. A tapestry needle is advisable because it will not split yarn. Edges to be joined must be neat and have equal numbers of stitches; otherwise use methods at top of the facing page.

Stocking stitch – side seams. Lay sections right side up, stitches aligned. Attach yarn at right end. *Insert needle under next horizontal loop adjacent to edge stitch on one section, then under corresponding loop on the other.*

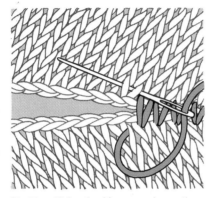

Stocking stitch – shoulder seams. Lay sections right side up, corresponding stitches aligned. Attach yarn at right end. *Take needle under next knit stitch adjacent to casting off on one section, then under next knit stitch on the other.*

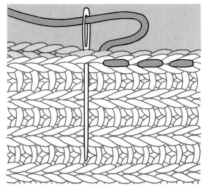

Ribbing – side seams. Hold sections right sides together, corresponding stitches aligned. Attach yarn at right end. *Bring needle up through centres of next 2 corresponding edge stitches, then down through centres of next 2 stitches.*

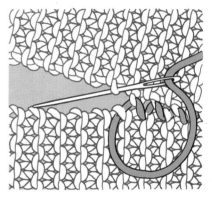

Garter stitch – side seams. Lay sections right side up, corresponding stitches aligned. Attach yarn at right end. *Insert the tapestry needle through lower loop on one edge, then through corresponding upper loop on the other edge.*

Grafting

Grafting is a way of joining sections horizontally so that the seam is smooth and elastic. It is accomplished by weaving stitches together, directly from the needles.

To graft, both edges must have the same number of stitches. Grafting is always used to join the side of a sock heel to the body; it is also suitable for joining shoulders that were shaped by turning.

There are two ways to position the work for grafting; use whichever feels comfortable. (1) Hold both needles in the left hand with wrong sides of the work facing each other. (2) Lay the two sections face up on a table, as illustrated below. To sew, use a tapestry needle and one strand of yarn, removing each stitch from the needle only after yarn has been pulled through.

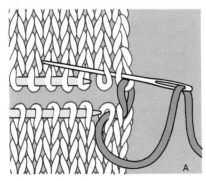

Stocking stitch. To start, bring needle *purlwise* through bottom and top end stitches; re-insert *knitwise* in bottom stitch, *purlwise* through next stitch on needle. *Insert needle *knitwise* in top

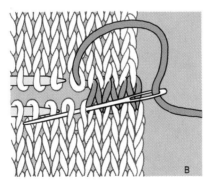

stitch where thread emerges, *purlwise* through next stitch on needle (A). Insert needle *knitwise* through bottom stitch where thread emerges, *purlwise* through next stitch on needle (B).*

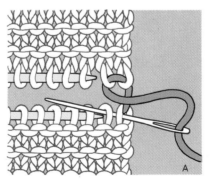

Garter stitch. To start, bring tapestry needle *purlwise* through bottom and top end stitches, then insert *knitwise* through next top stitch. *Insert needle *knitwise* in bottom stitch where thread

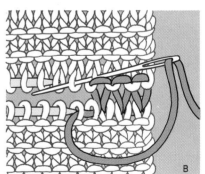

emerges, then *purlwise* through next stitch on needle (A). Insert needle *purlwise* through top stitch where thread emerges, then *knitwise* through next stitch on needle (B).*

Joining sections with seam allowances

Joining with seam allowances is ideal for sections on which edges are uneven, such as a shoulder that has been cast off in steps. It is also suitable for taking in a garment or shaping curved seams, as the stitches can be made any distance from the edge. Two methods are shown below. Both make sturdy and neat joins with any yarn type, but are best suited to fine or medium weights.

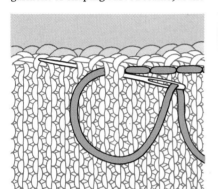

Backstitch. Using tapestry needle and matching yarn, bring needle up 2 stitches ahead of edge. *Insert it 2 stitches back (within row, at the point where thread emerged for previous stitch); bring it out 2 stitches ahead of emerging thread.*

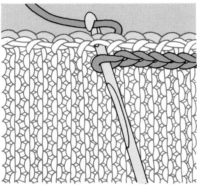

Slipstitch. Using a crochet hook of appropriate size and matching yarn, draw a loop through a corresponding stitch on each section; *insert hook through next 2 stitches; draw a loop through both stitches and the loop on the hook.*

Setting in a sleeve

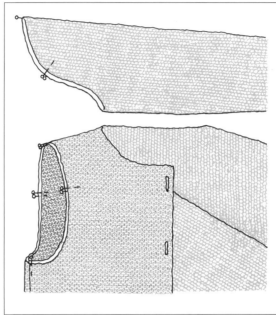

A sleeve cap is curved differently from the armhole and is sometimes slightly larger. Follow these steps to ensure a smooth join. First, join garment side and shoulder seams and the sleeve underarm seam. Fold sleeve in half; place a pin in centre of cap. Set two more pins on each side halfway between centre of cap and underarm seam. On the garment, place pins at shoulder and halfway between shoulder and underarm seams. With sleeve and garment right sides together, pin sleeve to armhole, matching pins and underarm seams. Insert more pins if needed. Sew seam inside sleeve with backstitch.

Joining an edge to a section

The joining of an edge to a section should be as inconspicuous as possible. Choose a method from those below; as you work, stretch the knit gently occasionally to prevent puckering.

Oversewing is used for most flat edges; it makes a firm join and, at the same time, keeps the edge from curling. **Slipstitch** is suitable only for a folded edge. You would use it, for example, to sew on a patch pocket that has turned-under facings. A **stitch-by-stitch** method is an inconspicuous join for heavy yarns. It is used primarily when the hem or facing is formed at the end of work, but could be used with a looped cast-on. Stitches can be sewn in the same way as oversewing, or by the technique shown below, in which the knit and purl stitches are duplicated.

Oversewing. *Insert needle at a right-angle under 1 loop (purl stitch) on the garment, then under 1 strand of a corresponding stitch on the hem or facing edge; pull yarn through.*

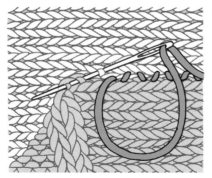

Slipstitch. *Insert the needle under 1 garment stitch (preferably a purl stitch if the fabric is stocking stitch), then under 1 or 2 stitches of the folded edge; pull yarn through.*

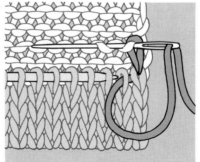

Stitch-by-stitch. To start, insert needle purlwise in 1st stitch on knitting needle, up through 1st purl stitch on garment and down through next purl stitch. *Insert the needle knitwise through knit

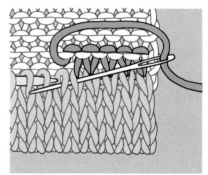

stitch where thread emerges, then purlwise through next stitch on knitting needle. Insert the needle up through purl stitch where thread emerges, down through next purl stitch.*

485

Assembling and finishing

Knitted buttonholes 481   Oversewing 485
Backstitch 485   Crocheted slipstitch 275

Inserting a zip

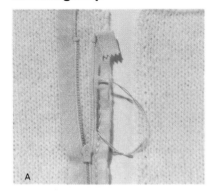

A

Sewing first half of zip with the backstitch

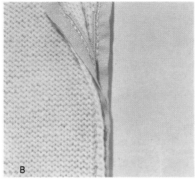

B

Second half of zip sewn in place

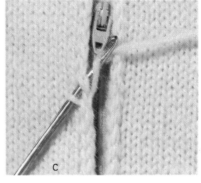

C

Finishing the edge with crocheted slipstitches

For a garment of fine or medium-weight yarn, adding crochet to the edges of the zip opening makes them flat, neat and firm.
To face the zip opening, work 1 or 2 rows of double crochet along each side.
To attach zip, open it and place half of zip face down against right side of garment, with edge of tape facing edge of garment. Sew tape to garment with a backstitch, placing stitches along the line where crochet meets the edge of the knitting (A). Fold garment right sides together with opening edges aligned so that second half of the zip can be sewn exactly as first half was (B). Close zip; press zip opening lightly from right side. Work a row of crocheted slipstitches along both edges of the zip opening (C).

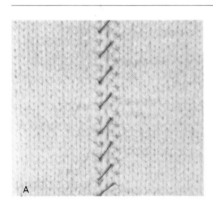

A

Garment edges tacked

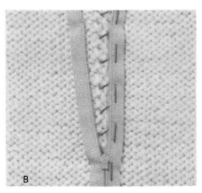

B

Tacking zip to the inside of the garment

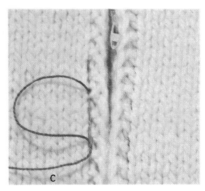

C

Backstitching zip to the garment

For a garment of heavy or tweedy yarn, a two-stitch selvedge makes a neat and firm finish for the edge of the zip opening.
To border the zip opening, substitute a selvedge for 2 stitches of the pattern. Double chain edge or double garter edge is suitable (see p. 424 for the methods). With large oversewing stitches, tack the border edges together on the right side (A).
To attach zip, tack it to wrong side of the garment, teeth aligned with centre of the opening (B). On the right side, sew zip to the garment with a backstitch, placing stitches along the line where border meets edge of the pattern stitch (C). Use buttonhole twist or a double strand of heavy-duty thread in a matching colour.

Adding tape

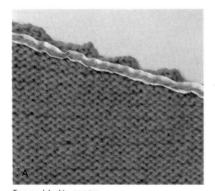

A

Tape added to a seam

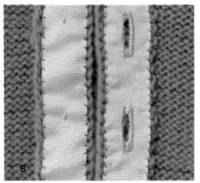

B

Ribbon backing for buttonholes on a cardigan

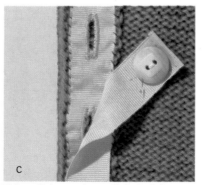

C

Ribbon with buttons, inserted in buttonholes

A seam can be taped when extra stability is needed, for example, on a jacket shoulder. Tape 5 mm to 1.5 cm wide is suitable.
To attach tape, centre it over the seam on one section; tack in place. Backstitch seam (A).
Buttonhole and button edges are often backed to prevent sagging; tape and corded ribbon are suitable. Cut 2 pieces to fit; oversew one to edge on which buttons will be sewn; tack other to buttonhole edge and mark buttonhole positions. Remove tape; work buttonholes in it by machine or hand. Re-tack tape, aligning buttonholes; oversew edges (B). On right side, finish buttonholes.
Buttons can be sewn to ribbon to make a child's cardigan suitable for a girl or a boy. Work buttonholes on both sides of cardigan; button the ribbon on to whichever side is suitable (C).

Adjusting fit

ADDING ELASTIC

Elastic thread woven into back of ribbing

Elastic thread inserted through ribbing back

Elastic inserted through a casing stitch

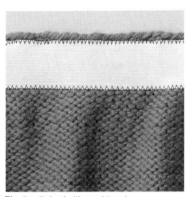

Elastic stitched with machine zigzag

A closer fit for a cap or socks is obtained by adding elastic thread to the ribbing, either weaving or threading it.
Weave in elastic as you knit, carrying it on the wrong side as if it were a second colour (see p. 460 for weaving technique).
Thread the elastic after ribbing is completed, using tapestry needle and inserting it under the vertical knit ribs along each row on the wrong side.
A close yet flexible fit at the waist is achieved by drawing elastic through a band or casing stitch, or stitching it in place; the last two methods are shown.
For casing stitch, use a crochet hook to form zigzag chain that is anchored to garment with slipstitches, and fits snugly over elastic.
For stitched elastic, cut elastic to fit waist; join ends. With pins, divide elastic and waistline in eight sections; pin them together, matching divisions. With machine zigzag, stitch top and bottom edges of elastic, stretching to fit garment.

TAKING IN WIDTH

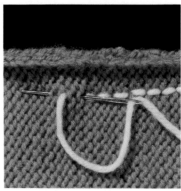

A seam taken in with a backstitch

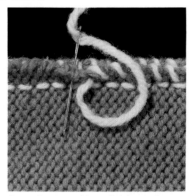

Seam allowances trimmed and oversewn

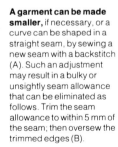

A garment can be made smaller, if necessary, or a curve can be shaped in a straight seam, by sewing a new seam with a backstitch (A). Such an adjustment may result in a bulky or unsightly seam allowance that can be eliminated as follows. Trim the seam allowance to within 5 mm of the seam; then oversew the trimmed edges (B).

SHORTENING OR LENGTHENING

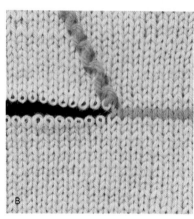

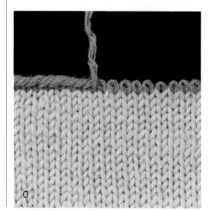

If necessary, a garment can be shortened after it is finished by separating the unwanted length from the garment. This can be done, however, only with a simple pattern, such as stocking stitch or garter stitch. Before beginning, open the seams to the cut-off point. Snip a yarn at one edge and start to draw it out (A). Snip the other end of the yarn at the opposite edge; draw yarn out completely. Both sections are now completely separated (B). Insert a needle through stitches along garment edge and knit a border or hem as desired.
If necessary, a garment can be lengthened after it is finished by removing the foundation yarn of the cast-on row (C), inserting a needle through the stitches, and knitting on the required length. This addition will show slightly. Since lengthening might be required for a child's garment, you can plan for it in several ways:
(1) Buy extra yarn; knit it into a large sample and wash it each time you wash the garment. When it is time to lengthen the garment, unravel the sample and use the yarn to knit the extra length; it should match perfectly.
(2) Cast on the garment stitches using the looped cast-on, as its foundation yarn is easily removed; or
(3) Knit the garment sections from the top down, as a cast-off row is easy to undo.

487

Assembling and finishing

Embroidering on knitting

Simple knitted patterns, such as garter, moss and stocking stitch, can be enhanced with embroidery. This is particularly suitable on a child's garment.

Embroidery techniques that work well on knitted fabric are chain stitches (pp. 28–32), in particular lazy daisy; detached filling stitches (pp. 42–43), especially bullion; and raised needle-weaving (p. 52), which permits the making of a solid motif without stretching the fabric. Basic cross stitch and its variations are also suitable, because a knitted structure lends itself naturally to any counted thread technique.

Duplicate stitch, also called Swiss darning, is another suitable embroidery form and one that is unique to knitting. It is a way of working over stocking stitches so that they are outlined precisely. Using duplicate stitch, you can, if you prefer, work a jacquard pattern over plain fabric instead of working in the additional colours as you knit. Use it also to embroider motifs, such as the letters shown opposite.

Transfer of a design should not be attempted with hand-knitted fabric. It is helpful, however, to mark the area to be embroidered by tacking around it with contrasting yarn. If a design has several parts, you could mark each with a different colour. When working from a graph (on which each stitch is represented by a square), remember that knit stitches are wider than they are tall and adjust proportions, if necessary, making them taller and narrower to compensate for this widening. To get an idea of the result, use the charting method below.

The most appropriate yarn for embroidery on knitting is one that matches the knitting yarn in type and thickness. If yarn is thinner, it tends to sink into the fabric; yarn that is thicker could stretch the knitting. If you have no yarn suitable for this purpose, you can buy small skeins of embroidery canvas work threads, such as crewel, tapestry and Persian wool; pearl cotton or stranded cotton. Use the number of strands that matches the knitting yarn weight.

To start the embroidery, thread yarn in a tapestry needle (this type will not split the stitches) and bring it through from the wrong side, leaving an end long enough to weave into the back later. For the basic cross stitch or the duplicate stitch, follow directions on this page; for other stitches, see appropriate embroidery pages. Take special care not to pull stitches too tight. After completion, a light steam blocking may be needed; do not press the embroidered area.

CROSS STITCHING ON STOCKING STITCH

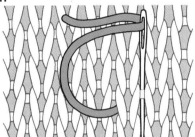

To form a basic cross stitch, bring needle up under a purl strand connecting 2 knit stitches; *cross right, take needle down behind the purl strand that lies between next 2 knit stitches.

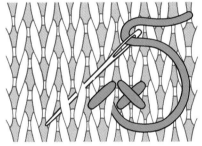

Cross left, insert needle above purl strand between the 2 stitches where thread emerges, then take it diagonally behind next knit stitch, and bring it out again under the next purl stitch.*

DUPLICATE STITCHING ON STOCKING STITCH

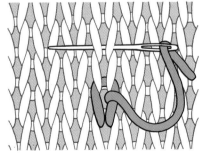

To form a duplicate stitch, *bring needle up under the connecting strand at the bottom of a knit stitch (where strands lie close together), then right to left behind knit stitch above.

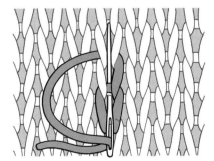

Insert needle bottom to top under same strand where thread emerges for 1st half of stitch.* As you work, take care to match the tension of the knitting, otherwise the fabric may pucker.

MAKING A CHART FOR EMBROIDERY

A charted embroidery design is usually represented on a graph in which one square equals one stitch. If you use such a chart to embroider on knitting, the design will flatten out because knit stitches are always wider than they are tall. To be sure that a design will work on knitted fabric, you can first adapt it to a rectangular chart like the one shown below. These rectangles nearly duplicate the proportions of most knit stitches. (Compare the chart with the embroidered samples on the left.)

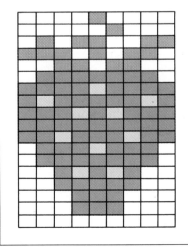

Alphabet to embroider

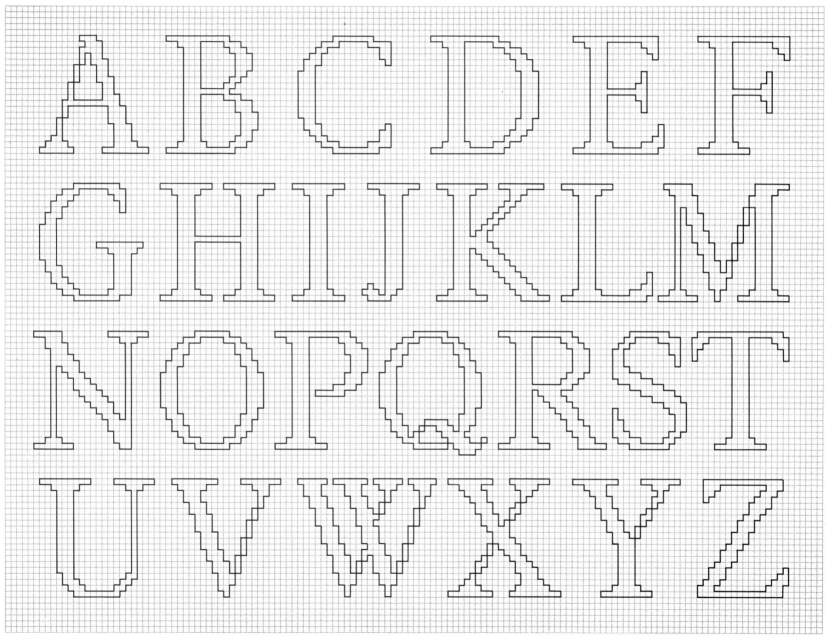

An initial or monogram can be added to your hand-knitted project, using duplicate stitch and the letters above (see the sock, p. 492, for an example).

Children's cardigans and hats

ALL-OVER-STRIPE SET

This pattern can be knitted from oddments of yarn to make an attractive and economical cardigan and hat for a child.

Size: Directions are for size 4 (chest 62 cm) and size 6 (64 cm).

Materials needed: Acrylic yarn in double knitting, such as Pingouin Madame: 150 (170) g each blue and white, 60 (90) g bright yellow, 30 (30) g each green and turquoise; knitting needles, 1 pair 3.75 mm, 1 pair 4.50 mm; crochet hooks size 4.00 and 4.50; 7 buttons, 10 mm in diameter; tapestry needle

Tension: 18 sts and 26 rows = 5 cm in stocking stitch

Cardigan back: Using 3.75 mm needles, cast on 56 (60) sts with blue yarn. Work 1 × 1 ribbing for 1 row. Attach white, leaving blue at the side. Work 2 rows of ribbing with white, 2 rows blue, 2 rows white, 2 rows blue. Change to 4.50 mm needles and work in stocking st, alternating 2 rows white, 2 rows blue until piece measures 21 (24) cm, ending with P row in blue; fasten off. Attach green and K 2 rows; K 2 more rows each of green, turquoise, green; fasten off. Attach yellow; K 1 row, P 1 row.

Shaping armholes: Attach white and continue in stocking st, casting off 3 sts at beg of next 2 rows; then alternate 2 rows yellow with 2 rows white, dec 1 st at each end every other row. Work straight on rem 44 (48) sts until armholes measure 10 (11) cm, ending with a K row. P next row, casting off centre 18 (20) sts.

Shaping neck: Working one half of neck 13 (14) sts, dec 1 st at neck edge every other row twice; work straight until armhole measures 12.5 (13.5) cm.

Shoulders: At armhole edge, cast off 6 (6) sts at beg of next row, 5 (6) sts at beg of following row; fasten off. Work other half of neck and shoulder to correspond.

Right front: Using 3.75 mm needles, cast on 28 (30) sts with blue yarn. Work as for back until the armhole measures 9 (9.5) cm.

Children's cardigans and hats shown on left are knitted from the same pattern. The all-over-stripe cardigan and matching hat (left) and the stripe-trimmed cardigan and matching hat (right) vary in the use of colour. You could knit the cardigan and hat in any colours you wish. Directions are for size 4; changes for size 6 are given in parentheses.

Baby coat and matching hat in photograph on right will fit a six-month to nine-month-old baby. Design of coat yoke and hat is alternating bands of stocking stitch and garter stitch. The coat and hat may be knitted in baby yarn as was done here, or in 3-ply sock or sweater yarn.

Shaping neck: At neck edge, cast off 9 (10) sts. Dec 1 st at neck edge every other row twice. Work until front is same length as back. Shape shoulder as for back.

Left front: Work the same as right front, with the shaping reversed.

Sleeves: Using 3.75 mm needles, cast on 36 sts with blue yarn and work 1 × 1 ribbing in stripes as for back. Change to 4.50 mm needles and continue in stocking-st stripes until sleeve measures 5 cm; inc 1 st at each end of next row, then every 5 (4.5) cm until there are 44 (46) sts. Work straight until sleeve is 23.5 (26) cm. Work green and turquoise garter-st stripes as for back. Attach yellow, K 1 row, P 1 row. **Shaping cap:** Attach white yarn; cast off 3 sts at beg of next 2 rows. Continue with yellow and white stripes, decreasing 1 st at each end of every other row 8 (9) times. Cast off 2 sts at beg of next 4 rows, 3 sts at beg of next 2 rows; cast off rem 8 sts.

Finishing: Sew shoulder seams; sew in sleeves; join the side and sleeve seams. With right side facing us, using 4.50 hook and blue yarn, begin at lower right front and *loosely* sl st along front and neck edges (for crochet abbreviations, see p. 278). With 4.00 hook, work second row in dc, making 3 dc in each corner st. Mark 7 buttonhole positions on right front for girls, left front for boys. **Next round,** with 4.00 hook and white, work 1 dc in each dc, making a ch-2 buttonhole at each marking and 3 dc in each corner st. Work 1 blue row, dec a few sts around neck for closer fit; fasten off. Attach buttons.

Hat

Using 3.75 mm needles, cast on loosely 86 (90) sts with blue yarn. Work alternate blue and white stripes in ribbing as for cardigan; fasten off. Change to 4.50 mm needles and garter st; work rows of green and turquoise stripes as for cardigan; fasten off. Attach yellow and white; work stripes in stocking st until

hat measures 11.5 (12.5) cm. [*For size 4 only:* When hat measures 10 cm, K 2 tog at one edge only (85 sts).] **Dec row 1:** *K 3, K 2 tog* across row; P 1 row, K 1 row, P 1 row. **Dec row 2:** *K 2, K 2 tog* across row; P 1 row, K 1 row, P 1 row. **Dec row 3:** *K 1, K 2 tog* across row; P 1 row. **Dec row 4:** *K 2 tog* across row; P 1 row. **Dec row 5:** K 2 (3) tog, *K 3 tog* across row; 7 (6) sts remain. Fasten off, leaving a 45 cm end. With tapestry needle, thread yarn through each st, then draw it up tightly; fasten securely. Sew back seam. Make a pompon with white yarn (see p. 493 for instructions).

STRIPED-TRIMMED SET

Yarn amounts: Same wool as previous pattern, both sizes: 260 g white, 90 g blue, 60 g green, 30 g each yellow and orange

Cardigan back: Using 3.75 mm needles, cast on 56 (60) sts with blue yarn. Work 1 × 1 ribbing for 7 rows. Attach white; work 2 rows of ribbing. Change to 4.50 mm needles and work in stocking st: 6 rows of green, 2 rows white, 4 rows yellow, 2 rows white, 2 rows orange. Continue in white until back measures 24 (27.5) cm. Shape underarm and neck same as for other cardigan.

Cardigan fronts: Work as for other cardigan, using stripe design given above.

Sleeves

Work stripes as described above. Work in white until sleeves measure 26.5 (29) cm; shape the sleeve cap as for other cardigan.

Finishing: Finish as for other cardigan, but work all three rows of trimming in blue.

Hat

Work as other hat, using stripe design.

BABY SET

Size: Six-month to nine-month-old baby; chest 48 cm

Materials needed: 100 g acrylic baby yarn, such as Sirdar Snuggly; 3.25 mm knitting needles; size 3.25 mm crochet hook; tapestry needle

Tension: 14 sts and 20 rows = 5 cm in stocking st

Pattern stitch. Row 1: knit. **Row 2:** purl. **Row 3:** knit. **Row 4:** purl. **Rows 5–12:** knit. This pattern is 4 rows of stocking st followed by 8 rows of garter st.

Coat back: Loosely cast on 124 sts. K 7 rows. Work in stocking st [K 1 row, P 1 row] until piece measures 15 cm, ending with a P row. **Next row:** K 8, *K 2 tog* across to within last 8 sts, K 8 (70 sts). K 7 rows.

To shape raglan armholes: Starting with Row 1 of the pattern st, dec 1 st each side every other row until 24 sts remain. Complete garter-st band, loosely casting off all sts on Row 12 of pattern.

Sleeves: Cast on 46 sts, K 7 rows. Work in stocking st, inc 1 st at beg and end of row every 2.5 cm 5 times; you now have 56 sts. Work straight until piece is 15 cm; end with P row. K 8 rows.

To shape raglan cap: Starting with Row 1 of pattern, dec 1 st each side every other row until 10 sts remain. Complete garter-st band, loosely casting off all sts on Row 12 of pattern.

Left front: Cast on 62 sts. K 9 rows. **Next row:** K 4, P to end. (Front border is garter st.) Work in stocking st with first 4 sts in garter st until piece measures 15 cm ending with a P row. **Next row:** K 8, *K 2 tog* across to within last 4 sts, K 4 (37 sts). K 7 rows. **To shape raglan armhole:** Starting with Row 1 of pattern, dec 1 st at *beginning* of Row 1 [to dec at beg of a row, sl 1, K 1, psso] and every other row thereafter until 14 sts remain. At same time, to work front border, K *first* 4 sts of the P rows. Complete the garter-st band, loosely casting off all sts on Row 12 of pattern.

Right front: Cast on 62 sts. K 9 rows.

Next row: P across to within last 4 sts, K 4. Work in stocking st with last 4 sts in garter st until piece is 15 cm; end with a P row. **Next row:** K 4, K 2 tog to within last 8 sts, K 8 (37 sts). K 7 rows. **To shape raglan armhole:** Starting with Row 1 of pattern, dec 1 st at *end* of Row 1 [to dec at end of a row, K 2 tog] and every other row thereafter until 14 sts remain. At same time, to work front border, K *last* 4 sts of the P rows. Complete the garter-st band, loosely casting off all sts on Row 12 of pattern.

Finishing: Join raglan seam, then side and sleeve seams, with backstitch or crocheted slipstitch (p. 485). For ties, make 6 double chains (p. 277), each 15 cm long; sew to yoke front.

Hat

Hat is knitted in T-shape. Cast on 100 sts. K 7 rows. Starting with Row 1 of pattern, work Rows 1–12 4 times. Piece should measure 11.5 cm from beg to last K row. Cast off 35 sts at each edge, leaving centre 30 sts on needle. Fasten off. Attach yarn to centre sts, and begin with Row 1 of pattern. Continue in pattern until piece measures 24 cm from beg, ending with Row 10 of pattern. Cast off. To assemble, backstitch the 35 cast-off sts on either side to sides of centre extension. For ties, make 2 double chains (see p. 365), each 25 cm long, and sew to cap at bottom edges.

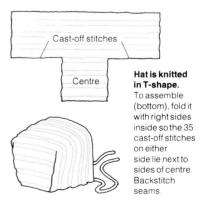

Cast-off stitches

Centre

Hat is knitted in T-shape.
To assemble (bottom), fold it with right sides inside so the 35 cast-off stitches on either side lie next to sides of centre. Backstitch seams.

Socks

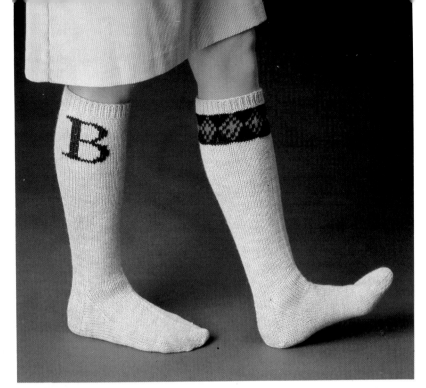

Sock pattern can be made with diamond band knitted in or with duplicate-stitch initial added later.

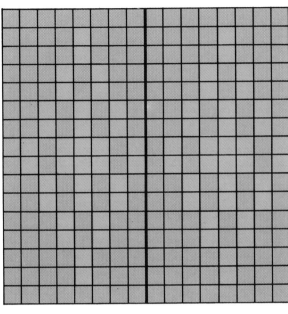

Follow this chart for the decorative band on the geometric sock. One square on the graph equals one knit stitch. See p. 457 for working from a chart. Because the sock is knitted in the round, the chart is read from right to left for each row. Diamond-shaped motif is repeated eight times around the top of the sock.

The same pattern offers you socks with a geometric design knitted in or an initial added in duplicate stitch after the sock is completed. Instructions for working from a chart are on p. 457. Directions for duplicate stitch appear on p. 488.

Size

Adjustable (see the foot instructions in column on far right)

Materials needed

170 g beige double knitting such as Sirdar Majestic for one pair of socks in either design; for geometric design, 30 g each green and red double knitting; for initials, 2 m green double knitting; 1 set 2.75 mm double-pointed knitting needles; tapestry needle

Tension

14 sts and 20 rows = 5 cm

Leg

Ribbing: With beige, cast on 64 sts, dividing the sts on to 3 needles (p. 439). Work in 1 × 1 ribbing for 2.5 cm. Change to stocking st, every rnd K.
Geometric design: K the next 16 rows

in the colour pattern, following the chart given above. (For directions on working with two colours of yarn, see pp. 457–8.)
Initial design: Work 16 rows of beige.
For either sock: With beige, continue to K around until sock measures 12.5 cm from cast-on row. **Next round:** Dec 1 st at beg of 1st needle and end of 3rd needle. Rep this dec every 2.5 cm, 7 more times. Work straight on 48 sts until piece measures 33 cm.

Divide for heel and foot

At beg of next rnd, K 12, sl 24 sts in centre on to a holder, turn.

Heel

P across 12 heel sts, then P across next 12 heel sts (24 sts on 1 needle), turn.
Row 1: *K 1, sl 1*. Repeat between * across row. **Row 2:** Purl. Rep these 2 rows for 6.5 cm, ending with Row 1.

Turn heel

Turning is the working of short rows in graduated lengths (see p. 469). **Row 1:** P 9, P 2 tog, P 3, P 2 tog, P 1, turn.

Row 2: sl 1, K 4, sl 1, K 1, psso, K 1, turn. **Row 3:** sl 1, P 5, P 2 tog, P 1, turn. **Row 4:** sl 1, K 6, sl 1, K 1, psso, K 1, turn. **Row 5:** sl 1, P 7, P 2 tog, P 1, turn. **Row 6:** sl 1, K 8, sl 1, K 1, psso, K 1, turn. **Row 7:** sl 1, P 9, P 2 tog, P 1, turn. **Row 8:** sl 1, K 10, sl 1, K 1, psso, K 1, turn. **Row 9:** sl 1, P 11, P 2 tog, P 1 (14 sts). Break off. Divide heel sts between 2 needles, 7 sts on each. With right side facing you, join yarn at top left of heel ribbing. Pick up and K 14 sts along ribbing side, placing sts on left heel needle; on to a 2nd needle, K 24 sts from holder; on to 3rd needle, pick up and K 14 sts along other side of heel plus 7 sts from other heel needle (21 sts on each heel needle).

Shape heel gusset

Start at centre of heel to shape gusset.
Round 1: On 1st needle, K to within last 3 sts, K 2 tog, K 1; on 2nd needle, K instep sts; on 3rd needle, K 1, sl 1, K 1, psso, K to end of rnd. **Round 2:** Knit. Rep these 2 rnds until there are 12 sts on

1st and 3rd needles.

Foot

K around until piece is 5 cm less than desired finished length from back of heel. (For a size 10 sock, work until piece measures 20.5 cm.)

Shape toe

Round 1: On 1st needle, K to within last 3 sts, K 2 tog, K 1; on 2nd needle, K 1, sl 1, K 1, psso, K to within last 3 sts, K 2 tog, K 1; on 3rd needle, K 1, sl 1, K 1, psso, K to end of needle.
Round 2: Knit. Rep these 2 rnds until there are 5 sts on each heel needle, then put all heel sts on one needle. Break off yarn, leaving a 30 cm end. Weave toe sts tog.

Finishing

Block socks lightly (pp. 482–3). For the sock with initial, use duplicate stitch using green double knitting to add desired initial (see p. 489). For a closer fit, weave a length of elastic into the ribbing at the top of the sock. To do this, see instructions on p. 487.

Mittens and hat

MITTENS

Size

Woman's medium or man's small (or equivalent in teen sizes)

Materials needed

4-ply, such as Patons Beehive, 90 g beige, 30 g each green and red; knitting needles, 1 pair 2.75 mm, 1 pair 3.25 mm, tapestry needle

Tension

14 sts and 18 rows = 5 cm

Cuff

With beige yarn and 2.75 mm needles, cast on 48 sts; work in 1 × 1 ribbing for 6.5 cm.

Hand

Change to 3.25 mm needles and work in stocking st for 6 rows, ending with a P row. K 23, put marker on needle, inc in each of next 2 sts, put marker on needle; work to end of row. **Next row:** Purl. **Next row:** K to marker, slip marker, inc in next st, K 2, inc in next st, slip marker, K to end of row. **Next row:** Purl. **Next row:** K to marker, slip marker, inc in next st, K 4, inc in next st, slip marker, K to end of row. Continue in this manner, increasing 1 st after first marker and 1 st before second marker on every K row until you have 22 sts between markers and 68 sts on needle. Work straight on all sts until you have 7.5 cm of stocking st, ending with a P row. **Next row:** K 43, turn. **Next row:** P 18. For thumb, work on these 18 sts *only* for 6 cm. End with a P row.

Thumb shaping

Row 1: *K 1, K 2 tog*. Rep between * across rows (12 sts). **Row 2:** Purl. **Row 3:** K 2 tog across row (6 sts); break off yarn, leaving a 30 cm end. Thread tapestry needle with yarn end and run needle through sts. Fasten off.

To complete hand

Attach beige to base of thumb; work to end of row. Work stocking-st rows as follows: 2 beige, 2 green, 2 beige, 4 red, 2 beige, 2 green. Work straight in beige until piece measures 21 cm from cast-on row; end with a P row.

Top shaping

Row 1: K 1, K 2 tog, K 19, K 2 tog, K 2, K 2 tog, K to within last 3 sts, K 2 tog, K 1. **Row 2:** Purl. **Row 3:** K 1, K 2 tog, K 17, K 2 tog, K 2, K 2 tog, K to within last 3 sts, K 2 tog, K 1. **Row 4:** Purl. Dec this way until 18 sts remain. Cut yarn, leaving 30 cm. Thread tapestry needle with yarn end and run through sts; fasten off. Weave cuff seam (p. 484) and backstitch hand seam (p. 485). Make second mitten same way.

HAT

Size

Adjustable

Materials needed

Same wool as mittens, 60 g beige, 30 g each green and red; 3.25 mm knitting needles; tapestry needle

Tension

12 sts and 26 rows = 5 cm in garter stitch

With beige, cast on 50 sts; K 2 rows. Hat is made in garter st in following colour pattern: 2 rows green, 6 rows beige, 4 rows red, 6 rows beige. Rep until piece fits snugly around head; end with 2 more beige rows. Cast off. Backstitch cast-on row to cast-off row. Thread separate yarn through one side edge; gather tightly (below). Turn other edge under 1.5 cm and hem. Make pompon (below) and sew to hat.

Mittens and matching hat are knitted in 4-ply yarn; you could choose any colours you wish.

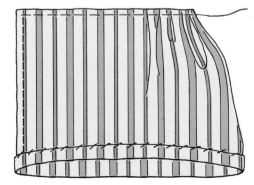

To assemble hat, sew cast-on row to cast-off row with backstitch. Thread separate length of yarn through one side edge; gather up tightly. To hem other edge, turn under 1.5 cm and sew.

To make a pompon, wrap yarn around a 5 cm piece of cardboard 180 times. Slip separate piece of yarn under threads at one edge and tie securely. Cut yarn at other edge. Shake the pompon vigorously; then trim yarn ends to shape pompon.

Evening skirt, top and shawl

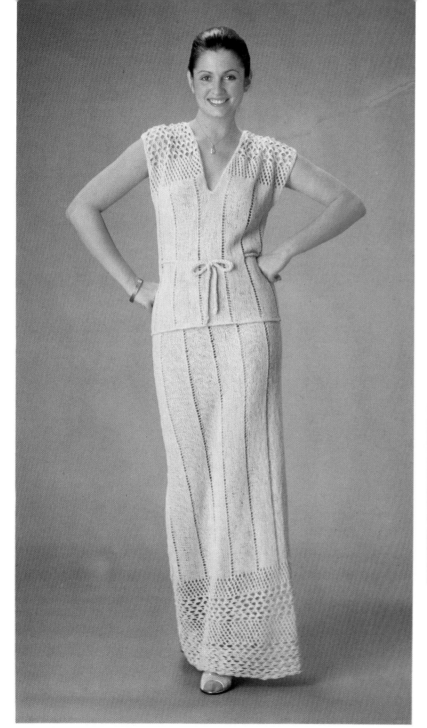

Evening skirt and matching top can be worn as a dress as shown, or over a blouse.

Co-ordinating shawl is worked in the same three knitted lace patterns as the skirt and top on left.

The skirt, top and shawl are knitted in a combination of three stitches: net and oblique openwork lace stitches are on p. 444; stocking stitch with rows of eyelet stitches is described in the instructions below.

The skirt may be knitted floor length – about 100 cm long – with a double border of net and oblique openwork stitches as shown on the left. Or it could be knitted in a shorter version – about 85 cm long – that reaches to mid-calf and has a single border of the lace stitches.

The top has a centre front slit that is formed into a V-neckline by gathering the front shoulders to fit the back. The side seams may be sewn up to the armhole or, for a tabard style, tacked together only at the waist. A drawstring belt is threaded through eyelets at the waistline.

The shawl is made with the same yarn type used for the skirt and top. You could choose a contrasting colour for the shawl as was done here (see photograph opposite), or you could use the same yarn colour for all three pieces. The shawl is square with a square centre and four flounce sections with mitred ends. The top edge of each flounce section is eased slightly to fit the sides of the centre square; sections are attached with double crochet (see p. 274) so the shawl has a finished look on both the right and wrong sides.

SKIRT AND TOP
Size
Directions for sizes 8–10 and 12–14
Materials needed
4-ply such as Patons Beehive or Jaeger Matchmaker: 500 g for skirt, 300 g for top; 1 pair 5 mm knitting needles; 5.00 crochet hook; stitch holder; ring stitch markers; yarn needle; 1 m of 25 mm elastic; 50 cm of 6 mm tape or satin ribbon; sewing needle; thread to match yarn; for lining (optional), 2.30 m lining fabric for long skirt, 1.90 m for shorter version
Tension
10 sts and 14 rows = 5 cm in stocking st
Skirt border
Cast on 116 (124) sts. For floor-length skirt, work 10 cm in net, 6.5 cm in oblique openwork, *7.5 cm in net, 5 cm in oblique openwork. Start at * for shorter skirt. (Additional length adjustments can be made at the top before beginning the waistband.)
Body of skirt
Change to stocking st with eyelets. **Row 1:** K 8 (12), 1 eyelet [to work eyelet: yrn, K 2 tog], *K 12, 1 eyelet*. Rep between * 6 more times, then end with K 8 (12). **Row 2:** Purl. Rep these 2 rows, dec 1 st at beg and end of every

10th row until there are 88 (96) sts. Work straight until skirt is desired length. For waistband, work 1 × 1 ribbing for 2.5 cm; cast off. Make second skirt piece like the first. Join pieces with weaving stitch (p. 484).
Finishing
If you line the skirt, fold it in half and pin to fold of lining fabric. Trace around skirt, allowing 1.5 cm for seams and 5 cm for hem. Cut out lining; stitch side seams; hem. Fold under 1.5 cm at top edge; put lining inside skirt with wrong sides facing. Stitch together at top edge; stitch again 2.5 cm from top, leaving 5 cm open. Thread elastic through casing formed by lining and knitted waistband. Stitch ends of elastic together; stitch opening closed. If you do not line skirt, sew elastic to wrong side of waistband with a zigzag stitch or anchor it with a crocheted casing (see p. 487).
Back of matching top
Cast on 84 (92) sts. Work stocking st with eyelets. **Row 1:** K 6 (10), 1 eyelet, *K 12, 1 eyelet*. Rep between * 4 more times, then K 6 (10). **Row 2:** Purl. Rep these 2 rows for 34.5 cm; put markers at each side for armholes. Work stocking st with eyelets for 6.5 cm, then oblique openwork for 6.5 cm, and net for 10 cm. Cast off.
Front of matching top
Work same as for back but after armhole markers, form a slit in centre front as follows: work to centre, place remaining unworked sts in row on holder, turn and continue up first half to shoulder. On other half, attach yarn at centre and continue to shoulder.
Finishing the top
Block pieces. With an extra length of yarn and a yarn needle, run a tacking stitch along each shoulder front on right side. Gather knitting along tacked thread until each piece measures 16.5 cm, pin to back shoulder, matching armhole edges. Sew shoulder seams with a weaving stitch, working from

wrong side, catching more than one st from front to accommodate gathers. Remove tacking thread. Hand-stitch tape or satin ribbon to front edge of seam with sewing thread. Sew side seams together, working from bottom up for 34.5 cm, leaving armholes open. Or, for a tabard, sew sides together for 2 or 3 cm at waist. To finish edges, work double crochet (p. 274) around neckline, armholes and bottom edge. For belt, make a 130 cm double chain (p. 277), using two strands of yarn; thread it through the row of eyelets nearest your waist.

SHAWL
Size
122 cm square
Materials needed
600 g same yarn as skirt; 5 mm knitting needles; 5.00 crochet hook; yarn needle

Centre section
Cast on 160 sts. Work in oblique openwork pattern st (see p. 444) for 92 cm. Cast off.
Flounce
Make 4 pieces. Cast on 212 sts. Work in network pattern st (see p. 444), dec 1 st at beg and end of every other row until you have 200 sts and piece measures 6.5 cm. Change to stocking st with eyelets (directions above), dec 1 st at beg and end of every row until you have 168 sts and piece measures 15 cm. Cast off.
Finishing
Block pieces lightly. Pin mitred edges of flounce sections together; join with double crochet (p. 274). With an extra length of yarn, run a tacking stitch along inner edge of flounce. Ease flounce slightly to fit sides of centre square. Pin flounce to square and attach with double crochet.

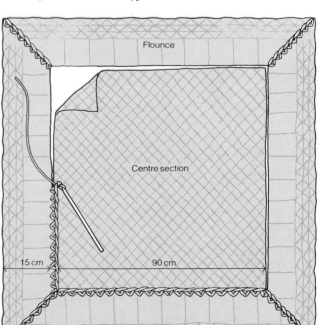

To assemble the shawl, pin the mitred ends of the four flounce pieces together; join with a double crochet stitch (p. 274). With an extra length of yarn, tack along inner edge of flounce sections. Ease the flounce slightly to fit sides of centre square. Pin together and attach with double crochet.

Knitted lace for sheets and pillowcases

A knitted lace border is added to a pillowcase: a knitted lace insertion decorates a plain sheet.

One band of knitted lace decorates the edge of a pillowcase; another lace band is inserted below top hem of a sheet.

Materials needed
Crochet cotton, such as Phildar Relais No. 8, 1.70 m per centimetre for border with crocheted edge, 1.90 m per centimetre for insertion; 1 pair 2.75 mm knitting needles, 2.75 mm crochet hook

Tension
Pillowcase border: 1 unit = 5 cm
Sheet insertion: 1 unit = 4.5 cm

Measuring the linens
To determine length of border, measure around pillowcase edge. Insertion length is width of top sheet. Add 2.5 cm to each measurement to allow for take-up in knitting. To estimate crochet cotton needed, multiply the length you will knit by amount per centimetre above. Block each piece before sewing.

BORDER
Cast on 20 sts.
Row 1: sl 1, K 2, yrn, K 2 tog, yrn, sl 1, K 1, psso, K 3, K 2 tog, yrn twice, sl 1, K 1, psso, K 2 tog, yrn, K 1, yrn, K 2 tog, K 1
Rows 2, 4, 6, 8, 10: yrn, P to within last 5 sts, K 2, yrn, K 2 tog, K 1
Row 3: sl 1, K 2, yrn, K 2 tog, K 4, K 2 tog, yrn, K 1, K 2 tog, yrn twice, sl 1, K 1, psso, K 2, yrn, K 2 tog, K 1
Row 5: sl 1, K 2, yrn, K 2 tog, K 3, K 2 tog, yrn, K 1, K 2 tog, yrn, K 2, yrn, sl 1, K 1, psso, K 2, yrn, K 2 tog, K 1
Row 7: sl 1, K 2, yrn, K 2 tog, K 2, K 2 tog, yrn, K 1, K 2 tog, yrn, K 4, yrn, sl 1, K 1, psso, K 2, yrn, K 2 tog, K 1
Row 9: sl 1, K 2, yrn, K 2 tog, K 1, K 2 tog, yrn, K 1, K 2 tog, yrn, K 6, yrn, sl 1, K 1, psso, K 2, yrn, K 2 tog, K 1
Row 11: sl 1, K 2, yrn, (K 2 tog) twice, yrn, (yrn, sl 1, K 1, psso, K 3, K 2 tog, yrn) twice, K 1, yrn, K 2 tog, K 1
Rows 12, 14, 16, 18, 20: yrn, (P 2 tog) twice, P to within last 5 sts, K 2, yrn, K 2 tog, K 1
Row 13: sl 1, K 2, yrn, K 2 tog, yrn, sl 1, K 1 psso, K 1, yrn, sl 1, K 1, psso, K 8, K 2 tog, yrn, K 1, yrn, K 2 tog, K 1
Row 15: sl 1, K 2, yrn, K 2 tog, K 1, yrn, sl 1, K 1, psso, K 1, yrn, sl 1, K 1, psso, K 6, K 2 tog, yrn, K 1, yrn, K 2 tog, K 1
Row 17: sl 1, K 2, yrn, K 2 tog, K 2, yrn, sl 1, K 1, psso, K 1, yrn, sl 1, K 1, psso, K 4, K 2 tog, yrn, K 1, yrn, K 2 tog, K 1
Row 19: sl 1, K 2, yrn, K 2 tog, K 3, yrn, sl 1, K 1, psso, K 1, yrn, sl 1, K 1, psso, K 2, K 2 tog, yrn, K 1, yrn, K 2 tog, K 1

Finishing
To finish border edge, work a crochet edging (p. 274) in picot loops on zigzag side of strip. To do this, attach new strand of thread in picot loop at one end of strip as follows. Holding thread at back of work, yarn round hook (yrh), then insert hook under loop and end of thread, yrh and draw up loop, yrh and through both loops on hook; one dc made. Work 1 more dc in same loop, work 2 dc in each loop to the end. Fasten off. Sew short ends of strip together. Pin straight edge of border to pillowcase; stitch in place with neat, small stitches.

INSERTION
Cast on 24 sts.
Row 1: sl 1, K 2, yrn, K 2 tog, K 1, 1 popcorn [(K into front and back of st) twice, then slip 3rd, 2nd, and 1st sts over 4th one], K 3, yrn, sl 1, K 1, psso, K 2 tog, yrn, K 3, 1 popcorn, K 3, yrn, K 2 tog, K 1
Rows 2, 4, 6, 8, 12, 14, 16: sl 1, K 2, yrn, K 2 tog, P 14, K 2, yrn, K 2 tog, K 1
Row 3: sl 1, K 2, yrn, K 2 tog, K 3, K 2 tog, yrn, K 4, yrn, sl 1, K 1, psso, K 5, yrn, K 2 tog, K 1
Row 5: sl 1, K 2, yrn, K 2 tog, K 2, K 2 tog, yrn, K 6, yrn, sl 1, K 1, psso, K 4, yrn, K 2 tog, K 1
Row 7: sl 1, K 2, yrn, K 2 tog, K 1, K 2 tog, yrn, K 8, yrn, sl 1, K 1, psso, K 3, yrn, K 2 tog, K 1
Row 9: sl 1, K 2, yrn, (K 2 tog) twice, yrn, K 3, K 2 tog, yrn twice, sl 1, K 1, psso, K 3, yrn, sl 1, K 1, psso, K 2, yrn, K 2 tog, K 1
Row 10: sl 1, K 2, yrn, K 2 tog, P 6, K 1, P 7, K 2, yrn, K 2 tog, K 1
Row 11: sl 1, K 2, yrn, K 2 tog, K 2, yrn, sl 1, K 1, psso, K 6, K 2 tog, yrn, K 4, yrn, K 2 tog, K 1
Row 13: sl 1, K 2, yrn, K 2 tog, K 3, yrn, sl 1, K 1, psso, K 4, K 2 tog, yrn, K 5, yrn, K 2 tog, K 1
Row 15: sl 1, K 2, yrn, K 2 tog, K 4, yrn, sl 1, K 1, psso, K 2, K 2 tog, yrn, K 6, yrn, K 2 tog, K 1

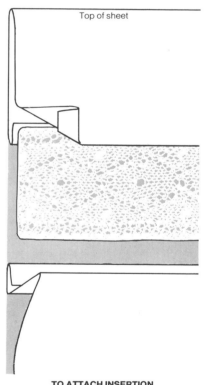

Top of sheet

TO ATTACH INSERTION
Cut off top hem of sheet 5 mm below stitched fold. Remove stitches from cut piece; press raw edge up 5 mm. Fold lace and hem in quarters; mark with pins; unfold. Insert one edge of lace into open hem edge (top); match markings; stitch in place. On cut edge of sheet, press 5 mm to right side twice; press doubled edge to wrong side (bottom). Fold and mark sheet edge in quarters. Insert other lace edge the same way.

Index

The projects are shown in *italics* throughout the index, and a complete list appears on page 501–2.

The names and addresses of some suppliers of needlework materials and equipment appear on page 504.

Bibliography

The publishers wish to thank the authors and publishers of the following books which were used for reference

Anchor Manual of Needlework, Batsford, 1974
Art of Cutwork and Appliqué, Herta Puls, Batsford, 1978
Batsford Encyclopaedia of Embroidery Stitches, Anne Butler, 1979
Book of Stitches, Constance Howard, Batsford, 1979
Canvas Work, Jennifer Gray, Batsford, 1974
The Complete Rug Hooker, Joan Moshimer, *New York Graphic Society*, 1979, available from Patrick Stephens Ltd, Bar Hill, Cambridge
Creative Knitting, Mary Walker Phillips, Van Nostrand Reinhold, 1971

Crochet Workshop, James Walters, Sidgwick & Jackson, 1979
Dictionary of Canvas Work Stitches, Mary Rhodes, Batsford, 1980
Easy Crochet, Creative Learning, DMC Library, 1977
Embroidery & Tapestry Weaving, Grace Christie, Pitman, 1979
Encyclopaedia of Needlework, Thérèse de Dillmont, DMC Library, Mulhouse, 1975
The Identification of Lace, Pat Earnshaw, Shire Publications, 1980
Inspiration for Embroidery, Constance Howard, Batsford, 1967
Introducing Macramé, Eirian Short, Batsford, 1970
Introducing Quilting, Eirian Short, Batsford, 1980
Machine Embroidery, Christine Risley, Studio Vista, 1980

Needlelace & Needleweaving, Jill Nordfors, Studio Vista, 1974
Needlemade Rugs, Sìbyl I. Matthews, Mills & Boon, 1960
Needleworker's Dictionary, Pamela Clabburn, Macmillan, 1976
Patchwork, Averil Colby, Batsford, 1973
Quilting, Averil Colby, Batsford, 1972
Quilting, Patchwork, Appliqué and Trapunto, Thelma Newman, George Allen & Unwin, 1975
Quiltmaker's Handbook, Michael James, Prentice-Hall, 1978, available from Quilter's Guild, Strawberry Fayre, Stockbridge, Hants.
Technique of Bobbin Lace, Pamela Nottingham, Batsford, 1979
Technique of Filet Lace, Pauline Knight, Batsford, 1980

Suppliers

American Museum in Britain, Country Store, Claverton Manor, Bath, Avon (hand rug hooks)
Bedford Wool Shop, The Old Arcade, Bedford (knitting and embroidery materials)
J. E. Beale Plc, 26/36 Silver Street, Bedford (needlework, canvas and knitting materials)
Cowling & Wilcox, 26 Broadwick Street, W1 (art materials, pounce)
Dryad, P.O. Box 38, Northgate, Leicester (craft, lacemaking and needlework supplies)
Handweaver Studio, 29 Haroldstone Road, E17 (embroidery threads, weaving and spinning yarns)

Harrods Ltd, Knightsbridge, SW1 (needlework materials, canvas and yarns)
Jacksons Rugcraft Ltd, Croft Mill, Albert Street, Hebden Bridge, W. Yorks (rug canvas, thrums and yarns)
John Lewis, Oxford Street, W1 (needlework and lacemaking materials)
Mace & Nairn, 89 Crane Street, Salisbury, Wilts (lacemaking and embroidery materials)
Ries Wools, 243 High Holborn, WC1 (knitting and crochet materials, tatting shuttles, crochet hooks)

Christine Riley's Embroidery Shop, 53 Barclay Street, Stonehaven, Kincardine (needlework, canvas, lacemaking materials)
Royal School of Needlework, Apartment 12A, Hampton Court, E. Molesey, Surrey (needlework materials, canvas, patchwork, yarns)
A. Sells, Lane Cove, 49 Pedley Lane, Clifton, Shefford, Bedfordshire (lacemaking materials, threads, books)
Spinning Jenny, Bradley, W. Yorks and Market Place, Masham, near Ripon, N. Yorks (embroidery, canvas, appliqué, patchwork, lacemaking, crochet materials)

Photographic credits

Page 12 Flower and bird design. The Bagshaws of St Lucia Ltd. Silk-screen bamboo-print wallpaper, Janovic/Plaza
Page 103 Alphabet, from *New Art Deco Alphabets* by Marcia Loeb, New York, Dover Publications, Inc.
Page 208 Rose design quilt, The Gazebo
Page 233 Baby Blocks quilt, The Gazebo
Page 234 Grandmother's Flower Garden quilt. Thos. K. Woodard

40/029/7